A6

STUDIES IN THE
INSTITUTIONAL HISTORY OF
EARLY MODERN JAPAN

STUDIES IN THE INSTITUTIONAL HISTORY OF EARLY MODERN JAPAN

EDITED BY

JOHN W. HALL AND MARIUS B. JANSEN

WITH AN INTRODUCTION BY

JOSEPH R. STRAYER

CONTRIBUTORS

Harumi Befu · Albert Craig · E. S. Crawcour

R. P. Dore · J. W. Hall · Dan Fenno Henderson

M. B. Jansen · Robert K. Sakai · Donald H. Shively

Thomas C. Smith

PRINCETON UNIVERSITY PRESS

PRINCETON, NEW JERSEY

For Serge Elisséeff

FOREWORD

THIS VOLUME had its origins in a panel organized for the annual meeting of the Association for Asian Studies in 1964 and chaired by President Hugh Borton of Haverford College. Parallel papers treating the development of daimyo rule in three provinces of seventeenth-century Japan were discussed in relation to the institutional development of medieval Europe by Professor Joseph R. Strayer. A number of our colleagues encouraged us to publish those papers together. As we prepared to do so, we became aware of the need to add to them further discussions of the institutional history of early modern Japan in order to provide an adequate base for comparison and coverage. Some of these have been written specifically for this volume, and others have been gathered from writings previously published by our colleagues and ourselves.

Few fields of study have undergone more dramatic change and development than that of Tokugawa Japan. It has been a center of activity and controversy in Japan since the 1930's. At that time the overwhelming emphasis was on social and economic trends. This has begun to give way, in more recent years, to a focus on institutional developments of shogun and daimyo rule. The interrelationships of political, institutional, and cultural history are only now beginning to come into view. Among Western historians in the past two decades work has been particularly stimulated by the abundance of data that Japanese specialists in local history have made available. This work has remained largely free from the controversies that continue to mark the field in Japan, but its reappraisals of Tokugawa institutions, often in the light of Japan's subsequent modernization, have frequently led to new areas of interest and contention among scholars.

Since much of the best work has appeared in a variety of journals which are often difficult to obtain, it seemed to us important to add to our papers others that would be representative of the strength and coverage of current scholarship in the West. This volume thus indicates the present state of our understanding of the institutional life of Tokugawa Japan, and it is meant to serve the needs of students of Japan as well as those concerned with parallel or contrasting patterns of institutional development elsewhere.

Of the twenty-one selections which follow, eight appear here for the first time. Eleven are by the editors and reflect, in their emphasis on the provinces of Bizen and Tosa, the impressive body of materials that have been made available by energetic local historians in Okayama and Kōchi. We have made no effort to change articles that appeared earlier. Such diversity in terminology as occurs is met by cross-indexing and occasional footnotes. We have also felt it necessary to limit our coverage to institutional history, and we have therefore

Foreword

excluded discussions of nineteenth-century personalities and movements of political protest.

It is our hope that this volume will serve to reflect and also to stimulate the development of Tokugawa studies. We acknowledge with gratitude the encouragement of our colleagues, of the authors and journals that have permitted us to reprint their articles, and especially the contribution of Professor Joseph R. Strayer, whose studies in European institutional development have long stood as model for students of other areas.

John W. Hall
Marius B. Jansen

June 1967

CONTENTS

Contents

STUDIES IN THE
INSTITUTIONAL HISTORY OF
EARLY MODERN JAPAN

PART ONE
INTRODUCTION

CHAPTER ONE

THE TOKUGAWA PERIOD
AND JAPANESE FEUDALISM

JOSEPH R. STRAYER

Most students of the European Middle Ages would now, I think, admit that feudalism existed in Japan. They would also admit that it was "real" feudalism, and not just a set of institutions that looked like feudalism on the surface but actually worked in a very different way. Japanese feudalism belongs to the same genus as European feudalism; it is not like the marsupial wolf which resembles a European wolf but in reality is a kind of ferocious opossum.

No matter what definition of feudalism is used, Japan can be brought under its terms. I happen to prefer a rather narrow political definition, on the grounds that feudalism simply ceases to have any specific meaning when it is used to describe economic and social conditions. Great estates cultivated by poorly paid, almost landless laborers can exist without feudalism (for example, collective farms), just as factories and an urban proletariat can exist without capitalism. It is true, of course, that the political structure necessarily affects the economic and social structure: the dominant group in any organized community will control and divert production to suit its own purposes and will impose its standards and values on society. But the methods and forms of economic control and the social values which are inculcated vary with the political system and not vice versa.

In political terms, feudalism is marked by a fragmentation of political authority, private possession of public rights, and a ruling class composed (at least originally) of military leaders and their followers. It is not necessary to demonstrate that these conditions existed in Japan, perhaps even more noticeably than in medieval western Europe. Indeed, while extensive areas in western Europe were never feudalized, none of Japan remained untouched by feudalism.

It is also clear that the early and middle stages of Japanese feudalism were not unlike the corresponding stages in Europe. At first, public authority and public officials continued to exist alongside of increasingly powerful feudal lords. The central government retained power in some areas while losing it in others, and only gradually faded away to a shadow. The peak of fragmentation of authority and of private control of rights of government came several centuries after the process of feudalization had begun. All this seems familiar and reasonable to a western medievalist.

It is the final stage—the reversal of the process of fragmentation—which is strange and puzzling. It is strange because devices which proved dangerous or ephemeral in Europe—such as the existence of large principalities—were used effectively in Japan by the shogun to increase his authority. It is puzzling because the final stage lasted so long, because the changes which took place in the Tokugawa period were so slow that at times they were almost imperceptible. I judge that my colleagues whose views are represented in this book are also somewhat puzzled by political developments between 1600 and 1850. It is a period in which the forms of feudalism were carefully preserved while much of the substance vanished. But if the substance was vanishing, why were the forms necessary? Conversely, if some of the substance remained (as I think it did), why was it not disruptive, why could it be safely tolerated by the shogunate?

Let me elaborate a little on these points. There are two periods in western European feudalism which bear some resemblance to Tokugawa Japan. The first comes at the very beginning, in the ninth and tenth centuries, when the last Carolingians tried to hold their realm together by establishing great commands—the duchy of Burgundy, the duchy of Gothia, the duchy of Francia, and so on. The men who held these commands were at first not unlike Tokugawa daimyos: they were officials of the king; they or their heirs could be moved from one district to another; they could be forced to surrender or exchange some of the counties they administered. But very soon the holders of the great commands became hereditary rulers practically independent of the king, and soon after that the great commands broke up into smaller units. Burgundy might be compared to Tosa: each province was about equally distant from central authority; each had aspirations to control neighboring areas. But Burgundy paid less and less attention to royal orders, and in turn the subordinate counts of Burgundy paid less and less attention to the orders of the duke. Tosa, on the contrary, remained united and obedient. In short, Japanese feudalism seems to be marching backwards; it ends in the pattern with which western feudalism began.

The other period in western history which has some parallel to Tokugawa Japan cannot be dated so precisely; it begins with the emergence of large feudal principalities in France and Germany in the eleventh or twelfth centuries and lasts until the principalities were either absorbed into a larger political unit or became independent states. But the difference is that in Europe the period of feudal principalities was a period of intense political competition. No one was satisfied with the status quo; no one thought that the principalities could continue indefinitely as autonomous but subordinate entities. Kings did not trust princes to remain obedient; they tried to add princely holdings to the royal domain. Princes did not trust kings to respect local autonomy; they did their best to reject all possibility of intervention by higher authorities. On the whole, the issue was decided fairly quickly. During the thirteenth century, the king of France annexed so many of the great principalities—Normandy, Anjou, Poitou, Toulouse, Champagne—that more than half the country was directly governed by him and his officials. The remaining principalities could be infiltrated with royal agents and absorbed at leisure. In the end only Flanders escaped. In Germany, during the thirteenth century the princes became prac-

Introduction

tically independent. From that time on the accidents of war and inheritance, not the will of the emperor, determined the fate of German principalities.

This is not to say that feudalism, as a set of political institutions, ceased to have any influence in western Europe after 1300. It took many centuries to create the apparatus of centralized government, to build up efficient, well-trained, and reliable bureaucracies. Meanwhile local lords handled many of the details of local administration, either in their own right, or as deputies of a king or sovereign prince. As late as the seventeenth century Louis XIV, like a Tokugawa shogun, found it advisable to make his nobles spend part of the year at his court. As late as the seventeenth century the English gentry, who were not unlike the upper-level samurai of Japan, controlled local government through their positions as Justices of the Peace. But this late European feudalism had lost its basic structure and its monopoly of power. The old hierarchy of direct vassal, rear-vassal, rear-rear-vassal, etc., had vanished. Orders were no longer passed down a chain of command from count to baron to knight. The central government dealt directly with local authorities, great and small. The central government also had its parallel organizations, especially in matters of justice and finance, which reached down to the lowest levels of the population. Lords were left with enough prestige and power so that they could keep order among the peasants and collect their rents. They did not, as a rule, inflict serious punishments on peasants nor did they collect enough revenues from them to maintain large provincial armies or bureaucracies. In all these respects late European feudalism differed from Tokugawa feudalism.

Two questions emerge from this preliminary discussion: Why was the final stage of Japanese feudalism so prolonged? Why was it so different from the Western experience?

Some obvious and familiar answers can be given at once. The pressures which force political change were either absent or at a low level during most of the Tokugawa period. There was no external threat and very little organized internal opposition. There was, for example, no Church to focus and justify discontent; the various religious groups were controlled by secular authority. There were almost no courts of justice, certainly no courts like the French *parlements* and English common law courts with their long traditions of independent judgment. Thus an inferior oppressed by a superior could not expect support from either religious leaders or legal experts. The rise of a business class would have been slow in any case; it was retarded even more by the virtual absence of the foreign trade which had strengthened and enriched European merchants. In the end the development of internal commerce may have been one of the most important solvents of the Tokugawa system, but this development was very gradual. Meanwhile merchants and bankers had no effective political organization and they could not use their limited economic power to oppose the government.

In short, the shogun and his advisers were less dependent on the privileged classes than a European king and Council. The shogun did not need officers from the feudal nobility to fight for him in foreign wars, nor bankers from

5

the business community to finance them. He did not have to waste his energy in coercing bishops, judges, assemblies of estates, or semi-independent town governments. He could concentrate on one task: keeping enough of the daimyos obedient so that he would receive his share (a very large share) of the rice crop. Even if he held only one-sixth or one-seventh of Japan, this was still far more than any daimyo possessed. He could always count on the support, or at least the inertia, of most of the daimyos. He could overwhelm scattered rebels; and in the absence of any ideologies or institutions which could be used to unite latent opposition, scattered rebels were all that he was apt to meet.

These differences are immediately apparent. Others may have run deeper. The sheer size of the Japanese feudal class is amazing to anyone who has studied European feudalism; and size created problems which Europeans never had to face. It has been estimated that the maximum number of knight's fees which ever existed in England was about 6,000. This does not mean that there were 6,000 knights, since many fees had been subdivided to a point where they gave no real service and others were held by tenants who were usually excused from service. A single han in Tokugawa Japan would have had a larger number of samurai than the largest possible number of English knights, and the samurai were all expected to perform some kind of service. There seems to be no doubt about these numbers; the records are clear, consistent, and comparable over extended periods of time. To deal with these hordes of minor vassals required a degree of planning and organization which was never necessary in Europe. Japanese feudalism had to be more structured, more impersonal, more bureaucratic than European feudalism. At least it had to have these qualities from the middle of the sixteenth century, when we have evidence of huge armies and large numbers of retainers under the control of a single lord.

Another factor which must have made Japanese feudalism, even in its middle period, more structured and bureaucratic than European feudalism was the difference in the arrangements for providing economic support to the vassal. Household retainers were common in early European feudalism and they never entirely disappeared, but they were not an important element of the feudal class after 1100. Most vassals by that time had fiefs, and very rapidly the vassal became the virtual owner of his fief. In these circumstances, it would have been difficult to change the value of a fief and utterly impossible to try to create classes of fiefs in which each member of the class had a more or less uniform income. In most countries records were so poor that no one could have ascribed an exact value to any one fief or group of fiefs. Even in England, which was unique in having a survey of feudal possessions (Domesday Book), estimates of income were not very precise. England was also unique in groping toward the idea that the value of one type of fief—the knight's fee—should be standardized. But the evidence suggests that some lords thought an annual income of 10 pounds enough for a knight, that others used 20 pounds a year as a standard, and that in fact there were great variations in the yearly income of knights. Above the level of the knight there was no standardization whatever. When the concept of peerage developed and it became important to know whether a vassal was a knight or a baron, the king and his minsters were obviously perplexed. A man might be summoned as a baron on one occasion and be omitted from the list of barons on the next. Personal ability and political influence were as important as wealth in determining status, and no one would have said that an income of say 100 pounds a year automatically made a man a baron. In other countries very little was known about the actual income of individual vassals and there could be extremely wide variations among the incomes of men who theoretically belonged to the same level in the feudal hierarchy. Even in the late stages of European feudalism, when more was known about the value of holdings, there was no attempt to fix maximum and minimum incomes for certain ranks. After meeting what were, by Japanese standards, the very modest demands of his superior, the lord could exploit his holdings as he saw fit and keep any surplus which he had created. He remained closely tied to his estates and the change from feudal lord to landlord still left him with great prestige and influence in local government.

The rice economy of Japan seems to have lent itself more easily to exact measurement of feudal incomes. The vassal was to have so many measures of rice, not so many villages, or ploughlands, or acres. Such a system would work only if there were careful and repeated surveys of rice production, surveys which were far more thorough than Domesday Book and a great deal more common. Such surveys could be made only by higher authority, and as evidences of this authority they immediately reduced the autonomy of the local fief-holder. More important, the Japanese system made it easy to break the ties between vassals and the land. If a vassal was to have only a fixed rice income, then it made little difference whether he took it directly from a village or the daimyo's storehouse. Thus it was possible to concentrate the majority of the feudal class in castle-towns and to keep close control over the minority which still lived in the country. There was not much chance for an independent, self-sufficient squirearchy to develop under this system. And just as the daimyo broke the ties between his vassals and the land, so the shogun weakened the ties between the daimyo and his province. If the daimyo had to spend half of his time and much of his income in Edo, he was scarcely a territorial lord.

Finally, the concept and nature of authority in Japan differed tremendously from the European pattern. In Europe, the symbol of authority was the right to hold a court. The growing power of kings and princes in the later Middle Ages could be measured by the degree to which their courts extended their jurisdiction. The feudal hierarchy was broken down through legal procedures; when the king's courts could protect minor vassals, the immediate superiors of minor vassals lost much of their authority. The first attempts to define sovereignty were bound to the idea of law: he is sovereign who can render final decisions without appeal in all law suits, or make law for the common welfare. It is true that there was an argument as to whether kings were bound by law, but it was a sign of true kingship to respect the law, whether it was binding or not. And, as a practical matter, it caused a considerable amount of inconvenience for kings when they did not respect the law, especially the law which protected the rights and possessions of the feudal class. The legal systems which had been built up in the thirteenth and fourteenth centuries were sufficiently complicated so that a man with wealth and status could be very annoying if he decided to defend his rights. A number of royal officials would have to conduct investigations, find witnesses, prepare briefs, argue about the meaning of documents, and hear appeals from preliminary decisions. It was not difficult for a determined man to keep a case going for ten or twenty years. As a last resort, European opinion condoned rebellion if the rebel could find any sort of legal justification for his act. Of course, the king could usually win the law suit or suppress the rebellion if he made a determined effort, but he had neither the time, the resources, nor the trained personnel required to carry every case to a successful conclusion. Open or tacit compromise was often the only prudent solution. In short, the states of late medieval and early modern Europe were, to use the German phrase, law-states. Authority was based on law.

The contrast with Japan is obvious. Authority in Japan was based on a social pattern which was, in many ways, simply an extension of the family pattern. The authority of a father is not based on law; it grows out of his status as a father and the beliefs which his society holds about the rights and duties of a father. The Confucian theories, which dominated Japanese thinking about social relationships during the Tokugawa period, stressed the responsibility of the father for the family welfare, his complete authority to do anything necessary to provide for that welfare, and the duty of the family to give him unquestioned obedience. These theories also controlled the feudal relationship. There had been some familial elements in very early European feudalism: a Merovingian king could speak of his retainers as his *"pueri"*—his "boys." But this practice was quickly abandoned; a twelfth-century vassal, no matter how lowly, would have felt deeply insulted if he had been called the "child" of his lord. In Japan, on the other hand, the filial relationship was the most highly honored of all. To be the "child," or an adopted member of the family of the lord, was highly desirable, even for great men.

If the feudal relationship in Japan is thought of in terms of the family rather than in terms of legal obligations and privileges, then many of its unusual characteristics can be more easily understood. The feudal family lives together in a castle or a castle town. The head of the family is bound to provide for his children, but he may do it in any way that seems good to him. He does not, for example, have to give them shares of his landed property. He may reward or punish his children as he pleases. A member of the family who objects to such acts is guilty of disrespect and impiety; he is subverting the social order. Nothing in the religion, the mores, the political theories, or the habits of thought of the people justifies resistance. The problem of authority is reduced to its simplest terms: does the daimyo or the shogun have the physical power to enforce his orders?

8

Introduction

There were, in short, very real differences between late European feudalism and Tokugawa feudalism, differences in external circumstances, internal organization, and underlying concepts of society. These differences are great enough to explain why Tokugawa feudalism lasted so long, and why, even when it began to weaken, Japan preserved an unbroken façade of feudal institutions clear into the nineteenth century. From the thirteenth century on, western Europe had—and openly admitted that it had—a mixed political system. Non-feudal institutions appeared, acquired legal status, and took over increasingly wide areas of responsibility. Feudal institutions gradually became less useful and less used, but they did not vanish completely. It is impossible to say when European feudalism ended; one could make a good argument for any century between 1300 and 1900. In Japan, apparently, there was nothing but feudalism until the Restoration and no feudalism at all after the Restoration. There was no attempt to push centralization beyond the stage reached under the early Tokugawa; no attempt to create parallel institutions which would penetrate and weaken the han. The daimyo, an autonomous but obedient prince, governed his province through his vassals, just as he had always done.

This is, of course, a very misleading generalization. As my colleagues point out in later sections of this book, it is difficult to believe that the old feudal relationships were the essential element of government in the last century of the Tokugawa period. The bureaucratic tendencies which were strong even in sixteenth-century feudalism had developed to a point where they made the official feudal hierarchy almost meaningless. Japan was actually governed by a class, or classes, of hereditary bureaucrats—a system not entirely unlike that which prevailed in the West at about the same time. Merchants and financiers had great, if unacknowledged, influence—again, not completely unlike the situation in some western countries in the eighteenth century. There was even, at the end, a sort of Enlightenment, which generated as much heat, if not as much light, as that of the West.

What is surprising is not that Japanese feudalism was changing into another type of government, but that it was possible to conceal the changes behind an apparently unchanging façade. Here again, the peculiar nature of Japanese feudalism made it easier to absorb and camouflage change than had been the case in the West. As we have already seen, Japanese feudalism required a degree of management and record-keeping which made bureaucratic growth seem natural. The samurai, divorced from the land, needing employment, furnished more than enough candidates for bureaucratic positions. There was no need, as there had been in the West, to recruit bureaucrats from business and professional groups. Japan was still governed by the feudal class, even if it was using non-feudal methods. The custom of assigning feudal revenues in rice, obligatory residence in Edo, and the heavy debts incurred by some daimyos had made merchants a necessary part of the politico-economic system from an early period. There had been an emphasis on education—even if unenlightened—as soon as retainers became an administrative rather than a fighting

9

class. Finally, the habit of deference to and respect for superiors reduced the impact of change. The daimyo might not actually govern, but the men who did govern did not try to displace him or undercut his prestige. The samurai might be bureaucrats rather than warriors, but they kept their status as feudal vassals. They could believe, with some justification, that they were obeyed as nobles rather than as officials. Altogether, a significant part of the transition to modern forms of government could take place within the framework of Japanese feudalism.

The final problem is the one which was once posed by Professor Reischauer. Does the long Japanese experience of feudalism explain the ease with which Japan made the transition from an oriental to a westernized society? It is certainly true that Japan modernized its government, its economy, and its educational system more rapidly and more successfully than any other non-European country. It is also true that Japan was the only non-European country in which feudalism had played as important a role as it had in the West. One could even go further, and say that in the West it was precisely the most feudalized areas—England, northern France, and the Low Countries—which took the lead in developing the modern state, modern science and technology, and modern methods of exchange and production. It looks as if a good case could be made for a connection between feudalism and receptivity to the ideas and institutions which are dominant in the world today.

On further examination, however, the connection seems tenuous. In the first place, the West created its new ideas and institutions largely out of its own resources. This was especially true in the field of government, where the sovereign state of the early modern period grew out of feudal courts and councils, not out of limitations of Byzantine or Moslem regimes. There were some attempts to imitate the Roman Empire (which was one of the sources of the western tradition), but these attempts were superficial and unimportant. For all practical purposes, the western European countries had no model to imitate; they had to create their own. Japan, on the other hand, had the European model and felt that it had to imitate that model in order to survive. Thus the question is not whether feudalism can inspire the development of new institutions (as it certainly did in England and France), but whether the fact that Japan had a feudal tradition made it easy for Japan to imitate institutions originally developed in western countries which also had a feudal tradition.

It is not difficult to find elements in Japanese feudalism which could be adapted to the needs of a modern state. The responsibility of the military class for government had created a large group of men who were technically vassals but actually bureaucrats. In fact, the transition from rear-vassal to bureaucrat went further in Japan and produced a larger number of potential public officials than it ever did in the West. These men had had at least as much formal education as their western counterparts; many of them had also had practical administrative experience. The lord-vassal relationship, even if it had become somewhat formalized, had created habits of loyalty and obedience to the superior—habits which were probably stronger in Japan than in the West. The feu-

Introduction

dal hierarchy had been consolidated so that there was an unbroken chain of command running from the shogun through the daimyo to the village administrators. Men who had wealth and power also had responsibility, even if the responsibility was sometimes more apparent than real. But Japanese feudalism at least discouraged the growth of a class of wealthy men who simply enjoyed their wealth without performing public duties. In short, Japanese feudalism had produced both a centralized government (even if centralization was incomplete) and a bureaucracy. All that was needed was to put them to work on new tasks.

The only trouble with this analysis is that many of the same things could have been said about China, a non-feudal state. China had a large and literate bureaucracy, a tradition of public service, and a highly centralized government. Perhaps there were more bureaucrats or potential bureaucrats per square mile in Japan than in China, but mere numbers do not explain Japan's success in transforming its government—in fact the large number of samurai was an embarrassment, not an asset. Chinese bureaucrats were probably somewhat more corrupt and somewhat less responsive to orders from the center than Japanese bureaucrats, but they were not hopelessly out of control. In fact, during their rise to greatness, most western European countries had more trouble with corruption and disobedience in their bureaucracies than did China. It could be argued that if China had made the same determined effort to modernize its government that Japan did, the Chinese political structure could have stood the strain.

Moreover, the underlying political theory of both countries (as far as one can speak of political theory at all in the Far East) was based on Confucian ethics. Confucianism had begun during a semi-feudal period in Chinese history; perhaps for this reason it proved equally satisfactory as a code for justifying a feudally organized government in Japan and a non-feudal government in China. The loyalties which held Japanese society together under the Tokugawa were not very different from the loyalties which held Chinese society together under the Ch'ing dynasty: filial respect for the head of the family, the local authorities, and the supreme authority at the center. Japanese loyalties in the eighteenth century rested on a broader base than pure feudalism—which was just as well, since both early Japanese and early European experience had shown that feudal loyalty by itself was a chancy thing. One can scarcely speak of feudal loyalty when the great majority of vassals had no personal contact with their lord. The daimyo was a symbol of authority, and loyalty went to the symbol rather than the man. As far as there was any element of feudalism left in Japanese thinking this should have made it more difficult for them than for the Chinese to think in terms of loyalty to an abstract ideal such as the state. In actual fact, there seems to have been little difference; both peoples needed a symbol—the emperor—to serve as a focus of loyalty during the nineteenth century.

Perhaps the defects of Japanese feudalism were more important than its merits as forces favoring change. The extreme rigidity of the Japanese feudal system and the degree to which it preserved its hierarchical structure long after this structure was necessary are almost unprecedented. This is not to say that there was no social mobility in Tokugawa Japan, but there certainly was not a career open to the talented, even to members of the feudal class. The Chinese examination system, with all its faults, at least held out the hope of a series of promotions to ambitious men. In Japan many samurai had no meaningful duties, and their situation was aggravated by demands that they relinquish some of their income. Even a samurai of the upper level could not be sure that he would ever get an administrative post, and once he had it, he might be stuck with it for life. For educated, relatively prosperous men who were not members of the feudal class, the prospects were even grimmer. In feudal Europe and non-feudal China merchants were integrated into the ruling group; they had status and privileges. In Japan they remained on the outer fringes of society. Thus it is likely that in Japan there was a larger group of talented but thwarted men than in China—men who felt that they could not make a place for themselves in the existing society and who therefore welcomed radical changes. But this is only a relative difference; there were malcontents in China too; and, while they may have been relatively less numerous, they were not an insignificant group. Moreover, the great change in Japan was not entirely or even primarily the work of men with thwarted aspirations; it was welcomed by men who had a secure position in the pre-Restoration political structure.

Another, and perhaps more significant weakness in late Tokugawa feudalism, was the fact that the central government had not developed institutions commensurate with the authority which it claimed. When the shogunate was strong, the autonomy of the han seemed illusory. Nevertheless, there was autonomy, in the sense that the Bakufu did not govern the han directly and that there were differences in the efficiency of provincial administration. Some han made better use of their economic resources, or were more successful in avoiding ruinous debts than others. When the shogunate weakened, the differences among the han were accentuated. There was a certain amount of competition, and competition could lead to experiments with new ideas and techniques. It was a han government, and not the Bakufu, which first bought significant amounts of foreign weapons. Here Japan had a clear advantage over China: it was easier to modernize (if only incompletely) the army of a province than the army of an empire.

This leads us to the final weakness of Tokugawa feudalism, its failure to improve its military techniques. This is a common failing in feudal societies; western knights also disliked the new weapons and new tactics which made their specialized training obsolete. But, as we have seen, the West had a mixed political system from the thirteenth century on, and this mixture was reflected in military organization by the growing use of mercenaries to replace feudal levies. Mercenaries, on the whole, welcomed new weapons and new tactics which increased their market value. In Japan mercenaries were unimportant; the army raised by the Bakufu in its last struggle was a feudal army, fighting

Introduction

with the weapons and tactics of the seventeenth century. On the other hand, the feudal tradition did emphasize military strength, and there were probably more members of the ruling class in Japan than in China who felt the need to modernize their armies.

Although the Tokugawa period was actually a rather peaceful age, the emphasis on military virtues was never forgotten. The descendants of the old feudal class still liked to think of themselves as warriors, even if they did little fighting. Tradition recorded that drastic steps had been taken in the past to ensure, by military action, the unity and security of Japan. Thus when Japan's security seemed threatened in the nineteenth century there were precedents for taking drastic steps. It is true—though hardly a matter for rejoicing—that modernization or westernization has often meant primarily the acquisition of modern weapons, and that military or militaristic governments have naturally been quick to see the advantages of this type of innovation. But modern weapons cannot be used effectively or sustained indefinitely without modernizing the administration, the economy, and the educational system—something which not all militarily-minded governments have had the wit to see. Moreover, the priority of modernizing the armed forces is not absolute; some countries have been more interested in the prospect of solving economic problems. In any case, modernization—military or economic—requires a readiness to modify many aspects of the social structure, and a feudal tradition does not necessarily create such a state of mind. The desire to strengthen the armed forces was a powerful influence for change in Japan, but it had to be supported by a general receptivity to a host of other new ideas.

This receptivity may be explained, in part, by a Japanese tradition older than the feudal tradition, the tradition of borrowing from the West—not the far West of Europe, but the near West of China. Like all borrowers, the Japanese had ambivalent feelings about their dependence on outsiders; some of them sought to minimize Chinese influence while others came rather close to the slogan of "equalling and surpassing the [Chinese] West." But the fact of borrowing could not be denied; it was apparent in every aspect of Japanese life. Nor could it be said that the borrowing had been harmful: Japanese culture had been enriched but traditional Japanese virtues had been preserved. If Japan had gained by adopting and adapting certain elements of Chinese civilization, it was at least possible that Japan could gain by imitating Europe.

China, on the contrary, had been much less affected by outside influences. The one clear case was Buddhism, and that was ancient history, and in many ways unhappy history. The Chinese believed, on the whole rightly, that they had created their own civilization without assistance from any other people. Their civilization was the only real civilization; it had absorbed the barbarians who entered China and it had spread to the barbarians who were neighbors of China. Traditionally other people imitated the Chinese; the Chinese did not borrow from other people.

This psychological block was much weaker in Japan. It did exist, however, and certainly there were elements of social autarchy in the Japanese feudal tradition. Feudalism was what distinguished Japan from its neighbors; feudalism best expressed the values which were peculiar to Japan. On the other hand, members of the feudal classes were among the first to realize the need for modernization; the feudal group as a whole was not unalterably opposed to change. Feudalism had created some of the institutions and some of the ideals which speeded Japan's transition to a modern state. But a factor of at least equal weight was Japan's ancient experience of borrowing from the dominant civilization in its world.

CHAPTER TWO

FEUDALISM IN JAPAN—A REASSESSMENT

JOHN WHITNEY HALL

Reprinted from *Comparative Studies in Society and History*, Vol. V. No. 1 (October 1962)

The question of whether Japan can rightly be said to "have had feudalism" is by no means settled. Although Westerners have been writing about "Japanese feudalism" for well over a hundred years, the acceptability of this practice is still a matter of controversy among professional historians, notably among those who make the study of medieval Europe their specialty. To a long line of Western historians ending with Herbert Norman, however, there was no question about the appropriateness of placing the feudal label on Japan. Nor does the contemporary Japanese historian question a term which has become so important a part of his professional as well as everyday vocabulary. In a Japan in which the reading public is daily reminded that the "struggle against feudalism" is still being waged, feudalism seems a present reality which by its very nature cannot be denied to have existed in Japan's past.

To the Japanese historian of today feudalism in Japan is not only real, it is also the same universal reality against which the "more progressive" Western peoples had to struggle before their eventual emancipation. As Nagahara Keiji has put it,

It is now generally accepted that capitalism in Japan developed upon a foundation laid in the semi-feudal land ownership pattern of the villages. The power of the feudalistic landlords and the bourgeoisie, though on the surface full of mutual contradictions, served fundamentally to reinforce each other, leading inevitably to the military defeat of August 15th. Although it appeared at first that the land reform had decisively revolutionized the self-reinforcement of these two groups, dissolving large-scale landlordism and high rent tenancy and thereby destroying the feudal relationships within the village, actually it did not produce any such fundamental change. To the contrary, recent studies have shown that it resulted in a re-strengthening of feudal relationships under colonial control.[1]

American historians who reject this view are apt to be reminded by their Japanese colleagues that they have been spared the onus of living under feudalism and hence cannot appreciate its reality. Certainly the American scholar does not commute through a countryside which to him constitutes a living reminder of "the feudalism of the village". But while we cannot deny the Japanese his emotions of social protest, we can question whether the

[1] Nagahara Keiji, *Nihon hōkenshakai ron* (Tokyo, 1955), 8.

object of his attack is the same feudal system against which our European forefathers railed. This surely is a problem which can be studied objectively.

The question of whether the idea of feudalism can be applied to Japan (or any other society outside Western Europe) has exercised the minds of scholars since the time of Voltaire and Montesquieu. The endless conflict between what we might term the "broad" and "narrow" approaches to this problem has led down to the present generation in which we find a Marc Bloch suggesting the existence of "feudalism as a type of society" or a Bryce Lyon insisting that Western European feudalism is "unique".[2] In the light of this controversy the general historian who has no special stake in the problem is apt to assume a double standard, accepting as popular but misguided the usage that generalizes the term beyond the confines of Europe, and retaining for his own professional purposes a usage which limits the term to Western European societies. Pressed on the issue he is apt to reply, "I have no objection to anyone calling Japan feudal so long as *that* feudalism is not confused with the real thing." But for two types of historians, the question of whether feudalism as a general concept is appropriately applied to Japan cannot be so easily circumvented. One is the student of Japanese history, be he Japanese or Western, who must eventually commit himself to whether he will use or reject the concept in his writings. The other is the comparative historian, whose subject matter is the very stuff of which the feudalism controversy is made.

In the final analysis the question of whether the concept of feudalism can be applied to Japan raises two basic historiographical issues: first the idea of feudalism itself and its appropriateness as a general category of social organization, and second the methodology of comparative history and its validity as a branch of historical study. The case of Japan, it should be noted, is critical to both of these issues. For it is in part the discovery of similarities between certain Japanese institutions and those of Medieval Europe which has given courage to some historians to formulate the idea of feudalism as a general concept and has helped support the comparative historian's view in the utility of his approach. The importance of the Japanese experience to the comparative historian is apparent in such a recent work as *Feudalism in History,* in which Japan is cited along with Europe as exhibiting one of "only two fully-proven cases of feudalism", or indeed, "the classic case of feudalism".[3]

How has it come about that Japan has bulked so large in the feudalism controversy, and furthermore that the practice of calling Japan feudal has

---

[2] Marc Bloch, *Feudal Society* (Chicago, 1961), 441ff.; Bryce Lyon, *The Middle Ages in Recent Historical Thought* (Washington, Service Center for Teachers of History, 1959), 13.

[3] Rushton Coulborn, *Feudalism in History* (Princeton, 1956), 185; 199.

been so widely accepted? One answer is provided by the nature of Japanese history itself which has yielded so many startling comparisons with the feudal institutions of Europe. But another, and deeper one perhaps, lies in the way in which Japanese and Western historians have tended to reinforce each other in their thinking on this question. During the eighteenth century the societies of Japan and Europe both arrived at the discovery of their "feudal past" along independent, but parallel paths. Marc Bloch has found the earliest example of the use of the term *féodalité* as a reference to a state of society to go back no farther than 1727.[4] Certainly the earliest Western writers on Japan, those who wrote before the concept of feudalism had taken shape in Europe, did not describe Japan as feudal. This applied to Kaempfer, Thunberg, and Titsingh, who wrote as late as the 1790's. Western writers were not to take up the practice of calling Japan feudal until the nineteenth century; significantly, not until the Japanese themselves had begun to show an awareness of the distinctiveness of the particular form of society which they were beginning to put behind them.

Japanese historians had long recognized the ascendancy of the military aristocracy as a pivotal event in their national history. Historians of the seventeenth century commonly referred to the epoch of Japanese history from the middle of the twelfth century down to their own time as the age of military houses (*buke-jidai*). During the eighteenth century, Japanese scholars began to apply to this period the word *hōken,* a term of Chinese origin referring to the decentralized form of government which characterized the Chou dynasty. By 1827, when Rai Sanyō completed his *Nihon gaishi* (Unofficial history of Japan), the term had gained general currency.[5]

It is not precisely certain when western observers first described Japan as feudal. Von Siebold writing shortly before 1841 may well have been the first when he wrote:

Japan is a feudal empire in the strictest sense of the term. The *mikado,* as being the successor and representative of the gods, is the nominal proprietor, as well as sovereign, of the realm, and the *ziogoon* is his deputy or viceregent. His domains, with the exception of the portion reserved to the Crown, are divided into principalities, held in vassalage by their respective hereditary princes. Under them the land is parcelled out among the nobility who hold their hereditary estates by military service.[6]

To other nineteenth century observers who followed von Siebold, it was with a real sense of excitement that they reported experiencing in Japan a condition of society so similar to the feudalism of their own remembrance. To Alcock in 1863 Japan presented "a living embodiment of a state of society which

---

[4] Bloch, *Feudal Society,* xvii.
[5] Kimura Motoi, *Nihon hōkenshakai kenkyū shi* (Tokyo, 1956), 4.
[6] Contained in M. M. Busk, ed., *Manners and Customs of the Japanese in the 19th Century* (New York, 1841), 142.

existed many centuries ago in the West; ... an Oriental phase of feudalism, such as our ancestors knew it in the time of the Plantagenets".[7] To William Griffis writing in 1870 the fit was even more striking:

Here were real gentlemen, who had served as pages in feudal mansions, had given the tokens of vassalage and had received their lord's beneficium. Their stories of the ceremonial gift of a flower, the presentation of an arrow, or some other emblem of feudal service—contemptible in market value, but priceless from the viewpoint of loyalty—touched the imagination. Men from the ends of the earth, who had heard of Europe only from books, told me of things which matched anything read about in the varied feudalisms of France, Germany, or England.[8]

By the 1880's knowledge of Japanese institutions was sufficiently widespread in Europe that Karl Marx could make his famous statement in *Capital:* "Japan, with its purely feudal organization of landed property and its developed *petite culture,* gives a much truer picture of the European middle ages than our own history books, dictated as these are, for the most part, by bourgeois prejudices."[9]

In a reverse manner, once Japan was exposed to knowledge of European feudal institutions it did not take long for Japanese historians to transfer the term *hōken* out of its previous context and to adopt it as a translation for the European concept of feudalism. The origin of this practice goes back at least to 1888 in the writings of Yokoi Tokifuyu. Japanese historians have continued this practice to the present, following two major lines of interpretation. The first group of Japanese scholars to use the word consciously according to a specified definition were the "legal historians" such as Miura Kaneyuki and Nakada Kaoru. These men, who published during the early 1900's, equated the Japanese *hōken* system with the feudalism of such Western legal historians as Maitland. They were followed after the early 1920's by writers, beginning with Hani Gorō and Hayakawa Jirō, who adopted the Marxist definition of feudalism.[10]

Characteristic of the Japanese use of the concept of feudalism has been a rather simplistic theoretical assumption of its universal applicability to all societies. Maki Kenji, dean of the legal historians today, expresses this straightforward approach in the preface to his *Nihon hōkenseido seiritsu shi* (History of the establishment of the feudal system in Japan):

In surveying the history of the rise of the civilized countries of the world today we can say that all have demonstrated a common three-stage development from a tribal antiquity through a feudal middle age to a bourgeois modern age. Japanese history has followed this same process ... It is useful to study the feudal system of Japan as a historic fact, and further to make comparisons with ancient China

---

[7] Sir Rutherford Alcock, *The Capital of the Tycoon* (London, 1863), 109.
[8] William Eliot Griffis, untitled manuscript, Rutgers University Library.
[9] Karl Marx, *Capital* (Chicago, 1912), 789.
[10] Kimura Motoi, *Nihon hōkenshakai,* 5.

and medieval Europe as a means of clarifying important aspects of Japanese history by pointing up common features and special characteristics.[11]

Marxist historians in Japan also have assumed without significant change the applicability to Japanese society of the general theory of feudalism set forth by Marx in his *Capital* or by Lenin in his *Development of Capitalism in Russia*.[12]

Outside Marxist circles, it was Kan'ichi Asakawa who gave academic respectability to the use of the idea of Japanese feudalism in the West. Asakawa, by his remarkable control of the primary data of both European and Japanese institutions, was able to develop a coherent and systematic methodology for the comparative treatment of feudalism in Europe and Japan. His essay "Some Aspects of Japanese Feudal Institutions" has long remained the standard interpretation of the subject.[13] Only in recent years has the French scholar Joüon des Longrais supplemented Asakawa's work, largely on the basis of Japanese scholarship of the legal school.[14]

In reviewing the literature on "Japanese feudalism", both in Japanese and Western languages, one is struck by large areas of disagreement over precise terms of definition and by a general lack of theoretical sophistication. Even among professional historians there has been too easy an assumption of comparability between Japan and Europe or too ready an acceptance of certain developmental schemes of history in which feudalism is considered a "stage". Among non-specialists the term is used quite loosely. Once the similarity between certain conditions in Japan and those of medieval Europe was pointed out, it became common for both Western and Japanese writers to refer to Japanese institutions quite indiscriminately as feudal, with little concern over the theoretical problems engendered by such a usage. The term has entered popular literature where it is applied to any of a wide variety of traits which seem to have counterparts in medieval Europe. In Japan today, feudalism has taken on a popular pejorative meaning which is applied to almost any aspect of contemporary life which seems old-fashioned or touched with the older social or family ethic—a term with which children criticize their parents, or socialists label their conservative opponents.

Such widespread abuses have naturally prejudiced serious scholars against the possibility of extending the idea of feudalism outside its European context. But the question of whether feudalism can be conceived of as a general category of social organization or must be considered an event unique to European history surely need not be avoided because of such abuses, however much they may exasperate the historian. The systematic comparative historian

---

[11] Maki Kenji, *Nihon hōkenseido seiritsu shi* (Tokyo, 1935), 1-2.
[12] V. I. Lenin, *The Development of Capitalism in Russia* (Moscow, 1956), 190-192.
[13] K. Asakawa, "Some Aspects of Japanese Feudal Institutions", *TASJ*, XLVI, Part 1 (1918), 77-102.
[14] Joüon des Longrais, *L'Est et L'Ouest* (Tokyo, Paris, 1958).

is not obliged to assume responsibility for these abuses, but rather must seek to devise an orderly treatment of the problem, so that it can be studied for what it is, a problem in comparative historical theory.

A systematic approach to the question of whether "Japan had feudalism or not" should begin with a clear understanding of what is being asked. The question which the comparative historian asks is not whether it is possible to identify in Japan a pattern of history identical with that of Western Europe. He is not seeking to find "European feudalism" in Japan. Nor is he trying to hitch Japanese history onto an assembly line of universal historical development in which feudalism is a fixed stage. His objective is both more modest and more ambitious. He is concerned, rather, with this question, "Has Japanese society at any time in its history exemplified a pattern of social organization which, along with that of Europe, may properly be labeled feudal?" This is a question which need not concern all historians, and its solution need not disturb those who are not intrigued by the question itself. It is a question asked by the historian who wishes to engage explicitly in the kind of theorizing and categorizing which arises from the analysis of broad segments of human development which may embrace more than one culture.

In the strictest sense, of course, the historian can never isolate himself from the comparative implications of his work. For to greater or lesser extent the historian, by his use of concepts of varying degrees of abstractness, is constantly involved in the process of comparison between the actual data as he finds them and the generalized vocabulary with which he must conceptualize them. But this hidden comparative element in historical judgment is seldom explicitly recognized. The historical profession in practice demands a choice between the commonly practiced work in which comparison is implicit, limited and short range, and the more overt, explicit, and generalized form of it. Comparison of the explicit type is usually regarded as a separate branch of historical activity dealing most often with more than one culture. Its objectives and conclusions are considered different from those historical endeavors which confine themselves to a single cultural tradition. The problem of "feudalism in Japan" is clearly one which lies within the field of comparative history.

What makes the concept of feudalism particularly difficult to handle for the comparative historian is, of course, the complexity of the phenomena about which it tries to generalize. The historian's vocabulary is full of terms which have cross-cultural relevancy and are used without exciting controversy. No voices are raised against the practice of calling the Japanese *tennō* an emperor or the Japanese *mura* a village. But it is equally evident that these terms do not carry the same causative significance for the historian; they do not "seek to explain" as much of a whole society or epoch as does the concept of feudalism. Here presumably feudalism enters the company of general ideas such as nationalism, absolutism, or imperialism, but with the

Feudalism in Japan—A Reassessment

disadvantage that no Norman landing touched Japanese shores and no crusading knights crossed swords with the men of Kamakura. If we conclude that Japan was feudal we must do so with the full realization that Japan *became feudal independently of Europe.* This is the kind of thought that seems either to excite or revolt the historian, depending upon his predilection to seek out patterns of social development or to hold to the uniqueness of individual events.

The large organizing concepts of the genre of feudalism as used by the comparative historian arise out of his conviction that, while the events of history may appear to be infinite and infinitely varied, the general patterns of organization and structure of human society, in other words, the ways in which mankind meets its problems of living, are not infinite. The historian naturally does not find human society neatly ordered in classifiable genuses, but neither did the botanist or biologist at the outset of his inquiry into the nature of his data. While pattern and structure are more apt to project themselves out of diverse social data than absolute individuality or uniqueness, the complexity of the patterns which interest the historian are such that the categories of classification are not readily apparent in the data. Thus, if pattern is to be found, it must await the generalizing capacities of the human observer. It is only as theory and concept are worked against historical data that pattern is identified and definition refined. The questions the comparative historian asks are whether feudalism may be adopted as a term of reference for one pattern of social configuration, and whether such a pattern is relevant to more than one unique historical situation.

As a category of human organization, feudalism should be definable as an ideal type. The kind of definition needed is a statement of certain sets of relationships within a social framework which distinguishes the feudal type of society from other types. In setting up such a definition the responsibility for what is included or excluded admittedly rests with the historian, but this does not depend by any means solely on the historian's whim or imagination. It should derive from the historian's systematic application of hypothesis to empirical data.

Too much argument over the definition of feudalism, and especially over the question of whether Japan "fits the feudal pattern", has lacked the benefit of methodological uniformity. Different historians have used different conceptions of feudalism, or often the same historian has varied his definition to suit different arguments. Broadly speaking historians have tended to fall into two particular habits of conceptualization which, from the comparative point of view, have interfered with the cumulative refinement of the idea of feudalism. The first of these results from the use of what we might call the overly particularistic definition, one phrased almost exclusively in terms of some specific set of "feudal conditions" found within some particular area of Western Europe. Now it goes without saying that a definition which constitutes little more than full description of one or another of the Western European societies during the ninth century through the thirteenth can be of very little use for comparative purposes. Such a definition lays itself open to revision by each new particularistic study. Each new community which is studied adds a cluster of new qualifications to the original definition or casts doubt upon the definition itself. A logical extension of this approach makes it difficult to agree upon any single definition of feudalism for the various regions of Western Europe alone.

Those who take the particularistic approach to feudalism thus find it all the more difficult to accept a general definition which might be extended beyond Europe. Having demonstrated that Japanese institutions were not exactly like those of Europe, they either resist the use of feudalism for Japan or suggest that Japan gave rise to a "different kind of feudalism", something which should be called "Japanese feudalism". As one recent writer has put it, feudalism "was a system peculiar to Western Europe and was not found elsewhere except in a few regions of the Mediterranean and in the Middle East, where it was introduced for a time by the crusaders. This does not mean that there were not other feudal systems in other areas of the world, but that Western feudalism was quite different from Byzantine, Moslem, Japanese, and Chinese feudalism. These feudal systems existed during different periods of world history, were organized on different principles, and were developed to meet demands peculiar to the regions in which they arose." [15]

This statement exposes the dilemma inherent in a definition which limits feudalism to Western Europe. For if feudalism is unique to Western Europe, how then can one speak of other feudalisms? And if other feudalisms are recognized, then what features of these other societies make it possible to consider them feudal? Is it semantically any different to speak of "Japanese feudalism" or "feudalism in Japan?" In other words either feudalism must be considered truly unique or it must be treated as a generalized phenomenon.

But the issues raised by the particularistic definers are nonetheless of crucial theoretical importance to a consideration of feudalism as a general concept. Their particular concern is with what we might call the vertical limits (or limits of generality) of definition. Any society or social institution may be described in various degrees of complexity and specificity. For comparative purposes it is most useful to conceive of a general type so as to cover more than an extremely narrow range of subject matter. The historian may choose his level of generality. But once his definition is arrived at, it can be used only at the level of abstraction for which it is designed. Too often the argument as to whether Japan "fits" the feudal pattern is decided by changing the definition as the argument proceeds. A generalized definition at the outset is made more and more specific until the historian, consciously or uncon-

[15] Bryce Lyon, *The Middle Ages*, 13.

sciously, is using a definition which is little more than a complete description of medieval France or England. The argument often goes as follows. Granted that Japanese society developed certain gross similarities to European society during the feudal age, this is not enough. For once one penetrates below surface likenesses, all sorts of differences can be pointed out. Hence Japanese feudalism cannot be likened to European feudalism. The argument is clinched by some such statement as "The Japanese oath of vassalage did not involve the same contractual relations as in Europe." But to argue in this way is to make comparative history impossible. For if at every point of apparent comparability one is to drop down into a lower level of specificity to look for differences, one can never get beyond a fascination with differences alone.

The fact that if a general concept is to be useful, the limits of generality at which the concept is defined must be agreed upon by the historian is often taken as a demonstration of the arbitrary nature of the concept. Under such circumstances, it is argued, is not one definition as good as another? Is not the comparative historian deciding in advance which societies he wishes to include under his type and then drawing a definition around them? Let us remember that the categorization of societies into general types is not easily done and requires the empirical working of hypothetical definitions back and forth against the data provided by many societies, as well as against definitions of other social types. The utility of a general definition of a social type is that it unites into a single integrated concept a number of separable elements of society. A general concept of feudalism makes it possible to draw together, around certain basic similarities, a number of societies which may differ in many other details. In other words, it makes it possible on a hypothetical basis to hold constant certain variables while studying others. Essentially, then, the criterion for setting the vertical limits of a general definition will depend upon the variables which the historian wishes to "hold constant".

The second unsatisfactory approach to the problem of definition results from what might be called a linear or developmental conception of feudalism. This method has looked upon feudalism as a stage in a process of political or social development which begins with certain specific preconditions and terminates in certain other specifically defined postconditions. A definition of this type contains, either implicitly or explicitly, a commitment to the kind of society which produces feudalism and the kind which results after it disappears. Societies are included or excluded from the feudal category on the basis of such prior or postconditions or on whether the pattern of internal development conforms to a norm. More specifically, a society is excluded from consideration if its process of entrance into or exit from the feudal state does not coincide with the European pattern.

The evolutionary view of feudalism like the particularistic one lays itself open to attack from individual histories of varying societies which may not coincide with what has been assumed to be the typical process. The attempt to find "uniformities in history" which motivated the Conference on Feudalism and resulted in the volume *Feudalism in History* illustrates many of the difficulties which beset the effort to base uniformity on parallelisms of specific chains of historical events. For while it is unquestionably true that certain types of society under certain conditions are more apt to contain the seeds of feudalism, these do not constitute the only conditions from which feudalism might emerge. While it is informative to inquire whether or not the "feudal periods" of China and Japan were preceded by the decay of a previous empire, this exercise does not constitute part of the necessary "proof" for the existence or nonexistence of feudalism in these countries. One need not strain to stretch out the "ghost" of the Han Empire of China as a prelude to Japanese feudalism, as Coulborn does in *Feudalism in History*.[16] Rather it was the particular administrative and legal conditions which existed in Japan in the twelfth century which provide the scaffolding upon which feudal institutions rose.

Nonetheless, certain questions raised by the advocates of the developmental approach to feudalism can help to clarify another important dimension of the conceptual problem inherent in general concepts. What the developmental approach does, essentially, is to ask questions about the boundaries of feudalism on a horizontal level. If feudalism is to be defined by a certain set of political and social variables, we must determine some manner of distinguishing the limits of these variables. And this can be done only as historians differentiate other patterns of government or society which appear to be distinct from feudalism. In other words it is difficult to conceive of feudalism without having come to grips more precisely with the concepts of what is not feudal. Without other possible categories of social organization in mind, we have little with which to determine the external boundaries of our conception of what is feudal, and we have little notion of how to describe the preconditions which give rise to feudalism. One of the reasons for the difficulty which historians have had with this and other terms of social generalization is the lack of a systematic nomenclature in contiguous areas. Yet this paucity of terminology is not a proof of the inappropriateness of the attempt to develop general concepts. It is only after extended periods of trial and error analysis that historians or sociologists can come to some sort of agreement on what are the most meaningful categories in which to differentiate the varied moments of social history and where best to place the boundaries between these types.

The historian today does not lack for existing efforts at defining feudalism. By now enough hands have been at work upon the problem of feudalism so that the "feudal condition" has been sufficiently isolated for definitional purposes. Yet there has been little agreement among historians, even among

---

[16] Rushton Coulborn, *Feudalism*, 246-247.

those working exclusively within the field of European history, on a common set of criteria. Instead there has been a rather persistent dispute between two varieties of definition: one "narrow" in that it limits its scope to the political or legal sphere, the other "broad" in that it takes in a wider consideration of the whole society. It is unfortunate that arguments over the appropriateness of these two types of definition have bulked so large in the treatment of feudalism, for in the final analysis there is no unresolvable difference between them. The two types in actuality describe two different sets of criteria, which themselves are not contradictory. Very often, in fact, the proponents of the narrow definition must rely on the broader concept of feudal society in the course of their writing.

A characteristic definition of feudalism from the narrow point of view is presented by Coulborn and Strayer in *Feudalism in History*. Their so-called "provisional description" of feudalism begins as follows: "Feudalism is primarily a method of government, not an economic or a social system, though it obviously modified and is modified by the social and economic environment. It is a method of government in which the essential relation is not that between ruler and subject, nor state and citizen, but between lord and vassal." [17] But the authors do not stop at this limited statement. Instead they continue to amplify their description until they have carried it into the social and economic fields. First they add to the core concept the criterion that "political authority is treated as a private possession", then further that "since political power is personal, rather than institutional, there is relatively little separation of functions; the military leader is usually an administrator and the administrator is usually a judge". From here they enter the social area by adding that while "the men who discharge political functions in a feudal society are not necessarily aristocrats when they first begin to gain power, ... they soon are recognized as an aristocracy," and this makes for "a strong, almost irresistible tendency towards heredity of function." The description goes on to point up the connection between feudalism and landed property. It concludes that "it seems likely that in a fully feudal society there will be an almost equal development of both vassalage and the fief." [18] The difficulties inherent in the historian's attempt to limit himself to the political or authority syndrome when dealing with feudalism are even more evident in the comparative sections of *Feudalism in History* in which Coulborn is obliged to carry on his analysis in terms of the broader, though never clearly defined, concept of feudal society.

This problem of comparison has not been forced upon Coulborn simply because he chose to deal with several cultures. It confronts even those who remain within the confines of European history or of a single European country, for studies across time within a closed system present the historian

[17] *Ibid.*, 4-5.
[18] *Ibid.*, 5-6.

with the need to establish criteria for differentiating "stages" of development, and this too takes the historian out of the purely political syndrome. This point is illustrated in a recent treatment of European feudalism by Bryce Lyon, in which he described different stages of feudalism, differentiating them in terms of changes in the lord-vassal nexus which were discernible mainly in the areas of economic and ideological change. As he explains,

The traditional system of feudalism declined in the thirteenth century and was of slight importance in the fourteenth and fifteenth century. Feudal thinking and behavior, however, remained strong and account for the feudalism of money and the indenture system, both prominent in the fourteenth and fifteenth centuries. When speaking of the decline of feudalism, we must evade the pitfall of keeping the traditional feudalism around until the end of the middle ages and must speak instead of a feudalism of money and of an indenture system that nourished variant forms of feudalism down to the sixteenth century.[19]

The historian's problem, once he moves out of the narrow confines of the political definition of feudalism, is to place boundaries around these "variant forms", and for this he must be prepared to draw a broad area of social activity into his purview.

The narrow definition of feudalism, since it limits its scope to the lord-vassal nexus and to the system of government derived from it, is essentially an effort to define "feudal government". As such it is a perfectly appropriate concept, but it should be understood for what it is. The narrow definition cannot serve as a description of feudal society as a whole. It is not logically possible to restrict the concept of feudalism to mean "feudal government" and at the same time expect it to serve as a description of "feudal society". Such phrases as "feudal England" or "feudal Japan", though used by those who profess the narrow definition, frequently carry connotations which imply a great deal more than the mere fact that England and Japan had "feudal governments" at the time. They imply that the whole societies can be wrapped up in the concept of feudalism.

Unquestionably, proponents of the narrow view of feudalism, by placing their emphasis on a relatively small set of cultural relationships, are correct in avoiding one major danger which besets the historian who would use feudalism as a general social concept. A total society cannot necessarily be subsumed under a single all-inclusive concept. Thus while a model of feudalism expressed as a comprehensive social system may be conceived of as an ideal possibility, the elements of which such a model is composed will not necessarily embrace a whole society at any given time. In any specific society, it is possible that feudalism, as a form of government and as a set of social and economic organizations relating to it, may exist in equilibrium with other forms of social organization. Moreover, it is possible that in a given society,

[19] Bryce Lyon, *The Middle Ages*, 17.

certain relationships which by definition are part of the feudal system will be more typically developed than others. By definition then, feudalism as an ideal type need not be exemplified by the totality of a society at any given time.

It is also well to heed the words of the proponents of the narrow definition of feudalism that one should be cautious in ascribing non-political elements to the feudal model. A model of feudal society should be constructed so that its parts are logically related to the political core. Too broad a definition can be as destructive of useful analysis as too narrow a one. In moving outward from the crucial lord-vassal nexus the historian must be careful to bring into his definition only what appear to be the necessary concomitants and not a host of other irrelevant cultural traits.

But how is the historian to establish criteria for the inclusion or rejection of traits in his definition of feudalism? Here again we must return to the proposition that the historian is dependent upon the full state of inquiry into the comparative structures of society, for it is only as the various elements of societies in general are classified and the combinations studied that, as K. A. Wittfogel has expressed it, the "essential, specific, and nonspecific" elements of a social type can be differentiated. Actually the study of feudalism has attracted the attention of historians for such a length of time that there is a large area of agreement over the general categories which should be included in the concept. There is in fact no lack of existing definitions which agree in all but secondary characteristics or in emphasis. In the main these differences are the result not of stubborn details which refuse to yield to generalization, but rather of the different operational interests of the scholars proposing them.

It will be helpful to review a number of "broad" definitions of feudalism to see how various theorists have conceived of feudalism and whether some form of composite definition is feasible. One of the broadest, and a good one with which to start, is found in the following statement by K. A. Wittfogel:

The feudal system of limited and conditional service (not unconditional sub-servience), vassalage (not bureaucracy), and fief (not office land) is essential to the medieval societies of Europe and Japan. It occurs so rarely elsewhere that it may be considered specific to these societies.

Corvée labor is an essential element of hydraulic and feudal societies, and serfdom (the attachment of the peasant to his land or village) is essential to the helotage-based societies of ancient Greece, to feudal society, and to most simple and semicomplex Oriental societies. That is, both institutions are essential to more than one type of society and specific to none.

Innumerable elements of technology, custom, art, and belief occur widely and without being either essential or specific to the conditions of power, status, and property—that is, to the crucial relations within any society ... Recognition of these facts should go far in correcting the idea of a 'necessary relation between all possible aspects of the same social organism.'[20]

---

[20] K. A. Wittfogel, *Oriental Despotism* (New Haven, 1957), 414-415.

The interesting feature of Wittfogel's statement is that it defines feudal society along with a number of other types, thus providing some measure of the horizontal limits of feudalism. It also groups the elements of the definition into essential and non-essential categories, making it possible to classify a number of types of society in terms of a limited number of variables. But Wittfogel's definition is useful chiefly for the purposes for which it was devised, namely the most general kind of theorizing about whole cultures or civilizations.

For a more characteristically political definition we can turn to Max Weber who includes feudalism as a category in his discussion of "types of authority".

1. The authority of the chief is reduced to the likelihood that the vassals will voluntarily remain faithful to their oaths of fealty.

2. The political corporate group is completely replaced by a system of relations of purely personal loyalty between the lord and his vassals and between these, in turn, and their own sub-vassals (sub-infeudation) etc. Only a lord's own vassals are bound by fealty to him; whereas they in turn can claim the fealty of their own vassals, etc.

3. Only in the case of a 'felony' does the lord have a right to deprive his vassal of his fief . . .

4. There is a hierarchy of social rank corresponding to the hierarchy of fiefs through the process of sub-infeudation . . . This is not, however, a hierarchy of authority in the bureaucratic sense . . .

5. The elements in the population who do not hold fiefs involving some element of patrimonial or other political authority are 'subjects'; that is, they are patrimonial dependents. They are dependent on the holders of fiefs, on the one hand, in that their traditional status, particularly class status, determines or permits it, or on the other so far as the coercive power in the hands of the possessors of military fiefs compels it, since they are to a large extent defenseless . . .

6. Powers over the individual budgetary unit, including domains, slaves, and serfs, the fiscal rights of the political group to the receipt of taxes and contributions, and specifically political powers of jurisdiction and compulsion to military service—thus powers over free men—are all objects of feudal grants in the same way . . .[21]

While there are no profound differences between this definition by Weber and the fuller "description" contained in *Feudalism in History*, Weber has couched his statement in more general and structural terms. Furthermore in other portions of his analysis of authority he provides criteria which make it possible to place feudalism in context with other political systems such as patrimonial government and bureaucracy.

[21] Max Weber, *The Theory of Social and Economic Organization* (Glencoe, Ill., 1947), 375-376.

Feudalism in Japan—A Reassessment

One of the most elegantly simple definitions of feudalism is in actuality one of the oldest and reflects the particular legal biases of F. W. Maitland. According to Maitland, feudalism was "a state of society in which all or a great part of public rights and duties are inextricably interwoven with the tenure of land, in which the whole government system—financial, military, judicial—is part of the law of private property".[22] Such a conception neatly draws together the relationship of land rights and political authority, but it misjudges the extent of private authority permissible in a non-contractual society. One of the chief characteristics of the feudal system was the very non-existence of private property as such, for there was no possession free and clear without reciprocity. For this reason it would be better to reverse Maitland's proposition so as to emphasize the submersion of private rights within the government system.[23]

While Weber and Maitland stress governmental relationships in feudalism, the sociologist is more in need of a definition which clarifies the social structure of feudalism. Such a one is provided by Marion Levy:

a) closed social classes,

b) a well-defined hierarchy of power-holders,

c) identification, at least ideally speaking, of each individual as responsible to some particular individual higher than himself in the hierarchy and related to others outside of that direct line by virtue of his overlord's relations to them, and

d) a distribution of goods and services, most especially land ownership and control, primarily on the basis of the ranks distinguished in the hierarchy of power and responsibility.[24]

Levy's definition is also distinguished by structural simplicity and generality. For the historian, however, it is unquestionably too general. Specifically it does not provide for the aristocratic nature of the ruling groups and their monopoly of military power, although these features may be deduced from the conditions stated in Levy's model. It says little about the relationship between public and private exercise of authority and nothing about the economic and technological level of the society.

Yet another approach to feudalism puts its stress upon economic relationships. A standard version of this approach is found in Lenin's definition of "corvée economy" in his *The Development of Capitalism in Russia*:

Firstly, the predominance of natural economy ... Secondly, such an economy required that the direct producer be allotted the means of production in general, and land in particular; moreover, that he be tied to the land, since otherwise the

---

[22] F. W. Maitland, *The Constitutional History of England* (Cambridge, 1931), 22.

[23] I am indebted to Professor Karl Deutsch of Yale University for this point.

[24] Marion J. Levy, Jr., "Contrasting Factors in the Modernization of China and Japan", *Economic Development and Cultural Change* II. 3 (Oct., 1953), 193, n. 3.

landlord was not assured of hands ... Thirdly, a condition for such a system of economy was the personal dependence of the peasant on the landlord ... There was required 'extra-economic coercion', as Marx calls it ... Fourthly, and finally, a condition and consequence of the system of economy described was the extremely low and stagnant condition of technique, for the conduct of husbandry was in the hands of small peasants, crushed by poverty and degraded by personal dependence and by ignorance.[25]

This statement, though clearly limited to a description of the economic features of "feudal Russia", has been taken by some scholars as a sufficient definition of feudalism in its entirety. Its inadequacy for such a purpose stems from the limitations of the purpose for which it was set forth and in particular for its failure to take into consideration the political and social aspects of the system.

Finally, let us return to a definition of a more descriptive nature specifically devised to serve as a tool of comparative study for European and Japanese institutions. This is the noteworthy formulation by Asakawa:

In a feudal society:—(1) The ruling class should consist of groups of fighting men, each group chained together by links of an exhaustive personal bond of mutual service—a bond so personal that, in the last analysis, it should obtain, in each link, between two armed men only, lord and vassal: and so exhaustively personal that the one should swear to the other fidelity even unto death. Although the vassal's service is usually rewarded with a grant of land, land enters into this relation only as a secondary factor, the primary motive power being the personal agreement in arms between the lord and his man. (2) There, however, being other classes of people also, the division of all the classes, including the warrior class, should coincide with their private tenures of land,—the private land law of this peculiar society recognizing no absolute ownership, (except perhaps in the supreme overlord, if he did exist), but only a series of relative tenures. (3) In the general political life of the society as a whole, these private tenures of land should condition the exercise of public rights and obligations; and the superior rights of land should fall into the hands of the privately armed men, who should accordingly assume all the public functions of State;—in other words, the ruling class having secured the control of arms and land, there should result the singular spectacle of the private usurpation of public rights, and the public utilization of private institutions; that is, in government, in finance, in military affairs and in the administration of justice, there should be a complete confusion or coalescence of the public and the private.[26]

Asakawa's definition is close to those of Weber and Strayer. It puts its emphasis upon the bond uniting lord and vassal and on the fief which links private status with public authority. It offers an explanation for the conditions which gave rise to serfdom though it does not mention it specifically. Its major defect perhaps is its assumption that the exercise of authority by the ruling class was a "usurpation" of public rights.

It would be possible to pile more definitions on top of the ones we have

[25] Lenin, *Capitalism in Russia,* 191-192.
[26] Asakawa, "Some Aspects", 78-79.

already selected, but we have certainly reviewed a representative group. It should be evident also that the above definitions, though differing in their operational purposes and in specific details, serve to outline a fairly consistent core of essential features of feudalism as a social system. These features can be grouped into three general categories: political, social, and economic. Within each of these sectors of society the definitions tend to agree on certain particular types of essential relationships, though they differ over the manner and specificity with which they should be described. In the final analysis, then, the problem of definition hinges upon a limited number of questions of sub-definition at a secondary level of generalization.

One of the weaknesses of the common style of definition, such as those just cited, is that each is stated in static, two-dimensional terms. Such a style of definition tends to obscure the hypothetical nature of general concepts and the dynamic conditions within real societies to which a concept such as feudalism refers. A more useful model of feudalism, therefore, would be one expressed in two parts: first a statement of essential variables within each of several related sectors of society, and secondly a statement regarding the limits of variability of these elements. Let us conclude this inquiry into definition by attempting to restate the agreed upon elements of feudalism contained in the definitions cited above into a hypothetically and dynamically conceived statement of this sort.

Within the political sector, it is generally agreed that the essential feudal element is located in the lord-vassal complex, a relationship which shades on the one hand with the patrimonial structure of authority isolated by Weber and on the other hand with the bureaucratic structure of authority (at least in more technologically advanced societies). The essential feature of this lord-vassal complex is not a specific form of contract but rather the personal nature of the association (symbolized by homage in Europe) and its military origin. To say the relationship is voluntary (as Weber does) is to misjudge the role of the "consensus of conduct" based on knowledge of or remnants of a former legal system.[27]

In the social sector the feudal condition contrasts with aristocratic or slave-based societies on the one hand and the more freely mobile modern societies on the other. An important element of feudalism is arms-bearing as a class-defining profession. The feudal condition is distinguished by a relative closing of the social status system in which (for these groups dependent primarily on the land) the distribution of goods and services is closely integrated with the hierarchy of social statuses. There may be some disagreement over whether the fief is an essential feature of the political and social sectors, but the manner of distribution of rights and privileges over land and the workers of the land is certainly an essential ingredient.

[27] Conversation with Professor Karl Deutsch.

J. W. Hall

Within the economic sector we begin with certain technological conditions, noting that feudal government and society appear uniformly to rest upon a landed, or locally self-sufficient, economic base as distinguished from pastoral, commercial, or industrial. The merchant community, though it may play a significant role in the economy, is essentially outside the feudal nexus. It is readily observable that the appearance of certain technological features of government and economy, notably centralized communications and means of large-scale political organization, serve to make feudal government unnecessary and break down feudal social hierarchies. The condition of serfdom may not be specific to the feudal model since it calls for a particular form of attachment of a cultivator to land which is found in only certain parts of Europe. On the other hand we must postulate a long-term restriction on the mobility of the bulk of the population. The direct personal relationship of the land manager over the cultivators is also an essential feature which places the cultivator under feudalism somewhere between slavery on one side and free tenancy on the other.

Such a set of propositions cannot presume to constitute a final and sufficient definition of feudalism. But a definition of this type can be seen to consist of two parts. Of these, one (the theoretical or structural) can be left open. In other words, we can agree from a structural point of view that there are only a limited number of variables which require inclusion in the feudal syndrome and that the locus of these variables is by now well established. Further clarification of the feudal model requires no further debate over its major parts but rather a continuing effort at precise definition of the *essential features* of the agreed upon variables and beyond that a clarification of the limits of acceptable behavior within each of the sets of relationships of which the variable consists. Ideally, of course, a feudal society would be conceived of as comprising the essential elements stated above in their purest form. But no society has ever possessed a government in which authority in every instance was based upon a lord-vassal relationship, in which the hierarchy of social statuses coincided perfectly with the military and political hierarchy of ranks and with possession of land, and in which the economy was totally agrarian and all cultivators were serfs. Each of the elements of the feudal syndrome must be studied and compared with similar elements of other social conditions so as to determine the limits of permissible variability within which the feudal essential resides. That at this point in our historical study no such systematic effort has been made is in large part the reason behind the continued failure of historians to agree on a definition of feudalism. For in the absence of precise criteria of this kind, historians are prone to leave the boundaries of what they consider "feudal behavior" quite diffuse or are apt to insist on extremely particularistic conditions. The work of Max Weber in which he tries to differentiate feudal, bureaucratic, and patrimonial systems of authority illustrates the kind of further study necessary if we are to achieve, with any degree of refinement, an agreement on the boundaries of the several elements of the feudal syndrome. So long as such studies are lacking, the effort to "prove or disprove" the existence of feudalism in any society on the basis of highly specific criteria will be open in some degree to individual judgment.

But let us proceed with the definition at hand as a tool of inquiry into Japanese history. Did Japan at any given time sufficiently exemplify the feudal model, as defined by us, to be classed as feudal? If we stay within the limits of generality of our model, the fit would seem acceptably close. It is possible to identify in the fabric of Japanese society as early as the eleventh century elements of feudal authority relationships, although not linked with other social and economic concomitants contained in the model. It is also possible to trace as late as the nineteenth century certain survivals of feudal governmental practice as well as survivals of feudal social organization and ideology. During the early sixteenth century Japanese society gave every indication of conforming in general outline to the ideal type itself. It is this moment in Japanese history, from roughly 1500 to 1550, that requires the most careful comparative analysis.

In order to confirm this observation we must compare Japanese practices with those ideal practices which we have adopted as the basic variables of the feudal syndrome. We can begin with the *tono* and *gokenin* relationship which in Japan coincided functionally with the lord-vassal relationship of our model. Described in general terms there is little question that the *gokenin* assumed towards his *tono* a posture of subordination to authority deriving from agreement in arms. On the basis of our theoretical model, however, we shall wish to apply further tests of equivalence. In particular we must know whether the *tono-gokenin* relationship was voluntary and honorable, and whether it was combined with the granting of land (conditions which are referred to in our model as homage and the fief). Both Asakawa and des Longrais have noted remarkable similarities between the practice of homage and the Japanese custom of *genzan*, between the swearing of the oath of allegiance and the signing of the *seishi*, between the fief and the *chigyōchi*. These practices appear to be sufficiently similar both in their individual parts and in their relationships to satisfy our test for equivalence. Yet, there are a number of specific differences between Japanese and European practices which must be taken into consideration before a final answer may be given. The most crucial difference appears as part of the specific bond which united superior and inferior in these different cultures. In Japan the relationship rested strongly on unwritten custom publicized by ceremonial observance; it relied less on written or oral contract which specified individual duties or privileges. The obligations of the Japanese *gokenin* were fully understood as part of a concensus of common behavior, and were set down in the lord's house regulations. The duties of the *tono* were left vague, although the responsibility of protection was commonly assumed. The lord in Japan tended to exert greater paternalistic powers over the vassal, who had no recourse to an extra-feudal source of legal protection. The question of whether these differences contradict the existence of the essential political features of feudalism in Japan refers us back to the problem of definition itself and to the limits of specificity which have been set by the model. If homage is not homage unless it is accompanied by certain practices found mainly in France or England, if allegiance is not allegiance unless sealed by a contract of a certain type, then these elements must be added to the model and Japanese practices may then be judged too divergent to be considered feudal. But unless we choose to redefine the model itself, these specific differences fall into the level of traits which are not essential to feudalism but are specific to the different cultures of Europe and Japan.

Turning to the social sector, it is obvious that Japanese society, over a fairly lengthy period of history, coincided in general outline with the pattern of social structure defined in our model. The relative closure of classes was a common phenomenon during most of pre-modern Japan. The separation of an aristocratic class dedicated to the professional bearing of arms was also specific to the age of the military houses (*buke*). It is in Japan of the sixteenth century, particularly, that the condition in which a "hierarchy of social rank corresponding to the hierarchy of fiefs"[28] became prevalent.

Students of Japanese feudalism have been less critical in their citation of differences between Japanese and European social structure, yet this is not due to a lack of observable dissimilarities. No doubt it stems from the paucity of comparative studies in the social field. No adequate attention has been given, for instance, to the significance for comparative purposes of the perpetuation in Japan of an imperial court and a civil nobility into the world dominated by the military aristocracy. Certainly this tended to dilute the truly feudal aspects of Japanese society for several centuries. What is the significance of the particular form of Japanese family organization characterized by the strong concept of "house" *(ie)* in which a main family (*honke*) exerts primacy over its branch families (*bunke*)? This social pattern was especially widespread among *buke* houses and was extended, through fictive or ritual kinship practices, so as to form an underlying principle in the lord-vassal nexus. Thus vassalage in Japan was more apt to be symbolized in ritual kinship terms; the vassal might call himself a child (*ie-no-ko*) or adopt the lord's surname. These points of peculiarity, though they have excited relatively little attention in the West, reveal a number of divergences in the substance of social organization in Japan and Europe. Yet, at our present state of understanding, these differences would appear to fall below the level of generality at which we have described our feudal model. They reveal only that feudal relationships may be colored by a variety of cultural traits.

[28] K. Asakawa, *The Documents of Iriki* (Tokyo, 1955), 29.

Feudalism in Japan—A Reassessment

Within the economic sphere there also is little doubt about the basic similarity of the Japanese economy and that of our feudal model. Land economy with a minimum of commercial activity characterized Japan until the seventeenth century. Thus land became the chief basis for distinguishing differences in social and political status. By the fifteenth century, public rights and duties met Maitland's dictum that they be "inextricably interwoven with the tenure of land". The worker of the land and the holder of the fief were (at least during the sixteenth century) closely interdependent. By this time fief rights (*chigyōken*) carried the privileges of free extraction (within customary limits) of land rent, corvée labor, and military service from the workers of the land, but they also carried the reciprocal responsibility of sound administration and protection of the fief.

Admittedly many of the precise forms of serfdom and manorialism typical of Europe did not appear in Japan. Both Asakawa and des Longrais have been careful to point out the difference in the nature of peasant dues. In Japan such dues were apt to be paid as portions of the produce of a land holding or in terms of an assessment figure abstracted from the cultivator's holdings. There was some, but less, provision for specific service dues such as work on the lord's demesne or corvée service. Asakawa explains this in terms of the difference between the intensive form of rice agriculture in Japan and the more extensive dry cultivation in the West. The differences between the Japanese *shō* and the European manor have been described by Asakawa in some detail.[29] But unless we are prepared to revise our definition of feudalism to include the particular details of manorial organization, the above variations do not affect the relevance of the feudal model to Japan.

The foregoing argument has affirmed the possibility of applying the concept of feudalism to Japan under certain specific definitional controls. What precisely does this signify? In actuality we have said nothing more than that certain Japanese institutions, notably during the sixteenth century, bore a generic resemblance to a set of theoretically defined institutional relationships which we have seen fit to call feudal. We have not "proved that Japan had feudalism" in its particular European guise, but rather that Japan during a certain period of its history developed a pattern of society which bore a specific resemblance to the essential features of an admittedly theoretical social model. But where do we proceed from here? What are the legitimate lines of inquiry which are opened up as a result of our argument so far?

Perhaps we should return again to a basic premise of this inquiry, namely that the use of the kind of general concept represented by the term feudalism takes the historian into a special realm of historical inquiry. We have shown that the historian must choose between a concept of feudalism defined in such limited terms that it is applicable only to certain areas of Western Europe or

[29] K. Asakawa, "The Early Shō and the Early Manor", *Journal of Economic and Business History*, 1.2 (Feb., 1929). Also des Longrais, *L'Est et L'Ouest*, 7-103.

that he must define his term so that it stands for a generalized, ideal type of society. These two methods are fundamentally distinct, since they involve two radically different aspects of the historian's methodology. Feudalism probably suffers more than other general concepts because from the start the term was so rooted in a particular European context. The term itself does not provide a means of differentiating the various levels of generality to which it may be applied. As a general concept, FEUDALISM (should we capitalize it in order to distinguish its specific nature?) must be recognized as a tool of historical inquiry with certain prescribed areas of application. It helps in the investigation of certain types of problems and can yield certain varieties of findings, but its proper sphere is limited. Certainly there is no special magic which can result from conceiving of Japan as feudal. The concept will not by any means unlock all the mysteries of Japanese history nor provide an explanation for specific events. In particular we are not justified in borrowing directly the explanations of European history into Japanese history. There should be no expectation on the part of historians "that having mastered western feudalism they can understand all feudal systems," including Japan's.[30]

Much of the objection we must raise against the voluminous literature on "feudal Japan" is that it contains too many assumptions that once feudalism is identified in Japan its very existence carries with it certain causal and explanatory necessities. The common literature on Japanese feudalism too frequently loses sight of the abstract nature of the concept and begins to use it with its full load of European connotations. The Marxists are not alone in conceiving of feudalism in almost anthropomorphic fashion as a living social organism which can be described as "taking over" a society, as "bringing" certain institutions into being, as "resisting" change or "leading" to other stages of society. This unfortunate practice of viewing feudalism almost as a foreign body which a society can "have" or "not have", a substance which once "had" inevitably leads to certain consequences, is at the core of a large number of the misuses of the feudal concept with respect to Japan.

In its strictest sense, the value of setting up a general model of feudalism (as with any other general concept) is that it can serve to focus attention upon a certain nexus of relationships within a given culture and, beyond this, to point up the essential ways in which these relationships "belong together." By studying a particular set of related traits in Japan, and by reference to a general model which embraces them, it is possible to place Japanese history (or at least a portion of it) into a genre of ideas of broad scope which have been generated out of the study of the model itself or from related studies. Such ideas, or hypotheses, may derive both from the analysis of the structural relationships within the model or from empirical studies of historical societies in actual fact. In either case they help to pose questions or frame hypotheses

[30] Bryce Lyon, *Middle Ages*, 13.

about institutional relationships and changes which can lead to more penetrating explanations of historical change in Japan. But it must be remembered that the juxtaposition of the model against Japanese historical data can only lead to points of hypothetical insight. The historian is not thereby provided with laws or necessities but rather with probabilities that a pattern of organization in one society or a process of change in another can help to identify pattern or process in Japanese history. Moreover the level of generality at which the model is defined sets the limits of types of hypothetical insight which can result from the comparative technique.

If this is the limit of the legitimate usage for a general model of feudalism, the question may well be asked: why attempt to define a model at all? For if comparisons leading to probabilities and hunches are the only result of the pains required in setting up an abstract model, cannot hypothetical comparisons be made at any point in history on an *ad hoc* basis between Europe and Japan? What is the point of "going through" an abstract model rather than applying comparative European data directly to that of Japan? The answer is, of course, that the use of the model helps to systematize comparative judgments. The model stands, as it were, in the midst of a set of observations of a generalized nature derived from the study of many societies and (hopefully to be sure) of a more general relevance than the casual observation which might result from comparisons intuitively picked out of the historian's experience.

At this point it becomes obvious that the kind of rigorously controlled comparison or hypothetical analysis which we have advocated has seldom been put to practice. Historians dealing with what they have termed Japanese feudalism continue to accept loose or ambigious definitions, borrow value judgments from European data, or assume that patterns of European historical development should provide norms for Japanese history. The difficulties inherent in the methodology of comparative history are indeed enormous. Few historians have acquired the necessary depth of experience in more than one society which will permit them to engage in systematic comparative procedures. Within the historical profession at large the inability of groups of historians, Western and Japanese, to communicate with each other on comparative lines has frustrated the possibility of combined attack upon problems of general conceptualization. This is borne out by the fact that the historical literature on feudalism in English and in Japanese today contains few points of useful coincidence.

Such is the rather unhappy situation which confronts the historian who would seek some solution to the problem of feudalism in Japan. Such in fact is the situation which has induced many a serious scholar to ask whether it would not be best to abandon the use of the term in writing about Japanese history. Clumsily or improperly used, the concept of feudalism unquestionably obstructs rather than aids the historian in his attempt to understand Japanese history. Used within its proper limits, on the other hand, the term is far from providing a universal explanation. Should we not avoid the large errors and misunderstandings by foregoing the seemingly small advantages of using the term in a comparative sense? The answer to this query is probably dependent as much upon the temperament and basic conviction of the individual historian as upon any rational argument. The historian who holds that his work deals fundamentally with the unique and the non-quantifiable will instinctively shun the broader comparative problems inherent in the feudalism controversy. Those who incline towards the general, or are obliged to generalize in the course of their writing, will seek to gain cumulative knowledge about general processes of social change or patterns of institutional behavior. Few historians have managed both tasks equally well, and few, it would seem, who are of one sort have tolerance for the other. Ironically it would seem that the most significant contributions to our understanding of Japanese history appear to have come from a dialectic process operating between these two extremes. On the one hand, the exaggerated over-generalizations of comparative historians while rejected by more cautious scholars have nonetheless obliged historians to look afresh at their materials and frequently to acknowledge the modicum of truth contained in the over-generalization. On the other hand the work of constant and meticulous digging into the data of Japanese and European history has provided the basis for new levels of hypothetical inquiry. The problem of what to do with the concept of feudalism falls therefore between the historian's innate skepticism toward "general systems" and his need to have categories for the organization of his observations with respect to human behavior.

Let us agree then that there are legitimate areas within which a general concept of feudalism may be applied to Japan, but that this must be done with full recognition of a number of qualifying propositions. First, it is obvious that an analysis of feudalism *in* Japan is an operation which must yield results of a quite different sort from the usual narrative history of "feudal Japan". The former is a technical undertaking, the latter is a conventional form of historical exposition in which the use of the term feudalism often obscures more than it clarifies. Secondly we should expect that in contrast to Europe, feudal practices in Japan would differ considerably in origin, pattern of development, and manner of disappearance. Thirdly that these very differences are important in pointing up basic cultural contrasts between Japan and Europe.

In reassessing the subject of feudalism *in* Japan our first task must be to retrace the origins and developments of feudal institutions in Japanese society and to assess the area of Japanese history which can be "explained" by reference to the feudal concept. Here the early and late phases of the process require our special attention, for it is at the ends of the process that the greatest discrepancies between concept and data seem to appear.

Feudalism in Japan—A Reassessment

The "origin of feudalism" in Japan is most often identified with the establishment of the Kamakura shogunate by Minamoto-no-Yoritomo in 1192. But in the strict sense of our definition this date marks neither the origin of feudal practices nor of feudal society in Japan. For while vassalage and enfeoffment may have originated considerably before the twelfth century, it is also clear that only a small portion of Japanese society was organized around these practices by 1192.[31] To try to explain Kamakura Japan as a "feudal society" exaggerates beyond acceptability the prevalence of the feudal nexus. In Kamakura Japan the legal government was still centered upon the emperor. It operated through the traditional civil administration (greatly weakened to be sure) and an expanding system of semi-public domains (*shōen*). In terms of volume, while the bulk of the personnel of the lower administrative and managerial apparatus had taken up the military profession, the greater portion of this personnel served as hereditary agents within the civil domains. Their relationships to their superiors could not be described as that of vassal to lord but rested upon the customary administrative practices left behind as the centralized imperial system of government gradually declined. On the other hand, independent of these administrative and fiscal relationships based upon the *shōen,* there were numerous informal hierarchies built upon clan ties and military allegiances. Military hierarchies tended to form around the leadership of local magnates. They were most often not based upon the reciprocal grant of land rights or official title. It was primarily within the hierarchy of such allegiances as they came to center upon the office of shogun (or certain other high military posts) that the essential feudal element was added to the military clique.

The power structure created by Yoritomo and assembled at Kamakura was first of all based on the military band of which he was chief. The band was eventually extended to include the majority of military (*bushi*) families in eastern Japan (the *Kantō*) and then spread out more thinly to the rest of the provinces. While we have no exact count of the numbers of Yoritomo's vassals (*gokenin*), the most common estimate is that he started with approximately 2,000, a rather small number when one considers the entire size of the managerial class of the provinces.[32] The members of Yoritomo's band were naturally of various capacities. Some were proprietors of considerable proportions with authority over lands which embraced entire counties. Such great provincial families had typically held regional offices of importance in the imperial system. They were located mostly in the eastern provinces, which formed the geographic base of the Kamakura hegemony. In the main,

---

[31] An excellent survey of the problem of Yoritomo's rise to power is found in Minoru Shinoda, *The Founding of the Kamakura Shogunate 1180-1185* (New York, 1960), especially 114-144.

[32] Senō Seiichirō, "Hizen-no-kuni ni okeru Kamakura gokenin", *Nihon rekishi,* 117 (March, 1958), 35.

however, the rank and file of Yoritomo's housemen (*gokenin*) were *bushi* of the petty land managing variety. The tie between Yoritomo and these housemen became technically feudal as Yoritomo gained in authority and was able to grant confirmation or protection of land holdings in return for pledges of loyalty.

Yoritomo's importance to the development of feudalism in Japan is that he regularized and extended the practice of combining pledges of military allegiance with protection over land holdings. At first this action was at best extra-legal. Yoritomo's public authority to make appointments and to interfere in the *shōen* system was based on his emergency assertion of supreme military command in a time of national crisis. But by the time he became shogun, his legal powers had vastly increased.[33] He himself held directly a large agglomeration of *shōen* granted to him by the emperor. This made him a power within the imperial system comparable to the court aristocracy and the great temples. In these *shōen* he held rights of appointment over subordinate officials. In addition, the shogun was made "proprietor" (*kokushu*) of the nine provinces of eastern Japan. In these areas he was empowered to make his own appointments of administrative officials. Throughout vast regions of Japan, then, he had the authority to appoint governors, civil officials, *shōen* officials, and stewards (*jitō*). All such appointments carried with them both title and income in the form of land tenures (*shiki*).

While the legal rights to make appointments and confirm *shiki* came to the shogun from the central civil government, Yoritomo's use of these rights was in the main personal and military. Appointments were made to his followers who had pledged service as housemen. It is in this respect that the power to appoint *shugo* and *jitō* was so important to Yoritomo's system. Justified originally in 1186 over the need to clean up remnants of military resistance, Yoritomo secured the right to set *shugo* (or military governors) over all provinces, where they would exercise control over provincial military and police affairs, and *jitō* (or stewards) over the land system in order to assure regular tax collection and to collect an emergency military tax for the prosecution of the war. The *shugo-jitō* system was not conceived of as replacing imperial local administration but rather as supplementary to it. Its importance to Yoritomo was that it provided the shogun a network of provincial connections which extended over the country. It was this network which gave Yoritomo's Kamakura headquarters its national character. For as Yoritomo appointed his housemen to posts of *shugo* and *jitō* in distant provinces, he built his band of followers into a national organization.

The degree to which Japan has been considered "feudal" during the Kamakura depends in large measure upon the extent to which the authority

---

[33] Satō Shin'ichi, "Bakufu ron", *Shin Nihonshi kōza* (Tokyo, 1951), 14-17; Ishimoda Tadashi, "Kamakura seiken no seiritsu katei ni tsuite", *Rekishigaku kenkyū*, 200 (Oct., 1956), 15.

of the *shugo-jitō* system is believed to have taken over in Japan. Until recently, scholars (such as Asakawa and Japanese legal historians) tended to exaggerate the power exercised by the shogun. This is perhaps a natural outcome of the studies of Kamakura institutions which took their material largely from shogunal records. More recent studies have put the shogunate in better perspective.[34] Unquestionably the establishment of the shogunate was a major turning point in Japan's political history. Yet since the country shifted only slowly from its customary administrative and legal practices, the bulk of the people continued to be governed through a non-feudal apparatus; the bulk of the land was controlled under the *shōen* system centering on Kyoto. The same may be said about the social and economic sectors of Japanese society. Socially, the military aristocracy was only beginning to differentiate itself from the general mass of upper and lower aristocracy which still adhered to the court system of ranks and official titles. What in later centuries became merely a convenient system of titles and rank designations to demarcate statuses in the military hierarchy was in these days still a meaningful apparatus for the exercise of authority. Thus the Kamakura *bushi,* though basing much of their actual power upon the force of arms, nonetheless depended for legitimacy upon the possession of posts and ranks within the imperial system. Their functions were as yet limited chiefly (except in the Kantō area) to the police and military sectors of Japanese society. The fief as an economic concomitant of political organization was still not fully developed. The benefice (*onkyū*) was granted in terms of rights (*shiki*) to income from *shōen.* They were held under conditions set by *shōen* law which derived in turn from the imperial system. Public and private law had not by any means coalesced.

While we must be careful not to see feudal practices where they did not exist during the Kamakura period, it is also clear that as the period progressed the feudal nexus in government and society steadily encroached upon the imperial-*shōen* complex. It is this process of encroachment which Asakawa has explained chiefly in terms of the shift from *shōen* to *chigyō* (fief) within the land tenure system.[35] But the process was both more complex and more gradual than revealed in Asakawa's studies, and must be traced at several levels within both the political and social sectors.

To begin with, at the apex of the state structure, military authority gradually overreached civil authority. During the thirteenth century the balance between civil and military power shifted steadily in the direction of Kamakura. A turning point in this shift took place in 1221 when the Kamakura forces

---

[34] This perspective has been gained chiefly through local studies in regions other than the Kantō and southern Kyushu. A notable study of the balance between civil and military authority in the province of Bizen is contained in Kanai Madoka, "Kamakura jidai Bizen kokugaryō ni tsuite", *Nihon rekishi,* 150 (Dec., 1960), 36-54.

[35] K. Asakawa, "The Life of a Monastic Sho in Medieval Japan", *Annual Report of the American Historical Association for 1916,* I (1919), 311-346.

quickly routed an army mustered against them by the emperor Go-Toba. With this victory the Kamakura shogunate completed its extension of the *jitō* system into all territory and acquired the power of direct interference in court and imperial household affairs.

At the provincial level of government, military interests gained over civilian as the *shugo* increasingly took on the stature of military governors.[36] Locally the *shugo* were able to build up their economic support largely through the plural holding of *jitō* rights to numerous *shōen*. They used their superior status in the shogunal hierarchy to assert their influence among local *bushi*. Before long the *shugo* had absorbed many civil administrative powers at the same time that they achieved personal leadership of province-wide military bands which they organized increasingly on a lord-vassal basis.

Below the *shugo*, the step by step expansion of the *jitō*'s land rights also served to extend the feudal element in Japanese society.[37] At the outset, *jitō* had been given limited police and fiscal powers within the *shōen*, for which they received the rights to specified incomes or units of salary land (*kyūden*). Soon, however, they began to take over tax collection rights for entire *shōen* on a contract basis, though without securing additional proprietary rights. A further encroachment occurred during the mid-Kamakura period when the *jitō* obliged the civil proprietors to acquiesce to a division of the *shōen*, generally on a half-and-half basis. This procedure, known as *shitaji-chūbun* had been carried out in a large percentage of the *shōen* by the middle of the fourteenth century. It gave to the *jitō* proprietory rights (*chigyōken*) over the newly acquired portion of the *shōen*. Thus by the end of the Kamakura period many of the *jitō* had become true proprietors with the right to sub-divide or to grant to their followers the lands they held.

The implications of this last development were most profound. For as local *bushi* became proprietors (*ryōshu*) endowed with lands at their disposal, they began to divide these lands among family members or retainers, extending the practice of linking grants of land to bonds of military loyalty. The new military bonds forged between *shugo* and proprietory *jitō* or between *jitō* and vassal families became the basis of an ever widening system of social and political organization which was essentially feudal and which continually encroached upon civil authority in the provincial areas.

A comparison of Japanese society of the fourteenth century with that of the twelfth in terms of composition and stratification shows numerous contrasts. The *bushi* as a class had increased in self-consciousness and in numbers. The first attempts at the formulation of a legal code for military

---

[36] For an example of the rise of a powerful *shugo* house see Matsuoka Hisato, "Ōuchi-shi no hatten to sono ryōkoku shihai", in Uozumi Sōgorō, ed., *Daimyō ryōkoku to jōkamachi* (Tokyo, 1957), 24-98.

[37] Nishioka Toranosuke, "Chūsei shōen ni okeru jitō", in *Shōenshi no kenkyū* (30, Tokyo, 1956-1957), 3. 783-857.

houses (1223) was followed by a growing awareness of the social and political importance of the military man in Japanese society as revealed in the later writings of the Ashikaga period. The shift toward primogeniture, though only incidental to the feudal condition, was clearly visible by this time.

For the common cultivator, the major change affecting his life during these years was the final disappearance of territory administered as "public domain" (*kōryō*). Throughout Japan land management, whether of civil or military proprietors, had been reduced to private customary arrangements between the proprietor (*ryōshu*), his agents, and the rent producing cultivator (now designated as *myōshu*). Ties of personal bondage were becoming more common.

The warfare which embroiled most of Japan during the middle of the fourteenth century hastened the above trends in all parts of the country. The establishment of the Ashikaga shogunate radically altered the former balance between civil and military authority in favor of the military-feudal complex. Under the Ashikaga shogunate in effect there ceased to be two governments in Japan. The shogunate, now located in the very seat of the imperial court in Kyoto, absorbed most of the powers and functions of the civil government, though even now the emperor continued to play a crucial role as the ritual symbol of sovereignty and the source of the shogun's delegated authority. The tenacity of civil fiscal practices is evident as well, for it was not until the end of the fifteenth century that the *shōen* completely disappeared in central Japan.

In the provinces the key figures were the *shugo,* now vastly more powerful than their Kamakura predecessors. By the end of the fourteenth century the *shugo* had developed into true regional overlords, having acquired the combined powers of the former civil and military governors.[38] In other words they held title, under the shogun, to territories the size of entire provinces, serving as the ultimate authority in both civil and military affairs. But it must be pointed out that they did not hold these provinces as unitary fiefs. Although within a province the *shugo* family was the most powerful, this was only relative to a number of other powerful families. In no province did the *shugo* count all military men his vassals, and within the province he held but a fraction (perhaps a tenth) of the land in fief. Thus, in asserting authority over the province, the *shugo* was still obliged to rely upon remnants of imperial authority. This is the prime reason that the *shugo* protected, to a point at least, the *shōen* interests of court or religious establishments within their provinces.

The government of the early Ashikaga period was to this degree a hybrid organism in which military government still depended upon remnants of the imperial administrative system. Under the Ashikaga shoguns the feudal

---

[38]   Sugiyama Hiroshi, "Muromachi bakufu", in *Nihon rekishi kōza* (Tokyo, 1956), 3. 49.

authority structure was still to some extent obliged to function through the machinery of the imperial system. In fact the discrepancy between the coercive power of the *shugo* and the administratively specified areas of local jurisdiction over which they were placed, was in essence a measure of the discrepancy between the effectiveness of the feudal system and the national hegemony it claimed for itself. During the fifteenth century, as the *shugo* extended their claims over more and more territory, they found the task of organizing and holding their territories increasingly difficult.

By 1500 most of the jurisdictional territories of the *shugo* had been broken into fragments and a wave of new magnates of local origin had inherited the pieces. The *shugo* had disappeared and with them not only a generation of *bushi* leaders but also the last remnants of imperial law and civil land management based on the *shōen*. The new group of local magnates owed nothing to external sources of power. Their domains had been built from the bottom up on strictly military principles.[39]

The local magnates of the sixteenth century, the largest of whom were called daimyo, represented new conditions of local government and social configuration. Their territories were no longer scattered but were concentrated in single contiguous domains, which in most instances they had won through conquest. Their followers were closely clustered around them in compact territorial units. By now the distinction between the boundaries of legal jurisdiction and outright mastery had been largely obliterated. The complex division of *shiki* rights among several layers of *shōen* proprietorships had given way to the consolidated fief. A daimyo held his land through his own capacity to fight for it and could dispose of it as he pleased. He wielded absolute power over his vassals as the lord who granted and guaranteed them their fiefs. Within his domain all "warriors were vassals and rear-vassals".[40]

A description of the unitary domain of the sixteenth century reveals how close to the feudal model Japanese society had developed by this time. As an example let us take the territory of the house of Urakami in the province of Bizen. During the 1550's this unit, covering a geographical area of roughly six hundred square miles, consisted of 172 separate fiefs held directly by lord Urakami or by his 59 major vassals. Each of these vassals maintained a castle which dominated his major holding and subinfeudated his land to his own followers. Between lord Urakami and his vassals there passed oaths of loyalty sworn in the names of Shinto and Buddhist deities, and grants of fief defined in terms of villages or parts of villages. Within the domain, administration and enforcement of justice was undifferentiated from the lord-vassal system of authority relationships. At the village level, individual cultivators

---

[39] J. W. Hall, "Foundations of the Modern Japanese Daimyo", *JAS*, XX.3 (May, 1961), 322-323.

[40] Asakawa, *Iriki*, 29.

owed rent, corvée duty, and loyal service to lord Urakami, his vassals or rear-vassals. Although villages were organized into semi-selfgoverning communities, *bushi* retainers of the Urakami lived close enough to the villages to maintain direct ties of supervision over individual peasant families, thus making for a peasant status approximately like that of serfdom.[41]

The condition of extreme political decentralization resulting from the appearance of the elemental fief lasted for a comparatively short time in Japan. In quick succession Japan came under the dominance of a few powerful overlords who grasped control of large regional coalitions of daimyo, and then between 1582 and 1590 under a national hegemony of daimyo led by Toyotomi Hideyoshi. The movement towards centralization on the national level was matched by a similar integration process within the daimyo domains. In particular, the daimyo in order to achieve more effective adminstration of their territories, began to eliminate the small fiefs into which their domains had been subdivided. The great civil wars which engulfed Japan from the 1530's through 1590 and which culminated in the formation of a new national hegemony gave rise to conditions which served to eliminate the most typical feudal practices from many sectors of Japanese society. Ironically, when Japan was for the first time brought completely under the rule of "feudal lords", those very lords had begun to divest themselves of the most fundamentally feudal aspects of their means of governance.[42]

The Tokugawa regime, established in 1603 with its headquarters at Edo, rested at least superficially upon a fulfillment of some of the trends which we have traced up to now as indices of the growth of feudal practices in Japan. The entire country was now governed by daimyo who in turn were the shogun's vassals. The "military band" had by now apparently taken over the entire operation of government. Furthermore, the seemingly artificial efforts of the Tokugawa regime to create a closed caste out of the samurai and to tie the peasantry to the land, support the view that Japan was at long last feudal through and through.[43]

Historians have recognized, however, the danger of too sweeping a characterization of Tokugawa Japan as feudal. Most writers have tended to soften their judgment by referring to the Tokugawa age as a period of "late feudalism", "centralized feudalism", or "national feudalism". Asakawa was also careful to point out that the Tokugawa system was "no longer purely feudal, either on the whole or in its parts, either in its warrior class or in its peasantry".[44] Unfortunately Asakawa never fully amplified these views except

---

[41] Shimizu Mitsuo, *Nihon chūsei no sonraku* (Tokyo, 1942), 121-166.

[42] Asakawa, *Iriki*, 44.

[43] The recent trend among Japanese historians to view the seventeenth century as the culmination of feudalism in Japan rests largely on economic grounds. The foremost advocate of this view is Araki Moriaki (see his "Taikō kenchi no rekishiteki igi", *Rekishigaka kenkyū* 167 (Jan., 1954), 12-23).

[44] Asakawa, "Some Aspects", 101.

in his study of the peasantry under Tokugawa rule, a task for which he was not the best suited. Since Asakawa's time it has been more common for Western writers to subscribe to the "re-feudalization" theory, in other words that the Tokugawa rulers took over a Japan that was rapidly moving away from feudalism and returned it to a more strictly feudal condition.[45]

The most obvious reason why Tokugawa society has been looked upon as a feudal throwback stems from a misreading of the evidence of what was happening in Japan during the sixteenth century. The assumption that Japan was about to "throw off" feudalism before 1600 and was "re-feudalized" thereafter results from the exaggerated significance assigned to certain purportedly "anti-feudal" trends such as increased social mobility, growing foreign trade, the use of firearms, and the like. There is no denying that many of these accepted symbols of the "decline of feudalism" in Europe did appear in sixteenth century Japan. But both their appearance and later disappearance were incidental to the main stream of institutional development in Japan at that time. The truly significant developments of these centuries were of another order and were closely tied to the growth of daimyo authority.[46] The feudal element in Japanese government, social structure, economy, and climate of thought did indeed begin to shrink in importance after the mid-sixteenth century, but this tendency was both slow and continuous, extending well beyond the beginning of the Tokugawa regime. The trend was not noticeably arrested by the cessation of foreign trade or the proliferation of social class legislation.

Tokugawa government is best described by the term coined by Japanese historians for the purpose, the *baku-han* system. This view of the machinery of Tokugawa government as a balance between shogunate and daimyo domains (*han*) should be thought of neither as a frustrated national unity nor as an agency of re-feudalization. Nor should it be assumed that the system was somehow given its perfect and final form by Tokugawa Ieyasu, the first shogun, in the early 1600's to be perpetuated unchanged thereafter. The beginnings of the *baku-han* system go back to the middle of the sixteenth century; its full maturity did not come until at least the beginning of the eighteenth.

How feudal was the *baku-han* system? Admittedly the bond between the shogun and daimyo took the form of that between lord and vassal. Up to the very end of the Tokugawa period the larger daimyo retained an independence in policy and military affairs unthinkable in a fully centralized state. On the other hand the actual means of communication between daimyo and shogun had become highly impersonal, and shogunal authority had increased markedly in its control over the daimyo and their domestic policies. This was

[45] E. O. Reischauer, "Japan", in Coulborn, *Feudalism in History*, 36-37.
[46] J. W. Hall, "The Castle Town and Japan's Modern Urbanization", *FEQ*, XV.1 (Nov., 1955), 41-45.

especially true of the *fudai* daimyo who never really gained sufficient independenc to function as more than local administration agents for the shogun.

If the relationship of shogun to daimyo exhibited a balance between feudal and bureaucratic techniques, the trend toward centralized bureaucratic procedures was conspicuous within the *han*. The key institution in this regard was the *kashindan,* or the assemblage of retainers, which comprised the staff of the shogun and the daimyo. In the early years of the Tokugawa period, the relationship of housemen to daimyo was still in the main personal and voluntary. Though many of the retainers were stipended, the upper strata were individually enfeoffed. But later, with the nearly complete withdrawal of the samurai from the land to live in the castle headquarters towns of the daimyo, the members of the *kashindan* lost their individual identity. Grouped by rank into an army-type organization they were placed under appointed leaders and assigned freely to civil and military duties. Throughout the Tokugawa period the tendency within the shogunal and daimyo administration was for the central authority to gain at the expense of the independent vassal. Within the *kashindan* the number of landed and high salaried officers was constantly reduced while the number of dependent and stipended men increased. Eventually even the remaining land allotments were fictionalized. In certain instances daimyo without territory received rice incomes from the shogun's granary.[47] In the han, supposedly enfeoffed retainers actually received only stipends, losing all powers of interference in the affairs of the villages which once comprised their fiefs. By the beginning of the eighteenth century nearly ninety per cent of the daimyo had forced their entire retinues to draw their subsistence from the domain granaries.[48]

These changes were accompanied by important changes in the nature of the bond which tied samurai to daimyo. The pledge of loyalty, once so sacred as to be sealed in blood, became increasingly formalized and perfunctory. In many instances the personally sworn oath was dispensed with and required only when a retainer took an important post in the daimyo's service. Thus, in most areas of Japan "personal vassalage privately rewarded by enfeoffment was giving way to a system of military statuses which fed into a civil and military bureaucracy. Loyalty was becoming a principle rather than a private commitment."[49] The daimyo became more a legal symbol than a personal despot.

In other sectors of Tokugawa society also authority was being exerted less as a personal right than through institutional or legal channels. The authority of the samurai class, asserted under the feudal system as a privately exercised prerogative over fiefs and cultivators, gave way to a more impersonal

---

47 The Hitotsubashi branch of the Tokugawa house received 100,000 *hyō* (bales) of rice.
48 See Kanai Madoka, "Dokai kōshūki ni okeru bakuhan taisei no ichi hyōgen", *Shinano,* 3.6 (June, 1951), 37-47.
49 J. W. Hall, "The Modern Japanese Daimyo", 327-328.

and public administrative system. For the farming class the condition of personal bondage gave way to the status of taxpaying tenant of the daimyo. Local administration was absorbed into the daimyo's bureaucracy and no longer subdivided among the daimyo's retainers. Corvée labor and personal indenture was increasingly replaced by paid labor and paid domestic service.[50]

How useful is it to call Tokugawa Japan feudal? The historian meets in seventeenth and eighteenth century Japan many of the same conceptual problems that he did in the Kamakura age. Here was a time when only a dwindling portion of the structure and process of Japanese government and society conformed to the requirements of the feudal model. Yet the tendency has always been to stress the importance of this feudal remnant. And understandably so, for the period was obviously dominated by the *bushi* class, the prime agents of feudal practices in Japan from the twelfth century on. In fact, Japan of Tokugawa times was probably more thoroughly dominated and saturated by the samurai than at any other time in its history. And yet the samurai class itself was becoming less characteristically feudal in its manner of exercising political authority and in the social and economic institutions which it nourished.

The task of identifying the essentially feudal from the non-essential remnants of traditional practices is made the more difficult for the historian of the Tokugawa period because the samurai themselves were so loath to part with their memories of the past. As in Europe, the "idea of feudalism" lingered much longer than the substance. The forms, rituals, and speech of feudalism continued in much the same way in Tokugawa Japan as did the fief in its fictionalized form. Certainly if Tokugawa institutions are to be called feudal, this must be done with a full realization of the declining feudal content of many political and social practices.

Feudalism as a concept of explanation for Tokugawa history thus has serious limitations. The tendency of the historian of post-Tokugawa Japan to explain Tokugawa institutions as feudal obscures too much. Such phrases as the "death agony of feudalism" or the "abolition of feudalism" are suggestive of much more change than actually took place. The common failing of historians to keep more of the old system around than the facts justify permits them in the end to kill off a healthier old regime that actually existed. The abolition of the *han* and of the samurai status after 1871 or the granting of land ownership certificates in 1873 symbolize the passing of institutions which had only a superficial resemblance to the criteria of a strictly defined feudal model.

In the foregoing paragraphs we have been able to narrate the story of feudalism *in* Japan without any necessary reference to European experience.

[50] See K. Asakawa, "Notes on Village Government in Japan after 1600", *JAOS*, XXX-XXXI (1910-1911), 259-300; 151-216. Also T. C. Smith, *The Agrarian Origins of Modern Japan* (Stanford, 1959), 24-25.

Feudalism in Japan—A Reassessment

A study of feudalism *in* Japan can be carried through, then, completely within the confines of Japanese history itself. Since the Japanese data contain terms for each of the specified relationships which make up the feudal model, it would have been possible, in fact, to have written the whole story in Japanese. What, then, has been the value of setting up a model of feudalism as a backdrop to Japanese history? The answer must be found not in the story we have just narrated but elsewhere; it lies in the comparative and causal questions which can now be asked, and perhaps answered, about Japanese history.

The variety of questions which the comparative historian may ask of his data can only be suggested in the pages which follow. These questions may obviously take off from positive or negative premises, from observed similarities or differences, and they may have as their objective the further clarification of the *general concept* of feudalism or of a given historical situation in Japan, Europe, or elsewhere. Now is the proper time to inquire about the differences and similarities between the origin of feudal practices in Europe and Japan, or in the way feudalism declined. What about the "ghost empire" or the "barbarian frontier"; are these necessary ingredients of the pre-feudal environment? Should the emphasis be placed on *empire* of the variety of ancient Rome, or only on a pre-existent system of civil law and administration? Could a modern society adopt a feudal form of government?[51] Or again we may wish to ask about the role of religion in feudal society. How is it that in both Europe and Japan universal religions (Christianity and Buddhism) functioned so importantly as the intellectual guiding force in an otherwise decentralized society? How important to feudalism was the religious establishment? We may wish to ask about the significance of technology. Must the military aristocracy in a feudal system always wield a sword and clothe itself in armor, or is it a matter of the monopoly of superior arms (of any variety) that counts? Turning to the end of the feudal spectrum we may enquire into such matters as the effect of money economy upon feudal government, the relationship of "feudal patterns of loyalty" to national consciousness, and like problems of transition from feudalism to other forms of society. Such questions and many more have been asked by historians for many generations, but seldom with the necessary openness of approach. The pursuit of hypotheses which ramify from the feudal concept do not yield new criteria which then must be added to the feudal model itself. New observations about the relationship of religion or of money economy to feudalism are useful hypothetical statements to associate with the feudal concept, but they do not constitute part of the model itself.

Turning our comparative process in another direction, we can open up a range of possible insights into Japanese history by inquiring into the reasons

[51] For an attempt to apply the feudal concept to Nazi Germany see Robert Koehl, "Feudal Aspects of National Socialism", *The American Political Science Review*, LIV.4 (Dec., 1960).

for significant differences between European and Japanese institutions. The identification of such differences and studies of their causes help to point up many aspects of Japanese history which have given it its special quality. Asakawa was not the first but certainly one of the most incisive in posing questions regarding differences between Europe and Japan in such areas as international relations, social organization, law, and agriculture. One characteristic of Japan's international position, to take up one of these avenues of inquiry, was its isolation. Isolation protected the Japanese islands from foreign invasion and the easy interference of foreign powers. Does not this condition help account for the slow evolutionary nature of the process of the change in Japanese institutions and the simultaneous continuation of seemingly contradictory institutions (for instance, civil and military systems of government) over long periods of time? Isolation and the homogeneity of the Japanese populace also meant that warfare was always civil war, a condition which may account for the frequent lack of completeness in the outcome of great power struggles in Japan. Thus, Japanese military government seldom achieved a complete degree of centralization, but was generally based on a balance of forces resulting from military compromise. Does this factor also explain the unique relationship in Japan between feudal organization and the source of ultimate sovereignty, the Emperor? How do we account for the continued importance of the imperial institution despite its loss of political power? Why did not the feudal hierarchy ever seek to displace the emperor? Certainly answers to these questions will reveal a great deal about the manner in which power was held and legitimized in Japan.

In practices pertaining to the feudal syndrome itself numerous points of difference between Japan and Europe intrigue the historian into asking for underlying explanations. Is it not possible, for instance, that the Japanese have consistently maintained a more strongly clan-like social organization, especially within the families which comprised the political elite? And does this not account for the fact that the leader-follower relationship has so often been expressed in paternalistic, family-based forms? The historical vocabulary signifying lord and vassal in Japan is full of familial terms such as *yori-oya* (parent = lord), *yori-ko* (child = vassal), *kachū* (the household, meaning all vassals), *kenin* or *kashin* (housemen), *higo* (dependent child, meaning serf). Does this heavy emphasis on family concepts not help to account for the lack of clearly spelled out provisions of lordship and vassalage in Japan?

Numerous other questions come to mind, the answers to which are far from being certain. What has been the influence on Japanese government, especially at the local level, of an economy which places such heavy emphasis on rice as the staple crop and on intensive cultivation based on intensive labor and intricate irrigation techniques? How has Buddhism, so different in its social ethic from Christianity, affected the pattern of thought and behavior of the various Japanese classes, especially of the warrior elite? Is it possible to identify the distinctive influence of Chinese legal systems and social philosophy upon the ideas of the governing class and in the development of judicial institutions in Japan? For each of these questions, comparison with relevant European experience helps to clarify the problem and point to possible areas of explanation.

Comparative interests have encouraged still a bolder line of inquiry regarding large scale processes of social change in Japan. Questions of this type have not always been posed on valid premises, but they have turned the attention of the historian nonetheless to new areas of investigation. Even those who have pursued the "re-feudalization" theory have asked significant questions which, when answered, will reveal a great deal that is yet unknown about Japan. Why did not Sakai develop as a free city? Why did not Hideyoshi, or at least Ieyasu, destroy the daimyo and establish a centralized national state? Why did the Tokugawa "reaffirm" the samurai class? These are questions the comparative historian asks, though perhaps with little hope of answer. And he asks them for the very reason that he is struck by contrasts or similarities with what he knows of other histories. It is from such a speculative frame of mind that one of the most intriguing of all comparative questions has been posed, first by Asakawa and most recently by Reischauer. In a discourse on "the feudal legacy" in Japan Reischauer suggests that the feudal experience in Japan "which so closely paralleled that of Europe, may have had something to do with the speed and ease with which the Japanese during the past century refashioned their society and government on European models."[52] Such factors in Japanese society as the aristocratic military tradition, the code of honor, national consciousness, concepts of law, styles of economic and social organization, all of which contrasted with parallel Chinese institutions, he suggests, may well account for Japan's early lead in modernization. Speculations of this last type do not necessarily depend for their existence on the perusal of a systematic comparative technique. But any attempted answer must rest upon the disciplined use of terms and procedures of comparison.

Note: The author wishes to acknowledge the support of the Carnegie Corporation of New York to the project on the Political Modernization of Japan at the University of Michigan for aid during the preparation of this essay.

[52]   E. O. Reischauer, "Japan", in Coulborn, *Feudalism in History*, 46. See also E. O. Reischauer, "Our Asian Frontiers of Knowledge", *University of Arizona Bulletin, Riecker Memorial Lecture No. 4,* (Tucson, 1958) for a fuller treatment of this idea.

PART TWO
THE ESTABLISHMENT
OF DAIMYO RULE

CHAPTER THREE

THE NEW LOOK OF TOKUGAWA HISTORY

JOHN WHITNEY HALL

THE Tokugawa period in Japanese history has suffered a bad press from modern historians both in Japan and the West. As the "old regime" against which the new Japan sought to measure its progress, or as the last dark age of feudalism and despotism before the saving touch of Western influence, Tokugawa Japan has appeared to embody for most writers all that was undesirable in Japan's past. In recent years, however, this predominantly negative view has begun to change. As with the Dark Ages in Europe or the Old Regime in France, historians have begun to treat the Tokugawa period less as something to deplore than to explore.

Changes in historical interpretation can result from a variety of circumstances. C. Vann Woodward, commenting on the fact that "Our Past Isn't What It Used To Be," has suggested that historical revisionism "arises mainly out of new readings of old evidence in the light of changed conditions by historians with new preoccupations, sensitivities, identifications, methods and moods."[1] New interpretations of Tokugawa history have arisen from precisely such factors. Some new evidence has been added, to be sure, but of greater significance have been the new preoccupations and identifications of the current generation of Tokugawa scholars.

It is interesting to reflect that this is not the first time that opinions have changed regarding the Tokugawa period. The writings of the seventeenth-century Jesuit missionaries or of the Dutch traders at Nagasaki frequently contained quite favorable accounts of Tokugawa government and society. To these early European observers the shogun and daimyo appeared to rule with no greater severity than the kings and princes of Europe. The Englishman, Will Adams, for instance, could say of the people of Tokugawa Japan: "their justice is severely executed without any partialitie upon transgressors of the law. They are governed in great civilitie. I meane, not a land better governed in the world by civill police."[2] And the Japanese of the time appear to have endured the rigors of a tightly regimented social and political system periodically to raise their voices in praise of the "great peace" which sustained them.

But the undercurrent of resentment against the Tokugawa regime which built up during the long years of shogunal domination, and the hostility which arose during the hectic decades after 1830 when Japan came into con-

---

[1] C. Vann Woodward "Our Past Isn't What It Used to Be," *New York Times Book Review*, July 28, 1963, 1.

[2] As quoted by Basil Hall Chamberlain, *Things Japanese* (4th ed. revised; London, Kobe, 1939), 273.

tact with the British, French, and Americans, turned Japanese opinion deeply negative. The Restoration of 1868 became a revolt against the Tokugawa order in more than a narrow political sense. The Charter Oath of 1868 spoke of the need to purge Japan of "base customs of former times." The Tokugawa memory became an evil dream—a repository of all that Japan must be rid of before it could embark upon the way of progress and national success.

To the Japanese of the Meiji enlightenment little good could be found in the Tokugawa period. Fukuzawa Yukichi railed against the feudal regime and its restrictive social code, its minute gradations of rank and privilege, and the servility it inculcated in the lower classes. To him the Tokugawa rulers provided "the worst government in the whole world."[3] And he spent a lifetime trying to educate the Japanese out of their acceptance of social inequalities and the Confucian values upon which the old attitudes rested. Japanese historians of a later date continued to find reasons to disparage their immediate past. As the "defeated dynasty" the Tokugawa regime was carefully scrutinized for its weaknesses. And once the models of the French and English revolutions were placed before the Japanese, the Tokugawa period was probed for answers to why Japan remained "retarded" by comparison to Europe or why it failed spontaneously to develop popular government. Marxist historians drew adverse comparisons with Europe even more sharply. Since the 1930's, the Tokugawa policy has been looked upon as embodying the culmination of feudalism, whose contradictions and tensions provided the motive power for the Restoration, but whose backward features accounted for the inadequacy of the social revolution which might have assisted Japan into the modern world. Thus as historians followed Japan's course of military expansion, the Tokugawa legacy became identified in their minds with that "fatal flaw" in the historical traditions which brought their country into suicidal war in the Pacific.

One would expect Western scholars to have approached the Tokugawa period with fewer negative biases. But they too found themselves committed to certain preconceptions and cultural prejudices which served to play down many of the genuine problems which the Tokugawa age willed to modern Japan while exaggerating others. The late nineteenth-century foreign observers of Japan, obsessed with the mission of bringing progress and enlightenment to a recently "opened" country, viewed the values and institutions of the Tokugawa period as benighted and backward. By the 1850's the Western image of Japan was far from favorable. Seclusion had led to Western ignorance; and ignorance had led to fantasy. The Japanese were considered remote, exclusive, hostile, "a species of semi-cannibal race who indulged in an annual practice of 'trampling on the cross.'"[4] Upon closer observation the image was tempered: the Japanese people were found to be courteous, alert, and open; it was rather

---

[3] Carmen Blacker, *The Japanese Enlightenment, A Study of the Writings of Fukuzawa Yukichi* (Cambridge, 1964), 9.

[4] Quoted in Akira Iriye, "Minds Across the Pacific: Japan in American Writing (1853–1883)," *Papers on Japan,* Harvard (June 1961), 3.

their social and political institutions which were to be blamed for the arrogance and suspiciousness of the Japanese official. Vistors from the England of Victoria now spoke with alarm of the police state methods of the "Tokugawa dictators" and the corruption of the samurai officials. To Sir Rutherford Alcock the Edo regime was a "feudal form of government, . . . an administration based on the most elaborate system of espionage ever attempted . . . a discivilising agent . . . an impediment to progress intellectual and moral."[5]

If to Western observers the Tokugawa period had become the night from which Japan had been awakened, the Meiji Restoration came to stand for the dawn of that new awakening. William Griffis hailed the year of the abolition of the daimyo domains in the most enthusiastic terms. "Japan's record of progress for 1871 is noble. . . . Feudalism is dead. . . . The swords of the samurai are laid aside. . . . Progress is everywhere the watchword. Is not this the finger of God?"[6] Ernest Clement welcomed the Meiji constitution as a document which "took Japan forever out of the ranks of Oriental despotisms and placed her among the constitutional monarchies."[7] Progress, to these writers, was the measure of Japan's willingness to reject the past and to acquire enlightenment from the West. The Tokugawa period passed further into ill repute.

And so later Western writers joined Japanese historians in looking critically upon the Tokugawa period. To Edwin Reischauer, Tokugawa policy was "reactionary" even in the early seventeenth century.[8] Herbert Norman considered the regime "the most conscious attempt in history to freeze society into a rigid hierarchal mold."[9] Most general accounts were content to see Japan in 1850 as feudal, isolated, and asleep to progress. Modernization was the gift of the West.

Of course Japan was, to an extent, all of these things: feudal, backward, regimented, isolated, and economically weak. But it was the *extent* that made all the difference, and it was the *context* within which these terms were applied to Japan that mattered to the historian. Thus it has been in large part the willingness of writers since World War II to look back upon the conditions of Tokugawa life without negative precommitment that has produced the most recent revisions of interpretation.

Oddly enough the postwar change in Japanese attitude toward the Tokugawa period has been most noticeable, not among scholars, but among the general public. The popular imagination has recently turned back to the Tokugawa age and to the heroic wars which preceded it with new curiosity surprisingly devoid of prejudice. Television serials have taken up the lives of Nobunaga, Hideyoshi, and Ieyasu, making idols of men once scorned for their

---

[5] Sir Rutherford Alcock, *The Capital of the Tycoon: A Narrative of a Three Years' Residence in Japan,* 2 vols. (London, 1863), vol. II, 250.

[6] William Elliot Griffis, *The Mikado's Empire,* (5th ed., New York, 1906), 540.

[7] Ernest W. Clement, *A Handbook of Modern Japan* (9th edition, Chicago, 1913), 120.

[8] Edwin O. Reischauer, *Japan Past and Present,* (2nd edition, New York, 1963), 80–81.

[9] E. Herbert Norman, *Japan's Emergence as a Modern State* (New York, 1946), 12.

militarism. Yamaoka Sōhachi has stretched his best-selling novel based on the life of Ieyasu to well over twenty volumes and a sale of over ten million volumes. Recently even the business world has taken to recommending this work to its young executives. The Old Badger, as Ieyasu was known in history, has apparently found a new place in the Japanese imagination, not because of his stubborn military capacities, but because of his exemplification of the qualities of the modern organization man.

Elsewhere in Japan today there is evidence of a rising boom of interest in the Tokugawa period. The great Nikkō mausoleum, dedicated to Ieyasu, has recently been refurbished at national expense. Tokugawa castles which were bombed during World War II are now being busily rebuilt—in ferro-concrete and usually together with plans for a museum, amusement park, or some other tourist attraction. Japan's great age of castle building, the Keichō era of the 1590's, has been matched by a second age of construction as the "Castles of Shōwa" have sprung up during the 1950's and 1960's. The Japanese people, now separated from their Tokugawa past by both the Restoration and the Occupation, are finding it possible to look back, less in anger than with nostalgia and even pride, to discover in Tokugawa Japan heroes or symbols of power and grandeur which can excite their modern sensibilities.

This boom of interest and willingness to forego resentment toward the past is still largely a phenomenon of the popular mind. It is less evident in Japanese academic circles, for which the Tokugawa period remains a dark age. Japanese historians immediately after the war noticeably hardened their attitude toward the Tokugawa regime by developing the theory that feudalism in Japan came to its repressive culmination under the Tokugawa shogunate and that this condition bequeathed to Meiji Japan a political absolutism which successfully repressed the desires of the Japanese people for political and economic freedom.[10] For Japanese scholars it has been hard to look back to the Tokugawa era through the rubble of the Pacific War with any sense of forgiveness.

Yet the last decade of Japanese scholarship has given evidence of certain changes in attitude. For one thing, the Edo era has recently become a major

---

[10] Nakamura Kichiji in *Nihon hōkensei saihenseishi* (History of the reestablishment of feudalism in Japan) (Tokyo, 1939), has presented the classical statement of the "refeudalization" theory. His later work, notably his "Kokudaka seido to hōkensei—Bakuhan taisei no seikaku" (The *kokudaka* system and feudalism—the nature of the shogunal-daimyo system) in *Shizaku zasshi,* LXIX, nos. 7–8 (July, August 1960), has developed the theme that Tokugawa government was not fully feudal. Suzuki Ryōichi's *Shokuhō seiken ron* (On the governmental structure of the Shokuhō period) in *Nihon rekishi kōza, Chūseihen,* vol. 2, Tokyo, 1953, develops the idea that Tokugawa institutions represent "pure feudalism." Araki Moriaki, "Taikokenchi no rekishiteki igi" (The historical meaning of the Taiko cadastral survey) in *Rekishigaku kenkyū,* 167, 1954, and Miyagawa Mitsuru, *Taiko kenchi ron* (On the Taiko cadastral survey), 2 vols. (Tokyo, 1957), have developed the theory that the Tokugawa government was the only true feudalism. Hatori Shisō in his *Zettaishugi ron* (*The Theory of absolution*) (Tokyo, 1948), and Tōyama Shigeki, *Meiji Ishin* (*The Meiji Restoration*) (Tokyo), have linked Tokugawa institutions to the "absolutism" of the Meiji period.

focus of scholarly attention. Important collections of source materials are being published on a wide variety of subjects. The Historiographical Institute's *Dai Nihon Kinsei Shiryō* (*Historical Sources of Early Modern Japan*), which began publication in 1953, now consists of over 30 volumes of village records, shogunal personnel registers, official diaries, and the like. The Hampō Kenkyūkai (Society for the Study of Han Statutes), organized in 1954, has already brought out several volumes of legal records from some of the major daimyo domains.[11] And in almost every locality archivists are at work collecting the remaining Tokugawa materials into libraries or for publication.

By comparison with the state of affairs just a decade ago, there has been a literal transformation in the field of Tokugawa studies nurtured by the availability of new materials and a new interest in local history.[12] Characteristic of the new work in the field has been a tendency to play down the pronounced anti-establishment biases of the previous decade in favor of a greater degree of empiricism in selecting problems and in drawing conclusions. Closely researched monographic works now abound for every level of Tokugawa institutional study.

Most of the significant work on the Tokugawa period in recent years has in fact been institutional in its prime focus. Moreover, scholars have begun to direct their attention to the secondary levels of the political structure—to the daimyo domains and the local organs of *bakufu* administration—as against the shogunate in its national political role. Studies of the "power structure" of shogunate or the composition of the daimyo domains—what is referred to as the *baku-han* system—have begun to appear in profusion. The formation in 1958 of the Hanseishi Kenkyūkai (Society for the Historical Study of Han Government) under Professor Itō Tasaburō of Tokyo University has set the stage for a genre of studies which is now coming into full view.[13] Kanai Madoka's *Hansei* (*Han Government*), published in 1962, was the first effort to synthesize the new field of han studies. Fujino Tamotsu's *Bakuhan taiseishi no kenkyū* (*Historical Study of the baku-han System*), published the year before, was the first analytical study of the political institutions and configurations of political powers within the *bakufu* using the newly available primary materials.

The existence of these new and empirically structured studies does not necessarily signal a conscious interpretive break with the early postwar style of negative evaluation. When it comes to making generalizations or comparisons with Europe, the Japanese historian is still apt to describe the Tokugawa period as being feudal and retarded. Yet fewer scholars are devoting their careers

---

[11] Hampō Kenkyūkai, ed., *Hampō shū* (Tokyo), vol. 1 (in 2 parts), *Okayama han*, 1959; vol. 3, *Tottori han*, 1961; vol. 4, *Kanazawa han*, 1963; vol. 4, *Shohan*, 1964.

[12] Compare the present state of Tokugawa studies with an assessment made in 1956 in my "Materials for the study of local history in Japan," HJAS, vol. 20, Nos 1–2 (June 1957), 188–91.

[13] The first monograph produced by this group is: Hanseishi Kenkyūkai, *Hansei seiritsu shi no sōgō kenkyū, Yonezawa Han* (*A synthetic study of han government, Yonezawa Han*) (Tokyo, 1962).

to explaining the "negative" side of Tokugawa life, and some, such as Tsuji Tatsuya and Minamoto Ryōen, have begun to call for a revaluation of the Tokugawa age as one which contained the determining factors—good and bad—for modern Japan.[14] Something of a "new look" in Tokugawa history has begun to appear in the Japanese academic world.

Such a new look has been in evidence among Western historians for some years. And this has resulted in large part from certain new premises which Western scholars since the war have adopted in their study of Tokugawa Japan. There has been, first of all, a general change in outlook among historians of the English speaking nations with regard to historical causation and historical theories as a whole. Noticeably weakened in the postwar decades has been the economic interpretation of history. On the one hand, scholars have looked with increased skepticism on simplistic or deterministic solutions to historical problems. Old formulas and explanatory concepts such as feudalism or money economy are being questioned or broken down into component parts. On the other hand, with the aid of new theories from the social sciences, they have been looking for new and more complex explanations of human behavior. Economic or class motives are not neglected, but they no longer are accepted as being primary or exclusively scientific in their revelation. All of this has led to a tendency among historians to see history in less black and white terms—to write in "muted contrasts and low moral voltage," as Professor Woodward put it. In the interpretation of diplomatic history, for instance, there has been a tendency "to let up on the search for villains and the passing of moral judgments."[15] The new approach takes some of the color and much of the fire out of historical writing. But while it does not view history as the handmaiden of political reform nor point the finger of shocked concern at the iniquities of past institutions, it is not without a sense of problem.

Aside from the general change in historical approach to causality, Western historians in the Tokugawa field have shown a sensitivity to the work being done on the periods which lie adjacent to the Tokugawa period. No longer, in other words, is Tokugawa Japan being studied in isolation but rather in the context of the broader sweep of Japan's institutional development. The achievements of the Tokugawa regime are evaluated by comparison with the conditions which preceded the establishment of the Edo shogunate. Tokugawa institutions are studied as they relate to the transformation of Japanese society which came after 1868. Viewed from either of these vantage points—one looking down from the Sengoku era and the other looking backward from the present—the Tokugawa period has taken on increased importance as a time of institutional development.

By far the major source of reinterpretation, of course, has come from the approach which looks upon Tokugawa Japan in the light of Japan's experi-

[14] Tsuji Tatsuya, "Tokugawa sambyakunen no isan" (The legacy of the Tokugawa three hundred years), *Chūōkōron,* No. 923 (1964.9); Minamoto Ryōen, *Meiji no gendōryoku (The motive power of Meiji), IDE kyōiku sensho* no. 89 (Tokyo, 1965).

[15] Woodward, *op. cit.,* 24.

ence at modernization. And it is largely over the evaluation of that experience that Western scholars have differed with Japanese. Western scholars, on the whole, have looked upon Japan's modern development as being comparatively successful—particularly when compared with other countries of Asia and Africa. They have been impressed by Japan's success at "nation-building" and industrialization, though admitting that the Japanese citizen was slow to acquire his civil rights. By contrast Japanese scholars have been more inclined to believe that Japan's economic development was too slow, and that the failure to acquire civil rights and to maintain international peace was an inevitable result of the unhappy legacy of the Tokugawa period. Thus the most recent Western scholarship has taken a rather different course from the bulk of Japanese scholarship. Much of it, at any rate, has been distinguished by the effort to discover "dynamic elements" in the Tokugawa age, to identify if possible "the sources of Japan's modern condition." Thomas Smith's study of Tokugawa village life is entitled *The Agrarian Origins of Modern Japan.*[16] Ronald Dore in his book, *Education in Tokugawa Japan* asks the question "What role did education play in the modernization of Japan?"[17] Where heretofore the transition from Tokugawa to Meiji was seen as a sequence of fossilization, decay, and revolution (or revitalization) under Western influence, the emphasis is now more apt to be placed upon the factors of institutional growth and ideological continuity which bridged Tokugawa and Meiji Japan. And beyond the Restoration there is an increased recognition of the possibility that, as Sir George Sansom put it so well at the beginning of this whole recent trend in interpretation, "many of the important changes that took place in [Meiji] political and social life came about not by direct imitation of Western models but by a natural process of evolution which produced results similar to those which had arisen in the West out of similar circumstances."[18]

To say that Tokugawa history has been given a new look in the works of leading Western scholars should not imply that there has been any conscious attempt to rewrite Japanese history or to form a new school of interpretation. Whatever has happened has come about gradually as scholars have questioned certain longstanding interpretations, or have pursued new lines of interest on the basis of their new premises. The identifying marks of the new look are best revealed, therefore, by examining certain specific points at which the newer scholarship takes exception to the older historiography. The following list of propositions, together with the objections which the recent literature has raised against them, is not comprehensive, but is indicative of the kinds of reinterpretations which make up the new look.

1. *The Tokugawa period was basically feudal.* Feudalism is a much overworked term. The danger in labeling the Tokugawa period feudal is that the concept becomes a blanket characterization of every feature of Tokugawa life. Feudalism, in other words, is used to "explain" events and motivations. One

[16] Thomas C. Smith, *The Agrarian Origins of Modern Japan* (Stanford, 1959).

[17] Ronald P. Dore, *Education in Tokugawa Japan* (Berkeley, 1965).

[18] George B. Sansom, *The Western World and Japan* (New York, 1950), 314–15.

notices in the new works on the Tokugawa period much less reliance on the term as an explanatory device; similarly with such terms as fief, serf, bourgeoisie, and the like. To some extent this makes for a less dramatic historical analysis. What was formerly treated as the "struggle against feudalism," for instance, is drained of emotional overtones. And one can no longer exclaim over what happened in 1871 as "the end of feudalism."

2. *The Tokugawa regime was simply the result of Ieyasu's effort to perpetuate the power of the Tokugawa family.* Certainly Tokugawa Ieyasu did his utmost to assure the continued preeminence of his succession. Still, to maintain that the political institutions of the Tokugawa period were simply the outcome of a dogged attempt at grasping power and perpetuating a family hegemony downgrades the importance of the shogunal and daimyo regimes brought together in 1600. The Tokugawa regime, for all of the special qualities given it by the Tokugawa House, rested on certain basic institutions which had been taking shape across the nation for several decades. Had it not been for Tokugawa Ieyasu, some other leading daimyo would have taken over as hegemon in the early years of the seventeenth century, and his style of governance would not have been markedly different.

A corollary to the above proposition is the claim that the techniques used by the early Tokugawa leaders were essentially reactionary at the time they were adopted and ran counter to the more progressive alternatives offered Japan in 1600—in other words, that the Tokugawa leaders "refeudalized" Japan. On the contrary, the new writers say, the *baku-han* system rested upon the more dynamic of the institutional ingredients available to the Japanese at the end of the sixteenth century. It was, in fact, a major organizational achievement and nothing of which Japan need be ashamed. Over two hundred years of domestic peace is a major achievement under any circumstance.

3. *Tokugawa Japan, by isolating itself from the rest of the world, shut itself off from important stimuli from abroad and therefore stagnated.* It is true that the Japanese of the Tokugawa period reduced to a minimum their contact with the outside world. But the conclusion that this resulted in stagnation does not necessarily follow. Seclusion did not deny the Japanese people the possibility of cultural and intellectual growth. It was not necessary that Japan have direct contact with China for a new wave of Chinese learning to spread through the country and literally transform the intellectual life of the people. Total seclusion against Europeans was never achieved, nor perhaps even attempted. Closure was never so complete that Dutch studies could not be pursued by dedicated private scholars. Even in official circles knowledge of world geography, Western cosmology, astronomy, and military and agricultural science was sought for, once the practical value of such information was appreciated.

4. *Changes which occurred during the Tokugawa period happened "in spite of" the system.* The assumption that fundamental changes in institutions and ways of thought, being unwanted, could only take place behind the "feudal façade" deals with the element of change in too oblique a manner. It plays

down evidence of the internal dynamics of Tokugawa institutional history and hence leads to the interpretation that Japan was literally waked from a deep sleep in 1853. Or it plays up all signs of change as being "contrary to the system" and hence subversive.

The question of whether or not the Tokugawa period was simply a vast two and a half centuries of undifferentiated stagnation as the result of an unparalleled effort to legislate against change has not received sufficient attention from historians. But the common periodization which conceives of the age in terms of a series of routs and rallies down a long path of dynastic decline is obviously off the mark. Changes did take place, and these were not simply destructive in nature. Implicit in the more recent literature is a more dynamic periodization that conceives of the long Tokugawa era as falling into three distinct phases: an early "creative phase," a middle "phase of maturity," and a later "phase of crisis and innovation."

The initial growth phase of Tokugawa institutions must be seen to last well beyond 1600, roughly to 1720. The Tokugawa system, as an integrated set of institutions and policies, was less a straightjacket tightened upon a reluctant country in 1600 than a set of loosely fitting garments. During the first century or so there was still room for growth: political, social, and economic institutions were still being systematized, and the people were still adjusting to new circumstances. For instance, in government the administrative bureaucracy was still being perfected and the samurai were still busy adapting to new bureaucratic values and to life in the castle cities. The social class structure was still being clarified according to function and elaborated by law, while Confucian ideals were brought forward to assure responsible government and social stability. The limits of economic growth and structural development were not yet reached, though urbanization increased immensely and land improvements extended the land under cultivation. In terms of population alone Japan nearly doubled in size.

We can think of the middle century of the Tokugawa period, from roughly 1720 to 1830, as one during which the structure as perfected in the seventeenth century ran out of elasticity. The institutions and precedents which had been adopted earlier could no longer accommodate to the pressures for further change, and the regime was thrown on the defensive. The limits of easy agrarian expansion and population growth were reached. And as a consequence, disturbing inequities began to show up. While certain levels of the samurai class were unable to make economic ends meet, for instance, certain levels of the commercial sector were able to live well and even with conspicuous display. Some of the daimyo domains were able to improve their economic status, while the shogunate and other daimyo were frustrated by debt. Wealthy members of the peasant class acquired land surreptitiously, while the vast majority of the peasantry found their livelihood deteriorating. Such "differential development" continued unchecked and gave rise to both the problems and the dynamics of the late Tokugawa period.

By the 1830's a sense of crisis was gripping much of the country. The turning point probably came in 1837 with Ōshio's rebellion. A realization that the system was running into difficulty now spread widely. The sense of crisis was accentuated during the 1840's by the failure of the shogunal efforts at reform. Of course by this time the Japanese were becoming aware of the dangers of Western encroachment as well. But the essential point is that an internal sense of crisis had come into being and had activated a number of critical attempts at remedy.

5. *Japan in 1835 required the prod of Western influence to rouse it into action.* The "sleeping beauty" theory of Japan's modern awakening is not tenable if we accept the periodization described above. There is no denying, of course, that the influence of the West upon Japan after 1853 was critical. But neither should we deny the evidence of internal changes which served to "prepare" Japan for rapid modernization and which helped to account for the ease with which the Japanese absorbed Western influence after 1853. The attention of recent scholarship has been directed toward what was indigenous to the Tokugawa environment yet which helped to account for the course and pattern of Japan's development as a modern society: in continuities rather than elements of failure.

6. *The Tokugawa "legacy" to modern Japan was ultimately one of political authoritarianism and lingering feudal remnants.* This proposition is perhaps the most difficult to assess with any balance. Marius Jansen has put the problem in sophisticated context in his article "Tokugawa and Modern Japan." But historians have not studied the period from the 1830's to 1900 with sufficient care to enable us to say how much conditions at the turn of the century owed their substance to a direct Tokugawa legacy. Our assessment can only be tentative in terms of a "balance sheet," to use Ronald Dore's phrase. And it is significant that Dore concludes his work on Tokugawa education with the following balanced statement. "The same features of the legacy bequeathed to modern Japan by Tokugawa educators probably helped to promote both economic growth and militaristic expansion, and it is doubtful if Japan could have had the one without the other." [19]

---

[19] R. P. Dore, *Education in Tokugawa Japan,* 315.

CHAPTER FOUR

FOUNDATIONS OF THE MODERN
JAPANESE DAIMYO

JOHN WHITNEY HALL

Reprinted from *Journal of Asian Studies,*
Vol. XX, No. 3 (May 1961)

THE institutional foundations of the Tokugawa daimyo have been obscured by the lack of insight which historians have traditionally shown into the history of the Ashikaga period and, in particular, into the late Ashikaga, or Sengoku, age. Like the Dark Ages in Europe, this chapter of Japanese history has been accepted in historiography as a dark and formless era of war and trouble. Japanese historians have dismissed the Sengoku period as a time of *ge-koku-jō* when the political order was capriciously turned upside down by unworthy leaders. The colorful Western historian, James Murdoch, has heaped his most caustic invectives upon the main figures in Ashikaga history. Of the founder of the Ashikaga shogunate he claimed, "Takauji may indeed have been the greatest man of his time, but that is not saying very much, for the middle of the fourteenth century in Japan was the golden age, not merely of turncoats, but of mediocrities."[1] To Murdoch the Sengoku period was a "vile" age when the Japanese people showed, as he put it, a "lust for war and slaughter . . . utterly beyond human control," and only the timely arrival of the "great trio" of daimyo, Nobunaga, Hideyoshi, and Ieyasu, saved the day for Japan.[2]

Walter Dening, Hideyoshi's biographer, is even more eloquent in depicting the contrast between the Sengoku age and the peace which Hideyoshi brought. "The history of this time," he wrote, "is a history of successful usurpation age after age. . . . The whole country was a scene of desolation unprecedented in Japanese annals. By the genius, indomitable courage, and resolution of one man, the whole aspect of affairs was transformed."[3] To historians such as Murdoch and Dening the daimyo of the late Sengoku age were heroes who brought peace and stability to a chaotic world.

But not all writers have drawn the pre-Tokugawa centuries so darkly nor the daimyo so brightly. Even Murdoch recognized some redeeming features in the Ashikaga period. Recently a brighter side to this dark age has been found by Japanese historians. Nakamura Kichiji was the first to develop this new view, and subsequently it has been included in Western literature.[4] The Sengoku period was a time of hopeful signs, we are told, characterized by the emergence of lightfooted peasants who, as *ashigaru,* vaulted into the ranks of the samurai; by the emergence of free cities; by an expanded foreign trade; and many other purportedly "anti-feudal" tendencies.

---

[1] James Murdoch, *History of Japan* (3 vols., Kōbe and London, 1903–1926), I, 580.

[2] Murdoch, I, 636.

[3] Walter Dening, *The Life of Toyotomi Hideyoshi (1536–98)* (Kōbe, 1930), pp. 6–7.

[4] Nakamura Kichiji, *Hōkensei saihenseishi* [*History of the Re-establishment of the Feudal System*] (Tokyo, 1939).

J. W. Hall

Justified or not, this picture of the Sengoku age is paradoxical to the historian. For, in proportion to the emphasis placed upon the supposedly hopeful or "progressive" signs in Sengoku society, the work of Murdoch's "great trio" is minimized and the daimyo are less admired. For when it is discovered that Hideyoshi, after his unification of Japan, did not complete these trends, and, as one recent writer puts it, did not "respond with a plan of integration which would have placed Japan on the threshold of progress as a modern state and world power,"[5] the question arises "Why not?"

The answer most frequently given is that Hideyoshi was a spokesman of conservative feudal interests. Nobunaga's reduction of Sakai, Hideyoshi's slamming of the door in the face of those who would have followed him out of the peasantry, and Ieyasu's purported return to outgrown feudal institutions have been held against Murdoch's heroes. Japanese historians have gone further. Suzuki Ryōichi has called the social settlement under Hideyoshi a "betrayal" perpetrated by a victorious coalition of feudal groups against the struggling *nōmin*. In his words, "The new absolute feudal hegemony . . . suppressed the further anti-feudal struggle of the peasantry . . . ."[6] What are we to believe: that the dark ages were dark or bright, that the "great trio" were heroes or traitors?

The answer to this question lies in the study of the daimyo who emerged as the new political masters of Japan and of the methods by which they gained and governed their domains. Of all the institutional products of the Ashikaga period, the daimyo were without question the most significant. A study of the Ashikaga period in the light of the evolution of the daimyo as the representative figures of Japanese local and national government, rather than as individual heroes, can illuminate this enigmatic chapter of Japanese history, divorced from the labels of *ge-koku-jō* or of hero-worship. Conversely, it is only as we trace the institutional origins of the daimyo back into the Ashikaga period that their true significance as the molders of local government in Tokugawa Japan can be understood.

In recent years, Japanese historians such as Nagahara Keiji, Satō Shin'ichi, Toyoda Takeshi, Itō Tasaburō, and Nakamura Kichiji, have directed serious attention to the institutional origins of the daimyo. Although these scholars have not always agreed upon the interpretation of their data, their studies have given us a useful periodization and nomenclature for this field of study. Basically, what these men have done is to make a series of cross-sectional analyses of the structure of Japanese local administration at four points in time from, roughly, the middle of the fourteenth century to the end of the seventeenth century. This admittedly artificial segmentation of the continuum of social change has provided the data for the postulation of four ideal daimyo types, each building successively upon the institutions of the previous, and each embracing larger and more effective areas of hegemony. They are: (1) the *shugo-daimyō* type which characterize the period from mid-fourteenth century to somewhat beyond the Ōnin wars, approximately until the 1490's, (2) the *sengoku-daimyō* type which emerged before 1500 and continued into the 1560's and 1570's, (3) the *shokuhō-*

---

[5] Ryusaku Tsunoda, Wm. Theodore de Bary, Donald Keene, comp., *Sources of the Japanese Tradition* (New York, 1958), p. 322.

[6] Suzuki Ryōichi, "Shokuhō-seiken ron" ["On the Shokuhō Political Structure"], Rekishigaku Kenkyūkai and Nihonshi Kenkyūkai, *Nihon rekishi kōza* [*Lectures on Japanese History*] (8 vols., Tokyo, 1952), IV, 86.

daimyō type which came into being under Nobunaga and Hideyoshi and lasted until the early seventeenth century, and (4) the *kinsei-daimyō* type which became dominant during the Tokugawa period and matured by the end of the seventeenth century.[7] Each of these types exhibited certain distinctive patterns of social and political organization within several levels of government: (1) the level of ultimate authority and sanction for the exercise of legal or administrative powers, (2) the level of power organization among the local elite, and (3) the level of relationships between local power holders and the various subordinate groups of local inhabitants.

The possibility that the military confusion of the Sengoku period masked many fundamental and even revolutionary social and political changes has not been ignored completely by historians. The traditional emphasis upon the "reunification" of Japan has implied the adoption of certain new practices of military and political organization. G. B. Sansom has laid considerable stress on the shift in social organization from clan to family and on the changing nature of feudal law.[8] K. Asakawa has studied the evolving patterns of land tenure and fiscal administration.[9] What has been lacking has been a recognition of the full magnitude and variety of the institutional changes which accompanied the emergence of the modern daimyo and the capacity to describe these changes comprehensively. A structural study of the daimyo domain provides the materials for such an integrated treatment.

It may be argued, of course, that a single pattern of daimyo evolution cannot possibly emerge from the diverse local histories of the scattered regions of Japan. And it is unquestionably true that, in terms of timing and pattern, social change in Japan has shown considerable regional variation. On the other hand, enough work has been done by Japanese historians to show that there is a "main stream" of daimyo evolution illustrated by the progression of the four ideal types described above. The following amplification of the institutional origins of the modern daimyo combines this recent work of Japanese historians with data taken from the case study of a single locality: the province of Bizen, which occupies today the southeastern third of Okayama Prefecture. The history of the rise of the modern daimyo in Bizen follows rather closely the main stream of daimyo development. Admittedly, it contrasts with the pattern in some of the fringe areas of the Japanese islands, as those familiar with Asakawa's work on Satsuma will recognize.[10] But the Bizen case is close to the norm

---

[7] For a selection of the more accessible and generalized writings of these historians see: Nagahara Keiji, "Shugo ryōkokusei no tenkai" ["The Changing Structure of the *Shugo* Domain"], *Shakaikeizaishigaku*, XVII (Feb. 1951), 103–104; Satō Shin'ichi, "Shugo ryōkokusei no tenkai" ["The Changing Structure of the *Shugo* Domain"], *Shin Nihon rekishi taikei [New Series on Japanese History]* (6 vols., Tokyo, 1952–1954), III, 81–127; Toyoda Takeshi, "Sengoku-daimyō-ryō no keisei" ["The Structure of the Sengoku Daimyo Domain"], *Shin Nihon rekishi taikei*, III, 197–223; Toyoda Takeshi, "Shokuhō seiken" ["The Shokuhō Political Structure"], *Nihon rekishi kōza*, III, 185–208; Itō Tasaburō, "Kinsei daimyō kenkyū josetsu" ["Introduction to the Study of the Modern Daimyo"], *Shigaku zasshi*, LV, nos. 9 and 11 (Sept., Nov. 1944); Nakamura Kichiji, "Kokudaka seido to hōkensei—Bakuhan taisei no seikaku—" ["The *kokudaka* System and Feudalism—The Nature of the Shogunal-Daimyo System—"], *Shigaku zasshi*, LXLX, nos. 7–8 (July, Aug. 1960).

[8] George B. Sansom, *Japan—A Short Cultural History* (rev. ed., New York, 1943), pp. 362–365.

[9] Asakawa Kan'ichi, tr. and ed., *The Documents of Iriki, Illustrative of the Development of the Feudal Institutions of Japan* (New Haven, 1929).

[10] Satsuma, the scene of the Asakawa's study of the Iriki house documents, is one of the few regions in which a *shugo* family of Kamakura origin, the Shimazu, managed to retain its power and continue as a daimyo under the Tokugawa hegemony.

J. W. Hall

of the process as it unfolded throughout central Japan, and it was this area which provided leadership both in social change and political unification.

Bizen, one of the original 66 provinces established in the eighth century, had a history of relatively stable administration with strong ties to the center of court influence at Kyōto. Comprising an area of about 670 square miles, it supported a population of just under 400,000 persons by the end of the seventeenth century. During the Tokugawa period, it was totally dominated by the daimyo of Okayama, hereditarily assigned to the house of Ikeda. Although Bizen did not provide the base of support for a major *shugo-daimyō* power during the early Ashikaga period, it eventually gave rise to an indigenous daimyo family, the Ukida, which gained national prominence under Nobunaga and Hideyoshi. The Ukida were succeeded by the Ikeda during the early years of the Tokugawa hegemony, and it was the latter house which perfected the institutions of the modern daimyo in Bizen.

The shugo-daimyō

The wars of the dynasties during the last half of the fourteenth century witnessed the emergence of a group of powerful local families bearing the title of *shugo* and given appointment by the Ashikaga shogun. These *shugo* were essentially military governors, for they served both as the military subordinates of the shogun and exercised the remaining civil functions of the former imperial provincial governors.[11] These military governors were, in effect, the institutional forerunners of the later daimyo, although in only rare instances, such as the Shimazu, Ōtomo, or Date, did *shugo* families manage to perpetuate their power to become daimyo at a later age.

The units of *shugo* jurisdiction and appointment were provinces (*kuni*) such as Bizen, over which they exercised prescribed legal powers vested in them by the shogun, who derived his authority in principle from the emperor. In most provinces, however, a sizeable discrepancy existed between the jurisdictional authority of the *shugo* and the area of their enforceable authority. The imperial bureaucratic system was nearly dead, but the system of military allegiances and controls had not yet fully taken its place. This, in essence, was the weakness of the Ashikaga policy, and not Murdoch's turncoats and mediocrities.

Bizen, during the early Ashikaga period, was divided into some 105 *shōen* units, administered under a confusing welter of resident and absentee proprietorships. Of these, 4 were held by the imperial family, 4 by court families, 26 by centrally located temples or shrines, and 12 by the Hosokawa family whose head served as deputy shogun (*kanrei*). Thirty or more small *shōen* were held, probably under resident proprietorships, by military families, most of them former *jitō*.[12] One of these houses,

---

[11] Itō Tasaburō, *Nihon hōkenseido shi* [*History of Feudal Institutions in Japan*] (Tokyo, 1951), p. 142; Yoshimura Shigeki, *Kokushi-seido hōkai ni kansuru kenkyū* [*A Study of the Decline of the System of Provincial Governorships*] (Tokyo, 1957). For a case study of a *shugo* family in the vicinity of Okayama see: Matsuoka Hisato, "Ōuchi-shi no hatten to sono ryōkoku shihai" ["The Emergence of the Ōuchi House and its System of Territorial Control"], in Uozumi Sōgorō, *Daimyō-ryōkoku to jōkamachi* [*Daimyo Territories and castle towns*] (Kyōto, 1957).

[12] These figures were compiled by Madoka Kanai from the following sources: Nagayama Usaburō, *Okayama Ken nōchishi* [*History of Agricultural Land in Okayama Prefecture*] (Okayama, 1952), 394–452; Nakamura Naokatsu, *Shōen no kenkyū* [*Studies on shōen*] (Tokyo, 1939), 601–643; Takeuchi Rizō, *Jiryō shōen no kenkyū* [*Studies on Temple Shōen*] (Tokyo, 1942), 63–64, 77, 471–472; Nishioka Toranosuke, *Shōenshi no kenkyū* [*Studies on Shōen History*] (3 vols., Tōkyō, 1956–1957), III, 882–886; Shimizu Masatake, *Shōen shiryō* [*Documents on Shōen*] (2 vols., Tōkyō, 1933), 1121 ff.

the Matsuda, briefly held the appointment of *shugo* of Bizen, but lost the title to a stronger power, the Akamatsu of the neighboring province of Harima. The Akamatsu served as *shugo* of Bizen for most of the years from 1364 to 1522.[13]

From almost any point of view the basis of Akamatsu power was precarious. In Harima, the family held 12 *shōen* in varying degrees of completeness, and other holdings were scattered over 6 other provinces. In its home province the Akamatsu may have controlled a tenth of the land and counted a majority of the *bushi* families as their allies or vassals. But the interests of absentee court and religious proprietors were still evident in the province. In Bizen the Akamatsu held but two of the 105 *shōen*, so that their authority rested almost entirely on the uncertain submission of the Matsuda house which dominated western Bizen and on the services of the Urakami, who, as *jitō* of one of the Akamatsu *shōen*, fought for a precarious hold over eastern Bizen. To both of these houses, the Akamatsu assigned titles as deputy-military-governors (*shugodai*).

The existence of a gap between the area of enforceable authority and that of legal jurisdiction accounts for the importance the *shugo* placed upon their participation in the affairs of the Ashikaga shogunate and the reliance they placed upon the shogun's support in their own local affairs. It is an historic irony, however, that this reliance upon central rather than local sources of power was to be their undoing. The necessity the *shugo* felt for the legal authority of the shogunate and the court involved them more and more in the affairs of the capital. But as the *shugo* families turned their attention to Kyōto, they found the task of organizing and holding their territories increasingly beyond their means. The network of relatives and trusted vassals on whom they depended became scattered and divided in loyalties and interests. Neither the force of the oath of allegiance nor family solidarity based on primogeniture had been perfected.[14] Competition on the national stage drew the *shugo* and their armies away from their power bases, so that they gradually lost their hold over the lower echelons of their own subordinates. Real initiative in the provinces began to pass to another level of local families, very often to the *shugodai* who had been able to put down stronger roots in the local soil. In the Ōnin war, the *shugo* families exhausted themselves opposing each other, so that nearly all disappeared or became the puppets of their stronger vassals. Between 1467 and the 1530's, the far-flung jurisdictional territories of the *shugo* broke into fragments, and a second wave of families of local origin inherited the pieces.

The sengoku-daimyō

In Bizen, the collapse of the Akamatsu between 1483 and 1522 brought the two *shugodai* families, the Matsuda and Urakami, to the fore. Theirs was not a simple case of inheritance from the Akamatsu, however. The territories controlled by these

---

[13] Mizuno Kyōichirō, "Shugo Akamatsu-shi no ryōkoku shihai to Kakitsu no hen" [The Territorial Administration of the *shugo* Akamatsu House and the Kakitsu Incident], *Shirin*, 42 (1959), 254–281.

[14] For an analysis of the institutional weaknesses of a *shugo* house similar to the Akamatsu see: Koyamada Yoshio, "Muromachi jidai no Mōri-shi ni tsuite" ["On the Mōri House during the Muromachi Period"] *Rekishi kyōiku*, 7.8 (1959), 24–26; Fukui Sakuji, "Mōri-shi no daimyō ryōshusei no hatten" ["The Development by the Mōri House of its System of Daimyo Territorial Control"], *Geibi chihōshi kenkyū*, V–VI (1954), 17–24. Sugiyama Hiroshi, *Shōen kaitai katei no kenkyū* [*Studies on the Dissolusion of the Shōen*] (Tōkyō, 1959), 138–192.

emerging *sengoku-daimyō* were of a new and more rugged type. In them, the gap between legal and effective control had been wiped away, or, more correctly, it had become impossible to lay claim to jurisdictional authority unsupported by actual military force.

In the region of Bizen today, the remains of over 200 small hilltop fortifications, dating from the Sengoku period, stand as evidence of a new kind of political-military organization based on entrenched military power.[15] At the bottom of Bizen elite society, small *bushi* landowners, asserting themselves in their immediate neighborhoods, built up small but strongly consolidated units each consisting of a fort and surrounding fiefs, unifying within the protection of the fort the many *myōshu,* or cultivators, of these fiefs. These were the building blocks of the power structure of a new warring society, the individual leader of which was the mounted fighter, or *ki.* Such leaders were gradually and systematically organized into larger valley-wide hierarchies of loyalties under the leadership of the former *shugodai* during the wars of the Sengoku era. But while it was primarily upon military coercion that the former *shugodai* relied for their regional hegemony, they utilized as well the residue of prestige and legal authority which remained from their previous official titles.

In Bizen, two competing centers of military power came into existence led by the Matsuda and Urakami.[16] Each of these longstanding powers had entrenched themselves in mountain fastnesses from which they could extend control over the lesser military houses within small but defensible geographical regions. The Matsuda, controlling the Asahi River valley of western Bizen, counted 350 *ki* among their vassals in the 1490's and could muster 5000 men in emergency. Their domain, or, rather, sphere of influence, was an area of relatively fluid boundaries including 20 major tributary-valley forts and many smaller ones. The Urakami sphere of power which embraced the Yoshii River of eastern Bizen did not reach full maturity until the 1550's. By that time it consisted of some 172 separate fiefs (*chigyōchi*) held by 59 major vassals.[17] Each vassal was enfeoffed directly, and few held less than what was later the equivalent of 500 *koku.* Thus we can visualize the majority of these 59 vassals as petty castle-holders, each possessing his own followers and land-holdings of long standing. *Sengoku-daimyō,* such as the Urakami and Matsuda, were in effect leaders of separate coalitions of local families (generally referred to as *kokujin*), most of which had grown up within the *shōen* system as *jitō.* These coalitions had been drawn together over a long period of time and were characterized by a heavy reliance on kinship and marriage relationships in addition to bonds of vassalage and enfeoffment for purposes of solidarity. This was particularly true of the Matsuda, the majority of whose supporters were heads of branch families or were linked to the Matsuda by direct marriage ties.[18]

As a general rule, at least until after 1530 or so, the daimyo of the Sengoku period did not acquire jurisdiction over territories which approached in size those of the

---

[15] Nagayama Usaburō, *Okayama Ken tsūshi* [*Survey History of Okayama Prefecture*] (2 vols., Okayama, 1930), II, 987–1011.

[16] Okayama Shiyakusho, *Okayama Shi shi* [*History of Okayama City*] (6 vols., Okayama, 1938), II, 1195 ff. Tanaka Seiichi, ed., *Kibi gunsho shūsei dai san shū (Senki bu)* [*Collected Writing on Kibi, Volume 3, (Military Chronicles)*] (Tokyo, 1921).

[17] *Ikeda-ke monjo* [*Ikeda-house Archives*], *Urakami Ukida ryōke bugenchō* [*House Rolls of the Urakami and Ukida*], doc. Zatsu, 717.

[18] *Okayama Shi shi,* II, 1325.

shugo. But their grip was more secure and complete. Their holdings and those of their followers were closely compacted into contiguous domains which, in most instances, had been won or defended in battle. Thus the distinction between boundaries of legal jurisdiction and outright control had been largely obliterated. Within this area, the complex division of rights which characterized the *shōen* system had given way to the holding of land in fief. By now the absentee interests of courtiers or distant temples had been almost entirely squeezed out. In other words, the vertical lines of authority and control had been pulled short and taut. Very little administrative and almost no fiscal contact existed between the provinces and Kyōto. The individual daimyo domains were essentially independent. Within them the power and authority relationships consisted of a hierarchically structured system of allegiances in which military service was exchanged for grants of fief. Furthermore, the exercise of the functions of government, coincided with those relationships. It is this situation which can be compared most closely with the model of decentralized feudalism in Europe.

The shokuhō-daimyō

In Bizen as elsewhere, no sooner had the new local powers consolidated the domains from which they could draw extensive military and economic support, than they began to contest for territory among themselves. Beginning during the 1530's and reaching a crescendo after 1560, the struggle raged for local and, eventually, national hegemony. In most locales—and this was true of Bizen—the original *sengoku-daimyō* did not survive the devastating wars of the 1530's to 1560's. Again they were replaced by a new group of families which showed still greater capacities for leadership and organization under the strenuous requirements of warfare. This was the heyday of *ge-koku-jō,* when, according to the traditional view, military upstarts displaced their legitimate superiors by treachery and trickery. In actuality, however, it is clear that these new leaders, who inherited the domains of their former lords and proceeded to carve out even larger territories, built their successes upon certain clearly defined institutional advances.

The basic weakness of the daimyo of the early Sengoku period was that, as time went on, their vassals became increasingly powerful and insubordinate. The new daimyo of the late Sengoku period were able to impose a sufficiently effective control over the fighting men and the resources of their domains, a special capacity that kept them relatively free of such centrifugal forces. This capacity was well illustrated in the growing concentrations of military and economic might which the new daimyo assembled in the great castle headquarters of their domains.

In Bizen, this new stage of organization was achieved by the military leader Ukida Naoie.[19] The history of Ukida's rise is remarkably similar to that of the better-known military figures of this age, such as Oda Nobunaga, Toyotomi Hideyoshi, or Ikeda Terumasa, who eventually took over Bizen. In 1545, Ukida Naoie, a minor vassal of the Urakami, was given command of a small fort on Bizen's sea frontier. He was assigned 30 men for its defense and a small fief nearby. Here were the in-

---

[19] The Ukida House has left behind only a very few documents relating to its rise as the first great daimyo of Bizen, perhaps due to its violent demise in 1600. The available records are fairly well assembled in *Okayama Shi shi,* II, 1403 ff. A few house rolls recovered from the archives of the Ōoka family are found in the Okayama Kenritsu Toshokan (Okayama Prefectural Library).

gredients of a new power structure which was eventually to take over all of Bizen and parts of neighboring provinces. There were two important innovations in authority relationships. Ukida Naoie was in effect the commander of his 30 men. In the words of the day, he was their *yorioya* (parent) and they his *yoriko* (children). Between them was a chain of command relationship differing fundamentally from the previous marriage or oath of vassalage tie. Secondly, these men were maintained on Naoie's fief. They lived in his castle and lived off his land which adjoined it. Thus the degree of dependence between these men and their leader was more complete.

As Naoie and his men fought their way out of the corner of Bizen, he added to his fiefs and began to set out some of his own *yoriko* as commanders of outlying castles. About half of his original band became unit commanders (*kumigashira*) possessing their own vassals, and five of these became major castleholders within Naoie's territory. The granting of such privileges involved certain risks which a leader like Naoie must have recognized. In a sense, it meant a return to the older form of less dependent lord-vassal status. But it was unquestionably necessary because Naoie had not yet developed a sufficiently effective centralized control over his expanding territory. As it was, Naoie worked hard to maintain his dominance over his men, rotating commands frequently, and periodically pulling back his major vassals to his own castle headquarters. Moreover, he maintained a large force of troops under his own direct command, so that the military center of gravity of his holdings was clearly located in his main castle. Thus Naoie moved his own headquarters to successively larger castles until in 1573 he entered Okayama castle, newly built to house his swelling corps of fighters. By this time Naoie was mustering from 10,000 to 15,000 men in his frequent campaigns. His fiefs extended over nearly a tenth of Bizen.[20] Although he was nominally still vassal to the head of the Urakami house, he was beginning to have ambitions of his own.

After the middle of the sixteenth century, while local leaders such as Ukida Naoie were perfecting strongly centralized military organizations within their own territories, the older regional lords, such as the Matsuda or Urakami, held to their systems of extended coalitions of independently enfeoffed vassals. Continuing to rely on the presumed invulnerability of their mountain castles, they came to depend more and more upon their own subordinates to do their fighting. As a consequence, they were obliged to permit their vassals a dangerous rate of growth and freedom. During the 1560's and the 1570's, the many *kokujin* vassals of the Urakami were showing signs of restlessness. It was now increasingly possible for such local families to make alliances outside of Bizen with neighboring powers such as the Mōri to the west, the Amago to the north, or even with Oda Nobunaga, who had begun to push westward from Kyōto. By this time, however, the head of the Urakami house could only depend upon Ukida Naoie to keep his restless vassals in line. While Urakami Munekage sat in his mountain citadel of Tenjinyama, the Ukida reduced, one after another, the tributary-valley powers of the Urakami vassals for disciplinary reasons. One by one, the small hilltop castles of this area were put to the torch. In 1568, the Matsuda were wiped out under Ukida Naoie's generalship. While this was going on, the Urakami, depending on the loyalty of the Ukida and other close vassals, failed to expand their landed and military resources to keep pace with the process of consolidation. By

---

[20] *Urakami Ukida ryōke bugenchō.*

Foundations of Modern Daimyo

1573, when Ukida Naoie moved into Okayama castle, he, not Urakami Munekage, commanded the majority of Bizen's military forces, and his castle at Okayama was larger than that of his overlord. In 1577, Naoie, using the pretext of a succession dispute in the Urakami house, stormed Tenjinyama and displaced his lord. Bizen was now unified under his command. Within a generation, the network of small hilltop castles which had stood for the independently enfeoffed *kokujin* had been superseded by the consolidated domain commanded by the Ukida at Okayama.

The Ukida domain, centering on Okayama, was typical of those brought under control by Nobunaga and Hideyoshi. It rested, not only on a generation of military conquest, but on extensive redistribution of land rights and simplification of tenures. Productive land was being systematically surveyed and converted to a uniform measure (*kokudaka*). Naoie held some 400,000 *koku*. His retainers, or housemen (*kashin*), were organized in chain of command fashion. A band of some 1400 retainers of officer status were organized into 14 groups (or *kumi*) each headed by a trusted commander.[21] Seven of these were set up as subsidiary castle holders guarding the frontiers of Bizen and the approaches to Okayama. Each held lands producing over 10,000 *koku*. In other words, they were embryonic daimyo. But they were obliged to reside in Okayama. The unit commanders (*kumi-gashira*) of lesser status were officers who commanded their men on a *yorioya-yoriko* basis. This was essentially an army type of organization in which there was a minimum identity of family to locality or dependence upon family ties for loyalty. A significant source of the daimyo's power in this system was the balance between daimyo's lands and those of his retainers. In the Ukida domain, some 25 per cent of the territory was now held directly by the daimyo as *chokkatsuchi*.[22] This made the maintenance of standing mercenary divisions controlled by the daimyo (the daimyo's own *kumi*) possible and useable to maintain loyalty if needed. Such troops were frequently paid, not in fiefs, but in rice stipends.

From the point of view of local government in Bizen, two significant developments accompanied the consolidation of the Ukida domain. First of all, despite the Ukida acquisition of complete proprietary and administrative authority over Bizen on the basis of conquest, this conquest was capped eventually by the acquisition of legitimacy from higher authority. In Bizen, this legal authority was acquired, first from the Mōri who had secured legitimacy as *shugo* from the Ashikaga shogun, then from Oda Nobunaga whose control of the capital and of the powers of the shogunate gave him *de facto* if not *de jure* legitimacy. When Ukida Naoie died in 1580, his son secured confirmation of his status in Bizen by receiving Nobunaga's red seal certificate (*shuinjō*), a token of complete legal jurisdiction over Bizen under the new structure of sovereignty emerging in Kyōto.[23] The use of the *shuinjō* as the capstone of a new national political order was further extended by Hideyoshi.

The other important development related to the more general structure of society.

---

21 See *Ōoka-ke monjo* [*Ōoka House Archives*], *Ukida Chūnagon Hideie Kyō kashi chigyōchō* [*Roll of Fiefs of the Housemen of the Middle Counsellor, Lord Ukida Hideie*], Okayama Kenritsu Toshokan, doc. 692.8/132.

22 Taniguchi Sumio, "Bizen hansei no kakuritsu katei," ["The Establishment of the Bizen Domain Administration"], *Okayama Daigaku Kyōikugakubu kenkyū shūroku* [*Collected Research Papers from the School of Education, Okayama University*], II (1956), 1–3.

23 *Okayama Shi shi*, II, 1492, 1504. The significance of the *shuinjō* is discussed in Okuno Takahiro, *Nobunaga to Hideyoshi* [*Nobunaga and Hideyoshi*] (Tōkyō, 1955), 61–63. But the technical study of the

J. W. Hall

Because of the disappearance of the *shōen* and the weakening of the decentralized system of enfeoffment, it became increasingly common to find the inhabitants of the domain, both samurai and commoners, treated as functional groups and classes. The Ukida band of retainers, as we have seen, was not a cluster of individually enfeoffed and locally independent vassals, the typical organizational pattern for the *sengoku-daimyō*. It was organized into *kumi* within which the daimyo's men were assigned statuses which were commonly differentiated according to military rank and function.[24] Thus the family-based categories of vassal classification—cadets (*kamon*), or vassals (*fudai*)—became less important than military rank terminology—generals (*karō*), group commanders (*bangashira*), unit commanders (*kumigashira*), officers (*heishi*), petty officers (*kachi*), or foot soldiers (*ashigaru*). Status, once achieved, was still largely inheritable, but there was also considerable mobility, partly because of the constant displacement through military defeat of daimyo and their retainers at the top and the need for those below to fill out the positions evacuated above them. The *kumi* method of securing the loyalty of retainers to the daimyo through intermediary group leaders (*kumigashira*) may be thought of as something of a transition system. Retaining some features of the previous practice of independent enfeoffment, it nonetheless yielded increasingly to the direct interference of the daimyo.

Within the domain at large, also, the vertical chain of fiscal or loyalty relationships between enfeoffed proprietor (*jitō*) and subordinate cultivator (*myōshu*), were beginning to give way to large, horizontally structured, functional class relationships between the "daimyo's men" (*kashin*) and groups such as farmers, merchants, and artisans.[25] This change was accompanied by the increasing reliance on class or group legislation and the use of bureaucratic methods of military and civil administration to replace the older reliance on personal allegiances and kinship ties. Hideyoshi's social policy was to a large extent an extension of these trends. In particular, by taking leadership in carrying out a nation-wide cadastral reassessment, he laid the foundation for a new system of rural administration and taxation. It is to these new techniques of political and military organization that we can attribute the success of the *shokuhō-daimyō* in recruiting armies of tens of thousands and in building and maintaining citadels of grandiose size. Bizen saw not only the erection of a great castle at Okayama but an intensive resurvey of the land and an accompanying reordering of the agricultural population under the Ukida.[26]

---

legal issues involved in the transfer of authority from the Ashikaga Shogun's consent to the "red seal" of Nobunaga and Hideyoshi has yet to be made.

[24] This is revealed in the structure of the Ukida house rolls. See especially: *Ukida Chūnagon Hideie Kyō kashi chigyōchō.*

[25] Disregarding the controversy over whether the resulting condition should be interpreted as more "feudalistic" than the previous situation, Japanese studies have agreed upon the importance of certain basic changes in the organization of rural and urban communities. See Shimizu Mitsuo, *Nihon chūsei no sonraku* [*The Medieval Village in Japan*] (Tokyo, 1942); Miyagawa Mitsuru, *Taikō kenchi ron* [*On the Cadastral Survey of Hideyoshi*] (2 vols., Tokyo, 1957); Shakaikeizaishi Gakkai, *Hōken ryōshusei no kakuritsu—Taikō kenchi wo meguru shomondai* [*The Establishment of Feudal Proprietorship—Various Problems Related to the Hideyoshi Cadastral Survey*] (Tokyo, 1957); Araki Moriaki, "Taikō kenchi no rekishiteki zentei" ["The Historical Foundations of the Hideyoshi Cadastral Survey"], *Rekishigaku kenkyū,* 163 and 167 (1954).

[26] For studies of the effects of the reorganization of the land system under the Ukida see Kanai Madoka, "Shokuhō-ki ni okeru Bizen" ["Bizen during the Shokuho Period"], *Chihōshi kenkyū,* XLII (1959), 9–20; Shibata Hajime, "Sengoku dogōsō to Taikō kenchi" ["The Sengoku Local Gentry and Hideyoshi's Cadastral Survey"], *Rekishi kyōiku,* VI, No. 8 (1958), 52–63.

Foundations of Modern Daimyo

The ķinsei-daimyō

Despite the marked improvement in technique of political and military organization evolved by the daimyo who fought to a standstill under Hideyoshi's hegemony, these new techniques were to prove insufficient for the more stable age which followed. Thus, despite the outward resemblance between the daimyo of the Shokuhō age and those of the Tokugawa, many institutional differences lay between them. Between 1600 and 1700, the process of internal evolution of the daimyo domains was accelerated by two factors: the frequent shifting of daimyo from locale to locale, and the predominant atmosphere of peace. Bizen was typical of most Japan in this respect. Immediately after 1600, five different daimyo houses governed Bizen in short succession. It was not until 1632 that Ikeda Mitsumasa, moving to Okayama from Tottori, set up the line which continued until 1871.[27] These changes, it should be emphasized, were made, not as a result of local wars or battles for Bizen, but by order of the Tokugawa shogun. The period of adjustment to peaceful conditions was, for most parts of Japan, a traumatic experience. For, once the fighting ceased, the threat of war, which had acted as a powerful justification for the exercise of harsh military discipline, ceased to exist. It now became necessary to devise new theories of government based on new sanctions of power, to clarify administrative practices, and to work for the social and economic security of the people.

In their search for a new theory of government commensurate with their new-won powers, the *ķinsei-daimyō,* as is well known, adopted a number of Confucian-based principles of sovereignty and social morality. In Bizen, this adoption awaited the pioneer work of Ikeda Mitsumasa, whose enunciation of the daimyo's position as an agent of heaven under the guidance of the shogun, placed the daimyo securely in a "naturally ordained" political order and justified the social structure which he ruled.[28]

After 1600, the daimyo continued to improve their methods of administration on a more bureaucratic basis, amplifying their legal codes in the process. Within the domain, the centralizing power of the daimyo was increased over his retainers and subjects, while, at the same time, he became less a personal despot and more a legal symbol. In Bizen, by the end of the seventeenth century, all subsidiary castles had been eliminated, and the practice of direct enfeoffment of high ranking retainers was displaced by the stipend (*hōroķu*) system in all but name only. The daimyo's men were now considered his officers (*ķashin*). Within the domain a uniform local administrative organization, staffed by the daimyo's officers, was placed over the urban and rural sectors alike. The daimyo's retainers were now strictly ordered according to 12 ranks (*ķakyū* or *ķakushiķi*) in ascending order from *ashigaru* to *ķarō*. Although for disciplinary purposes these retainers were still grouped into *ķumi,* their real relationship to the daimyo was on the basis of service in rank within the military and civil bureaucracy. Though certain ceremonial remnants of feudal practice, such as audiences and investitures, still remained, their importance diminished. Oaths of loyalty were now tied to posts in the bureaucracy. Within the samurai class in Bizen, then, a shift from personal vassalage privately rewarded by enfeoffment was giving

---

[27] For an analytical treatment of the stabilization of the Bizen domain under the Ikeda see Taniguchi, "Bizen hansei," pp. 4–14.

[28] See J. W. Hall, "The Confucian Teacher in Tokugawa Japan," David S. Nivison and Arthur F. Wright, *Confucianism in Action* (Stanford, 1959), pp. 272–277.

way to a system of military statuses which led to a civil and military bureaucracy. Loyalty was becoming a principle rather than a private commitment.[29] Changes of a similar sort affected the lower levels of society in Bizen. Under the impact of Confucian theory, the people (*tami*) were distinguished by class or function and placed under broad legal codes.[30] For the farmers especially, the change from personal indenture to membership in the village as taxpaying tenants of the daimyo was a major change. After 1600 in Bizen, first the direct hold of the samurai, then of the *shōya* or village heads, over the villagers was replaced by a bureaucratic system of local government.[31] It has been claimed that the strict class structure adopted by Hideyoshi and perfected by the Tokugawa constituted a "refeudalization" of Japanese society. Somewhat the reverse is probably closer to the truth. For the establishment of legally defined statuses (*mibun*) freed many sectors of Japanese society from the more restrictive and more personally conceived relationships based on private vassalage or indenture.[32] These trends were not, of course, uniformly characteristic of all Japan. They constituted, however, the dominant pattern of the institutional change which accompanied the rise of the daimyo of Tokugawa times. Moreover, they involved changes not easily made nor successfully carried out in most of Japan until well into the Tokugawa age. In fact, the Tokugawa daimyo did not mature institutionally until at least 1700.

The Sengoku age was indeed a time of significant social change in Japan, but not simply of the capricious kind implied by the phrase *ge-koku-jō*. Bizen saw not only the rise and fall of a procession of military houses, but also a radical change in the methods of local government and in the structure of relationships which joined government and society. In this the daimyo were both participants and products.

1. At the highest level of political organization, that which provided the sanctions for exercise of power, Bizen passed from the shaky jurisdictional authority of the *shugo-daimyō*, resting on uncertain military support and a weak legacy from the imperial tradition, to a nearly absolute authority vested in the daimyo by virtue of the shogunal charter (*shuinjō*), the imperial consent, and Confucian principles of morally exercised authority.

2. At the level of the organization of power, Bizen passed from the system of extended family relationships, utilized by the *shugo-daimyō*, to the Sengoku system of decentralized direct enfeoffment, to the military group (*kumi*) system of the

---

[29] Taniguchi Sumio, "Han kashindan no keisei to kozō—Okayama-han no baai" ["The Structure and Organization of the *han* Houseband—The Case of Okayama"], *Shigaku zasshi*, LXVI, No. 6 (June 1957), 594–615.

[30] See Hampō Kenkyūkai, ed., *Hampōshū, 1, Okayama-han* [*Collected han laws, 1, Okayama-han*] (2 vols., Tokyo, 1959–1960); *Okayama Shishi*, vols. III and IV, for the most extensive published sources on Okayama legislation.

[31] Hampō Kenkyūkai, *op. cit.*, I, 186, 263; Kanai Madoka, "Ōjoya no gyōseki kuiki ni tsuite—Bizen-han no baai" ["On the Administrative Jurisdiction of the *ōjōya*—The Case of Bizen-han"], *Shigaku zasshi*, LXII, No. 1 (Jan., 1953), 66–71.

[32] Nakamura Kichiji, in his article "Kokudaka seido to hōkensei" (cited in note 7) has recently reversed the dominant academic trend in Japan led by Araki and Miyagawa who have taken the stand that the Tokugawa period brought a true serfdom to the Japanese peasant and therefore represents the final attainment of feudalism in Japan. Nakamura has emphasized the many "non-feudal" aspects of the Tokugawa political and social structure.

Shokuhō period, to the rank (*kakyū*) or status (*mibun*) structure utilized by the daimyo of the Tokugawa period.

3. At the level of the common inhabitants of Bizen, there occurred a gradual shift from a condition characterized predominantly by vertically structured personal relationships to one based increasingly on administrative and class-defined relations between government and individual. Large segments of Japanese society were developing new horizontal relationships within the boundaries defined by such social concepts as rank and status.

To return to our question of interpretation regarding Japan's dark ages, it is obvious that one of the common fallacies of historians has been the assumption that the daimyo and the system of local control he represented remained constant throughout the several centuries preceding 1700. Changes in the nature of the daimyo establishment in fact represented a dynamic theme which ran through the Sengoku and early Tokugawa periods. These changes underlay the confused condition of warfare during the Sengoku era and continued to affect Japanese government and society even after the supposed freezing of society by Tokugawa Ieyasu. Hindsight criticism has been heaped upon Hideyoshi and Ieyasu for their failure to unify Japan completely and for their "return" to a restrictive, status-bound society cut off from foreign contact. A more accurate analysis of the state of local government and social organization shows that Japan underwent many major internal changes after 1590 and that these changes can by no means be characterized as retrogressive.

CHAPTER FIVE

THE IKEDA HOUSE AND ITS RETAINERS IN BIZEN

JOHN WHITNEY HALL

SOMETIME between the seventeenth century and the 1870's the common term by which foreigners referred to the daimyo's band of retainers changed from some such expression as "servants of the prince" to "clan." The word clan is still with us, casting vague shadows of misconception upon the Tokugawa scene. The early English observers who first imagined the similarity between the groups of daimyo retainers and the Scottish Highland clans may have done so with some justification—at least if we recall their experience with the sword swinging and fanatically motivated Satsuma and Chōshū retainers. Yet even a Satow used the word sparingly in his writings (perhaps as it intruded from his later editing).[1] And it was only later that the practice became sufficiently universal that Chamberlain could write in his *Things Japanese* under the heading "Clans":

> "This is the usual English translation of the Japanese word *han* (藩), which may also be rendered "daimiate," that is, the territory and people subject to a *Daimyo,* or territorial noble, in feudal Japan. The Japanese clans differed from the Highland clans in the fact that all members of a clan did not claim a common origin or use the same surname. But they were equally bound to their lord by ties of love and implicit obedience and to each other by a feeling of brotherhood. This feeling has survived the abolition of feudalism in 1871." [2]

We can see, in this groping for an English equivalent of a Japanese reality, certain obvious uncertainties about the look of a daimyo domain and also perhaps the influence of certain changes in nomenclature adopted by Japanese of the Restoration era. One wonders, for instance, whether the similarity in pronunciation between *"han"* and "clan" (as rendered by the Englishman in Japan) had anything to do with joining the two words in the English mind. And if so, did the coiners of the clan-*han* equivalence understand the origin of the term *han*. For *han* was actually a late arrival in Japanese official vocabu-

---

[1] Sir Ernest Satow, *A Diplomat in Japan* (London, 1921), 37–38, remarked, "Thus arose in each daimiate a condition of things which may be compared to that of the Highland clan, where the ultimate power was based upon the feelings and opinions of a poor but aristocratic oligarchy." But this was clearly a later observation. The parts of his narrative based upon diary notes is sparing in the actual use of such phrases as "Chōshiū clan."

[2] Basil Hall Chamberlain, *Things Japanese* (2nd ed.; London, Yokohama, etc., 1891), 84–85.

lary, necessitated by the change in conception towards the old domains after 1868. With the abolition of the shogunate, the daimyo domains became true subdivisions of the state, consisting of territory, subjects, and government. It was to this old entity newly conceived that the term *han* was applied. As Kanai Madoka has pointed out, while the character for *han* was used in literary references to certain daimyo domains (largely as a classical affectation), it was never once used by the shogunate for official purposes.[3] The separate elements of Tokugawa local rule which were combined to form the idea of *han*—i.e., the territory (*ryō*), the daimyo's retainers (*kachū*), and the people (*tami*)—these remained separate in the Japanese mind until after 1868. The bands of retainers who served the daimyo of the Tokugawa period were generally referred to by the daimyo of the day, either collectively as their *kachū* (their household) or individually as their *kashin* (their house officials) or *kerai* (their housemen). Presentday Japanese historians have coined the phrase *kashindan* (houseband) to handle this institution.

Every student of Japanese history is familiar with the greatest of the Tokugawa *kashindan* (though he may not have thought of it in quite that way), namely, the shogun's band of retainers comprised of the *fudai* daimyo, the *hatamoto,* and the *gokenin.* Like so many Tokugawa institutions, there was, of course, no typical form which such groups took, for a rather wider range of patterns could be found. The shogun's own band, characterized by the territorial independence of his greatest retainers (the *fudai*), illustrated the extreme in decentralization among the retainers. At the other extreme stood the highly centralized and dependent bands of some of the smaller *fudai.* Satsuma and Tosa illustrated variant examples on the side of decentralization. But the norm—and this is the closest we come to typicality—was the pattern exemplified by the larger *fudai* and more dependent of the *tozama.* The example of the Ikeda house of Bizen which I shall cite in this paper is fairly close to this norm.

It is a simple axiom that every samurai of the Tokugawa period was either a member of a daimyo's *kashindan* or was obliged to count himself a *rōnin.* The organization of samurai into separate service units began during the civil wars of the mid-sixteenth century and took roughly a hundred years to complete. There were two prime ways by which these bands came into being: one through *consolidation,* whereby powerful local houses reduced their neighbors to submission and enlisted them under their expanding authority; the other through *accretion,* as minor military figures drew more and more followers into their commands while they rose through the ranks in the service of Nobunaga, Hideyoshi, or Ieyasu. It is obvious that, after the smoke of Sekigahara had cleared, the daimyo who survived were overwhelmingly of the latter pedigree and not of the former. Both styles of formation had their effect upon the structure and operation of the bands so formed, particularly upon the strength of authority which the daimyo could exercise over his retainers, and upon the rights or privileges which the retainers could exercise over the

[3] Kanai Madoka, *Hansei* (Tokyo, 1962), 6–7.

daimyo's territory and its inhabitants. The Ikeda houseband was of the accretion type, similar in its pattern of growth and ultimate organization to that of the *fudai,* but differing from them in having taken shape under all three overlords (Nobunaga, Hideyoshi, and Ieyasu), not simply under Ieyasu.

The Ikeda house began the climb, which in the decade after Sekigahara was to make its chief one of the two or three greatest daimyo in Japan, in 1536, largely through the fortuitous circumstance that the mother of the future Ikeda Nobuteru became the wet nurse of the future Nobunaga.[4] Nobuteru and Nobunaga became from birth "bosom companions." Reaching manhood, Nobuteru rose rapidly in Nobunaga's service. In 1560 he received his first independent assignment as a company commander (*samurai taishō*) at the head of 30 men. Six years later he was in command of his first castle (Kinota). In another four years he was shifted to the strategic castle of Inuyama, and then in 1580 to the command of Osaka castle with a territory of 100,000 *koku.* By this time Nobuteru was frequently ordered by Nobunaga to join his forces under the military command of Hideyoshi. Thus when Nobunaga was assassinated in 1582, Nobuteru made an easy transfer to Hideyoshi's suzerainty.

Hideyoshi moved the Ikeda house to Ōgaki castle in Mino in 1582. Two years later Nobuteru was killed in battle against Ieyasu. He was followed by his second son, Terumasa, a worthy successor to the Ikeda name. When the Tokugawa were transferred to the Kanto in 1590, Terumasa was moved into former Tokugawa territory and received Yoshida castle in Mikawa with a holding of 152,000 *koku.* In this way Hideyoshi hoped to use the Ikeda to counterbalance the Tokugawa, but no real rift was intended between the houses. In 1594 Terumasa acquired one of Ieyasu's daughters in marriage. And this, as it turned out, paved the way for a quick switch of allegiances after Hideyoshi's death in 1598. At Sekigahara, Terumasa fought on the Tokugawa side and helped to rout the Chōsokabe forces. Rewarded as one of the most worthy of Ieyasu's *tozama* allies, he was granted the strategic castle of Himeji in Harima, with a domain of 520,000 *koku.* In a few years, branches of the Ikeda house were settled in Awaji, Bizen, and Inaba. All together the main house and its three branches controlled some 1,000,000 *koku,* and Terumasa was respectfully spoken of as "shogun of western Japan" (*saigoku no shōgun*).

But Terumasa's death in 1613 was followed by a series of untimely deaths among the next generation of Ikeda males. The Tokugawa hastily moved in to break up the holdings which had by now begun to appear dangerously large to the masters of Edo. By 1632 the house was reduced to two branches of nearly equal size: one controlling 320,000 *koku* centered upon Tottori castle of Inaba-Hōki, the other controlling 315,000 *koku* based on Okayama in Bizen.

---

[4] The history of the Ikeda House which follows is covered in more detail in John Whitney Hall, *Government and Local Power in Japan 500-to 1700: A Study Based on Bizen Province* (Princeton, 1966), 381–402.

(Harima and Awaji had been lost.) It was in 1632 that a final transfer of castles took place, and Ikeda Mitsumasa of the Tottori branch was ordered to exchange territories with his cousin in Bizen. Thereafter the two Ikeda lines remained in their territories until after the Restoration, ranking number 17 and 18 in order of size in the Tokugawa hierarchy of daimyo. After 1632 then, Okayama became the headquarters of the houseband which is the object of our attention.

So much for the history of the Ikeda house. What are the lessons it revealed? First, note the humble origins of the house and the manner of its growth—not by conquest of neighbors but by the accumulation of rewards from successive overlords. Thus the original core of the Ikeda houseband was not a family or a feudal band, but a unit of assorted fighters assigned to Nobuteru in 1560. Nobuteru's relationship to this group was essentially one of command. Yet these original 30 men became identified with the Ikeda house, providing the nucleus of a houseband which grew with every promotion in the meteoric careers of Nobuteru and Terumasa. When Terumasa died in Shirasagi castle (one of the great remaining monuments of this period to be seen in Japan today), he was mourned by perhaps 6,000 retainers of samurai rank. Seven of these held territories assessed at from 10,000 to 33,000 *koku* (in other words, they were the equivalent of daimyo) and of these 5 were members of the original band of 30.[5]

Note, secondly, the fantastic geographic mobility (6 moves in 30 years; 8 in 60 years), and this not by calculation but by capricious command from superior authority. And each move except the last two took the Ikeda into new territory and larger commands. The moves from one castle headquarters to another were always strenuous and costly affairs. (There was some obvious limit to the stretch expected in any transfer.) The moves occurred, as we can imagine, under two rather different conditions: one confusedly, under the unsettled circumstances following victory in battle; the other calculatedly, during the more peaceful years after 1600, as the overlord made strategic or political shifts among his chief retainers. In the first instance, the incoming Ikeda band would find a resentful or demoralized remnant of the defeated daimyo's forces, some hopeful perhaps of securing service under the Ikeda command, but others, despairing of favorable treatment, having fled into the countryside in an attempt to salvage a living in the villages. The best-documented example of the first variety of entrance into unfamiliar territory occurred at the time of the initial Ikeda takeover in Bizen in 1603. In that year, Bizen was added to Terumasa's holdings and placed under the command of his eldest son Toshitaka.

The Ikeda entrance into Bizen was undoubtedly similar to the Yamauchi takeover in Tosa. The early orders by Terumasa and Toshitaka indicate that their first concern was to restore order: "There shall be no indiscriminate cut-

---

[5] See the roster of Terumara's retainers (*samurai-chō*) in Nagayama Usaburo, *Ikeda Mitsumasa Kō den (Biography of Lord Ikeda Mitsumasa)*, 2 vols. (Tokyo, 1932), vol. I, 196–216.

ting of bamboo and trees," his first command stated. "No seizure of abandoned houses or land will be permitted. Wives and children of the previous daimyo's retainers will not be seized and put into service. Farmers pressed into service shall be returned to their villages."[6] Gradually the strategic (or defensive) distribution of the Ikeda forces within the new territory was worked out to Toshitaka's satisfaction. Subsidiary castles were occupied or built new. Major vassals were placed in strategic locations to guard the approaches to Okayama. This was followed by a completely new and comprehensive land survey after which fiefs were distributed. (The daimyo, though relying on his retainers to govern these fiefs, nonetheless attempted to standardize and regulate the powers of the retainers with respect to their lands and the peasantry.) Finally, the main castle was expanded and the castle town of Okayama enlarged both for the quartering of more samurai and to provide for more commercial facilities.[7]

Of the subsequent moves demanded of the Ikeda daimyo, the one which followed the exchange of territories in 1632 is the best-recorded.[8] Here was an excellent example of a peacetime move, fully prepared for on both sides. The operation took six months in all, beginning with orders in the two domains that everything be put in good order for the next occupants. Roads and bridges were repaired, buildings and residences of the samurai were cleaned and patched, even the *shōji* were freshly papered. Soon advance teams of officials were exchanged between the two territories to check on the condition of the castles and the samurai quarters, to study the tax records, and to negotiate the point at which local taxes would terminate for the outgoing daimyo and begin for the incoming. The actual transfer of retainers, either overland or by sea between Tottori and Okayama, occupied a month's time. The daimyo provided loans to retainers to ease the burden of the trip. A total of 3,873 families left Okayama for Tottori, and probably a somewhat larger number entered Okayama under Mitsumasa's command.

In Okayama the first task undertaken by the new daimyo was the assignment of quarters. To this day there remains in the Ikeda house archives a large map of Okayama prepared by Mitsumasa's predecessor in which all of the residences were labeled with the names of their occupants. Over these names are now pasted the names of the new assignments made by Mitsumasa. Mansions, houses, barracks-like quarters, graded according to size, were appropriately distributed to Mitsumasa's retinue, each according to his status. Having thus solved the housing problem, Mitsumasa set about organizing his administration and finances. The first assignments were to 10 district administrators and 3 city administrators. A committee of 6 officers was given the task of distributing fiefs. Crews of inspectors were sent into the villages and within three months the daimyo was able to hand out stipendiary and enfeoffment

[6] In Nagayama Usaburō, *Okayama-ken tsūshi* (*General History of Okayama Prefectures*), 2 vols. (Okayama, 1952), vol. II, 191.

[7] Hall, *Government and Local Power*, 393–96.

[8] *Ibid.*, 400–02.

certificates. Shortly thereafter basic rules for the conduct of the several classes were issued and the transfer was complete. By 1633 Ikeda Mitsumasa settled down to govern the province of Bizen with a band of retainers organized for civil and military service, a band made up of samurai brought into Ikeda service by two generations of daimyo before him at widely separate times and places, and by himself in Tottori and most recently in Okayama. From the time of his grandfather the head of the Ikeda family had moved 8 times, taking their retainers, servants, and baggage with them. Okayama was the end of a long journey from the Ikeda family birthplace in Owari.

Let us look at the Ikeda houseband as it came to rest in Okayama, first as to numbers. The Ikeda establishment in Okayama was a large affair. A census of 1707 lists a total of 22,628 individuals inclusive of family members, servants, and menials who were in one way or another part of the Ikeda organization.[9] But the houseband proper was only a portion of this. Of the 22,000, only 10,029 were samurai (*ashigaru* and above) and their families. And this accounted for something over 3,400 families. Subtracting from this number the lowest class of retainers, the *ashigaru,* we have left a body of just over 1,600 families of officer and petty officer status which comprise the daimyo's *kashindan* proper.

What was the composition of this group of families; when did these retainers enter Ikeda service, and where did they come from? A study by Professor Taniguchi and his associates of the service records of the Ikeda retainers provides the answers for 1,294 out of roughly 1,600 families in the year 1694:[10]

244 (about ⅕)   had been in service since before 1600,
271 (another ⅕) joined the Ikeda between 1600 and 1613 in Harima,
67   joined between 1613 and 1632 in Inaba,
602 (nearly ½) were added to the registers after 1632,
100   gave insufficient information.

If we analyze these families according to their places of origin we find that:

384 (or ⅓)   came from Owari,
233 (or ⅕)   came from provinces between Owari and Osaka,
84   came from Harima,
48   came from Inaba or Hōki,
333 (or ¼)   came from Bizen or adjacent provinces,
124   were of other miscellaneous origins.

These figures confirm our picture of the Ikeda houseband, taking shape orginally in Owari and adding retainers in order to govern larger and larger territories or to replace the families which died off or fell by the wayside. The main process was accretion, but replenishment was also common. The process

---

[9] Sō-ninzu no kakitsuke (Complete census register), Hōei (1707) 4/16/15, ms in *Ikedake monjo* (Ikede House archives, Okayama).

[10] Taniguchi Sumio, "Han kashindan no keisei to kōzō" (The formation and structure of a *han kashindan*), in *Shigaku zasshi,* 66.6, 596–600.

of accretion is of course simple to imagine. There was obviously a considerable absorption of manpower from the disbanded retinues of defeated diamyo, especially at lower ranks where they could be watched. And even in Bizen under peacetime conditions the Ikeda band grew by some 500 families.[11] The process of replenishment is less immediately apparent. Yet as time passed, the addition of new retainers to fill the places left vacant by losses among the daimyo's staff became a prime factor affecting the composition of the band. The flow in and out of the Ikeda houseband remained remarkably active.

The pattern of movement and expansion experienced by the Ikeda daimyo in the early years obviously had profound effects upon the structure of the houseband, particularly in defining the relationship of retainers to the daimyo and to the daimyo's territory. The fact that the Ikeda houseband was assembled by accretion meant that from the first the daimyo had strong powers over his retainers. Housemen were all joined to the daimyo by some form of oath of allegiance. But these were more in the nature of pledges of loyal service rather than reciprocal compacts. No retainer could claim special privilege through prior rights over some hereditary fief. To Mitsumasa his retainers were "his men" who had voluntarily sought service with him and hence had accepted a position of strict accountability. Over them he claimed complete and absolute authority. As one of Mitsumasa's advisors stated, "the *kashin* are indeed the lord's personal possessions."[12] The *kashin* were increasingly considered to be the daimyo's staff, living on stipends and in housing provided by him.

One of the critical indices of this growing power of the diamyo was seen in the dwindling authority which the retainers were able to exercise over their fiefs. In the early days of the Ikeda rise, enfeoffment of retainers was standard practice—in fact, it was probably essential to the daimyo's ability to hold his territory. But in later years this practice was curtailed as much as possible. Nonetheless Mitsumasa was obliged to apportion the villages of Bizen among his *kashin* in 1632. Yet he was careful to interpose between his retainers and their fiefs the supervisory authority of his own rural intendants. Then in 1654 a flood and famine produced emergency conditions which gave Mitsumasa the opening he needed to cut the *kashin* completely away from their lands. Claiming that the *kashin* had abused their rights and had squeezed the peasants for their own interests, he placed the entire machinery of tax collection and village administration in the hands of his intendants. The *kashindan* became a captive corps of officers hereditarily tied to the Ikeda house and supported from his granary.[13] If there had been any possibility that the *kashin* might have put down roots in the countryside, it had now been checked. As Ogyū Sorai so aptly put it, henceforth the samurai lived "as if in an inn." Their entire reason

---

[11] *Ibid.*

[12] Hōkōgaki, Tsuda-ke, Tenna 1/12/27 (Service record, Tsuda house, 1681), ms in *Ikedake monjo*.

[13] Biyōkokushi ruihen, Shōō 3 (1654) 8/11, ms in *Ikedake monjo*.

for being was contained in the world of the castle town and in the service of the house of Ikeda.

Another indication of the lessening individual freedom of the *kashin* was seen in the way in which the daimyo's authority over them became routinized and systematized. There was a time when the head of the Ikeda house could know all his retainers intimately. In Okayama that day was long past. By Mitsumasa's day only the upper levels of the houseband had audience privileges and so from time to time had business with him or came before his presence in ceremonial functions. For the rest, the houseband was a list of names on the service rolls or faces in the long lines of assembled retainers who mustered on New Year's Day in the daimyo's park. Increasingly then the relationship between daimyo and retainer became formal, impersonal, and bureaucratic. Control was exercised through rank, group, and functional commands. In fact, except for the top two levels, the daimyo's retainers were all conceived of as belonging to personnel units under the superintendence of superior officers. Thus the daimyo when he invoked the attention of all his retainers merely needed to call in his elders (*karō*), commanders (*ban-gashira*), and unit heads (*kumi-gashira*) to make sure that all would eventually hear his wishes.

There is much that could be said about the Ikeda houseband beyond this point: the way, for instance, the retainers became adjusted to life in the castle town, to the conditions of peace, and to the bureaucratic routine. I should like to comment on only one effect of the passage of time upon the internal organization of the *kashindan*. We have described the household as a hereditary group. This it was to a certain extent, but it would be a mistake to assume that the band somehow became completely frozen as to membership, rank, and function. For one thing the process of growth and renovation which we noted during the years of mobility continued even after 1632. Between the data and the end of the shogunate 1,102 families either died out or left Ikeda service and were replaced.[14] While in principle the daimyo's retainers served him generation after generation, in fact, membership continued to be remarkably fluid.

There is another aspect of the operation of the principle of heredity in Tokugawa Japan, that is that rank or status tended to be hereditary to the family (*ie*) but the function of an individual retainer depended in some measure on his own abilities or aspirations. By the time of Mitsumasa, the rank structure of the Ikeda houseband was already formalized. There were 10 ranks of an essentially military nature beginning with the elders (*karō*) and divisional commanders (*bangashira*), and running down to lower petty officers (*keihai*) and footsoldiers (*ashigaru*). Now, as a general rule, within this hierarchy, the head of a house inherited rank but not office or function. Office was assigned to heads of houses as they proved themselves in the daimyo's service. In the entire domain, therefore, there was only one house for which office was by definition hereditary, and that was the family of the daimyo. Even among the highest level of retainers, the *karō*, there were 7 houses eligible

---

[14] Taniguchi, "Han kashindan," 596–97.

for 3 assignments to the high council. As one went down the hierarchy of ranks the possible assignments for each rank became more and more numerous. And hence the usual career pattern of a middle ranking retainer showed considerable movement among posts within the level appropriate to his rank.[15] Promotions or demotions in rank were not out of the question either, especially if the change represented only a single step up or down the scale of ranks.

But an important distinction has to be made on this point. Changes in membership in the houseband were more apt to occur at the lower levels of the hierarchy than at the higher. Hereditary perpetuation of a given house was more secure at the top than at the bottom of the samurai rank scale. In fact in the early years the *ashigaru* were brought into service for one generation only.[16] There was no automatic succession to this rank, though as time went on the class tended to become self-perpetuating. At the other extreme, however, the families of *karō* or *bangashira* rank continued to maintain their identity and status generation after generation, by adoption when necessary. Among the *karō* families at the end of the Tokugawa period, 6 had been in the Ikeda service since 1600—and 3 were descended from the original band of 30. Among 14 houses of divisional commander rank, 10 had achieved their status before 1613. On the other hand, of 671 houses in the lowest officer status (*heishi*), only 165 had been in Ikeda service before 1600 while 231 joined the house after 1632. Among the 527 families of the petty officer class (*kachi*), only 42 had continued since 1600 whereas 354 had joined after 1632.[17]

Thus time had a markedly differential effect upon the Ikeda *kashindan*. For it is evident that "feudal" or hereditary authority tended to be more characteristic of those at the top of the *kashindan*, becoming weaker at the lower levels of the hierarchy. What this meant was that the Ikeda *kashindan* was becoming divided between authority-perpetuating or legitimizing families and service families (though perhaps the Japanese of the time failed to see it this way). The *karō* and *bangashira*, like the daimyo, served increasingly not as policy-makers but as ceremonial sub-symbols of the daimyo's authority. In a time when family status meant political prestige in the eyes of the people, the perpetuation of these high-ranking families aided in the maintenance of the authority structure. It is no accident then that as time went on the Ikeda house tended to patronize these families, granting them their sons to fill in successions and in this way cementing closer relations with them. By the nineteenth century 4 of the 7 *karō* houses and 5 of 13 *bangashira* houses bore the surname Ikeda.[18] Each one of these resulted from the adoption of an Ikeda heir at some time in the past.

---

[15] Examples appear in John Whitney Hall, "The Nature of Traditional Society: Japan," in Robert E. Ward and Dankwart A. Rustow, eds., *Political Modernization in Japan and Turkey* (Princeton, 1964), 30.

[16] Tottori-han shi kōhon (Draft history of Tottori *han*), ms Shokusei, Part III, photocopy tkb 110.

[17] Taniguchi, "Han kashindan," 597.

[18] Samurai-chō (Roster of officers), ms compiled 1838, privately owned.

J. W. Hall

The Tokugawa *kashindan* when carefully scrutinized was obviously not a simple homogeneous organism but had its internal separations and differences—especially between upper and lower levels. And we should be careful about making unitary judgments or generalizations about such an organism. Much that recent scholarship has been saying about the comparative mobility within daimyo bureaucracies or about the high political achievement orientation of the Tokugawa samurai applies to those levels of the *kashindan* which engaged in functional services. Conversely much of the harsh language which late Tokugawa writers heaped upon what they described as stupid and incompetent leadership in the shogunate and the domains would apply chiefly to those fixtures whose very function it was to live as symbols of inflexible authority. As time went on then, it is understandable that many *kashindan* pulled apart increasingly between these groups. But this was not simply a matter of rift between high and low—between those with power and those without. So long as the Tokugawa political system relied more on family prestige than on legal concepts for the maintenance of the structure of legitimacy, it made a virtue out of hereditary succession and aristocratic pedigree. The "stupid men in high places" were as much a part of the system as were the restive men below them.

In summary then, the Ikeda houseband in Bizen consisted of a group of retainers assembled at various times in the history of the Ikeda house and continuously undergoing change; hereditary only in the sense that service once entered into was in principle renewable generation after generation; clannish perhaps only at the very top of the hierarchy where the daimyo and his close retainers became literally interrelated. The bulk of the *kashindan* consisted of a group, utterly dependent upon their service towards the daimyo, living in quarters assigned by him and on stipends over which they had no control. Once drawn together from the ends of Japan under the leadership of the Ikeda military commanders, the band settled down after 1632 to a sedentary life in Okayama. There it was as much the factor of living and growing up together in barracks-like quarters that instilled the sense of personal comradeship within the ranks of the *kashin*. Loyalty to the daimyo continued to be a pervasive factor. The daimyo came to personify the territory and the service in which the samurai found themselves. And since at the highest level, authority and family coincided, that loyalty was focused upon the daimyo's house. Yet the ultimate tie was that of service, and hence the ease with which it was switched to other symbols and services once the daimyo ceased to exist.

CHAPTER SIX

TOSA IN THE SIXTEENTH CENTURY:
THE 100 ARTICLE CODE
OF CHŌSOKABE MOTOCHIKA

MARIUS B. JANSEN

Reprinted from *Oriens Extremus,* Vol. X, No. 1 (April 1963)

The latter decades of the sixteenth century witnessed sweeping institutional changes in all parts of Japan. In each geographic area new military leaders arose who were unwilling to accept the restrictions of earlier systems of tenure, revenue, and authority. Instead they groped toward new patterns of social and political organization, for which they also worked out new justifications and codes. The over-all dimensions of the process are best studied in the central provinces, and they have recently been summarized and discussed by John W. HALL[1]. From this development emerged the full consolidations of bureaucratic and territorial institutions of Tokugawa times[2].

In more remote areas of southwestern Japan a comparable process was at work. In some respects better documented through the survival of early records, it permits specific illustration of the manner in which the new daimyo built upon the institutions they inherited as well as illustrating the social cost of the process for some of the men who helped bring it about. Examination of such a case also shows the way developments in relatively distant provinces were affected and channeled by policies worked out by the contenders for hegemony on a nation-wide scale, men who anticipated the national, yet decentralized, order of Tokugawa times. Such a case, described with a minimum of cultural translation of institutional terminology, in its own vocabulary and on its own terms, may also contribute toward the discussion of institutional uniformities in history without prejudging the issue.

The province of Tosa, a fan-shaped realm on southern Shikoku and supported from the narrow band of land that runs along the Pacific with its additional food supplies, contained perhaps three hundred thousand inhabitants in the late sixteenth century. Bounded by mountains on all land borders, the province divides into the central Kōchi plain, which gives the modern prefecture its name, and the districts of Hata to the west and Aki to the east. Of these the central plain, more populous and fertile, has

---

[1] "Foundations of the Modern Japanese Daimyo", *The Journal of Asian Studies* XX, No. 3 (1961/May), 317—329.
[2] A process admirably and succinctly described by KANAI MADOKA, in: *Hansei* (Tōkyō, 1962), 150 p.

been most contested and most strategic, and the outlying areas more secure and less developed. Sources for the institutional transformations in early modern Tosa are unusually full. The sixteenth century land survey, which will be noted below, survives in its entirety and is now available in a printed edition. *Shō* records provide continuous documentation of at least one territorial and administrative unit into Tokugawa times. The 100 Article Code of CHŌSOKABE MOTOCHIKA, one of the nine major codes of this period, is also one of the richest and fullest, and, taken together with the land survey, gives both the goals and the achievements of one of the most important realm builders of sixteenth century Japan[3]. From this picture, assiduously studied and analyzed by a group of able local historians in recent years[4], one can see the emergence of local peculiarities and attitudes which survived through Tokugawa times and remained alive to provide additional fuel for nineteenth century revolutionary theory and practice[5].

Chōsokabe Motochika (1539—1599)

Although the name Chōsokabe[6] belongs in any list of "new" daimyo of the sixteenth century, the family possessed a much longer pedigree of office than was the case with most daimyo of the Sengoku Period[7]. The family name appears in Tosa records from Kamakura times on as a holder of the *jitō* rank, and it rose in prominence during Ashikaga times as supporter of Ashikaga Takauji and later as subordinate of the Ashikaga deputy for Shikoku, Hosokawa. Chōsokabe's loyalty was rewarded with appointment as Temple Commissioner *(tera bugyō)*, with responsibility for the important Kyūkoan, on Godaisan, near present Kōchi City. The seat of Chōsokabe power was in the central Kōchi plain, in Nagaoka district. Here the slight eminence at Okō provided the site for an early fortification under whose protection the Chōsokabe organized a group of about sixty *myōshu* as *kokujin* or *kunizamurai*.

When the ōnin wars broke out at the imperial and shogunal capital of Kyoto in the late fifteenth century deputies of distant authority were everywhere summoned home to defend their masters. In Tosa, as elsewhere, the lapse in Hosokawa attention provided opportunity for the

---

[3] Printed sources include *Kinsei sonraku jichi shiryō-shū*, Vol. 2, *Tosa no kuni jikata shiryō* (Tōkyō, 1956); *Chōsokabe chikenchō* (Kōchi, 1957—60), 5 vols., *Nanroshi* (Kōchi, 1959).

[4] Among them: YOKOGAWA SUEKICHI, *Ōsato shō no kenkyū* (Kōchi, 1959); YAMAMOTO TAKESHI, *Chōsokabe Motochika* (Tōkyō, 1960); INOUE KAZUO, *Chōsokabe okitegaki no kenkyū* (Kōchi, 1955).

[5] Marius B. JANSEN, *Sakamoto Ryōma and the Meiji Restoration* (Princeton, 1961), p. 20 foll.

[6] The Tosa preference is for C h ō s o g a b e, but since contemporary evidence is no longer available these pages follow Tōkyō usage.

[7] The most ambitious claim for Chōsokabe had them descended from Ch'in Shih Huang Ti. For other daimyo of the period, ITŌ TAZABURŌ, *Nihon hōkensei shi* (Tōkyō, 1959), p. 212 foll.

development of local ambitions. Earlier institutions were by no means abandoned; the *shō* set up centuries earlier continued to exist, but needs of law enforcement and self protection accelerated the importance of the bands of armed field holders, the *myōshu*, and the *jitō* who vied for leadership. The provincial scene also attracted people of eminence from the center. The court noble Ichijō Norifusa, *kampaku* or "Chancellor" since 1458, fled the warfare around Kyoto in 1468 to take refuge on his estates in western Tosa, Hata. Here he settled on his *shō*, and laid out a small town, Nakamura, on the approximate lines of the Kyoto he had abandoned. Its ambitious and unfulfilled street and temple plans long remained as evidence of his nostalgia for the capital. The Ichijō line was for some time the most important of the seven families which competed for primacy, each in its own sphere of interest; it was more remote and secure than were the Chōsokabe at the center, but it provided no leaders of the stamp of the two Chōsokabe family heads who built modern Tosa.

This process began in the middle of the sixteenth century. Chōsokabe Kunichika, beginning with a small band of rustic warriors, very nearly suffered total eclipse when he lost his fortification at Okō. Through the help furnished by the Ichijō, who gave him sanctuary, he managed to rebuild his following, regained his hill and his standing. Like his six principal competitors, he was secure only as long as his neighbors and subordinates failed to attack him in the rear while he aggressed against his adversary of the moment. It required an adroit sense of tactics and timing, the right combination of promises and justifications for breaking them, for him to enlarge his sphere of interest. Yet given his abilities his central position, in one sense a disadvantage, was also an advantage. By the time of his death in 1560 Kunichika had eliminated his immediate neighbors and established substantial, though not complete, control over the vital center of the Kōchi plain.

Chōsokabe Motochika succeeded to the family leadership and responsibilities in 1560, and immediately set out on a series of battles that gradually grew in size and complexity from armed raids to military campaigns[8]. Within half a decade he had come to dominate virtually all of the central plain, so that his primacy was contested only by the Aki to the East and the Ichijō to the west. He had secured a minor court rank *(Kunai no shō)*, he had converted several rivals into collaterals by forcing them to adopt his relatives as heirs, he had utilized a loose alliance with the Ichijō to checkmate their subordinates on his west flank, and he had begun the preparation of his emerging "realm" to increase his military capabilities for defence and offence.

In 1569 Motochika was ready to attack to the east. An affront to his Ichijō allies provided him with pretext for war, and the army of some seven thousand men he led against the Aki showed his new potentialities.

---

[8] The biographical account below is taken from the excellent recent work by YAMAMOTO, *Chōsokabe Motochika.*

The Aki were crushed. Meanwhile Motochika's preoccupation had tempted Ichijō supporters on his rear to molest his subordinates, so that the provocation for punitive measures to the West lay ready at hand. Domination of Hata district required another five years. It was made easier by the degeneration of Ichijō leadership, which had advanced so far that vassals changed sides. The extinction of that line, and the reduction of isolated areas of further resistance, brought Motochika undisputed control of Tosa in 1574.

Up to this point Motochika had not made any fundamental changes in the systems of allocation or privilege in the areas he had conquered; he had, indeed, defeated leaders and won over subordinates, but he had not conquered land with a view to administering or exploiting its resources. Hata district he had allotted to his younger brother, the adopted head of the Kira family. Yet the number of Motochika's followers and their expectations of reward for their services had increased dramatically. It was always easier to reward them with some one else's land, and inevitably thoughts of conquests beyond the borders of Tosa arose. The provinces of Sanuki (modern Kagawa Prefecture), Awa (Tokushima), and Iyo (Ehime) offered hopes of richer harvests and participation in national leadership, and it was to conquest of them and hegemony of all Shikoku that Motochika now bent his efforts. The armies he now led were larger than any he had yet assembled; he led a reported twelve thousand men in the invasion of Sanuki in 1579, and for Awa and Iyo the numbers rose, according to some sources, to 36,000 men. Although there were some setbacks and numerous compromises with local leaders involved, Motochika's forces were everywhere successful; by 1585 he had emerged as hegemon of Shikoku.

Motochika was now involved in national politics, whether he wanted to be or not. There is evidence that he was willing to face this, and that he even considered backing the last Ashikaga pretender to shogunal authority. But his more immediate problems were the major contenders for national leadership, Oda Nobunaga (d. 1582) and Toyotomi Hideyoshi (d. 1598). On the larger scene the situation was as fluid as it had been on the Kōchi plain when Motochika began his conquests, and his adversaries regularly implored help from, and promised subordination to, other military figures. Motochika had succeeded in taking Iyo because the neighboring daimyo on the main island of Honshū, Mōri, had been hard pressed by Nobunaga and unable to respond to pleas for assistance, and Motochika had taken the precaution of sending envoys to Nobunaga before his excursions from Tosa to explain his purposes and win his approval. Nobunaga is said to have described Motochika as a "bat on a birdless island", and he seems to have approved Motochika's moves in the confidence that he could appear as a greater bird of prey whenever it suited his convenience to do so. In 1582 Nobunaga was in fact preparing an expedition to take Iyo and Sanuki away from Motochika, but his death in that year instead led to a period of uncertainty in which Motochika was able to consolidate his gains in Shikoku.

Tosa in the Sixteenth Century

In national affairs Motochika showed little of the adroitness and timing that had marked his rise to power in Tosa. During the prolonged jockeying between Ieyasu and Hideyoshi he sided with the former, only to have his "ally" make peace with Hideyoshi. It was now Hideyoshi's turn to carry out Nobunaga's pattern and to demand Sanuki and Iyo of Motochika. Motochika tried to hold on to one of these provinces, and instead lost Awa in addition when he proved unable to withstand the invasion that Hideyoshi mounted. In 1585 he swore fealty to Hideyoshi and found himself restricted once again to Tosa.

The rest of Motochika's life was spent fighting Hideyoshi's wars. As symbol of his entry into Hideyoshi's family he took the name Hashiba and styled himself *Tosa no kami*. He contributed wealth and lumber to Hideyoshi's building plans. He led an army — and lost a favorite son — in the Kyushu battles against Shimazu. He led an army against the Hōjō at the siege of Odawara in 1590, and in 1592 and again in 1597 he led armies to Korea. He died at Fushimi, where he had taken his son and successor Morichika to pledge loyalty to Hideyoshi's young son Hideyori, in 1599; the following year that son lost his realm after his commitment to the losing side in the battle of Sekigahara which ushered in the years of Tokugawa hegemony.

Organizing the Realm: the *Kashindan*

After the unification of Tosa, Motochika's first thought had been further conquests to reward his men. Hideyoshi's invasions of Korea, following the unification of Japan, had some of the same motivations. An end to foreign conquest brought the careful management of status, office, and income that characterized the Tokugawa polity; in the Tosa case, the failure to retain other Shikoku provinces made it necessary to set about the reorganization of the realm. The difficulties Motochika experienced with the rationalization of his military bureaucracy served to forecast the finality of the separation of samurai and land that was prerequisite to the stabilization of social classes of Tokugawa times.

The immediate impetus to Motochika's reorganization of his warriors seems to have been the rough handling his armies received from the Hideyoshi and Shimazu generals. There was, indeed, a considerable difference between the professionals who blocked his path to power and the part-time warriors who had served and opposed him in Shikoku. A retainer summarized the difference in these terms during the discussions which led to the surrender to Hideyoshi; the mainlanders, he said, had immensely superior arms and equipment; their big horses were elaborately fitted with hardware of carved gold and silver, enough to make one's eyes pop out; when in formation, with their carefully made pennants fluttering behind their ranks, they made a majestic appearance. In contrast, of the Shikoku men "seven out of ten are mounted on Tosa ponies, wooden stirrups dangling from crooked saddles. Their coats of armor are cut of

93

wool so rotting that it is held together by hemp twine, and their pennants are thrown across their laps. They cannot be compared to the *kamigata* warriors." It had, he went on, been a futile effort to try to resist the enemy, as Tosa could not match one tenth of the strength the other had[9].

Nevertheless the unimpressive, poorly mounted and equipped Tosa figure had been the basis of Motochika's rise to power. He owned his horse and weapons, and possessed enough land to support himself, so that he was known as *ichiryō gusoku*[1]. Usually drawn from the *myōshu* and *jitō* groups, he was independent in means and attitude, however shabby in appearance. The *ichiryō gusoku* was part farmer, part fighter. As a Tokugawa Tosa gazeteer, the *Nanroshi*[10], put it, "The *ichiryō gusoku* of Chōsokabe times had a few paddies as *ryō* and performed almost no duties. They stayed secluded on their own property and did their own cultivating; they didn't mix with other samurai, and they knew nothing about propriety and courtesy. The only thing they prized was fighting courage. Even when they went into their paddy to cultivate, they tied their sandles to the handle of their lance and stuck it in the ridge between paddies; if someone gave the word, they would drop sickle and plow and dash off[11]."

No doubt they entered their paddies more to supervise than to plow, for their local standing and the requirements of paddy agriculture provided them with a good chance to conscript labor. Their *ryō* was in any case seldom an integrated holding, and its varied plots required much care. An early seventeenth century work on agronomy compiled in Iyo describes *ichiryō gusoku* holdings there as averaging 1 *chō*, two and one quarter *tan* (in modern terms, slightly over three acres) and describes the total days of duty labor required for such a collection of wet and dry fields at 811 per year[12][2]. But whether or not such landlord-warriors tilled with their own hands, their personal involvement in farming with dependents and followers[13] meant that they, and not the daimyo, controlled the countryside and its income. In the Shikoku wars, where they met their counterparts from neighboring provinces, their enthusiasm and courage

---

[9] Quoted by Irimajiri Yoshinaga, *Tokugawa bakuhansei kaitai katei no kenkyū*, (Tōkyō, 1957), p. 208, from *Kainan jiranki* (1913).

[10] A gazeteer of Tosa compiled by Mutō Munekazu (1741—1813), of which a partial published edition began to appear in Kōchi in 1959.

[11] Quoted by Irimajiri, op. cit., p. 209. One is reminded of R. R. Palmer's recent description of Polish nobles who, "possessing a few acres and a horse, made a shabby living by doing the farm labor themselves. Travelers saw them going into the fields wearing their swords, which they hung on trees as they went about their plowing or their digging." *The Age of the Democratic Revolution* (Princeton, 1959), p. 415.

[12] The *Seiryōki*[2], written in 1628, is described as the oldest work on agronomy in Japan. A published edition, edited by Irimajiri Yoshinaga, appeared in Tōkyō in 1955. See also Irimajiri in *op. cit.*, p. 218.

[13] The *tezukuri* system, described by Thomas C. Smith, *The Agrarian Origins of Modern Japan* (Stanford, 1959), p. 5 foll.

---

[1] 一領具足   [2] 清良記

had suited Motochika's needs admirably; in the case of an attack on Awa, when Motochika met separately with his most powerful retainers and with the farmer-warriors, the enthusiastic urging of the latter for the proposal to attack led him to ignore the reservations their superiors had raised against it [14]. But since they had proven inadequate in battles with Hideyoshi's full-time warriors, and since their holdings stood to prevent the buildings of a corps of professionals in Tosa, changes were in order. The *kumi*, or band, of *kokujin*, landsleute, began to give way to the retainer corps, or *kashindan* [3].

Motochika had prepared the top brackets of this organization by his absorption of early neighbors and adversaries through their adoption of his relatives and heirs. The *ichimon*, as they were known, came to be headed by two of Motochika's younger brothers and two of his younger sons. Since these families came to have considerable holdings and importance, a firm division was next made between their retainers, Motochika's rear vassals *(baishin)*, and his direct retainers *(jikishin)*, who numbered, at the time of Motochika's death, 9,736. The *ichimon* were prestigious, but (like the Tokugawa *gosanke* and *kamon)* they were kept outside of the main decision forming process; when the Kira house head (Motochika's brother) tried to protest Motochika's selection of his fourth son as heir and successor, he was condemned to death and his lands declared forfeit. Active counsel was kept within the ranks of the top-ranking *jikishin.* *Karō* (lit. house elders) were military leaders and also furnished from their ranks the three Commissioners *(san bugyō)* with over-all administrative responsibility. Under them served magistrates *(sho bugyō)* to regulate shrines, appeals, award lands, travel, communications, land, wells and moats, and materials [15]. Below these, the soldiers were organized in groups familial in name but not in fact; *yorioya* (unit commanders) instructed and led their *yoriko.*

In terms of national patterns, Motochika had taken only the first steps on the road to organization and rationalization of his military and administrative force, and there is evidence that by the end of his career a considerably greater rank differentiation was being worked out [16]. Additional steps would require modification of the *ichiryō gusoku* into professional soldiers or full-time agriculturalists. Only professional soldiers maintained by their daimyo could be expected to give proper attention to the endless campaigns that vassalage to Hideyoshi had involved for Motochika, and absent soldiers could not long continue the direction of agriculture and village subordinates. In any case, it was Hideyoshi's desire to achieve a

---

[14] Yamamoto, *Chōsokabe Motochika*, p. 93.
[15] Yamamoto, op. cit., p. 176. Later Motochika showed his respect for Hideyoshi's enthusiasm by appointing a Tea Ceremony Commissioner as well. p. 222.
[16] Inoue, *Chōsokabe okitegaki no kenkyū*, p. 186 foll., provides details of ranks and holdings of the principal retainers.

---

[3] 家臣團

clear separation between agriculturalist and soldier. What was needed, therefore, was a clear demarcation, and shift, from estate through fief to salary; or, in the terms of the Tosa land survey, from *honchi*[4], through *kyūchi*[5] until the warriors, separated from their holdings, resided in Kōchi and received a regular *hōroku*[6]. The first steps in this process can be followed through Motochika's land survey and efforts to develop a castle town.

The Chōsokabe Cadastral Survey

Hideyoshi ordered all his vassals to conduct cadastral surveys and prescribed uniform measures and methods to be used and followed. These surveys had as one goal the identification of a class of producing farmers permanently separated from martial callings who would be solely responsible for the tax yield of the fields they worked. They were also an essential prerequisite to efficient local administration. Population increase and the growth of specialty products had placed in dispute boundaries between areas and villages; mountain and woodland areas, poorly demarcated, could also go untaxed. The goal of clarifying local administration was in large part achieved, and it could be maintained with strenuous warnings against "hidden" fields like those contained in the Chōsokabe 100 Article Code. The social stratification, however, could be speeded, but not carried out, by such surveys; they accelerated, but first recorded, the trends of their time.

Chōsokabe Motochika, like other daimyo, had conducted earlier, less intensive surveys, basing them upon documents *(sashidashi)* accepted from subordinates at the time of surrender or fealty. Immediately after the Kyushu fighting of 1587, in which he fared badly, Motochika returned to inaugurate the new survey. He instructed his officials that they were not to show partiality, they were to keep their pledges, to abstain from liquor while the survey was in progress, to work a full day, to resist all invitations to entertainments by village heads and farmers; they were not to be swayed by arguments or evidence of precedents, but they were to measure fields and grade them, efficiently and accurately[17]. The main work for the survey was done between 1587 and 1590; several years later supplementary surveys were conducted to tap newly reclaimed lands that had come into cultivation.

The Chōsokabe survey is one of the few of that period to survive in its entirety, largely because it served as basis for taxation and local administration throughout Tokugawa times. It lists every house, field, and taxpayer of its day, and in its completeness it permits studies of personal

---

[17] Some of the instructions quoted by HIRAO MICHIO, "Kaisetsu", in *Chōsokabe chikenchō*, Vol. I (Kōchi, 1957), p. 670.

---

[4] 本地　　　　　　　　[5] 給地　　　　　　　　[6] 俸禄

holdings of members of Motochika's staff. The arable fields of the realm were listed as producing 248,000 koku of rice; of this acreage approximately one tenth was in the hands of the daimyo[18]. The greater part of this, however, lay in Hata and Aki, the areas most recently subdued, whose earlier rulers had been most completely destroyed. For his chief retainers, as for Motochika himself, the survey provides evidence of rapid increase of wealth after the last stage of conquests within Tosa had begun. Thus one of his chief officials, Hisatake, began as a myōshu with slightly over 4 chō; to this he added 97 as award lands (kyūchi) and smaller amounts through purchase and for residences to make a total of about 125 chō. Hisatake's kyūchi, however, were scattered in five districts and 26 villages, and were far from an integrated sub-fief. On his original lands, or honchi[19], he worked with his own tenants and subordinates, in the tezukuri style of extended family cultivation; for others he was clearly dependent upon the development of patterns of rural administration. Thus Hisatake, a "modern" administrator for his daimyo who filled a variety of posts, held lands both in the pre-survey manner and in the post-survey pattern of dependence upon the new autocrat[20].

The Chōsokabe survey listed by name mostly persons of substances in the countryside; myōshu, jitō, or established farmers with tenure rights. In the case of a large landholder like the afore-mentioned Hisatake, dependents in positions of agricultural responsibility might also be listed. But most members of semi-free categories — genin, hikan — mentioned in the Code do not appear at all. When they do appear, they are so listed; at other times, gradations of importance are conveyed by the size and location of the characters with which the name is recorded[21]. Rural inequality is further documented in the fact that more houses, (for the which the count is presumably complete) are listed than families to live in them. Frequently these are ascribed to kage no mono — literally "shadow people" — who live in subordination, or under the shadow of those whose names do appear[22]. Thus gradations of land (good, average, poor; jō — chū — ge), of status, and of tenancy, are all indicated in the survey, which offers a unique opportunity to study the complex pattern of institutional development that had survived into the sixteenth century.

It is striking to note that of the names that do appear, almost 80% hold less than 5 tan of land (one and one quarter acres). From this it has been suggested that the survey documents land fragmentation and inequality;

---

[18] YAMAMOTO, op. cit., p. 197. Contemporary computations were made at the basis of one koku per tan; Chōsokabe fields totalled 2, 375 chō.

[19] The honchi-kyūchi distinction is worked out by YOKOGAWA SUEKICHI, Ōsato shō no kenkyū, p. 97 foll.

[20] YOKOGAWA SUEKICHI, "Chōsokabe chikenchō: Hisatake Kuranosuke no kenkyū", Tosa shi'dan: (New Series, No. 16) No. 95 (Kōchi, 1959), p. 1—14.

[21] YOKOGAWA, in Kōchi Shi shi (Kōchi, 1958), p. 253, 258; in Ōsato shō no kenkyū, p. 93—97; for the national scene, SMITH, op. cit., p. 3 foll.

[22] YOKOGAWA SUEKICHI, "Chōsokabe chikenchō no yashiki nauke ni tsuite", Tosa shi'dan (New Series No. 6), No. 85 (Kōchi, 1955), p. 1—5.

for every *myōshu* listed there are seemingly independent, but probably semiindependent, followers who also appear[23]. In time, no doubt, facts caught up with appearances, so that the subordinates grew into the petty landholders who emerged as Tokugawa village members. If, as authorities agree, petty holdings of this size distinguished men of some substance in the village, one can imagine the degree of welfare that faced those too lowly to be listed.

The Chōsokabe survey permits the historian to note Motochika's goals and his degree of success. By scattering the rewards in land for his warriors in small, diverse plots, he kept them from being able to exploit and farm them by the *tezukuri* system, forced them to accept an annual produce tax, and took them one step away from their status as *ichiryō gusoku*. On the other hand, the warriors' retention of their *honchi* despite larger *kyūchi* also tells something of the tenacity of traditional holdings and customs in Tosa. Motochika, who had risen to power with such men, could only with difficulty force them to give up their bases. He himself, when offered Ōsumi by Hideyoshi after the death of his son in action against the Shimazu armies in 1587, begged to be allowed to retain Tosa, perhaps because of his retainers' urgings. That some progress had been made toward the establishment of a countryside rationally administered by civilians is, however, indicated in the language of the 100 Article Code with its underlining of the authority of village and coastal headmen (*shōya, tone*). The entrustment of specific powers to such men, who were to be obeyed because charged by their daimyo and not because they were also samurai, began here, and it developed until by Genroku times the Tosa *shōya* was fully responsible for his area of administration.

The Castle Town

Given the tenacious retention of the warriors' original land holdings and the modest dimensions of most warrior grants, it is evident that the effort to move all retainers to the castle town would meet with difficulties. Yet the attempt had to be made, for hopes of centralizing rural administration had no chance of success unless the soldiers could be placed under discipline and kept in economic dependence. Moreover Motochika needed and wanted a populous and thriving castle town, of the sort then growing around the fortresses of his peers elsewhere in Japan.

Motochika's first efforts at developing a castle town were at Okō, where he organized artisans and merchants and tried to attract retainers, but without success. In 1588 his new national responsibilities made it seem appropriate to try again at a new site, and he moved his capital to Ōtakazaka, on the site of the present city of Kōchi. This time his town was more obviously dominated by the administrators who laid it out. Motochika set aside some seven and one half acres for commerce and artisans, and again set about urging his retainers to move to town. Again

---

[23] YOKOGAWA, in *Kōchi Shi shi*, p. 254 foll.

the response was poor. The land survey, which had listed 125 houses for Okō, records 132 for Ōtakazaka. There is evidence of some disaffection among the *ichiryō gusoku,* who were least able to stretch their resources to finance the move, and one source reports a brief rebellion. Whether or not the rising took place, it is not hard to imagine that the petty warriors were by this time hard put to make ends meet in view of the expensive allegiance to Hideyoshi which Motochika had taken up [24].

In 1591 Motochika moved his castle and tried again, this time at Urado, directly on Kōchi Bay. Here his sea connections to Osaka and Hideyoshi were excellent, and here, too, he could build on the fortifications of an earlier rival family. Again special efforts were made to attract and reward merchants. Of the specially honored "official" merchants *(goyō shōnin)* several came from outside of Tosa, including one from the province of Harima whose place of business later provided downtown Kōchi with its best known name [25]. The 100 Article Code went to considerable effort to set wages for artisans and services, and it added encouragement for trading ventures by Tosa shippers. Yet retainers continued reluctant to make the move. The land survey, compiled before Motochika's efforts had had their full effect, could list only 64 houses for Urado, and even the most favorable view of the contemporary population of all villages comprehended in which might be called Greater Kōchi can estimate only 3100 residences with a possible 20,000 people in the area [26]. No doubt, too, some of the merchants who were present came as dependents of samurai families; some retainers, like Hisatake, were themselves active in business activities of a primitive sort [27].

There is abundant evidence that this urban growth was far less than the daimyo desired. As late as 1600, edicts warned of extra labor for retainers who failed to come and promised exemptions from duty for those who complied with instructions; wives and families, it made clear, should also be brought [28].

Ichiryō gusoku who could not afford to comply with such instructions had little real alternative to giving up their warrior status. The clauses in the 100 Article Code that regulate such transactions clearly tried to slow the process, but they could not fail to approve its long run effect of separating warrior from farmer.

The daimyo as lawgiver

One can sense in these changes the way in which the fundamental nature of the relationship between Motochika and his retainers had been altered.

---

[24] Yamamoto Takeshi, "Chōsokabe seiken no henshitsu to ichiryō gusoku", in *Nihon Rekishi,* No. 117 (Tōkyō, March 1958), p. 69—77.
[25] Yamamoto, *Chōsokabe Motochika,* p. 207.
[26] Yokogawa, in *Kōchi Shi shi,* p. 261.
[27] Yokogawa, "Hisatake Kuranosuke", *Tosa shi'dan,* p. 95.
[28] Quoted in *Kōchi Shi shi,* p. 238—240.

M. B. Jansen

The squirarchy whose bellicose advice before his entry into Awa had seemed so admirable to Motochika a decade earlier had become a limitation on his wealth and power of manouver. Increasingly aloof from his retainers, Motochika became also more despotic and arbitrary in his dealings with his counsellors; he was concerned to become ruler in fact as he was in name. His survey and his administrative measures showed the effort to overcome his handicaps and achieve the kind of dominance and wealth that characterized his contemporaries in the more populous and economically advanced areas along the Inland Sea.

Bit by bit Motochika put himself into the role of Confucian ruler and moralizer as well. During his early campaigns he had often gone out of his way to protect, restore, and support Buddhist temples. Like his father, he took Buddhist orders in his advanced years. But Confucianism too made its impression upon him as the path for the proper ruler, and the moral tone he adopted in his Code brought him to the threshold of the Tokugawa daimyo ideal[29]. The outstanding product of this is his 100 Article Code, which shows Motochika's goals and some of his problems.

The Code was not meant to be a public document. In all probability it was read to the principal Chōsokabe retainers as guide to their activities when in office. It sets forth in great detail regulations for officials, priests, and samurai, and establishes the line for social morality that is to be observed. Twenty-nine articles deal with infractions of law and punishments, fifteen deal with taxes, another fifteen regulate officials procedures, and others spell out minor regulations. Six articles stipulate samurai services, and others apply to Buddhist priests. Relations with Hideyoshi and the Imperial Court come for early attention. Longer than Takeda Shingen's, which predates it by four decades[30], Motochika's code has sometimes been described as its only true parallel.

Like the land survey, the 100 Article Code survived into Tokugawa times. After Yamauchi replaced Chōsokabe in 1600, the new daimyo, without the intimate knowledge of the past that characterized his predecessor, and without the corps of administrators which Motochika had been developing, naturally relied fully upon the land survey. A copy was in the hands of each District Commissioner, who was expected to use it as the basis of his work, and it was praised highly as the one essential work by the early Yamauchi daimyo[31]. Gradually its distinctions between *honchi* and *kyūchi* became meaningless, and the *ichiryō gusoku* became a rural gentry of headmen and leading farmers. A few, not content to accept this fate, provided the only resistance that met the Yamauchi entry into Tosa in

---

[29] Which ideal also cost his son his realm. When Morichika's retainers, in 1600, killed an elder brother the father had ordered placed in seclusion to strengthen Morichika's hold on the succession, they provided the Tokugawa administrators with the occasion for removing Morichika from authority as a person devoid of proper familial attitudes.

[30] Translated and annotated by Wilhelm Röhl, "Das Gesetz Takeda Shingen's", *Oriens Extremus*, (Hamburg, 1959), Vol. 2, p. 210—235.

[31] Hirao, in *Chōsokabe chikenchō*, Vol. I, p. 669, 672.

1600. Still other Chōsokabe retainers fled to Sakai to take up merchant careers, further illustrating the lack of hard class lines in early Tokugawa times[32]. As with the survey, so with the Code; it became the basis of early Yamauchi codes, and dissident and fearful Chōsokabe retainers and supporters were assured that "the laws (of Chōsokabe) are to remain in force[33]".

Despite these assurances, the Yamauchi entry inevitably speeded the changes which Motochika had contemplated. Motochika, who had grown with his realm and with his retainers, could not undo the past; he tended to be cautious and conservative in his measures. His successor, who inherited a situation in which many *ichiryō gusoku* had rebelled and others had fled, could deal with them as Motochika could never have done. His changes were, ultimately, sweeping, and although the Chōsokabe cause survived as symbol for anti-Tokugawa resistance in the 1860's by rustic samurai, now known as *gōshi*, it could never become a more than the romantic invocation of a primitive, virtuous past.

The Hundred Article Code[34]

1: Services and festivals of (Shintō) shrines must be carried on in the manner that was prescribed in earlier years. Furthermore, wherever possible maintenance costs of shrines should be met from their own lands and endowments. In the event of great damage that makes this impossible, the Commissioner must be consulted. Failure to report in this manner will be construed as an offence on the part of the shrine priest authorities and families[35].

2: The functions of (Buddhist) temples must be continued in the way they have come down from the past and must not be allowed to deteriorate. Furthermore, temples should meet their maintenance expenses by relying on income from their own domain[36].

---

[32] *Kōchi Shi shi*, p. 230, 246.

[33] *Kinsei sonraku jichi shiryōshū*, p. 18.

[34] In preparing this translation I have had the advice and assistance of my former colleagues at the University of Washington, particularly Noburu Hiraga, who assisted in the preparation of an earlier translation which was presented to the Japan Seminar at the University some years ago. Subsequently I have had the advantage of consultation with HIRAO MICHIO and INOUE KAZUO. The recent works by Yamamoto and Yokogawa have helped to clarify further the setting of Chōsokabe times. The standard source and authority is the magistral work of (Judge) INOUE KAZUO, *Chōsokabe okitegaki no kenkyū* (Kōchi, 1955, p. 648, to which the reader is referred for discussions of texts and variations, a synoptic text with punctuation, (p. 132—166) and an exhaustive commentary. The Code has also been reprinted in many books of sources, among them *Nihon keizai taiten*, Vol. 1, p. 659—672, and *Kinsei sonraku jichi shiryō-shu* (Tōkyō, 1956), p. 303—308.

[35] Earlier instructions here declared still in force doubtless refer to ordinances issued by KIRA, ICHIJŌ, HOSOKAWA, and similar authorities, as well as earlier Shogunal conventions. They are mentioned in a total of six other articles (2, 14, 31, 45, 58, 75) covering a wide range of subject matter.

[36] Father and son the Chōsokabe, who had for a time held the office of Temple *bugyō*, exerted themselves to protect, restore, and regulate the Buddhist establishments under their control; they both entered orders toward the end of their lives.

3: As soon as an order affecting matters of state is issued it must be carried out conscientiously. Any sign of laxity will naturally be punished immediately[37].

4: It is of course absolutely forbidden for anyone, high or low, to make use of the chrysanthemum-paulonia crest (of the Imperial family).

5: In regard to the reception accorded an emissary or deputy (from Hideyoshi) who comes to our province: every effort must be made to receive him properly. Those who excel in the pains they take in regard to receptions or farewells shall be rewarded. Furthermore, at such a time care must be taken to report everything which the guides or attendants in the emissary's party may have said.

6: Lords and vassals, priests and laymen, noble and mean, high and low, must all keep from allowing the rules of humanliness, righteousness, and propriety to suffer disgrace, but should on the contrary keep them constantly in mind.

7: It should be the primary concern of everyone to train himself unceasingly in military accomplishment. Those who tend to excel their fellows in this should be given additional income. Particular attention should be paid to musketry, archery, and horsemanship. The military code is contained in a separate document[38].

8: Strive to develop accomplishments appropriate to your status. Furthermore, you must keep always in your mind the study of books and pursuit of arts insofar as these are consistent with your duties.

9: You should try to live up to the teachings of the various (Buddhist) sects. In things like literary studies, those who excel their fellows, according to their achievements, can nourish hopes in whatever their area, whether worldly prosperity or religious life.

10: With regard to (Buddhist) priests: (a) those to return to lay life without reporting this to the lord of the province will promptly be executed. (b) They will no longer go out at night unless there is a compelling reason, and (c) their misconduct, when reported, will bring special reward for the informer. Violations of these points will bring punishment of exile or death, depending on the gravity of the offence[39].

---

[37] Motochika took his duties to Hideyoshi very seriously, and in provision of wealth, lumber, or armies showed his respect for *kōgi*-matters of state.

[38] Of muskets, in which the Tosa armies were far behind their Honshū contemporaries, YAMAMOTO writes, "muskets were first ordered from other provinces, but from Keichō years (1596 on) there were workers known as musket blacksmiths. Manufacture was not restricted within the retainer corps, but it was absolutely forbidden to non-(Tosa) nationals; orders hat to be reported, and secret manufacture was a crime punishable by death". *Chōsokabe Motochika*, p. 210. INOUE notes that the above-mentioned military code has never been found. *Chōsokabe okitegaki no kenkyū* p. 438.

[39] In these three articles one finds much of the Tokugawa ethic incorporated; emphasis on status, itself as yet imperfectly worked out in Tosa, emphasis on the study of books and civilized and military arts, respect for Buddhist teachings, and encouragement in the struggle for distinction and achievement in walks secular and religious. And, as the last shows, respect for Buddhist teachings did not necessarily extend to Buddhist clerics; no doubt it also reflected experience as *tera bugyō*.

11: The Three Commissioners have been appointed to administer throughout the seven districts of this province, and no objections are to be raised against any decisions the Commissioners make. Furthermore, shōya have been appointed for each community, and the instructions they announce must not be neglected in any way[40].

12: The words of the yorioya and other unit commanders are to be respected at all times, and no one should ever raise the slightest objection to them.

13: As regards law suits throughout the realm, they should first be taken up with the unit commander (yorioya) and thereafter submitted to the lord. Those who have no unit commander should take it up with the magistrate. Suits can not be taken up during periods of military service, duty in Kyoto, or absence, although exceptions can be made in cases of emergency. Furthermore, cases will be heard three times a month, on the tenth, twentieth, and last day. Urgent matters requiring immediate attention may be submitted at any time.

14: The official responsible for forwarding cases to the lord should have both parties discuss the issue together and only then submit it to the lord. But, as in the past, he should not interfere with the rōjū[41].

15: Any interference by wives in legal action is strictly forbidden.

16: Once a verdict has been reached the case cannot be submitted to the lord a second time, even if additional arguments exist.

17: It is only natural that services are demanded of those who hold fiefs, and they must be carried out to the letter regardless of whether they are large or small. Anyone late for logging or construction work will be required to repeat the duty period as punishment. And anyone who comes short of the food and provisions requested of him for work details without excuse will be required to supply as much again.

18: In regard to those who abscond: offenders must be punished whatever their excuse and so also their relatives. Proper reward should be given neighbors or friends who report anyone whose behavior causes suspicion that he is planning to desert. Those who have knowledge of such

---

[40] Throughout these pages the distinction between the san bugyō, a group with overall responsibility chosen from the top karō families, and the sho bugyō, officials with specific responsibilities who numbered, according to one source, 138, is suggested by rendering the former as commissioners and the latter as magistrates. It is possible, however, that the code may in places mean one of the 3 instead of one of the 138 when it says only bugyō. For make-up, renumeration, and duties of bugyō, see INOUE, 380—394. Shōya normally supervised a single village, but where feasible and appropriate they might administer several, while a large population might justify appointment of two or three shōya. A late sixteenth century account credits Chōsokabe Tosa with 174 shōya and 63 tone, the comparable office for coastal (fishing) villages. INOUE, p. 398—403.

[41] Here, as in civil suits for commoners, the administrators made every attempt to have cases settled out of court, since they had no particular interest in the outcome and much preferred the compromise settlement consonant with Confucian harmony. For persistence of this, Dan F. HENDERSON, Patterns and Persistence of Traditional Procedure in Japanese Law, unpublished dissertation, University of California Berkely, 1955.

intent and fail to report it will receive the same punishment as the offender. Furthermore, a man who reports late for lumbering or construction and leaves without getting permission from the magistrate will have his land declared forfeit. If a man deserts directly to another province, punishment will also be imposed on his relatives. Similarly, if a man's servant *(hikan)* deserts (from labor duty), the master will be penalized threefold[42].

19: Anyone who performs more service *(kyūyaku)* than required should take it up with the magistrate to obtain the proper reduction. In case of emergency, not only in event of military service, one should increase the number of laborers and exert himself to the utmost. Thereafter it can be taken up with the magistrate for appropriate reductions in services. But in no case can such reductions be divided or shared.

20: Unless there is an explicit statement of release from the authorities, no one can be excused from services, whatever the reasons that are advanced.

21: When a man is sent somewhere on a mission or named as a magistrate, he will be excused from providing personnel for service duty as follows: If he goes to another province, 5 men less; to Hata or Aki, 3 men less; to the 5 central districts, 2 men less. This has no bearing on men of low status.

22: A man who desires to surrender his fief may be permitted to do so if it is clearly beyond his capacity. But to do so from choice and not from necessity is punishable. When cases are under consideration the applicant will in any case be required to perform his obligations until the twelfth month of the year, after which he may be permitted to give up his fief[43].

23: As regards crossing the borders of the province by people of any rank, in either direction: Under no conditions will any one who does not have a signed permit from a magistrate or village elder *(toshiyori)* be permitted to pass a mountain or coastal check point. *Shōya* have been appointed in the mountain areas and *tone* have been appointed in coastal areas, and anyone who disregards their instructions and tries to leave or enter without authority shall be punished. If someone without the proper

---

[42] *Hikan* was originally a designation of subordination, with *jitō* acting as *hikan* of the *shugo*. The term gradually came to have a more specific connotation of semi-free, indentured service, and signified the hands whereby the extended family carried out agriculture on the *tezukuri* system. In the above instance, *hikan* are sent off to perform the labor which is required of the fief holder, who stands responsible for their performance.

[43] Of this YAMAMOTO writes, "in the 1590's evidence of *ichiryō gusoku* who seek to renounce their award fiefs *(chigyō chi taru kyūchi)* becomes plentiful . . . such release of land and surrender of fiefs had its origin in economic reasons expressed as "incapable" and "faltering", but at the same time this must frequently have contained the idea of escaping the burdens of fief-incurred service *(kyūyaku)*". "Chōsokabe seiken no henshitsu to ichiryō gusoku", *Nihon Rekishi*, loc. cit., p. 71—72.

permits boards a ship, the person in charge of the ship will also be punished [44].

24: As to horses: Anyone with three *chō* should keep (his mount,) saddle and other equipment in a state of readiness. Naturally those with more land should perfect themselves in military arts, and those with less than three *chō* also will, if they keep up their military training, receive reward.

25: Quarreling and bickering are strictly forbidden. Whether in the right or wrong, begin with restraint and forbearance. If instead of this men resort to violence, then both parties should be punished, regardless of the right or wrong of the matter. If one party only raises his hand against the other, regardless of his reasons for having done so he will be punished.

26: With regard to thieves: They should be captured immediately and the magistrate informed. If there is no question about guilt, they will of course be beheaded. If the thief resists arrest, he will be slain. If these rules are not carried out, the *shōya* responsible will be held punishable.

27: As to cutting and wounds: Whatever the circumstances, whoever strikes or hits a fellow retainer must be punished. However, this does not apply to those serving as magistrate.

28: With regard to someone who injures another without reason: The nature of the death penalty which is to be imposed will be determined after careful examination. Further, if punishment is extended to the offender's relatives, the details of the investigation should be made clear.

29: As to cutting a man and then running away: Anyone doing this will be crucified. The *jitō, shōya,* and people of the vicinity should immediately pursue and capture the criminal and then report. If they cannot capture him, they should (try to) strike him down. If he escapes the whole community will be punished. If the murderer's relatives had any knowledge at all of the matter they will receive the same punishment as the criminal. If it is clear that they knew nothing, an appropriate verdict will be found. Anyone who was at the scene and failed to intervene will also be punished. Furthermore: with respect to (punishment for) relatives, the exact degree of relationship will be taken into account [45].

30: With regard to hitting (with shot or arrows) men in hunting areas, at construction sites, and elsewhere, without provocation: Anyone guilty of this will be punished immediately. If he had a prior grudge against his victim he will be sentenced to death, and punishment will extend to his relatives.

31: With regard to bandits and pirates: As has been the rule in the past, it is the responsibility of the area nearest to their hideout to search for and produce these people. If this is not done, the area in question will be penalized.

---

[44] Punishment, *seibai,* could include death, INOUE, op. cit., p. 132.

[45] *Jitō,* which is used six times in the Code (29, 47, 52, 60, 72, 79), meant little more than enfeoffed proprietor in this period, and seems to have been interchangeable with *chigyō* samurai, *kyūnin.* INOUE discusses variant interpretations, p. 396.

32: Heavy drinking is prohibited for all people, high and low, to say nothing of all magistrates. Furthermore: With regard to drunkards, the fine for minor offenses will be three *kan* of coins, and appropriate punishment *(seibai)* will be imposed for severe offenses. A man who cuts or strikes others (while drunk) will have his head cut off.

33: As to illicit relations with another's wife: Although it is obvious, unless the guilty pair kill themselves, both of them should be executed. If approval of relatives is obtained, revenge may be undertaken, but unnatural cruelty will constitute a crime. If the husband fails to kill the man, or if he is away the time the offense becomes known, the people of the village should kill the offender. In addition: If a woman has a reputation, the (marriage) contract is to be broken.

34: When there is not a man in the house, no males — masseurs, peddlers, travelling *sarugaku* performers and musicians, solicitors for religious contributions *(banjin)* or even relatives — shall set foot in the house. If someone is ill and if the relatives approve, a visit may be made, but then only in daytime. Even the magistrate must carry on his business outside the gate. However, this does not apply to parents, sons, and brothers (of the household head) [46].

35: Also, when a man is not present, a woman is not to go visiting Buddhist temples or Shintō shrines or sightseeing. Furthermore: The annual and monthly rites (for deceased relatives) should be held at the temple.

36: Also, in the absence of a man: It is absolutely forbidden for a priest to go in and out of the house. Furthermore: This does not apply to devotional services.

37: With regard to regulating *fudai* (hereditary servant) status: Men and women who have served their masters for ten years without having been discharged will be considered *fudai*. Similarly their children will naturally be considered *fudai* also. A male child will go with his father, and a girl goes with the mother. Even though a servant may have been told by his master that he is dismissed, unless there is written evidence of this no other master is to take him as his servant. If a master violates this rule the servant's former master should report this and claim his servant again according to law. It will then be his responsibility to decide whether to put the man in service again or to put him to death. If a servant ran away and his whereabouts were unknown, no matter how many years ago it was he should (if discovered) be reported and returned to his master. Furthermore: But if such a servant's whereabouts in a neighboring area were known to the master for more than ten years without his having taken any action, this will not apply. Similarly, as to *fudai* attached to

---

[46] YAMAMOTO, noting the instructions to retainers in the *Tenshō shikimoku* of 1574 to "develop arts such as dancing *(rambu)*, flute and drum, football, and tea; you should be ashamed to feel inferior on visits to other provinces", suggests that such efforts to popularize the culture of the Kyōto nobility among the ruling class were accompanied by the modest numbers of itinerant performers who toured the countryside. "The attainments of the commoners did not reach a very high level, but this (article 34) illustrates the general trend of the period". *Chōsokabe Motochika*, p. 226.

fiefs: If the proprietor *(jitō)* has gone to another province, even though he return, if he does not receive reinstatement of his original fief, he will not regain his powers over the *fudai* [47].

38: Debts of rice must be returned in the exact amount that was borrowed. It is a crime to return an insufficient measure of rice as though it were the full measure.

39: With regard to loans to petty retainers throughout the realm: Where the retainer, without his master's knowledge, has already been paying out his whole income and has had to give up his house and become a burden on his master, he should not be pressed for payment any longer [48].

40: In cases in which borrowed goods or things held in trust, or the lord's (tax) rice, are lost by fire or theft while in someone's possession, if that person's own possessions are also lost, he will not be required to make restitution. But if only the goods in his custody are lost, then he will have to make restitution. Also: It is forbidden to lend to others things which have first been borrowed.

41: With regard to pawned articles: Once it is established that an article has been lost because of theft or fire, claims for the borrowed money for which it served as security will be considered forfeit.

42: With regard to delinquent loans: If the borrower makes difficulties after having been pressed to pay, the matter should be reported to the magistrate, and the loan reclaimed without fail. But if the lender has for years failed to press for payment only the principal need be repaid.

43: Law suits over *kōryō* (daimyo domain) and *myōden* (private, name fields) must stop. Furthermore: land purchases will be validated by special decree, while the quality of service performed will be the criterion for (transfer) of land for which no validation papers previously exist [49].

44: It is a punishable offense to convert rice paddy field into dry field or house sites. Where this has been done the taxes will be kept at the same rate as those for paddy.

45: With regard to purchasing land: Even if someone has a contract providing for transfer in perpetuity, if the rice produced (by the plot) is less than ten *hyō* (about one acre of normal paddy) the land remains

---

[47] INOUE, p. 256 foll., discusses the significance and setting of this in the status arrangements of the period, and YOKOGAWA *(Ōsato shō no kenkyū,* p. 202—3), says of this article, "According to this, in the original fiefs *(honchi)* the medieval type of personal servitude of the *hikan* relation went almost unchanged under Chōsokabe rule, while on the new or award fiefs one sees the development of farmers' relations growing from a more modern type of land system. On the new fiefs one can see the first instances of a direct tax system expressed in the rule, "two thirds of the yield for the *jitō,* one third for the farmer" beginning to change the tax-tribute relationship centering on corvee labor which characterized the previous period".

[48] The word here is *matahikan. Mata* ("again, next") was a prefix added to terms for petty retainers to indicate they were attached to rear vassals, *baishin,* e. g. *matahikan, matakomono, matawakato.* INOUE, p. 186 foll.

[49] *Tokusei,* here rendered as "special decree", was normally an edict cancelling retainer debts; in this instance it permits alienation of land already registered in another's name, and hence also constitutes special intervention in the retainer's interest. INOUE, p. 281; for discussion of the fact that both retainers and the daimyo himself purchased land, YOKOGAWA, "Hisatake Kuranosuke", loc. cit.

redeemable (by the seller). Even if it is claimed that a plot was clearly sold permanently, if there is no documentary evidence to support this the plot can be reclaimed by its seller (with restitution of price). And if despite claims there is no documentary evidence to establish even such redeemable status for land, the land will be considered as *toshige* (redeemable from crop yield). The above rules are established in accordance with previous regulations. When a contract provides that land will be held in pledge at the rate of 1 *tan* per borrowed *hyō* of rice (about one fifth the yield of average paddy), if the lender has enjoyed crop rights for three years the original owner will no longer be required to repay the loan; he is also entitled to the return of his land. Furthermore: Land alienated under provisions of perpetual or of conditional sale will revert to the original owner if the purchaser's family dies out. But if someone succeeds to this family within ten years the land must again be returned to the purchaser. If, however, it is more than ten years before a successor takes over, their claims lose effect and the land will be considered part of the original ower's fief. The same rule holds for lenders and loans. Furthermore, if the seller's family dies out, except for lands specially registered earlier, all three classifications — perpetual sale, conditional transfer, and terminal option — are to be declared forfeit and confiscated[50].

46: With regard to abandoned and waste land throughout the realm: *Shōya* in the area must warn their people against letting it grow rank. If the *shōya* is unable to deal with it alone he should consult the magistrate about initiating reclamation measures. If the abandonment has been caused by negligence, the *shōya* of that place must assume responsibility for paying the tax in place of the tillers.

47: As to fiefs throughout the realm: The crop yield, as ascertained by the fall survey of fields ready for harvest *(kemi)* should be apportioned, two-thirds to the vassal samurai *(jitō)* and one-third to the farmer. If farmers object to this, the samurai will have to use his own judgment. He must, at any rate, take care lest the land be abandoned and ruined.

---

[50] It is not surprising that sixteenth century Japan, in which land was the chief form of wealth, had a vocabulary rich in terms to indicate degrees of ownership and tenure. The terminology adopted above is for the terms *kyūchi* [7] (permanently alienated land), *honmono* [8] conditional transfer, which can return to the principal *(hon)* owner, and *toshige* [9], at present "yield", but then used in the sense of land "purchased" under an arrangement whereby the seller-borrower paid interest and principal in kind from the fields, so that after a given period of time — usually ten years — it returned into his possission. Violation of this "option" would presumably result in loss of land. Furthermore, the sudden use of the word "fief" *(chigyō)* half way through the article makes it clear that Motochika's concern here lies with his samurai, probably with the *ichiryō gusoku*. It may be noted that this article is included in a volume of excerpts from feudal land law by the Ministry of Agriculture *(Dai Nihon Nōshi*, Tōkyō, 1891, II, p. 156, 7.) The net effect of these regulations would be to discourage and slow alienation of land, so that the article is as INOUE (p. 287) points out, a step in the progress toward the Tokugawa prohibitions on alienation of any kind.

---

[7] 永地   [8] 本物   [9] 年毛

Furthermore: Cultivation rights applying to lands which have changed hands in recent years will be determined at the discretion of the vassals holding the fiefs[51].

48: With regard to forestation, reclamation of abandoned land, development of waste land, and salt fields: Such reclamation must be reported to the lord, and work may be started after receiving his approval. The practice of keeping the existence of reclaimed land secret must absolutely be stopped. Supplement: The first year after reclamation the *tanmai* tax will be paid, and from the following year on regular taxes will be levied. Such fields are, after all, the lord's lands[52].

49: With regard to the waste land of fief holders *(kyūnin):* There can be no excuse for having allowed land to go to waste since the land survey.

50: As for the paddy, dry, and dwelling fields which came in dispute at the time of the land survey: As long as these are unresolved, the *shōya* of those areas will have to deliver the exact amount of tax due.

51: With regard to irrigation duty: The irrigation magistrate and *shōya* of the areas concerned must place particular emphasis on allowing nothing to obstruct the irrigation channels. If large-scale damage beyond the capacity of the people dependent on the water takes place, it should be reported to the magistrate, who, after consultation, should call out all the people to repair the damage.

52: Whoever discovers that anyone, whether vassal or farmer, is concealing the existence of (untaxed) fields and reports it to the lord, will be rewarded strikingly. Acting on such information, the magistrate will base his ruling on the land survey register. If it becomes clear that a vassal concealed the field, he will be severely punished. And if it was a farmer who concealed it, he will be made to pay double the tax due since the land survey, after which he will be banished. If he pleads hardship at this, he will have his head cut off.

53: With regard to disputes over property lines: In all cases such disputes will be decided in accordance with the register of the land survey. After a case has been heard with the arguments of both parties stated, the person found to be at fault will be fined five *kan* (i.e. 5000 copper coins) to punish him for his carelessness. If both parties refuse to listen to reason, the disputed area will be confiscated.

54: Within the lord's own domain, not even one grain of rice may be taken away in payment for loans or purchases before the date set for the

---

[51] "Although the Chōsokabe were unable to make a really thorough change", YAMAMOTO writes, "their aim, as seen in Motochika's Article 47, must surely have been to change the nature of the *ichiryō gusoku,* protect their fief holders, and build a new retainer corps on the basis of the separation of soldiers and farmers", *Chōsokabe seiken no henshitsu to ichiryō gusoku,* loc. cit., p. 74.
[52] Salt fields, *shiota,* can refer either to salt flats or reclamation of marsh land. Around Urado much reclamation took place, and as can be seen its profits ended in the daimyo's coffers. *Tanmai* [10] was a tax levied on rice paddies in addition to the regular tax.

---

[10] 米反   [11] 代名少幼

M. B. Jansen

payment in full of the fall harvest tax. If this ruling is not observed, both the *shōya* and the farmers involved will be severely punished.

55: In regard to the annual tax *(nengu)*: It must all be paid in hulled rice. The decision to plant *taimai* or *kichimai* rice will depend upon the soil. Planting *taimai* on soil more suitable to *kichimai* is strictly prohibited. If this order is violated the tax will be collected at the *kichimai* rate[53].

56: With regard to units of measure: Throughout the realm measures will be standardized to *kyōmasu*. However, long measure will be used for the annual tax and loan repayments, and short measure for private transactions[54].

57: Throughout the realm, *tanmai* must be paid each year as assessed.

58: In certain areas the tithe must be paid exactly as it was done in the past[55].

59: Whether it is hulled or unhulled rice, one *hyō* must contain five *to*.

60: With regard to farmers throughout the realm: The *jitō*, *shōya*, and magistrates must foster them solicitously in their official capacity. Do not require extra taxes and work in addition to the regular exactions from them. But of course, the regular annual tax must be paid strictly. If it comes even a little short, *shōya* and land owners of the lord's own domain will receive prompt and severe punishment.

61: It is strictly prohibited for a magistrate to develop private or abandoned fields.

62: If anyone discovers that a magistrate who has been sent to some part of the realm speaks irresponsibly or shows favoritism he should report the facts of the case, and, no matter how low his position, he will be rewarded handsomely as a result. After receipt of this report and in the light of an examination of the matter, that magistrate will be punished severely.

63: With regard to a magistrate or *shōya* anywhere in the realm who shows favoritism or partiality or indulges in any other unjust practices whatever, it makes no difference whether complaints come from someone in the offender's area (of jurisdiction) or not. Details should be forwarded to the authorities, and they will be rewarded. After an investigation, punishment will be meted out.

---

[53] *Kichimai*, standard paddy rice, was superior to *taimai*, a southern, soft rice with higher yield. *Kichi* was considered syonymous with rice, and paddy land was often referred to as *kichi chi*. See the articles by YAMAMOTO TAKESHI, in *Nihon rekishi daijiten* (Tōkyō, 1956), Vol. 5, p. 316, and Vol. 12, p. 69.

[54] In this article one sees Motochika following Hideyoshi's orders for standardization of weights and measures. The *kyōmasu koku* was more than 10% smaller than that earlier in use, and the unit measure also smaller, so that the traditional generalization that Hideyoshi's smaller unit measure meant higher taxes requires further examination in the case of Tosa.

[55] Both the *tanmai* and the tithe *(jūbunichi)* were traditional taxes continued by Chōsokabe; the former had its origins in a tax on paddies inaugurated by Kamakura *shugo* and was designed as additional income for enfeoffed retainers, while the tithe survived into Tokugawa times as an impost on goods and especially shipping. YOKOGAWA discusses the *tanmai* and related problems in *Ōsato shō no kenkyū*, p. 187—191.

64: A magistrate is forbidden to post or issue regulations for even a single area without reporting it.

65: Throughout the realm, if messengers for officials such as magistrates request horses or labor services on their way, they should be accommodated, provided they have official authorization with them. If they do not, they do not have to be obeyed.

66: It is absolutely forbidden to sell horses of this province to other provinces. If anyone attempts to send out horses illegally, the horses will be confiscated. The barrier keepers (at border crossings) must keep particularly close watch in view of this.

67: Artisans should have confidence in the things that magistrates and group leaders say and should not raise any objections to their instructions.

68: Wages for artisans including carpenters, sawyers, cyprus bowl makers, blacksmiths, silversmiths, sharpeners, lacquerers or painters, dyers, leatherworkers, tilers, cyprus dyers, wall plasterers, mat *(tatami)* makers, armorers and the like should be, per day, 7 *shō* of unhulled rice, *kyōmasu* measure, for skilled workers, 5 *shō*, *kyōmasu* measure, of unhulled rice for average workers, and 3 *shō* of unhulled rice, *kyōmasu* scale, for unskilled workers. The classification into skilled, average, and unskilled categories must be approved by the magistrate. Supplement: The wages for a boat-builder will be one *to* of unhulled rice, *kyōmasu* scale, per day [56].

69: The standard length of cotton cloth, irrespective of quality must be 7 *hiro*, taking one *hiro* as 4 feet 5 inches *(shaku, sun)* on the carpenter's measure. Coarse sacking will be standardized at 6 *hiro*.

70: With regard to trading boats: They should operate as much as possible, but the traders should realize how important it is that they stay within the borders of the province.

71: With regard to runners: The local *shōya* should dispatch or reserve them with due regard to the distances involved. If, when there is urgency, the runner is late, he should be decapitated.

72: The width of the main roads is to be 2 *ken,* each *ken* being 6 feet, 5 inches *(shaku, sun)*. In regard to roads, *shōya* must see to it that they are maintained, whether in mountain, countryside, or coastal areas. If a road is bad, it is the *shōya's* responsibility to collect one *kan* of coins from the landed samurai and farmers as a fine and turn it over to the magistrate's office.

73: With regard to linear measurements: In castle construction and all other work, use the standard *ken* of 6 *shaku* 5 *sun*. However, rice paddies are an exception.

74: It is strictly forbidden to travel along side roads. Anyone who breaks this regulation will be fined 1 *kan* of coins.

75: As for the fishing tax *(katsura zeni)*: It will be maintained as in the past.

---

[56] As was noted above Motochika's efforts to attract merchants and artisans to his castle town were not very successful, and it is apparent in this article that the Code is directed largely to *goyō shōnin*, merchants favored by the regime, as it is the magistrates who make the key decisions about quality and pay.

M. B. Jansen

76: It goes without saying that it is strictly prohibited to cut bamboo, cedar, cypress, camphor, pine and all other trees which have been registered for official use. It is also forbidden to cut down a bamboo of which one has need, even though it is within the confines of his own fief, without first reporting it to the magistrate's office. It is an important resource for all areas, country, mountain and coastal, to have bamboo trees growing.

77: It is strictly prohibited to break off bamboo shoots. Anyone who violates this rule will be fined 1 *kan* of coins, which will be given as reward to the informer who reports the offense.

78: It is forbidden to let cattle and horses wander freely at any season. Anyone who violates this rule will be fined 100 *mon* of coins. If there has been damage caused to harvest in the fields, an additional 100 *mon* will have to be paid to the owner.

79: If a man builds a house on leased land and moves away, if he has paid the annual tax, the house, whether board or thatched roof, belongs to him. But if he has been sentenced for a crime then the master (land owner) will take over his property as well as the house. If there is some question about his having paid his tax, the landowner will have to pay it to the enfeoffed proprietor in his stead. If, however, a landless laborer is convicted of a crime his house and property will be confiscated. In such a case the annual tax, if still outstanding, will be remitted to the (enfeoffed) land owner[57].

80: Between father and son, if either acts against the will of the lord, he will receive separate punishment according to his offence and what it deserves. But each case should be considered on its own merits.

81: With regard to transferring the headship of a temple throughout the realm: Suitable persons should be recommended to the lord and the transfer arranged in accordance with his instructions. Even though the candidate is a disciple (of the head), selection must necessarily be based on capability.

82: With regard to family succession: It is necessary to notify the lord and receive his permission, even if the heir is the head's real child. It is strictly forbidden to decide succession matters privately. Furthermore: One must also request and receive permission to become a guardian for a minor[58].

---

[57] This important article shows gradations of tenure and dependence among non-samurai. The first case, of the man who leases land from another, finds the Code giving the tenant substantial rights provided he has had no record of punishment; it represents, in other words, a step toward an undifferentiated body of agriculturilists. Yet the tenant is still subordinate *(hikan)*, as seen from the compulsion on his landlord the tenant is still subordinate *(hikan)*, as seen from the compulsion on his landlord *(shunin)* to pay his tax to the enfeoffed proprietor *(jitō)*. On the bottom rung, the landless laborer *(mōto)* gets less consideration, and the concluding phrase (for the interpretation of which this follows INOUE, p. 309) seems to protect the fief holder against loss. YAMAMOTO discusses this article at some length in "Chōsokabe seiken —", *Nihon Rekishi*, loc. cit., p. 73—74. A general view of stratification in village life of the period can be found in T. C. SMITH, "The Japanese Village in the 17th Century", *Journal of Economic History*, XII, 1, (1952).
[58] Alternatively, the last phrase could refer to selection of a child as heir or of a temporary family head. INOUE, p. 161 and 270, prefers "name a child as heir". The code, which reads yōshō myodai [11], permits either construction.

83: Anyone who succeeds to two houses without getting the approval of higher authority will be punished as soon as it becomes known.

84: As regards family name and succession designation for loyal retainers: If a vassal commits a crime and has to be punished, his family name will not be affected if the offence was a minor one. But if he commits a major crime, his punishment should include the loss of his family name.

85: With regard to the marriage of samurai: It is strictly prohibited for samurai who receive over 100 *koku* to arrange a marriage without the lord's approval. Supplement: Whether one's status be high or low, matters of marriage must not be broached at any time if the understanding of both families has not been arranged.

86: Private contract is prohibited in all matters[59].

87: It goes without saying that anyone who speaks or proposes evil things without regard for what is in the interest of the realm will be punished; in addition anyone in his company will receive the same punishment.

88: Those who start groundless rumors shall immediately be punished by death by crucifixion. It is also wrong to write irresponsible things on walls or gates. Anyone discovered to be doing this will be put to death.

89: It is absolutely forbidden to employ *rōnin* without notifying the lord and obtaining permission.

90: As regards *matawakato* and *matakomono:* they are strictly forbidden to associate in public or in private with the lord's own retainers[60].

91: With regard to documents concerning paddy and dry fields: precedence (between conflicting documents) will be established by the date indicated.

92: As to false accusations: Punishment will depend on whether the offence is minor or serious. If it is a minor matter, the fine will be 3 *kan* of coins.

93: Regardless of rank, the practice of dismounting (in deference to a superior) should be stopped. However, when an envoy or deputy from above (i.e., Hideyoshi) passes, he should receive this courtesy.

94: In matters large or small and good or bad, the lord's chamberlain must at all times transmit the sentiments of all the people, whatever their status to the lord. When there is an urgent matter and there is no one to transmit it, it should be submitted at once on paper. If an official fails to transmit anything, regardless of what it is, he will be punished immediately.

---

[59] This provision would operate both to reinforce the previous article and, more particularly, to guard against the organization and consolidation of new power groups in the countryside. In the fifteenth century contractual agreements among groups of *myōshu* led to the formation of semi-military bands out of which the *ichiryō gusoku* developed. For examples drawn from the Ōsato Shō, YOKOGAWA, *Ōsato shō no kenkyū,* p. 58—62, discussed also by IRIMARIJI, op. cit., 212—213. By the 1590's, YAMAMOTO concludes, "it is probable that remnants of the old *myōshu* alliances had ceased to exist". "Chōsokabe seiken no henshitsu", op. cit., p. 75.

[60] This separation of rear vassals from direct vassals would contribute both to peace and order and to consciousness of class and status distinctions.

M. B. Jansen

95: Anyone who has something on his heart should report it freely, whether his status is high or low. If he keeps it within himself until he develops evil ideas, he will be punished severely.

96: No one, high or low, is permitted to change his seal[61].

97: No one may change his family name, his official title or office, or his given name. However, an official title may be changed once in accordance with provisions with the lord's permission[62].

98: With regard to fire, it is essential to be vigilant at all times. If fire breaks out in a neighborhood, the owner of the house in which the fire first started will be fined according to his status. If the fire is confined to one house, the owner will be banished. Furthermore if responsibility for arson becomes clearly established, severe punishment will extend even to the relatives of the incendiary.

99: When someone in this realm, whatever his social standing, takes a long trip, there should be no objection raised against providing him a night's lodging. If a man of low rank steals or damages some of the things in his lodgings, he must make restitution. Supplement: The fee for the accommodations shall be determined by both parties.

100: With regard to the division of family property among relatives: Allocate one-tenth of the property to the father, and one-twentieth to the mother. But if both father and mother live together they should be satisfied with the father's share. The service *(kyūyaku)* required of a man who retires must be performed carefully by his successor. However, an exception can be made if different arrangements have been made by agreement between parent and son. Settlement of rights of brothers, uncles, nephews and other family members will be decided on the basis of their degree of relationship. But in all cases, whether between elder and younger brothers, or uncles and nephews, or others with the same surname, judgments will be handed down on the basis of propinquity of relationship.

These articles will provide the rule throughout this realm from this time on. All people, whether noble or base, must observe them strictly and in good faith. Any violation, even one word, is subject to immediate and severe punishment. Accordingly, it is promulgated as here set forth.

Twenty-fourth day of the Third Month,

Second Year of Keichō (1597)

Morichika
Motochika

---

[61] MIURA HIROYUKI, *Hōseishi kenkyū*, (Tōkyō, 1924) p. 1089, explains that seals were substituted for hand-written signatures at about this time.

[62] These references to official title and office are to the honorific designations awarded by the imperial court, in return for service or payment. For a brief review of the way in which territorial titles like "lord of ... " became separated from place and function, see INOUE, op. cit., p. 164—5. Similarly family names, which had their origin in place, were by this time disassociated and therefore changeable.

CHAPTER SEVEN

TOSA IN THE SEVENTEENTH CENTURY: THE ESTABLISHMENT OF YAMAUCHI RULE

MARIUS B. JANSEN

DURING the Meiji period Japanese who wrote about the Tokugawa years usually emphasized the stultifying effect of rule by precedent and custom. From the perspective of changes made in the nineteenth century, all that had gone before seemed stationary and without interest. But the work of modern historians has shown how inconstant a factor Tokugawa "custom" was, and how constant were the changes behind the ritual invocations of precedent. It is particularly during the seventeenth century that one sees the speed with which policies were transformed. Political transfer, samurai resentment, and peasant terror seemed to threaten the consolidation and centralization of the age of the unifiers, until corrective measures resulted in far greater central control.

The province of Tosa provides in microcosm the problems of much of Japan during the formative century of Tokugawa, but its history is also full of particularities that derived from its geographical situation and historical setting. It is of special interest because a transfer of rule occurred at the very beginning, just after the victory at Sekigahara, and because that transfer was the first change of power the province had known since the reunification. The main routes of Honshu had known many battles and changes of command. But Tosa warriors had for the most part done their fighting outside the province, and they were deeply rooted in their own society. As a result the entry of a new daimyo with a relatively small force of his own men required cautious planning; and it was many decades before a two-strata system of retainers, "loyal" and "outside," was worked out. The manipulation of one group against the other offered unusual opportunities for the advancement of centralized control, and the economic problems the new rulers faced encouraged their more imaginative administrators to take full advantage of such possibilities.

The administrative and organizational pattern of Tosa is well recorded in contemporary documents, particularly in three great codes of law that span the century. The first of these is Chōsokabe Motochika's Hundred Article Code of 1597, the first document to illustrate in detail the administrative goals of Tosa's daimyo in the days of Hideyoshi. Motochika's son Morichika lost his realm after Sekigahara, and the new rulers who followed him issued a Seventy-Five Article Code in 1612. In this document we see the new administrators, still aliens in their realm, trying to restore order in a confused social and political sit-

115

M. B. Jansen

uation. The third document, the great Genroku Code of 1690, contains 569 articles that show the institutional structure fully matured.[1] Comparisons between provisions of these codes offer unusual opportunities for observing political and social developments.

I. POLITICAL TRANSFER AND THE YAMAUCHI ENTRY

Tokugawa Ieyasu allotted the province of Tosa to Yamauchi Kazutoyo, an ally at Sekigahara, who had been lord of a small fief in Tōtōmi rated at one-fourth the assessed income of Tosa. Kazutoyo faced the problem of dealing with Chōsokabe retainers and especially a rustic squirarchy of farmer-soldiers known as *ichiryō gusoku*. These were men supposedly able to equip themselves from their own resources, usually mounted on Tosa ponies, and possessed of excellent fighting skills. They had begun to be displaced by professionals, for the Chōsokabe daimyo had done his best to develop a full-time retainer band that would live near him in his small castle town. His Code of 1597 makes it clear that many of the rustic samurai were unable to afford the move to town and were petitioning to give up a samurai status that was bringing them chiefly opportunities to fight Hideyoshi's wars in Kyūshū and Korea. The Chōsokabe reluctantly permitted resignations; Article 22 reads, "A man who desires to surrender his fief may be permitted to do so if it is clearly beyond his capacity. But to do so from choice and not from necessity is punishable." The majority were still farmer-fighters, however, and they numbered about 9,000 in 1600.

To deal with them, the Yamauchi had only a small force. One source credits Kazutoyo with only 158 mounted warriors when he arrived, and several decades later his total was still below 400. Even if one allows 10 men per knight (including *ashigaru* units of musket, bow, and lance), this was still a small army. Kazutoyo therefore petitioned Ieyasu for help in claiming his reward, and the latter delegated the task to his vassal Ii Naomasa, who in turn sent his retainer Suzuki Hyōe from Ōsaka with eight ships, less than a month after Sekigahara.

Upon Suzuki's arrival in Tosa, he was met by a host of angry *ichiryō gusoku* who refused to consider his call for the surrender of the castle unless he could promise that half of the realm would be set aside for their former lord. The resistance was put down, not so much by Suzuki as by senior Chōsokabe retainers who still commanded part of the army. Their grounds for doing so were fear that continued resistance might imperil the life of Morichika,

---

[1] For the Chōsokabe code, see M. B. Jansen, "Tosa in the Sixteenth Century: The 100 Article Code of Chōsokabe Motochika," above, pp. 89–114. The Code of 1612 can be found in *Kinsei sonraku jichi shiryōshū*, Vol. II, *Tosa no kuni jikata shiryō* (Tokyo, 1956), 315–28. The Genroku code is available in several printed works, among them the *Kōchi ken shiyō* (Osaka, 1924), 105–87. A recent photographic reprint has made available again the standard 1940 work on Tosa law of Inoue Kazuo, *Han hō, Bakufu hō, Ishin hō*, 3 vols. (Tokyo, 1965).

who was living in Ōsaka. The resistance delayed Suzuki's occupation of the castle, which he entered five weeks after his arrival in Tosa. To show that he had not been idle he sent 273 heads, in two boatloads, back to Ii Naomasa. Final disposition of the resistance came in the third month of 1601, after the arrival of Kazutoyo. *Sumō* matches were held on the beach at Katsurahama to mark the inception of his reign, and all village heads and rural samurai were urged to show their respect by attending. From those who did so, 73 leaders of the resistance were selected for crucifixion; several others who failed to appear were later seized in their villages and sentenced to the same fate. In 1603 there was a minor rising at Motoyama led by a former Chōsokabe retainer, now village head, who refused to institute new taxes. But after this was crushed with comparable severity, direct resistance from Chōsokabe retainers came to an end.[2]

Kazutoyo's first administrative decisions showed that a new daimyo making a fresh beginning could greatly accelerate the cautious moves toward centralization that had begun earlier. His measures separated farmers from samurai, and also samurai from samurai. The senior Chōsokabe retainers were exiled, and the *ichiryō gusoku* were treated as farmers. This done, a sweeping allocation of lands divided the province into *chokkatsuchi*, land reserved for the Yamauchi and overseen by *daikan*, and *ryōchi*, or fiefs, for his chief retainers. These, placed in Sagawa, Sukumo, Kubokawa, Motoyama, and Doi, now averaged double the income they had known in Tōtōmi.[3] Through intermarriage and adoptions with the main Yamauchi house they became the elite of the new social and bureaucratic structure. Kazutoyo's younger brother Yasutoyo received the district of Nakamura as a sub-fief, with daimyo status. But while Chōsokabe *chokkatsuchi* had been concentrated in Aki and Nakamura, areas at the extremities of the fan-shaped province last conquered by the daimyo and his original allies, the Yamauchi holdings were in the heart of the Kōchi plain. And, at 20% of the rated income of Tosa, they were double those that had been reserved for Chōsokabe.[4]

After a tour of his new realm and its resources, Kazutoyo decided on a new castle at the headwaters of Urado Bay. Once Ieyasu granted his petition to build, he selected one of his retainers, Dodo Yasuyuki, as Commissioner General, and construction began in the fall of 1601. A special bureaucracy of con-

[2] For a survey of Kōchi upon the Yamauchi entry, see Ozeki Toyokichi, "Tosa hansei shoki no jōsei," *Tosa shidan* #32 (Kōchi, 1930), 76–97. Other accounts in Hirao Michio and others, *Kōchi Shi shi* (Kōchi, 1958), 283–88; Matsuyama Hideo, "Urado kō no kaikaku to sono shiseki," *Tosa shidan* #21 (1927), 1–14; Irimajiri Yoshinaga, "Tosa hansei sōsōki to gōshi seido no kaikaku," *Waseda shōgaku*, Vol. 12, #3 (1936), 239–71. Motoyama Rebellion materials are brought together in *Dai Nihon shiryō*, Section 12, Vol. 1 (Tokyo, 1901), 734–49. For the Yamauchi background, see Yamamoto Takeshi, "Kazutoyo izen no Yamauchi uji no keifu to rekidai no dōkō," three articles concluded in *Tosa shidan* #102 (1962), 31–35.

[3] Ozeki, *op. cit.*, 79.

[4] Yokogawa Suekichi, the authority on the Chōsokabe holdings, cites these changes in his *Nonaka Kenzan* (Tokyo, 1962), 20–21.

struction, materials, carpentry, blacksmith, and samurai service commissioners and magistrates was set up. Stones and lumber were brought in by boat, and construction gangs impressed 1,200 to 1,300 men into service each day. The work was carefully organized with daily subsistence rations in rice and small payment in coin. Even children, the accounts have it, were rounded up to help carry rock and sand. *Sake, shōyu,* vinegar, and oil were shipped from Ōsaka, and tea and vegetables were brought from all parts of the realm. Kazutoyo and five of his top retainers visited the work daily in the daimyo equivalent of work clothes (bamboo hat and sleeveless *haori*), their appearance greeted by Chōsokabe loyalists with some acerbity as "the six big shots" (*roku dai shū*) The main part of the job was done by the summer of 1603, when Kazutoyo moved in with proper fanfare.[5] Around his residence he placed his principal retainers and relatives in declining order of importance. Modern Kōchi would grow around the eminence he had crowned with his keep.

Kazutoyo had needed help from the central political power in taking possession of his new realm, and he was soon equally obligated to mainland (Honshu) economic centers for help in his new activities. His decision to place his castle at the headwaters of the bay indicated the importance he attached to water communications with other parts of Japan. Outside contacts were numerous and obligations heavy. *Sankin-kōtai* involved the expense of trips to Edo and the maintenance of several mansions there. The Yamauchi also contributed to the building of the Edo castle in 1606, Sumpu in 1607, Sasayama (Hyōgo) in 1609, Nagoya in 1610, Edo in 1613; they helped destroy the outer moat in the Ōsaka campaign of 1614, did guard service between Ōsaka and Fushimi in 1615, contributed to the rebuilding of the Ōsaka castle in 1620, and contributed lumber for many other *bakufu* building projects.

Almost from the first, Tosa economic relationships under the Yamauchi were more complex and more closely related to the national scene than they had ever been before. Ōsaka merchants provided important assistance at all points. It was an Ōsaka merchant who loaned Kazutoyo the ships with which he came to Tosa; some accompanied him there, and others provided essential services for storing and selling Tosa products in Ōsaka and purveying outside products to Tosa.[6] Much of the lumber in the Ōsaka market was from Tosa. Throughout most of the seventeenth century there were Tosa interests in trade with Nagasaki, conducted for the domain by merchants. Tosa imported rice from presentday Ōita Prefecture in Kyūshū. Kōchi itself came to have a small community of powerful, well-connected merchants, whose social standing and contacts were with the *han* officials whose needs they served.[7] Production

---

[5] The fullest account of the work, including a sketch map, is in *Dai Nihon shiryō,* Section 12, Vol. 1, 449-60. See also, for the daimyo's participation, *Kōchi Shi shi,* 290.

[6] Hirao Michio, *Tosa han shōgyō keizai shi* (Kōchi, 1960), 237-46.

[7] Yokogawa Suekichi, "Katsurai Soan 'Mannichi chōkaku' ni shimesareta: Kinsei shoki 'jōkamachi fushō' no seitai," *Tosa shidan* #104 (1963), 5-9, draws on fragments of a merchant family diary of the 1660's to illustrate social contacts between large merchants

within the realm and debts outside it became objects of Yamauchi policy and planning within the first decades of their tenure as daimyo of Tosa.

II. The Restoration of Order

The first obstacle to production was the turbulence that resulted from the dispossession and flight of the Chōsokabe retainers. The take-over of fiefs and villages by new samurai masters resulted in flight by agriculturalists of all sorts, and the new rulers had to make the recovery of confidence and stability their first concern.

Early announcements tried to slow the exodus of men and alienation of goods by ordering exact surveys. Ii Naomasa, in a proclamation he sent to Tosa with Suzuki Hyōe, ordered village heads and farmers to prepare a careful inventory of "workers, post horses, and other things in your land," and he warned against concealing or damaging anything. At the same time, assurances were issued that no general upheaval was planned and that past surveys and patterns would continue to be followed. "The laws of this realm," Yamauchi Yasutoyo announced on his brother's behalf, "are to remain in force . . . we are willing to consider anything brought to our attention anywhere and will handle any matter"; the *ichiryō gusoku,* too, were told that they should return without rancor, and "if you desire to serve us we will receive you in any way you wish, and treat you accordingly. Therefore your hearts should be at rest." [8]

In practice things worked out less happily, and during the decade that followed neither hearts nor legs were at rest. A dismaying proportion of the farm population seems to have headed for neighboring villages, valleys, and provinces. This can be seen most clearly from the Regulations issued by the second Yamauchi daimyo, Tadayoshi, in 1612.[9] Its seventy-five articles show that farmers and servants, whether from fear or from desire to better themselves, had taken advantage of the disorder to move. Flight and vagrancy became major problems for administrators anxious to reinstate a productive normality. The problems were further complicated in that, by 1612, many of the farmers who had fled were beginning to return, demanding their share of lands that had been allocated in the paddy areas of the plains,[10] while others, farmers

and samurai, and contrasts the early merchants to the merchants that appeared during and after the Genroku period. Further illustration of the same point also in *Tosa shidan* #104 (1963), by Hiroya Kijūrō, "Tosa hansei chūki ni okeru shōgyō shihon no dōkō," 10–15.

[8] *Kinsei sonraku jichi shiryōshū,* Vol. II, *Tosa no kuni jikata shiryō,* Introduction, 18–19, and documents, 312–13.

[9] Tadayoshi was Kazutoyo's nephew, the son of the Yasutoyo who had preceded Kazutoyo to Tosa. Born in 1592, he inherited the realm in 1605, ruled until 1656, and died in 1664 at the age of 72. His wife was a daughter of the Matsuyama lord Matsudaira Sadakatsu, himself a younger brother of Tokugawa Ieyasu. Tadayoshi is described as a typical early Tokugawa daimyo; vigilant, tough, blustery, coarse in his tastes and pleasures. Yokogawa, *Nonaka Kenzan,* 24–27.

[10] A discussion of the way *honden* fields were allocated by lot (*kuji*) can be found in Hirao Michio, *Tosa han nōgyō keizai shi* (Kōchi, 1958), 97 foll.

and samurai, were seeking return of servants and tenants who had been located in other areas. The Yamauchi administrators had no fondness for litigation, but they had to provide some guidelines for procedure. Justice was less important to them than order and stability.

Runaways, of course, were a violation of both, but even here common sense required a distinction between those who remained inside the realm ("After all," as Article 32 admits, "the main thing is to keep them from leaving the province") and those who tried to get away for good. Thus Article 12 noted that "our Tōtōmi law forbade movement under any circumstances, but if we do not allow some moving around people who suffer distress may go to another province." Again, says Article 26, harboring a runaway "probably deserves the death penalty, but if we become too severe the result would only be to make them flee all the way to the next province." For those with that intent, however, the law was without pity. "It is a very serious offense to desert to another province. Those who assist in the getaway are equally guilty. Both ears and nose must be cut off. If, at a later time, the runaway is caught and brought back, he will be punished by death, and so will those who helped him . . . If a person is a fugitive, his offense is less serious if he hides within the borders of this realm. But fleeing to another province must be absolutely forbidden." [11]

Every effort was made to limit the damage done to a village or sub-fief through desertion. Article 47 declared children of deserters bound to their village, and procedures outlined for the recovery of runaways were designed to prevent altercations between their original and their more recent masters. On the other hand, unlimited rights of repossession could threaten the very order that was the principal purpose of those who wrote the laws. Therefore they discouraged dredging up old complaints, warned against appeals (Article 23), ruled that negative judgments in appeals would bring punishment to those who brought them (Article 4), and stressed that it was "pointless to change things now even though an old document may have some facts about the past. If we bring up evidence from the past there will be no end to it" (Article 7). For those who insisted on doing so, the code expressed exasperation: "It is completely unreasonable to bring the matter up seven years later . . . this is truly too late for a ruling" (Article 70).

Tadayoshi had little reforming intent. Article 46 notes the prevalence of samurai's seizing and keeping peasant children as hostages for unpaid rent, but frowns on the further possibility of using the child as part payment of a debt due someone else. *Ichiryō gusoku* were welcome to continue as farmers, but required to submit records of their holdings and subordinate dependents

---

[11] All references to the 1612 code are from the version found in *Kinsei sonraku jichi shiryōshū*, II, *Tosa no kuni jikata shiryō*, 315f. A good discussion of the desertion problem in early Tosa can be found in Hirao, *Tosa han nōgyō keizai shi*, 5f. Article 34, quoted above, is one of several in which payment of a silver coin is the alternative to loss of an ear. Japan was of course still close to Hideyoshi's *mimizuka* of 1598.

and servants (Article 41). Had it been possible to resume agriculture in the sixteenth-century manner, with multiple hierarchies based upon unfree and semifree labor throughout the countryside, the immediate Yamauchi purpose would have been adequately served. But mass flight and rearrangement of personal and property rights confused that system beyond its full restoration. There are indications that deserters sometimes made release from their unfree status a condition for their return.[12] The code therefore had to be concerned with protection of subordinates from their masters, and had to provide regulations for the forms and length of servitude. It becomes, then, a step between the rigor of the Chōsokabe regulations and the restrictions on indenture and servitude that are to be seen in the Genroku Code of 1690. Excessive severity was depopulating the realm, and the only way to put an end to this was to regulate the conditions of bondage. Article 36 made a distinction between those who had entered service after 1610, who were entitled to request discharge after giving proper notice, and those who had served uninterruptedly since before 1605 and could be presumed to have permanent (*fudai*) servant rank.[13] And even in the latter group, Chōsokabe artisans (whose skills were in particularly short supply) "should consider their old master-servant bonds terminated" (Article 17). By 1621, a new set of regulations calling for reports of excess labor demands made by (samurai) masters shows that their situation had stabilized and that the *han* was now fully aware of the necessity of protecting its farmers from its vassals.[14]

The 1612 regulations also prepared the way for Tokugawa emphases upon the family system. An only female child had to succeed the family, and could not be given away; a husband selected for an only child had to remain in the village as farmer even after the wife's death (Articles 14, 15). Peasants should keep two sons before giving others out for adoption. Again, the mutual responsibility that would be worked out in detail later is prefigured by the provision of guarantors for servants, men who, "although it is a great deal of trouble," stand accountable for their work and debts (Articles 51, 53, 54).

The conditions that produced the laws of 1612 thus operated to bring some order and moderation into the arbitrary brutality of an earlier day, and the social redistribution it tried to regularize tended to even out some of the mutiple levels of inequality in Tosa. Gradually the problem of deserters was brought under control.

As order returned, it became harder to get away. By 1634 extradition treaties were negotiated with neighboring areas that, like Awaji, had been the principal goals of runaways. And along the borders of Tosa, coastal and inland,

---

[12] Yokogawa, *Nonaka Kenzan,* 143.

[13] Hirao, *op. cit.,* 17, notes that under the Genroku Code of 1690 (Article 255) children assigned to service during the first seven years of life still had permanent status, those eight and over did not. By then *bakufu* provisions limited indentured service for those over twenty to ten years.

[14] Hirao, *nōgyō keizai,* 9; the Genroku code provisions for protection of peasants from excess demands represented the conclusion of this process.

sekisho (barriers and check stations) multiplied until they numbered 86 in the eighteenth century.[15]

III. Recruitment and reclamation: Nonaka Kenzan

If the first part of Tadayoshi's reign was dominated by the problem of restoring order and putting an end to vagrancy and desertion, the second part centered on efforts to increase income. Debts incurred in the course of services ordered by Edo and building the new administration became a problem within two decades of the Yamauchi entry into Tosa. Efforts to solve them meant a new kind of competition between the *han* government and its retainers, one in which increased centralization channeled more of the province's revenue into the coffers of the Kōchi administration. This required new devices to control the countryside, and new emphasis was put on the recruitment of local leaders.

Bakufu directives were part of this process. In 1615 the fall of Ōsaka (and death of Chōsokabe Morichika) was followed by orders to all fiefs to destroy all but one castle, and it was symbolic of the decreased autonomy of sub-fiefs that the keeps at Sakawa and Sukumo were dismantled by their holders. In 1621 Edo officials warned the Tosa administration to prepare ways to reimburse its Ōsaka creditors, and in the next year the so-called "reform of Genwa" inaugurated measures to make fief-holders contribute 3% of their assessed rating in rice, and farmers to provide more labor, for *han* finance. The fief-holders criticized the Kōchi chief administrator (Fukuoka Tamba) as unjust to farmers, while he retorted that the fief-holders were at fault.[16]

In the years that followed the *han* gradually regularized first its own and then its retainers' tax systems to bring about uniformity and to guarantee itself a share of the fief-holders' income.[17] Beginning in 1674 tax rates on *honden* paddy were revised in the cultivator's favor, from 66⅔% to 60%. Fief-holders were limited further by requirements that they set aside part of their yield as support for members of the military establishment attached to them; the allotment of a fief might mean status, but hardly wealth.[18] Alienation of *honden* to retainers became less frequent, and stopped in 1681, after which grants in rice became the usual retainer salaries. Most early fiefs were allowed to stand, but no new grants of *honden* land were made after 1681.[19]

---

[15] Hirao, *op. cit.*, 5, for text of treaty with Awaji. The *sekisho* are dealt with in detail and enumerated in Hirao Michio, *Kinsei shakai shi kō* (Kōchi, 1962), 151–73.

[16] Yokogawa, *Nonaka Kenzan*, 31–37.

[17] Moritsuni Sansaburō, "Byōdōmen no seiritsu ni tsuite," *Tosa shidan* #98 (1960), 32–39, describes ordinances of 1681 as completing a *han* effort to control its retainers that began with the "Genwa reforms."

[18] Hirao, in *Kinsei shakai shi kō*, 72, cites as example a fief of 200 *koku*: taxes came to 70 *koku*, from which the holder was required to set aside 40 *koku* for the support of 10 *ashigaru* leaving him with 30 *koku*. For tax rates, Hirao, *nōgyō keizai shi*, 122–27.

[19] Sekita Hidesato, "Tosa han ni okeru jikata chigyō," *Tosa shidan* #81 (1952), 10–14, gives an eighteenth-century figure in which 439 out of 4,001 Yamauchi retainers held

Tosa in the Seventeenth Century

The measures of the 1620's were only preliminary to a drive for more pro-duction and greater Tosa self-sufficiency in order to cut imports. These began in earnest with the appointment to top administrative office of Nonaka Ken-zan in 1631. Until his discharge in 1663 this man dominated his daimyo and his fief. He stands as one of the great administrators during the formative pe-riod of Tokugawa rule.[20]

Nonaka relied upon local elite whom he recruited for leadership. The Yamauchi retainers were too few, too inexperienced, and too involved in the life of the castle town and Edo to provide effective direction in the country-side. This was true in most parts of Japan, for within a half-century samurai became rarities in the countryside,[21] but it was particularly the case in Tosa where recent entry and difference of speech made them virtually foreigners. Effective local control lay with the village heads, the *shōya*. Undoubtedly many of them were former *ichiryō gusoku* of Chōsokabe days. They were a tough and forceful lot, but they also needed the cooperation and respect of the villagers among whom they lived, especially during a period of disorder.[22] Their ranks and remuneration were set by the *han,* and many documents itemize the powers and responsibilities they bore.[23] The *shōya* were never more essential to samurai rule than in areas where commercial and managerial relationships were relatively complex, and it comes as no surprise to find many of them attaching themselves early to the Yamauchi cause, serving it well, and receiving speedy reward. Thus a *shōya* of Aki district, a lumber area, could

---

fiefs. This, he notes, was relatively high for Japan as a whole. A samurai count for 1853 gives a total of about 6,000, of whom 700 to 800 could be considered "upper" samurai. Hirao Michio, *Kōchi han zaisei shi* (Kōchi, 1953), 12.

[20] Nonaka's origin illustrates some of the crosscurrents of early Tokugawa times. His father had been promised a 1,500 *koku* fief by Kazutoyo shortly before his death, but the promise was not honored by the *han.* He therefore left Tosa, living in the Osaka area as a *rōnin* on an income of 200 *koku* provided by his father-in-law, an Ikeda retainer in Himeji. The Ikeda lost Himeji, however, and Nonaka's father his income. His second wife, and Nonaka's mother, was descended from Osaka merchants. Upon his father's death, Nonaka returned to Tosa as an adopted son to an uncle, and rose swiftly in the samurai hierarchy.

[21] Ogyū Sorai in *Seidan,* a memorial he wrote for the Shogun Yoshimune early in the eighteenth century, notes that "At present members of the military classes are forbidden to go into the country for a distance of more than five ri, for it is feared that they might behave in a disorderly manner because there are no members of the military class resident there." J. R. McEwan, *The Political Writings of Ogyū Sorai* (Cambridge University Press, 1962), 60.

[22] *Shōya* are discussed in Hirao, *Tosa han nōgyō keizai shi,* 30–49. Most had the privilege of surname and swords, as well as clothing and ceremonial evidences of status; they were given "office fields" as well as, usually, 1% of the income of the area they administered.

[23] Yasuoka Ōroku, "Shōya no mibun, shokyū oyobi shokushō," *Tosha shidan* #98 (1960), 27–31, discusses the ranks (*sanbangashira ōjōya, sanbangashira retsu ōjōya, ōjōya, omemie shōya, banjin shōya, shōya*); and lists, from a *sashidashi* one Kitakawa, the Karahama *shōya,* submitted, 104 duties for which he considered himself responsible. These range from overseeing public morality to fire prevention, seeing to it that farmers keep two or three children, to local justice, etc.

become an agent for *han* lumber contracts with Ōsaka merchants, travel to the Sakai-Ōsaka-Kyōto area on official business, and rise swiftly to samurai rank.[24] And even where roles were less specialized, *shōya* cooperation shortly became essential to the massive projects that were set in motion.

Nonaka made reclamation his main goal. This involved him in constantly greater need for corvee labor. New channels for rivers, dikes to control them, and dams to impound them increased the productive and particularly the paddy area. Nonaka's waterworks irrigated 3,872 *chō;* new fields (*shinden*) which had grown about 600 *chō* up to 1634 and 483 *chō* between 1635 and 1646 jumped by 7,020 *chō* between 1647 and 1676, until the total came to one-third the *honden* of the original Chōsokabe land survey.[25] These efforts were accompanied by a succession of edicts to *shōya* that stand as models of Tokugawa attempts to get the most out of the countryside. Thus in 1643: "Although a farmer may get one-third of his crop for himself, he is expected to eat whatever is available during autumn and winter and keep rice in stock until spring. If he fails to do this, or if he brews *sake,* he is to be punished. *Shōya* will report breaches of this rule; if it is kept secret, the *shōya* will be punished. No one is to buy and drink *sake.* No one should be a late riser. Violators will be charged three *momme* of silver for laziness. . . . Tea trees, paper mulberry trees, or any other trees that help one in paying his annual tax may be planted; a useless tree should never be planted." And in 1662: "Magistrates will consult with *shōya* and elders to decide on annual duties for farmers. Even if a farmer gets official orders, he may not be able to distinguish good from evil. Therefore each farmer's behavior should be examined monthly by the magistrate, *shōya,* and village elder. His deeds during the first month will be reviewed on the fifth day of the second month. . . . Each village will do this in one unit, and the magistrate and *shōya* will give a reward to the people of a place where edicts are well observed. . . . A notice, 'As this is a leisurely time for the farmers, they should do such and such work and produce such and such an amount' should be sent to the *shōya* and village elders at the beginning of each month." [26]

Nonaka rewarded local officials' cooperation with grants of "office fields," which the *shōya* were permitted to work with tenants and dependents. More important, in 1644, the year after the announcement of unprecedentedly harsh labor demands, he enlisted local support through a new program of recruitment of local samurai (*gōshi*).

Gōshi rank was first created in 1613, the year after Tadayoshi's code. It was

---

[24] Hiroya Kijūrō, "Nonaka Kenzan shiseiki ni okeru shōya no ichi dōkō: Aki gun hōmen no keizai hatten no ichi kōsatsu," *Tosa shidan* #111 (1965), 10–12, and #113 (1966), 10–18, illustrates several cases.

[25] On *shinden*: Hirao, *Tosa han nōgyō keizai shi,* 58–66; above figures from Yokogawa, *Nonaka,* 68, and Hirao Michio, *Kōchi han zaisei shi,* 2.

[26] From the famous proclamation to the farmers of Motoyama. In *Kinsei sonraku jichi shiryōshū: Tosa no kuni jikata shiryō,* 339 f.; also quoted and discussed in Irimajiri Yoshinaga, *Tokugawa bakuhansei kaitai katei no kenkyū,* 251 f.

as a measure of rural stability that a small number of Chōsokabe retainers were given small holdings, rated at 30 to 250 *koku,* with honors comparable to those of middle-ranking samurai, and ultimately rated just between the line of "upper" (and enfeoffed) and "lower" samurai. *Gōshi* were to be rusticated, and to help pacify the countryside. They were first under the supervision of local *shōya,* and then became independent of them and constituted a parallel network of eminence in the countryside.

Nonaka greatly expanded the numbers of men holding this rank and tied it to reclamation. In 1644 the *han* announced that one hundred certificates of *gōshi* rank would be available for those who could establish descent from Chōsokabe retainers and who had reclaimed fields producing the minimum of 30 *koku* annually. (This would mean about 3 *chō* of paddy, or 7½ acres.) Later announcements issued by the *han* for recruitment of *gōshi* emphasized Chōsokabe descent less and reclamation more. *Rōnin* as well as farmers could qualify.[27] The *gōshi* became a significant element in the Yamauchi retainer corps. Nonaka expanded the number of men holding this rank, and shortly before his fall, army figures for 1662 showed 613 *gōshi* as against only 296 mounted *bushi.* In time, their numbers augmented by additional reclamation campaigns in outlying parts of the *han* in the eighteenth and nineteenth centuries, *gōshi* came to number between 800 and 900. By the end of the seventeenth century *shinden* holdings totaled 81,080 *koku;* of these *gōshi* held 23,930, samurai 13,420, and commoners 43,730. Favorable tax rates reflected both the lesser quality of land and the *han*'s eagerness for reclamation.[28]

The importance of the *gōshi* can scarcely be exaggerated. They formed an important addition to *han* military strength, especially in view of the prolonged absence of much of the regular retainer corps. Nonaka was anxious to add to the military establishment, for calls to help in the Shimabara rebellion in 1637, coupled with directives to guard against all foreign ships that followed, seemed likely to require constant expenditure of men and money.[29] The *gōshi* were therefore treated with honor. Nonaka himself trusted and used many of them as foremen for public works projects, as magistrates, and even at times in higher administrative posts, practices that did little to raise his popularity

---

[27] Standard accounts of the *gōshi* system are Ozeki Toyokichi, "Tosa han no gōshi ni tsuite," *Tosa shidan* #48 (1934), 117–54; Irimajiri, *Tokugawa bakuhansei kaitai katei no kenkyū,* 221–50; and most recently the carefully documented work by Hirao Michio, *Tosa han gōshi kiroku* (Kōchi, 1964), 279 pp. It should be noted that in Tosa *rōnin* rank was a regular grade, carefully regulated, and not without honor. Of some 400 registered in the seventeenth century, some had considerable property in land. Hirao, *Kinsei shakai shi kō,* 91–103.

[28] For *gōshi* numbers, Hirao, *Tosa han gōshi kiroku,* 75; Ikeda Yoshimasa, "Tempō kaikaku no saikentō: Tosa han o chūshin ni shite," *Nihonshi kenkyū* #31 (Kyoto, 1957), counts 742 for the 1860's. For *gōshi* holdings, Hirao, *nōgyō keizai shi,* 55. *Shinden* were usually tax exempt for five years after reclamation, and a tax rate of 33 1/3% was raised to 40% in 1690. Thereafter the rates (4–6) were the reverse of *honden* (6–4) until the end of the Tokugawa period. Hirao, *nōgyō keizai shi,* 125.

[29] Yokogawa, *Nonaka Kenzan,* 98.

with the regular retainers. Perhaps it is because of this that one finds changes in ritual honors enjoyed by the *gōshi*. A good number of *gōshi* administrators went down with Nonaka when he fell from power.[30]

These measures solved the last problems of conciliating Chōsokabe retainers and integrating them with the new administration. *Gōshi* formed a network of power parallel to, but independent of, that of the *shōya,* and became with them the rural elite of Tosa. They had of course been drawn from that elite originally. For the ability to develop new fields in areas where public works projects had provided water or drained land usually signified accessibility to wealth, whether in labor of dependents or through hire. Moreover holdings were seldom integrated into one parcel. Inevitably the *gōshi* titles reflected previous patterns of local eminence. In later decades, as the local economy changed further in response to marketing practices, *gōshi* and *shōya* stood to profit. *Gōshi* titles could be transferred through purchase (with *han* permission), and by the nineteenth century there were 82 *gōshi* resident in the castle town itself, as absentee landlords.[31]

Nonaka's years of power also marked the rise of Confucian scholarship and political philosophy in Tosa. It is significant that his search for an ideology of authoritarian and monolithic state control led him to the code of imperial China. Although he began as a student of Zen, he recognized in Chu Hsi Confucianism a superior code for the governance of the realm. Under his sponsorship Yamazaki Ansai, Tani Jichū, and other scholars developed the southern school (*Nangaku*) of Confucianism. At his orders books from China and Korea were sought in Nagasaki, Tsushima, and Satsuma. Students were sent to Nagasaki to study Chinese. Nonaka's was a single-minded determination that brooked no opposition. He welcomed the denunciation of Buddhism by Yamazaki Ansai. He observed with humorless rigor Confucian regulations as he understood them for the funeral of his mother, despite criticism from many, and observed the three years' mourning period strictly.[32]

Nonaka's drive to increase Tosa self-sufficiency led him to tighten control over economic activities and to abandon the favoritism toward merchants that had characterized the early part of Tadayoshi's reign. More and more forms of enterprise were brought under *han* control. Edicts fixing the price of rice were designed to establish a predictable official income which could be used in barter with parts of the realm that specialized in salable products. Imports were reduced by the introduction and encouragement of honey, clams, carp, trout, textiles, paper, and dried bonito techniques from other parts of Japan. Mining consultants came from Satsuma, pottery specialists from central Japan. And lumber, Tosa's most important resource, was carefully regulated with a sustained yield and reforestation policy that was implemented by using army foot

---

[30] *Ibid.,* 108. Hirao, *gōshi kiroku,* 59, for the manner in which *gōshi* participation in the daimyo's New Year review was reduced in the 1660's.

[31] *Kōchi Shi shi,* 330–37, gives their names and locates their holdings.

[32] With the important exception that he remained in office. Nonaka had also banned *sumō,* which did not endear him to Tadayoshi, who enjoyed it.

soldiers (*ashigaru*) as part of the ever-larger labor force that was required. The castle town of Kōchi grew in size and importance as its residents came to direct the economic life of the realm. Within it, however, restrictive laws limited the commercial profits to the large official merchants who served the *han* purpose. Smaller establishments were forced or legislated out of business.[33]

Nonaka's fall illustrates some of the constraints on Tokugawa statesmen, virtually all of which he had violated. He had alienated many of the upper samurai in creating and favoring the *gōshi,* and then angered the latter by his restrictions on commercial activities in the countryside. Peasants had borne unprecedented demands for corvee, and they had never been supervised as closely. Merchants had seen a period of *han* favor followed by restrictions. All were alarmed by an issue of *han* notes in 1663 that were supposed to eliminate the use of specie in local transactions. And in the 1650's Nonaka managed to annoy the *bakufu* itself by the headstrong manner in which he conducted two boundary disputes with the neighboring domain of Uwajima. In both cases— one involving a lumber area, the other a fisheries ground—he was sure that the Chōsokabe survey was on his side, while his Uwajima opponents had recent custom or other documents on theirs. Nonaka refused compromise and resisted both local and *bakufu* attempts at conciliation. When the two *han* filed suit (through *shōya*-farmers resident in the disputed areas) in the Edo court,[34] Nonaka lobbied with the *rōjū* and Tadayoshi approached the *bakufu* directly, a practice that was expressly forbidden. The *bakufu* judges, more interested in balance than in justice, ruled that each side was right on one issue, and Nonaka lost his second case. Soon after, senior *karō* in Tosa petitioned that Nonaka's policies were harming the people. Invitations to complain brought a flood of laments from the countryside and from merchants. Bureaucratic enemies reported that the Edo councillors were suspicious and irritated by the persistence with which Nonaka, a Tokugawa rear-vassal, had presumed to influence the court of jurisdiction in the boundary case.[35] Nonaka was dismissed and sent into retirement. He died later in the year. A de-Nonakaization policy followed which ended the use of *han* notes, freed merchant activities, lightened corvee, and replaced a single administrator with a rotation system of *han rōjū.* Neo-Confucianism was temporarily treated as a form of dangerous thought, and Nonaka's scholars driven out, in the process spreading Nangaku Confucianism to other parts of Japan. Nonaka's administrators were dismissed and punished, and marriage ties with Nonaka relatives were dissolved.

---

[33] Figures on *sake* shops, as well as other illustrations of the effects of Nonaka's policies on merchants, in Hirao, *Tosa han shōgyō keizai shi* (Kōchi, 1960), 102–09.

[34] Documents in *Tosa no kuni jikata shiryō,* 339–40. Excellent discussion of the procedure can be found in Yokogawa, *Nonaka Kenzan,* 199–217. When direct negotiations failed, petitions were filed before the *bakufu Hyōjōsho* (see Henderson, below), by *shōya* from both sides as farmer' suits (*hyakushō kuji*). In this way official prestige was less openly involved, and the *bakufu* relieved of the necessity of ruling against one of its vassals.

[35] Tadayoshi was retired by this time, and made no move to shield his long-term administrator. His Matsuyama (Tokugawa collateral) relatives were the avenue for reports of *bakufu* displeasure.

M. B. Jansen

Nonaka's last descendents were sent to an outlying part of Tosa and kept under close surveillance. The family line was allowed to die out, and his last male heir died in 1703.[36]

IV. TOSA AT THE END OF THE CENTURY

Although Nonaka's fall was as spectacular as his rise, it would not do to overlook the permanence of his contribution to the administrative policies of the domain. He had pushed people too hard and overstepped the bounds of prudence, but he also made it possible for his successors to follow his lead without seeming so demanding. His measures to raise productivity became a permanent part of the Tosa program. Tosa lumber and bonito, as well as paper and lacquer, became and remained standard exports. Merchant restrictions were relaxed upon Nonaka's death, but by 1704 the basic monopolies of his day (paper, tea, lacquer, oil) had been reinstituted. Merchants were never again the object of legislation as stringent as Nonaka's, but by the time of the Genroku Code of 1690 *sake* shops were once again limited in number.

The seclusion and protection of the Tosa economy from products of other areas continued without a break. If Nonaka sought to stop all except officially needed imports, his successors were more generous in motive but hardly in execution. The Genroku code lays out in great detail the restrictions on leaving and entering the realm by ship, and specifies appropriate custom duties for all permissible articles of import. *Shōya* were charged with the management of the 86 border and port stations. Identification and travel papers were to be carefully checked. Special permits were required for residence in the castle town. Urbanization, which had been a policy of the early daimyo who wanted a flourishing commercial center, was now seen as something that competed with an agricultural surplus. On the other hand, new legislation imposed some of its sharpest restrictions on "outside" merchants who had been providing consumer needs in Tosa. In 1685 outside merchants were forbidden entry, and a plantive petition by a Bizen merchant whose livelihood had for thirty years depended upon his Tosa markets survives to record the success of the move. Interestingly enough, the new restrictions were not explained as anti-merchant in origin, but rather out of regard for the provincial merchants, who were felt to be less modern, less able, and less crafty than the outsiders.[37] Shades of the discussions over unrestricted residence for foreigners in the 1880's!

New issue of *gōshi* titles stopped for a time after Nonaka's fall, and although they were offered again for specific reclamation drives in the Hata and Niida districts (in 1763 and 1822 respectively) and in the rearmament campaign of late Tokugawa days, most entrants to the rank came through transfer or purchase of existing titles, and not through official recruitment practices. Recruitment nevertheless remained a basic way of filling vacancies in the

---

[36] Nonaka's fall is referred to as *"Kambun no kaitai"*; the political overturn of the Kambun era. I have followed Yokogawa, *Nonaka Kenzan* 226–69.

[37] Hirao, *Tosa han shōgyō keizai shi,* 162–64.

lower ranks of the military structure, and the Genroku code makes clear the provisions for entry and selection. At the bottom level of *ashigaru*, the Genroku code makes clear that the use of such forces for labor in lumbering, which remained the most basic of the *han* monopolies, continued a constant in policy.[38]

In other respects the control over the periphery by the central administration in the castle town grew ever stronger. After 1681 no further fiefs were granted; instead rice stipends became the rule at, as the Genroku code makes clear, 40% of rated income. The Genroku code further specifies the tax (*yakugin*, technically a commutation of service) levied on retainer and *gōshi* holdings according to their rice assessments. The main retainer group was to be found in the castle town or on duty in Edo, and by Genroku, provisions for housing arrangements (plot sizes, and constructions appropriate to rank) were spelled out in detail. Throughout the countryside the *gōshi* and *shōya* remained the instruments of *han* policy. *Shōya* were instructed to organize five-man units (the *goningumi* system) in the 1660's, and by the time of the Genroku code the regulations for these organizations were fully worked out. But while *shōya* could be expected to enforce regulations of this sort, their eagerness to assist in channeling the agricultural and extractive wealth to the castle town without sharing in that surplus was less marked, and their ability to obstruct posed a problem for *han* administrators of the future.

By Genroku the rough and ready fief-holder of the early codes was well on his way toward becoming an educated town-dweller. The third article of the Code of 1690 instructed him to devote himself above all "to the study of literary and military arts, always bearing in mind proper decorum. Even in temporary associations behave yourself appropriately according to your rank, and be proper in your morals." By that time, too, the administrator's consciousness of the *bakufu* presence (through inspection missions) and wishes (through directives) was far greater than it had been before.[39] The 1690 codifiers stress at every point the importance of conformity with *bakufu* instructions, which they cite as authority for everything from rules for defense works to personal servitude.

Despite its seclusion and remoteness, Tosa had thus been swept into the main stream of Japanese developments in the Tokugawa period. It was up to date in technology, agronomy, and administrative practices. Its daimyo was served by a two-strata corps of retainers, the one urbanized and followers of long standing, the other based upon the land and upon the memory of an earlier day. Taken together these conditions outlined the limitations on future policy and administration.

---

[38] Section 51, "Ashigaru shihai okite," Article 515.

[39] Yokogawa, *Nonaka*, 255, feels the *bakufu* decree settling the border dispute was a milestone in determining future *bakufu-han* relationships. Certainly the Genroku tone of obedience is quite different from occasional references to the *bakufu* in earlier codes.

CHAPTER EIGHT

THE CONSOLIDATION OF POWER
IN SATSUMA-HAN

ROBERT SAKAI

THE FIRST of the Shimazu rulers, Tadahisa, came to Satsuma in 1196 with an appointment from Kamakura as *jitō* of Satsuma-shō and *shugo* over all of Satsuma, Hyūga, and Ōsumi. By the fourteenth century the Shimazu had emerged as one of the early daimyo families of Japan. They displayed a burst of energy in the last quarter of the sixteenth century, invading and conquering nearly the entire island of Kyushu except for the state of Bungo. Their headlong progress was checked in 1587 by Toyotomi Hideyoshi, who pushed back the southern army to its original base. The Shimazu daimyo quickly made peace with Hideyoshi, and the latter confirmed the Shimazu claims to Satsuma, Ōsumi, and part of Hyūga. Kan'ichi Asakawa has described this setback to Satsuma as a blessing in disguise, "for it shattered their unnatural ambitions and threw them back to their proper sphere of power." [1]

In 1600 the Satsuma forces opposed and were defeated by Tokugawa Ieyasu at the Battle of Sekigahara. Shimazu Yoshihiro fled precipitously to Satsuma where his brother put him under confinement while two vassals beseeched the Tokugawa for clemency. Ieyasu wisely granted this, allowing the Shimazu family to retain their southern states virtually intact. [2] Yoshihiro, however, was forced to retire in favor of his third son, Tadatsune, who became the eighteenth head of the Shimazu dynasty.

Tadatsune in 1603 made a special trip to Edo and Fushimi to apologize to the new shogun and to pledge him his future allegiance. Ieyasu in turn displayed his magnanimity by permitting Shimazu Tadatsune to assume the name of Matsudaira, the surname of branch families of the Tokugawa. Moreover, Tadatsune was permitted to change his personal name to Iehisa, thus incorporating the first character of Ieyasu's name. Documents sent to the Satsuma daimyo often were addressed to *"Matsudaira Satsuma no kami dono"* or *"Matsudaira Satsuma no kami Iehisa sama."* [3]

Among all the daimyo of the Tokugawa period only the Shimazu family could claim continuous control over its territory since the Kamakura period when Yoritomo had appointed Tadahisa as *jitō* and *shugo*. [4] Despite their long

---

[1] Kan'ichi Asakawa, *The Documents of Iriki* (reprint by the Japan Society for the Promotion of Science, Tokyo, 1955), p. 11.

[2] *Kagoshima no oitachi* ["We of Kagoshima"], (published by Kagoshima City, Kagoshima, 1955), p. 264.

[3] See e.g., Asakawa, p. 337.

[4] The uniqueness of the Satsuma daimyo's political lineage was pointed out to me by Professor Haraguchi of the University of Kagoshima.

rule over Satsuma, however, the Shimazu prestige and authority had suffered from the results of the recent wars. It was necessary to restore this authority and to demonstrate the justice and propriety of Shimazu administration. This study will be limited to a discussion of some of the key measures adopted toward this end by Iehisa during his tenure as daimyo, 1602–1638.[5]

The consolidation of Shimazu power in Satsuma-han after the Battle of Sekigahara depended, first of all, upon the toleration, if not the assent, of the *bakufu*. Iehesa thus went to great lengths to allay suspicions and demonstrate his good faith to the shogun. The latter put him through many tests. In 1606 Satsuma and Choshu-han were ordered to contribute men, material, and money for the reconstruction of the Edo castle. According to a contemporary memorandum, Satsuma built 300 large boats to transport the huge stones required for the fortifications. The number of masons and stonecutters provided by the *han* is not recorded, but 150 pieces of gold were turned over by Iehisa to the shogun.[6]

The Osaka campaign of 1615 and the Shimabara Rebellion of 1637–1638 also tested the loyalty of Satsuma. In the former campaign 13,800 warriors of the Shimazu embarked upon 500 ships to give support to the Tokugawa, but by the time they arrived at Hirado, word reached them that the Osaka castle had fallen to the *bakufu*. The troops returned home while Iehisa continued on to Fushimi to congratulate Ieyasu.[7] To suppress the Shimabara Rebellion 11,200 Satsuma troops participated, using Amakusa Island as the point of embarkation.[8]

Historians of Satsuma suggest that the *sankin kōtai* system was institutionalized for the Tokugawa by the actions of the Shimazu daimyo. Although lords Fujitaka and Asano had left their families in Edo as early as 1605, it was not until a few years later, when Shimazu Iehisa brought his wife and three children to reside in Edo, that the example was followed by all other daimyo. The idea of leaving wife and children as a guarantee of loyalty to the shogun was suggested by the Shimazu *karō* (councilor) Ise Sadamasa to the Tokugawa *rōju* (councilor) Doi Toshikatsu. It is said that the shogun Iemitsu was so gratified by the Shimazu daimyo's action that he presented him with the gift of his horse.[9]

---

[5] In 1631 Iehisa's title was changed from *"Satsuma no kami"* to *"Ōsumi no kami,"* though he retained control as daimyo of the three states of Satsuma, Ōsumi, and Hyūga. His son, Tadayuki, having attained his majority, became *"Matsudaira Satsuma no kami Mitsuhisa-sama."* Go chisei nempyō ["A chronology of (Satsuma) political rule"], p. 5a. This document was recorded by a certain Iwakiri, perhaps in the An'ei period (1772–1780). A copy was made for the Tamasato branch of the Shimazu family in 1887. A second copy was made available to me by Professor Haraguchi.

[6] *Ieyasu jidai gaikan* ["Survey of the Ieyasu period"], (*Kinsei Nippon kokumin shi* series ["History of the Japanese in Recent Times"]), Vol. XIII, 55–60.

[7] *Go chisei nempyō*, p. 3; *Kagoshima no oitachi*, p. 265.

[8] *Kagoshima no oitachi*, p. 266; Kagoshima Ken (ed. and pub.), *Kagoshima kenshi* [*Kagoshima Prefectural History*] (Tokyo, 1940), Vol. II, 192–95. Hereafter *Kenshi*.

[9] *Kagoshima no oitachi*, pp. 265–66; *Kenshi*, II, 187–88.

Consolidation of Power in Satsuma

Scholars have noted the similarity of the Satsuma control system to that of the Tokugawa.[10] The hostage system was a well-established practice in Satsuma long before the Tokugawa came to power. In the time of Shimazu Iehisa all the lords of private domains (*shiryō shu*) within the *han* were required to establish residence in or near the castle town of Kagoshima where they and their families could be kept under surveillance. In *The Documents of Iriki*[11] Asakawa provides the example of Shigetaka, lord of Iriki-in. He was granted a piece of residential land in Kagoshima by the daimyo in 1611, but Shigetaka could not afford to maintain his residence there until 1613. It was intended that the residence requirement keep rival families in a state of financial embarrassment. The domain of Iriki, for example, was poorly situated and had more dry fields than paddy fields. The *taka* (rice income) was 6,287 *koku* in 1614, supporting about a thousand families, roughly 700 of which were samurai. By the beginning of the nineteenth century approximately the same population size was being maintained with less than half of the above income. According to Asakawa, "There probably were few other instances in the entire Shimadzu *han* of so many unproductive persons living upon so few peasants or on so small a domain supporting so great a number of vassals."[12] Yet the lord of Iriki was forced to make a show of opulence in his Kagoshima residence where more than 50 people were in constant attendance.

One of the benefits derived from Iehisa's policy of mollifying the Tokugawa was the latter's consent to allow the Shimazu to maintain a much larger proportion of samurai than in any other *han*. In 1615 Ieyasu had decreed that there should be but one castle in each *han* and that all samurai within the *han* would reside in that castle town. The Shimazu pleaded for an exception in the case of Satsuma, which had lost territory in the recent wars, leaving thousands of samurai without means of support. With the *bakufu's* consent these extra warriors were permitted to concentrate in some 100 district seats, known as *tojō*, or "outer castles."[13] It should be recalled, however, that the presence of large numbers of samurai throughout the *han* constituted a major factor in the stability of the Satsuma countryside. The *gōshi* assumed the administrative chores in the district and leadership over the daily activities of peasants, fishermen, rural merchants, and artisans. The link between the *gōshi* and the daimyo were the *jitō*, general supervisors of the districts. Like the private domain

---

[10] Asakawa, pp. 11–12.

[11] *Ibid.*, p. 341.

[12] *Ibid.*, p. 365.

[13] *Rekidai seido* ["Regulations of successive generations"], Vol. VII, section on *tojō* ("Outer castles"), 27–31. This is a document in the Shimazu collection of the Shiryō Hensanjō, University of Tokyo. See also Robert K. Sakai, "Feudal Society and Modern Leadership in Satsuma-han," *Journal of Asian Studies*, Vol. XVI, No. 3, 365–76; also Haraguchi Torao, *Sappan hōken shakai no kōzō ni kansuru ichi kōsatsu* ["An investigation concerning the structure of Satsuma feudal society"], (Kagoshima, n.d.), pp. 1–6; and *Kagoshima ken no rekishi* ["History of Kagoshima Prefecture"], (*Kyōdo no rekishi* series) (Tokyo, 1959), pp. 387–452.

lord, the *jitō* were later made to maintain their residence in Kagoshima and made only occasional trips into their districts.[14]

The total land area of Satsuma-han was estimated to produce an annual revenue of about 729,000 *koku*, which included about 90,000 *koku* from the Ryukyu Islands.[15] This total income, or *taka*, which belonged to the daimyo, was divided into two broad classifications, the *kura-iri taka* and the *kyūchi taka*. The *kura-iri taka* was the revenue which came directly from the land to the *han* granaries located either at the castle town of Kagoshima or in the *tojō*, or "outer castle," districts. The *kura-iri taka* was used by the daimyo for his household expenses and for general administrative expenses, including the payment of periodic stipends to samurai who were assigned to minor functions.

The *kyūchi taka* were actually grants of land by the daimyo to powerful vassals, to temples and shrines, and to lesser samurai. The taxes from such land went directly to the holders of *kyūchi taka*. Such land grants, regardless of size, were considered to be sub-fiefs. The possession of such *taka* carried certain social prestige as well as tax and military service obligations. The largest of the sub-fiefs were called *shiryō* or *issho* and their possessors were called *shiryō shu* ("lord of private domain") or *issho mochi* ("holder of one locality"). To qualify as *issho mochi* or *shiryō shu* one had to be in control of an entire *tojō*, or outer castle, district. Powerful lords whose holdings were scattered and did not embrace an entire *tojō* were designated as *issho mochi kaku* ("having the rank of one who holds one locality").[16] Many of the vassals who were given large private domains were members of the Shimazu family; some were former rivals who had submitted to the will of the Shimazu. These vassals provided troops to the daimyo in time of war and served as *karō* (councilors) or in other important capacities in time of peace. Although detailed analysis remains to be done, perhaps 20% to 25% of the total *han* income went directly to large fief holders. A document of 1620 shows that 2 men were assigned more than 10,000 *koku*, 25 men between 1,000 and 10,000 *koku*, and 41 men between 500 and 1,000 *koku*.[17]

The majority of the samurai receiving *kyūchi taka* were given very modest or miniscule income. Some received *taka* amounting to about a handful of rice, but the fact that they were registered as *taka mochi*, holders of *taka*, gave them more prestige than that of samurai who might possess more income, but were not registered as *taka mochi*. The *taka* of these lower-ranking samurai

---

[14] *Rekidai seido*, Vol. VII, 27.

[15] Kagoshima-ken shiryō kankōkai, *Sappan seiyōroku* ["Digest of Satsuma han administration"], (Kagoshima, 1960), p. 5. This invaluable reference lists the *taka* given by the shogun to Iehisa in 1634 as 605,000 *koku* from the states of Satsuma, Ōsumi, and Hyūga, and 123,000 *koku* from the Ryukyu islands. The Ryuku *taka* as of the survey of 1610, however, is listed as 113,041 *koku*. *Ibid.*, p. 7.

[16] For the distinction between the *issho-mochi* and the *issho-mochi kaku* I am indebted to Professor Haraguchi. See Asakawa, pp. 340–49, for fixed assignments of military obligations.

[17] Asakawa, pp. 350–52.

was referred to as *karoku*, or permanent annual salary. This *karoku* came from three types of land: *kado daka*, *kakechi*, and *ukimen*. The *kado daka* was cultivated by peasants while the other two types of land were reclaimed and usually self-cultivated by the samurai, though peasant labor was often used. Samurai who were given any of these three types of land were obligated to turn over as much as 80% of their income to the *han* government as *dashimai*, or rice tax. (The high rate of taxation is concealed by the fact that in Satsuma the gross rice income was computed to be in terms of unhulled rice, whereas the *han* government demanded 40% of the gross figure to be turned over in polished rice.) Samurai were given permission to farm land classified as *eisakuchi*, *mizoshita*, *mikake*, and *oyamano*, but owners of these categories of land were not considered to be *taka mochi*.[18]

The most powerful warrior families, the *issho mochi*, were placed in territories of strategic importance, such as Izumi and Ibusuki in the northwest and southwest corners of Satsuma *kuni;* Ijuin, which guarded the western coastal route; Shigetomi and Kajiki, which protected the northern approaches to Kagoshima; Tanegashima, the island immediately south of Ōsumi; Kokubu and Tarumizu, which looked out on Kagoshima Bay; and Miyako-no-jō, situated on an important road near the western border of Hyūga.[19]

It may be expected that the daimyo was ever on the alert for signs of disloyalty or unseemly ambition on the part of the large private-domain holders in the *han*. Besides requiring them to maintain family residences in Kagoshima, the daimyo often made marriage alliances which linked potentially dangerous families more closely to Shimazu interests.[20] While these private lords enjoyed a considerable measure of autonomy, they were constantly subject to the daimyo's displeasure, and they might suffer expropriation, transfer to other areas, or even capital punishment in extreme cases. Such a fate was meted out to *karō* Hirata Masumune by assassination in 1610 for allegedly plotting against Iehisa. Hirata's son had already been killed for taking the part of Lord Ijuin who had been assassinated in 1603. One of Hirata's brothers was exiled to Iwojima and another was forced to enter the Buddhist order, exiled to the Ryukyus, and eventually assassinated in 1634.[21] Assassination was a common procedure for disposing of potential rivals, since a prolonged trial and formal execution might excite unrest among the samurai followers of the intended victim.

The exercise of feudal authority and effective *han* administration required exact information about the land area and its productive capacity. On the basis of such information the daimyo made assignments of sub-fiefs and fixed the income and the tax obligations of his retainers. For the gathering of such data

[18] Haraguchi, *Kagoshima ken no rekishi*, pp. 387–452; also, Robert K. Sakai, "Landholding in Satsuma, 1868–1877," *Studies on Asia, 1963*, (University of Nebraska Press, Lincoln, 1963), pp. 55–68.

[19] Asakawa, pp. 350–63.

[20] *Ibid.*, p. 364.

[21] *Kenshi*, II, 178–79.

land surveys were essential. Such surveys were required from time to time also to correct inequalities which developed as a result of population changes, variations in the quality of the soil, the opening up of new arable and taxable land, and shifts in ownership of land rights. (In Satsuma the sale and purchase of land rights was permitted within limits prescribed for each rank within the samurai class.)

Toyotomi Hideyoshi had carried out a land survey in Satsuma-han in 1594–1595. Complaints of injustices arising therefrom resulted in certain adjustments in 1596. It was not until 1611 that Iehisa made his own general land survey. Such a survey undertaken by the *han* was called *naiken* "domestic survey"), to distinguish it from *bakufu* supervised surveys known as *kyōzao* or *kōken*. ("Kyoto rod" or "public survey"). The Tokugawa did not attempt a survey of Satsuma, but four *naiken* were carried out by the Shimazu in 1611–1614; 1632–1633; 1657–1659; and 1722.[22] It is to be noted that these surveys were carried out in the early part of the Tokugawa period, two of the four being ordered by Shimazu Iehisa.

It may be assumed that the announcement of a land survey was cause for uneasiness among those who possessed private domains or who otherwise had reasons to conceal their actual economic status. As a prelude to the survey of 1611 Iehisa called attention to prevailing quarrels, disorders, and charges of injustices throughout the *han* which made necessary a more equitable distribution of land. He impressed upon the survey teams the need for honesty and fair play. Detailed instructions were given on the organization and duties of the survey teams and the procedures and methods to be followed.[23]

The overall supervision of the project was entrusted to 3 high officials of the *han* administration, perhaps a precaution against the high-handed action of any one official. Each survey team was composed of 19 men headed by the rod chief or rod captain, *sao bugyō* or *sao taishō*. The latter usually was the *jitō*, or the district administrative deputy of the daimyo. He was assisted by 2 secretaries, 2 calculators, 2 inspectors of sowing, and 2 men in charge of the rod. Each of these officials in turn were accompanied by their assistants. The secretaries and calculators were sent from Kagoshima, the inspectors of sowing (*maki-mi*) and the rod men were samurai of the *tojō*, and the petty assistants were recruited from among the local peasantry.[24] (It might be noted that in the third general survey of 1657–1659 the inspectors of sowing and the rod men were selected from samurai in the local district, except when the survey was of a private domain, in which case these officials were chosen from some other area.)[25]

The rod which Hideyoshi used for his survey was 6 feet 3 inches long (Japanese measure), but the Satsuma standard adopted in the survey of 1611 and thereafter was 2 inches longer.[26] The *maki-mi* (inspector of sowing) mea-

---

[22] *Ibid.*, II, 52–53; *Sappan seiyōroku*, p. 7.
[23] *Kenshi*, II, 53.
[24] *Ibid.*, II, 53.
[25] *Ibid.*, II, 56.
[26] *Ibid.*, II, 59.

sured the amount of seed which the peasant used per plot of land. This served to check the accuracy of the rod measure. Though there were slight regional variations, the *maki-mi* was guided by fixed equations of so many cubic measure of seed per measured unit of land. (The Satsuma peasants looked upon their land from a different point of view. Instead of describing the land as of so many rods, or so many ounces or pints of seed, the peasant referred to so many "bundles" or sheaves.)[27]

The *naiken,* or general *han* land survey, produced basic information concerning the increase of rice paddies and fields, the number of trees, and the amount of salt fields. The names and the number of people in the local villages were recorded in the *nayosecho,* or name registry.[28] Statistics were also gathered for horses and cattle. The conclusion of the first survey of 1614 was followed by a general redistribution and allocation of fiefs and *taka* (rights to the rice crop). These assignments took account of the location of the land in relation to transportation routes and granaries.

Effective administration depended upon accurate surveys, but political considerations sometimes dictated the allocation of land. After the land survey completed in 1614 the lord of Iriki's domain had been reduced from 15,000 *koku* to 6,287 *koku.*[29] The powerful lord of Miyako-no-jō, Kitago Tadayoshi, was ordered to return to the daimyo the three districts of Takajo, Katsuoka, and Yamanoguchi in exchange for certain other areas designated by the daimyo. The administrative responsibility for Yamanoguchi was assigned to Shikine Yorikane, as *jitō,* but on his way to assume the post he was assassinated.[30] Land distribution often was the occasion for fierce political struggles.

The land survey was not unrelated to the economic difficulties of the *han.* Since the defeat at Sekigahara the *han* debt mounted rapidly. It is said that even on his first trip to Edo in 1603 Iehisa had found it necessary to borrow money.[31] Thereafter the demands of the daimyo, costly fires at Edo, the Ryukyu military expedition of 1609, and the *sankin kōtai* obligations continually left the *han* treasury short of funds. Satsuma hoped to balance expenditures by increasing profits from the Ryukyu trade, but in the time of Iehisa it is probable that profits from this commerce did not meet expectations.[32] Iehisa, like other daimyo in Japan, was forced to obtain extra contributions from his vassals and retainers. The land survey provided the daimyo with a realistic picture of what the traffic could bear. By 1618 the samurai were contributing an additional 10% of their income to the regular tribute they submitted to the lord.

In 1619, confronted with a financial crisis, the daimyo was forced to tighten

---

[27] *Ibid.,* II, 60.

[28] *Ibid.,* II, 59.

[29] By 1632 the *taka* of the lord of Iriki is listed as 4,489 *koku.* Asakawa, p. 264.

[30] *Kenshi,* II, 191.

[31] *Ibid.,* II, 177.

[32] Robert K. Sakai, "The Satsuma-Ryuku Trade and the Tokugawa Seclusion Policy," *Journal of Asian Studies,* Vol. XXIII, No 3 (May 1964), 391–403.

his control over the produce from the land. The samurai of various ranks as well as temples and shrines were ordered to return to the *han* from one-fourth to two-thirds of their land allottments.[33] The directive declared that the ever-increasing debt necessitated this action, but promised that the fiefs would be returned to their original size as soon as the *han* financial obligations had been cleared. Frugality was ordered especially for the higher-status samurai. The sale and purchase of land was strictly prohibited and the building of new temples and shrines was halted. Artisans, craftsmen, and others performing such special services for the *han* were instructed to relinquish any land which had been allotted to them as salary and henceforth they were to be paid out of the *han* granary.[34]

While the daimyo was constantly confronted with large expenditures, particularly for his residences and offices in Edo, Kyoto, and Osaka, some large landholders in Satsuma were in positions to enhance their wealth and prestige. They monopolized the highest offices in the *han* administration, and with the lord away in Edo for so much of the time, inevitably the responsibilities of *han* administration were assumed by these land-holding aristocrats.

Iehisa was alert to the possible erosion of his own authority. In 1628 Hishijima Kunitaka, who had been a *karō*, or councilor, since 1623, was ordered to commit suicide for alleged arrogance, arbitrariness, cruelty, and obstruction to *han* administration. Hishijima's close associates and relatives were placed under surveillance or exiled. His family fortune, a sum which in terms of silver, gold, and rice alone totaled to 350 *kan* silver, was confiscated.[35] With this the *han* debt of the time was paid up with 50 *kan* left over to spend on the construction of roads, bridges, temples, and shrines. It was reported that Hishijima had profited by lending money to the *han* through a Kyoto moneylender.[36] The revelation of Hishijima's cruelty to the people within his private domain was made the occasion for a general order to reform the conduct of civil administration. In 1631, when Kitago Tadayoshi, lord of Miyako-no-jō, died, Shimazu Iehisa issued a stern warning to Kitago's son and successor not to behave like his late father, who had reputedly killed 600 people in his domain.[37] Henceforth capital punishment or confiscation of property within private domains were to be reported to the *han* government. Apparently the Kitago had not adequately heeded the daimyo's warning for three of its leading members were subsequently executed on charges of cruelty to the people.[38] Such punishments and confiscations of private domains gradually diminished the power of rival families and enabled the Shimazu daimyo to reward his own relatives and loyal supporters.

---

[33] In 1619 Shimazu Iehisa was required to contribute three thousand pieces of lumber for use in the construction of Edo castle. *Kenshi*, ii, 187.

[34] *Ibid.*, ii, 184–86.

[35] *Ibid.*, ii, 189–90.

[36] *Ibid.*, ii, 190.

[37] Kitago Tadayoshi had been stripped of much land earlier in 1614. *Kenshi*, ii, 178.

[38] *Ibid.*, ii, 191–92.

In 1632 the *han* debt had again risen to a new high of 7,000 to 20,000 *kan* silver.[39] It was probably no coincidence that another land survey was ordered by the daimyo in this year. The announced purpose was to correct injustices which had developed in recent years. Along with the survey teams, inspectors were sent from Kagoshima into the districts to observe and listen to the complaints of the people. Where the results of the survey were deemed unfair by the people, new measurements were to be taken. Where injustices or discrimination were suspected, the samurai and *jitō* of the district were to submit separate reports. Overall supervision of the land survey of 1632–1633 was placed in the hands of three members of the Shimazu family, and the completion of the survey was quickly followed by another general redistribution of land and land rights.[40] Though evidence is scarce, in view of the disposition of the Hishijima and the Kitago cases, whose private domains were confiscated on various charges including cruelty to the people, it may be suggested that the solicitude of the daimyo for the welfare of the people was a convenient way of consolidating his own power at the expense of the private domain-holders.

By 1634 the *han* debt was 8,000 *kan* silver. This was further reduced by an order forcing samurai to return part of their fiefs to the *han,* to make gifts of gold and swords, and to lend silver to the *han*. By 1637 the *han* debt stood at 181 *kan* silver, but further economies were ordered and more land was returned by the samurai to their daimyo. The *Kagoshima Kenshi* suggests that this rapid debt reduction is attributable to the development of the Ryukyu trade, but evidence for this is lacking.[41]

The measures described in the foregoing account strengthened the political position of the Shimazu daimyo. Shimazu Iehisa must be credited for initiating a program for solidifying the power of his dynasty, but it remained for his successors to carry it out so thoroughly as to preclude any internal challenge to the Shimazu authority. By the eighteenth century a roster of the 20 *issho mochi,* holders of large private domains, included 12 with the Shimazu surname, and of the remainder most were related to the daimyo by marriage.[42] These measures which consolidated Shimazu control over land rights, however, did not solve more basic economic problems. More constructive economic reforms for the increase of production and revenue were not to be carried out until the Tempō reforms of the nineteenth century. In the meantime, the Shimabara Rebellion had broken out in 1637, for which Satsuma was called upon to contribute thousands of troops. Iehisa died just prior to the collapse of this rebellion.

---

[39] In the same year Satsuma contributed 10,000 pieces of silver on the occasion of the shogun Hidetada's death. *Kenshi,* II, 188.

[40] *Ibid.,* II, 55; also *Go chisei nempyō,* p. 5a.

[41] *Kenshi,* II, 189.

[42] *Rekidai seido,* Vol. VII, section 5 on *shiryō,* 32–35.

PART THREE
DAIMYO RULE IN CASTLE
TOWN AND VILLAGE

CHAPTER NINE

MATERIALS FOR THE STUDY OF LOCAL HISTORY IN JAPAN: PRE–MEIJI *DAIMYŌ* RECORDS

JOHN WHITNEY HALL

Reprinted from *Harvard Journal of Asiatic Studies,*
Vol. 20, Nos. 1 and 2 (June 1957)

The history of Japan during the two and a half centuries prior to the opening of the country in 1854 has traditionally been told as a story of the rise and fall of the Tokugawa central government. It is natural, of course, for historians to view a national history in this fashion, that is, in terms of the political and cultural center of affairs. Yet in the case of Tokugawa Japan, this approach has certain serious shortcomings. We have only to follow the course of events which transpired after 1854 and culminated in the downfall of the shogunate to see that they were shaped in large part by forces originating outside of the political center of Japan. The men who emerged to lead the modern Japanese state were, for the most part, products of the *daimyō* domains, or *han*, which existed as semi-independent entities within the Tokugawa system. To gain a balanced picture of the Tokugawa period, therefore, it is imperative that the historian bring into his view the local areas represented by the *daimyō* domains.

The study of Tokugawa local history, especially if concentrated upon the domains, can reveal much that would escape the attention of the historian preoccupied with the problems of the center alone. In a very real sense the *han* constituted the basic unit of Tokugawa political, social, and economic life. Numbering some two hundred and sixty-five at the conclusion of the Tokugawa period, each was a microcosm, its structure mirroring in miniature the institutions of the national macrocosm. For this reason the *daimyō* domain offers to the historian a convenient example of Tokugawa society, small enough to be studied as a complete entity, yet large enough to retain the features of the whole.

Despite the importance of the *han* in early modern Japanese history, we have only fragmentary and imperfect knowledge of what one was like in its totality: that is, as a geographical, political, social, economic, and cultural organism. This is not to deny that Japanese historians have written and compiled a great deal in the field of local history. But unfortunately their work in this area is of limited use. The pre-modern local histories, such as the eighteenth and nineteenth century provincial gazetteers and *han* histories, are antiquated in their conception and methodology. They consist for the most part of chronologically arranged quotations from sources which are often of a secondary nature and frequently unreliable. Recent works in this field, such as the great multi-volume prefectural or city histories, are often poorly organized and lack a sufficiently analytical approach. Many of them, like their predecessors, are scarcely more than chronologically arranged extracts from primary or secondary sources or from statistical materials. While such works can be useful for reference purposes they are not designed to meet the needs of the contemporary historian.

It must be admitted that this situation has changed somewhat in more recent years as the analytical attention of Japanese historians has begun to turn towards local history and *han* studies. The concern of Japanese historians of the 1930's in the social and economic aspects of their history invited their attention to locally defined historical problems. The issues of two journals in particular, *Keizaishi kenkyū* [*Studies in Economic History*] [1] and *Shakai keizai shigaku* [*Journal of the Social and Economic History Society*], [2] contain a large number of historical studies of local problems of the Tokugawa period. More recently local historical research of the type reported in the journal *Chihōshi kenkyū* [*Studies in Local History*] [3] has begun to appear. Yet it is characteristic of these studies that they deal with limited problems or are based on fragmentary materials. Field studies most often

---

[1] *Keizaishi kenkyū* 經濟史研究, published monthly from 1929 to 1944 by the Nihon Keizaishi Kenkyūjo of Kyōto University.

[2] *Shakai keizai shigaku* 社會經濟史學, published monthly since 1931 by the Shakai Keizaishi Gakkai of Tōkyō.

[3] *Chihōshi kenkyū* 地方史研究, published three times a year since 1951 by the Chihōshi Kenkyū Kyōgikai of Tōkyō.

are confined to single villages. Thus the comprehensive picture of an entire *han* is yet to emerge.

Aside from the size and complexity of the *han* which defies easy analysis or description, the chief reason for the lack of comprehensive studies of the Tokugawa feudal domain is unquestionably the difficulty of securing adequate source materials. Again this is a condition which persists despite the existence of what appears on the surface to be more than an adequate supply of published documents. Nearly every prefecture has published in the last few decades some form of documentary historical series. A number of former *daimyō* houses have also made available selections of house records. Yet, as in the case of local histories, these collections are fragmentary or overly selective. Except in one or two instances no attempt has been made to make available on an extended scale the basic source materials for the study of an entire *han*. Even in these instances materials are chronologically arranged and hence difficult for functional use.[4] Thus it is safe to say that no systematic attempt has yet been made to evaluate, organize, and make generally accessible the documentary resources upon which a complete institutional study of a *han* might be based.

Written documents which remain from the Tokugawa period are voluminous and bafflingly varied. The historian will find at his disposal private papers relating to the lives and private activities of the former domain residents of all classes; semi-public

[4] The outstanding examples of published records of *daimyō* houses are the compilations of the MAEDA House 前田家, *Kaga-han shiryō* 加賀藩史料 [*Historical Materials of the Kaga Domain*], Tōkyō, Ishiguro Bunkichi, 1929-, 15 v., and the work of HORIUCHI Makoto 堀內信, *Nanki Tokugawa shi* 南紀德川史 [*History of the Tokugawa Branch Family in Kishū*], Wakayama, Nanki Tokugawa Shi Kankōkai, 1930-1933, 18 v. The Tōkyō Daigaku Shiryō Hensanjo 東京大學史料編纂所 is also publishing a documentary series entitled *Dai Nihon komonjo, iewake monjo* 大日本古文書家わけ文書 [*Ancient Documents of Japan, Documents Arranged According to Ownership*], Tōkyō, 1904-. Most of the collections published to date are of pre-Tokugawa origin, the major exception being ten volumes of records from the DATE House 伊達家. An excellent list of published sources on *daimyō* domains of the Tokugawa period is found in SHIMONAKA Yasaburō 下中彌三郎, *Sekai rekishi jiten, dai nijūni kan, shiryō hen, Nihon* 世界歷史事典第二十二卷史料篇日本 [*Encyclopedia of World History, Volume 22, Source Materials, Japan*], Tōkyō, Heibonsha, 1955, pp. 277-278.

documents relating to such non-governmental organizations as temples, shrines, commercial houses, and landed families; and public records which were produced by the governmental agencies of the *han*. Admittedly the first two categories of papers can be of importance in certain aspects of the historian's work, since they shed light on a number of specific historical problems. But the unpredictable nature of private and semi-public materials and their limitation to certain specific institutions detract from their usefulness as souces of general information on the structure and development of the *han* of Tokugawa times. For this purpose the public records are both better preserved and more extended in coverage. Despite their bias in favor of authority and law, the public records will be the historian's first concern.

By the Tokugawa period, government in Japan had given rise to a complex bureaucracy activated by a vast and complex system of paper work. Beginning at the top with the formal contracts of feudal investiture, the laws and ordinances of the *shōgun* and the *daimyō*, the memorials of officials, records concerned with military planning and taxation, down to the petty matters of village administration, papers of all sorts circulated up and down the chain of administrative command. It is these records, coming to rest in the hands of public officials or in the official storehouses of the domain, which remain to us today. While in Tokugawa times there were numerous resting places for such public documents, today most documents have disappeared except those relating to the two extreme ends of the official hierarchy: village records retained by former village heads, and *daimyō* records retained by the descendants of former domain chiefs. Yet these two groups of documents, if they exist in any quantity, can provide the basis of a comprehensive understanding of an entire *han*.

The nature of village documents has been extensively commented upon both in Japanese and English literature.[5] But

---

[5] Cf. Kinsei Shomin Shiryō Chōsa Iinkai 近世庶民史料調査委員會, *Kinsei shi shomin shiryō chōsa narabini mokuroku kisai yōkō* 近世庶民史料調査並に目録記載要項 [*An Investigation of Popular Records of the Early Modern Period Together with a System for their Classification*], 1950, 8 pp.; cf. additionally FURUSHIMA Toshio 古島敏雄 and ŌISHI Shinzaburō 大石慎三郎, "Chihōshi

daimyō records are yet to be thoroughly evaluated and categorized. Of the two groups, unquestionably the latter is more important to the historian. In general it is safe to say that *daimyō* records were kept more systematically and in greater volume than corresponding village records. Furthermore, since the domain administration touched not only on political matters but social and economic affairs, education, religion, and even morals, the records of the domain government can shed light upon nearly every facet of *han* life.

The major problem faced by the historian who would use *daimyō* records is that of availability. After the abolition of the *han* in 1871, local administration quickly shifted out of the castle headquarters of the domains into modern prefectural seats. The *daimyō* for the most part took up permanent residence in Tōkyō. The old records, rather than becoming the property of the new prefectural governments, remained in the possession of the former *daimyō*. In the years following many of the bulkier items in these collections were disposed of. What remained gathered dust in family storehouses, or, in some instances, was put at the disposal of house historians for the compilation of family or domain histories; access by the public was rarely permitted.

There were exceptions. In a few instances *daimyō* archives were presented to city or prefectural libraries where they were made accessible for public use. Pre-war examples of this were the SHIMAZU collection at the Shiryō Hensanjo of Tōkyō University, the KAGA archives of Kanazawa and the MŌRI archives of Yamaguchi. Since the Pacific War, as a result of the abolition of the Japanese nobility, there has been a further liberalization of access to *daimyō* archives.[6] Yet despite this fact there is a considerable

kenkyū-hō" 地方史研究法 ["Methodology for the Study of Local History"], *Nihon rekishi kōza* 日本歴史講座 *[Japanese Historical Series]*, Tōkyō, Kawade Shobō, 1952, v. 8, pp. 172-230; MARUYAMA Jirō 丸山二郎 and KODAMA Kōta 兒玉幸多, *Rekishigaku no kenkyū-hō* 歴史學の研究法 *[Historical Methodology]*, Tōkyō, Yoshikawa Kōbunkan, 1952, 164 pp. KANAI Madoka 金井圓, "Kinsei shiryō no seiri ni tsuite" 近世史料の整理について ["On the Classification of Early Modern Documents"], *The Nippon-Rekishi*, v. 77 (Sept. 1954), pp. 58-63; and John Whitney HALL, "Materials for the Study of Local History in Japan: Pre-Meiji Village Records," *Occasional Papers*, Center for Japanese Studies, v. 3, pp. 1-14.

[6] A partial list of archival collections of *daimyō* records and their present location can be found in SHIMONAKA, *op. cit.*, pp. 284-286.

lag in the use of these materials by Japanese historians. One reason is that most of these collections have yet to be catalogued and their contents classified. Much remains to be discovered about the nature of these collections, their value as historical sources, and the types of questions which may be answered by their study.

One of the most complete collections of *daimyō* records in Japan was owned by the IKEDA family of Okayama. This collection was presented to the newly founded Okayama University in 1949 and moved to its present location in the University's main library in 1950. Here it is being catalogued by qualified historians and librarians. When in 1950 the University of Michigan Center for Japanese Studies established a field station in the city of Okayama, negotiations were undertaken to secure permission to photostat a selected portion of the IKEDA archives. It was the good fortune of the Center not only to obtain permission to do so, but also to secure the support of a number of historians and librarians at the University. Photostating of the IKEDA collection was begun in the fall of 1951 and still continues. In the course of these operations, the author together with members of Okayama and Tōkyō Universities conducted a survey of the entire collection in an attempt to determine approximately what it contained and to formulate a working analysis of the materials.[7]

Naturally it cannot be claimed that *daimyō* archives throughout Tokugawa Japan were so similar that the study of one would reveal the contents of the others. Each of the two hundred and sixty-odd *daimyō* conducted his affairs according to inherited tradition. There was no enforced uniformity; *tozama* and *fudai daimyō* in particular differed markedly in their procedures. Yet the conditions which gave rise to the writing and preservation of documents in the domains were in nearly all cases similar. While details differed, fundamental practices remained constant. Thus

---

[7] The author is particularly indebted to Professor TANIGUCHI Sumio 谷口澄夫 with whom he is currently engaged in a full-scale study of the Okayama domain. Others who have participated in the task of classification are: Professor FUJII Shun 藤井駿 of Okayama University; Mr. KANAI Madoka 金井圓 of the Shiryō Hensanjo, Tōkyō University; Mr. HATTAN Kōhachi 八丹幸八; and Dr. Gaston SIGUR of the Asia Foundation.

it is possible to arrive at a general conception of the main types of documents which one would normally expect to find in the archives of a Tokugawa *daimyō* through the study of the IKEDA collections.

The IKEDA archives comprise nearly 4,000 different items tightly packed in boxes occupying about 2,000 cubic feet of space.[8] They contain records accumulated by the *daimyō* of Okayama over a period of nearly 250 years. Most of them relate to the administrative process of the Okayama domain. In approaching the problem of classification of these documents, a number of possibilities presented themselves. One obvious way was by subject content. But while this method might appear most logical, it was considered impractical for several reasons. Many documents touch on a variety of subjects. A classification by subject would require an elaborate cross reference system. Furthermore, such a method of classification would not help to provide general insight into what other *han* collections might contain. It seemed more practical and useful, therefore, to analyze the materials in terms of the functions and agencies within the *han* administration which produced them. Since the administrative machinery of most *daimyō* domains was approximately uniform, such a method would reveal the types of documents which could be expected to remain in the *daimyō* archives of other domains.

It should be admitted before proceeding further that the functional categorizations here proposed will necessarily neglect certain features of the IKEDA collection. Since we shall be dealing in only the major categories, much of the unique must be overlooked. No system can do justice to the collection as a whole, to the signed letters by the great historic figures of the past such as TOYOTOMI Hideyoshi and TOKUGAWA Ieyasu, the beautifully

---

[8] A draft catalogue of this collection, prepared primarily by Professor TANIGUCHI, is available in mimeograph: Okayama Daigaku Fuzoku Toshokan 岡山大學附屬 圖書館, *Ikeda ke bunko kari mokuroku* 池田家文庫假目錄 [*Draft Catalogue of the Ikeda House Library*], 1953, 87 pp. A brief description of the main items in the collection was also mimeographed in 1954: Ikeda Ke Bunko Seiri Iinkai 池田家 文庫整理委員會 *Ikeda ke bunko kaidai* 池田家文庫解題 [*Annotated Bibliography of the Ikeda House Library*], 48 pp.

painted maps and charts, the elaborately illustrated heraldic
designs, and the thousands of memoranda and memorials. All
these must be subsumed under the somewhat colorless titles of
administrative and operational categories.

The Okayama domain of the IKEDA family may be considered
a typical *tozama han* of medium size. Occupying the entire
province of Bizen and parts of Bitchū, it sustained a population
of nearly four hundred thousand. Assessed at a normal production of 315,200 *koku* of rice, the domain rapidly extended its
agricultural base by land reclamation. At the mid-point of the
Tokugawa Period, the domain had a real productive capacity of
454,000 *koku*. The center of this domain was the castle town of
Okayama, with a population of over 38,000 people by the beginning of the eighteenth century. Here resided the *daimyō* and his
retinue of vassals together with members of the service classes
of artisans and merchants. Outside of the *han*, the IKEDA, in
conformity with Tokugawa procedure, maintained an official
residence in Edo for attendance upon the *shōgun*, they placed their
representatives in Kyōto and Fushimi, and their office in Ōsaka
handled the domain's financial dealings with the areas outside
of Okayama proper. Within the domain, the *daimyō* created out
of his retinue a military and civilian bureaucracy for the protection and administration of his domain. Capping this bureaucracy
were the ceremonial functions of the *daimyō*'s own court which
drew together the entire administration in service and allegiance
to the *daimyō*. Under the *daimyō* his administration, both military and civil, descended in orderly progression down to the level
of the individual domain inhabitants. It was this hierarchy of
vassals and the bureaucracy they staffed that gave rise to the
voluminous records retained by the *daimyō* of Okayama.

As in all bureaucracies, the paper work generated by the *han*
authorities was broadly separable into two types: records related
to personnel matters and those concerned with governmental
operations. The first dealt with matters of fealty, feudal status,
official rank, salary, and promotion. The latter recorded the activities of military and civil bureaucratic personnel and documented
actual operation of the bureaucracy in terms of decisions, regu-

lations, memorials, reports, statistics, and the like. Our first functional division, therefore, will be in terms of these two main categories.

I. Personnel Records

Under the Tokugawa political system while the *daimyō* was vassal to the *shōgun*, the *daimyō*'s vassals were directly accountable to him alone. The feudal relationships between *shōgun* and *daimyō*, *daimyō* and vassals gave rise to an elaborate documentation involving contracts of investiture, acknowledgment of fealty, regulations, and personnel reports.

Records Concerning the Shōgun-Daimyō Relationships: Not all of the intricate relationships between *shōgun* and *daimyō* need be our concern, for many of these produced records which were retained chiefly at the shogunal level and left little mark in the *daimyō* archives. Furthermore such items as the basic code governing *daimyō* and *samurai* conduct, the *buke shohatto* 武家諸法度, are generally accessible in the commonly available printed collections of Tokugawa documents. More specifically concerned with the *daimyō* side of the *shōgun-daimyō* relationship were documents of the following types:

1. The Contract of Investiture (*ryōchi hammotsu* 領知判物), a document bearing the *shōgun*'s signature and testifying to the original domain (*ryōchi*) grant made to the *daimyō*.

2. The Domain Inventory (*ryōchi mokuroku* 領知目録), a document describing in detail the location by village and assessed rice yield of the *daimyō*'s domain. This document, signed by members of the *shōgun*'s corps of Masters of Ceremony (*sōsha ban* 奏者番), was renewed for each successive *daimyō* when he inherited his domain.

3. Documents granting titles, special honors, and posts within the shogunal administration.

In return for the above documents which descended from *shōgun* to *daimyō* were others submitted to his superior by the *daimyō*. Aside from the *daimyō*'s oath, most of these were of an informative nature, resulting from the desire of the shogunate to keep fully informed of the affairs of the various *daimyō*. In this category we find:

1. The Oath (*seishi* 誓詞) of the *daimyō* to the *shōgun*, repeated by each *daimyō* in succession.

2. Genealogical Tables (*kafu* 家譜) and other genealogical information concerning the *daimyō* family.

3. Domain Maps (*kuni-ezu* 國繪圖), Village Rosters (*gōchō* 郷帳), and Cadastral Records (*kenchi-chō* 檢地帳), all of which presented basic statistical data on the size, topography, and tax assessment of the domain.

4. Reports on the Investigation of Religious Preference (*shū-mon aratame kakiage* 宗門改書上), a yearly guarantee of the nonexistence of Christians in the domain. Only a few scattered examples of these documents remain.

5. Census Reports (*sōninsū no kakitsuke* 惣人數之書付) compiled periodically by the *daimyō* for presentation to the *shōgun*. In the Okayama domain these reports took several forms of which the above variety is only one. After 1721 census figures were required on a regular six-yearly basis by the shogunate.

6. Special reports on topics requested by the shogunate, especially with respect to domain procedures or upon the completion of some public or military service for the *shōgun*. In the IKEDA collection one such report entitled " O-tazune no shinajina kakiage chō " 御尋之品品書上帳 [" An Answer to Various Questions Asked by the Shogunate "] provides a thorough summary of information on political and military organization, taxation, population, and economic development of the *han* as of 1764.

Of the documents stemming from the *shōgun-daimyō* relationships, the most significant from the historical point of view are the special reports, the reports on religious investigation, and the maps. Much of the information contained in the other personnel records is available in more accessible form in the published materials of the Tokugawa shogunate.[9] The actual papers passed

---

[9] Cf. SHIMONAKA, *op. cit.*, pp. 273-284.

between the *daimyō* and the *shōgun* are thus of prime importance in revealing the local details of the structure and articulation of the *daimyō-shōgun* relationships.

Records Concerning the Daimyō-Vassal Relationships: Documents defining the relationships of vassals to the *daimyō* in terms of status and service were of the following main types. First, passing from *daimyō* to vassal were:

1. The Contracts of Investiture (*origami* 折紙) which designated the feudal status of each vassal, the size of his income, and the location of his sub-fief by village, if such were granted. While these documents were retained by the vassals themselves, models (*shitagaki* 下書) were kept by the *daimyō*. Documents also recorded the granting of new fiefs (*shinchi* 新知) and the bestowal of additional fief increments (*gokazō* 御加增).

2. Appointment to posts within the civil or military bureaucracy came in the form of Assignments (*jirei* 辭令).

Fortunately the information supplied in both of the above categories of documents is available in complete and classified form. The *Samurai* Rosters (*samurai chō* 士(侍)帳) and Stipendiary Rosters (*kirimai chō* 切米帳) recorded on a yearly basis the status and income of all vassals. The Registers of Appointments (*shoshiki kōtai* 諸職交代) at regular intervals listed the personnel changes for all major offices within the *han* bureaucracy. A Register of Appointments compiled in 1865 gives the names and terms of office of all official personnel in the *han* bureaucracy from the year 1603 on. In addition other registers keep minute records of the special assignments of the *daimyō*'s vassals. For example there is the Record of Vassals on Missions to Other Domains (*takoku e sankin chō* 他國江參勤帳).

Paralleling the various personnel documents which descended from *daimyō* to vassal were a host of documents which proceeded in the other direction from vassal to *daimyō*. Among these were:

1. Oaths of Allegiance (*seishi* 誓詞, *kishōmon* 起請文).

2. Genealogies (*kafu* 家譜), conveniently brought together in the *Kachū shoshi kafu go-on yose* 家中諸士家譜五音寄 [Col-

lected Genealogies of Housemen Arranged by the Five Sounds]
compiled in 1669 in 18 volumes.

3. Service Statements (*hōkō-gaki* 奉公書). These records, one
of the largest items in the IKEDA collection, consist of five-yearly
statements on the activities of the vassal families. The practice
of submitting reports was begun in 1644. Nearly 3,000 volumes of
Service Statements remain to provide a vast personnel file on the
more than 1,200 families of higher rank in the *daimyō*'s retinue.

4. Reports on the Investigation of Religious Preference (*shū-
mon aratame kakiage* 宗門改書上) presented to the *daimyō*
through the Inspector of Religion (*shūmon bugyō* 宗門奉行).
These were submitted by the heads of each personnel unit. Each
such officer was obliged to prepare a yearly report listing all
personnel under his jurisdiction and guaranteeing that there
was no Christian among them.

Taken together, the above varieties of records make possible
the intimate reconstruction of the personnel structure of the *han*
bureaucracy. They define the relationship between *samurai* and
daimyō, the connection between feudal status and office, the
nature of the process of selection for office, the role of heredity,
and the amount of flexibility or rigidity in the system. The
Service Statements in particular are available in such volume as
to make possible a thorough statistical study of the career patterns of the *samurai* class in the *han*.

II. OPERATIONAL RECORDS

The administrative and defense organization of the *han* which
emerges from its personnel records was complex but reasonably
logical in its structuring. At the head of the status and operational hierarchy stood the *daimyō*. The domain chief, as is well
known, divided his time between his castle headquarters at Okayama and his residence at Edo. The *han* also maintained establishments at Ōsaka, Kyōto, and later at Fushimi. Below the
daimyō, the chief decision-making body of the *han*, the Council
(*hyōjōsho* 評定所), served both the civil and the military branches
of the *han* affairs. It was staffed by two of the *daimyō*'s senior

vassals (*karō* 家老 and *bangashira* 番頭) and by an indeterminate number of chief civil administrative officers.

The military organization of the domain was closely linked with the social hierarchy of the *daimyō's* vassals. In theory, of course, all *samurai* were accountable for military service. However, due to the limitation placed by the *shōgun* upon the size of the *daimyō's* military forces and the heavy shift of emphasis towards civil administration during the years of Tokugawa peace, a specialized military branch of service to the *daimyō* came into being. A number of vassal families retained hereditary membership in the Guards (*ōban* 大番) under hereditary Commanders (*bangashira* 番頭). Specialized branches of the armed forces were maintained by such officials as the Superintendent of Naval Affairs (*funate bugyō* 船手奉行), Superinendent of Works (*fushin bugyō* 普請奉行), and Superintendent of Flags (*hata bugyō* 旗奉行), the last being a sort of communications officer.

The civil administration, though poorly organized at the outset of the domain's history, eventually occupied the efforts of the majority of *han* vassals. Senior administrative responsibility rested with the three Councilors (*shioki* 仕置) and three Junior Councilors (*kojioki* 小仕置), officials appointed from among the *daimyō's* highest ranking vassals. Under them a number of service and supervisory functions were performed by such officials as the Chamberlains (*ō-koshō-gashira* 大小姓頭), the Chief Inspectors (*ō-metsuke* 大目付), the Secretaries (*yūhitsu-gashira* 右筆頭), and the Recorders (*tomegata* 留方). The main administrative duties were performed by the Magistrates of County Affairs (*gundai* 郡代), Financial Affairs (*sakumaigata* 作廻方), Town Affairs (*machi bugyō* 町奉行), Temple and Shrine Affairs (*jisha bugyō* 寺社奉行), School Affairs (*gakkō bugyō* 學校奉行) and by a host of other officials. Each one of these magistrates headed a staff of appropriate size to execute the functions of his office. Some *han* officials, notably the Recorders and the Magistrates of County, Financial, and Town Affairs, were given permanent office space either within the castle or in the town of Okayama.

This then was the bureaucracy which produced the operational records of the *han*. Such records are conveniently divided into two varieties as a result of two separate but closely associated practices within the bureaucracy. First of all, officials in the *daimyō*'s service kept detailed records of the day-to-day activities of their offices. For every office there existed a record book in which daily notations of officially transacted business were jotted down. Besides these relatively static documents were the more mobile papers which transmitted decisions and orders (variously known as *tasshi* 達, *oboe* 覺, *ofure* 御觸, etc.) down the chain of administrative command, and the memorials, recommendations, petitions, and reports (*kakiage* 書上, *kōjō* 口上, *negai* 願, *ikken* 一件, etc.) coming up from below. Such individual documents formed the bulk of the paper work of the *han* government. It will be easily seen, however, that there exists a considerable area for duplication among the static and mobile documents, as we have called them, since in nearly every case the mobile papers were copied in whole or in part in record books of one or another of the *han* officials. These record books, variously called *chō* 帳, *tome* 留, and *nikki* 日記, are without question the most important of the operational documents for the historian. Furthermore, since a number of the administrative offices were in the habit of periodically combining and classifying the information contained in their yearly record books, the work of the historian has been greatly simplified in these instances.

Even a cursory glance at the documents retained by a *daimyō* such as the IKEDA of Okayama impresses one with the seriousness with which the *daimyō* and his officials kept records. Scribes and secretaries were constantly on hand recording minutes and noting the comings and goings of officials. Requests and decisions were carefully noted. Furthermore, after the establishment in 1666 of the office of Recorders (*tomegata* 留方) in Okayama, a clear policy was developed with respect to the collection, classification, and selective retention of essential documents by the domain authorities.

Records Related to the Office of Daimyō: An important, though relatively small, part of the records of the IKEDA *han* is concerned with what might be called the external relations of the domain. As chief of the *han*, the *daimyō* was involved in a number of channels of official communication, with the *shōgun* and other *daimyō*. Thus for each IKEDA *daimyō* there exists a collection of Correspondence (*shokan* 書翰). In a more routine fashion, the *daimyō* was a constant recipient of shogunal injunctions and regulations which required integration into the *han's* administrative and judicial procedure. A record of such official communications was kept in the form of a Communications Register (*otodoke dome* 御屆留), twelve volumes of which cover the years 1691 to 1866. Documents such as the Registry of Circulars (*kaijō dome* 廻狀留) and Registry of Town Regulations (*machifure dome* 町觸留) exist for the years 1833 to 1868. Such matters as disputes with other domains, domain problems requiring shogunal action, and the performance of military and public service for the *shōgun* also required a goodly amount of paper work. But these in their variety and irregularity cannot easily be grouped into categories.

Within the domain, the *daimyō's* participation in civil and military affairs gave rise to other documents. As administrator of the domain, the *daimyō*, although delegating the execution of policy, was frequently called upon to give expressions of general policy and make statements of ultimate decisions on disputed problems. Such statements, seldom of great length, were duly recorded and carefully preserved for each *daimyō* in the form of Directives (*oboegaki* 覺書) and as items in Diaries (*nikki* 日記) or other official records. The most prized of such statements and decisions were those made by the first of the Okayama *daimyō*, IKEDA Mitsumasa 池田光政 (1609-1682). These are preserved as a form of house tradition in:

1. *Hōretsu-kō otedome* 芳烈公御手留 [*The Private Register* of Lord *Hōretsu*], a five-volume work containing the decisions and statements of IKEDA Mitsumasa from 1637 to 1669.

2. *Gozen otomechō* 御前御留帳 [*Record of Decisions Made by the Lord*], a classified record in two volumes of the personnel, military, legal, and administrative decisions by the founder of the Okayama domain.

Another important function of the *daimyō* was to serve as ceremonial head of the *han*. The following records relate to this aspect of his work:

1. The Yearly Ceremonial Register (*nenjū gyōji* 年中行事), a work in which the *daimyō*'s ceremonial duties and his comings and goings are minutely recorded. From it one gains a full picture of the pressure of ceremonial duties on the *daimyō*.

2. Documents concerning protocol, exemplified in the Clarification of Precedence for Processions (*gyōretsu sōgi* 行列裝儀). This document provides valuable insight into the hierarchy of official status relationships.

3. Records of funeral and commemorative ceremonies for past *daimyō* (*hōji* 法事).

As the official procedure of the *daimyō* domains became stabilized, one of the prime functions of the *daimyō* became that of holding audiences for his vassals or representatives from outside the domain. The *daimyō*'s performance of this function both at Okayama and Edo was voluminously recorded by his Secretaries and Recorders in various diaries. The following are the most important:

1. *Otemoto nikki* 御手許日記 [*The Private Diary*] was a detailed record of the *daimyō*'s private and public activities. Seven hundred and eighty volumes of this document cover two hundred and thirteen years from 1663-1875.

2. *Tōsei hiroku* 東政秘錄 [*The Secret Record of Domain Affairs at Edo*] is a classified summary of important ceremonial and administrative activities recorded at the IKEDA Edo residence. It covers the years 1764 to 1834 in seventy-eight volumes.

3. Travel Diaries. The *daimyō*'s actions while on the road to and from Edo were carefully recorded in the Diaries of Travel for Attendance at Edo (*go sampu ki* 御參府記) kept regularly from 1663 to 1862. Detailed accounts of the *daimyō*'s activities while engaged in special inspection tours were set down in Inspection Registers (*gojunken goyō chō* 御巡見御用帳).

Records of the Council: Next to the *daimyō* the most important authority in the domain was the Council. This group consisting of two chief vassals and a varying number of top administrative officials of the domain met regularly in the Council Room of Okayama Castle. On the 5th, 14th, and 23rd of the month it conducted hearings (*tachiai* 立會) on personnel matters while on the 9th, 19th, and 28th of the month it conducted civil, judicial, and military deliberations (*hyōjō* 評定) of non-routine importance. Its records were extremely varied since it both received and dispersed a great many documents. Only a fraction of this paper work has been retained in its raw form, but the following will serve to illustrate the nature of the records of the Supreme Council:

1. Registers of several varieties were kept to record the sessions of the Council. Since only a few of these remain it is difficult to reconstruct Council procedure with certainty. Detailed proceedings of the Council appear to have been kept in a document entitled Register of Hearings and Deliberations (*tachiai gohyōjō tomechō* 立會御評定留帳). Records were kept of such routine matters as Hearings on Requests for Building Permits (*tachiai sagyō negai dome* 立會作業願留), and Hearings on Requests Concerning Adoption, Marriage, etc. (*tachiai yōshi kon'in . . . negai dome* 立會養子婚姻 . . . 願留).

2. Council decisions or actions taken in acquiescence to shogunal direction were recorded and made public in several ways. Documents such as the Registry of Decisions (*otomechō hyōjō-gaki* 御留帳評定書) and Registry of Judicial Decisions (*sengi dome* 穿議留) appear in the IKEDA collections but are available for only a few years. They undoubtedly were kept on a regular basis. The Registry of Injunctions (*otasshi dome* 御達留) and Registry of Regulations (*ofure dome* 御觸留) are also available for a few years during the 1850's and 1860's.

3. Case Reports. A large number of reports on specific incidents requiring administrative or judicial action were prepared for the Council. These reports each differ in title but all end with the words *ikken* 一件 or *shidai* 次第 (case).

4. Special Dossiers. Most of the special events of the domain

were recorded in lengthy reports or collections of documents known as *shimatsu* 始末 (report of circumstances). Dossiers exist for such affairs as military operations, public works, and inter-*han* negotiations.

5. Collected Laws. Undoubtedly one reason for the scarcity of Council records is that they were used in preparing the Collected Laws (*hōrei shū* 法例集). This document, the single most important work related to the Council, is a series of three compilations running to thirty-six volumes. The series sets down under classified headings the major decisions of the Council together with other laws and ordinances adopted by the Council as the law of the domain. Laws, ordinances, administrative and judicial decisions made from the 1620's to 1871 are brought together under eighty headings of which the following are the most important: cultivated land, forest land, land tax, tax assessment, tax relief, payment of produce tax in silver, highways, ports, ships, public works, labor service, administrative posts, administrative offices, the County Affairs Office, irrigation administration, the *han* college, officials, salaries, servants, pariahs, vassals, military affairs, uniforms and clothes, food, ceremony, currency, commercial taxes, trade, inspection of religious preference, temples and shrines, house laws, travel, passports, judicial practice, punishments, *rōnin*.

6. Collected Punishments (*keibatsu kakinuki* 刑罰書抜) is a selection in eleven volumes of criminal case judgments made between the years 1642 and 1795.

Documents Concerning Military Affairs: As stated above, the military side of the organization of the *daimyō* domain had been drastically curtailed and formalized after the cessation of civil war in the early 17th century. The duties of the *daimyō*'s chief vassals had become more civil than military, while the function of the Guards had become increasingly ceremonial. On the other hand military arts continued to be highly regarded, and the *han* maintained an active though small functional military organization headed by the various superintendents of the specialized branches of military service. It was this military bureaucracy which gave rise to most of the military documents retained in the IKEDA collection. The following are some of the main categories of military documents:

1. Military Regulations (*gumpōsho* 軍法書) which recorded the basic military regulations of the domain and the rules for military conduct of the IKEDA vassals.

2. Collected Camp Regulations, Military Orders, and Assignments of Military Duties (*ojinbure, hōrei, gun'eki-no-sadame* 御陣觸, 法令, 軍役之定). The remaining documents of this variety relate largely to military operations during the 1860's.

3. Rosters of Men and Equipment (*jimba yosechō* 人馬寄帳). A few of these are drawn up for actual military operations which took place at the beginning and end of the Tokugawa period.

4. Charts, maps, drawings of Okayama Castle, troop encampments, defense works, harbors, sea lanes in the Inland Sea and other such material.

Of the documents relating to specialized branches of military service the following two collections are the most complete:

1. The Register of the Office of Naval Affairs (*funate dome* 船手留) deals with the affairs of the port of Okayama and other naval, transport, and shipping matters.

2. Records of the Superintendent of Works (*fushin bugyō* 普請奉行) contains detailed reports on the construction and repair of military establishments and public buildings within the domain, civil engineering works, land reclamation and water control projects, and the like. Included also are a number of detailed drawings of construction plans.

Documents Related to Civil Administration: It is in the category of civil administration that the bulk of the documentary material sought by the social and economic historian will be found. As previously mentioned, the officials in this branch of government performed both service and administrative functions. The service officials such as the Chamberlains, Inspectors, and Protocol Officers obviously were engaged in duties which required a minimum of paper work. Nonetheless they did have secretarial assistants, and records of their performance of official services appear to have been kept in the conventional register form. There are unfortunately few remnants of such materials. But an example is found in the Register of the Inspector (*ometsuke dome* 御目付留), a document in fifteen volumes dated 1765.

Records of the administrative officials such as the magistrates of the various civil affairs offices are available in greater volume. They are treated below under the appropriate offices:

A. *Records of the Office of County Affairs:* These represent one of the most important sections of the IKEDA archives. Nearly 90 per cent of the residents of the domain lived in the rural area and came under the jurisdiction of the County Affairs Office. A nearly equal percentage of the domain's tax income came from the rural sector and was collected by this office. The raw records of the Office of County Affairs consisted of papers coming up from the village administrative units for information to, or action by, the Magistrate of County Affairs, and decisions and orders descending from the Council and the Magistrate of County Affairs to the County Magistrates (*kōri bugyō* 郡奉行) and the villages. Undoubtedly the office kept registers, but these have not remained. The reason may be that they were destroyed when the *han* prepared, in 1823 and again in 1868, classified summaries of the activities of the County Affairs Office. These compilations, the *Satsuyōroku* 撮要錄 in thirty volumes and its successor *Satsuyōroku kōhen* 後編 in eight volumes, contain documentary materials arranged chronologically under the following main headings: forests, bodies of water, ships, water gates, bridges, reclaimed land, salt fields, land and cultivators, public buildings, granaries, inspection points, administrative offices, official posts, trade, temples and shrines.

While the registers and other raw documents of the Office of County Affairs are not preserved in the IKEDA collection, a number of types of statistical materials relating to rural affairs are available. These are largely concerned with rural taxation, land reclamation, and population census. Some typical documents of this kind follow:

1. Cadastral Registers (*kenchi chō* 檢地帳). Copies of the original land survey cadastral records of the domain were made on a village by village basis. These records were preserved only in fragmentary fashion by the Ikeda *daimyō*, although at the village level they still remain in abundance.

2. Register of Village Assessment for the Domain (*ryōchi gōson takatsuji chō* 領知郷村高辻帳). This document gives total figures by village on original assessment, reclaimed land, added assessments, and other related matters.

3. The Tax Register (*men chō* 免帳), a consolidated document compiled for each county (*gun*) which recorded by village the grades of land, the tax assessment for each grade, and the method of calculating the total tax assigned to each village. Volumes covering only five counties for the year 1868 remain.

4. Register of Fief Allocations by Village (*chigyō daka murawake chō* 知行高村分帳), a document listing by village the division of fields according to whether they delivered taxes to the *daimyō*'s granary or to one or another of the vassals. Registers covering the Ikeda domain in Bitchū give fuller information and list not only the parcels of land but the cultivators working the parcels.

5. Register of New Fields for Bizen and Bitchū (*Bizen-Bitchū shinden sōdaka mokuroku* 備前備中新田總高目錄), a convenient listing as of 1866.

6. Census data collected by the Office of County Affairs were quite extensive and complete. Unfortunately raw census records which remain in the Ikeda archives are too fragmentary to reveal the exact procedure by which the office compiled its data. Official census figures for rural Okayama are available in the annual census summaries contained in the Combined Registers described below. These provide the following information: total population, male population, female population, horses, houses, cattle. For each category the increase or decrease over the previous year is indicated.

7. Maps (*ezu* 繪圖) drawn up of counties provide excellent

visual documentation on the location of villages, roads, and canals, and on the history of land development.

It will be seen from the types of the above documents that the records of the Office of County Affairs provide a reasonably complete coverage of the structure of the rural political and social organization, the tax and allocation systems, and even the physical features of rural Okayama.

B. *Records of the Office of Financial Affairs:* The most fragmentary among the office records in the IKEDA collection are those of the Office of Financial Affairs. The reason for this is not altogether clear. It is well known, of course, that the financial data of the domains were jealously kept from public view. On the other hand it is obvious from the attention given to financial affairs by the IKEDA *daimyō* and from our indirect knowledge of the workings of the Office of Financial Affairs that the office must have kept books of the *tome-chō* variety together with separate collections of records dealing with the several branches of taxation and finance. For some reason such documents have not been systematically preserved. Consequently the historian must look for financial documentation in such works as the Combined Register described below or in chance finds among the special reports prepared for the *daimyō*. Fortunately one section of the yearly register compiled by the *daimyō*'s Recorders contains a gross financial summary of the *han*'s tax intake and expenditures. But for more detailed statements of income and expenditures in Okayama and Edo only a few documents of the following kinds are to be found:

1. *Jibun katte sakumai tsumori mokuroku* 自分勝手作廻積目録 [*A Budget for the Management of the Domain's Finances*], a plan drawn up in 1676.

2. *Omononari harai subete tsumori chō* 御物成拂凡積帳 [*A Budget for Disbursement of Tax Income*] drawn up in 1683.

C. *Records of the Office of Town Affairs:* This office was concerned with the administration of the town of Okayama. Despite the fact that its operation required the keeping of numerous record books, only a few scattered records now remain. Two of these worth mentioning are:

1. *Okayama machijū gokenchi sedaka jishigin chō* 岡山町中御檢地畝高地子銀帳 [*Register of Land Survey and Tax Assessment for the Town of Okayama*].

2. *Okayama machijū jimba on-aratame chō* 岡山町中人馬御改帳 [*Census of Men and Horses for the Town of Okayama*].

Despite the lack of raw documents on town affairs, this whole field is admirably covered by the Summary of Town Administration (*shisei teiyō* 市政提要). This work in twenty-five volumes is a classified collection of basic documents relating to town affairs and covering the years from about 1660 to about 1860. Documents are arranged chronologically under seventy-five headings of which the following are examples: sumptuary laws, inns, manufacture of wine, oil, etc., wholesale houses, commodities, domestic service, sale of rice, town guards, fires, shipping, river ships, bridges, occupations, religious inspection, the Office of Town Affairs.

D. *Records of the Magistrate of Temples and Shrines*: For the Office of Temple and Shrine Affairs the IKEDA collection is unusually complete. Of the original Temple and Shrine Registers (*jisha dome* 寺社留) some eighty volumes remain covering about one third of the years from the 1630's to the 1860's. Furthermore this office also prepared during the 1840's a complete classified documentary collection of temple and shrine affairs. This is the *Shaji kyūki* 社寺舊記, a work in forty-seven volumes covering the years from the 1680's to 1840.

E. *Records of the Domain College*: Documents related to the IKEDA Domain College have been conveniently brought together into the compilation entitled *Biyō kokugaku kiroku* 備陽國學記録. A chronological documentary collection, it covers the years 1666 to 1871 in sixty-nine volumes. This work provides the materials for a complete reconstruction of the operation of the *han* college, its administration, its student body, and its curriculum.

III. Documents of the Office of Recorders

The above categories of personnel and operational documents represent the bulk of the collection's original records. While it is possible to extend the list of official functions and their related records, the preservation of materials dealing with the less important activities of the *han* has been extremely unsystematic. Furthermore the need to inquire into further types of *han* records has been made less necessary because of the existence of a remarkable document compiled by the Recorders. This is the Combined Register (*tome-chō* 留帳) already referred to above. Shortly after the establishment of the Office of Recorders in 1666, the Recorders began the practice of compiling an annual Combined Register which would extract material from all possible sources within the *han* administration. Over 200 volumes of *tome-chō* are in existence for the years from 1673 to 1894, compilation having gone on even after the abolition of the *han*. Each year is covered by one or two volumes. Material is arranged chronologically under the following categories: shogunal relations, funeral ceremonies, shrines, temples, *daimyō* affairs, external affairs, the college, laws and orders, personnel assignments, new stipends, stipend increases, new assignments, retirement, succession, rural affairs, taxes, commendations, public works, hunts, naval affairs, absconders, punishments, and miscellaneous.

The fact that the Combined Register is compiled on a yearly basis makes it difficult to use as a research source on any given topic. Yet the existence of the document is in every other respect a boon to the historian. Beyond this the *tome-chō* is a tribute to the conscientiousness of the IKEDA archivists and an excellent indication of the seriousness with which the Tokugawa period *daimyō* regarded the keeping of records.

IV. Works of Official and Semi-Official Historians

The historical-mindedness of the *daimyō* and officials of the Tokugawa period is revealed in yet another way by the numerous historical works prepared either at the behest of a *daimyō* or privately under semi-official auspices. While works of this nature found in the IKEDA collection take us somewhat afield from the strictly documentary sources for the study of the domain, they are nonetheless of prime importance to the historian and their existence needs to be fully explained. Moreover, since these works were written under the influence of Chinese methods of historical compilation, most of them are in effect documentary histories. In the official and semi-official compilations listed below the historian will frequently find important original documents now lost in the main IKEDA collection.

1. *Ikeda-ke rireki ryakki* 池田家履歷略記 [*History of the Ikeda House*] was compiled in thirteen volumes by SAITŌ Kazuoki 齋藤 一興 and covers the history of the rise of the IKEDA family from 1555 to 1795. It is chronologically arranged and makes liberal quotations from primary sources. Although the chief emphasis is on members of the IKEDA family, the work affords a comprehensive view of the history of the IKEDA domain, its official personnel, its laws, and its relations to the shogunate. Later compilations amounting to thirteen volumes bring the history down to 1863.

2. *Biyō kokushi* 備陽國史 [*History of Biyō*]. This work of uncertain date and authorship is a carefully compiled documentary history of the Bizen domain during the twenty-year period from 1654 to 1673. It runs to twenty-four volumes. Because the years it covers constituted one of the most formative periods in the history of the Bizen domain, the work is especially important as a reference to early laws and decisions which set precedent for later administrative practices. A topical reworking of the material in this compilation is also available.

3. *Biyō kokushi* 備陽國志 [*Biyō Gazetteer*]. Compiled at official request by six scholars in the service of the IKEDA house, this work was completed in 1737 in sixteen *kan*. Organized in traditional gazetteer fashion, it gives geographical and historical information on each of the counties under IKEDA control.

4. *Kibi onko* 吉備溫故 [*Kibi Miscellany*]. A privately compiled miscellany of documents, historical works and geographical information, it was left unfinished during the 1790's. The work is arranged in topical fashion and thereby provides convenient

access to information on basic domain laws, geographical data, and main incidents in domain history. At present only 113 volumes of a total of 120 volumes are extant.

*

* *

The foregoing survey of the IKEDA *daimyō* documents, though touching only the important points, will demonstrate the richness of the historical materials available for the study of a Tokugawa *daimyō* domain. Again it should be pointed out that the kinds of documents contained in the IKEDA collection will not be duplicated in any exact form for other domains. Yet the method of classification used in our analysis has wide application. In the domains, administrative practices were similar, and depending upon the conscientiousness of the domain chiefs in maintaining archival completeness, similar categories of documents can be looked for. The historian who has in mind the functional approach to the classification of domain archives will find the task of documentary search made easier and more meaningful.

CHAPTER TEN

THE CASTLE TOWN AND JAPAN'S MODERN URBANIZATION *

JOHN WHITNEY HALL

Reprinted from *Far Eastern Quarterly,*
Vol. XV, No. 1 (November, 1955)

JAPAN'S role in Far Eastern history has been unique in many respects. Traditionally an integral part of the Chinese zone of civilization, Japan has nonetheless demonstrated a marked ability to remain independent of continental influence. In recent years Japan's remarkable record of adjustment to the conditions imposed upon her by the spread of Western civilization to the Orient has raised the provocative question of why Japan, of all Far Eastern societies, should be the first to climb into the ranks of the modern industrial powers. Is it possible, as one scholar has suggested, that Japan "has been the country which has diverged the most consistently and markedly from Far Eastern norms, and these points of difference have been by and large, points of basic resemblance to the West"?[1]

To seek an answer to this fascinating problem in culture comparison is beyond the scope of this short article. Yet with this question in mind it may be profitable to pursue an approach to Japanese history through one of its key institutions. Perhaps by confining our attention to a single facet of historical development it will be possible to gain some useful insights into the process of cultural evolution in Japan, particularly into the historical factors which were so influential in the years of transition which followed the "opening" of the country to the West in 1854. For such purposes the city presents itself as a convenient object of study.

The city has been a distinct and important segment of society in both East and West. Characteristically it has constituted, in the words of Mumford, a "point of maximum concentration for the power and culture of a community."[2] Most often the city has served as a source of progressive leadership, the center from which forces of innovation and change have spread into the community as a whole. The city as a cultural institution is both universally prevalent and historically significant. In the case of Japan it affords an especially rewarding object of study not only for the measure it provides of Japan's internal social and economic development but for the light it sheds on Japan's relative position between the cultural extremes of East and West.

Japanese cities prior to the impact of industrialized civilization upon them were essentially "oriental" in their composition and their social and economic func-

---

* Material contained in the article is in part the result of research supported by the Horace H. Rackham School of Graduate Studies of the University of Michigan.

[1] Edwin O. Reischauer, *The United States and Japan* (Cambridge, Mass.: Harvard University Press, 1950), 184.

[2] Lewis Mumford, *The Culture of Cities* (New York: Harcourt, Brace and Co., 1938), 3.

J. W. Hall

tions.[3] As in China such cities were larger by far than their European counterparts. But they seldom attained their size on the basis of trade alone. As in the case of most Eastern cities, a prime reason for their existence was that of civil administration and military defense. Yet while the morphology of Japanese cities and their role in national life reflected their oriental environment, it is also apparent that in their evolution they followed a pattern much more similar to that of the West than of China. In contrast to China where, since Han times, the function and structure of cities remained comparatively unchanged dynasty after dynasty, Japan presents a picture of continuing urban modification and expansion. Thus in Japan the major cities which succeeded in making the transition to modern times were, with few exceptions, completely undeveloped at the beginning of the sixteenth century. Furthermore, most of these did not reach maturity until the early eighteenth century and even then did not settle into a static, unchanging mode of existence. The city in Japan may be viewed as a constantly growing and evolving organism which, while it may never have constituted the dramatic challenge to the traditional land-based political and economic order as in Europe, was capable of rapid modification under the impetus of Western influence.

Before pursuing these observations further, however, it would be well to point out some of the limitations which must attend a study of this kind. Even within a society as comparatively homogeneous as that of Japan, cities have seldom been identical either in type or structure. Cities and towns have arisen from many diverse causes. Their historical evolution has followed several distinct paths according to the complex interweaving of changes in political, economic or religious conditions within the country. Geographic regionalism, especially in the contrasting features of the highly advanced central core of Japan and the generally retarded fringe areas, has provided a constant factor of diversity.[4] Thus any attempt to trace the course of urban development as a single uniform process must run the risk of oversimplification. On the other hand, during many periods of Japanese history, one or another type of town has tended to predominate, and hence has stood out as the representative urban institution of its era. This is especially true of the period which immediately preceded the appearance of the modern industrialized city in Japan. During roughly three centuries, from the 1570's to the 1870's, the castle town, or *jōkamachi*, assumed an importance out of all proportion to other types of urban communities. The story of the rise of the castle town and its eventual modification under the forces of internal decay and Western influence may be taken as the central theme of Japan's modern urbanization.

The story of the castle town has its origins in the early Middle Ages in Japan,

---

[3] For an interpretation of the historical Chinese city see Rhoads Murphey, "The City as a Center of Change: Western Europe and China," *Annals of the Association of American Geographers*, 44.4 (Dec. 1954), 349–362.

[4] On regional factors influencing the distribution and types of Japanese cities see R. B. Hall, "The Cities of Japan: Notes on Distribution and Inherited Forms," *Annals of the Association of American Geographers*, 24.4 (Dec. 1934), 175–200.

in the era of transition from the classical age of aristocratic rule to the feudalism of the rising military class.[5] In medieval Japan, the Sinified monolithic government adopted from China during the seventh century and the old style administrative towns which housed the court bureaucracy fell into decay. After the twelfth century both Nara and Kyoto lost their significance as centers of political authority and fell apart into a number of loosely clustered towns: Nara as a locus of temples; Kyoto as a place of residence for court families.[6] The provincial capitals, the *kokufu*, for the most part, reverted to the villages from which they had sprung. Lacking the massive walls of the Roman outposts in Europe, even the remains of their public buildings quickly disappeared from sight. This decline of the central government left few large concentrations of political or ecclesiastical power, since early feudal society in Japan was decentralized and its constituents were individually weak.

Beginning with the twelfth century, Japan entered a new phase of urban development along lines which followed the rise of new religious or military centers and the new economic requirements of a decentralized feudal society. Growth was slow. Kamakura appeared momentarily as a flourishing administrative seat but faded with the fall of the Hōjō. Not until the late fourteenth century did new towns of any consequence make their appearance. Fed by an expanding manorial economy, Nara and Kyoto began to recover some stature as commercial centers. Muromachi flourished as the location of the Ashikaga shogunate. Beyond these, local feudal headquarters such as Kagoshima, Yamaguchi, and Bingo Funai, religious centers such as Ishiyama, Sakamoto, and Ujiyamada, and commercial towns such as Hakata, Muro, Hyōgo, and Sakai attested to the expansion of the power of feudal and religious institutions and to the growth of domestic and foreign trade.

Scholars who have attempted to identify this phase of urban growth in Japan with comparable stages in the rise of European cities are uniformly agreed that the fourteenth-century Japanese towns remained far more dependent for their support on the agencies of political or ecclesiastical authority than did the newly emergent towns of Europe.[7] Whether this was the result of some basic "charac-

---

[5] In applying the term feudalism to the institutions of Kamakura, Ashikaga, and Tokugawa Japan I follow K. Asakawa, "Some Aspects of Japanese Feudal Institutions," *TASJ*, 46.1 (1918), 76–102.

[6] Several recent studies have been made of the transformation of the classical cities of Nara and Kyoto into medieval towns. See Nagashima Fukutarō[a], "Toshi jichi no genkai —Nara no baai" (The limits of urban self-government—the example of Nara), *Shakai keizaishigaku*, 17.3 (1951), 27–51; Matsuyama Hiroshi[b], "Hōken toshi seiritsu ni tsuki no kōsatsu" (On the establishment of feudal towns), *Rekishigaku kenkyū*, 180 (Feb. 1955), 12–22; Murayama Nobuichi[c], "Nikon toshi seikatsu no genryū" (The source of urban life in Japan) (Tokyo: Seki Shoin, 1953) 69f.

[7] For some general studies of the medieval Japanese town in addition to Murayama, see Endō Motoo[d], *Nihon chūsei toshi ron* (*Medieval cities of Japan*) (Tokyo: Hakuyōsha, 1940); Harada Tomohiko[e], *Chūsei ni okeru toshi no kenkyū* (*A study of cities in the middle ages*) (Tokyo: Dai Nihon Yūbenkai Kōdansha, 1942); Toyoda Takeshi[f] "Toshi oyobi za no hattatsu" (The growth of cities and guilds), *Shin Nihonshi kōza*, 4 (1948).

teristic" of Japanese society[8] or merely a product of the tardy development of commercial economy is hard to determine. But for whatever reason it is apparent that the medieval town and the commercial and service community in Japan looked for security not in the building of walls, but in the patronage and protection of the aristocracy or the politically powerful temples, shrines, and military houses. More clearly a result of economic backwardness was the relative lack of differentiation of the town from the surrounding agrarian community. In fourteenth-century Japan traders and artisans continued to maintain strong ties with the land, functioning both as landlords and as members of trade or craft guilds. Self-government was slow to develop and in most areas was inspired by a more vigorous movement towards village self-rule.[9]

During the fifteenth century, however, with the breakup of the Ashikaga hegemony and the consequent wars of succession and feudal rivalry, a growing spirit of freedom became evident in both countryside and town. The troubled times of Japan's civil wars provided the lower classes with both the occasion for independence and the opportunities for self-advancement. While the feudal wars brought destruction and turmoil, they served also to encourage social mobility and widespread economic growth. The causes of such growth are not easily enumerated, but the accompanying signs were clearly visible in technological improvements affecting agriculture and mining, the increase in foreign and domestic trade, the spread in the use of currency and in the agencies devoted to the handling of credit and exchange, and in the gradual absorption of the fragmented manorial economies into the larger blocks of feudal or ecclesiastical holdings.[10]

By the sixteenth century such factors of economic growth and feudal competition had accounted for the emergence of the town into new prominence. New bonds of dependence were forged between castle and trading town as the shogun or the great *shugo* lords attempted to buttress their economic positions against the lesser feudal barons of the countryside. Notable was the attempt of the Ashikaga shogunate to maintain its superiority over its vassals through its use of the merchants of Sakai. In the ensuing years Sakai, Hirano, Hakata, and a few other port cities of central Japan won a degree of freedom from feudal control. Sakai in particular, the "Venice of Japan" to the Jesuits of the late sixteenth century,[11] took on the form made familiar by free cities of Europe: a port governed by its chief burghers, protected by walls and moats, and by its own militia.

[8] Horie Yasuzō states in his "The Life Structure of the Japanese People in Its Historical Aspects," *Kyoto University Economic Review*, 21.1 (April 1951), 20–21, ". . . in the case of Japan the feudal system was a manifestation of the traditional family-like structure of life. . . . Thereby it prevented the healthy maturing of urban society and caused the development of urban society to be deformed."

[9] This is brought out clearly in Harada Tomohiko, "Chūsei toshi no jichi teki kyōdō soshiki ni tsuite." (On the self-governing communal organization of the medieval town), *Rekishigaku kenkyū*, 156 (Mar. 1952), 1–13. See also Harada, *Chūsei ni okeru toshi*, 253–255; Nagashima, 47–51; Murayama, 124–132.

[10] Many of these developments have been summarized by Delmer Brown, *Money Economy in Medieval Japan* (New Haven: Far Eastern Monographic Series, No. 1, 1951).

[11] Note the descriptions of Sakai in 1561–1562 by the Jesuit Vilela. Quoted in James Murdoch and Isoh Yamagata, *A History of Japan* (London: Kegan Paul, 1925), 2:147.

Castle Town and Modern Urbanization

The appearance of such cities as Sakai has occasioned considerable speculation among Japanese and Western historians regarding the direction which Japan's social and economic institutions were taking in the mid-1500's. Early writers such as Takekoshi were extravagant in their views, claiming to see in the rise of trading cities the beginning of the end of feudalism in Japan.[12] But more considered studies have demonstrated the weakness of these independent urban communities.[13] Sakai was, after all, the achievement of a relatively unique region of Japan which, especially in its economy, had advanced far beyond the rest of the country. It is obvious that Japan as a whole lacked the basic requirements which could support a more widespread growth of free cities as Europe had done. Furthermore, the conditions which had favored such a growth in central Japan were to diminish in subsequent years. In sixteenth-century Japan religious organizations, which in Europe helped counterbalance feudal authority, were on the decline. Foreign trade, that source of vital energy for a free commercial class, was at best a precarious activity for the Japanese, placed so far from Chinese and Southeast Asian ports. Even in its most prosperous years much of the foreign trade carried on by Japanese adventurers was made possible only through the use of capital supplied by feudal or religious institutions.[14] The ease with which the feudal authorities were able to control and then to monopolize foreign trade before the middle of the next century was a clear indication of the failure of such trade to become the support of urban freedom in Japan.

The "freedom" of such cities as Sakai was indeed illusory, based, as it was, less upon any prolonged struggle against feudal authority or on any overwhelming economic resources than upon the accidents of feudal rivalry and the weakness of the Ashikaga shogunate. Once the crumbling shogunate was replaced by new military coalitions, once Nobunaga and Hideyoshi turned towards the "free" cities, they fell, and Sakai among them.[15] Perhaps the surest commentary on the "free cities" of the sixteenth century Japan was their subsequent history. Not one was to continue its dominant role through the succeeding Tokugawa period into the modern age.

In Japan of the sixteenth century the truly significant institutional development was not the free city nor the rising merchant community, but rather the maturation of a new type of feudal ruler, the daimyo. The rise of the modern daimyo produced one of the major turning points in the history of Japanese political and social institutions. During the late years of the civil war period the daimyo had been increasing constantly in size and effective strength. Then after

---

[12] Takekoshi Yosoburo, *The Economic Aspects of the History of the Civilization of Japan* (London: George Allen and Unwin, 1930), 1:362.

[13] Harada, *Chūsei ni okeru toshi*, 259–264.

[14] Nishida Naojirō[g], *Nihon bunkashi josetsu* (*An introduction to the cultural history of Japan*) (Tokyo: Kaizōsha, 1932), 480.

[15] The story of the fall of Sakai is told by Takekoshi, 1:363–364. For a penetrating analysis of some of the weaknesses of the Sakai merchants see Sakata Yoshio[h], *Chōnin*, (*Merchants*) (Tokyo: Kōbundō, 1939), 156–158. A detailed study of the fall of Nara under Hideyoshi's feudal control is contained in Nagashima Fukutarō, "Toyotomi Hideyoshi no toshi seisaku ippan," (An example of Toyotomi Hideyoshi's policy towards towns), *Shigaku zasshi*, 59.4 (Aug. 1950), 58–64.

J. W. Hall

the mid-sixteenth century, as the daimyo joined ranks in far-reaching military alliances, and eventually in an overall national unity, all opposition to feudal authority fell before them. The cities as well as the Buddhist church submitted. Japan was, in the words of her own historians, thoroughly "refeudalized".[16]

But the word "refeudalization" is hardly adequate to describe the radical changes which swept Japan during the late sixteenth century. These years were distinguished not by some conservative retrogression within Japanese society but by a dynamic burst of activity which had few parallels in the history of Japanese institutions. The new feudal lords and the domains, or *han*, which they held represented the harnessing of social and material energies on a new unprecedented scale.[17] Forged out of the great civil wars of the fifteenth century, the daimyo domains were the product of a process of military and political consolidation which brought increasingly large areas under the unified control of individual feudal rulers. They were supported by new advances in agricultural technology and by extensions in the area under cultivation which released into the hands of the feudal lords new potentials of wealth and military power. They won their way by the perfection of new developments in the art of warfare: the mastery of the use of muskets and cannon, the improvement of the means of fortification and the shift to the use of large mass armies.[18] Finally, they were both the result and cause of far-reaching changes which affected the social organization of the peasantry and of the feudal ruling class. Characteristic of the daimyo was their ability to devise new means of social control which enabled them to draw increasingly on the manpower resources of the countryside and on the loyal services of their military vassals.

It has been suggested that the larger of the daimyo domains resembled petty principalities.[19] Needless to say, however, not all Japan was consolidated into domains of sufficient size to warrant such a description. Many parts of the country remained politically fragmented, either because of adverse geographical conditions or because they occupied buffer zones lying between large rival concentrations of feudal power. By 1560 over two hundred daimyo had made their appearance, and the major plains of Japan had been reduced to stable

---

[16] The standard exposition of this thesis is found in Nakamura Kichiji[i], *Nihon hōkensei saihenseishi* (*A history of the refeudalization of Japan*) (Tokyo: Mikasa Shobō, 1939).

[17] Japanese scholars have recently devoted considerable attention to the subject of the emergence of the *kinsei daimyō* "modern daimyo." For an analysis of the feudal lords who preceded the daimyo see Nagahara Keiji[j] and Sugiyama Hiroshi[k], "Shugo ryōkokusei no tenkai," (The development of the *shugo* domain), *Shakai keizaishigaku*, 17.2 (1951). On the modern daimyo themselves, the outstanding author is Itō Tasaburō[l]. Of his many writings see "Kinsei daimyō kenkyū josetsu" (An introduction to the study of the modern daimyo), *Shigaku zasshi*, 55.9 (Sept. 1944), 1–46; 55.11 (Nov. 1944), 46–106. His *Nihon hōkenseido shi* (*A history of Japanese feudalism*) (Tokyo: Yoshikawa Kōbunkan, 1951), is useful as a brief survey. The establishment of the Bizen domain of central Japan is being made the theme of joint study by members of the University of Michigan Center for Japanese Studies.

[18] Delmer M. Brown "The Impact of Firearms on Japanese Warfare, 1543–98," *FEQ*, 8 (May 1948), 236–253.

[19] Edwin O. Reischauer, *Japan Past and Present* (2nd ed., New York: Knopf, 1952), 77.

174

blocks of control by the more powerful of these feudal lords. Although much fighting remained to be done, the contours of daimyo control had been established and the basis was laid for the movement towards "national unification."

The story of Japan's political unification in the last years of the sixteenth century is well known. Beginning with the formation of regional alliances among daimyo, it progressed under the leadership of the "three unifiers," Oda Nobunaga, Toyotomi Hideyoshi, and Tokugawa Ieyasu. By 1603 a national hegemony had been effected by the ascendancy of a new shogunal power able to reduce the competing daimyo to vassalage. The resultant political structure, referred to as the *baku-han* system by Japanese historians,[20] was a curious blend of centralization and local feudal autonomy. In it direct shogunal authority extended from the powerful Kantō base of the Tokugawa house to include much of central Japan and most of the buffer zones, while the daimyo proper, though acknowledging their obligations of vassalage and subservience to the basic laws of the land, retained a generous amount of independence in local affairs.

The completion of this daimyo-based centralized feudalism had a profound effect upon the subsequent character of Japanese society, particularly upon its urban development. For the next three centuries all the cities of Japan were brought firmly under feudal control. Former religious centers or commercial and post station towns shared the common experience of incorporation into shogunal or daimyo territories. Those which survived as important cities saw the erection of huge castles in their confines or found themselves placed under the direct authority of feudal magistrates. Thus Kyoto, Sakai, and Nagasaki became nonmilitary cities within the shogun's territories. But the most numerous urban units of the time were the castle towns which made up the military and administrative headquarters of the shogun and daimyo.[21] Among these the vast majority were completely new cities occupying locations which, up to the time of their selection, supported little more than farming or fishing villages.[22] The erection

[20] For some recent analytical studies of the *baku-han* system see particularly: Itō Tasaburō, "Baku-han taisei" (The *baku-han* structure), *Shin Nihonshi kōza*, 11 (1947); and Imai Rintarōⁿ, "Baku-hansei no seiritsu" (The establishment of the *baku-han* system), *Nihon rekishi kōza*, 4 (1952), 103–121.

[21] Japanese interest in the castle town is indicated by the fact that the 1954 symposium of the Jimbunchiri Gakkai of Kyoto dealt with this subject. A mimeographed bibliography prepared for this symposium entitled *Jōkamachi kankei bunken mokuroku* (*A bibliography of materials on the castle town*) has been extremely helpful in the preparation of this article. Among the general works consulted on the subject the following have been found most useful: Ono Hitoshiⁿ, *Kinsei jōkamachi no kenkyū* (*A study of the modern castle town*) (Tokyo: Shibundō, 1928); Ono Terutsuguᵒ [Hitoshi], "Kinsei toshi no hattatsu" (The growth of the modern town), *Iwanami kōza, Nihon rekishi*, 11.4 (1934); Harada Tomohiko, "Toshi no hattatsu" (The growth of cities) in Tsuchiya Takaoᵖ, *Hōken shakai no kōzō bunseki* (*An analysis of the structure of feudal society*) (Tokyo: Keisō Shobō, 1950), 95–124; Toyoda Takeshi, *Nihon no hōken toshi* (*Feudal cities of Japan*) (Tokyo: Iwanami Shoten, 1952).

[22] Many of the so-called "new castles" were built on sites previously occupied by minor fortifications of one kind or another. But the fortresses built after 1575 were seldom dependent upon these earlier structures. In terms of size and conception they were literally new creations. The most familiar example is Edo which was converted from a small fortified outpost into the greatest fortress in Japan from 1590 to 1606.

of the castle towns of the late feudal period out of the undeveloped countryside required a tremendous outlay of resources on the part of the daimyo. The achievement was made all the more remarkable by the dramatic suddenness with which these operations were carried out. Most of the first-ranking castles and castle towns such as Himeji, Osaka, Kanazawa, Wakayama, Tokushima, Kōchi, Takamatsu, Hiroshima, Edo, Wakamatsu, Okayama, Kōfu, Fushimi, Takasaki, Sendai, Fukuoka, Fukui, Kumamoto, Tottori, Matsuyama, Hikone, Fukushima, Yonezawa, Shizuoka, and Nagoya were founded during the brief span of years between 1580 and 1610.[23] It would be hard to find a parallel period of urban construction in world history.

The castle town naturally derived its location and structural arrangement from the requirements laid down by the daimyo and the central shogunal authority, for the same forces which had given rise to the new combinations of feudal power gave shape to the castle towns. Thus as wider and wider domains were consolidated, the daimyo moved their headquarters from the narrow confines of mountain defenses to larger moat-and-tower fortresses placed at the strategic and economic centers of their holdings. In most instances the daimyo selected locations from which their castles could dominate the wide plains which formed the economic bases of their power and from which they could control the lines of communication stretching into the countryside. Here the daimyo was able to assemble and support his growing corps of officers and foot soldiers. In almost every instance the final establishment of the daimyo's castle town headquarters was preceded by the erection of less spacious establishments which were abandoned as the daimyo increased in power and stature. Oda Nobunaga's progress from Gifu to Azuchi and his subsequent attempt to acquire Osaka as his headquarters is merely the best known of such moves.[24]

The new *jōkamachi* symbolized first of all the new concentrations of military power achieved by the daimyo. In the domains, defenses formerly scattered in depth were now pulled back to single central citadels where the massed resources of the daimyo could be held in readiness and where protective walls could be thrown up at sufficient distance from the vital nerve centers of military operations to protect them from musket and cannon. The shogunal edict of 1615 which ordered the destruction of all but one castle in each province was merely the culmination of a lengthy process of consolidation in which the functions of many

[23] This list includes the major castles built or rebuilt in new style between these years. The order is chronological according to the dates on which construction was begun. Data is taken from Ōrui Noboru[q] and Toba Masao[r], *Nihon jōkakushi* (*History of Japanese castles*) (Tokyo: Yūzankaku, 1936), 528–533; and Toyoda, *Nihon no hōken toshi*, 89–90.

[24] Imai Toshiki[s], *Toshi hattatsushi kenkyū* (*Studies in the history of urban development*) (Tokyo: Tōkyō Daigaku Shuppambu, 1951), 206. In establishing the castle town of Sendai in 1591, the Date daimyo abandoned a former site at Yonezawa which was too far removed from the center of domain communication and too circumscribed in space. Yonezawa had a population of about 6,000. Sendai attained a population of over 60,000 within a generation after the erection of the new castle. Sendai Shishi Hensan Iinkai[t], *Sendai no rekishi* (*The history of Sendai*) (Sendai: Sendai Shiyakusho, 1949), 23–28.

Castle Town and Modern Urbanization

smaller installations were combined into a limited number of oversize estab-lishments.[25] In the province of Bizen, to take a typical example of an area which eventually came under the control of a single daimyo, there were at times during the fifteenth century between twenty and thirty castles. Yet by the time of the 1615 order only four remained. Of these, the lesser three were destroyed, leaving Okayama, which commanded the entire Bizen plain, as the headquarters of the daimyo of Bizen.[26] The citadels which resulted from this process were huge by any standards of their day. It is probably no exaggeration to say that the greatest of the Japanese fortresses, Edo and Osaka, had no peers in terms of size and impregnability.[27] For Japan, no clearer indication was needed of the ascendancy of feudal military might than these castles which at regular intervals towered over the Japanese countryside.

Intimately associated with the construction of the new consolidated fortresses of the late sixteenth century were a number of major changes in the structure of feudal society. In the first place the elimination of the numerous smaller castles had resulted in the decline and eventual elimination of numerous petty baronies scattered throughout the shogunal and daimyo territories. Within the new do-mains the daimyo became increasingly absolute as they consciously diminished the independence of their vassals. For this reason, and as a result of new military and tactical requirements, it became the policy of the daimyo to draw their vassals and retainers, both high and low, more and more into residence within the confines of the central citadel. The pattern made familiar by the enforced residence of daimyo in the environs of the shogun's castle at Edo had already become established practice at the daimyo level.[28] The citadel thus of necessity became a town.

This physical displacement of the feudal class from countryside to castled towns held even more fundamental social implications. As the petty lords and feudal gentry left the land and congregated at the center of daimyo authority, a new line of distinction was drawn between the cultivators, those remaining on the land, and the feudal aristocracy, those members of the daimyo's retinue gathered at his castle headquarters. The process was not sudden, but continuous over several decades. It was most dramatically brought out by Hideyoshi's nationwide land resurvey begun in 1582, and the "sword hunt" of 1588. There-after the privilege of wearing two swords had become the badge of social distinc-tion which gave to its possessor life and death power over the subject classes. By the end of the sixteenth century the castle and its attached feudal military elite had become a distinct unit and the chief reason for the existence of large

---

[25] Takayanagi Mitsutoshi[u], "Genna ikkoku ichijō rei" (The Genna law restricting one castle to a province), *Shigaku zasshi*, 33.11 (1922), 863–888.

[26] Okayama Shiyakusho[v], *Okayama shishi* (*History of Okayama*) (Okayama: Gōdō Shim-bunsha, 1937), 3:2042.

[27] For detailed descriptions of these and other Japanese castles see Ōrui and Toba; and Furukawa Shigeharu[w], *Nihon jōkakukō* (*A study of Japanese castles*) (Tokyo: Kojinsha, 1936).

[28] The Sendai domain maintained a system of alternate residence between castle town and fief for the major fief-holding vassals. Sendai Shishi Hensan Iinkai, 28–29.

concentrations of people in the years to follow. The *jōkamachi*, at first fundamentally garrison towns, had become the home of an entire class, the *bushi* or samurai. The castle towns thus individually and collectively became the physical embodiment of the Tokugawa feudal elite. Edo, the shogun's capital, symbolized the hierarchal unity of the daimyo under the Tokugawa house, as the several daimyo built residences in the shadow of the castle and proceeded on a regular basis to pay yearly homage to the supreme feudal authority. The daimyo's castle towns were but miniatures of this pattern. The morphology of the castle town was in essence a cross-section of the pattern of Japanese feudal society. The castle town was built by and for the daimyo and his vassals.[29] The castles, which occupied the center of these cities, were built to protect the aristocracy. No outer wall enclosed the whole community as in Europe, although outer moats were not infrequent. Around the central keep lay the residences of the daimyo's vassals, generally in two zones. The higher officials were placed in a group closely strung around the keep within the security of the main rampart and inner moat. A second belt, farther removed, lay unprotected except perhaps by the outer single moat and sometimes an earthen barricade. Here were the quarters of the lesser vassals. Between the two groups of vassals resided the daimyo's privileged merchants and artisans, while at the edge of the outer belt lay a ring of temples and shrines whose substantial buildings provided a sort of outer cordon of defense points controlling the major roads and points of access to the city. In such a community the lines of feudal hierarchy were clearly drawn and strictly maintained.

One of the most distinctive features of the castle town was the large number of samurai resident in it. On the average they accounted for approximately fifty per cent of the town's entire population. But the figure was frequently greater; for instance, in Sendai it was near seventy per cent and in Kagoshima it was over eighty per cent.[30] What this meant in total numbers of samurai and family members will be evident from a few examples. In Okayama, a city of slightly over 38,000 inhabitants in 1707, 10,000 were of the samurai class, another 8,000 were hangers-on of one kind or another. The census of 1872 for the city of Sendai listed 29,000 inhabitants of a total of 50,000 in the samurai class. In Tottori, a city of approximately 35,000 in 1810, 25,000 were of this category.[31]

The *jōkamachi* were built first and foremost as garrison towns and military headquarters of their domains. But they rapidly became points of concentration

---

[29] On the morphology of *jōkamachi* the following specialized studies have been found most useful: Obata Akira[z], "Kyū jōkamachi keikan" (A view of former castle towns), *Chiri ronsō*, 7 (1935), 31–76; and Nago Masanori[y], "Okazaki jōkamachi no rekishichiri teki kenkyū" (A study of the castle town of Okazaki from the point of view of historical geography), *Rekishigaku kenkyū*, 8.7 (July, 1938), 71–103.

[30] Harada, *Toshi no hattatsu*, 107; Sekiyama Naotarō[z], *Kinsei Nihon jinkō no kenkyū* (*A study of Japanese demography for the early modern period*) (Tokyo: Ryūginsha, 1948), 235; Toyoda, *Nihon no hōken toshi*, 147–154.

[31] Toyoda, *Nihon no hōken toshi*, 148–154; Sendai Shishi Hensan Iinkai, 156–157; Kanai Madoka[aa], "Hitotsu no han no sōjinkō" (On the total population of one *han* [Okayama]), *Nippon rekishi*, 67.12 (Dec. 1953), 38–39.

for many other functions important to the feudal rulers of the day. Thus as civil war gave way to a new political unity, the daimyo's headquarters became increasingly concerned with matters of local administration. It has been pointed out that one of the outstanding features of Tokugawa feudal administration was its "public character," in which a regular bureaucracy managed the affairs of taxation, judicature and maintenance of law and order.[32] This public bureaucracy was eventually achieved by the conversion of an essentially military hierarchy of officers and men, which constituted the daimyo's corps of vassals and retainers, into an administrative officialdom.[33] The great castles of Japan came to house the central and local administrative headquarters of the nation. From them political authority radiated outward into the countryside.

The castle towns also quickly assumed importance as points of economic accumulation and consumption. The degree of economic concentration achieved in the *jōkamachi* is perhaps best understood in terms of the tremendous outlay of manpower and material required to construct the fortress and its accompanying residences and temples. The castle town symbolized from the first the ability of the daimyo to draw from his domain vast productive resources and to recruit the services of numerous commercial and industrial agents. Once having accomplished the initial task of castle construction, moreover, the need for economic concentration did not disappear. The daimyo and their vassals, having taken up permanent residence in the new towns, became dependent upon their commercial agents who could supply the sinews of warfare and the necessities of daily living, agents able to bridge the gap between town and countryside. The feudal aristocracy of the Tokugawa era, living in cities at a level of subsistence and consumption far above that of the meager self-sufficiency of the village, was made increasingly dependent upon the services of a merchant class.

Thus the same movement which brought the samurai to the castle headquarters of the daimyo also brought merchants out of the older port or religious cities and scattered trading towns. The result was a radical rearrangement of commercial activity in Japan. Daimyo, eager to attract to their castles the services of merchants and artisans, offered liberal conditions to those who would join them. The old guild system of medieval Japan was broken down as merchants took advantage of "free" markets provided in the castle towns. Thus as the daimyo rose to power the older centers of trade declined and new communities, surrounding the new castles, began to flourish.[34]

This process, whereby the merchant community of the sixteenth century became increasingly attached to centers of feudal authority, has generally been described as coercive. It would be hard to deny the coercive aspects of the measures taken by the great centralizers such as Nobunaga and Hideyoshi as they clamped

---

[32] K. Asakawa, *The Documents of Iriki* (New Haven: Yale University Press, 1929), 46.

[33] On the shogunal bureaucracy see John W. Hall, *Tanuma Okitsugu, Forerunner of Modern Japan* (Cambridge, Mass.: Harvard University Press, 1955), 21–33. On the administration of the Bizen (Okayama) domain see Okayama Shiyakusho, 3:2135–2312.

[34] Toyoda Takeshi, "Shokuhō seiken no seiritsu" (The establishment of the political power of Oda Nobunaga and Toyotomi Hideyoshi), *Shisō*, 310 (1950), 237–247.

restrictions upon the merchants of Sakai or Hakata. But for most of Japan coercion was not the key factor. In the less economically advanced areas the daimyo provided local merchants and artisans with new and attractive opportunities. Under the stimulus of the insatiable demands for military supplies and food stores made by the warring feudal lords there came into being a new and more aggressive service class, many of whose members were actually drawn from the warrior class.[35] By allying itself with the rising feudal aristocracy, this new class of merchants was able to break the restraints of the medieval guild system and meet the daimyo's needs for an expanding economy. In the early years of their ascendancy the daimyo counted their commercial agents among their most valuable resources. It was even customary for a daimyo to take his merchant adherents with him when he moved the location of his headquarters.[36] Thus as the castle towns took shape, they became the economic centers of their domains. In them were concentrated the service groups which in turn acted as exploitive agents for the daimyo and *bushi*. In the *jōkamachi* the other half of the population consisted of merchants, artisans, and service personnel. These were the *chōnin* of Tokugawa times.

In both the shogunal territories and daimyo domains, castle town merchants had the advantage of patronage and protection. Within the domain, the daimyo drew a sharp line between castle town merchants and the residents of the countryside. Commerce was strictly limited to the central city and, under special circumstances, to the few towns which had functioned as urban centers before the emergence of the daimyo.[37] The villages were confined to agricultural and handicraft production. Within the domain the castle town merchants performed two prime tasks: the wholesale accumulation of produce from the hinterland, and the linkage of the domain economy to the national market. The first function gave rise to monopoly associations under daimyo patronage. The second brought into existence the class of rice merchants and domain financiers who maintained the produce warehouses at Osaka or other exchange centers. The desire of every daimyo to make his domain self-sufficient and prosperous was a constant stimulus to the castle town merchants.

As with the *bushi*, disposition within the castle town revealed graphically the relative status of the *chōnin* within the community.[38] In such towns the early commercial settlers, those first to enter the daimyo's service, constituted a privileged group. Among them the daimyo's chartered merchants, the *goyō shōnin*, enjoyed a degree of tax exemption and social advantages which belied the low status eventually assigned to the merchants as a class. For the sake of convenience and protection these groups were located in the belt between the two main zones of samurai residences. Late arrivals were obliged to take up

---

[35] Matsuyama, 20.

[36] Yamori Kazuhiko[ab], "*Jōkamachi no jinkō kōsei*" (On the demographic structure of a castle town), *Shirin*, 37.2 (Apr. 1954), 180–181.

[37] Ono Hitoshi, 232–280.

[38] Yamori, 181; Toyoda, *Nihon no hōken toshi*, 188–204; Sendai Shishi Hensan Iinkai, 35–38; Nagao, 75.

positions on the outskirts, along the main roads leading to and from the town. It is sometimes maintained by Japanese historians that the Tokugawa period merchants lived under a system of local self-government. But the self-government they enjoyed consisted of little more than the privilege of managing certain private areas of their activity under their own headmen. In fact it is hardly possible to distinguish any fundamental difference between the procedures utilized by the Tokugawa rulers in their administration of the village and of the town.

From their castles most daimyo divided their realms into two distinct parts, the villages (*mura*) and the city blocks (*machi*). The same sort of control mechanism was used to govern both parts. Within the city, each block was supplied with guards and gates which converted it into a separate administrative unit. Each block like its counterpart, a village, was responsible for its own good conduct under its own representatives, whose titles of office often corresponded to those used in the villages. Individual citizens were made subordinate to the laws of the daimyo and shogun under the system of joint responsibility, the *gon'ngumi*. The merchant community as a whole was managed by its own headman or headmen who performed their duties under the scrutiny of the shogunal or domain magistrates. In Tokugawa Japan all cities were administered ultimately by the city magistrate (*machi bugyō*) placed there by either shogun or daimyo.

It was inevitable, perhaps, that as the feudal authorities perfected their administrative machinery, the *chōnin* were brought under an increasingly heavy burden of legal responsibilities and social restrictions. Relegated increasingly to a low status as the Tokugawa adopted the concepts of Confucian social theory, the *chōnin* found almost every aspect of urban life and commercial activity placed under the scrutiny and regulation of the administrative class. Thus the merchant community passed from an early period of relative freedom to one of increasing regimentation. The protected location in the shelter of the castle turned into a prison. And even foreign trade, which might have offered an escape from feudal oppression, became a shogunal monopoly. Yet it must be remembered that there was always a limit to such oppression. In the final analysis, daimyo and shogunal policy towards the merchants was tempered by the degree to which the feudal class had become dependent upon their services. After the mid-seventeenth-century merchants were permitted to organize themselves into new guilds and protective associations. In this way, the Tokugawa merchants, though deprived of foreign markets, continued to prosper as the middlemen between castle town and countryside.[39]

A final aspect of the centralization achieved by the daimyo in their castle towns was attained at the expense of local religious institutions. The story of Nobunaga's dramatic conquest of the Buddhist church in Japan is well known. Less familiar is the history of the clash of ecclesiastical and feudal interests at the level of the local domain. Yet for the daimyo, the conquest over hostile religious bodies in his locality was also a prerequisite for secure possession of the

[39] John W. Hall "The Tokugawa Bakufu and the Merchant Class," *Occasional Papers, Center For Japanese Studies*, 1 (1951), 26–33.

J. W. Hall

domain. In each locality, as formerly independent religious centers were brought under daimyo control, we find the local headquarters of Buddhist and Shinto sects being moved to the castle town.[40] There the priests came under the direct patronage and surveillance of the daimyo and his magistrate of religious bodies. Even the location of religious buildings was frequently a matter of decision based on the strategic needs of the daimyo. In its growth the castle town became the focal point of the domain's religious institutions.

But of even greater importance in focusing religious sentiment upon the castle town was the adoption of the tenets of Confucianism, under which the shogun and daimyo became the divinely ordained rulers of the people.[41] By weakening the hold of Buddhism over the minds of their subjects and by emphasizing the spiritual foundations of loyalty to the feudal authorities, the new rulers of Japan were able to achieve a new degree of popular support and solidarity within their domains. The feudal lords of the Tokugawa period, supported by their Confucian advisors and all the pageantry of aristocratic life, were able to exalt themselves in the eyes of their subjects. The cities in which they maintained their castled residences became in essence local capitals for the populace of the domain.

These, in profile, were the castle towns which sprang up with such vitality during the late sixteenth century to become the major cities of the Tokugawa period. Created by the newly ascendant feudal leaders in the course of their militant march to local and national unification, the jōkamachi were a unique institutional product of the new political and social organization consummated under the baku-han system. In terms of their total numbers, the jōkamachi were not necessarily more numerous than other types of towns and cities of the Tokugawa period.[42] The commercial communities which continued to serve the major monasteries or which grew up around the ports and post-stations of the internal transportation network were far more prevalent. But most such communities were small and still largely rural in their orientation. In the final analysis all such towns were held under administrative and economic controls which emanated from the nearby castle town.

The supremacy of the jōkamachi in Tokugawa times is best demonstrated by a review of the size and number of those which attained a population of over 10,000. Admittedly, population data for the Tokugawa period are of uncertain accuracy. For one thing census figures, though assiduously kept, seldom listed the samurai population. Thus an exact population list is hardly attainable. Besides the incomplete statistics which do exist, however, students of Tokugawa population figures have suggested a rough rule of thumb to aid in gaining a general picture of the size of jōkamachi. Under this formula the inhabitants of castle towns would generally number somewhat more than ten per cent of the

---

[40] Sendai Shishi Hensan Iinkai, 25.

[41] A classical statement of this concept is found in Kumazawa Banzan's *Daigaku wakumon*: "The lord of a province is appointed by Heaven to be the father and mother of that province." Quoted in Galen M. Fisher, "Kumazawa Banzan, His Life and Ideals," *TASJ*, 2nd Ser., 14 (1938), 267.

[42] Maps of the Tokugawa period record between 148 and 164 active castles. R. B. Hall, 184. Orui and Toba list 186 castles at the end of the Tokugawa period (pp. 694–705).

total population of the domain, which in turn was roughly equivalent to the assessed size in *koku* of the domain.[43] Thus it would take a *han* of 100,000 *koku* assessment, of which there were just under fifty, to support a town of 10,000 inhabitants. A conservative estimate would place between thirty and forty castle towns, each the center of an extensive agricultural region, in the 10,000-or-more class.[44] And this should be compared with the ten or so cities of non-castle origin which had population of the same size.[45]

The above population figures do not, of course, apply to the early years of the Tokugawa period when the castles were still in construction and the city inhabitants not fully assembled. But under the peaceful conditions which followed the cessation of civil warfare, Japan's economy expanded rapidly, and with it her feudal cities. By 1700 most cities had reached their maximum growth. The pattern of Tokugawa urban development had fully matured. Edo was approaching the one-million mark. Osaka and Kyoto stood at around 300,000. Kanazawa and Nagoya had populations of nearly 100,000. Perhaps ten per cent of Japan's population lived in cities of over 10,000 inhabitants. The city had become a major factor in Japanese life, in the government and economy, and in the formation of popular cultural and intellectual attitudes. In this respect the continued dominance of the castle town among the cities of Tokugawa Japan was to become increasingly significant. In the years after 1700 the pattern of urbanization created by the feudal aristocracy was to place a deepening imprint upon the evolution of Japanese urban society.

First of all we must acknowledge the continuing effects of the strong centralized feudal authority symbolized by the castles. The *jōkamachi* were, as we have noted, primarily garrison towns, the loci of shogunal and daimyo military power. They were secondarily administrative centers, seats of feudal political authority. The high percentage of aristocracy—of military and official personnel—resident in the castle towns was a constant indication of the degree to which government served the interests of the elite and impinged upon the lives of its subjects. Yet, while in many ways the ascendancy of feudal authority must be looked upon as a stifling and restrictive influence, this is not the whole story. The city-centered local administrations established by the daimyo represented important advances in the technique of local administration. Life in Tokugawa Japan became infinitely more regularized and subject to written law than under earlier feudal regimes, and this in turn was a step in the direction of more modern public administration.[46]

This standardization of governmental procedures and policies had yet another

[43] Sekiyama, 100–106; Toyoda, *Nihon no hōken toshi*, 146–152.

[44] With the promulgation of the new law of local administration in 1888, 39 legal cities (*shi*) were created. Of these 33 were former *jōkamachi*.

[45] Sekiyama, 232–233. In the above calculations the cities of Kyoto and Fushimi have been listed as administrative towns.

[46] For a study of local administration based on materials in the archives of the former Bizen (Okayama) daimyo see John W. Hall, "Tokugawa Local Government and Its Contributions to the Modern Japanese State," Paper read at the annual meeting of the Far Eastern Association, 1953.

important effect upon Japanese society. The establishment of domain capitals became a powerful force in bringing about a uniform cultural and economic development throughout Japan. It was characteristic of the *jōkamachi* that their size depended not upon their proximity to the more developed core region of Japan but upon the size of the domain. Kagoshima, Kanazawa, and Akita, cities on the fringe, were in the same relation to the size of their domains as Nagoya or Hiroshima. No doubt a certain provincialism was inevitable in a feudal society such as that of Tokugawa Japan. But we find that throughout the nation the castle cities took on a remarkable uniform guise as the necessities of alternate attendance of the daimyo and their retinues at Edo circulated the ideas and practices of the center to the periphery, and as the enforced trade through Osaka and Edo knit the merchants of the realm more closely together.[47]

But the elements of systemization and uniformity were not the only significant products of the urbanization which occurred under feudal stimulus. The factor of urban growth itself was to have far-reaching influence upon the various levels of Japanese society. Eventually it was to call into question the very ability of the feudal authorities to maintain their existence. The city, its life and its institutions, was in reality basically antagonistic to the type of land-centered military regime envisaged by the Tokugawa authorities. The urban environment, from its inception, was destined to have a contradictory effect upon the feudal class. With respect to the daimyo this became evident as they succumbed to the amenities of a life of ease in their castle towns and in the great metropolis of Edo. Certainly it was hard to recognize in the daimyo who gave up their domains to the Meiji government in 1869 the descendants of the hardy warlords of the late sixteenth century. As for the *bushi*, the establishment of castle towns served to complete their final separation from the land. In the cities the gentry warriors of the earlier days became increasingly removed from the actualities of the countryside both in their way of life and in their legal relationship to the land. By the eighteenth century, except for a few locations, the *bushi* had been stripped of any direct jurisdiction over their fiefs by the expanding power of the daimyo.[48] Though as a class they nostalgically clung to the concept that they were a landed aristocracy, they had been converted, in reality, to little more than salaried officials of the daimyo. As their bureaucratic functions multiplied, their security became increasingly identified, not with the land, but with governmental service. Separated from the duties of actual land management, they became a thoroughly urbanized group living increasingly in sedentary style.

The assembling of the daimyo's vassals in the castle towns reflected yet another condition which was to have a depressive effect upon the morale of the *bushi* class. As peace and prosperity permeated the Japanese islands, as the settled life of the cities took the place of the more rugged life of the country, the military

---

[47] Even in 19th century Europe few cities other than national capitals rose to over 100,000 population. The evenness of Japan's urban growth was thus remarkable. Imai Toshiki, 208.

[48] Kanai Madoka " 'Dokai kōshūki' ni okeru baku-han taisei no ichi hyōgen" (A view of the *baku-han* system as seen in the "Dokai kōshūki"), *Shinano*, 3.6 (June 1951), 37–47.

services of the *bushi* became increasingly superfluous. Large numbers of urbanized *bushi* were obliged to maintain themselves in mock military readiness. The shogunal and domain bureaucracies were overstaffed manyfold as peacetime occupations were provided for a class whose numbers had been determined by the necessities of civil warfare on a grand scale. The result for many was a life of hypocrisy and indolence. For the country as a whole it brought into being the curse of *"yakuninerie,"* as one observer so colorfully described Japan's particular brand of over-bureaucratization.[49]

The economic hardships faced by the populous feudal class of Japan as it was obliged to maintain itself on fixed land incomes in the face of the mounting costs of urban life have been amply dealt with in Western literature.[50] We need observe here only that these difficulties and the counter-efforts made by the authorities, whether in the nature of establishing new domain-sponsored commercial monopolies or of providing household handicraft opportunities for the distressed samurai, had the net effect of driving the *bushi* towards a more commercialized existence and of undermining the traditional way of life of the feudal aristocracy.

The story of the spread of money economy and the remarkable growth in commercial and craft activities which occurred during the Tokugawa period is also well known and requires no elaboration here. Few aspects of Tokugawa society were to remain unaffected by the rise in wealth and numbers of the *chōnin* communities in the feudal cities. Yet the fact that throughout these years the strength of feudal authority remained high forced upon the Japanese merchant a political passivity not generally seen in the West. Certainly it is undeniable that the urban commercial segment in Japan failed to become, at least by European standards, a significant antifeudal force. If anything, the leading merchants became, as time went on, more strongly allied with the feudal order, more dependent upon feudal privilege, and hence less inclined to oppose the dominant political order.[51]

But if the Tokugawa merchant did not awaken to his possibilities of revolutionary leadership, the indirect effects of his enterprising commercial activities were great. In each locality the castle city with its core of merchants constituted a powerful stimulus to the economic development of the countryside, encouraging the spread of commercial agriculture and handicraft production. As commercial production interfered with land economy or was substituted for it, as trade became an alternative to agriculture, the feudal economic order was weakened. By the end of the Tokugawa period signs of fundamental change were beginning to appear in the structure of the Japanese urban economy. Within the administrative cities the machinery of feudal control began to weaken. Within the do-

---

[49] William Elliot Griffis, *The Mikado's Empire* (New York: Harper and Brothers, 1906), 2:526, rejoicing at the changes which followed the abolition of the Fukui *han* wrote: "The local officials of Fukui are to be reduced from *five hundred to seventy*. The incubus of *yakuninerie* is being thrown off. Japan's greatest curse for ages has been an excess of officials and lazy rice-eaters who do not work."

[50] Takizawa Matsuyo, *The Penetration of Money Economy in Japan and Its Effects Upon Social and Political Institutions* (New York: Columbia University Press, 1927).

[51] J. W. Hall, "The Tokugawa Bakufu," 28–32.

mains new towns of primarily economic importance began to compete with the privileged merchants of the castle towns.[52]

Nor can we overlook the importance of the many cultural and intellectual innovations which accompanied the establishment of the *chōnin* communities of the Tokugawa period. The bourgeois culture, particularly of the three great cities of Edo, Osaka and Kyoto,[53] became increasingly self-contained and sophisticated. In the art and literature of the *chōnin* and in the development of practical sciences and "Western learning," it was possible to discern the first stages of intellectual revolt against the feudal order and the Confucian system of thought. Such developments, moreover, were to carry an impact beyond the confines of the *chōnin* class. The *jōkamachi*, by bringing the *bushi* and *chōnin* into close proximity, eventually provided the basis for a fusion of interest between merchant and samurai. It was in this zone of fusion that the origins of the modern Japanese bourgeoisie were to be found.

Perhaps the fundamental reason why the feudal cities of Japan did not play a more clear-cut role of political leadership is to be found in their structure. Combining, as they did, military, administrative, economic, and religious functions, they did not represent a single unified social group or aspiration. Yet by the end of the Tokugawa period such a unity of aspiration was being forged under the pressure of political crisis and economic distress. The city had become a point of maximum concentration for those many tensions which were eventually to break the bonds of feudalism in Japan. By the mid-nineteenth century, the feudal city had reached an obvious impasse, a limit in its ability to develop under the conditions imposed upon it by the Tokugawa regime. Bound by the rigid political, social, and economic doctrines of the daimyo system, limited by the technology of transportation, manufacture, and finance, the Japanese castle city was in unhealthy decline. The daimyo were in debt, the samurai ill-fed, the city poor in rebellious spirit. The ties between city and countryside were dangerously strained. Decay was everywhere visible.[54] Yet it was in the depths of such decay that Japan's new leadership was stirring. In the zone of fusion of interest and outlook between the merchant and samurai resentment against the Tokugawa regime was mounting.

The revolution of the Meiji era brought in its wake political and economic changes of greatest consequence. The conditions which supported urban populations changed almost overnight. With the abolition of the shogunal and daimyo systems and the establishment of universal conscription, the large concentrations of *bushi* in remote areas ceased to be a necessity. With the abolition of the *han* and the opening of the entire nation to free economic development, with the creation of new ports of foreign trade, Japan's economic centers shifted rapidly.

[52] Ono Hitoshi, 281–298, describes the growing competition which rural towns presented to the central castle towns towards the end of the Tokugawa period.

[53] For a recent and novel approach to this subject see Ishida Ichirō[ac], "Kinsei bunka no tenkai" (The development of early modern culture), *Shin Nihonshi taikei*, Vol. 4: *Kinsei shakai* (Tokyo: Asakura Shoten, 1952), 308–415, esp. 410–415.

[54] Griffis (p. 430) describes his first impression of Fukui in 1871 as follows: "I was amazed at the utter poverty of the people, the contemptible houses, and the tumble-down look of the city. . ."

Castle Town and Modern Urbanization

In this era of sudden change the Tokugawa city and the institutions it had fostered played a noteworthy role.

Fundamental to the remarkable flexibility demonstrated by Japanese society in the transition period was the fact that in the castle towns the feudal ruling class had been largely removed from the land. Thus it was assured that there could be no politically powerful landed class remaining after the abolition of the daimyo. The *bushi* did not constitute an entrenched land-based gentry as in China, able to back up their interests in the face of modern change.[55] Without an economic base, the resentment they felt toward the reforms which deprived them of their feudal privileges was soon dissipated. Instead, they were forced to ride with the times, to join the new government or to seek security in the new economic opportunities which were offered them. They became the backbone of Japan's modern civil, military, and police bureaucracy, of her industrial management and labor force, and of her modern urban intelligentsia. In other words, they were a leaven for change rather than an obstacle.

Released from the inertia of social conservatism which a landed gentry might have provided, Japan after the Restoration moved swiftly in the direction of modern reform. In this process the castle city of Tokugawa times represented both an element of continuity with the past and a point of departure for far-reaching changes. In the first instance the *jōkamachi*, seats of feudal power, remained in modern Japan the local centers of national authority. Edo, the capital of the Tokugawa shogun, renamed Tokyo, was to remain the capital of new Japan. Today thirty-four of the forty-six prefectural capitals were *jōkamachi* in Tokugawa times, and in most instances the modern prefectures have taken the names of their capital cities rather than the old domain or provincial names.[56] Throughout Japan prefectural capitals still constitute the major cultural and educational centers of their locales. Here are concentrated the schools, hospitals, newspapers and radio stations. Before the War many of them also acted as divisional military headquarters. Thus the castles which dominated the cities of Tokugawa Japan continued to stand as symbols of strong centralized bureaucratic power in the modern Japanese state.

But the great cities of Tokugawa Japan were also to lead in the process of adjustment to the new economic requirements of the modern state. From the economic point of view not all of the major *jōkamachi* were able to shape their own destinies. After the Restoration certain areas, notably along the line running through the center of Japan from Tokyo to Fukuoka, developed almost to the exclusion of the rest of the country. As Japan's modern transportation system took shape, areas rose or fell in economic importance as they were serviced or bypassed by railroads or shipping lines. Thus those castle towns on the Japan Sea or in the extreme north tended to make a slower adjustment to

---

[55] I do not ignore the fact that in some *han* the *bushi* still retained their landholdings or that in the late Tokugawa and early Meiji periods a considerable number of *bushi* were "returned" to the land.

[56] Tōkyō Shisei Chōsakai[ad], *Nihon toshi nenkan* (Japan municipal yearbook) (Tokyo, 1952); Orui and Toba, 694–705.

modern conditions.[57] When given the chance, however, the *jōkamachi* demonstrated that they were in possession of the requirements necessary for modern commercial and industrial expansion. Situated at the major communication nodes, located on large rivers or close to the sea, in possession of land capable of cheap reclamation for industrial use, and linked to a large hinterland already closely tied to the city, the chief castle towns of the Tokugawa period made the transition to modern times to stand among the major urban centers of the new era. Today, more than one hundred years after the opening of Japan to the West, half of the sixty cities of over 100,000 population are former *jōkamachi*.[58]

a 永島福太郎	*l* 伊東多三郎	*v* 岡山市役所
b 松山宏	*m* 今井林太郎	*w* 古川重春
c 村山修一	*n* 小野均	*x* 小葉田亮
d 遠藤元男	*o* 小野晃嗣	*y* 長尾正憲
e 原田伴彦	*p* 土屋喬雄	*z* 關山直太郎
f 豐田武	*q* 大類伸	*aa* 金井圓
g 西田直二郎	*r* 鳥羽正雄	*ab* 矢守一彦
h 坂田吉雄	*s* 今井登志喜	*ac* 石田一良
i 中村吉治	*t* 仙臺市史編纂委員會	*ad* 東京市政調査會
j 永原慶二	*u* 高柳光壽	*ae* 伊藤郷平
k 杉山博		

---

[57] Itō Gōhei[ae], "Toshi no tatechi narabini hattatsu to chiri teki seiyakusei" (On the geographic conditions which influenced the founding and development of cities), *Toshi mondai*, 32.3 (Mar. 1941), 1–16.

[58] *Nihon toshi nenkan*; Orui and Toba, 694–705.

CHAPTER ELEVEN

CHANGES IN JAPANESE COMMERCE IN THE TOKUGAWA PERIOD

E. S. CRAWCOUR

Reprinted from *Journal of Asian Studies,*
Vol. XXII, No. 4 (August 1963)

THE development of commerce and the rise of a merchant class in Tokugawa Japan have deservedly received considerable attention from both Japanese and Western scholars. In Japan that interest would seem to have been prompted by the problem of the rôle of the pre-Restoration merchant class in the development of the modern capitalist Japanese economy. The study of this problem was characterized by a long controversy in which the Tokugawa merchants were depicted as either "progressive" or "feudalistic," depending on the historical philosophy of the participants. The argument was conducted at a high level of generality and on both sides within frameworks derived from the leading European (mainly German) schools of economic history. For some time neither side seems to have doubted the applicability of these frameworks to Japan's experience, but the controversy did eventually lead to valuable detailed studies of Tokugawa commerce and to attempts to interpret Japan's economic development in its own terms. Among the first to do this were the members of the so-called "Kyoto School" under Professor E. Honjō.

The early work of the Kyoto School, particularly that published in English, was itself on a very general plane, and in the light of subsequent factual studies now seems rather simplistic. One thinks in particular of its view of a monolithic merchant class first freeing itself from dependence on the feudal government, then consolidating its strength through internal organization and, after a bit of seesawing of the balance of power, gaining control of economic life. While the merchants were threatened (or should it be "re-inforced"?) by rural economic developments, they eventually created conditions under which feudal government became an anachronism. A fair statement of this view has been transmitted to English readers through C. D. Sheldon's *The Rise of the Merchant Class in Tokugawa Japan.*[1]

This interpretation has, however, tended to underemphasize the diversity within the merchant class and to attribute to the class as a whole characteristics and motives which would, at a less general level, be properly applicable only to particular groups and at particular periods. In Tokugawa political theory, all those who gained their livelihood through commerce were members of the same legal and social category. In practice, however, this vague theoretical community of interest was far outweighed by stratification along income or regional lines. The merchant class included not only the wealthy and economically powerful leaders of wholesale trade and the great financiers who held the purse strings of the feudal lords, but also the pedlars and small shopkeepers and the whole range between these extremes.

Much of the work for this study was done under the auspices of the Saionji Memorial Society.
[1] (New York: J. J. Augustin, 1958.)

E. S. Crawcour

But it is with changes over time that this article is primarily concerned, specifically with changes in the top echelons of the merchant ranks in response to changing economic and political conditions. Although the Tokugawa period is famous for its stability, it is only to be expected that considerable changes should have occurred between its opening at the end of the military struggles of the sixteenth century and its close with the restoration of imperial rule in 1868. We need only remind ourselves that this era coincides with a stretch of British history extending from the reign of Queen Elizabeth to that of Queen Victoria to see the appropriateness of Hall's phrase, "the changes behind the façade of seeming permanence in the Tokugawa polity." [2]

The daimyo of the "Warring Barons" period had sought to control commercial as well as other economic activity in the interests of their respective war efforts, and the development of free commercial communities had been choked off as obstructing rather than furthering their military ambitions. To prosper under a warring baron, a merchant had to be first and foremost a thoroughly reliable quartermaster. With the end of the "Warring Barons" period and the establishment of the system of a central shogunate and local daimiates known as the *bakuhan taisei* around the 1630's and '40's, these requirements changed substantially. The main economic concern of a daimyo was no longer how to provision an army, but how to raise enough cash to cover the heavy expenses which his new status involved. The old quartermasters were relegated to various odd jobs, while the daimyo turned for commercial services to a new group of Osaka merchants who were better able to provide such services as bulk storage and marketing of tax rice, and who were able to make available lines of credit when and where they were required. By the second half of the seventeenth century, these merchants had become a privileged group and were the undisputed leaders of the merchant community. They continued with remarkably little change in membership to occupy an important position until the *bakuhan taisei*, which was their *raison d'être,* collapsed in 1868.

With the rise of large centers of consumption, the growth of geographical specialization of production, and the development of national markets, this group of merchant financiers, although still the leaders of the banking system, failed to maintain its share of the country's commercial business. From about the start of the eighteenth century, wholesale interregional trade became important and was handled by a new group of merchants, the *tonya* or wholesale distributors. In many parts of eighteenth-century Japan, the growth of production was running ahead of the development of commercial facilities. The only alternative to a marketing system organized by the *han* government—a method rarely employed at this time—was to rely on substantial *tonya* from outside, usually from the three main cities of Osaka, Edo, and Kyoto, but often originating from such economically advanced provinces as Ise and Ōmi, and in any case having only an indirect connection with the Osaka banker/rice merchants. The *tonya* flourished throughout the eighteenth century, and by its end were generally incorporated into the official scheme of things as privileged groups. By this time, however, the development of commercial facilities in production centers was already catching up, and it proceeded rapidly in the first half of the nineteenth century. Despite official protection, the *tonya* who had once monopolized interregional trade were being increasingly bypassed. By 1841, the much-criticized but probably

---

[2] John W. Hall, *Japanese History—New Dimensions of Approach and Understanding*, Publication No. 34, Service Center for Teachers of History (Washington, 1961), p. 39.

realistic Mizuno Tadakuni appears to have decided that there was no point in continuing the association any longer. His inability to replace it with an alternative control mechanism at a time when potentially hostile *han* were successfully moving towards direct control of the economic activity of their fiefs proved fatal.

The following sections discuss four groups of merchants and relate their activities to Japanese development in general and to connections between government and commerce.

Privileged Merchants of the Early Tokugawa Period

In the *Sengoku* (Warring Barons) period, the requirements of the leading warlords for munitions, provisions, other commodities, and cash were far greater than could be supplied by the existing commercial facilities. The management of the commissariat was therefore entrusted to someone with the capital and experience to handle it. Takeda Shingen was supplied by a man called Sakata Gengo of Shinano, and Uesugi Kenshin by Kurata Gorozaemon of Echigo Funai and Arahamaya Sōgorō of Kashiwazaki. Oda Nobunaga employed the Itō family of Kiyosu.[3] These official merchant quartermasters, who were usually of samurai origin, were generally granted exemption from taxes and services, given monopoly rights to conduct certain kinds of trade or even all major trade within the baron's territory, and were often appointed as leaders and supervisors of the merchant community.

At the opening of the Tokugawa period, the leaders of Japanese commerce were all of this type. After it became clear in the 1630's that the *Sengoku* period was at an end, they lost their economic pre-eminence but retained their social prestige for a long time. In these early years the three great merchants [4] of Kyoto were Suminokura Ryōi, Gotō Mitsutsugu, and Chaya Shirojirō. All had been closely associated with Tokugawa Ieyasu during the campaigns that culminated in the battle of Sekigahara, and all were fully fledged samurai as well as merchants. Chaya had fought for Hideyoshi and Ieyasu under his family name of Nakajima Kiyonobu. In the same group were Kameya Einin (the former Kitasumi Hisamasa), Sueyoshi Magozaemon, Suetsugu Heizō, Hirano Tōjirō, and Yodoya Keian. All of the group held various licences and privileges, including licences to engage in foreign trade.[5] How these *Sengoku* merchant princes fared once the *Pax Tokugawa* became an established reality is best illustrated by following the careers of two or three of them.

Suminokura Ryōi [6] was born in 1553, the son of a successful doctor, and his family was closely associated with the leaders of the day. He was granted a licence for foreign trade by Hideyoshi and later by Ieyasu, who seems to have backed his trading ventures to Annam. In 1611 his son, Yoichi, presented silks and spices to Ieyasu through Gotō Shōzaburō (Mitsutsugu), and these may well have represented Ieyasu's share of the venture. The family continued to trade with Annam until 1634, amassing a huge fortune. From 1605 to 1611 Ryōi developed river navigation on the Hozu,

---

[3] Toyoda Takeshi, "Sengoku shokō no shōgyō tōsei" [Control of commerce by barons of the Sengoku period], *Rekishigaku Kenkyū*, XI (July–August 1941), 15–27.

[4] San Dai-chōja.

[5] Go-shuin. See Kawashima Motojirō, *Shuinsen Bōeki-shi* [History of Red Seal Ships Trade], 4th ed. (Osaka: Kōjinsha, 1942).

[6] His original family name was Yoshida. See the inscription on his tombstone composed by Hayashi Dōshun and given in Yamazaki Yoshishige, *Kairoku* [Records of the Sea], (Tokyo: Kokusho Kankōkai, 1915), p. 514. For his career in foreign trade see Kawashima, pp. 210–256.

Tenryū, Takase, and Fuji rivers and was in return granted certain navigation rights. A grandiose plan to lower the level of Lake Biwa by two or three feet by diverting the Uji River and so reclaim a large area of good rice-growing land apparently came to nothing. Ryōi died in 1614. His son Yoichi (Genshi) was an accomplished scholar who had performed distinguished service in the campaigns against Osaka. In the year after their conclusion, he was rewarded with the post of inspector of shipping on the Yodo River between Fushimi and Osaka, a post which carried the right to levy an inspection charge. With the end of foreign trade opportunities, the Suminokura income dwindled and the river and reclamation schemes must have consumed a good part of their wealth. Many of his contemporaries were ruined by similar grandiose schemes.[7] The family fortunes went steadily downhill, and they continually petitioned their old patrons, the Tokugawa, for an official position. Times had changed, however, and it was not until the end of the seventeenth century that they were given a small post which they did not keep long. By the late eighteenth century Suminokura, once one of the three millionaires of Kyoto, was described as "once a merchant, but now barely anything." [8]

The career of Chaya Shirojirō was similar. His ancestor had been lord of a castle in Owari Province and his father was a friend of the Ashikaga Shogun Yoshiteru. As Nakajima Kiyonobu, the first Shirojirō served Tokugawa Ieyasu when he was lord of Okazaki, and is said to have fought in fifty-three battles. He settled in Kyoto and was appointed official draper and general factotum to Ieyasu. He was offered the post of daikan of Moriyama in Ōmi Province but declined it, and instead was given a stipend of 200 koku. In 1591 he received a licence from Hideyoshi to engage in overseas trade, and like Suminokura he made a fortune out of the Annam trade. He died in 1596 and was succeeded by his son, Shirojirō the second, Kiyotada. He too maintained very close connections with Ieyasu, was his official draper, and was granted land in Kyoto and Edo. After Ieyasu's victory at Sekigahara, he was appointed head of all the merchants in the Kansai area, with particular jurisdiction over the business community of Kyoto. The family fortunes were now at their peak. With the prohibition of overseas trade they received a severe blow, but the family was able to make a fair profit from the Itowappu or silk-importing monopoly of which they were foundation members. The profits of this organization, however, declined and in 1655 it actually incurred a heavy loss. The monopoly was abolished the same year; although it was restored in 1685, profits again fell, and by the 1720's there was again a loss.[9] In 1700 the members of the Kyoto Itowappu were granted the privilege of minting iron coins to help them out of their financial difficulties, but they even managed to lose on this operation.[10] Chaya's other iron in the fire was also getting rather cold at about this time. By 1700 the official drapers had lost their raison d'être. The Shogunate could get better and cheaper service from the "professional" wholesalers who were by then flourishing in Edo and who got most of the government orders. Chaya and

[7] See E. S. Crawcour, "Some Observations on Merchants—a translation of Mitsui Takafusa's Chōnin Kōken Roku," Transactions of the Asiatic Society of Japan, VIII (December 1961), 55–56.

[8] Kanzawa Tokō, Okinagusa, Sect. 195 in Nihon Zuihitsu Taisei, Third series, XIII, 826.

[9] Nakada Yasunao, "Itowappu no hensen" [Changes in the Itowappu] in Itō Tazaburō, ed. Kokumin Seikatsu-shi kenkyū [Studies in the History of the Life of the People], II, Seikatsu to Shakai Keizai [Life and Social Economy] (Tokyo: Yoshikawa Kōbunkan, 1959) pp. 369–429.

[10] Sekiyama Naotarō, "Kyōto Itowappu nakama no chūsen jigyō" [The minting operations of the Kyoto Itowappu], Keizaishi Kenkyū, XIV (October 1955), 20–28.

his colleagues were reduced to a 10 per cent commission on special orders for ceremonial clothes for the Shogun's own use or to be given as official presents. Efforts to help them out involved a robbing-Peter-to-pay-Paul arrangement whereby the official drapers were given a share in the profits of the Itowappu. With the death of the Shogun Tsunayoshi, this too was eliminated and the austerity measures of his successor proved to be the final blow.[11]

Of the great merchants and overseas traders of the late *Sengoku* and early Tokugawa periods, Gotō Nuinosuke, once chief supplier and confidential ambassador of Ieyasu, suffered the same fate as Chaya. Gotō Shōzaburō[12] became master of the gold mint, an honourable but poorly paid position. An attempt to make use of the obvious opportunities to supplement the salary brought dismissal in 1810, but the family were government servants rather than merchants over a hundred years before that. Sueyoshi (Hirano) Kambei became a *daikan* and an official of the Fushimi silver mint. The family seems to have remained prosperous enough, but left the ranks of the merchant class.[13]

The decline of these carry-overs from the *Sengoku* period was due largely to the prohibition of foreign trade, but also to the changed political situation and the development of organized commercial facilities in the major cities, particularly in Osaka. With the end of the wars and the establishment of the *bakuhan taisei,* the commercial and financial requirements of the daimyo changed. By the 1650's most daimyo were dependent on the services of a new group of Osaka merchants. Outside of the major cities, however, commercial development was far less advanced. In the provincial castle towns, there was still a function for privileged merchants who provided services for the *han* and regulated local commerce under the supervision of the *han* administration. It was clearly to the interest of these privileged merchants to delay general commercial development as long as possible, since such development threatened them with decline. In this their interests coincided with those of the feudal authorities, who for other political reasons consistently aimed to prevent the commercialization of rural life. In the end, the continuance of the *status quo* depended as much on the geographical position and state of economic development of the *han* as it did on the policies and strength of the *han* government. In the more advanced areas of central Japan and around the Inland Sea, it was becoming difficult to hold the line as early as the first half of the eighteenth century. In the more backward areas of northern Honshu, the position of the privileged merchants was not seriously challenged until the nineteenth century.[14]

The BAKUHAN TAISEI and the Osaka Merchant Financiers

With the end of the wars, the incomes of the daimyo were more or less restricted to their agricultural taxes, and their financial problem was to convert this tax revenue, which was levied mainly in rice, into a more readily expendable form. Cash was required partly for the running of the fief, but mainly for the expenses of biennial

---

[11] Nakada Yasunao, "Edo jidai no gofukushi" [The official drapers of the Edo period], *Rekishi Kyōiku,* IX (October 1961), 12–22.

[12] No relation to Nuinosuke, who was known as "Gofuku Gotō" to distinguish him from Shōzaburō, known as "Kinza Gotō."

[13] The fate of a number of others of the same sort is recorded in *Chōnin Kōken Roku.*

[14] See Andō Seiichi, *Kinsei Zaikata Shōgyō no Kenkyū* [A Study of Rural Commerce in the Tokugawa period] (Tokyo: Yoshikawa Kōbunkan, 1958), especially pp. 388–402.

residence in Edo. Since there was no market for such large amounts within their own domains, most *han* made arrangements to market their rice in Osaka. In the first twenty years of the Tokugawa Shogunate, most major *han* arranged for warehouse facilities there, and senior retainers were appointed to handle the marketing. With the exception of two *han* which had presumably owned land in Osaka since an earlier period, daimyo were not permitted to own land in this city, which was administered directly by the Shogunate. The warehouses and associated offices were therefore built on land held in the names of Osaka citizens. The samurai officials in charge of the warehouses were, moreover, heavily dependent on the services of Osaka merchants. At first the tax rice was sold by tender, and a good deal of it seems to have passed through the hands of the famous Yodoya, whose huge rice-broking business apparently started before the beginning of the Tokugawa period. By about the 1650's, most *han* put the management of their Osaka warehouses into the hands of Osaka merchants,[15] who were then known as *kuramoto*. They usually acted as financial agents (*gin-kakeya*) also and received a salary and various social and economic privileges. When the Osaka banking system was organized in 1670, most of the ten members of the controlling group (*Jūnin ryōgae*) were active as *kuramoto* and/or *kakeya* for the various *han*. None seems to have been prominent before the beginning of the Tokugawa period.

The relations of this group with the Shogunate and *han* were not limited to the handling of tax rice.[16] Other products marketed by the *han* passed through the hands of these agents. The financial services provided included not only the handling and remittance of the proceeds of rice sales, but to an increasing extent the provision of advances in anticipation of revenue. These advances developed into long-term loans, in many cases of amounts equivalent to several years' revenue. The loans usually bore interest at the rate of between 15 and 20 per cent a year, and accumulated interest often raised the amount of the advances carried by the Osaka merchants to very high levels. When the property of Yodoya Saburoemon was confiscated by the Shogunate in 1705, his outstanding loans to daimyo were estimated at the incredible total of 100 million *ryō,* or several times the total national income of Japan at the time. All of the daimyo of western Japan are said to have been heavily in his debt. The whole story of Yodoya is, however, thickly overlaid with fiction. If the famous inventory of his wealth were anywhere near accurate, he would have been at least a thousand times richer than any of his merchant contemporaries. The "nice profit" of 121,867,610 *ryō* which the Shogunate is supposed to have made out of the confiscation of his property and which Sheldon regards as "possibly an exaggeration"[17] would have been equivalent to the total ordinary revenue of the Shogunate for about two hundred years![18] It is odd, to say the least, that the name of Yodoya does not even

---

[15] See *Dōjima Kyūki* [Records of Dōjima] in *Tokugawa Jidai Shōgyō Sōsho* [Collection of Writings on Tokugawa Period Commerce] (Tokyo: Kokusho Kankōkai, 1913) II, 27. See also Suzuki Shōhei, *Dōjima Kome-ichiba Shi* [History of the Dōjima Rice Market] (Tokyo: Nihon Hyōronsha, 1940).

[16] An account of the way in which Hiranoya Gohei acted as *kuramoto* and *kakeya* for the Tokuyama *han* is given in Takekoshi Yosoburo, *The Economic Aspects of the History of the Civilization of Japan* (London, 1930), III, 97–101.

[17] Op. cit., p. 103.

[18] Taking as a rough guide the figures given for shogunal revenue for 1716 in Ōkurashō [Ministry of Finance] ed. *Nihon Zaisei Keizai Shiryō* [Materials on Japanese Finance and Economics] (Tokyo: Zaisei Keizai Gakkai, 1922), I, 31.

figure prominently in the records of the business community after the middle of the seventeenth century. Evidence and common sense strongly suggest that the traditional accounts of the fall of this famous house should be treated as fiction.

The extent of the loans made to daimyo by these Osaka merchants is far better documented in the case of Kōnoikeya Zen'emon, one of the foundation members of the *Jūnin ryōgae*.[19] In 1684 his loans to daimyo totalled 3445 *kamme* (about 57,500 *ryō*) out of a total amount lent of 3858 *kamme*. By 1706 loans to daimyo had risen to 16,160 *kamme* (about 278,600 *ryō*) out of total loans of 18,258 *kamme*, and by 1795 the figure had risen again to 26,660 *kamme* (about 416,300 *ryō*) out of total loans of 33,470 *kamme*.[20]

Kōnoikeya is a good example of the merchants closely associated with the *bakuhan taisei* who are often thought of as the Tokugawa merchants *par excellence*.[21] The family may or may not have been of samurai origin. The story that they were descended from the famous sixteenth-century warrior Yamanaka Shikanosuke was denied by the family when approached for financial assistance by an unemployed samurai claiming to be of that family. The surname Yamanaka was used from time to time, but of itself this proves nothing. In any event the family was not of samurai status at the beginning of the Tokugawa period. About 1600 they were brewing and selling *sake* (rice wine) in the village of Kōnoike. From the Middle Ages on, *sake* brewers were among the richest members of the rural community and usually combined pawnbroking and moneylending with their manufacturing activities. About the 1660's, the family hit upon a technical innovation which revolutionized the brewing industry by making possible large-scale production of clear (as opposed to cloudy) *sake*. According to the traditional story, the discovery was made accidentally when a disgruntled employe tossed a bucket of ashes into a vat. Their improved product became famous, and to fill the demand for it in the growing city of Edo, they went into the shipping business. This too prospered, and by 1690 the firm owned over a hundred vessels. Shipping operations included the transport of rice to Osaka for the daimyo of western Japan. As early as the 1630's Kōnoikeya began advancing money to these daimyo, at first through the banking pioneer Tennōjiya Gohei. Through this connection he became, from about the 1670's, *kuramoto* and *kakeya* to many of the western *han*. In 1656 Zen'emon gave up brewing and opened an exchange shop (ryōgaeya) or bank modelled on that of Tennōjiya. When the *Jūnin ryōgae* were set up in 1670 to handle the financial transactions of the Shogunate and to supervise the Osaka money market, Zen'emon was one of the number. As a fully fledged banker, Zen'emon's relations with the *han* became closer, and by the end of the seventeenth century the firm had established business connections with thirty-two *han*.

It was merchant financiers like Kōnoikeya, Tennōjiya, and Hiranoya who were the undisputed leaders of the merchant class in the period following the establishment

---

[19] The annual accounts of Kōnoikeya Zen'emon have been analyzed by Yasuoka Shigeaki in "Zenkiteki shihon no chikuseki katei" [The process of accumulation of pre-modern capital], *Dōshisha Shōgaku*, XI, No. 5 (1960) and XII, Nos. 2, 4 and 5 (1961).

[20] I have excluded loans to other branches of the Kōnoike family which were more in the nature of subscriptions of capital. Conversions from *kamme* to *ryō* are at the rate of exchange used in the accounts for the year in question.

[21] The following is taken mainly from Miyamoto Mataji, *Kōnoike Zen'emon* (Tokyo: Yoshikawa Kōbunkan, 1958).

of the *bakuhan taisei*, which we may date from about 1640. As the leaders of the banking system, they controlled the credit system not only of Osaka and its environs, but of all the major centers of Japan. Through their exchange and remittance business, they controlled the market in which the relative values of gold and silver—and thus in effect the rate of exchange between Edo and Osaka—were set, and acted as the financial agents of the Shogunate. They thus collectively performed some of the functions of a central bank.[22] As commercial and financial agents and major creditors of the various *han,* they had considerable influence on *han* economic policy and a practical monopoly of the main exports of the *han*. Through their handling of tax rice, which amounted to about three-quarters of the supply, they controlled the Osaka rice market and thus the wholesale rice market for the whole country. When *han* began to issue paper currency for circulation within their territory, the issue was often underwritten and backed by members of this group and when, early in the eighteenth century, *han* sought to increase their revenues by developing new agricultural land, these merchant financiers often financed and carried out major reclamation projects. In this way most of them became large-scale landowners. Through their work for the Shogunate and the *han,* they became essentially civil retainers or quasi-samurai, with permission to use surnames and wear two swords when on official business. They also received stipends which, in the case of the Kōnoikeya, totalled 10,000 *koku,*[23] as much as a minor daimyo. The same type, though on a smaller scale, can be found in the so-called *fudasashi* of Edo, who began as agents for the direct retainers of the Shogunate, collecting and marketing their rice stipends for them and later advancing substantial amounts to them.

This group was obviously very closely tied to the *bakuhan taisei*. Although they took part in financing private commercial and even industrial undertakings, most of their business was with the *han* or the Shogunate. This demand for their services arose out of the political system, and the demand for cash advances in particular was largely for the expenses of the *Sankin Kōtai* system. Consequently they retained a leading position in the national economic life as long as the *bakuhan* system lasted. Although, as we shall see, economic development tended to be mainly outside their sphere of influence after the second half of the eighteenth century, Osaka nevertheless retained its paramount position. Cracks began to appear in the *bakuhan* system at least as early as the arrival of Commodore Perry, but the relaxation of the *Sankin Kōtai* requirements in 1862 gave a concrete indication that the system could not continue without considerable modification. The shogunal protection which the Osaka merchant financiers enjoyed by virtue of living in a city under direct shogunal administration proved to be a broken reed well before the Chōshū revolt exposed the Tokugawa Government's weakness. The financial position of most of the group was shaken when silver was drastically devalued to bring it into line with the gold/silver ratio in the outside world.[24] Since their assets were expressed in silver, and the group as a whole was holding a large part of the country's silver specie, the devaluation involved enormous losses. For most, the Restoration itself proved to be the final

---

[22] See E. S. Crawcour, "The Development of a Credit System in Seventeenth-century Japan," *Journal of Economic History*, XXI (September 1961), 342–360.

[23] That is, the right to receive the tax income on land rated at 10,000 *koku.* 1 *koku* = approximately 5 bushels.

[24] See Takekoshi, III, 329–337.

blow. One of the first acts of the new government was to demonetize silver, close the Osaka gold/silver exchange, and order conversion of all assets and liabilities expressed in silver at the current rate, which was very unfavourable to silver. There ensued a run on the Osaka banks which they were unable to meet, and most closed their doors, never to re-open. Furthermore, most of the assets of these merchant financiers, which were held in the form of advances to the *han*, were now no longer recoverable. Although the Restoration Government agreed to take over a part of the *han* debts, all such debts contracted before 1843 were repudiated. Almost half of the total claims of 74,130,847 yen were repudiated in this way.[25] Debts contracted between 1844 and 1867 amounting to about 11 million yen were to be repaid over fifty years free of interest. Some 12.5 million yen of debts contracted by the *han* between the Restoration of 1868 and 1872 were to be repaid at 4 per cent interest over twenty-five years with a respite of three years.[26] Most of these "New Loans" were probably held by people other than the old-established merchant bankers of Osaka.

With the collapse of the *bakuhan* system, therefore, the group of merchants who were so closely associated with it, and whose prosperity had depended on it for two hundred years, was thus practically wiped out. The few who survived, like Kōnoikeya and Mitsui, did so because of special circumstances. Since the Restoration was such a catastrophe for them, it is hard to understand why this group should have worked for the overthrow of the Tokugawa system on which they were so dependent. In fact, there is very little evidence that they did. Some sections of the merchant class did actively support the Restoration movement, but these were mainly wealthy rural entrepreneurs, not the class with which we are concerned here. It is true that they paid the levies or forced loans (*goyōkin*) demanded by the Shogunate with considerable reluctance, but probably with no more reluctance than they would have shown towards a similar demand from any other quarter. The famous contribution by the firm of Mitsui to the Imperial cause on the eve of the battle of Toba-Fushimi seems to have been an exception. After the setbacks of the 1860's, few of the other Osaka financiers had the ready cash to support the new government even if they had wanted to. Mitsui were tied to the central government, whatever form it might take, rather than to the *bakuhan* system, and they were fortunate or farsighted enough to have cash on hand in the form of a special reserve fund created by setting aside annually a percentage of profits, to be used only in an emergency such as a fundamental change in economic or political conditions.

Interregional Trade and the City TONYA *Merchants*

The last quarter of the seventeenth century and the first quarter of the eighteenth saw a very rapid growth of interregional trade. Several factors contributed to this development. On the demand side, the growth of large consumption centers, particularly Edo, was important. From about 1650, Edo developed rapidly as the administrative capital of Japan. Its population roughly doubled in the second half of the seventeenth century and reached a peak of about one million in the 1720's. With

---

[25] In the case of Kōnoikeya, the Meiji Government assumed responsibility for only about a quarter of the claims, which totalled close to 1.5 million yen. Miyamoto, pp. 233–234; Nihon Rekishi Gakkai, ed. *Jimbutsu Sōsho Furoku*, No. 13 (September 1958), Yoshikawa Kōbunkan.

[26] *Hansai Shobun Roku*, in Ōuchi and Tsuchiya, ed. *Meiji Zenki Zaisei Keizai Shiryō Shūsei* [Collected materials on finance and economics in the early Meiji period] (Tokyo: Kaizōsha, 1932), Vol. IX.

large and lavish establishments of the military aristocracy, free-spending citizens, and fluctuating but usually heavy government deficits, Edo enjoyed the reputation of having by far the highest propensity to consume in Japan. Here was a market far too big to be supplied from local sources, and from about the middle of the seventeenth century Osaka developed a growing export trade to the eastern capital. Payment for Edo's imports from western Japan was usually effected by setting it off against the flow of feudal tax revenues to be remitted from the Western Provinces to Edo. Interregional trade was also promoted by improvement of communications. The system of national roads converging on Edo and slow but steady improvement in local roads facilitated land travel, although land transportation was still limited to coolies and packhorses. Consistent attempts were made to improve inland waterways, and in the 1670's the coastal shipping routes all around the main island of Japan were greatly improved.[27] On the supply side, rising agricultural productivity permitted greater regional specialization and the development of simple rural industries.

These conditions combined to provide new opportunities for trade which were grasped by a new group of wholesalers and shippers known as *tonya*. The term refers to an occupation (not an organization), and was originally applied to forwarding agents. In the 1680's this group of merchants, based mainly on Kyoto or Osaka, vigorously developed wholesale trade between Kansai and the Western Provinces and Edo. Wholesale drapers like Tomiyama (Daikokuya), Izukura, Shirokiya, and Echigoya (Mitsui) had large purchasing establishments in Kyoto and often contracted for the textile production of whole districts. By their practice of advancing working capital to the producers, they were able to buy on very advantageous terms, and when they opened their wholesale and retail stores in Edo, the established local traders were unable to compete with them. Competition from this new group with its "modern" trading methods was a major reason for the final disappearance of the privileged or official merchants like the *gofukushi* from the ranks of active businessmen.[28]

The formation of the *Tokumi-donya* or "Ten groups of *tonya*" in Edo in 1694 and their successful struggle with the major shipping combines mark the arrival of this group as captains of commerce. The new merchants dealt in soft goods, ginned cotton, haberdashery, sake, paper, rice, matting, pharmaceuticals, lacquerware, crockery, ironmongery, builders' hardware, and various other goods. The granting of official monopoly privileges to these and other similar groups did not come until the time of Tanuma Okitsugu in the 1760's and 1770's,[29] although unofficial combination amongst themselves and with similar groups in Osaka and Kyoto seems to have been practiced for some time before that. In the period in which the new *tonya* were coming to the fore, between 1680 and 1720, however, competition among their own ranks seems to have been fierce. At this time they were independent, adventurous entrepreneurs, with no particular ties with the government and ready to try anything that promised a profit. It was members of this group who developed trade with

---

[27] See E. S. Crawcour, "Kawamura Zuiken—A Seventeenth Century Entrepreneur," to be published in *Transactions of the Asiatic Society of Japan*, Vol. IX.

[28] See Nakada Yasunao, "Tenna nenkan shinkyū shōnin-sō no kōsō" [The struggle between old and new merchants during the Tenna era], *Nihon Rekishi*, LXXI (May 1954), 21.

[29] See John W. Hall, *Tanuma Okitsugu, Forerunner of Modern Japan* (Cambridge: Harvard University Press, 1955).

Hokkaido. During their period as government-licensed monopoly companies from the 1760's to 1841, their spirit of enterprise seems to have ebbed away, and when their monopoly privileges were withdrawn, many were unable to meet the challenge of vigorous outsiders or to adjust to the development of local as opposed to interregional trade. Nevertheless, they still had an important function and many of the old *tonya* survived the Restoration and are still in business, although not as a rule among the leaders.

The Development of Local Commerce and the Rural Merchants

Although some local commerce existed in Japan from the beginning of the Tokugawa period, it was with the great increase in the production of industrial crops and the accelerated development of rural industries after 1800 that it became nationally important. Industrial development in the Tokugawa period was characterized more by the geographical spread of industry than by any marked advances in technique or industrial organization. The spread of industry was prompted in part by the desire to escape from the restrictive practices of the city industrial and commercial guilds, and partly by an enormous increase in demand for industrial products for which new sources of supply had to be sought. The spread of industry into the villages was permitted by increases in agricultural productivity, the existence of fairly large numbers of villagers either owning no land or needing to supplement their agricultural income, and the growing need of peasants for cash income. The initiative in introducing industries in rural areas sometimes came from city or Kinki (Ōmi, Ise) merchants seeking bigger and cheaper supplies to meet rising demand.[30] This was the case particularly in the districts surrounding Kyoto, Osaka, and the larger castle towns. Sometimes new industries were introduced by *han* to help solve local balance of payments problems and to increase revenue. Funds for such projects might be procured by raising a loan in Osaka, or by entrusting the operation to privileged castle town merchants who financed the project in return for a share of the profits or the right to collect fees. In many cases, however, industries were introduced by local entrepreneurs, usually substantial farmers with interests in moneylending, commerce, and such ubiquitous industries as brewing and the manufacture of soya sauce.

When the initiative came from city merchants, marketing was naturally taken care of by them. In many cases, however, particularly in the more remote and economically less advanced areas, the growth of production tended to run ahead of the development of commercial facilities. This was one reason for the establishment of *han* monopoly marketing organizations. Some official marketing boards may have represented an attempt to use the political power of the *han* to come between the producer and the market, but such monopolies were very hard to maintain and there was invariably a great deal of evasion. Quite often a marketing board organized by the *han* was the only possible method of obtaining outlets.[31] By marketing such products through its officials warehouses, moreover, a *han* was able to circumvent the powerful monopolistic commercial organizations (*kabunakama*). This practice led to disputes

---

[30] In 1815, for example, Ōmi merchants introduced sericulture to the Tanabe *han* in return for the exclusive right to buy the product. See Andō, pp. 189–190.

[31] A peasant uprising in Kii in 1855 protested against, among other things, the abolition of the *han* monopoly marketing board in its area. Andō, p. 392.

between *han* marketing organizations and merchant groups sponsored by the Tokugawa Government as early as the late seventeenth century.[32] In the nineteenth century such disputes became very frequent and usually the *han* got its way.

By the 1820's or 1830's local commerce was developing, at least in the geographically better placed and economically more advanced areas of Kinki, Chūgoku, the Kantō Plain, the districts bordering the Inland Sea, and parts of the Japan Sea coast. This development saw something similar on a provincial scale to the competition between protected merchants-by-appointment and a new class of professional businessmen in the major cities a century earlier. This time, however, competition was for the purchase of industrial materials and products rather than for markets. The lead was taken by prosperous farmer/businessmen who had by this time accumulated a good deal of capital and had largely replaced the old farming families as the leaders of the village community.

Official policy was to restrict these developments to protect peasant morality from corruption by the merchant ethic and in the interests of the castle town merchants associated with the *han*. By the 1830's (or earlier or later according to the region), this policy was becoming increasingly difficult to maintain, and rural merchants were being brought into the official system as peasant officials and agents of *han* marketing boards.[33] In Chōshū many businessmen were *shōya* by the mid-nineteenth century,[34] and the same was true of Tosa where this class was entering the lower ranks of samurai as *gōshi*.[35] In the Tottori *han* in 1861, rural businessmen were put in charge of silk cocoon marketing and given permission to wear two swords and use surnames;[36] at about the same time, they were entrusted with the marketing of iron,[37] successfully by-passing the Tokugawa Government-sponsored organization which had been set up in Osaka in 1780. In Okayama, rural businessmen played an important part in the economic life of the *han* as early as the 1830's.[38]

The way in which this new class challenged the established commercial channels is described by Sheldon.[39] Zeniya Gohei of Kaga, whom he gives as an example, would in the scheme adopted here be more typical of the *tonya* who exploited interregional trade around the beginning of the eighteenth century than of the local businessmen who were so active in the nineteenth. Kaga was, economically speaking, relatively backward with little spontaneous development of commercial agriculture, and this probably accounts for the late emergence of *tonya* like Zeniya. When the Kaga authorities began to encourage the production of industrial crops in the nineteenth century, they had to rely on people like Zeniya to provide commercial facilities which had not yet developed locally.

In more advanced areas, however, local businessmen were already very active. Local linen cloth dealers of Echigo, for example, challenged the Edo drapers as early

---

[32] See Yasuoka Shigeaki, *Nihon Hōken Keizai Seisakushi-ron* [History of Japanese Feudal Economic Policy] (Tokyo: Yūhikaku, 1959), pp. 45–78.

[33] Andō, pp. 390–391.

[34] Albert M. Craig, *Chōshū in the Meiji Restoration* (Cambridge: Harvard University Press, 1961), pp. 285–295.

[35] Marius B. Jansen, *Sakamoto Ryōma and the Meiji Restoration* (Princeton: Princeton University Press, 1961), p. 29.

[36] Andō, p. 230.

[37] Andō, p. 236.

[38] Andō, p. 200.

[39] Sheldon, pp. 144–161.

as 1814, and by the 1850's had gained direct access to the Edo market.[40] In 1859 only 10 per cent of the silk fabric coming into Edo was from Kyoto, which had once had almost a monopoly. The rest was from rural districts.[41] The history of one probably typical local merchant, Aburaya Yahei of Yamashiro, has been treated in detail by Professor Adachi.[42] Shibusawa Eiichi's father was no doubt fairly representative of this class on the edges of the Kantō Plain. By the 1850's, one or two businessmen of this type were to be found in almost every village outside of the backwoods areas.

It was this group which often, as in Tosa and Chōshū, supported reform movements in the *han* from about 1850 and which supported the Restoration movement.[43] The same group was active in the early Jiyū Minken movement and formed the majority of the propertied classes eligible to vote at the first general election of 1890. In the formation of industrial capital and the promotion of modern industrial enterprises, they were as active as the privileged financiers and merchants of Osaka, Kyoto, and Edo were passive. They would seem to have provided about 40 per cent of entrepreneurship and perhaps over a quarter of national domestic capital formation over and above a substantial contribution to investment through tax payments. Their prominence in the Meiji period may have been due partly to the collapse of older merchant groups, but it must be attributed mainly to the fact that is was they who had least difficulty in adjusting to a free enterprise capitalist economy.

Conclusion

When changes in pre-modern Japanese commerce are analysed, relations between commerce and government no longer appear as a two-and-a-half-century-long struggle between *the* merchant class and feudal authority. Although official opinion was generally hostile to commercialization, some degree of commercial development was essential to the working of the Tokugawa system. In their dealings with commerce, the authorities sought to keep it within the bounds of what they considered necessary and to control it within established channels. With the exception of a few ultra-conservative outbursts, the authorities do not seem to have been much worried by development within those channels. Relations between government and commerce, therefore, took the form of a series of associations between government and established merchant groups. By granting exclusive privileges to these groups, the authorities hoped to control them and to prevent what they regarded as the pernicious spread of commerce elsewhere. For their part, these established groups were willing enough to accept controls which could in any case easily be evaded; and they regarded the more or less token tax payments as a small price to pay for the protection which they received. The arrangements with the authorities made in this way, however, usually involved merchant groups whose interests were already being threatened, and with slow but steady economic change, it became from time to time impossible to hold

---

[40] Andō, pp. 255–258.

[41] Thomas C. Smith, "Landlords and Capitalists in the Modernization of Japan," *Journal of Economic History*, XVI (1956), 169.

[42] Adachi Masao, *Kinsei Zaigō Shōnin no Keieishi* [The business history of village merchants in the Tokugawa period], (Kyoto: Yūkonsha, 1955).

[43] Thomas C. Smith, *Political Change and Industrial Development in Japan: Government Enterprise 1868–1880* (Stanford, 1955), pp. 13–22. See also the same author's *Agrarian Origins of Modern Japan* (Stanford, 1959).

the line against outside economic development. The Shogunate itself was thus frequently in the position of being associated with sections of the merchant class for whom time was running out, and in the closing years of the period it lost control altogether, just when its vastly increased fiscal needs made access to commercial sources of revenue more necessary than ever. Most *han* faced similar problems, but in the end some were able to do on the smaller scale of their own fiefs what the Shogunate was unable to accomplish.

CHAPTER TWELVE

THE EVOLUTION OF TOKUGAWA LAW

DAN FENNO HENDERSON

DURING THE PAST century, the gradual expansion of Japanese law has occasioned remarkable changes in the general concept and role of law in shaping Japanese social and even political activity.[1] To follow this legal evolution, particularly since 1868, requires at each stage careful correlation of the consistently *avant-garde* legal prescriptions with the underlying and sometimes intractable social tradition;[2] it also requires an adequate historical perspective beginning at least with late Tokugawa law. For, of course, one cannot understand Japanese legal modernization without knowing first what from the Tokugawa past had to be changed and what was found to be usable by the builders of modern Japan. My concern here is mainly with Tokugawa law after 1742. The emphasis is on civil rather than criminal law because the civil litigation process in some ways represented the highest legal development in over a millenium of indigenous Japanese law. Unfortunately, the criminal law was marred by its discretionary quality, the harshness of its penalties and its torture techniques, which have often distracted modern scholars and still tend to obscure those aspects of Tokugawa criminal law, which had also begun to show signs of legal refinement and evolution.[3]

Historical Perspective

Such positive Tokugawa law as there was was produced by its own peculiar government, the Edo shogunate, established at the end of a thousand years (ninth–nineteenth century) of indigenous Japanese legal evolution. This millenium of largely unwritten, native law in turn occurred between two eras of foreign influence in Japanese legal institution—first, in the form of the Chinese-

---

[1] See Takayanagi Kenzo, "Kempō chosakai ni okeru kempō rongi no shisoteki haikei," *Jurisuto*, No. 309 (1964) 36–46, for the observation that the new, postwar constitutionalism is beginning to influence politics, as the political leaders of both parties gradually begin to realize that there is a fundamental *legal* difference between the Meiji (1889) and Showa (1947) constitutions, in that the former only afforded an opportunity to criticize official conduct as "unconstitutional" for whatever persuasive effect it might have on political allegiances, but now the fact of unconstitutionality as proclaimed by a proper court causes the official action so condemned to be in fact officially *invalid*.

[2] See Maine, *Ancient Law* (1st ed., 1861), 7–25. For later classifications and correlations between social and legal types and their development, see Vinogradoff, 1 *Historical Jurisprudence* (London, 1920), 148; Pound, *Outlines of Lectures on Jurisprudence* (1943), 40–48; Stone, *The Province and Function of Law* (Sydney, 1946), 466. For a list of modern schemes see Cairns, *The Theory of Legal Sciences* (North Carolina, 1941), 25–28.

[3] See Hiramatsu, *Kinsei keiji soshōhō no kenkyū* (1960).

D. F. Henderson

style (T'ang) *ritsuryō* codes, adopted just after 700 A.D. and largely drained of their effects after the ninth century. The second era of massive foreign legal influence did not occur until the end of the nineteenth century in the form of the European style codes, mostly German and French. In the long interim, Japanese society, often virtually headless without an effective government, regulated itself in the private sector largely by its own growth of customary law attuned to its rice culture and peculiar feudal institutions. The resultant customary law sometimes referred to in Tokugawa times as *taihō* was rather diverse from locality to locality and almost exclusively in unwritten form, overlaid by a country-wide politico-legal tradition in the public law consisting of the Confucianistic social stratification and family hierarchy, the feudal devices of vassalage and enfeoffment to organize larger areas, and the symbolism enshrouding the Imperial Court in Kyoto.

The general statement that the pre-modern Japanese law of private relations was unwritten customary law requires surprisingly little qualification throughout the entire thousand years involved. There were, however, some written recordings of customs, precedents, or piecemeal decrees. Also, there was some written public law of the feudal periods, notably the *Goseibai shikimoku* (1232). Some of the later laws even had a certain legislative quality in the sense that they sought to cause (or reflect) a change in social or political arrangements; for example, the house codes of the warring period [4] and the various *jomoku* and *sho hatto* of Hideyoshi and the first three Tokugawa shoguns. The high point of written, native law in Japan was Yoshimune's *Kujikata osadamegaki* (1742), a code in two books of some 184 articles.

The Osadamegaki in some minor ways also ran counter to the indigenous quality which had dominated Japanese law for centuries. It contained some renewed foreign (Chinese) law influences, both in content and format, although they are subtle and difficult to measure. We do know, however, that Yoshimune, the driving force behind the codification for two decades, was a serious student of the Ming law. Some innovations in the Osadamegaki such as the use of whipping and fines as penalties and the use of tattooing in lieu of cutting off ears, fingers, or noses may have been drawn from similar Ming (1368–1644) practices. But the most obvious Chinese feature was the revived *ritsuryō* format of the Osadamegaki. Despite these exceptions, it is generally true, though, that between the ninth and nineteenth centuries, the mainstream of Japanese law was indigenous and embodied in unwritten customs.

As noted, the relatively refined body of justiciable law in the criminal and commercial fields, which was both produced and enforced by the Edo bureaucracy in the latter half of the Tokugawa period (1742–1868), is of special interest to students of modern law and governance. With it, Japanese law was becoming for the first time professionalized in the modern sense. In civil cases this law appeared within the constricted and shallow jurisdiction of the Conference Chamber (*hyōjōsho*) and the three Edo commissions (*sanbu-*

---

[4] Jansen, "Tosa in the Sixteenth Century: The 100 Article Code of Chōsakabe Motochika," above, pp. 89–114.

Evolution of Tokugawa Law

gyō) in private diversity disputes (*shihai chigai*), which were tried in Edo because they transcended feudal boundaries. Except in these interesting diversity cases (described below), Edo law did not reach deep into the society, nor did shogunal civil law extend territorially beyond its own lands (one-seventh of Japan).

Concepts of Law and Their Significance

Even a preliminary attempt to deal with Tokugawa legal evolution will end in confusion without specific attention at the outset to categories and concepts —both our own and those of Tokugawa officialdom.[5] For example, in the recent literature we encounter, among other kinds of Tokugawa "law," (1) unlimited official power; (2) status authority and privilege; (3) family relationships; (4) village custom; (5) customary law; (6) traditional state theory and symbolism; (7) written law of various sorts—orders, decrees, and precedents. Of course, this entire mass of Japanese "law" can hardly be true to a single formulation which would correspond at the same time to our modern ideas of law. No doubt the present diversity of scholarly thought about basic "lawness," in the Tokugawa as well as other contexts, will be with us for some time to come, which is perhaps as it should be. So, our purpose here is simply to recommend several analytical concepts for convenience of communication. Particularly, clear language is needed to deal with two central problems of Tokugawa legal evolution. The first is the changing relationship between (1) concepts of law, (2) social behavior, and (3) "justice" (i.e., the purpose of law or its underlying political values), as traditional society progresses toward its modern condition. The second problem is a narrower one presented by the expansion of the *political* role of law as governmental techniques and controls become more effective and as (or if) society becomes liberal and sophisticated enough to develop and use the legal devices of a democratic constitution to institutionalize the process of orderly social change.

Law (justiciable or positive)

The major obstacle to understanding law-in-general is that modern analysis generally distinguishes justiciable law from administration, from social practice, and also from "justice"[6] (i.e., political values), whereas Tokugawa legal

---

[5] The following from my prior musing on the subject have been drawn upon for this summary: I. Henderson, *Conciliation and Japanese Law* (1965), chaps. 3 and 4; and "Law and Political Modernization in Japan," in Ward, *Political Development in Modern Japan* (1967); and "Some Aspects of Tokugawa Law," 27 *Wash. L. Rev.* (1952), 85–109.

[6] We use the term *justice* to refer to the purpose of law, which, especially when the law itself is vague, often means the judge's own values, drawn in to interpret ambiguous standards or gaps in the law for a specific case. Some writers use the term *natural law* in a similar fashion. Kelsen, *General Theory of Law and State* (Cambridge, 1945), xiv; Bodenheimer, *Jurisprudence* (Cambridge, 1962 126–57. Note that we have used the term *natural law* in a more classical sense to refer specifically to political values held as absolutes of nature such as those of the Tokugawa orthodox Confucianists.

205

thinking did not differentiate these categories. Our everyday, lawyers' kind of law is a hypothetical norm with the sanction of state power. Its distinctive features are that it is manmade and justiciable,[7] meaning that the rights given by law can be cashed in, so to speak, in independent courts supported by a professional bar and bench, special procedural safeguards, substantive rules, and by reasoned decision and written records. This whole specialized articulate process is, of course, a modern achievement, which we would not expect to find full blown in Edo. The concept of modern, made-law thus differs from what is simply going on in society or what is simply normative, and yet the differentiations say no more to scholars than that it is more useful than not, in analysis of modern social problems, to treat law, its purpose and its efficacy, as separate but related hypothetical categories of thought. They do, of course, blend into or overlap each other in reality.

Natural Law

As opposed to our differentiated, court-enforced (justiciable) law, the Tokugawa concept of law was a species of natural law, which did not distinguish law from behavior, administration, or "justice," but treated them all as a part of a cosmic system of principle believed to be inherent in the nature of things. This kind of "law" is given and immutable. It pervades all of nature, including man and his society. Thus, it is neither made by men, nor dependent upon human institutions for its validity or enforcement.

We must note here also that the concept of "natural law" is still used by some modern writers to refer to the idea of abstract justice or the purpose of law. This often means no more than the writers' own criterion for evaluating the law, which he may hold as an absolute as did the Tokugawa "courts,"[8] or he may recognize, more generously, that it is simply his personal political preference. We use "natural law" hereafter in the more classic sense to refer to the evaluative criterion, used rather unconsciously by the Tokugawa judges and devised largely by the orthodox Confucianists (*shushigaku-sha*). These judges assumed that no rule could be "law" unless it conformed with their concepts of "justice," or more precisely, law and justice (legal purpose) are the same thing, and both natural.

Customary Law

The nexus of social behavior and law lies where social custom and customary law meet. Again, however, the precise point of connection is inevitably a

---

[7] See on justiciable law, Kantorowicz, *The Definition of Law* (A. H. Campbell, ed.), 1958), 79; Stone, *Legal System and Lawyers' Reasoning* (1964), 166, 175–77; Marshall, "Justiciability," in *Oxford Essays on Jurisprudence* (1961), 265; Summers, "Justiciability," 26 *Mod. L. Rev.* (1963), 530–38.

[8] "Court" has been placed in quotation marks to remind us that the Tokugawa judicial offices were also the chief administrative agencies and had little of the attributes of modern courts (i.e., independence from the executive, judicial tenure, etc.). We use the term court hereafter with those reservations in mind.

gray area in real life, if not in concept. Social customs are ways of doing things in a certain group. Often they become normative; that is, the way things should be done, perhaps for no other reason than that they have long been done that way. "Customary law" is a form of justiciable law, which originates in custom, but has since been "positivized" and enforced by the courts' recognition of its binding effect on the community. We should advert here to the difficulty much debated by anthropologists and lawyers, as to whether or when custom becomes "law" without formal court recognition. Of course, custom which is enforced in formal courts, thereafter, becomes law embodied in precedent. But does custom have the force of law before there are articulate courts with written records and professional judges? This is a critical problem of Tokugawa village "law," and the recent works of certain anthropologists [9] have made a convincing case for the view that custom observed by primitive, even illiterate, groups is "law," not different in kind, from our modern law. This is because, they say, the primitive group has its "courts" (chief, wise man, strong man, etc.) and its sanctions (ostracism, approved self-help or violence such as the vendetta, etc.) to bring violators to "law." The only problem is that it takes a professional anthropologist to get this "raw-law" out where we hyper-civilized specialists in made-law can see it, especially where a group has no articulate "government," much less an independent court as a part thereof. Since we are concerned only with positivization of custom by literate "courts" in the Edo bureaucracy, this issue (i.e., whether custom is to be regarded, with the anthropologists, as "customary law") is therefore not of critical importance here.

All four of these analytical concepts—law (justiciable), natural law, custom, and customary law—plus the law-administration distinction will be discussed below in the Tokugawa context and in sketching out the evolution of justiciable law as it was created by the Tokugawa courts. Essentially our theme below will be as follows: the apparatus of justiciability grew up gradually in Edo, as a gloss on the natural-law thinking of Edo officialdom and as an overlay on centuries of accumulated custom; but significantly this new law, created by the superceding authority and dispute settlement function of the shogunate, remained socially shallow and territorially limited throughout the

---

[9] For a progression of anthropological analyses of primitive "law," see Hoebel, *The Law of Primitive Man* (1954), 18–28: (1) Hartland, *Primitive Law* (1924), 5, "Custom is king"; custom is spontaneously observed; tribal custom is primitive law; (2) Seagle, *The Quest of Law* (1941), 33, Custom is king, but not law; primitive man is lawless because he has no courts; he is under the "automatic sway of custom"; (3) Malinowski, *Crime and Custom in Savage Society* (1926), 14, suggesting that there is primitive law which is not followed spontaneously, but is enforced by the "law of reciprocity" of mutual services and by withholding services from a culprit who fails to contribute his share; (4) and finally Hoebel, *Law of Primitive Man*, 23, quoting Max Radin: "But there is an infallible test for recognizing whether an imagined course of conduct is lawful or unlawful. This infallible test, in our system, is to submit the question to the judgment of a court. In other systems exactly the same test will be used, but it is often difficult to recognize the court. None the less, although difficult, it can be done in almost every system at any time."

period down to the restoration of Imperial rule (1868). The relationship between the emergent Tokugawa government and the Tokugawa society, which was already highly regulated at its extremities (villages) by social custom, remained dualistic; they were separate in the sense that the shogunate recognized, as a world to itself, an enormous sphere of activity for society to regulate; conversely most of society regarded the shogunate and its law as generally alien to it. The consequence was that neither the rulers nor the people could comprehend the idea of law as anything more than the concern of shoguns, daimyo, and their officials. Fukuzawa Yukichi,[10] famous founder of Keio University, upon making a visit to the West in 1860, commented that, although they were truly amazing, he could nonetheless understand our scientific devices; but western law—he could not fathom that it was something that scholars could treat as a subject of scientific study or that professionals could learn in order to protect the rogues of society in criminal trials. Rather the Osadamegaki in stipulating that it was for the use of the highest officials only was more expressive of the social concept of law in Edo and in the countryside as well; it was an art of power maintenance for the expert manipulation of self-interested rulers in a society which was in the private relations of the subjects largely self-regulated. Law was an instrument to be used by rulers but not to limit their actions. And, as we shall see, even when the shogunate later came to handle private suits in considerable number the theory remained that the trial was a matter of beneficient grace offered by the shogunate only because of the inadequacies of the people in fulfilling their obligations to live harmoniously. In theory the people never had a *right* of access to the Edo courts.

This brings us to the second major problem which requires specific concepts to insure effective communications; namely, the expansion of the political role of Japanese law; in this expansion, of course, Tokugawa law was the starting point. Generally, modern law has come to limit government action in varying degrees in Japan as elsewhere in the course of the past century. To gain perspective, it is useful to distinguish between the roles which justiciable law plays in the public and private law fields. For, despite respectable argument to the effect that the public law/private law schism may be unsound in modern governmental theory,[11] such a distinction has considerable utility in describing the historical relationship between law and politics in Japan from Tokugawa to modern times. The public/private distinction was a basic principle borrowed by the Japanese from German law, no doubt because it was congenial to their Tokugawa experience of separating warriors and commoners in the administration of justice. Public law (constitutional, administrative, procedural, etc.) deals, of course, with relations between government (or officials) and sub-

---

[10] Osatake, *Ishin zengo ni okeru rikken shisō* (1925), 195.

[11] Kelsen's early analysis has called attention to the theoretical difficulties of the public/private law dichotomy in the modern state. Kelsen, *The General Theory of Law and State* (Cambridge, Mass., 1945). See also Friedmann, "Public and Private Law Thinking: A Need for Synthesis," 5 *Wayne Law Review* (1959), 291.

jects, while private law deals with relationships between private parties (contracts, property, torts, etc.). The western literature on general legal development beginning with Maine [12] (1860) has a certain relevance to the evolution of law-over-power in Japan, but once we stretch our analysis to cover both sides of 1868, the Japanese experience requires its own specific framework.

In Tokugawa experience, public "law" was simply structural and administrative; and such structural law was not justiciable. It created a power pyramid, imposing duties on the inferiors at each level of the power hierarchy, but it conferred no correlative justiciable rights on them or the subjects. Abuses of official authority might be redressed at the initiative and by the authority of a superior, but not on the basis of an inferior's "rights" invoked in court. Only after the Meiji Constitution (1889) did officials become bound in theory, but only nominally in practice, by justiciable law in the exercise of their powers granted by statute; and only after 1947 did policy formulation, especially legislative, come to be limited in favor of basic individual rights embodied in the Showa Constitution (1947), which in turn made popular elections more meaningful choices. Thus, in Japan such a basic thing as the political roles of law itself, not just its doctrinal form and content, have changed with each of three periods in the past century. For convenience, in the administrative and public-law area, these legal roles and periods might be conceived as follows: (1) rule-of-status (discretionary power of superiors within a multi-status, feudal structure), 1742–1868; (2) rule-by-law (generalized authoritarian law in a *de facto,* dual-status society—i.e., governors and governed), 1868–1945; and (3) rule-of-law (limited government of modern constitutionalism) in the postwar period 1945–1968. But against this background we are primarily concerned hereafter with the starting point of this progression—the rule-of-status; for an administrative, structural role was all the law achieved in the Tokugawa public "law," as we shall see. Only in the private law was there justiciable legal growth discernible in the decrees and precedents in the Edo bureaucracy. With the foregoing terminology—law, natural law, custom, customary law; public law, private law, rule-of-status, rule-by-law, rule-of-law—we can perhaps deal understandably with the complexities of Tokugawa legal dynamics.

PART II: TOKUGAWA LEGAL EVOLUTION

The Dynamics of Law: Modern and Tokugawa

We have noted preliminarily the conceptual discrepancy between how we view our made-law today and how Tokugawa officials viewed their natural law. These conceptual differences need further elaboration stressing the dynamics of modern law as contrasted with the statics implied by Tokugawa legal thinking. Then using our own concept of law as an analytical tool, we can observe the beginnings of modern legal dynamics in Edo.

---

[12] See citations above, n. 2.

D. F. Henderson

The Uses of Modern Law

Our modern idea of law is based on a convenient (and like all analysis somewhat unrealistic) differentiation between individual behavior, social practice, law (statutes and regulations), and basic political values ("justice"). Dynamically conceived, then our modern law has simply an instrumental role by which the state attempts to achieve its program (i.e., justice)—leaving aside the questions of the merit of the program or how democratically based the rulers' claim to power may be. This kind of positive, instrumental law, which has emerged from the early European idea of territorial sovereignty (Hobbes, Bentham, Austin, Kelsen, etc.), can and has served a variety of programs, "just" or "unjust," and has been employed by either elite or democratic juristic methods.

Thus, modern law is man-made law, typically legislation or a statute. It is envisaged by some human ideal, forged by some kind of politics, publicized by the modern media, tinkered with by legal professionals, applied by officials, sanctioned and enforced to a degree at least by state power. Its growth has moved from a multi-status law to a single legal status (subject or citizen); that is, the discrete, equal, juristic individual comprised, in democratic states, of a cluster of fundamental, justiciable personal rights (rule-of-law). In authoritarian states the individual also may have some justiciable rights, but only to the extent granted by the ruler (rule-by-law); there are no "inalienable or fundamental rights" immune from the ruler's fiat. By these same trends, the relationship between society and government has shifted toward more and more conscious permeation of society by government and more coverage by the national statutes, leaving less to be resolved by local, parochial, social control ("law"), administered by the inarticulate "courts" of the village. Justiciable law in modern states has thus become more universalistic and impersonal with an ever-widening and deepening range and specificity in the justiciable rules, and with an ever-more conscious, flexible, and purposive use of made-law (as opposed to cosmic natural law; or social customary law) in positive economic and social planning on a country-wide basis. Law has thus become a creative tool with which man can organize his society so as better to control his environment by the powers of collective action. He need not accept nature just as he finds it; there is a new efficacy in human effort when it becomes collectively channeled by made-law.

Uses of Tokugawa Natural Law

Of course, the Tokugawa perspective of the world (and therefore of law) was different, and although it produced some nascent law, which as scholars we can identify as approximating our own concepts, the dominant Tokugawa concepts were a species of natural-law thinking. For successive generations of Tokugawa bureaucrats and "judges," Japan was almost everything; other vague lands furnished curiosities, but really did not matter much. The whole country was one big rice estate, with daimyo sub-estates. Every bag of rice was precisely allotted before it was planted; each person was classified before he was born and registered soon thereafter. After the chaos and strife of times past, peace and security seemed quite enough to give one's retainers. All was now administration; there was no political activity worth noticing, just a bit of graft and intrigue to be rooted out by an occasional confiscation or by diligent application of ancestral moral precepts. Movement was slow, change imperceptible; efficacy of human effort to refashion any aspects of their world in a short generation was negligible. Such a caricature of the shogunate structure and thinking is of course over-simplified, but I suggest that it does nevertheless capture the mainstream and general tone of official thought in Edo.

Understandably then, the natural-law order of the Tokugawa shogunate represented quite a different conception of the nature, sources, purposes, and efficacy of law than our current concepts of justiciable, "made" law, or even the nineteenth-century concept of law as social excreta. However, it is interesting to note the structural similarities between Tokugawa natural law and western scholasticism [13] including its modern successors today.

To Tokugawa officialdom the concept of law included in one massive system the four things which, as we noted earlier, are commonly differentiated in modern analysis—individual behavior, social practice, positive law, and justice. In Tokugawa thinking, law and justice were synonymous, and both existed in society and nature. Humans did not make law, but rather must try to understand and comply with preexistent law of nature larger than governors and encompassing the whole of society. Courts and even "legislators" also simply discovered the extant law in nature. Decrees and judicial decisions alike were declaratory; the wise governors taught lessons in reality; human law was thus didactic and merely sought to reflect the extant natural law. Such a comprehensive idea of "law" was difficult to grasp all at once; perhaps the most advanced shogunate formulation of it was the principle (*ri*) of Orthodox Confucianism (*Shushigaku*), although it was implicit in the adjudicative [14] and legislative process, even when it was not fully articulated. The political utility of such a static kind of rationalism to preserve the shogunate intact is too clear to require elaboration here.

---

[13] Maruyama, *Nihon seiji shisōshi kenkyū* (Tokyo, 1952), 185, notes the resemblance to western scholasticism.

[14] There is, of course, an extensive literature on the poverty of juristic method to cover prospectively all of the real eventualities of social activity, and on how the gaps should be filled by drawing upon officials' and judges' apprehension of legislative intent or community values or the officials' own preferences. See, *e.g.,* Pound, *The Task of the Law* (1944), 48. For another approach to the relation between law and justice in the case of "gaps," see Kelsen, *General Theory of Law and State* (Cambridge, 1945), 145.

Modern administrative law, as it has developed in the past few decades, raises these questions most urgently, for the whole idea of th separation of power and judicial function is up for reappraisal or circumvention by the process. See Stone, "The Twentieth Century Administrative Explosion and After," 52 *Calif. L. Rev.,* No. 3, (1964), 513.

D. F. Henderson

If the Tokugawa concept of "law" did not differentiate between individual behavior, social practice, positive law, and justice, then of course many other differentiations and categories of modern, positive-law systems were not discernible in the Tokugawa legal system. Administrative and judicial functions were not clearly distinguished; indeed, in the early years the central bureaucracy itself was barely in the process of formation in Edo. Criminal and civil law overlapped to considerable extent; procedural and substantive laws were inextricably intertwined in much the same way that they were in the forms of action at common law. Public and private law, to the extent that those concepts are ever meaningful, were more distinct than in the prior periods, but by and large still feudally coalesced by way of the land tenure and household management of the warrior overlords. Consequently, we must affect a case of astigmatism in order to see clearly the lack of clear conceptual distinctions in Tokugawa legal thinking.[15] Yet there was an emerging system of justiciable law, which is discernible to us as twentieth-century observers. Indeed, the Japanese legal experience since say 1850 in building by steps a mercantile, industrial, and democratic society is perhaps the best proof that a system of justiciable law is not just a western ethnocentricity but rather a necessary component of such a society and of the division of labor upon which its trade and industry depends. In brief Japanese experience seems to indicate a sequence in legal evolution as follows: initially in Edo after 1600 there arose a country-wide power structure (rule-of-status); then a criminal law was created to support it; these were followed by court recognition of certain private claims in civil and commercial relations; only much later (after 1868) did administrative officials become subject, in applying the law, to justiciable legal limits in the public law field; and finally in a recent democratic phase (after 1945) law has even begun to overlap policy formulating power to protect basic individual liberties and principles of popular governance (a rule-of-law). It is the Tokugawa beginnings and limitations of this unusual Japanese legal evolution which we will examine more fully below.

Growth of Tokugawa Justiciable Law

Modern law evolved from the functioning of the shogunal bureaucracy. For indeed a body of justiciable law was produced in Edo, and it has come down to us in the form of brush-written and now worm-eaten volumes of decrees and precedents. Unfortunately, the Tokyo earthquake (1923) destroyed the only copy of the most valuable source of the private civil law, the case reports of the Conference Chamber (hyōjōsho), which were called the Saikyo-dome. However, a small portion of the Saikyo-dome was saved, and it is now printed in one volume.[16] Also, most of the collected reports of the Tokugawa criminal

---

[15] Boorstin, "Tradition and Method in Legal History," 54 *Harv. L. Rev.* (1941), 424–36.

[16] Forty-five volumes of the *Saikyo-dome* existed for the years between 1702 and 1867. Unfortunately all of the original forty-five volumes were lost in the Tokyo earthquake of

rulings *Oshioki reisuishū*,[17] as well as the major collection of decrees, *Ofuregaki shūsei*,[18] have been laboriously copied and printed recently by thoughtful Japanese legal historians so that, to considerable extent, we in this generation are spared the "worm's-eye view" of Tokugawa law which only a few decades earlier was the only way to see the primary sources of shogunate law.[19]

Perhaps as a general proposition we can suppose that law starts with bare

---

1923. At the time of the earthquake there were extracted copies of only two parts. One copy, covering the period from 1720 to 1729, is now at the Kyoto University Library. It has, however, a large gap from 1721 to 1727. The other copy is at Tokyo University and covers the period 1781 to 1782. These remnants were printed by the Ministry of Justice as *Shihō shiryō, Bessatsu*, No. 19, (1943), 607 pp., along with those parts of the *Saikyodome* which fortunately had been quoted at length in the *Tokugawa kinreikō kōshū*. These cover four parts of the *Saikyodome* for the period from 1796 to 1865. Although the loss of this major source of civil decisions is irreparable, these remnants in the printed volume give a sampling for the period from 1720 to 1865.

[17] As might be expected, criminal precedents of the Tokugawa period are more voluminous because of the usual preponderance of criminal law in early stages of positive, legal growth. The *Oshioki reiruishū* contains collections of Conference Chamber opinions rendered in response to questions put to the Chamber by the Senior Council concerning requests (*ukagai*) originally referred to the Council by other lesser shogunal officials and Commissioners. These criminal opinions were compiled by the Chamber itself on five different occasions in order to have the precedents in ready form for reference. The five compilations are as follows:

1. *Koruishū*, sometimes referred to as *Chahyōshi zenshū*, covering the period from 1771 to 1802; compilation began in 1804.
2. *Shinruishū*, or *Aobyōshi*, covering 1803 to 1814.
3. *Zokuruishū*, sometimes referred to as *Kibyōshi*, covering 1815 to 1826.
4. *Tempo ruishū*, sometimes called *Chahyōshi kōshū*, covering 1826 to 1839.
5. The fifth compilation was destroyed in the Tokyo earthquake of 1923. No copies remain.

Copies of the first four of these compilations may be found at Kyoto University and at the Naikaku Bunko. Only the *Koruishū* (1771–1802, 4 vols.), and the *Shinruishū* (1803–1814, 2 vols.) have been printed as *Shihō shiryō, Bessatsu*, Nos. 8, 10, 11, 12, *18, 20* (1941–1946).

[18] The *Ofuregaki shūsei*, now conveniently printed in five large volumes under the editorship of Takayanagi Shinzō and Ishii Ryōsuke, *Ofuregaki Kampō [Hōreki; Temmei; and Tempō] shūsei* (Tokyo: Iwanami Shoten, 1934), is another important source of Tokugawa law applicable to the commoners. In order to understand the character of these collections, it must first be remembered that *ofuregaki* were proclamations of the Senior Council (*rōjū*) or town commission promulgated through fixed channels of authority to the people in general (see text *infra*). The *Ofuregaki shūsei* then are decrees rather than court precedents. Furthermore, the *ofuregaki* were a special type of decree, in general promulgated at large as distinguished from *kakitsuke* or *tatsu* which were usually administrative memoranda to the officials. The first compilation of *ofuregaki* (Kampō, 1741–1744) was ordered by Yoshimune, and the other three compilations were continuations of the practice in Hōreki (1751–1764), Temmei (1781–1789), and Tempō (1830–1844).

[19] See Henderson, "Japanese Legal History of the Tokugawa Period: Scholars and Sources," *University of Michigan, Center of Japanese Studies, Occasional Papers*, No. 7, (1957), 100–21.

power which then somehow structures and rationalizes itself for security and convenience, by means of a kind of non-justiciable skeletal law to facilitate administration. Then justiciable law is later generated from either authoritative persons or regularized dispute settlement processes within the administrative structure. At any rate it does seem that Edo law emanated from two such sources—from (1) authority in the form of decrees and (2) from the regularity of the trial process in the form of recorded precedents, remembered and applied to later cases. We will discuss both of these sources of law later, but it is critical to deal first with another aspect of legal development in general which is well-illustrated by the Tokugawa experience. This is the importance of the quantitative overlap of authority by regularity to the eventual attainment of a rule-by-law or a rule-of-law. Much confusion can be avoided in studying Tokugawa law by accepting a rather obvious fact; namely, that this refinement never appeared and therefore the public-law relations between officials and individuals were not limited by justiciable law. The overlap of power by the regularity imposed by law never developed in Edo governance, though power was intricately structured by non-justiciable law (rule-of-status). The Edo shogunate was a minimal sort of government that had at great risk and effort managed to impose itself upon a largely hostile society, and understandably in the formative years its chief function was the basic task of maintaining peace and security by maintaining the shogunate itself—something not to be taken for granted in the light of the preceding century. Accordingly, the shogunate's use of law was, perhaps necessarily, self-centered, to define its structural (or "constitutional") aspects—the social hierarchy and warriors' feudal ties, etc.—and to protect itself by means of a harsh criminal law from its enemies and detractors.

As in emergent regimes in European history and even in many developing states today, this kind of self-serving criminal law was the core of the legal tradition in the courts of both Japan and China on the country-wide level during their respective traditional periods. Simply stated, in the *ritsuryō* legal format of Japan, adapted from the Chinese T'ang models and of varying influence from the seventh century onward, the criminal law (*ritsu*) was little more than a repressive auxiliary to maintain official power and policy (*ryō*). Beyond this there was little "national" law of any practical consequence. All else was of such a lower order of priority and concern that the weak and superficial state could give it practically no attention at all. So, society existed separately and was largely self-regulated; private relations and private "law" were local matters to be dealt with by customary accumulations of folk-law [20] without the intervention of the new "national" law or courts. Thus, al-

---

[20] See *Minji kanrei ruishū,* Takimoto Seiichi ed. (Tokyo: Hakutōsha, 1932), 390 pp.; *Shoji Kanrei ruishū* Takimato Seiichi ed. (Tokyo: Hakutōsha, 1932), 1130 pp.; *Zenkoku minji kanrei ruishū* (Shihōshō comp.), 50 *Nihon keizai taiten* (1880); *Zenkoku minji kanrei ruishū,* Kazahaya Yasoji comp., (Tokyo: Nihon Hyōronsha, 1944), 353 pp.

In the field of Tokugawa customary law it is fortunate that the Ministry of Justice, in preparation for the Meiji codification, compiled these sets of local customary law which

though the traditional regime in Japan was thoroughly authoritarian, it was not totalitarian because the governmental and administrative techniques were not developed to the point where private relations of society could be controlled by legal fiat from the center. The failure of Tokugawa law to effect society deeply has been explained as a preference of the regime for moral rather than legal controls; law was said to be a second-best method, to be used only as a last resort. In a sense this is true, but whether it was the reason or, instead, the rationale after the fact for such a shallow legal penetration is an interesting question. It may well find its answers in the necessities of underdevelopment rather than moral preferences of Chinese philosophy.

Tokugawa Proclamations

Nevertheless the shogunate issued a large quantity of decrees of various sorts, some of which sought country-wide observation. Most of them were analogous to the traditional regulatory laws (*ryō*) and they were thus supported by a criminal penalty provided in a separate decree (*ritsu*). In fact, the most important legislative project in Tokugawa times, the *Kujikata osadamegaki* (1742), was consciously compiled in *ritsuryō* format. Besides the Osadamegaki many piecemeal decrees were issued every year for various distributions. These were gathered together in major compilations called the *Ofuregaki shusei* in the Kampō (1741–1743), Hōreki (1751–1763), Temmei (1781–1788), and Tempō (1830–1843) periods, and, of course, in their printed form they comprise a convenient survey of over a century of late Tokugawa legislation.[21]

Although in modern law all regulations must be promulgated to be effective, in Tokugawa times there were two kinds of regulations: notices (*tatsu*) and proclamations (*ofuregaki*). The *tatsu* were addressed from a higher to a lower shogunal office and were not promulgated; the *ofuregaki* were addressed to the public at large or a segment of the public and were therefore promulgated by the Tokugawa methods described briefly below. Although called the *Ofuregaki shusei*, the major compilations mentioned above included both *tatsu* and *ofuregaki*, as well as such major legislation as the regulations for daimyo (*Buke shohatto*). The compilations were probably called *Ofure-*

---

have since been printed. More recently the *Minji kanrei ruishū* and *Zenkoku minji ruishū* have been consolidated into a single volume based primarily on the *Zenkoku minji ruishū*, but using whatever superior features the compiler felt were contained in the classification system of the *Minji kanrei ruishū*. The consolidated version seeks to avoid overlapping and at the same time to provide a better geographical coverage and index than the originals (see Kazahaya Yasoji, *Zenkoku minji kanrei ruishū*, 1944).

These collections were made by traveling commissions from the Ministry of Justice, which recorded practices in the various provinces of Japan as related to them by the local officials. Although the gathering of these records was begun in 1875, well into the Meiji period, they may be considered fairly representative of the prior Tokugawa local practices and are indeed an unusual set of materials.

[21] See n. 18.

D. F. Henderson

gaki compilations because of the predominance of the *ofuregaki* in their contents. These *ofuregaki* were largely those issued from the Senior Council in Edo. There is a similar compilation of decrees of the Edo Town Commission in thirty-two Japanese volumes (*kan*) of which the first three have been edited and printed.[22] Much about the efficacy of Tokugawa regulatory, public law can be learned by examining the shogunate's methods of publicizing and distributing its regulations by proclamation through its major offices, the three commissions in Edo.

First, we will consider the case of the Edo town commission.[23] The promulgation of proclamations (*ofure*) in Edo was made to the townsmen by the headmen of the towns. In the city of Edo there were more than a thousand towns, but there were many cases where one headman covered several towns. So, in all there were some two hundred headmen. Because of the large numbers, it was necessary for the government to devise a system of delivering its official notices to each headman through the town commission (*machi bugyō*). In 1722 the headman were divided into 17 groups, and toward the end of the shogunate the number increased to 21 groups, plus two exceptions, *Shin-yoshimura* and *Shinagawa*. Among these groups, the first and the second groups were called the Northern Group (*kita no koguchi*) and the fourth group was called the Southern Group (*minami no koguchi*). The headman, who belonged to these special groups, took turns by the year in delivering to each town-head the official notices which were received from the Town Commission through the city elders. Thus, the chain was: Town Commission, city elders, headman-on-duty, finally each individual headman to his people.

In Edo, the proclamations distributed by the Town Commission were of two kinds: general proclamations (*sōbure*) and town proclamations *machibure*). The former conveyed the written regulations of the Senior Council down through the Town Commission, while the town proclamation was originated by the town commissioners themselves. The fundamental difference between the two in terms of coverage in Edo lies in the fact that it was necessary to deliver the town proclamations, not only to the townsmen (*chōnin*) but also to Shinto priests and other religious persons registered in the Edo personal registry and therefore under Town Commission authority; but in the case of general proclamations the Town Commission's distribution had no concern with Shinto priests, ascetics, diviners, and the like in Edo, because they would be informed in the usual channels by the Temple and Shrine Commission (*jisha-bugyō*) which was responsible for them vis-à-vis the Senior Council, which issued this kind of proclamation. At first some town proclamations were ambiguous as to whether they were actually general *or* town proclamations. Thus, the term "Senior Council" was added later to the general proclamations to distinguish the two types.

[22] *Kyōhō senyō ruishū*, Ishii ed., (1944), 236 pp.
[23] The following account is based on Ishii Ryosuke, "Hō no koshi hohō no enkaku," *Hōgaku kyōshitsu*, No. 2, published by *Jurisuto* 80–84 (July, 1961); and Miura Kaneyuki, "Rekidai hōsei no kōfu to sono kōfushiki," *Hōseishi no kenkyū* 63 at 106–157 (1925).

Evolution of Tokugawa Law

In the next step the town headman then summoned to his house the land- and house-owners (*jinushi* and *yanushi*) in each block and informed them of the contents of each proclamation (*ofure-gaki*) received; he also had the house-owners inform their tenants of the contents. In case the proclamation was of special importance, the house-owner made his tenants sign jointly and return the copy to the headman, who also signed on the registry book at the office of the town elders. However, the joint signatures later became a matter of form only, and in 1791 during the tenure of Matsudaira Sadanobu, this system was abolished, and the headmen were thereafter obliged to give instructions directly to all tenants in their jurisdiction.

In Osaka, there was a general system which required that each person acknowledge proclamations by affixing his seal as evidence of compliance. In 1787, the regulation provided that all the proclamation be delivered to the general assembly of the town elders (*sōkaijo*), where the elders announced it to the headmen, who in turn distributed it to the townsmen at each town meeting, or a copy was circulated. There were also towns where the house-owners were obligated to inform their tenants. However, since this system was considered to be inconvenient and ineffective, a new method was instituted, whereby all townsmen were called together at the assembly where the proclamations were announced by the town elders and the headmen were required to affix their seals upon them; the same was demanded of the tenants. Furthermore, in 1822 even a proxy had to affix his seal, and it was called to his attention that he must inform his principal.

The townsmen organized their own groups according to their line of business, and the groups had their own system of handling announcements of proclamations. It was the usual procedure for the yearly duty officer to deliver the proclamation to each member upon receipt from the authorities; besides there was a special post called Proclamation Chief (*fure-gashira*) whose duty it was to deliver the proclamation to the group members. Examples are: the proclamation chief of the bean curds dealer (*tōfuya*); and the *fure-nagare,* a person who announced the proclamations at large on the streets for the painters (*e-shi*).

Next is the method whereby the proclamation was announced to shrines and temples through the temple and shrine commission. The shrines and temples had a system of proclamation chiefs (*fure-gashira*). Here, the proclamation chief was the unit (or temple) which conveyed the proclamation of the shogunate to all shrines or temples under the control of the main temple in the sect, and which also conveyed the petitions of the shrines or temples to the government. Each religious sect had its own proclamation chief, though with differing names: *sōroku* in both the *Sodo* and *Rinzai* sects, *rinban* in the *Shinshū* sect, and *yakuban* in the *Jōdoshū* sect. The temple or shrine serving as proclamation chief was usually selected from among those located in Edo. To illustrate the process more specifically: first, the Temple and Shrine Commission promulgated the proclamation to each proclamation chief for each religious sect, and then each proclamation chief saw to the delivery of the proclamation to the other temples of his own sect. In case a sect had no proclamation chief, the main temple of the sect was appointed to that position.

Finally, we will examine the process of promulgation from the Finance Commission (*kanjō-bugyō*) to the villages under its control: the Finance Commission sent copies of the proclamation to each District Deputy (*gundai*) and Deputy (*daikan*), who assembled his village headmen (*nanushi* and *shōya*) and gave them copies; then, the headmen after returning to their villages, held village meetings at which they read the copies aloud and explained the contents; when the proclamation was of particular importance, they sometimes had the villagers present a sealed receipt.

The above methods show the types of promulgation used to publicize proclamations issued by the shogunate. In spite of these various devices, the common folk were doubtless unable to remember the contents of each proclamation very long, even though the headmen had read them aloud and explained them to his villagers, and here, of course, lies the key to understanding the repetitive character (as well as the inefficacy mentioned above) of the shogunal legislation. In order to help people remember the content of the major regulations, the government contrived the system of the notice boards and the five-man-group registry (*goningumi-chō*).[24] One of the shogunate decrees of 1722 stated that, although the previous decrees had already instructed the farmers to obey the proclamations, there were only a few who could remember the contents on hearing the proclamation only once, and that, since there must be some writing instructors, even in the country, towns, and villages, those teachers ought to help the people learn to read and write the chief laws by assisting them in reading and writing their five-man-group registry. The five-man-group registries were first drafted by the deputies (*daikan*), and then certain villagers were entrusted with impressing the plan on each farmer's mind. According to a model of such a registry dated 1734, there were sixty-six articles, including one to the effect that each village had to organize itself into five-man-groups, and, if one of the group members commit a crime, the other members must report it immediately. Following the sixty-six articles, there was a note which requested each of the members, the chief of the group, the elders, and the headman to sign and to jointly seal the following acknowledgement:[25]

"With regard to the purport of the above proclamation the villagers will make copies and keep them; we also will have a meeting once each month at the headman's office and have the proclamation read aloud to all the main farmers as ordered, and we will strictly observe the proclamation. Should anyone violate its purport, he will have no complaint against punishment.

[24] The chief materials are: Hozumi Nobushige, *Goningumi-hōkishū* (1921); 705 pp.; Hozumi Shigeto, *Goningumi hōkishū*, 2 vols. (1944); Nomura Kentarō, *Goningumi no kenkyū* (1944), 682 pp.

[25] Ishii and Takayanagi (ed.), *Ofuregaki Kanpō shusei* (1934).

To this effect, we the headmen, elders and members of five-man-groups affix our seals jointly on this certificate."

To wit: Seals and Signatures

In this manner, the headman had to hold a village meeting of the main farmers at his place once a month and to read aloud the contents of the five-man-group registry. There were some registries that stipulated meetings every two months; so the frequency was not entirely uniform in all villages. But it seems to have been the shogunates' desire to have these meetings at least once a month.

It is curious that five-man-group registries did not exist in the towns; none existed in Edo, or Osaka or Kyoto. In Osaka, however, there was a kind of five-man-group registry for temples. It is not clear why the townsmen had no registries, but the fact that the shogunate did not desire to control the towns as closely as the villages was doubtless one of the main reasons.

Although there was no such system as the five-man-group registry in towns, the reading of major laws to townsmen was put in practice. One of the most remarkable examples was the Proclamation of the Second of the Month (*futsuka-bure*) in Kyoto; this *futsuka-bure* meant that on the second of each month, each town held a meeting called *Futsuka-bure* and at the meeting the town elders (*machi-toshiyori*), who were the counterpart in Edo of the village headman, read aloud the draft receipt certificate concerning town administration which was to be presented to the Town Commission and swore jointly to obey the decrees.

Besides the proclamations just described, the shogunate publicized its major regulations throughout the period by means of wooden notice boards which were posted permanently at Nihonbashi and five other well-known places and some thirty-five other places in Edo, as well as at certain places on all of the five major highways leading to Edo.[26] The following seven notices, posted at Nihonbashi, cover the typical subject matter:

1. A regulation requiring proper Confucian relationships.
2. A regulation prohibiting poisonous drugs.
3. A regulation about firearms.
4. A regulation against Christianity.
5. A regulation about weights.
6. A regulation about freight charges from Edo to various places.
7. A regulation against arson.

Also paper bulletins were often posted at the headmens' residences to announce temporary rulings, and wall-writings (*kabe-gaki*) were often used to

---

[26] Text of the major *kosatsu* can be found in the *Osadamegaki,* Book I, Articles 13 through 18 in 1 *Kinreiko koshu* 84 (Ishii ed., 1959). English translations: John C. Hall, "Japanese Feudal Law: III Tokugawa Legislation," 38 *T.A.S.J.* (pt. IV) (1911), 320–31. Also see Harafuji, "Kosatsu no igi," *Kanazawa daigaku hobungaku-bu ronshu; hokei-hen* No. 10, (1963), 12.

D. F. Henderson

publicize shogunate regulations. For example, the important *Buke shohatto* were posted as a wall-writing at the shogunate offices. Finally, we should note that where shogunate interest required regulation in the daimyo domains, these orders were distributed to the daimyo from the Senior Council through the Great Inspectors (*Ō metsuke*). Most daimyo also used the notice boards and *ofuregaki* systems in their domains to pronounce their regulations.

Although the Tokugawa regulations were numerous and systematically distributed to the farmers, townsmen, religious orders, etc., we can conclude from the nature of the system and the repetitive contents of the decrees that the efficacy of many of the rules was not very high or at least would fade away soon after the announcement. Thus, one gets the impression that the proclamations were ancilliary to the basic natural law and customary structure of the regime; much of the total volume of legislation of this sort seemed to be reminding the populace of rule presumed to be already laid down but being somehow ignored. Nevertheless, there were periods of creative remedial activity in the regulations; the most notable cases were of course the Kyōhō (1716–1735), Kansei (1784–1800), and Tempō (1830–1843) reforms identified with Yoshimune (eighth Shogun), Matsudaira Sadanobu (Regent), and Mizuno Tadakuni (Senior Councillor) respectively. The Osadamegaki (1742) compiled under Yoshimune had a substantial quantity of new regulations in it. Aside from these major reforms the decrees seemed to be used to scold or jog the memories of the populace and were often not intended to be justiciable on their face, though penalties were prescribed elsewhere to guide the discretion of the criminal administrators. Indeed, discretion was the essence of the process, and much of the written law was simply intended to guide the discretion of officials. This explains, too, the policy of not distributing the Osadamegaki to anyone except the major "Judges." But, of course, the customary and natural law were both well known; it has been well-said that the Osadamegaki was secret; but the law was not. To emphasize the non-justiciable character of the regulations in the sense that legal excesses of official conduct were not challengeable in court, we will review briefly the legal meaning of the rule-of-status.

Rule-of-Status and the Criminal Law Auxiliary

The rule-of-status was essentially a structured power concept, thus political and administrative rather than justiciably legal. The definition of the hierarchical social statuses (warrior-farmer-artisan-merchant: *shi-nō-kō-shō*) and the power of status-group officials to govern their own group (fief, town, village, family, etc.) comprised the basic structure upon which the centralized power of the Tokugawa state was based: it required absolute obedience of status inferiors and absolute power of superiors over the members of their group. As noted, in the early stages of legal growth, the chief legal implement of the new state to reinforce its power position was the criminal law, which was harsh and predominant in the work of the "courts." From the shogun at the top to the member of the smallest unit (the family) at the bottom, this thread of status rule ran by successive delegations of power, unpoliced by justiciable law. But the criminal law auxiliary was employed to reinforce the central power in court, of course, and in time, the law of crimes, penalties, and the execution thereof developed prescribed limits and legal procedures akin to elemental justiciable rights. We can take the shogunal domain as an example, although presumably the daimyo domains were similarly organized but with the added vassalage relationship with the shogun at the top. The shogun delegated to the senior council (*rōjū*), which delegated to the finance commission (*kanjō bugyō*), which delegated to the deputy (*daikan*), who looked to the village headman (*nanushi*), who looked to the chief of the five-man-group (*gonin-gumi kashira*), who looked to the househead, who controlled the family members.

As drawn, the foregoing unilinear chain-of-command penetrates both the feudal ruling (warrior) and nonfeudal, ruled (commoner) layers of society. The most important nexus of the feudal and nonfeudal was the headman, for the village was the standard unit of enfeoffment and its farmers comprised 80% to 85% of the Tokugawa populace. The villages were under bureaucratic (not feudal) tax control by the headman who delivered the rice to the enfeoffed lord. Intramurally the village had some degree of autonomy. Its character and extent are an important and highly controversial matter.[27] But it seems clear enough that the village as a unit had some autonomy, although it was constricted by the heavy rice tax and innumerable sumptuary rules to encourage maximum yield, so that the individual villager was usually not free to dispose of much leisure time or excess resources. Our point here is a little different, however, because we are adverting to *how* the intramural autonomy was exercised, not its overall scope vis-à-vis the lord.

The critical fact of the rule-of-status was that against the authority of any of the superiors (feudal, village, or family) there was no legally justiciable right either before a court or even before the next higher official superior. Indeed, there were no courts separated from the administrative offices (except, in a sense, the conference chamber [*hyōjōsho*]), and all of these offices were proscribed by shogunal law from accepting a petition by a Confucianistic inferior against a superior without his permission. All review and redress was from the top down, even the *ukagai* (sometimes translated "appeal") was simply a query to the next higher office[28] by a lower office for its own edification.

---

[27] See the controversial literature on this point cited in Ōde, "Kinsei sompō to ryōshu-ken," *Hōsei ronshū*, No. 18, 1–32, and No. 19, 73–128 (1962).

[28] See Ishii, *Nihon hōseishi gaisetsu* 480, n. 13 regarding rejection of a *daikan*'s decision (*saikyo kobami*). *Ukagai*, sometimes translated "appeal," was used technically to designate the situation where the lower shogunate official, not the party, requested instruction from a higher official. Kobayakawa, "Futatabi kinsei soshō ni kankatsu oyobi shinkyū," 33 *Hōgaku ronsō* 635 (1935), notes that using a modern term, *shinkyū*, as an equivalent for *ukagai* may have been confusing in his prior article: 32 *Hōgaku ronsō* 110 (1935).

D. F. Henderson

In this respect the authority of the state was analogous to the authority of the feudal master and also of the father, because the feudal state and the family were the same thing on different levels; and the duty of loyal subordination, first to the overlord (*shukun*) and secondly, the househead (*koshu*), combined to become the chief instruments of social discipline. Consistently, the concepts of loyalty to master (*chū*) and filial piety (*kō*) were considered inseparable. In most of the Tokugawa schools of Confucianism can be found phrases similar to the following by Fujita Tōko: "Letters and swords are inseparable; loyalty and piety indivisible." [29] Kaibara Ekken's words epitomize the official thought of his time, requiring complete subordination to Confucian superiors: "To criticize superiors—to criticize the country's administration, that becomes a serious breach of loyalty and piety." [30]

Turning specifically to the attitude of the shogunate toward suits against superiors, the "courts" asserted a strong policy against such actions, backed up by prescribed penalties. That this attitude prevailed at an early date in Tokugawa law covering the commoners as well as the warriors is shown by a section of a regulation circulated throughout Edo in 1655, tenth month, thirteenth day: [31]

> "In suits between townsmen and their servants, those who submit complaints and go to trial do not understand the proprieties of the master and servant relationship. When the servant is at fault, he will be imprisoned. Furthermore, the complaint is a matter to be entrusted to the master's discretion."

In the same regulation, suits between parents and children are discouraged. The family suits to be discouraged were not limited to those between father and son, but also included other suits against family superiors. The wife's incapacity to sue for a divorce, except through the colorful divorce temple (*enkiri-dera*), is another example.[32]

The law thus left settlement of such disputes to the will of the master, father, teacher, or other superiors as a matter of power or "jurisdiction." Suits were accepted only if the shogunal interest was involved and the superior was found to be seriously at fault,[33] or in some cases concerning household or property succession.

Tokugawa law did not stop at simply prohibiting suits against superiors

---

[29] See *Kōdōkan-ki* in 3 *Kinnō bunko* 119, and see Kobayakawa, 39 *Hōgaku ronsō* (1938), 534–35, for similar quotations from Yamaga Sokō and Nakae Tōju.

[30] Kaibara Ekken, *Kadōkun* in 3 *Ekken zenshū*, 423 (upper).

[31] 5 *Kinreikō zenshū*, 292 (bottom; third *hitotsugaki*).

[32] See Hozumi Shigeto, *Rienjō to enkiridera* (Tokyo, 1942), 209; Ishii, "Enkiridera—Tōkeiji no baai," 76 *Hōgaku kyōkai zasshi* (1959), 401, and vol. 77, pp. 127 and 413 (1961). Two temples, Nantokuji in Nitta and Tokeiji in Kamakura, were recognized as asylums for runaway wives, who after three years of life in the temple as a nun were legally regarded as divorced.

[33] This policy is clearly stated in *Tokugawa jidai minji kanreishū, Soshō no bu*, 216 *Shihō shiryō* (1936), 60, *Meue no mono o aitedori sōrō sojō no koto*.

(*shujū sōshō*). In the traditional *ritsuryō* format, it also supported these prohibitions with harsh criminal penalties in the *Osadamegaki*, Book II.[34] Transcendent petitions[35] (*osso, kagoso,* etc.) wherein the inferior petitioned over the head of his superior were severely punished, even by crucifixion if the petition was false. In passing, we should also note the venerable oriental principle that criminal liability to support administrative responsibility expanded to relatives (*enza*) and to the whole village or group (*renza*) of which the offender was a member.[36] It is well known that a regulated schedule of torture was an institutionalized part of the conviction procedure. True to its *ritsuryō* conception and early legal evolution generally, the criminal law, as a whole, was primarily an auxiliary of the power structure and administration, epitomized by the rule-of-status as outlined above.[37]

Perhaps the only procedure which might be regarded as an exception to the basic principle of rejecting complaints against authority was Yoshimune's plaint box[38] established in Edo in 1721, but the practice was not to give direct replies to the plaint-box petitioners. Also, the petitions could only be submitted to report a public matter; complaints concerned merely with private or personal mistreatment were not authorized. Even public complaints, if submitted without permission of the petitioner's superior were out-of-channels (*suji chigai*)[39] and punishable.

We have dwelt upon the concrete workings of the rule-of-status and the consequent lack of "public law" redress against authority in Tokugawa administration somewhat at length because in this all-pervading feature clearly lies the outstanding political characteristic of the Tokugawa public-law order. There was virtually no justiciable law in the field of administration (or public law in our terms), where power relations were defined. In general western jurisprudence, it is a much-mooted question whether unreviewable official authority for arbitrary, *ad hoc* exercises of official power should be included in the concept of basic "lawness" at all, or whether law and arbitrary power (however official) are not opposites. Some scholars feel that the essence of law is its generality of prospective application.[40] Surely, such a distinction between law and discretionary official acts is a useful one, and certainly it also

---

[34] See *Osadamegaki*, Book II (*Hyakkajō*), Article 65, which gives some qualifications, too.

[35] Kobayakawa, "Kinsei minji saiban no gainen to tokushitsu," 45 *Hōgaku ronsō* 372–402 (1941) for the fullest discussion of transcendent petitions; *Osadamegaki*, Book II, Article 19.

[36] Miura mentions the softening of the use of vicarious liability (*renza* and *enza*) after Yoshimune. Miura, "Edo jidai no saiban seido," in *Hōseishi no kenkyū* (1925), 345.

[37] Hiramatsu, *Kinsei keiji soshōhō no kenkyū* (1960), 3–244, is the standard work on Tokugawa criminal proceedings.

[38] *Osadamegaki*, Book I, Articles 8–12.

[39] *Osadamegaki*, Book II, Article 4, in 17 *Shihō shiryō bessatsu*, 29, provides for confinement (*oshikomi*) for a priest or warrior who does not observe channels and handcuffing (*tejō*) for commoners.

[40] Bodenheimer, "Reflections on the Rule of Law," 8 *Utah L. Rev.* (1962), 2, criticizes Kelsen and Stammler for considering such official acts "law."

D. F. Henderson

continues to be one of the major problems of modern jurisprudence, but the unique and highly structured status hierarchy of the Tokugawa regime is difficult to classify on such a criterion. Often these hierarchical status relationships of man-over-man have been characterized as a rule-of-man,[41] and Confucianistic philosophy has also given some support to such a term.[42] Hence, the "legal" system has been viewed as a power structure with nothing more than authoritarian duties for subordinates, without any correlative rights. Indeed this view is quite correct and one might say rather obvious in proper historical perspective whereby one can readily see that power always precedes the refinements of limited power (i.e., rights of individuals). However, what is easy to lose in this emphasis is that Tokugawa status had rather important social and natural-law (moral) limiting aspects.

Here we have preferred to use the term "rule-of-status" in order to emphasize the limiting quality of status and for the reasons which will appear more fully below. All individual persons at the bottom did have social *status* as members of hierarchical group, even though they had no legal status as individual, in the modern sense, under shogunate law. And, as noted, society and its controls loomed large in the private life of the village in comparison with the alien legal emanations from Edo. Thus, these Tokugawa statuses had their "legalistic" limitations for superiors and were observed socially even though not enforceable legally. The Tokugawa inter-status relations (*shi-nō-kō-shō*), and even intra-status relations, were minutely defined, and every daily routine was so ordered by rules of proper procedure and conduct for both inferiors and superiors that paradoxically the society was uncommonly legalistic, although without positive, justiciable legal remedies from the bottom up. Still it would be a grave error to suppose that the rules of society, fief, village, or family were not effective and largely observed. The social expectations of proper status-conduct of superiors and the downward surveillance of superiors by their superiors to ensure observance, plus the intimacy of village life doubtless mitigated the rigors of arbitrary power, especially during the later years. It is, therefore, useful to characterize this system, which was not without its legalistic social controls and yet which is not readily comprehended by our legal categories, as a rule-of-status. Again, it is most easily understandable if we always bear in mind the early stage of development, the superficiality of the shogun's law and the shallow limits of his concern for only peace, security, and the tax. This way of viewing Tokugawa social legalisms takes into account the regime's ideal of governance by moral, wise, and disciplined men, predating any justiciable law and auxiliary court system, but at the same time it underscores the fact that there was power discipline from the top down, and social discipline from the bottom up, and that western (and modern Japa-

[41] An early use of the term is Wainright, "Japan's Transition from a Rule of Man to a Rule of Law," 48 *Transactions of the Asiatic Society of Japan* (1919), 155.

[42] Junshi [Hsun-tsu] Kundōhen (see the phrase: "Osamuru no hito ari; osamuru no hō nashi"), in *Kokumin bunko kankōkai* (ed.), 8 *Kokuyaku kanbun taisei,* 32 (separate paging for Chinese), p. 124 (Japanese).

nese) right-oriented, juristic method was not available to review aberrant official conduct. Such justiciable law as there was, outside the criminal field, was administered as a matter of grace in the field of private relations as discussed below.

Justiciability of Diversity Cases

As sketched above, the status law with its criminal law supports was the basic core of the shogunate public law, and presumably of the daimyo as well. But in some ways the later refinements of the private law, worked out in litigation, were the more interesting aspects of Tokugawa law for lawyers. There was a positively antifeudal accretion of justiciable, commercial law building up in the central offices of Edo in the latter half of the Edo period [43] in response to the growing commerce and money economy. This commercial, judge-made law was anti-feudal because first the suits were mainly money suits (*kane-kuji*) arising from the growing commercial activity of lowly merchants, and secondly, because they involved parties registered in different fiefs, thus evading the intra-fief jurisdiction of the feudal lord. Therefore, since the lord of neither party had the normal feudal jurisdiction requiring the registry of both parties, these cases involved diversity-of-jurisdiction (*shihai chigai*), and the shogunate, as a central super-lord (or government), was pressured into settling them.[44] When we remember that there were hundreds of fiefs, many composed of noncontiguous parts (*tobi-chi*), and that commerce had no respect for such petty boundaries, especially in the Kanto and Osaka/Kyoto complexes, it is easy to understand why, with the rise of commerce, these suits became by far the most numerous kind of litigation in Edo. By the early eighteenth century they had become a serious burden on the "courts." [45] The shogunate tried to discourage them by mutual settlement decrees (*aitai sumashi-rei*),[46] which required private settlements; by discard decrees (*kien-rei*), which extinguished the debts outright; by dilatory procedures and centralized jurisdiction in Edo; and by stringent requirements of impeccable documentary proof from plaintiff.[47] Still by the mid-eighteenth century a fixed and refined formulary system in hierarchical arrangement was developed for civil suits as follows: (1) land and water disputes (*ronshō*); (2) main suits (*honkuji*, i.e., secured claims without interest); (3) money suits

---

[43] Kabayakawa, *Kinsei minji soshō seido no kenkyū* (Maki Kenji, ed., 1957) contains the most advanced work on Tokugawa civil litigation.

[44] Koabayakawa, "Iwayuru 'shihai chigai ni kakaru deiri' ni tsuite," 34 *Hōgaku ronsō* (1936), 408, 756.

[45] See a chart of statistics for Osaka in Haruhara, *Osaka no machibugyōsho to saiban* (1962), 12–13, and Takayanagi and Ishii, *Ofuregaki* (kanpō) *shūsei* (1934), 1196, for decrees noticing the problem of numerous *kanekuji* suits in 1702.

[46] Harafuji, " 'Aitai sumashi' rei kō," *Kanazawa daigaku hōbungaku ronshū hōkei-hen*, No. 2, (1955), 1–29.

[47] Harafuji, "Kinsei saikenhō ni okeru shōsho no kinō," 4 *Kanazawa hōgaku*, No. 2, (1958), 77; *id.*, vol. 5, No. 2, (1959); *id.*, vol. 6, No. 1, (1960), 35.

D. F. Henderson

(*kanekuji*, unsecured claims with interest);[48] (4) mutual affairs (*naka-magoto*); (5) "Confucian" suits (*shujū sōshō*, claims against family or feudal superiors). These types of claims were handled by a corresponding hierarchy of procedures of varying adequacy depending on the importance attached by shogunate to each type of underlying interest. Land suits were important to the tax so they were handled most promptly and adequately; main suits somewhat less adequately; money suits, being unimportant merchant claims, were handled largely by didactic (as opposed to voluntary) conciliatory techniques and toothless judgments, if conciliation failed. Mutual affairs were always rejected summarily; and Confucian suits as noted above were not only rejected but ordinarily the petitioner was penalized for complaining against his superior.

This hierarchical formulary system[49] for handling *shihai chigai* cases produced the only substantial body of truly national and justiciable law for civil cases in Tokugawa Japan. As we have seen, all other civil law was a local customary law with much diversity derived from long-established practices of the particular community. And the method of applying local law was by local conciliatory techniques, which we have called didactic conciliation because the settlement technique was neither strictly voluntary nor formally judicial, although they may have often approached the standards, which students of primitive law have seen as a kind of inchoate adjudication. In addition some local (nondiversity) suits were taken to the shogun's deputies (*daikan*) for a more judicial hearing, but little is known about the actual handling of civil cases by the shogunate at that level.[50]

Yet as a judicial process, it is easy to overrate Edo litigation[51] and this becomes clear in reviewing its salient characteristics. First, until 1875 Japan had never known an independent court as such. In Edo, the Conference Chamber was largely judicial in function, but its "judges" were the members of the three commissions (minus the two *katte-kata kanjō bugyō*). Perhaps the specialization of the judicial officers (*kuji kata*), two of the four finance commissioners, should also be mentioned as quasi judicial. Other "courts" were even more obviously administrative offices with concurrent power to settle disputes. As for the "bench," we should note the legal specialists of the three commissions: the *yoriki, tomeyaku;* and *gimmimono shirabeyaku* of the Town, Finance, and Shrine-and-Temple Commissions respectively. Although

---

[48] The mature form of the *honkuji-kanekuji* division was fixed in a Conference Decision of the Conference Chamber (*hyōjōsho ichiza hyōketsu*) in 1767. *Tokugawa jidai minji kanreishū, soshō-no-bu* in 216 *Shihō shiryō* (1936), 80.

[49] Kobayakawa, "Kinsei minji saiban ni okeru mibunteki seikaku to tōkyusei ni tsuite," 46 *Hōgaku ronsō* (1942), 20, 388, sets out this hierarchy of procedure. Cf. Maitland, *The Forms of Action at Common Law* (1936).

[50] Ishii, *Nihon hōseishi gaisetsu*, 480, n. 13, says that by rejection of a *daikan's* decision (*saikyo kobami*), a litigant could get a hearing in Edo, under certain circumstances.

[51] Cf. 2 Wigmore, *Panorama of the World's Legal Systems* (1928), ch. 8; and Takayanagi, "A Century of Innovation: The Development of Japanese Law, 1868-1961," in *Law in Japan* (von Mehren ed.) (1963), 5 at 23.

some of these petty underlings were highly skilled in law and trial practice, and presided at most of the trial hearings as examiners, they were not the responsible judges as such and had nothing akin to judicial tenure or independence. Finally, the almost total lack of private practicing lawyers was a striking deficiency which has still not been entirely overcome in modern Japan. The suit innkeepers (*kujiyado*) had an important concurrent role as legal advisors but these colorful specialists lacked most professional attributes and were not allowed to represent clients.[52]

Shogunal trial procedures were rather nonjudicial.[53] Even in diversity cases the Edo procedures never quite broke free from feudal concepts of administration. For example, the claimant could not sue in Edo without the approval of both his village and his feudal lord. Thus, suits were still group, not individual matters; they were still not free from a vestigial administrative orientation, which thoroughly smothered the individual even in "private" litigation. Perhaps the most picturesque manifestation of this mode of thinking was the requirement that the itinerant litigant in Edo (and, of course, at least one party was always an itinerant in diversity cases) obtain his house-owner's (innkeeper's) approval, for in Edo all tenants were required to get the approval of their superior (house-owner) for various "private" transactions. Naturally enough the suit inns (*kujiyado*), which catered to litigants, became experts in Edo litigation, hence their role as legal advisors.

If the civil suit in Edo never quite emerged from the group and administrative trappings of feudal authority, neither did it achieve during trial complete freedom from lapses into criminal procedures. The *deiri suji* was essentially a civil procedure between adversary private parties as opposed to the inquisitorial proceeding (*gimmi-suji*) which was generally of a criminal nature. If a party was slow to compromise or was otherwise offensive during an otherwise civil trial, the officials could proceed to treat the party as a criminal and place him in jail or subject him to torture to bring him into line. This, too, was a habit which Meiji officials were unable to give up until 1879. We have also seen that substantive and procedural law were coalesced in a formulary system in much the same way they were in the forms of action at common law.

Two other features of Tokugawa trials were highly significant to legal evolution: (1) the policy to individualize in deciding cases, and (2) the continual pressure exerted on the parties to compromise their disputes by conciliation even after the suit was accepted. The policy to individualize was encouraged by the fact there were few written rules in the field of civil law, which was governed largely by ancient local custom, called the great law (*taihō*).[54]

---

[52] See Takigawa, *Kujiyado no kenkyū* (1959); and Hiramatsu's review thereof in 12 *Hōseishi kenkyū* (1961), 243. For practices of a Kyoto *kujiyado*, see Takigawa (ed.), *Nijōya no kenkyū—kujiyado no kenkyū* (*zoku*) (1962).

[53] For concrete descriptions of several actual trials in Edo, see Nakada, "Tokugawa jidai minji saiban jitsuroku," in 3 *Hōseishi ronshū* (1943), 753–832, 833–904.

[54] Nakada, "Kōhō zakkō," 1 *Hōseishi kenkyū* (1951, 1–44; and *id.*, "Taihō,' 3 *Hōseishi ronshū* (1943, 1096.

But in ajudication the Osadamegaki and other basic decrees provided that reason (*dōri*) should override the great law as found in custom and precedents.[55] And as noted, even statutes were not usually effective prescriptions but were most often moral exhortations, reminders of the natural-law obligations or simply convenient guides to the exercise of official discretion. These features fostered the pronounced policy in favor of individualization in deciding each case, thus creating a basic kind of equity known as Ōoka justice, after the famous judge, Ōoka Echizen-no-kami, the father of many trial legends of presentday Japan.[56] Needless to say excessive individualization tended to minimize the effectiveness of legal prescriptions, as we understand them today.

Conciliation was even a stronger anti-legal feature of Tokugawa justice.[57] As noted earlier, the vast majority of Tokugawa civil disputes were settled by didactic conciliation on the village level, without a suit, or more significantly without a right to sue. But in addition, as records of the proceedings show, even in those cases which because of diversity could be brought to Edo, the trials were often little more than a series of hearings given over to pressures by the judge to obtain a compromise settlement. We should not overlook the fact that both the conciliation pressures and the tendency to individualize had the effect of stunting the growth of law through the development of precedent, because neither technique produced decisions that could be publicized and remembered as precedents in future conduct and cases. Furthermore, the coercive character of didactic conciliation resulting from the social differences between the parties and between parties and officials or conciliators, plus the lack of appeals and other alternative remedies, all make us wonder if this conciliation process did not serve well the established authority of the community and tend to perpetuate tradition. Conciliation may have been itself traditional and a conduit of other substantive traditions.

In summation surely the first insight which comes through clearly is that the highest achievement of the Tokugawa was administration and not justiciable law. The administration at all levels was efficient, surprisingly well-recorded and above all superlatively authoritarian in concept and implementation. No doubt this remarkable efficacy of administration was based to some degree on the immobility and mutual dependence of rice farmers, all captives of the demands of the rice cycle itself, strapped to the land by the registries, and defenseless in a world of sword-wielding warriors. These administrative

---

[55] *E.g.*, Ishii, *Nihon hōseishi gaisetsu* (1960), 370, n. 1. Shimada, an Edo town commissioner, had requested permission to make available to his successors compilations of precedents which he had built up during his tenure in office. The second Shōgun, Hidetada (tenure 1605–1622), denied permission on the grounds that such a reliance on precedents would dull the judge's sense of justice.

[56] The strong popular admiration in Japan for this basic equitable type of justice is called *Ōoka saiban* after a famous Tokugawa "judge (*bugyō*), Ōoka Echizen-no-kami (1677–1751), is an important part of the jural tradition illustrative of this point. See *Ōoka seidan* in the series, 1 *Kinsei monogatari bungaku* (1960), which though partly fictional, nevertheless gives the feel for this tradition.

[57] I, Henderson, *Conciliation and Japanese Law—Tokugawa and Modern* (1965), chap. 6.

elements were later useful: the basic authoritarian family and village, the registries, the ingrained attitudes of samurai leadership and authority, complemented by "creative obedience" not only in official relations, but also built into all tenant, employment, and other contractual relationships and business enterprises.

But there was no tradition of a separate judiciary or an independent bench and only a beginning of a bar, even to handle private litigation. And, of course, the idea of justiciable law to control the making or execution of official policy is a concept from another world.

CHAPTER THIRTEEN

BAKUFU VERSUS *KABUKI*

DONALD H. SHIVELY

Reprinted from *Harvard Journal of
Asiatic Studies,* Vol. 18, Nos. 3-4 (December 1955)

The *kabuki* drama of the Tokugawa period was an art form
which represented the taste and interests of the class of townsmen.
Deprived of political and social opportunities, the townsmen
tended toward grosser pleasures, and evolved a theater which
was gaudy, graphic, and emotionally unrestrained. It contrasted
with the drama of their social superiors, the military class of
shogun, feudal lords, and upper samurai, who patronized *nō*
drama: subtle, symbolic, a form already made static by tradition.
Of all the lively forms of entertainment and art for which the
culture of the townsmen is well known, none excited so much
interest in all classes of society as early *kabuki*. Certainly there
was none which ran so blatantly counter to the social and moral
principles espoused by the Tokugawa government, the *bakufu*,
nor which was more disruptive to the structure of Confucian
relationships which the *bakufu* strove to maintain.

The traditional date for the first performance of *kabuki* is 1603,
by coincidence the year Ieyasu received the title of shogun and
the Tokugawa *bakufu* began officially. From the start, the government was appalled at the popularity of *kabuki* and its disruptive
influence, and took steps to control it. The running duel between
the *bakufu* and *kabuki* lasted the entire 250 years of the Tokugawa period, the *bakufu* constantly thrusting with restrictive
laws, the *kabuki* parrying with ingenious devices.

Of particular interest is the nature of these restrictions and the
effect they had on the development of *kabuki* as a dramatic form.
As might be expected, the harassing measures of the *bakufu*
circumscribed *kabuki* in some respects, and forced it into some
strange avenues. But most extraordinary, in some ways the effect
was artistically beneficial.

A review of the origins of *kabuki* will help to explain the government's attitude. It began as open-air performances of dances

and farces by women, who used it to advertise their secondary, if not primary, profession of prostitution. Among the most popular themes for the skits of the early period were those demonstrating techniques used by prostitutes in accosting clients, or by clients in accosting prostitutes, and scenes of revelry in brothels [1]—all matters in which the actresses had professional competence. Contemporary notices leave no doubt that the dialogue was alive with indecent lines, the dances with suggestive movements. In most of the troupes of *onna kabuki* 女歌舞伎 (" women's *kabuki*,") there were male actors, but distressingly enough, they often took the female roles while the actresses played the male roles, providing the opportunity for much improper pantomime. The young actors were involved in homosexual prostitution, which had become widespread in Japan during the campaigns of the medieval period, and particularly during the century and a half of intermittent warfare which ended in 1600. Among the early *kabuki* actors and promoters there were other dubious types—ruffians, gamblers, and panderers. The government seems to have been fully justified in considering those connected with *kabuki* an undesirable element in society.

The *kabuki* troupes were an immediate success, not only with townsmen, but perhaps even more with military personnel. With the close of the Korean campaigns and the restoration of peace after the battle of Sekigahara, the large numbers of men who had entered the military profession craved abandoned entertainment, and they had money to pay for it. The early *kabuki* performances, tailored to attract them, were crude and down to earth. As might be expected, the famous Confucian scholar HAYASHI Razan 林羅山 (1583-1657) was not complimentary in his description of these shows:

The men wear women's clothing; the women wear men's clothing, cut their hair and wear it in a man's topknot, have swords at their sides and carry purses. They sing base songs and dance vulgar dances; their lewd voices are clamorous, like the buzzing of flies and the crying of cicadas. The men and women sing and dance together.[2]

---

[1] TAKANO Tatsuyuki 高野辰之, *Nihon engeki shi* 日本演劇史 2(1948).20, 39.
[2] *Razan bunshū* 羅山文集, quoted in TAKANO 2.23.

An early seventeenth-century work provides a description of an actress-dancer's stage entrance in Edo:

When a high placard was put up at Nakabashi announcing that there would be a *kabuki* by Ikushima Tango-no-kami, people gathered, and the high and the low thronged to it. After they had waited impatiently for her appearance, the curtain was flung up, the leading dancer appeared and came along the runway. She was gaily dressed, wore a long and a short sword worked in gold, and had a flint-bag and gourd hung from her waist. She had Saruwaka as a companion. The figure, as it sauntered on in high spirits, did not appear to be that of a woman but of a true-hearted man: it was indeed the image of Narihira,[3] who long ago was called the spirit of *yin* and *yang*. The people in the pit and in the boxes craned their necks and, slapping their heads, rocked about forgetting themselves. When she reached the stage, her face, which when seen more closely was even better, was indeed that of a YANG Kuei-fei. It was as though you could say that one of her smiles would throw the six Imperial consorts into the shade. The outer corners of her eyes were like the hibiscus, her lips like red flowers. . . . Anyone who would not fall in love with such a beautiful figure is more to be feared than a ghost.[4]

Then fifty or sixty people danced on the stage, while the samisen accompanied songs meant to arouse a desire for dissipation with such words as:

> Be in a frenzy
> In this dream-like floating world.
> Even the thunder
> That rumbles and rumbles
> Cannot put you and me
> Asunder.[5]

There is no doubt about the excitement that *kabuki* created during its early years. The same book says: "Although there are many different things which are popular in Edo now, there is nothing to compare with the *kabuki* women of Yoshiwara-chō." [6] A guidebook of Kyōto, *Kyō-warabe* 京童 (1658), describes the effect of the actresses on the audience at the height of women's *kabuki*:

---

[3] ARIWARA no Narihira 在原業平 (825-880), whose amorous exploits are the subject of the *Ise monogatari*.

[4] *(Keichō) kemmon shū* (慶長) 見聞集 by MIURA Jōshin 三浦淨心 (Shigemasa 茂正) (1565-1644); *kan* 5, in *Shiseki shūran* 10 (1901), "Sanroku" ["Miscellaneous *Notes*"] No. 42, p. 144.

[5] *Ibid.*, 145.

[6] *Ibid.*, 143

They afflicted the six sense-organs of people, they captivated their hearts by appealing to their six senses. Men threw away their wealth, some forgot their fathers and mothers, others did not care if the mothers of their children were jealous. Day and night they had their hearts on [the actresses], and exhausted the money-boxes in their godowns. They did not tire of dallying as long as their wealth lasted. Although they concealed this from their parents and deceived their wives, it became known, [just as nothing escapes] the meshes of the many nets pulled up on the beach of Akogi. Because this was so disturbing to the country and an affliction of the people, the *kabuki* of prostitutes was banned.[7]

A guidebook to Edo, the *Edo meishoki* 江戶名所記 (1662), in reviewing the history of women's *kabuki*, says:

. . . . when theaters were built for the prostitutes to give *kabuki* performances, the impetuous eccentrics among the high and the low became infatuated with them and thronged and jostled one another in the boxes of the theaters. Still unsatisfied, they constantly engaged them, consummated their trysts, squandered their inheritance, and ruined their names. Some, engaging in brawls and arguments, were taken to court. Women's *kabuki* was banned because it disturbed the country, caused deterioration in various ways, and was the cause of calamities.[8]

Where the heavy-drinking, pleasure-bent veterans congregated, trouble was quick to flare up. These samurai, foot-soldiers, and *rōnin* (unemployed samurai), were pugnacious and unruly. In the crowd around the stage the accidental brush of sword scabbards or an unintentional touch with a foot might be enough to set off a brawl among the quick-tempered warriors. Heckling of a favorite actor often started quarrels. Sword fights broke out because of rivalries and jealousies over the attentions of actresses and young actors. Because *kabuki* performances so often led to disorders and even to bloodshed, TOKUGAWA Ieyasu himself ordered the troupes expelled from his base at Suruga in 1608.[9]

In other areas local reform measures were taken in the attempt to halt the subverting of public morals by actresses and actors. They were so much the rage in the capital that even court ladies were said to have been influenced by their style of behavior. In

---

[7] By NAKAGAWA Kiun 中川喜雲 (1636-1705); in *Kyōto sōsho* 3 (1914) .7.

[8] By ASAI Ryōi 淺井了意 (d. 1709?); in *Zoku zoku gunsho ruijū* (Kokusho Kankōkai ed.) 8 (1906) .756.

[9] IHARA Toshirō 伊原敏郎, *Nihon engeki shi* 1 (1904) .28-29.

1608-1609 five ladies of the Imperial court, of whom two were favorites of the Emperor, went strolling about the city after the manner of prostitutes and *kabuki* actresses, and holding a rendezvous with nine courtiers, drank and made love with them. The Emperor was so displeased that he sent a messenger to Ieyasu, asking him to punish the participants; the principals were executed or banished.[10]

In 1628 the *kabuki* dancer Azuma was ordered out of Edo when her performance resulted in a fight, and all women *kabuki* performers, women dancers, and women *jōruri* reciters were banned.[11]

When such local measures failed to solve the problem, and when women appeared in *kabuki* in Edo again the next year, in 1629 the Tokugawa government took the decisive step of prohibiting women's *kabuki* and banning all women from the stage.[12] At first this ban was not always strictly enforced, for there are reports of women appearing on the stage in Edo as late as 1642 or 1643.[13] This is also evident from the fact that the ban was repeatedly reissued, as in 1630, 1640, 1645, and 1646.[14] The next year, when women appeared again on the stage of KASAYA Sankatsu's 笠屋 三勝 theater, the manager was thrown in prison.[15] After this time the ban was more rigorously enforced, and in effect, women were kept off the *kabuki* stage in the principal cities for 250 years—until after the Meiji Restoration. Only in some provincial areas and around Ise did women continue to appear on the stage.

[10] TAKANO 2.45.

[11] IHARA 29.

[12] The law of the 10th month, 1629 read: " In theater performances we hear that heretofore men and women have been mixed. As this is improper, it will not be done henceforth." Cf. IHARA 30-31.

[13] TAKANO 2.45.

[14] SEKINE Shisei 關根只誠 (1825-1893), *Tōto gekijō enkaku shi* 東都劇場沿革 誌 (Chinsho Kankōkai ed.) 1 (1916).31b; IHARA 87-88. The law of 1645 said: " Although notification was given during the year 1640 that it is a misdemeanor for men and women to appear together in *kabuki* dancing, lately not only were women dancers being employed and subjected to a bitter life [i. e., prostitution], but men and women were being mixed in *kabuki* performances, and consequently the employers and dancers were punished. Hereafter those who violate this law will receive severe punishment." (IHARA 87.)

[15] IHARA 88.

Dancing girls were repeatedly proscribed in the principal cities, but the authorities were unable to check entirely their appearance for private entertainment.

More than a decade before women were banned from the stage, at least as early as 1612 there had appeared troupes composed entirely of young men, performing what was called *wakashū* 若衆 *kabuki* (" youth's *kabuki* "). The popularity of the young actors is attested to by the *Kyō warabe*:

> From the time that " youth's *kabuki* " began with youths beautifully gotten up, there was homosexual dallying. Still again [as in the instance of actresses] men had their souls so stolen by them that when they ate their meals they did not taste them. Moreover they became partners of the thighs and arms. Some young women asked to marry these beautiful youths, or were watchful for an arrow shot from Aizen's bow. How much more the monks of the various temples, who, wishing to get them, decided to use the *mameita* coins they received as offerings for theater tickets, and gave these bewitching creatures as gifts the *chōgin* coins received as subscriptions. . . .[16]

The description in the *Edo meishoki* says:

> . . . " youth's *kabuki* " began, with beautiful youths being made to sing and dance, whereupon droll fools again had their hearts captivated and their souls stolen. As they rapturously gave themselves up to visiting the youths in high spirits, the early depletion of even substantial fortunes was like light snow exposed to the spring sun. How much worse it was for those whose fortunes were slight to begin with. There were many of these men who soon had run through their fortunes and who, making for Nambu Sakata, concealed their tracks; others became novice monks although their hearts were not in it, and clothing themselves in black robes, wandered about the various provinces. I have heard that men of the capital have also done this. . . . Even though the lineage of every one of the youths was extremely base, these beautiful youths were respected by the stupid; they flapped about like kites and owls and, going into the presence of the exalted, befouled the presence; and these were scoundrels who, saying insolent things as it pleased them, ruined men and held them in contempt; moreover, they polluted the high-born on the sly. This made them a canker twice over. . . .[17]

It is said also that the sons and grandsons of the military heroes of the campaigns of Hideyoshi and Ieyasu had lost their interest in the martial arts, and were not as familiar with the names of

[16] *Kyōto sōsho* 3.7. A silver *mameita* piece was 1 to 5 *momme* (which is 3.75 grams), and a *chōgin* was 43 *momme*.

[17] *Zoku zoku gunsho ruijū* 8.756.

the feudal lords as they were with those of actors and prostitutes. The passion of both the military and townsmen for the young actors so alarmed the authorities, that in 1642 they banned all female impersonation from the stage.[18] In 1644, upon the petition of the theater people, they relented to the extent of permitting female impersonations on condition that a clear distinction would be made between the actors who played female roles and those who played male, that the gender of their roles would be clearly made known, and that there would be no action on the stage which would confuse the audience as to this distinction.[19] In 1648 and repeatedly thereafter decrees forbade homosexual practices by dancers and actors.[20] Although the government looked upon the theater as an evil influence, and upon the actors as little better than the pariah class, there was no denying the fascination they held. Occasionally troupes were even called to the shogun's castle for command performances, as in the ninth month of 1650 and three times early the next year, on each occasion receiving money and gifts in compensation for their services. However, with the death of the third shogun Iemitsu (1604-1651) in the fourth month, the new regime under Ietsuna (1641-1680), as part of its sweeping reform movement, dealt severely with *kabuki*. The authorities were concerned not only with the effect of the young actors on the morality of the public at large, and on the morale of the samurai (which they considered to be waning from indulgence in luxuries and pleasures), but also with the fact that certain feudal lords and their retainers had become infatuated with the young actors.[21]

In 1652 the *bakufu* took steps considered second in importance only to the banning of women. "Youth's *kabuki*" was ordered stopped in the sixth month,[22] and in the twelfth month the more drastic action was taken of closing the twelve *kabuki* and puppet

[18] SEKINE 1.32a. The order of the 8th month, 1642, read: "To call *kabuki* plays 'sarugaku,' and for the men to play as women and act voluptuously, is prohibited."
[19] SEKINE 1.32ab; IHARA 88 says 1643.
[20] IHARA 92.
[21] *Tokugawa jikki* 徳川實紀 3 (1902) .55b, in *Zoku kokushi taikei*, vol. 11.
[22] SEKINE 1.34b-35a; cf. also TAKAYANAGI Shinzō 高柳眞三 and ISHII Ryōsuke

theaters in Edo.[23] As a result of repeated pleas by the troupe managers, a formula was worked out which enabled the theaters to reopen in the third month of the next year.

The chief concern of the *bakufu* seems to have been to reduce the attractiveness of the players of women's roles, the *onnagata* 女方, and the key reform it required to this end was to shave the actors' forelocks and require them to dress their hair like men instead of women. To the society of that day which took such interest in hair-styles, and in which the dressed forelock could be highly alluring, apparently this was a change of major importance. This and lesser reforms were the basic agreement under which *yarō* 野郎 *kabuki* ("fellow's *kabuki*"), as it was thereafter called, was permitted to operate for over two centuries until the Meiji Restoration.

The effect of the shaven forelock evidently was most disenchanting:

They somehow looked precocious, as a man who, at forty, would wear a persimmon-color loin cloth. The appearance of their faces was smooth and like cats with their ears cut off, and they were a sorry sight. It is said that these persons, sad, mournful, and plaintive, wept tears of blood. However true this was in the beginning, it seems that later they were not thought so ugly. They were accorded a welcome again, and they placed a wrap-around hood on their foreheads, arranging it so that they were not displeasing to look at, and so appeared on the stage.[24]

To hide their shaven forelock when playing women's roles, the young actors began to wear scarfs or small caps. At first scarfs of cotton or silk were draped over their heads to appear

石井良助, compilers, *Ofuregaki Kampo shūsei* 御觸書寛保集成 (hereafter *Ofure*) (1934) No. 2685 (p. 1239a).

The government's action was provoked, according to the *Tokugawa jikki* (3.55b), by a fight which broke out in the Ōsaka residence of a *daimyō*, HOSHINA Masasada 保科正貞 (1588-1661), arising from a drinking affair involving a young actor. According to another explanation, the order was issued by the Edo town commissioner when he found young actors at a banquet he attended (IHARA 93). Such explanations of what brought official action should be regarded more as symptomatic than as factual.

[23] IHARA 93-94. The explanation for the action in this instance is that the wife of a certain feudal lord had an affair with an actor, and the two planned to commit suicide together. It is also said that homosexual scandals were again prevalent.

[24] *Edo meishoki, Zoku zoku gunsho ruijū* 8.756.

like a casually-placed kerchief; even this practise was at times prohibited.[25] Some wore brocade caps, and later a close-fitting patch of purple silk was placed over the shaven area to give the illusion of a woman's lustrous hair. Within a few years they surreptitiously began to use wigs in place of the disenchanting cloth patches. The hair wigs used in *kabuki* before this time had been only the crude ones taken from *nō* and *kyōgen*, such as the ones used for demon roles or the drab wigs used for the parts of old men and women. In the latter years of the 1650's, the cloth patches began to be replaced by crude hair wigs called *maegami-gatsura* 前髪鬘, "front hair wigs." The use of any hair wigs was forbidden in 1664, but it was conceded at that time that there would be no objection to the use of cotton caps or scarfs.[26] That this order was not always strictly enforced is indicated by some contemporary woodblock prints which show actors wearing wigs. A book about Kyōto customs published in 1681 says: "Long ago when EBISUYA Kichirōbei and UKON Genza were popular, they wore on their heads pieces of silk like hand-towels, and they called themselves *onnagata*. Now what actors do is to use helmets of copper on which hair is attached, and these are called wigs (*katsura*)."[27] The copper-lined *kabuki* wig developed from this time, and references to wigs in the literature and art thereafter suggest that they were probably in continual use.

To make themselves appear more feminine off the stage, the actors let their forelocks grow as long as they dared. There is even mention of *onnagata* of the early 1670's whose forelocks were unshaven.[28] Periodically the actors were required to appear at a government office to pass inspection to show that their forelocks were not more than a half-inch long.[29] There were orders

---

[25] In the 8th month of 1641 MURAYAMA Sakondayū 村山左近太夫 appeared in a dance piece at the Saruwaka-za with a silk scarf draped over his head, carrying a branch of artificial flowers to which were attached poem cards. The performance was much applauded, but it was banned (SEKINE 1.32a).

[26] IHARA 436, 98. For illustrations of the styles of scarfs and caps used, see IHARA 99.

[27] *Miyako fuzoku kagami* 都風俗鑑 (1681), quoted in IHARA 458.

[28] IHARA 100.

[29] See for example one of the many orders of the 5th month, 1689, quoted in IHARA 437.

issued from time to time, directing the actors to shave their heads more closely or to shave a wider area.[30]

In " fellow's *kabuki* " the old abuses continued, if less openly, and the madness of the audience for the youths remained unabated. Describing the performances, the Edo guidebook says:

> When these youths, their hair beautifully done up, with light make-up, and wearing splendid padded robes, moved slowly along the runway, singing songs in delicate voices, the spectators in front bounced up and down on their buttocks, those in back reared up, while those in the boxes opened their mouths up to their ears and drooled; unable to contain themselves, they shouted: " Look, look. Their figures are like emanations of the deities, they are (?) heavenly stallions (天道馬)!" And from the sides others called: " Oh, that smile! It overflows with sweetness. Good! good! " and the like, and there was shouting and commotion.[31]

A book on actors entitled *Yarō mushi* 野郎虫 [*Fellow Bugs*] (ca. 1660), gives us a satirical account of the young ones:

> In these times in the capital there is a great number of what are called " fellow bugs " who eat away the bamboo and wood of the five monasteries and ten abbeys, the books of the learned priests, and even the purses of fathers and grandfathers. . . . " Fellow bugs " are about the size of a human being fifteen or sixteen years old; they are equipped with arms, legs, mouth, nose, ears, and eyes, wear a black cap on the head, fly around Gion, Maruyama, and Ryōzen, and have their eyes on people's purses. When I asked someone: " Are those not the young *kabuki* actors of Shijō-gawara? " he clapped his hands, laughed, and said: " You are right." These young *kabuki* actors have multiplied in number especially in the past year and this year. The handsome among the children of lowly outcastes and beggars are selected; and when, their faces never without powder, and dressed in clothes of silk gauze and damask, they are put on the stage to dance and sing, the old and the young, men and women, become weak-kneed and call out: " Gosaku! Good! good! I'll die! " Not only do they call to them, but seduced by their alluring eyes, after the performance they go with them to Higashiyama; borne away in woven litters and palanquins, they proceed in high spirits, calling: " Here, here! A palanquin, a palanquin." Ah! what grateful affection! Bilked of a large amount of gold and sliver for one night's troth, the droll priests of the temples, their bodies wasting away day by day, desire only to engage the fellows. Having no money, they sell the treasures of paintings and tea-ceremony utensils that have been handed down generation after generation in the temples, and if these do not suffice, they cut down the bamboo and trees, and with that money, engage fellows.[32]

---

[30] 8/1694 and 1/1697 (IHARA 438); 4/1699 (*Ofure* 2711).

[31] *Edo meishoki, Zoku zoku gunsho ruijū* 8.757-758.

[32] Quoted by TAKANO 2.57-58; facsimile ed. 1b-2b, in the Kisho Fukusei Kai 稀書

Bakufu versus *Kabuki*

The critical booklets on actors, the *yakusha hyōbanki* 役者評判記, give more attention to the physical attributes of the actors than to acting ability until the end of the seventeenth century; it was only by gradual stages that art gained ground on sex.[33] Those characteristics of early *kabuki* which were considered to have a corrosive effect on society and morals continued throughout the Tokugawa period, but were kept within certain limits by the intermittent harassing.

If the officials considered that *kabuki* constantly poured into society the poisons of immorality and extravagance, why did they not abolish *kabuki* outright? The attitude of the *bakufu* seems to have been that *kabuki* was, like prostitution, a necessary evil. These were the two wheels of the vehicle of pleasure, useful to assuage the people and divert them from more serious mischief. The document known as Ieyasu's legacy, a basic guide for *bakufu* policy, states:

複製會 Series, No. 3. Another account of the young actors, appearing in the *Edo meishoki* (cf. *Zoku zoku gunsho ruijū* 8.756-757), seems to draw some of its material from the *Yarō mushi*, to which it had referred earlier:

While [the fellows] parade down the runway, they sing songs in voices like that of Kalavinka, said to be a bird in Paradise; the sight as they open their fans and perform a dance leads one to think that the fluttering of the sleeves of the feather robe of the heavenly maiden who descended from the sky at Udo Bay long ago must have been like this. The blind eccentrics, who think nothing of spending great amounts of money, consummate frequent rendezvous as their memories of the floating world. It is especially the exalted and noble monks of the various temples, and in addition, the acolytes of the various monasteries who, each and every one of them, are captivated and lured by these youths and go to visit them with their hopes pinned on a meeting. Each time they see them they feel as though the three Holy Ones [Amida, Kannon, and Seishi] were coming to receive them. When they accomplish their end, they feel like the carp of Lung-men who have leapt up the three-fold falls. Since they are still unsated, they go again and again. In the end, lacking the money with which to engage them, they sell their sutras and holy teachings to raise the fee; they pawn Buddhist utensils and their surplices, steal and carry away the age-old treasures of the temples, and present them to the youths to curry favor with them for a thousand-year troth. It is sad that on account of this they receive scandalous reputations, their virtue is damaged, and they are reduced to flight. Although I may not indicate who they are, there are among the *kabuki* youths of today, those who are beautiful in face and form and resemble Narihira, but whose appearance when they take a fan and dance is like boars swimming. Or there are those who are gentle in voice and speech, but whose manners are coarse and movements unrefined like untrained, fledgling falcons, or like calves newly muzzled. Again there are those who have a fearful look about the eyes, being cross-eyed. Then there are those whose mouths are large with thick lips, resembling rain-water jars. They are all as foul-tempered as starving dogs, and in their greed for things they resemble cats guarding their food. Now the "way of youth" flourished in China and it has existed in Japan since ancient times, but the very name for the *kabuki* youths today is *onnagata* and in all ways they behave like prostitutes, having as their chief aim to seduce men and to take things. Furthermore, even though they contrive to sweeten their dispositions, their efforts easily fall apart, and they are like inexperienced foxes disguising themselves as beautiful women. When they reveal their tails from time to time, ridiculous things happen. Nevertheless the devotees are blind to their good and bad points, and indeed it is only after they have unswervingly spent everything that they finally awake from their dreams . . .

[33] TAKANO 2.57-59, 200-201, 304.

Courtesans, dancers, catamites, streetwalkers, and the like always come to the cities and prospering places of the country. Although the conduct of many is corrupted by them, if they are rigorously suppressed, serious crimes will occur daily, and there will be punishments for gambling, drunken frenzies, and lasciviousness.[34]

Although *kabuki* and prostitution constituted social problems, if they were suppressed completely—if the professionals were thrown out of work and their patrons were disgruntled—still more serious social, if not criminal, results would follow. If Edo became the deadest town in Japan, the professionals and many others would move elsewhere. There were also economic and political reasons for not suppressing *kabuki* and prostitution. Instead, the government segregated and isolated them in certain quarters of the cities so that society as a whole would not be contaminated.

The government went beyond geographical segregation and attempted to draw and maintain distinctions between the professions of the prostitutes, dancers, and actors. As these professions were traditionally one, it was difficult to check their continual tendency to drift toward each other. It was also an innovation for the government to regard prostitution and homosexuality as evils. These had long been accepted in Japan and the attempt of the Confucian-inspired bureaucrat to curb them resulted in a tiresome repetition of laws of limited effectiveness.

The *bakufu*'s laws concerning *kabuki*, like so many of its laws, were ordinances primarily for the city of Edo, but they stood as models which other areas were encouraged to emulate. Some concluded with the phrase: " The above is ordered sent also to Kyōto and Ōsaka." [35] In most cases, however, the commissioners in Ōsaka and Kyōto did not issue the Edo edicts at once, but waited for an opportune moment, when an incident occurred which would make the new restriction accepted with less discontent. The same month of 1652 in which the forelocks of the Edo actors were ordered shaven, a swordfight in an Ōsaka theater

---

[34] " Tokugawa seiken hyakkajō " 德川成憲百箇條, *Tokugawa kinrei kō* 禁令考 (hereafter *Kinrei*) 1 (1931) .88.

[35] *Ofure* 2707.

brought about the closing of the theaters there until the next year.[36] The Kyōto commissioner had to wait four years for an appropriate pretext; this was provided when a samurai, jealous over the favors of one of the actors, provoked a swordfight in a box of one of the theaters. It seems that the Kyōto theaters were closed longer than those of Edo and Ōsaka.[37] However, judging from the similarity of conditions in the *kabuki* theaters of the three cities, it is apparent that the prohibitions and the tacit permission were roughly the same.

The Tokugawa laws issued to the common people, known as *ofuregaki* 御觸書 , were to a considerable extent hortatory. The government's attitude was that the townsmen were "stupid people" (*gumin* 愚民) who had to be talked to like children. The officials summoned together all the theater managers and actors once a year and read them the regulations. When they considered that the customary infringing of a law had become too blatant, another was issued to the same effect, prefaced with some phrases, such as: "There are rumors of violations. If these occur again, there will be swift and severe prosecutions." The leniency that the officials generally showed in enforcing the laws, preferring to issue warnings rather than to prosecute, is illustrated by a passage in another *ofuregaki*: "... as this is most improper, if an investigation were made it would call for strict punishment; but since

---

[36] IHARA 95.

[37] IHARA 94-95. The precise year of the ban is in doubt. One tradition says the 2nd month of 1656, another 1657.

Typical of the fanciful tales associated with Tokugawa period literary and theatrical figures is the account that a Kyōto manager, MURAYAMA Matabei 村山又兵衞, petitioned so earnestly and tenaciously for the reopening of the theaters that he remained ten-odd years in front of the town commissioner's office, never returning home, ignoring rain and dew, until his clothes were in tatters. Many of the actors went into other trades or moved to other areas, but those who remained in Kyōto took food to him, and he persevered until at last in 1668 his plea was granted. However, whatever the basis for this story, the *Kyō warabe* (published in 1658) describes the Kyōto theaters as in thriving condition; the *Yarō mushi* (ca. 1659) mentions three theaters, and ASAI Ryōi's *Tōkaidō meishoki* 東海道名所記 (1662) (*kan* 6, *Onchi sōsho* 1[1891].243-244) mentions a fourth. Cf. TAKANO 2.356-357; also the "Gei kagami" 藝鑑 by TOMINAGA Heibei 富永平兵衞 in *Yakusha rongo* 役者論語 (1776), *Shin gunsho ruijū* (Kokusho Kankōkai ed.) 3 (1908).6b.

all this is known by rumor, it will not be made a legal case this time. . . ." [38] One order concluded with the curious statement:

In general, after there has been a prosecution, orders are issued; but in no time there are those who violate them, and it is not well that they have not been prosecuted. Since such has been the case, hereafter constantly and without remiss it should be kept in mind that investigations will be carried through.[39]

There is no comprehensive collection of these laws concerning the theater, and most of them must have been lost. However, there are well over a hundred still to be found in the collections of Tokugawa laws or scattered through Tokugawa encyclopaedias, guidebooks, diaries, and miscellanea. Those already discussed were largely intended to curb prostitution and homosexual practices. The remainder fall into three general categories: first, those designed to segregate the theater and its actors from the rest of society; second, sumptuary laws attempting to restrict the costumes and architecture of the theater to an austerity appropriate to the townsmen class; and third, those forbidding subject matter in plays which would have a subversive political or moral influence. All were designed to preserve the morality of the state and its people, since political, social, and ethical morality were considered one, all subsumed under proper observance of human relationships, with particular stress on conduct appropriate to one's status. The Tokugawa official, then, would consider these to be not repressive but reform measures.

Fundamental to the segregation policy was the concentration of the large theaters in two quarters of the city. This was facilitated in Edo by the fires of the 1650's, especially that of 1657, which leveled large areas of the city. Thereafter the government required that all the main theaters be located in a quarter comprised of Sakai-chō 堺町 and Fukiya-chō 葺屋町, or in Kobiki-chō 木挽町.[40] The same occasion was utilized to concentrate the houses of prostitution farther from the center of Edo by moving

---

[38] Undated law in *Kinrei* 5.700-701.

[39] 3/1714; cf. *Ofure* 2733.

[40] 12/1661: "Henceforth *kabuki* will not be performed except in Sakai-chō, Fukiya-chō [i. e., Upper Sakai-chō], and Kobiki-chō 5-chōme and 6-chōme." (*Ofure* 2690.) The former two were located northeast of Nihonbashi, the latter south of Kyōbashi.

the licensed quarter to Asakusa, where it became known as the New Yoshiwara. The number of large theaters (*ō-shibai* 大芝居) was restricted to four (not increased during the Tokugawa period), and there were allowed eight small theaters (*ko-shibai*), as well as those of temples and shrines, which could put on performances for limited periods of time upon receipt of a permit from the town commissioner (*machi bugyō* 町奉行). Punishment was threatened for the staging of unauthorized performances.[41] The number of actors in a troupe was also restricted, as in 1694 when each large theater was limited to twenty actors and ten apprentice actors.[42]

The same procedures were followed in Kyōto and Ōsaka. In Kyōto the large theaters were restricted to Shijō-gawara 四條河原, and were gradually reduced in number, as opportunities permitted, from seven to three. In Ōsaka there were three theaters in Dōtombori 道頓堀 and one in Horie 堀江.[43] In addition there were some medium- and small-sized theaters in both cities.

In order to protect society at large from the corrupting influence of actors, great care was taken to separate them professionally and physically from the rest of society. Just as prostitutes were restricted to their respective quarters of the cities, actors were not permitted to leave the theater quarters. They were required to live in the close neighborhood of the district, and could not reside in the homes of non-actors, nor allow those of other professions to live in their residences.[44] The authorities were interested primarily in preventing the actors from accepting invitations to entertain outside the quarter, particularly in the mansions of the feudal lords (*daimyō*) in Edo, or in the residences of samurai or wealthy merchants. It is evident that the actors were much in demand at private parties, and that the attempt to keep them restricted was a continuous and largely unsuccessful battle. Countless arrests, imprisonments and banishments seem to have

---

[41] 5/1708 (*Ofure* 2726); in 1662 the "bamboo-grass walled theaters" at temples and shrines were ordered not to stage performances for more than 100 days a year. See *Kiyū shōran* 嬉遊笑覽, *kan* 5b (ca. 1830), by KITAMURA Nobuyo 喜多村信節 (1784-1856), 1(1926).587 in *Nihon geirin sōsho* vol. 6.

[42] IHARA 438.

[43] IHARA 449.

[44] 3/1678 (IHARA 437).

been insufficient deterrents. That violations persisted is apparent from the fact that between 1648 and 1709 edicts ordering that actors should not leave the theater quarters were issued so repeatedly that the texts of at least twenty can be found.[45]

It is evident that even the second of these, issued in 1655, had been preceded by many others:

Laws have been issued time after time that even if *kabuki* actors are invited to feudal lords' residences, they must not go. Of course they must not wear sumptuous costumes. . . . Minstrels, if invited to residences, must not do imitations of *kabuki*, nor imitate the Shimabara style. Even if one or two *kabuki* actors are invited to residences, they must not go nor perform imitations of Shimabara.[46]

The order of 1668 said:

After the actors of Sakai-chō and Kobiki-chō finish the plays on the stage, they must not meet government employees [i. e. samurai]; farmers and townsmen must not visit them indiscriminately and stay long.[47]

That of 1678 said:

We hear that actors go to the homes of samurai and townsmen, and not only stay a long time, but also sometimes even stay overnight. This is most improper. Henceforth, even though they be summoned, they must not go.[48]

The edict of 1695 said:

It has been strictly forbidden by law over and over that *kabuki* actors, *rōnin yarō*, those with unshaven forelocks who do not appear as actors, women dancers, and homosexual youths, go out. It is hereby ordered that henceforth such people must not be sent out at all. We hear that recently there has been some going out, and that the above persons have also been sent out on boats. This is outrageous. Henceforth, more than ever before, it is prohibited to send the above persons anywhere. Of course they may absolutely not be sent out in boats. Anyone who violates this will, upon discovery, be arrested. . . .[49]

---

[45] 2/1648 (*Kinrei* 5.521), 5/1655 (*Ofure* 2688), 1/1661 (IHARA 436), 12/1661 (*Ofure* 2690), 1/1662 (IHARA 436), 3/1668 (*Ofure* 2695), 4/1671 (IHARA 437), 3/1678 (IHARA 437), 5/1689 (*Ofure* 2704), 5/1689 (*Ofure* 2705), 5/1689 (*Ofure* 2706), 8/1695 (*Kinrei* 5.695), 1/1697 (*Ofure* 2709), 4/1699 (*Ofure* 2711), 2/1703 (IHARA 438), 4/1703 (*Ofure* 2716), 3/1706 (*Ofure* 2793), 3/1706 (IHARA 438), 6/1706 (*Ofure* 2719), 6/1706 (*Ofure* 2720), 7/1709 (*Ofure* 2729).

[46] *Ofure* 2688.
[47] *Ofure* 2695.
[48] IHARA 437.
[49] *Kinrei* 5.695.

There were also orders warning actors not to disguise themselves as ordinary townsmen in the attempt to slip out of the
quarter to answer calls to residences. There were also numerous
prohibitions against those not registered as actors to dress like
them, or to put on performances, or to go to private residences
to entertain. There were such prohibitions concerning not only
youths but also women dancers.[50]

From time to time the government weeded out unauthorized
entertainers, as in an order of 1689:

Hereafter, as the law on actors provides, only actors of Sakai-chō and
Kobiki-chō, and with their forelocks shaved, are permitted to appear in
theaters. As to the other youths, the money paid for them will be their
master's loss, and they will be returned to their guarantor or parent. If they
should be sold again, it will be an offence.[51]

An order of 1706 said:

Although it has been ordered over and over that women dancers must not
be sent around, in recent years it has become rife, and this is outrageous.
Hereafter women dancers are prohibited. Some word has been heard to the
effect that they are being called " maids " and are being sent to feudal lords'
mansions and townsmen's homes. The same applies to this as to the preceding.[52]

In 1703 the following was issued:

As ordered repeatedly before, Sakai-chō and Kobiki-chō actors may not go
out, but it is heard that recently there has been lax observation of the
prohibitions against groups of townsmen who have entertaining skills going to
feudal lords' mansions, and also the employing of women dancers and sending
them about here and there. This is improper. . . .[53]

The distinction between actors and the rest of society was emphasized by prohibiting any amateur dramatics, except at those
two most important festivals, New Year and Bon.

In its efforts to enforce observance of laws concerning actors,
the *bakufu* utilized informers and the devices of group and cor-

---

[50] 6/1652 (*Ofure* 2685), 6/1666 (*Ofure* 2694), 5/1689 (*Ofure* 2703-2706), 5/1689
(*Kinrei* 5.694), 1/1697 (IHARA 438), 4/1699 (*Ofure* 2711), 4/1703 (*Ofure* 2716).
6/1706 (*Ofure* 2719), 6/1706 (*Ofure* 2720).

[51] IHARA 437-438.

[52] *Ofure* 2720.

[53] *Ofure* 2716.

porate responsibility on which it relied in much of its law enforcement. Most of the ordinances concerning the segregation of actors or prohibiting the keeping of female dancers and youths ended with clauses specifying the extent of responsibility, as for example:

> The contents of the above is to be passed throughout the quarters (*chō*) to house-owners and renters and all those on their premises. Quarter representatives (*nanushi*), five-man groups, and house-owner groups should investigate, and should leave no one at all of the above types. From this [office] men will be sent around, and if there are such people, as soon as they see them or hear of them they will arrest them, and so this should be strictly observed. If there are those who violate this they should be reported at once. If they are concealed and we learn of them from other sources, the person in question, needless to say, and even the house-owner, five-man group, and quarter representative will be strictly prosecuted for the offence. Hence the purport of this should continue to be observed.[54]

Because of the attention the *bakufu* gave to proper relations between classes, it was most anxious to stop the type of fraternization implied by the visits of actors to the residences of lords and samurai. As each class had its own professions, its style of living and amusements, *kabuki* was not supposed to be completely public theater, but was intended only for townsmen. The theater of the upper classes was *nō*, which was intended for them exclusively. When it was discovered that a special performance of *nō* was put on for townsmen in the Yoshiwara, those involved were punished. So that high personages could attend in secrecy, boxes were built in the Edo *kabuki* theaters in 1646, raised above the pit and screened with bamboo blinds. Three years later, and repeatedly thereafter, blinds and standing screens were prohibited.[55] The clever managers devised a means of slipping vertical lattices hastily in place to make sheltering partitions when a feudal lord or high-ranking samurai attended; they could be quickly dismantled when he left.

But men of such rank might lose status or even be punished for attending, and as *bakufu* surveillance increased late in the seventeenth century, they probably came rarely. The lords' wives, daughters, and ladies of the shogun's court were consumed with

[54] 6/1706 (*Ofure* 2720).
[55] IHARA 89; also law of 3/1668 (*Kinrei* 5.693).

248

eagerness to have a glimpse of actors on the stage. Most did not have the nerve to go in, but stopped their palanquins in front of the entrance and had their footmen part the curtains so that they could have a glimpse. This practice became so common that there was a law forbidding it. Such was the envy of the upper classes for the townsmen's *kabuki*. The lower samurai, although forbidden to attend the theater, seem to have gone quite openly—when they could afford the price of proper seats, which was considerable.

Adjoining the theaters or in their close vicinity were many small establishments called " theater teahouses " (*shibai-jaya* 芝 居茶屋). Here theater-goers could eat and drink, arrange for reservations at the theaters, check their wraps while they went to see the plays, or sit and visit with their friends. But " teahouse " was also a euphemism for a house of assignation. Since the actors were forbidden to leave the quarter, these establishments served as places to which their patrons could invite them. The furnishings of such teahouses become more and more luxurious, and the parties there were a concern to the authorities. They placed restrictions on the teahouses, but they did not abolish them outright because they also had their legitimate functions, and eating and drinking were considered to be an important part of theater-going. The actors were ordered not to meet patrons there, or backstage, or in the boxes, but such prohibitions were essentially unenforceable.[56]

The second category of prohibitions is related to the system of sumptuary laws by which the officials attempted to curb extravagance and conspicuous consumptions by all classes. It specified for each class what sort of clothes, personal adornments, houses, and furnishings could be used. The government was particularly anxious to prevent any show of high living by the merchants which would excite the envy of the theoretically superior samurai.

Many of the sumptuary laws " governing " the *kabuki* forbade the use of expensive costumes. The love of expensive clothes is

---

[56] 4/1671 (IHARA 437).

a dominating interest in traditional Japanese culture. Throughout Japanese literature from the *Genji monogatari* on, there are minute descriptions of clothes, their style, color, and texture. This interest increased as the art of weaving developed in Japan after the immigration of Chinese weavers into Sakai late in the sixteenth century, and the establishment by Hideyoshi of the Nishijin quarter of Kyōto as the major center of weaving. During the seventeenth century new developments in the arts of weaving and dyeing raised the interest in fine clothes to a passion.

Rich brocade and silk costumes were an essential part of *nō* drama, and, as the only colorful and luxurious element, were heavily relied on for effect. But *kabuki*, as the theater of the townsmen, was prohibited from using brocade or other expensive costumes. In addition to the sumptuary laws concerning the clothes townsmen could wear, specific orders were issued concerning *kabuki* costumes. In 1636 the manager and an actor of the Saruwaka-za 猿若座 were jailed for using costumes that were too sumptuous in a *kabuki* dance piece. The same year, when the manager of a puppet troupe, SATSUMA Koheita 薩摩小平太 , who had arrived in Edo advertising " the country's best, down from the capital," hung purple silk curtains bearing the crest of the Lord of Satsuma and used rich costumes on his puppets, he too was jailed.[57] The use of silk and other rich materials was forbidden repeatedly, as in 1649, 1650, 1655, 1662, etc.,[58] but it is evident that by 1668 the authorities were making concessions on this front also. The order of the third month of that year reads:

1. The shows in Sakai-chō and Kobiki-chō must not be extravagant. In general the actors may wear clothes of silk, pongee, and cotton, and on the stage, they may wear costumes of *hirashima*, *habutae*, silk, and pongee. Goods dyed to order, purple linings, red linings, purple caps, and embroidered articles are prohibited. Further, on the stage silk crepe and cotton curtains are permissible, but purple silk crepe is not permitted.

2. Puppet costumes must not be sumptuous. Gold and silver leaf must not be used on anything. But puppet generals only may wear gold and silver hats.[59]

---

[57] SEKINE 1.31b-32a; IHARA 89.

[58] 2/1649 (IHARA 89), 3/1650 (IHARA 89), 5/1655 (*Ofure* 2688), 1/1662 (IHARA 436), etc.

[59] 3/1668 (*Ofure* 2695).

Another order reads:

[The observance of] what has been ordered over and over has lately become lax. Actors' costumes have gradually become more gorgeous. Gold and silver threads have been used to embroider all over. Chinese-style weaving has been seen. It is improper for samurai costumes to use ceremonial kimono, long skirt and tunic, of course, and figured satin, *habutae*, and crests, and to have long and short swords and other articles of intricate work. . . . Actors' costumes should be of silk, pongee, and cotton, and should not be gorgeous. Long and short swords and other articles of intricate work must not be used.[60]

Theater managers were required to take oaths that they would not permit any of the prohibited materials to be used, and periodically a number of actors were given thirty days in jail for violations.[61] In certain periods there were annual, semi-annual, or even monthly inspections of the theaters and their properties.[62] The managers seem usually to have had prior intelligence of the inspection so that they were able to conceal the proscribed items. The officials, during most years, seem to have taken a generous attitude, not interpreting the law strictly. The inspection was an occasion to remind the managers and actors about the prohibitions and to warn them of the intention to give swift punishment for infractions in the future.

An example of the minuteness of the regulations is that realistic sword blades could not be used; it was prohibited to cover the wooden blades with silver foil or paper, but they could be painted.[63] Actors were forbidden to ride in palanquins or litters of any kind (as were all townsmen) or on horses, but the frequency with which this order was issued suggests the prevalence of violations.[64]

Concerning the architecture and furnishings of the theaters, the

---

[60] Undated (*Kinrei* 5.700-701).

[61] In 9/1708, for example, 4 actors were jailed for 30 days for wearing prohibited costumes (SEKINE 2.82b).

[62] 2/1726 (SEKINE 2.100b).

[63] 2/1704 (IHARA 438). The incident which provoked the law against the use of real swords, however, was of another order. In that month the great actor, the first ICHIKAWA Danjūrō 市川團十郎 (1660-1704) was stabbed and killed on the stage during a performance by another actor who had a grudge against him (TAKANO 2.258-259).

[64] 3/1650 (IHARA 89), 1665 (*Kinrei* 5.695-696) et al., 8/1695 (*Ofure* 2708).

bakufu fought a protracted rearguard action against the shrewd theater owners. The earliest *kabuki* was performed on a small, uncovered stage, the audience enclosed by a bamboo paling or a bunting on four sides after the manner of a sideshow tent without a top. Later just the stage was covered by a roof as in the *nō*. A drawing of 1639 shows the audience sitting on matting spread on the floor; overhead were installed reed blinds over which matting was placed, so that performances could go on even in a light rain. Despite the disapproval of the authorities the theater and its appointments steadily developed in size and elaborateness. A drawing of 1646 shows the bamboo paling replaced by a board fence.[65] Although the use of boxes, blinds, and screens was repeatedly forbidden, even periodic inspections of the theaters failed to halt completely the use of detachable partitions used to form boxes, or the use of blinds; and at most times permanent boxes seem to have been in use.

After the fire of 1657, the Edo theaters were rebuilt on a more substantial scale. In the next decade the evolution of longer plays with several acts led to the development of different types of drawn and drop curtains to separate acts and scenes, and to the designing of more elaborate stage sets. By 1677 the side runway (*hashigakari*) derived from the *nō*, developed into the runway through the audience (*hanamichi*). A picture of 1677 shows actors making up, seated about on the second floor of the greenroom much as they do today. We see boxes equipped with screens and blinds extending on three sides of the pit. The area that a theater was permitted to occupy was restricted by ordinances, and upon the petitions of the theater managers, was gradually increased as the Tokugawa period progressed. At the front of the theater stood a tower in which a drum was beaten from early in the morning on days when performances were to be given in order to draw a crowd. Townspeople were thus provided with a sort of weather forecast. This practice of drum-beating was forbidden in 1679 and again in 1684.[66] By the end of the century, despite laws to the contrary, the theater had a roof,

[65] TAKANO 2.62. [66] IHARA 454.

three levels of boxes, three stories of dressing rooms, and luxurious theater teahouses.[67] *Kabuki* was flourishing in defiance of the law when the greatest scandal in its history broke.

During the early years of the eighteenth century the most talked-about actor in Edo was IKUSHIMA Shingorō 生島新五郎 (1671-1743). A contemporary work on actors says that he specialized in love scenes, of which he was considered the founder, and that he played them "realistically" and provocatively.[68] Another book says he "presented love scenes on the stage, causing the ladies in the audience to be pleased." [69] He is said to have been extraordinarily handsome, and that the women of Edo were wild about him. The one among them most smitten was Ejima 江 (~繪) 島 (sometimes called Enoshima), one of the highest lady officials of the women's quarters of the shogun's castle, who served the mother of the seventh shogun, Ietsugu (1709-1716).

There are a number of differing accounts of the incident which brought this sensational affair to light, and they appear to have been so embroidered that the details of none of them are to be too seriously regarded. In essence what happened was that on the twelfth day of the first month of 1714, Ejima was ordered to make a proxy pilgrimage to the mausoleum at Zōjōji in Shiba, accompanied by a considerable number of attendants. The established precedent was that after they had attended to their duties, they would be feted in the abbot's quarters. However, on this day Ejima left the temple without stopping at the abbot's quarters, and with eleven others from the entourage, went to the Yamamura-za to see the plays. They called the actors to their box and drank with them. Among the actors was Ejima's lover, IKUSHIMA Shingorō. News of the theater party leaked out, and an investigation resulted in a full exposure, not only of the party,

[67] Miyako no Nishiki (1675-?1710) wrote in the *Genroku taiheiki* 元禄太平記 (1702): "The theaters of Edo, differing from those of Kyōto and Ōsaka, have three tiers of boxes, and are even more flourishing than has been heard. The ticket and seat charges are double those of Kamigata (Kyōto-Ōsaka), and you must even pay for fire for smoking." Cf. *Saikaku zenshū* 2(1893).1019 in *Teikoku bunko*, vol. 24.

[68] *Yakusha za furumai* 役者座振舞 (1713), quoted in TAKANO 2.337.

[69] *Yarō nigiri kobushi*, quoted in TAKANO 2.337.

D. H. Shively

but that a love affair between Ejima and IKUSHIMA had been in progress for nine years. All those implicated in the affair and the party were given punishments ranging from banishment to death. The lady officials were placed in the custody of different lords, and IKUSHIMA was banished to Miyake-jima, where he remained eighteen years until he was pardoned the year before his death.[70]

The most serious consequence for the history of *kabuki* was that the Yamamura-za, which had been the most popular among the Edo theaters for more than a decade, was closed on the sixth day of the second month, the building demolished, and the assets confiscated. For the remaining 150 years of the Tokugawa period there were three instead of four large theaters in Edo. All of the theaters were closed until the ninth day of the fourth month, when they were permitted to reopen under stringent conditions. The twenty-four leading actors of the Edo stage were required to submit written statements that they would not violate any of the orders of the *bakufu*. The regulations imposed upon the managers were set forth in a document of the ninth day of the third month:

---

[70] TAKANO 2.338-339. For a highly colorful, if undocumented, account of the Ejima-Ikushima affair, see *Chiyoda-jō ōoku* 千代田城大奥 by NAGASHIMA Imashirō 永島今四郎 and ŌTA Yoshio 太田賢雄, 2(1892).69-106. This work (pp. 86-94) quotes an unnamed source for a description of Ejima's theater party, which it claims included 130 persons:

The aspect of this day was a hubbub which cannot be described. In the boxes were spread carpets, and the theater owner, Nagadayu, IKUSHIMA Shingorō, and NAKAMURA Seigorō, wearing *hakama* and *haori*, were invited to be drinking partners. The uproar of the party was such that the sounds of the play could not be heard. . . . At this time in a lower box was a retainer of MATSUDAIRA Satsuma-no-kami, a person called TANIGUCHI Shimpei, watching the play with his wife. In the upper box, Ejima, quite intoxicated and not knowing what she was doing, spilled her *sake*, and it poured on Shimpei's head. He sent a messenger to the upper box. The *kachi-metsuke*, OKAMOTO Goroemon, made the apologies, but this did not satisfy Shimpei. Goroemon apologized over and over, and finally Shimpei accepted the apologies, and although it was about midday he and his wife left the theater. . . . Thereafter Goroemon several times urged Lady Ejima to leave, but she would not consent, and instead became very angry. At 2 P. M. a passageway was installed from the second-floor box by which they went to YAMAMURA Nagadayū's house, and the capers of the many maids who went were beyond words. . . . For the entertainment of Ejima, many actors, young actors, and youths were summoned to be drinking partners. . . . When it had become 4 P. M., they left Nagadayu's rooms and went to a teahouse on the street behind called Yamaya. On the second floor the maids and actors came and went and there was a great hubbub. . . . They finally left Kobiki-chō and returned by the Hirakawaguchi Gate [of the castle] at 8 P. M.

This account also says that some of the robes and money, which had been intended as offerings to the Zōjōji, were presented to the actors, youths, and teahouse people.

254

1. The boxes of the theaters have been made two and three stories in recent years. As formerly not more than one story will be permitted.

2. It is prohibited to construct private passages from the boxes or to construct parlors for merry-making backstage, in the theater manager's residence, or in teahouses and such places. Nothing at all should be done by the actors other than performing plays on the stage, even if they are called to the boxes or teahouses or the like. Of course pleasure-making patrons must not be invited to the actors' own houses.

3. In the boxes it is not permitted to hang bamboo blinds, curtains, or screens, and to enclose them in any way is prohibited. They must be made so that they can be seen through.

4. In recent years the roofs of theaters have been made so that even on rainy days plays can be performed. In this matter also roofs must be lightly constructed as was done formerly.

5. The costumes of actors in recent years have been sumptuous; this is prohibited. Hereafter silk, pongee, and cotton will be used.

6. It is strictly prohibited that plays continue into the evening and torches be set up. It should be planned so that they will end at 5 P.M.

7. Teahouses in the vicinity of the theaters should be lightly constructed, and parlor-like accommodations are entirely prohibited. Concerning those which are in existence at present, petitions should be submitted to the town commissioner's office, and upon inspection, a decision will be given.

The above must be observed without fail. If there are violations, the principals, of course, and even the representative of that quarter and five-man group will be considered offenders.[71]

Four years later, in 1718, when the theater owners pleaded that rainy days were bankrupting them, wooden shingle roofs were permitted over the stage and boxes.[72] Five years later, to reduce the fire hazard, the theaters were actually ordered to lay tile roofs and construct the outside walls of plaster.[73] The wily theater managers pleaded that they could not afford this construction unless their income could be increased by the construction of a second tier of boxes on three sides around the pit—a request which was grudgingly granted. The same year the Nahamura-za was permitted to enlarge substantially the size of its stage and the length of its runway.[74] It is of course conceivable that the officials

[71] *Ofure* 2734; see also 2733.
[72] Sekine 2.87b; Takano 2.340-341.
[73] Ihara 454-455. Because the Kobiki-chō theaters were situated near the Hamagoden, a detached residence of the Tokugawa family, they were directed in 1705 to have the buildings plastered and to cover the towers with copper sheeting as a fire-prevention measure.
[74] Takano 2.341.

were encouraged to sanction these steps by gifts or entertainment provided by the managers.

Another restriction which the theaters encountered came in 1707 when they were instructed not to hold performances on days when the shogun proceeded out of the castle. In replies to pleas that this worked a financial hardship, the theaters were permitted, the next year, to begin performances after the shogun's return to the castle. On these occasions the program would last until after dark, and pine torches were used to illuminate the stage. Because of the fire hazard, by 1716 performances were permitted daily regardless of the movements of the shogun.[75]

The practice of using torches to light the stage must have been recurrent. In 1707 an order said that on days when the wind was strong, *kabuki* performances must be stopped to reduce the danger of fire.[76] After wooden roofs were permitted, it was no longer required to stop performances on windy days. An undated order complains that there were rumors of performances lasting until midnight. Because of the danger of fire as well as the impropriety of the late hour, the theaters were instructed to begin their performances early in the morning if necessary so as not to continue after dark.[77]

The third type of restrictive law forbade the introduction into plays of subject matter which would have an undesirable political or moral influence. The same restrictions were applied to playwrights as to other kinds of authors, that matters concerning the government must not be published, that the names of contemporary members of the samurai class and above must not be mentioned,[78] nor any incidents involving samurai occurring after 1600. In 1644 the order was issued: " In plays the names of contemporary persons will not be used." [79] By " contemporary persons " was meant, of course, the people who counted. It is believed that this order was issued as a result of a fight which

[75] SEKINE 2.81b-82a.
[76] SEKINE 2.81b.
[77] *Kinrei* 5.700-701.
[78] 5/1673 (*Ofure* 2220).
[79] IHARA 90.

broke out in the Yamamura-za earlier that year when a living person of importance was mentioned in a play. An order of the second month of 1703 read:

1. As ordered repeatedly before concerning unusual events of the times, it is prohibited still more henceforth to make them into songs or publish and sell them.

2. In the Sakai-chō and Kobiki-chō theaters also, unusual events of the times or [action] resembling them must not be acted out.[80]

This ban of 1703 was issued when dramatizations of the revenge of the 47 *rōnin* were performed within a few months of the event. The playwrights were nimble in deceiving the censors, for they changed all the names and recast contemporary events in the Kamakura or Ashikaga period. It became a stock convention of the *kabuki* and puppet theater that when Hōjō Tokimasa 北條 時政 (1138-1215) appeared in a play he was really TOKUGAWA Ieyasu (1542-1616); Kamakura was substituted for Edo, the Inase River near Kamakura for the Sumida River, the Hanamizu Bridge near Kamakura for the Eitai Bridge in Edo, and so forth.[81] By such camouflage, some playwrights were clever enough to attempt political satire and get away with it. Of the several plays in which CHIKAMATSU Monzaemon (1653-1725) used this device, the most extensive use of contemporary materials was in his *Sagami nyūdō sembiki inu* 相模入道千疋犬 (*The Sagami Lay Monk and the Thousand Dogs*) (1714), in which he satirized TOKUGAWA Tsunayoshi (1646-1709) and his legislation protecting dogs.[82]

For moral reasons the *bakufu* disapproved of the too suggestive treatment of the gay quarters and its prostitutes. These quarters were the scene of much of the social life as well as entertainment of townsmen, and were much frequented by the samurai. They served as the setting of the most flowery scenes in practically all of the history plays as well as the domestic plays, providing the excuse to depict beautiful courtesans, romantic rivalries and

[80] 2/1703 (*Ofure* 2668); see also 4/1703 (*Ofure* 2716).

[81] IHARA 458.

[82] See the author's "Chikamatsu's Satire on the Dog Shogun," *HJAS* 18 (1955). 159-180.

intrigues, luxurious living, and riotous behavior. The types of action specifically proscribed were depiction of the style of walk and behavior of courtesans of the Shimabara quarter of Kyōto, or episodes demonstrating the techniques of accosting and winning the favor of high-ranking prostitutes. Such miming had been an important part of *kabuki* from the time of the earliest skits, and despite the bans of 1655 and 1664 forbidding such scenes in any type of theater, including the puppet stage,[83] they continued to be stock episodes in play after play. The effect of the ban seems to have been to prevent this action from becoming excessively salacious rather than to deny the audience the vicarious pleasure. Related to the sumptuary laws were the provisions that the houses of the gay quarter should not be made to appear luxurious. To make that life appear too glamorous would tend to undermine not only moral behavior but also the hierarchal social system.

Another favorite theme which was banned, but effectively only for a few years, was the double "love suicide." The sensational and romantic treatment of such suicides by playwrights like CHIKAMATSU seems to have been too suggestive to thwarted lovers. Rash young men and women anticipated that their deaths would be publicized, if not immortalized, in prose and drama. In addition to banning the publication of stories on this theme in 1723,[84] the *bakufu* attempted to discourage the acts by imposing punishments on those who survived unsuccessful attempts and by heaping dishonor on the corpses of those who succeeded. Within a few years, however, love suicide plays were again written and performed, and have continued to the present day to be a favorite theme of the *kabuki* and puppet theater; nor did the disapproval of the Tokugawa government by any means eliminate from Japanese life the practice of committing double suicides.[85]

In the foregoing survey of the laws with which the *bakufu*

---

[83] 5/1655 (*Ofure* 2688), 1/1664 (IHARA 436).

[84] 12th month, Kyōho 7[Jan. 1723] (*Ofure* 2022).

[85] On love suicide plays see Serge ELISSÉEV, "Le double suicide (Shinjù)," *Japon et Extrême-Orient*, 9 (Sept. 1924).107-122; and the author's *The Love Suicide at Amijima* (1953), esp. 18-29.

attempted to reform or restrict the development of *kabuki*, the
pattern which emerges is the tendency of the government to yield
to the persistent pressure of the theater interests. The officials
were subjected not only to the pleas and petitions of the theater
managers, but were constantly faced with non-observance of the
laws in varying degrees of flagrancy, not only by the managers,
but by the actors, playwrights, and even the audience. Since the
reason for permitting *kabuki* to continue to exist was to assuage
and divert the lower classes, it was only during certain determined
reform movements, when the leaders of the administration were
attempting to rally the moral fiber of the country, that the laws
were enforced as harshly as the letter might suggest. Because a
more permissive attitude generally prevailed, it was difficult for
the authorities to establish any specific line to hold against the
constant pressure, motivated not only by commercial interests,
but by the pleasure-loving, excitement-seeking propensities of
the irrepressible townsmen. The government lost ground on
almost every front: the increasingly substantial construction of
the theaters, the luxurious teahouses, the elaborate staging, the
use of wigs and rich costumes, and the introduction of " subversive " subject-matter into the plays. The appeal of *kabuki*
to all classes could not be checked. It is a symptom of the trend
that by the early nineteenth century the women attendants of
the lords' mansions and even of the shogun's castle were openly
sent to the theater to learn *kabuki* dances so that they could
perform them for their lords.

If we are to assess the effect of the *bakufu*'s measures on the
development of *kabuki*, we must give primary attention to the
banning of women, as it led to the development of players of
women's roles, the *onnagata*. Incredibly skilled in impersonating
women, they analyzed the characteristics of female motor habits,
and abstracting the essential gestures, developed in their acting
a peculiar type of eroticism never completely divorced from homo-
sexualism. After women's parts had been played by *onnagata*
for two and a half centuries, the conventions were so well established that the attempt to reintroduce actresses into *kabuki*,
following the Meiji Restoration, was a failure. Actresses seem

less feminine, in part because of certain conventions which men hold about what makes women attractive, and which women, of course, cannot be expected to understand. From the point of view of the aesthetics of acting, women seemed too natural, and so were incapable of emphasizing the essential characteristics of women. This required a more detached order of understanding and execution. The extent to which the institution of *onnagata* has affected the development of *kabuki* can be illustrated by saying that if actresses were now to be substituted for *onnagata*, they would have to play their parts, not as women imitating women, but as women imitating *onnagata* imitating women.

An effect of the laws which was more clearly to the disadvantage of *kabuki* was that the actors were despised, at least officially. There had been some patronage by the second and third Tokugawa shoguns, notably in 1633 and 1650-1651, but because of scandalous incidents and the increasingly rigid attitude of the government toward ethics, this patronage ceased. In 1719 a *kabuki* troupe was invited to perform at the castle, but when an official protested, citing the Ejima affair of 1714, the invitation was withdrawn, and a puppet troupe was invited instead.[86] The official attitude was that actors were a social group lower than merchants, and only a little above the pariah class. This type of social persecution prevented overt patronage by men of education and position, and gave the actors little opportunity or incentive to raise their art to levels which were potentially attainable.

The censorship eliminated any possibility of writing plays of real social or political significance. The isolated examples which touched on such subjects were intended more to electrify the audience with the playwright's daring, than to influence it with his criticism.

It is futile to predict what the development of *kabuki* might have been without government interference, because this repression was present from the time of the *kabuki*'s crude beginnings. We can only observe that the effect of the interference was beneficial in forcing *kabuki* to mature more quickly—that it separated

[86] IHARA 447.

kabuki from female prostitution, and that the continued super-vision made for more emphasis, for lack of choice, on art. The *bakufu* must be given credit for accelerating or even causing the turn from vaudeville and burlesque toward dramatic art, from one-act dance pieces at best toward dramatically structured plays of five acts or more. The banning of women also quickened the development of make-up, costuming, and staging.

We lack the information to be able to evaluate what potentialities for development *kabuki* might have had if it had been unrestricted in the environment of Tokugawa culture, and to weigh it against the *kabuki* which actually developed and which was so profoundly affected by the repression. In the balance it may be that the repression was beneficial to the development of *kabuki* as a dramatic form.

CHAPTER FOURTEEN

THE JAPANESE VILLAGE IN
THE SEVENTEENTH CENTURY

THOMAS C. SMITH

Reprinted from *Journal of Economic History,*
Vol. XII, No. 1, (Winter 1952)

I

A S IN the Middle Ages in the West, so in Tokugawa Japan
(1600–1868) men were fond of explaining the hierarchical society
in which they lived by comparing it to an organism. Social classes,
Confucian scholars said, were like parts of the body: each had a vital
function to perform, but their functions were essentially different
and unequal in value. In this scheme the peasants were second in
importance only to the ruling military class. Just as the *samurai* officials were the brains that guided other organs, so the peasants
were the feet that held the social body erect. They were the "basis of
the country," the valued producers whose labor sustained all else.
But, as a class, they tended innately to backsliding and extravagance.
Left alone they would consume more than their share of the social
income, ape the manners and tastes of their betters, and even encroach
upon the functions of other classes to the perilous neglect of their
own. Only the lash of necessity and the sharp eye of the official could
hold them to their disagreeable role. They had to be bound to the
land; social distinctions had to be thrown up around them like so
many physical barriers; and, to remove all temptation to indolence
and luxury, they had to be left only enough of what they produced
to let them continue producing.

What the Tokugawa writers were describing was their ideal of a
perfectly ordered and stable society. They were as far from giving a
realistic social picture as the medieval schoolmen who explained
European society by much the same sort of analogy. Nevertheless,
their descriptions had enough verisimilitude to convince later generations, which have largely drawn upon them and upon legislation
designed to enforce the ideal they express for historical material.

We still tend to think of the Tokugawa period in the absolute social categories of the Tokugawa schoolmen and to imagine the peasants as being what the lawgivers would have made them: a distinct and relatively homogeneous class at the economic base of society and, therefore, uniformly wretched, exploited, and impoverished.

This picture of the peasantry, if insisted upon strictly, creates a number of difficulties of historical interpretation, of which two examples may be cited here. The first concerns what is certainly one of the most arresting and significant features of Japanese history—the quiescence of the peasantry for centuries under conditions that would seem to favor revolt. Never did the Japanese peasantry stage the kind of general revolutionary uprising found in some other national histories: the Peasant Rebellion of 1381 in England, the Peasants' War in Germany, the Taiping Rebellion in China. Of course there were frequent peasant disturbances throughout the Tokugawa period and later, but they were sporadic, local, and largely devoid of political aims. This relative passivity seems incomprehensible if the peasants were roughly equal in their misery and, at the same time, left free from the immediate, local control of the military class, as they are supposed to have been.

The second difficulty concerns the Meiji restoration of 1868 which has long been interpreted as a nationalist, antifeudal revolution carried out by a dissatisfied wing of the *samurai* class. Historians have traditionally excluded the peasantry from participation in the restoration, presumably from the conviction that they were incapable of creative effort and that in any case their lowly social position forbade participation in a movement that was strongly aristocratic. There are several objections to this interpretation. First, there is some positive evidence of peasant leaders in the restoration movement. Second, granting that the low-ranking *samurai* had reason to rebel against the Tokugawa regime, why did they replace it with one that on the whole was even less favorable to their special interests? Third, how did it happen that an impoverished group of *samurai* succeeded in effecting so dramatic and sweeping a political change—unless they had powerful outside support?[1]

---

[1] E. Herbert Norman, *Japan's Emergence as a Modern State; Political and Economic Problems of the Meiji Period* (New York, 1940), pp. 49–70, argues that this support came primarily from the big-city merchants such as Mitsui. He cites as evidence particularly the loans made to the Meiji government in the critical years 1868 and 1869. However, these were

Japanese Village in the Seventeenth Century

In the last decade or so, Japanese historians have begun to study intensively new kinds of materials on the peasantry—land registers, household budgets, diaries, mortgages, bills of sale. From these studies a picture radically different from the one drawn by the Tokugawa philosophers is slowly being pieced together. Incomplete as the picture still is, it already suggests a solution to the two interpretive problems just mentioned. Here I shall attempt only to sketch the main lines of this emerging picture; and for reasons that will be clear later I will confine the sketch to the seventeenth century, before the rising tide of capitalism had begun to obscure traditional arrangements in the village.

II

Everywhere in seventeenth-century Japan the peasant population was divided into those who held land and those who did not. This was more than a purely economic distinction, for it ordinarily implied rights and obligations of different kinds. Only peasants listed in the village land register—that is, *hyakushō*,[2] or landholders—had the privileges and duties that went with membership in the village. Since taxes of all kinds were laid on land rather than on persons, only *hyakushō* were responsible for payment of the various dues the village collectively owed the lord.[3] In return, they alone could participate in a village assembly, hold village offices, draw shares of the common

forced loans of the kind merchants had long been accustomed to make at the order of any government powerful enough to require appeasing; they do not necessarily imply approval and support of the restoration government. Indeed, as late as 1866 the merchants made very large loans to the shogunate itself. *Meiji ishin keizaishi kenkyū*, ed. Honjō Eijirō (Tokyo, 1930), p. 359 ff., and *Nihon keizaishi jiten* (Tokyo, 1942), I, 596–97. Moreover, in the years immediately after 1868, the Meiji government did not show the degree of solicitude for the special interests of the great merchant houses that one would expect if merchant backing had been voluntary at the time of the restoration. (1) It promptly abolished the elaborate Tokugawa system of trading privileges of which these houses had been the chief beneficiaries; (2) it repudiated about 80 per cent of the enormous debts owed to them by its predecessors, the shogunate and the *han;* and (3) it adopted financial policies that were directly responsible for the bankruptcy, within seven years of the restoration, of Ono and Shimada, two of the three greatest merchant houses of the time, both of which had contributed heavily to the loans of 1868 and 1869. Takahashi Kamekichi, *Nihon shihon shugi hattatsu shi* (Tokyo, 1929), p. 89 ff.; and *Nihon keizaishi jiten*, I, 181, 742; II, 1351.

2 Throughout the Tokugawa period the term *hyakushō* was used in two senses: broadly, to designate the peasantry in general; technically, to mean a peasant who was enrolled in the land register. It is in the latter sense, as a synonym for landholder, that the term is used in this paper.

3 *Nihon keizaishi jiten*, I, 947–48.

lands of the village, address the village headman on official business, or take part in a legal act of the village such as the sale or acquisition of water rights.[4] The rest of the population of the village was without public rights and duties, aside from the general obligation to abide by the law. Indeed, the local and higher officials rarely took cognizance of them at all except in criminal cases. Such people were completely dependent, in one form or another, on some *hyakushō* who used their labor on his holding; for most purposes he stood between them and the law, and their obligations and rights were defined primarily by their relations with him rather than with any public authority.[5] But this class will be considered later; here we are concerned only with the *hyakushō*.

The land registers are the basic economic document on landholding in the village. Since they were compiled for the purpose of allocating taxes of all kinds, they list the names of the *hyakushō* and give a description of the holding of each. Too few registers from the seventeenth century have yet come to light to permit nice generalizations about the distribution of land among holders. It is obviously impossible from the number of registers tabulated below to guess, for example, what percentage of holdings were under one *chō* (2.45 acres),[6] considered by Professor Fujita, whose conclusions are based on the study of a large number of family budgets, as the minimum holding that would support a family of five in northeastern Honshu at this time.[7] But even the few registers we have leave very little doubt concerning the general picture of inequality among holdings. Although they come from widely separated areas, they all show holdings of less than one-half *chō*—some of them little better than gardens—or holdings whose annual yield was valued at less than five *koku* (one *koku* = 4.96 bushels) of hulled rice alongside holdings ten, twenty, or thirty times as large or productive.[8] Not infrequently we encounter *peasant* holdings that can only be described as estates. For example, we find a

---

[4] The fullest discussion of the evidence bearing on this subject is Furushima Toshio, *Kinsei nihon nōgyō no kōzō* (Tokyo, 1948), I, 1–55; for the author's conclusions, see pp. 50–55.

[5] *Ibid.*, p. 465 ff.

[6] There was no uniformity in Japanese land measure until the first part of the seventeenth century when the *chō* was generally stabilized at the present 2.45 acres. Even so, some local differences persisted, and complete uniformity was not achieved until the reform of the land tax in 1874. *Nihon keizaishi jiten*, II, 1067.

[7] Fujita Gorō, *Nihon kindai sangyō no seisei* (Tokyo, 1948), p. 218. It should be added that the minimum figure would be smaller for central and southern Japan where cultivation was more intensive and agriculture more commercialized.

[8] In the Tokugawa period the land tax was a percentage of the *taka*, or value-yield of the holding as expressed in *koku* of hulled rice.

TABLE I
DISTRIBUTION OF LAND AMONG HOLDERS: SIZE OF HOLDINGS IN *TAN* (10 *TAN* = 2.45 ACRES)

VILLAGE	PROVINCE	DATE	NUMBER OF HOLDINGS									TOTAL
			0-5 tan	5-10 tan	10-15 tan	15-20 tan	20-25 tan	25-30 tan	30-35 tan	35-40 tan	40 and over tan	
Higashi [11]	Iwashiro	1593	18	2	2	7	1		1	1	1	33
Kawachi [12]	Iyo	1657	6						15		4	25
Okada [13]	Echigo	1683	2	5	14		10				1	32
Koga [14]	Yamashiro	1697	118	11	6	4	5				4	148
Shimajima [15]	Aki	1705	33	30	12	6	9					90
Terayama [16]	Sagami	1706	16	12		11					11	50

TABLE II
DISTRIBUTION OF LAND AMONG HOLDERS: VALUE OF HOLDINGS IN *KOKU* (1 *KOKU* = 4.96 BUSHELS)

VILLAGE	PROVINCE	DATE	NUMBER OF HOLDINGS												TOTAL
			0-1 koku	1-2 koku	2-3 koku	3-4 koku	4-5 koku	5-10 koku	10-15 koku	15-20 koku	20-25 koku	25-30 koku	30-40 koku	40 and over koku	
Shimo [17]	Echigo	1587	3	5	5			4			1				18
Kinebuchi [18]	Shinano	1666				1				5		10	5	2	23
Okawara [19]	"	1677	9	11	6	10		12	5		1				54
Tsukiyama [20]	Yamashiro	1694	4	2	1	1	1	2	2						13
Makuuchi [21]	Iwashiro	1691	4	2				8	12	2	2				30
Nishihara [22]	Mikawa	1730	5	1		8		4	1	2					21
Kaminagada [23]	Mino	1734	16		8	30		27	9						90
Ikezaki [24]	Kaga	1750	22	8				4	9		3		5	6	57

11 Toya Toshiyuki, *Kinsei nōgyō keiei shiron* (Tokyo, 1949), pp. 21–22.
12 Ono Takeo, *Tsuchi keizaishi kosho* (Tokyo), p. 54.
13 Kitajima, p. 26.
14 Furushima, "Edo jidai ni okeru Kinai nōgyō to kisei jinushi," *Rekishi gaku kenkyū*, No. 144 (March, 1950), p. 3.
15 Furushima, *Nōgyō no kōzō*, II, 594.
16 Nakamura Shōnosuke, *Nihon kosaku seido ron* (Tokyo, 1936), p. 147.
17 Kitajima, p. 9.
18 Suzuki Hisashi, "Kinsei nōson no ichi keitai," *Rekishi gaku kenkyū*, No. 149 (January, 1951), p. 37.
19 Furushima, *Nōgyō no kōzō*, II, 594.
20 Fujita, *Nōminzō*, pp. 190–91.
21 Furushima, "Kinai nōgyō to kisei jinushi," pp. 8–9.
22 Furushima, *Hōken jidai kōki no nōmin no seikatsu* (Tokyo, 1948), p. 240.
23 *Ibid.*
24 Furushima, *Nōgyō no kōzō*, II, 593.

village headman in Iyo Province in 1682 holding 34 *chō* with an annual yield of 165 *koku*[9]; and, in the early eighteenth century, two families in Shinano Province with incomes from land of more than 100 *koku* each.[10]

It is not surprising that such extremes of wealth and poverty among *hyakushō* of the village were accompanied by marked social distinctions.[25] We may pass over differences of dress, food, and housing,[26] which directly reflected economic well-being, to distinctions of education and family with one comment. Two contrary complaints about the peasantry run through the economic writings of the whole Tokugawa period and, not infrequently, through the works of a single author. On the one hand, it is said that the peasants lived like beasts in the field; on the other, that they lived with the reckless extravagance of the merchant.[27] Since these are views persistently expressed by contemporaries who knew of what they spoke, they cannot be ignored; and they can only be reconciled if we understand them as comments on the way of life of two rather distinct economic classes among the peasantry.[28]

Although the law bound them to the land and treated them in other respects like ordinary peasants, the rich landholding families were not purely peasant in origin. Many could trace their ancestors back not many generations to petty warriors, some of whom collected taxes and administered justice in the village and, on occasion, even demanded military service from the peasants under them.[29] In the century of

[9] Kitajima Shōgen, "Echigo sankan chitai ni okeru junsui hōken no kōzō," *Shigaku zasshi*, LIX, No. 6 (June, 1950), 19–20.

[10] Furushima, *Nōgyō no kōzō*, II, 522. [For notes 11 through 24, see Table I.]

[25] Tanaka Kyūgū, "Minkan shōyō," *Nihon keizai sōsho*, ed. Takigawa Seiichi (Tokyo, 1914–17), I, 280–81.

[26] For evidence on the living standards of various groups in the village, see Koseki Toyokichi, "Hansei jidai ni okeru nōson ni kansuru seisaku to nōmin no seikatsu," *Tosa shidan*, No. 44 (September, 1933), pp. 92–128; Sekijima Hisao, "Tokugawa matsugo no nōson jinushi no shōhi seikatsu," *Shakai keizai shigaku*, XII, No. 9 (December, 1942), 69 ff.; and Kakayama Tarō, "Nōmin no kaikyū to minzoku—Edo jidai wo chūshin to shite," *Minzoku gaku*, IV, Nos. 10 and 11 (October and November, 1932).

[27] For examples of such comment, see Kobayashi Yoshimasa, *Nihon shihon shugi no seisei to sono kiban* (Tokyo, 1949), p. 18; and Fujita, *Kinsei ni okeru nōminzō kaikyū bunka* (Tokyo, 1949), p. 91.

[28] Not infrequently the existence of distinct economic classes in the village was explicitly acknowledged. Horie Eiichi, *Hōken shakai no okeru shihon no sonzai keitai* (Tokyo, 1949), p. 87; and Nakamura Hideichirō and Asada Kōki, *Nihon shihon shugi shakai keizai shi* (Tokyo, 1949), pp. 86–87.

[29] On the recent warrior status of many wealthy peasants in the early Tokugawa period, see Furushima, *Nōgyō no kōzō*, I, 125–26, and *Kazoku keitai to nōgyō no hattatsu* (Tokyo, 1949), pp. 101–02; Kitajima, p. 4; Fujita, *Kindai sangyō*, p. 200; and Nishioka Toranosuke, "Kinsei shōya no genryū," *Shigaku zasshi*, XLIX, No. 2 (February, 1938), 3–4.

anarchy before Nobunaga's time, there had been no clear distinction between soldier and landholder,[30] the very possession of land implied arms to defend it. "No arms, no land," the saying went.[31] Hence, Hideyoshi and the other barons had found no satisfactory distinction at hand for prying warrior and peasant apart when they sought to separate the two at the end of the sixteenth century, with the result that nearly everywhere a backwash of warrior families was left among the peasantry.[32]

No wonder that such families were at pains to maintain their traditions and past dignity by the only means the new order, which had dropped them legally into the peasant class, permitted: education and intermarriage with their kind. While the general run of peasant was illiterate, literacy in the more substantial families went far beyond the rudiments of reading and writing. What else are we to think when we find them maintaining private tutors in their homes,[33] keeping diaries, composing family histories, and making reports on conditions in the village in the exacting official style of the time,[34] or placing orders with the village headman going off to Edo on business for such books as the *Nihon shoki*? [35, 36] Even training in the use of weapons was not unknown among such families.[37]

They showed the same solicitude for the proper marriage of their children as for their education. The Hino family of Kamiyama village

[30] Nakamura Kichiji, *Kinsei shoki nōsei shi kenkyū* (Tokyo, 1938), p. 255.

[31] "Ichiryō gusoku" or "ichiryō ippiki," literally, "one holding and armour" and "one holding, one horse."

[32] I do not refer to *gōshi*, or warriors, who, while remaining on the land, retained *samurai* rank; but to former warriors who were incorporated in the peasant class. The best discussion of the separation of the warrior and peasant classes is Ono, *Nihon heinō shiron* (Tokyo, 1943), pp. 131–54. A detailed and important study of the application of this measure in Kai Province is Itō Tasaburō, "Iwayuru heinō bunri no jisshō-teki kenkyū," *Shakai keizai shigaku*, XIII, No. 8, 1–50; on warriors being dropped into the peasant class, pp. 31–32, 39, 45–48.

[33] Nishioka, p. 14.

[34] Furushima, *Nihon hōken nōgyō shi* (Tokyo, 1941), pp. 125–27; and Fujita, *Kindai sangyō*, pp. 240, 247

[35] The *Nihon shoki* or "Chronicles of Japan" was compiled in 720 and was written in the Chinese language. While it purports to be an authentic record of early Japanese history, it is in fact a skillful blending of myth and history in such a way as to enhance the prestige of the imperial family. This amalgam was later used by the restoration leaders as historical justification for their revolutionary activities; thus, interest in this text is as much a comment on political outlook as on literacy.

[36] This information is taken from the diary of a headman from a village near Niigata. The diary is dated 1867, considerably after our period, but appreciation for a book like the *Nihon shoki* was not likely to have come from less than several generations of literacy. Parts of this extremely interesting diary are published in Fuse Tatsuji, "Tokugawa matsugo nengu shūnō no kunan wo egaita Edo kikō," *Shakai keizai shigaku*, VII, No. 4 (July, 1937), 106–17 (esp. 111–12).

[37] Nishioka, p. 14.

in Iyo Province is a good example. The Hino had been warriors since the fifteenth century and had been reduced to *hyakushō* status in 1632. They had not, however, been deprived of their considerable holdings in Kamiyama, and the lord partly compensated them for loss of status by making them hereditary village headmen.[38] Not once in the seventeenth century did the Hino intermarry with a Kamiyama family, although there were well over a hundred families in the village.[39] The reason seems obvious: since the Hino were the only family in the village with a warrior background, except for their former military followers, and until 1587 had held the entire village as a fief from the shogun, to find suitable matches this proud family had to look to other villages. On occasion they even went as far afield as neighboring provinces. Of course this does not prove that the practice was general; but it would be surprising, when the histories of other families are studied, to find that there was anything unusual in the very strong preference the Hino showed for intermarriage with families of similar background and economic position.

The economic and social dominance of the larger *hyakushō* in the village was supported by a tight monopoly of local administrative and political power. Invariably the headman and his lieutenants came from this class,[40] and their monopoly of office was almost impossible to break —short of rebellion. Often the office of headman was hereditary in a single family and at best it rotated among a few qualified families, each holding office for a generation.[41] In rare instances, it is true, at least in the late Tokugawa, the headman was elected by the *hyakushō* of the village; but given the unequal stacking of the cards in other respects, it is not very difficult to guess how these elections ordinarily turned out.

The practice of restricting local office to the larger holders was not new. By the Tokugawa period it was already so firmly established in custom that legal enactments to support it would have been superfluous. For some four centuries before 1600 land, arms, and political power had been an inseparable trinity in the village. As early as the Kamakura

---

[38] Aruga Kizaemon, *Nihon kazoku seido to kosaku seido* (Tokyo, 1943), pp. 223–24.

[39] Nishioka, No. 3, pp. 76–77.

[40] Even if there were not an imposing array of cases to support this view (and none, to my knowledge, contradict it), we would be assured of its accuracy by a Bakufu law of 1673 stipulating that a holding could not be divided among heirs unless it were valued at more than 10 *koku* in the case of an ordinary peasant and *at more than twice that figure in the case of a headman*. Furushima, *Hōken nōgyō*, p. 109.

[41] *Ibid.*, p. 127.

period (1185–1333), the *myōshu*,[42] as the landholders were then called, were already securely in control of local affairs outside the fast-disappearing public domain. They were the armed officials of the *shō*[43] who saw to its defense, collected its taxes, directed the labor of its tenants, and maintained law and order in its precincts.[44] The local power of this class was greatly strengthened during the prolonged civil war that ensued on the collapse of effective central government in the first half of the fourteenth century; and when, in the sixteenth century, unity and order were at last imposed on the country by Nobunaga and his successors, those warrior-landholders who were left on the land were disarmed but not stripped of their local administrative power.[45] Nor could they be. They were the innumerable points of support scattered about the countryside upon which the whole machinery of government ultimately rested, for local government consisted of nothing more than the authority they had traditionally exercised in the village.

III

Thus far we have been considering only the *hyakushō*: that is, those peasants who were listed in the land registers. Until recent years it was believed that the land registers accounted for the whole peasant population and, accordingly, that the Tokugawa village was a community of small holders who were the virtual owners of the land they worked. Tenantry, so characteristic a feature of modern Japanese agriculture,

---

[42] In the light of other evidence bearing on the social origins of the village headmen, it is significant that the most common title they bore in the Tokugawa period, *nanushi*, was written with the same two Chinese characters as *myōshu*, and that *shōya*, the only other title that had wide currency, in the Kamakura period referred to an officer of the *shō*. (On the significance of the *shō*, see n. 43.)

[43] The *shō* was an institution that emerged after the eighth century with the gradual decline of the imperial government. It first appears after land had been nationalized in the seventh century, simply as a piece (or pieces) of privately owned land that had been separated by one means or another from the public domain. Later, as the power of the government failed, the *shō* became tax free and immune from the police power of the government. And new *shō* were continually being formed, until by the Kamakura period (1185–1333) scarcely anything remained of the public domain. The titular possessor of the *shō* at this time was usually a court noble or a Buddhist temple through whose influence the *shō* had won and continued to maintain its immunities and who drew revenues from its lands. The real possessors, however, were the local officials who managed the *shō* and held land within its confines. These landholders, or *myōshu*, had already armed themselves and had developed among themselves an intricate system of military relationships. Thus, at the height of its development, the *shō* was being transformed into a fief, a transformation that was completed during the protracted civil war that began in the fourteenth century.

[44] Shimizu Mitsuo, *Nihon chusei no sonraku* (Tokyo, 1942), p. 29 ff.

[45] Nishioka, No. 2, pp. 3–4.

could be explained, therefore, as the result of capitalism having invaded the village, thrusting this peasant up and that one down.[46]

This view is no longer tenable. The assumption upon which it rested was first called into question by Professor Imai's suggestion, made in 1940, that the land registers listed only holders and not the entire population of the village.[47] Imai's hypothesis has since been confirmed; there is now ample proof that part of the peasantry stood outside the land registers for the simple reason that they did not hold land. This class of peasants was not confined to any particular region. It is found in such widely separated places as Kyushu and northern Honshu, Shikoku, and the area along the Sea of Japan.[48] But if the evidence clearly points to this class as a general feature of Japan's institutional development at that time, and not as a local historical accident, it is less satisfactory on point of numbers.

Although the evidence available on the ratio of tenants to *hyakushō* in our period is too scanty to permit precise conclusions, tenants must have comprised a substantial part of the total population. In some areas the percentage of tenants runs very high indeed. The figures for Buzen Province, which are based on a detailed census during the years 1681–1684 that included even horses and oxen, show as tenants over 50 per cent of the total number of family heads. It is very difficult to believe that this ratio could have held for the country as a whole. Nevertheless, even in the ten villages of Kawachi Province, where the percentage is the lowest of any area for which we have figures, tenants comprised just under 25 per cent of the total population, and only two villages of the nine had no tenants at all.[49]

We shall probably not fully understand the significance of tenantry and precisely what it entailed until its institutional origins have been further explored. But this much seems certain: tenantry was already characteristic of Japanese agriculture in the seventeenth century before capitalism had invaded the countryside in any considerable force. Indeed, it seems to have been most firmly entrenched in remote or mountainous areas like Buzen and Shinano which were isolated to a high degree from influences of the marketplace. The inference seems ines-

[46] *The Documents of Iriki: Illustrative of the Development of the Feudal Institutions of Japan*, ed. K. Asakawa (New Haven, 1929), pp. 336–37; and Nakamura Shōnosuke, *Nihon kosaku seido ron* (Tokyo, 1936), I, 196 ff.

[47] Imai Rintarō, "Kinsei shotō no okeru kenchi no ikkō-satsu," *Shakai keizai shigaku*, IX, No. 11 (March, 1940), pp. 116–21.

[48] The evidence bearing on the population outside the land registers is summarized in Furushima, *Nōgyō no kōzo*, I, 3–25.

[49] Nakamura, *Nihon Kosaku*, pp. 147–48.

TABLE III

TENANTS AND HOLDERS IN BUZEN PROVINCE, 1681–1684 *
(TOTAL PEASANT POPULATION OF FIVE COUNTRIES: 39,808)

| COUNTY | HOLDERS | | TENANTS |
	Village Officials	Other Holders	
Total	28	3353	4018
Kiku	6	831	697
Tagawa	7	982	1496
Chikujō	4	438	684
Miyako	7	622	373
Kamige	4	480	768

* Furushima, Nōgyō no kōzō, I, 48–49.

capable, therefore, that tenantry reflects some differentiation among the peasantry that antedates the Tokugawa period. Moreover, the overtones of personal dependence associated with tenant status suggest something more than a purely economic contract between the tenant and his landlord.

The tenant did not share any of the public rights and duties of the landholder. It has already been noted that his rights and duties, for the most part, were private in nature and that they were governed by his relationship to his landlord (for so we may now call the larger *hyakushō* whose holdings were worked wholly or in part by tenants). Although this was a customary and private relationship, it was respected and supported by the political authorities. There seems to have been no general legislation in the period regulating it, and administrative interference by the local magistrate, which did occur infrequently, was resisted by landlords as an invasion of a domain that was their exclusive concern.[50]

Certainly tenantry involved an economic dependence on the landlord that was very nearly complete. Although custom gave the tenant some measure of protection in his holding, he had no legal claim to the land he worked. The only right acknowledged by the village register, and consequently by the lord and his officials, was that of the landlord. The landlord sold or mortgaged or passed on to his heirs both land and tenants, without consulting the latter's wishes. No doubt in most cases he could also dispossess his tenants without cause or compensation if

[50] Mori Kaheiei, "Kinsei nōmin kaihō no shakai keizai shiteki igi," *Nōmin kaihō no shiteki kōsatsu,* ed. Shakai keizai shigakkai (Tokyo, 1948), p. 70.

only he were prepared to risk the censure of his neighbors.[51] Everywhere the plots assigned tenants were too small to have permitted them to accumulate any significant capital of their own.[52] There is good reason, moreover, to believe that when favorable economic or political factors, such as increased productivity or a low tax rate, made a higher income for the tenant possible, the landlord took the increment in higher rents.[53] But the tenant was dependent on the landlord not only for access to land; the house in which he lived and the tools with which he worked often belonged to the landlord. And he had access to the common forest and wastelands of the village, which provided much of the fertilizer [54] and all the fuel and building materials so essential to the economy of the peasant household, only because the landlord drew a share of the common as a village *hyakushō* and permitted the tenant the use of it.[55]

The personal relations of the tenant and landlord reflected the generally accepted criteria of the time for dealings between unequal parties. All relations of this kind in Tokugawa society between employer and employee,[56] teacher and pupil, lord and vassal tended to approximate the Confucian ideal of family relationships. All had their peculiar features, but all had in common distinctions of worth between the two parties and reciprocal but different sets of obligations—obedience and loyalty on the one side and benevolence and protection on the other —that ideally obtained between father and son. To the tenant the landlord was *oyakata* or "parent"; to the landlord the tenant was *kokata* or "child." [57]

---

[51] Arbitrary dispossession was not possible in the case of tenants called *buntsuke hikan*. For historical reasons that are not wholly clear, such tenants had exceptionally strong claims to the land they worked, and the landlord could only liquidate their claims by purchase. But this type of tenant has been found only in a few places, and even there in relatively small numbers. Furushima, *Nōgyō no kōzō*, II, 497.

[52] *Ibid.*, p. 594.

[53] Furushima, "Edo jidai ni okeru nōgyō to kisei jinushi," *Rekishi gaku kenkyū*, No. 144 (March, 1950), pp. 13, 15.

[54] Fertilizer was intensively used throughout the Tokugawa period. Surviving budgets show that in some cases as high as 34 per cent of the total outlay of peasant households went to buy fertilizer. Horie, pp. 58–59. However, the peasant provided most of his fertilizer himself, the chief sources being compost in the form of grass and leaves gathered from the common and manure from animals grazed on the common. Dried fish and night soil were also important. Furushima, *Nōgyō no kōzō*, I, 133–38, 183.

[55] *Ibid.*, pp. 183–94.

[56] The house laws and shop rules of most merchant families contained sections on the proper relationship between employer and employee; for examples, *see* Miyamoto Mataji, *Kinsei shōnin ishiki no kenkyū* (Tokyo, 1942), pp. 125–26, 139–41, 146–47, 166–68.

[57] *Nihon keizaishi jiten*, I, 183.

This system of values inevitably tended to turn economic dependence into intense personal subordination. There are a few scraps of evidence that throw some direct light on this aspect of the tenant's position. The tenants of Shinano Province, in addition to performing labor services for the landlord, were all subject to a class of obligations that seem more a signification of personal dependence than an economic payment. Some tenants were required to send their sons and daughters as unpaid servants to the landlord for a fixed term; others to deliver firewood to the landlord, or to provide a meal for him on specified occasions, or to attend him on occasions of personal sorrow or rejoicing; and still others to deliver a small quantity of rice and wine or such things as a wooden bucket or a piece of cloth at certain seasons of the year.[58]

The authority that landlords exercised over the lives of their tenants is suggested by the admonitions one of them laid down for his tenants in 1725. Tenants were not to leave the village on a visit or to put up relatives for more than five days without reporting the reasons to the landlord; they were strictly forbidden to lodge wandering priests, pilgrims, and other strangers even for a single night. They were to avoid ostentatious and expensive things. Specifically forbidden were *zōri, haori,* and *wakizashi.*[59] They were not to put new roofs on their houses or otherwise repair them without the landlord's permission. All "luxurious" things in their houses, such as *shōji*[60] and mats, were ruled out, but gables, which had been forbidden in the past, were now allowed. They were to show due respect at all times to the landlord and his family and servants and to the *hyakushō* of the village. They were not to wear footgear in the presence of the landlord, nor to adopt a family insignia resembling his, nor to use a character in a name that was in use in his family, and so on.[61] This document, which recalls a Tokugawa feudal lord lecturing his people on the virtues of frugality and proper behavior, is by no means unique; there are numerous other documents of this kind, some of them of much later date, that strike the same note.[62]

[58] Furushima, *Nōgyō no kōzō,* II, 480.

[59] *Zōri:* a particularly elegant type of straw sandal; *haori:* a type of coat, again very elegant; *wakizashi:* a dagger worn at the side.

[60] *Shōji:* sliding doors usually made of a fine, translucent paper mounted on a light wooden frame and used as partitions between rooms.

[61] Mori, pp. 65–68.

[62] See particularly an undated document from the Tokugawa period in Nakamura and Asada, p. 107.

But the degree of personal subordination which tenantry involved was not everywhere the same. There were two main types of tenantry at the end of the seventeenth century, one of which gave the tenant greater personal freedom than the other.

Over the greater part of the country, the landlord allotted a part of his holding in plots to his tenants for their support; the rest he exploited directly for his own profit with the labor services his tenants owed him in return. The cases of tenantry cited above were of this type. But, in the economically more advanced areas where trade was destroying the self-sufficiency of the village and spreading rural industry and commercial agriculture, this regime was giving way to the modern form of tenantry. Landlords were breaking up their entire holdings among tenants, except perhaps for what they could work with family labor and servants, and substituting rent in kind for labor services.

The reasons for this shift are not obvious. From the evidence at hand it seems likely that with the spread of rural industry and the development of the market,[63] the possibility of by-employment caused tenants to place a higher value on their labor, and the landlord was forced to make concessions to keep them on the land since emigration to the cities, although quite illegal, was impossible to prevent in fact.[64] On the other hand there are no grounds for believing that landlords lost by the new arrangement. Throughout the Tokugawa period the costs of production—the meals provided tenants on workdays, fertilizer and agricultural implements, the wages for hired hands at the planting and harvest—were constantly rising, making the old system of management less and less profitable.[65] Providing that labor services were commuted into rent in kind at a high enough rate, the new system could serve to transfer the increasing burden of these costs to the tenant; and this may have been the real reason for its adoption.

[63] A convenient short discussion of this subject may be found in Horie, pp. 37–67.

[64] There was a spectacular growth of urban population at the end of the seventeenth century: Edo grew from 353,000 in 1692 to 553,000 in 1731; Osaka from 345,000 in 1692 to 382,000 in 1721; and there was a proportionate increase in the population of port cities, castle towns, and stations along the main routes of overland travel. Furushima, *Hōken nōgyō*, p. 304, and *Nōgyō no kōzō*, II, 611. There is convincing evidence that this growth was owing primarily to the influx of population from rural areas. A census of Edo in 1721 showed a ratio of 100 men to 53 women, suggesting a heavy immigrant population in the city (*ibid.*). There were constant complaints from local officials at this time of a serious shortage of agricultural labor which they attributed to the movement of people from the villages to cities and towns. Oda Yoshinobu, *Kaga han nōsei shikō* (Tokyo, 1929), p. 578.

[65] For evidence on rising costs, *see* Furushima, *Nōgyō no kōzō*, II, 603–16. Regarding the causes of this rise: (1) the rapid expansion of commerce and industry created constant new demands for labor and materials; (2) more and more food was required to support the expand-

Although the change spread so slowly and unevenly that to date it for the country as a whole is impossible, it appears that the older form of tenantry remained dominant through the greater part of the seventeenth century.[66] The tenant was obviously less free under this form than under the one that was gradually displacing it, for it put a good part of his time and labor at the disposal of the landlord. The greater personal freedom of the new form of tenantry should not be exaggerated, however. While the tenant was no longer constantly at the beck and call of the landlord, his legal position was unchanged: he remained without rights in the village and dependent on the landlord for representing his interests, and there is no reason to believe that his economic position was much improved, if it was improved at all.[67] Moreover, there was nothing inherent in the new arrangement that required tampering with personal relations of long standing. The old habits of authority and obedience, while they were no doubt loosened in the course of centuries by the elimination of labor services, must have persisted unchanged for a very long time. Indeed, until very recent times they could still be found in some regions of Japan in forms that were familiar in the seventeenth century.[68]

There was a third type of tenant who may have been the most free, for he was a new tenant and not the legacy of an earlier time. This was the former landholder who, through poor husbandry or bad luck, or because his holding had become uneconomic, had lost his land and become a tenant. Capitalistic influences, which gave the wealthy peasant the means and incentive to acquire more land while undermining the

ing urban population; and (3) hardpressed feudal lords were continually resorting to various forms of currency inflation to meet their financial difficulties.

[66] So it would seem, at least, for it was not until after the Genroku era (1688–1703) that the writers of *Jikata no shu*, a kind of textbook on agricultural management and administration, took much notice of the newer type of tenantry; by the late eighteenth century, however, such books were concerned with little else. Furushima, *Nōgyō no kōzō*, II, pp. 602–03, 605.

[67] The scanty direct evidence we have on the economy of the tenant under this type of management shows him existing on an incredibly small agricultural income, sometimes not more than one *koku* annually. The evidence on this point is summarized by Toya, pp. 352–57.

[68] When, after the restoration (1868), tenants were given full legal equality, many of them submitted pledges to their landlords swearing not to abuse their new rights, "never to forget the way of master and follower," and binding their "children and children's children" to observe this pledge. For the text of such pledges, *see* Mori, p. 67. That these pledges were often observed, in some cases down to very recent times, was revealed by a series of field studies of landlord-tenant relations in the 1930's, the findings of which are summarized in Irimajiri Yoshinaga, *Nihon nōmin keizaishi kenkyū* (Tokyo, 1949), pp. 401–48. To cite but one case in point: in Ekari village, Iwate Prefecture, the tenants of M., in addition to paying rent on their holdings and houses, owed him an average of eighty workdays a year, and each tenant family was under the obligation to send two sons for one year each and two daughters for two years each to work as servants in M.'s household (p. 407).

position of the small holder, constituted the economic lever that produced this type of tenantry on a large scale. Such tenants were probably already numerous in the seventeenth century but they did not become the dominant type until well into the eighteenth.[69] Since the peasant did not relinquish his land until he was destitute, such tenants could have had no more economic independence than others. But whether they lost their rights in the village when they lost their land and became legally, as well as economically, dependent on the landlord to the same extent as other tenants is an open question of the greatest importance. Until this question is answered there is no way of knowing whether the slow growth of capitalism in the Tokugawa period was gradually altering the pattern of tenantry, or simply extending among the peasants the incidence of legal inequalities that date from an earlier time.

IV

High as the figures cited earlier on the ratio of tenants to *hyakushō* seem to be, they by no means show the whole peasant population that stood outside the land registers. Entirely omitted in these figures are the hereditary servants that were often found in the households of rich peasants.[70] This group appears in the documents under a variety of names, but perhaps the most common and certainly the most descriptive is *genin* or "low person." [71] It is impossible to guess how numerous the *genin* were, but there can be no doubt that they were an important source of agricultural labor under the older system of landlord management. For example, in Makuuchi village, where this system prevailed until well after the seventeenth century, 14 large holders used a total of 38 *genin* in 1691; and the number of *genin* to each varied roughly according to the size of the holding, with the largest holder in the village using 14 of the 38.[72] So far as our data on other villages go, these figures do not appear exceptional.[73] With the shift of landlords to the new type of management, there seems to have been a con-

---

[69] Since this type of tenant is clearly the product of the intrusion of money economy in the village, it is found most commonly in the more economically advanced regions—the area along the Inland Sea and in the vicinity of cities and towns.

[70] *Nihon keizaishi jiten*, I, pp. 470–71.

[71] Among others: *zusa, fudai, shojū, hikan, zōnin.*

[72] Fujita, *Nōminzō*, pp. 190–91.

[73] See the figures for twelve villages in Shinano Province in Ichikawa Oichirō, "Edo jidai no nōka no jinteki kōsei no henka," *Rekishi gaku kenkyū*, No. 147 (September, 1950), pp. 36–37.

siderable decline in the number of *genin*.[74] What generally happened to these people is unknown, but, sometimes at least, the landlord made them tenants. Since this appears to have occurred even under the older form of management, it is not unlikely that systematic investigation would reveal in this practice an important institutional root of tenantry.

Very little is known for certain of the evolution of the *genin,* and his status even in the Tokugawa period is shadowy. The most plausible theory is that the *genin* developed from the numerous class of slaves known to Japan's early history and that their more recent ancestors, at least in some cases, had been military servants.[75] That many landholding families in whose households they are found bore arms earlier, and that some of the various names by which the *genin* were called were common names for the lowest class of military retainer from the Kamakura period on, are facts that tend to confirm this theory. Like the tenant, the *genin* had no public standing in the village, and his rights were defined by his relations to his master. Although he was handed down in a single family from father to son like any other piece of property, it is the opinion of one of Japan's outstanding social and legal historians that he could not be transferred to a new master against his will.[76] Perhaps the best way of describing the *genin's* position is as an inferior member of the master's family. One of the distinctive features of the Japanese family is its capacity for almost indefinite expansion to include not only remote relatives within its lines of authority, but persons having no blood or marriage relationship to the family at all. Indeed, not infrequently the *genin* was formally incorporated in the family: he worshipped the family ancestors, owed loyalty and obedience to the head of the family, and in return received such protection as the family accorded members of inferior standing.[77]

V

Although the most recent Japanese studies have left important problems regarding the peasantry still unsolved, they have nonetheless

[74] For figures showing this decline in various villages, see: Furushima, "Kinai nōgyō to kisei jinushi," p. 10; Ichikawa, p. 34; and Suzuki, pp. 40–41.

[75] For this view, Takigawa Masajirō, *Nihon shakai shi* (Tokyo, 1946), pp. 214–15. Takigawa's study of family registers of the Nara period suggests that somewhere between 5 and 10 per cent of the population at that time were slaves. Ono, *Nihon shōen-sei shiron* (Tokyo, 1943), pp. 31–32.

[76] Takigawa, p. 219.

[77] Aruga, p. 354 ff.

established the main lines of a picture that is not likely to be radically altered. The peasants were not the homogeneous class depicted by the Confucianists. Peasant society itself was a pyramid of wealth and power and legal rights that rose from the tenant and *genin* at the bottom through small and middling landholders to what might be called a class of wealthy peasants at the top. Nor was this pyramid a recent structure, the work of capitalism in placing one peasant over another. Rather it was the survival from an earlier age in which men were raised and lowered in society by force of land and arms, not by the power of money.

I should like to suggest, in very general and tentative terms, the possible bearing of this picture of the peasantry on the two interpretive problems mentioned in the introductory section of this paper, with a warning to the reader that some of the inferences to be made go beyond the evidence available at present.

The persistent docility of the peasantry, in a country where peasants even today number almost half the population, is a fact of obvious and immense significance. Most students would agree, I believe, that this political and social passivity has provided an extraordinarily solid base for authoritarian government and support for social policies of the most conservative order for the past four centuries at least. To inculcate and enforce such discipline among peasants who, in general, have been held consistently at the ragged edge of starvation implies some extremely efficient system of social and political control. I would suggest that this system was composed in part of the following elements. (1) The peasantry was divided against itself by arrangements in which one peasant exploited the labor of another and in which the upper layer of the peasantry was in fact an adjunct of the ruling class, sharing in the economic benefits of the regime and in the administration of the country so that any prospective peasant uprising would find this group —the wealthy and literate families of the village—aligned solidly against it. (2) This group sprang partly from the warrior class: in its ranks were many men who had run local affairs by a combination of land and arms for centuries; and although it was disarmed at the end of the sixteenth century, its local authority was by no means weakened, for it was now supported by the armies of a feudal lord. (3) Despite the spectacular changes effected in other spheres, the Meiji restoration passed over the village without disturbing the distribution of power or the system by which land was exploited. Thus, the Japanese landlords of modern times, taken as a whole, were not a new and precariously dominant group thrown up by the impact of capitalism on the village but a class whose habit of power goes back to the formative period of Japanese feudalism.

The other interpretive problem concerns the need for finding a more satisfactory social and economic explanation of the Meiji restoration. Specifically, the participation of some other class than the low-ranking *samurai* is needed to explain both the nature and the success of the restoration. Without denying the leading political role to the *samurai,* it is possible to believe that decisive outside support came from the wealthy peasants.[78] That such a class existed and that it was accustomed to playing a political role is certain. Moreover, as rural industrialists, local merchants and moneylenders (roles the larger holders developed after the beginning of the eighteenth century), and as heavy taxpayers, the members of this class had cause to be dissatisfied with the Tokugawa system. Indeed, much of the "progressive" legislation of the restoration government—the abolition of legal classes, the removal of restrictions on the use and sale of land, the abolition of official trading monopolies, the commutation of *samurai* pensions—can most readily be explained as reflecting the interests and aspirations of this group. There is, moreover, direct positive evidence of the participation of a considerable number of peasant leaders in the restoration movement.[79]

But, it may be asked, how does one account then for the generally conservative character of the restoration? To put the question differently, why should this class of wealthy farmers have surrendered top leadership to the *samurai,* thus almost wholly excluding themselves from positions of power in the restoration government, rather than leading a popular revolutionary movement? Partly, the alliance with the *samurai* was a necessary stratagem (conscious or not) to split the military class. Partly, it was dictated by the nature of Tokugawa political institutions, which permitted the *samurai* alone the necessary freedom of movement to organize a nation-wide, conspiratorial movement. But as important as either of these factors was the interest of the wealthy farmers themselves. Socially, they were more nearly akin to

---

[78] Nobutaka Ike has emphasized the role of the wealthy peasants in the restoration, particularly those who had interests in rural industry. *The Beginnings of Political Democracy in Japan* (Baltimore, 1950), pp. 11–21.

[79] The evidence on this point has never been treated systematically, to my knowledge. There is, however, a good deal of very important scattered evidence; see particularly, Tōyama Shigeki, "Sonno jōi shisō to nashanarizumu," *Sonjō shisō to zettai shugi,* ed. Tōyō bunka kenkyūjo, (Tokyo, 1948), pp. 28–30; and Tanaka Sōgorō, *Meiji ishin undō jimbutsu kō* (Tokyo, 1941), pp. 111–31.

the *samurai* than to the ordinary peasant—the small holder and tenant. Moreover, if they were being forced by their expanding interests to free themselves from the conomic and social restrictions placed on them, they were under the necessity, at the same time, of conserving their hold on the land and the system of exploiting it. Thus they were simultaneously revolutionary and conservative. While they were intent on finding means of changing leadership and policy at the top, they were determined to avoid the violent overthrow of the regime from below with the terrible risk of social revolution that entailed.

CHAPTER FIFTEEN

THE LAND TAX IN THE TOKUGAWA PERIOD

THOMAS C. SMITH

Reprinted from *Journal of Asian Studies*,
Vol. XVIII, No. 1 (November 1958)

FEW notions are so widely held among students of Japanese economic history as the view that the land tax during the Tokugawa period was cruelly oppressive. It is thought to have left the peasantry no significant surplus after production costs, and moreover to have become heavier as time passed.[1] I propose in this paper to examine certain evidence bearing on this view, which strongly influences the interpretation of modern Japanese history.

It is commonly held that the increasing weight of the land tax impoverished the peasantry and drove it to rebellion, thus weakening the economic and political foundations of the Tokugawa regime and hastening its end. The tax burden also is thought to have deeply colored the society that emerged from the downfall of the Tokugawa. Having blocked capitalist development in the countryside, which consequently remained "feudal" in a social sense long after the Restoration, modernization in general and industrial development in particular were primarily achievements of the state. In the ultimate extension of the argument, this is held to account in considerable measure for the abortiveness of political democracy in Japan before World War II.

Of course no one attempts to explain any of the developments—or absence of them—wholly by reference to the land tax. Disproof of the assumptions made about the tax, therefore, would not necessarily make untenable any particular view of Japanese history. It would suggest, though, that the views outlined above bear re-examination.

Historians have been generally content to support their views about the severity of taxation by citing the proportion of the assessed yield of holdings that was normally taken by the land tax. But since nothing is said about the relation of assessed to actual yield, such figures mean very little and may even be misleading, as is suggested by the fact that agricultural productivity increased substantially in the two and a half centuries after 1600. This is evident not only from improvements in agricultural technology,[2] but from the notable increase in urban population during this period

---

[1] Representative statements of these views may be found in Toya Toshiyuki, *Kinsei nōgyō keiei shiron* (Tokyo, 1949), pp. 13–73; and Kajinishi Mitsuhaya *et al*, *Nihon ni okeru shihonshugi no hattatsu* (Tokyo, 1951), I, 13–23.

For help in collecting material for this article, I wish to express my gratitude to Professors Andō Seiichi, Egashira Tsuneharu, Harada Toshimaru, Harafuji Hiroshi, Tokoro Mitsuo, and Yasuzawa Shunichi. I am also indebted to the Rockefeller Foundation and the Social Science Research Council for support in gathering these and other materials. Finally, I wish to thank Professor William Capron for advice on statistical problems, and Professor Herman Chernoff for arranging for the computations.

[2] Chiefly by the development of new plant varieties and more intensive fertilization. Furushima Toshio, *Nihon nōgyō gijutsushi* (Tokyo, 1950, 2nd ed.), Vol. I.

T. C. Smith

without benefit of food imports.[3] Add to urban growth an increase throughout the population in per capita consumption of food and fibers such as unquestionably took place, and one is forced to conclude that there was a very sizeable increase in the productivity of agricultural labor. There was also an increase in crop yields; on individual fields for which we have production data it ran as high as 112 per cent in fifty years.[4] This may well have been an exceptional case, but even a much smaller increase would imply the existence of powerful incentives on the part of cultivators to increase yields, and, further, their ability to invest in commercial fertilizers and other means of accomplishing this. Neither condition suggests confiscatory taxation.

This is not to deny that the tax burden was uncomfortably heavy; but it was perhaps not as oppressive as is sometimes made out, and it became lighter with time— at least in some places for some people. Surviving tax records leave little doubt of this; but before considering the evidence of these documents a word needs to be said about the Tokugawa tax system.

The main tax levied on the peasants was the land tax, called $nengu^a$, which was based on the estimated productivity of land. With certain local exceptions (noted later), all other taxes were negligible by comparison. Like other taxes imposed by the lord this one was levied on village communities as a whole, rather than on individual proprietors or families. In order to levy the land tax, it was obviously necessary for the lord to know the extent and productivity of the arable land in every village under his control. For that purpose each field in each village was surveyed and assigned a grade which expressed its per-acre yield in normal years—yield being measured in units of unhulled rice, or rice equivalents in the case of other crops. Size times grade therefore gave the normal yield of the field—a datum called $kokudaka^b$, which might be translated as taxable, or assessed, yield. From the data on individual fields, it was of course simple to compute the kokudaka of holdings and villages.

The village kokudaka was the lord's basic referent in setting the land tax, which he announced annually to the village in a document called $menjō^c$. The menjō recorded both the assessed yield of the village and the percentage demanded as land tax. Upon receipt of this document the village, by consultative processes unknown in detail, allocated the tax bill among its individual holders. The register that recorded the resultant allocation ($waritsuke-chō^d$), along with the register of payments ($kaisai mokuroku^e$), and of course the menjō itself, were for obvious rea-

---

[3] It is exceedingly difficult to estimate the increase in the proportion of urban population, but some notion of its size is suggested by the fact that total population was nearly stationary from 1711 to 1748 but the population of towns and cities continued to grow. Edo grew from 353,000 in 1693 to 864,000 in 1801, and Osaka from 345,000 in 1692 to something over 400,000 near the end of the eighteenth century. See Sekiyama Naotarō, Kinsei nihon jinkō no kenkyū (Tokyo, 1948), pp. 231–232; also Furushima Toshio, Kinsei nihon nōgyō no kōzō (Tokyo, 1943), p. 611.

[4] This is not implausibly high, as the following quotation shows: "To illustrate, a project just now getting under way in India indicates that, for a set of 6 representative case-study farms in 2 districts in Uttar Pradesh . . . an addition of Rs. 321 cash expenditures per farm, mostly spent on fertilizer and seeds, would add Rs. 1,219 or 77 per cent to the gross value of output per farm." John D. Black, review in the American Economic Review, XLVII, No. 6, (Dec., 1957), 1033–34.

For increments in productivity during the Tokugawa period, see Gotō's figures on rice yields between 1787 and 1856 in Aki Province; Gotō Yōichi, "Jūku seiki Sanyo nōson ni okeru tōnō keiei no seikaku," Shigaku zasshi, LXIII, No. 7 (July 1954), 12. Also Imai's estimates for a holding in Settsu Province. Imai Rintarō, Hōken shakai no nōgyō kōzō (Tokyo, 1955), p. 47.

sons exceedingly important records for village administration. They were consequently preserved with special care and survive to this day in considerable number. Sometimes it is even possible to find a series of such documents recording the assessed yield and annual tax payments of a village for a period of well over a century.

The graphs in this article (pp. 15–19) record the tax data for a total of eleven villages, in each case beginning sometime before 1700 and terminating after 1850. The top line shows assessed yield and the bottom line what percentage of that figure was taken by the land tax. Note that the two lines refer to different scales and therefore might have been plotted on separate graphs; they were not, in order to make comparison of their gross contours possible, but the distance between them has no significance whatever.

The first feature of these graphs that strikes our attention is the astonishing stability of the top lines. Remember, these lines represent village *kokudaka,* the official assessment of productivity on which taxes were based. One therefore confidently expects them to move upward to reflect the increasing productivity of land —or, at least, to show frequent movements of *some* kind, reflecting successive assessments of productivity. But in fact there is no movement at all for long periods. Startling as the realization is, it is evident that in these villages at least, from about 1700 on, land ceased to be periodically surveyed; by the middle of the nineteenth century, therefore, taxes were based on assessments a century to a century and a half old.

This is puzzling. Why should the warrior class, always in need of additional revenue, have failed to revise the tax base at a time when yields were rising? One deterrent to revision was the massive administrative effort that was required to survey an entire fief. But the surveying could have been done village by village rather than all at once; besides, great though administrative inertia may have been, it can hardly have blocked a measure so patently advantageous. Is it possible, since the peasants would as patently lose as the warriors gain by reassessment, that the decisive deterrent was fear of resistance?

Whatever the reasons, reassessment was neglected. The graphs for nine villages show either no change in assessed yield, or negligible change only, from about 1700 to the middle of the nineteenth century; and several show no change whatsoever from some time in the seventeenth century. In the sole case (VI) of a considerable increase after 1700—from 719 *koku* in 1699 to 752 in 1732, after which there was absolutely no change—the entire increment was the result of an addition of new arable to the tax rolls, not of a reassessment of yields.[5] Despite appearances, then, this village conforms to the same pattern as the others.

Almost certainly there were villages that would present a very different picture if we but had the relevant data. But even if numerous cases of this type should subsequently come to light, the pattern shown by the villages for which we now have data must be judged a common one. The villages were widely scattered geographically (see map), all but two were located in different fiefs, and all were chosen for no other reason than the availability of material.

Since the tax base was not significantly revised in any of these villages, we would

---

[5] This is obvious since in this, as in most *menjō,* old fields (*honden*) and new fields (*shinden*) were listed separately.

expect to find the *rate* of taxation rising very sharply in compensation. The trend was supposedly upward generally, and it should have been especially steep in these communities to make up for assessments that fell ever further behind actual yields. But we find no such thing. Nine of the eleven villages show no significant long-term increase from 1700 or shortly thereafter until the end of the period; some show no change at all; a few register a long-term decline. Two villages only show a size-able increase; but in one of these (I) the rate of taxation was uncommonly low to begin with and the increase short-lived. In the other (III), the tax rate increased notably between 1700 and 1710, held firm from 1710 to 1780, but after that sank slowly to the original level. But the graphs speak for themselves.

Again we must resist the temptation to generalize too broadly from a few cases; but the similarities among the cases are impressive. It is difficult to understand fully why, with actual productivity rising and assessments static, the tax rate in these villages was usually not raised. Probably one very powerful reason was the technical difficulty of raising the tax rate without reassessment, for any considerable increase would then put an unbearable burden on peasants whose crop yields had not in-creased. This difficulty, incidentally, is one of the most cogent reasons for doubting

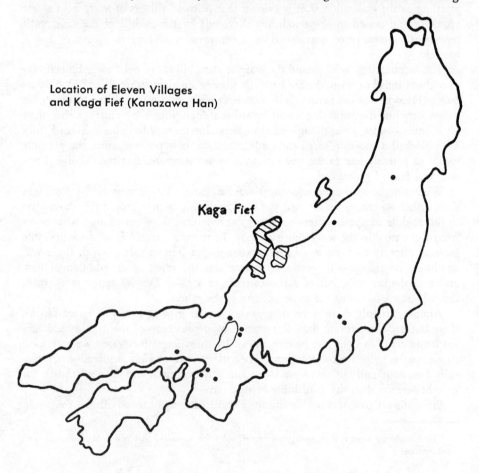

Location of Eleven Villages
and Kaga Fief (Kanazawa Han)

Kaga Fief

Land Tax in the Tokugawa Period

that the trend in the rate of taxation could have been significantly upward generally —assuming that the reassessment of land after 1700 was actually as rare as it seems to have been, which itself needs additional proof and explanation.

Evidence from the Kaga fief located on the Japan Sea confirms the impression the graphs give, that the tax burden did not necessarily increase with time. To understand the evidence it is necessary to speak briefly of the tax system of the Kaga fief, for it was different from the one typical of the rest of the country.

Instead of sending a tax bill down to the villages annually, the Lord of Kaga left permanently in effect in each village the basic tax rate set for it in 1651. It is true that the effective rate might be altered from time to time; but this was done by adding to or subtracting from the initial rate—so that, for example, if a 10% increase in a tax of 50% were decreed, it would be expressed as 50% plus 10%, not 60%. This system made it clumsy to compute a village's effective tax rate in places where the rate had undergone numerous alterations, but the system had the inestimable advantage, for the historian, of keeping in the expression of the current rate a permanent record of prior changes.

Table I shows the net change in taxation after 1651 in each of 424 villages in three counties of the Kaga fief. The table is based on a tax register for these villages that was copied in the early Meiji period from a late Tokugawa document. Since the register is a copy, and a copy moreover of a document that may itself have been compiled from other documents, it is probable that individual entries have been miswritten or dropped somewhere along the line. One cannot be certain, therefore, that the computations for all villages are precisely accurate; on the other hand, it is unlikely that they are generally erroneous or that they err consistently in one direction so as to exaggerate either increases or decreases.

TABLE I

CHANGES IN LAND TAX AFTER 1651 IN 424 VILLAGES IN KAGA FIEF

Per Cent Increase or Decrease	Decrease	No Change	Increase
0		64	
under 1%	7		151
1–5%	10		72
6–10%	25		11
11–20%	23		4
21–30%	15		3
31–40%	17		2
over 40%	20		0
Totals	117	64	243

Compiled from *Fugeshi kōri muramura takamen-ki'*. and *Haka ryōgun takamen-ki⁸* (both undated manuscripts) Nos. 164–99, Kanazawa City Library.

It will be seen that more villages experienced a net increase than a net decrease —243 to 117. But with very few exceptions the net increases were negligible: 151 were under 1% and 223 under 5%. On the other hand, a great majority of the net decreases were over 5% and more than half were over 10%. Since Kaga was a large, compact fief and one of the more backward in the country, we should expect to find here if anywhere that the tax burden was increasing through time.[6] What we discover in fact, however, is that from the middle of the seventeenth century to the end of the Tokugawa period, the land tax in most villages remained unchanged for all practical purposes, and in the remainder it was more often reduced than not.

Are we to conclude, then, that as time passed taxation left a larger and larger surplus[7] in the hands of the peasants in many if not most villages? This seems to have been the case as concerns the land tax; but there are three other categories of taxes or dues to be considered: the *corvée,* irregular exactions by officials, and a multitude of supplementary taxes generically called *komono-nari*[10]. Let us consider each of these categories briefly in turn.

(1) *Corvée* labor was used in three types of work: castle construction and other work that was exclusively for the benefit of the warrior class; road building, the construction of irrigation works and so on that were more generally beneficial; and overland transport. It is very important to remember that there was almost no direct use of peasant labor by the warrior class in agriculture,[8] though this accounted for the bulk of peasant labor services in medieval Europe and earlier in Japan.

Labor employed in the construction and maintenance of roads and irrigation works had a distinct benefit for the peasant; far from being an economic loss, such labor may properly be considered a form of involuntary investment that yielded long-run returns to him. But even labor on castle-walls and moats, though distasteful, was an economic loss only insofar as the peasant was compelled to forego a profitable alternative use for his labor, which was by no means always the case. This work might be done in periods when work was otherwise slack, and common sense would caution against commanding it during the busiest seasons of the agricultural year.

There was however one important type of *corvée* which did often reduce the peasant's surplus. Labor was taken regularly from villages along the main routes of travel to move official parties and their equipage from one posting station to another, over mountain passes and rivers and moor.[9] Since high-ranking warriors travelling with large retinues were constantly moving to and from the capital, the demands for transport placed upon the wayside villages were often exceedingly heavy; some communities were forced to maintain a larger animal population than would otherwise have been required. This was a burden which reduced the surplus left by the land tax; but communities subject to it, though numerous in absolute terms, accounted for no more than a small proportion of the perhaps 150,000 villages of that time.[10]

---

[6] The land tax is thought to have been generally more oppressive in such fiefs than in the small, fragmented fiefs in the Kinai. The reason is that the warrior class in the former had virtually no other important source of revenue and was in a stronger political and military position against the peasantry.

[7] By "surplus" is not meant, of course, what was left after all necessary expenses—that is, savings; but the difference between what was left after taxes now and earlier, whether used for savings or not.

[8] The only exception was the relatively few warriors known as *gōshi*[a], who lived on the land instead of in castle-towns; *gōshi* typically held land which they worked in part with the labor of neighboring peasants and were a survival from an earlier period. They were to be found chiefly in Satsuma, Tosa, and Chōshū.

[9] Villages too far away to provide labor and animals were taxed in money or kind for the support of posting stations; such taxes were included in *komono-nari*.

[10] Yanagida Kunio, *Nihon nōminshi* (Tokyo, 1931), p. 21.

Land Tax in the Tokugawa Period

(2) Bribes and gifts to tax officials were the main form of illegal exaction, but it is doubtful that they bulked large in the total economic burden of the village. They may actually have reduced rather than added to it, for bribes of all forms were offered in the hope of securing special consideration for the village in the matter of taxes. Significantly, complaints against the practice came not so much from peasants protesting an additional burden as from officials lamenting the loss of revenue to the lord and partiality in administration.[11]

(3) *Komono-nari* consisted chiefly of dues imposed on forests, moor, rivers, and ponds; taxes on handicrafts and other non-farming occupations; and a great number of miscellaneous taxes with little uniformity from one place to another. Frequently all these taxes were listed in the same document that announced the land tax (*menjō*). This was true of five of the eleven villages represented in the graphs (I-V); in these cases *komono-nari* has been added to the land tax in plotting the bottom line.[12]

If these villages may be taken as representative, no conclusion justified by study of the land tax would be materially altered by including *komono-nari*—for two reasons. *Komono-nari* was negligible in all cases, and it showed the same tendency to stability after 1700 as the land tax. This is reflected in the charts for the five villages which, despite the addition of *komono-nari,* show neither an unusually high rate of taxation nor any tendency for taxation to increase with time. It is always possible, of course, that our documentation is incomplete—that *komono-nari* in these villages was announced partly in the *menjō* and partly in other documents of which we have no record.

(4) Two other factors deserve mention since either could have eliminated any surplus seemingly left the peasants as effectively as a hidden tax. One was the commutation of taxes in kind; the other was population increase.

Though nearly always levied in kind the land tax was sometimes actually paid partly in money, especially on land planted in cash crops. Insofar as it is possible to tell from the documents,[13] this was not the practice in any of the eleven villages discussed earlier. But wherever it was the practice, clearly the rate of commutation could have the effect of increasing the peasants' tax burden. But it could also have the effect of lightening taxes, and moreover would have, if the commutation rate were not frequently altered, for money steadily lost value throughout the Tokugawa period. What the actual effects of commutation were, however, is a question that requires special study and cannot be confidently answered now. The most that can be said is that there seem to have been few complaints from the peasants about commutation, and that in most regions no more than a small fraction of the land tax was commuted.

The other factor to be taken into account is population increase. The surplus after

---

[11] Tanaka Kyūgū (1662–1729) expressed the standard reaction to official corruption when he described it as stealing from one's lord, going on to say: "If an official accepts a bribe of 1,000 gold pieces, it will infallibly cost the treasury 10,000." "Minkan seiyō," *Nihon keizai sōsho*, I, 394.

[12] Items of *komono-nari* expressed in money have been dropped since no index exists for converting them to units of rice; but in all cases the money payments dropped were infinitesimal and remained so during the entire period covered by the data.

[13] That is, the documents announcing the land tax did not stipulate that any part of it was to be paid in money. This omission seems the more significant since in comparable documents from at least one other village payments in money were stipulated. See documents on Nagatake Village, Meiji University.

T. C. Smith

the land tax may have been steadily expanding as our graphs suggest, but if farming population per acre of arable land were expanding at the same rate, the whole surplus would have been required just to maintain living standards at their former level.[14] Here we are on relatively certain ground. Rural population certainly increased during the Tokugawa period, and it may have increased more rapidly than the cultivated area; but the population engaged in agriculture did not. If anything it was decreasing, because farm labor was being steadily drawn into other rural employments (as well as to the city) by the rapid growth of trade and industry. The result was an acute shortage of farm labor that was felt nearly everywhere from about 1720 on and lasted into the Meiji period. A great many quotations from all parts of the country might be adduced as evidence of this fact.[15]

It would seem, then, that the size of the "surplus"—if one existed—was determined mainly by the land tax, except where the *corvée* was unusually heavy. The percentage of the *assessed* yield taken by the land tax was often fearfully high; fifty or sixty percent was not unusual, a fact frequently cited to illustrate the severity of taxation. But, as we have seen, the tax was based on a quantity that had less and less relation to actual productivity as time passed. How greatly productivity increased between 1700 and 1868, is therefore a critical question, but it is also an exceedingly complex one that we cannot hope to cope with here.

Although we must leave to one side this question and therefore that of the *size* of the surplus, it is pertinent to ask who received such surplus as there was. Was it spread through the village more or less evenly or did the greater part stick to the hands of some holders only? If the latter, the surplus would have been socially and economically more significant than if its effects were widely dispersed.

This brings us to the question of how the village allocated the land tax and *komono-nari* among its holders. If proportionately to the assessed yield of holdings, it is obvious that a cumulative inequity in taxation would result. Holders A and B would then be nominally subject to the same tax rate; but A, whose fields had gone unimproved for three generations, would be paying at twice the *actual* rate of B, whose crop-yields had doubled in the meantime. The point is that under such a system the surplus would have gone to improving peasants only, and to each only in proportion as the productivity of his land had increased. This would have given such holders an important advantage in further improving their land and presumably have led to even greater disparities in the incidence of taxation in the future.

But were taxes actually allocated in the village on the basis of assessments that went unrevised for generations on end? Perhaps the village made frequent assessments of its own to avoid the gross inequities of the lord's assessment, although I think it is fair to say no one knows for sure. Officials who wrote on such matters were interested in tax administration up to the boundaries of the village but no farther.

---

[14] This does not mean of course that the "surplus" would actually have been used for that purpose, especially if unevenly distributed.

[15] Typical is a village document from what is now Tottori Prefecture. "Since opportunity for by-employments is abundant in the countryside," it tells us, "labor is scarce and there are many villages which suffer year after year because, owing to want of labor, they are late finishing the planting." Mihashi Tokio, "Edo jidai ni okeru nōgyō keiei no henkan," in Miyamoto Mataji (ed.), *Nōson kōzō no shiteki bunseki* (Tokyo, 1955), p. 16. Also, Furushima Toshio, *Shōhin seisan to kisei jinushi-sei* (Tokyo, 1954), p. 88; Nomura Kanetarō (ed.) *Mura meisaichō* (Tokyo, 1949), pp. 26, 736; Oda Kichinojō (ed.) *Kaga han nōsei shikō* (Tokyo, 1929), p. 578; *Minkan seiyo*, pp. 260–261.

Land Tax in the Tokugawa Period

We consequently find a great many detailed descriptions of how land was surveyed and graded, of the various factors to be taken into account in setting the tax rate, of the comparative advantages of setting it annually or for a period of years—but nothing on how the villagers divided the annual tax bill among themselves.

There are reasons, nevertheless, for thinking the allocation was generally in proportion to the lord's assessments of yield. First is the sheer simplicity of this method. How easy it was to follow year after year the individual assessments of the land register, which bore the authority of the tax official and had once been more or less equitable; and how difficult for the villagers themselves to revise the assessments. Who, in the event of revision, would not claim that his fields yielded less than a neighbor's, and less than they actually did? That some concession ought to be made for their clumsy location, poor drainage, and so on? The possibilities of disagreement were endless. Agreement would be the more difficult, moreover, because the improving farmers, who on the whole were bound to be the most influential members of the village, had the most to lose by any revision at all.

Second, one encounters many contemporary statements to the effect that good land and good farmers were taxed less heavily than poor. These statements are very perplexing unless one assumes that assessments had gotten badly out of date and that consequently taxes were relatively low on improved land and high on unimproved. If this were the case, complaints like the following one in a memorial to the Lord of Matsuyama become quite understandable:[16] "Now one peasant whom we shall call Ichisuke is prosperous; since his fields are actually larger and their yield higher than registered, cultivation of his holding is profitable. But the holding of Nisuke is smaller and its yield less than registered, so however hard he works there is never profit but bitter suffering only. Within your lordship's domain *there are many cases like these two. . . .*" (italics supplied).

There is, additionally, quite specific documentary evidence on this point; though it consists of a single case, it is, I believe, the only evidence of the kind and deserves careful notice. The case is that of Renkōji village*y*, located in Musashi Province in the fief of a Tokugawa retainer named Amano.

There exists for this village, in the Shiryōkan in Tokyo, a very long series of *waritsuke-chō,* or registers of individual assessments.[17] Each of these documents records for a different year how the land tax and *komono-nari,* taken together,[18] were allocated among the holders of the village. It lists every holder in the village, the amount of land he owned in each of the various grades, and the amount of tax rice he owed on land in each grade. It is a simple thing to determine that land within each grade was uniformly taxed.[19] The critical question then is whether assessments of fields were periodically revised. If not, they were bound to have fallen behind actual productivity on some fields and inequities in taxation resulted.

We unfortunately cannot follow the assessments of particular fields through successive *waritsuke-chō*—if that were possible the question could be easily answered.

---

[16] Kan Kikutarō, "Matsuyama han ni okeru jōmen-sei no kenkyū," *Shakai keizai shigaku,* XI, No. 8 (Nov. 1941), 54.

[17] Tomizawa* family documents.

[18] Postface of the *waritsuke-chō* for 1693.

[19] For instance, in 1754, all holders paid a tax of .1920 *koku* of rice per *tan* on top-grade upland, .1610 on middle grade, .1320 on low grade, and .500 on residential land.

T. C. Smith

Land was not listed in these documents by field but by grade only—"upper paddy," "middle paddy," "lower paddy," and so on. It is possible however to follow the composition of individual holdings by grades, as Table II illustrates. It shows the amount of land in each of several grades owned by a certain Shimpei (and his successive

TABLE II
Holding of Shimpei, Renkōji Village, Musashi Province
(figures in *tan* of land) (" means ditto)

	Paddy			Upland			Residential
Date	upper	middle	lower	upper	middle	lower	
1753	.4726	.3920	1.1224	.7214	.5812	1.8726	.2015
1754	"	"	"	"	"	"	"
1755	"	.3012	.9729	"	.3401	"	"
1756	"	"	"	"	"	"	"
1757	"	"	"	"	"	1.8300	"
1758	"	"	"	"	"	1.8512	"
1759	"	"	"	"	"	"	"
1760	"	"	"	"	"	"	"
1761	"	"	"	"	"	1.8315	"
1762	"	"	"	"	"	"	"
1763	"	"	"	"	.5327	2.1324	"
1764	"	"	"	"	"	"	"
1765	"	"	"	"	"	"	"
1766	"	"	"	"	"	2.1525	"
1767	"	"	"	"	"	"	"
1768	"	"	"	"	.4802	2.1607	"
1782	"	.3118	.7829	"	"	2.0228	"
1783	"	"	"	"	"	"	"
1784	"	.3020	.6418	"	.4902	"	"
1785	"	.3012	"	"	"	"	"
1786	"	"	"	"	"	"	"
1787	"	"	"	"	"	"	"
1789	"	"	"	"	"	"	"
1790	"	"	"	"	"	2.040	"
1791	"	"	"	"	"	"	"
1792	"	"	"	"	"	"	"
1793	"	"	"	"	"	"	"
1794	.4606	"	"	"	"	"	"
1795	"	"	"	"	"	"	"
1796	"	"	"	"	"	"	"
1797	"	"	"	"	"	"	"
1800	"	"	"	"	"	"	"
1801	"	"	"	.7908	"	1.9720	"
1802	"	"	"	"	"	"	"
1803	"	"	"	"	"	"	"

heirs) from 1753 to 1804. Note, first of all, that there were very few changes in the amount of land registered in the various grades; consider next that such changes as are recorded can mean two things only. Either that land was bought or sold (or ownership otherwise transferred), or that it was moved from one grade to another without change of ownership. The first kind of change would indicate no regrading—no reassessment of land; but the second, if it occurred, obviously would.

Land Tax in the Tokugawa Period

The problem is, of course, to determine whether changes occurred in the second way and if so how often. Fortunately the problem is susceptible to a solution for which one can claim at least a rather high degree of reliability. Let us illustrate: in 1761, the amount of "lower upland" belonging to Shimpei decreased from 1.8512 *tan* to 1.8315—a decrease of 0.197. Since there was no increase in the other grades totalling that amount—in fact, in this particular year, no change in any of them whatsoever—it seems probable that the land in question was transferred to another holder: hence no reassessment of land is indicated. All changes throughout the table except two seem[20] to be of this kind, as the reader may confirm by studying the figures carefully.

The two exceptional changes—one in 1784 and another in 1794—clearly did result from reassessments, for in both cases there is a notation in the *waritsuke-chō* to that effect. In the one, .0100 *tan* of lower paddy was regraded as middle upland, and in the other .0120 of upper paddy was taken off the tax rolls because it had "gone to waste." Since these are the only reassessments noted, it seems probable that the other changes occurred by transfer of ownership. Moreover, there are good grounds for believing that these two particular changes were made for exceptional reasons and not as part of periodic, general reassessments. One plot of land had presumably gone out of production entirely, a fact which could not simply be ignored in allocating taxes; and the other had been transformed from paddy to upland—a circumstance that may have been occasioned by a community decision with respect to water and one that in any case would have been registered by a notable physical change in the appearance of the field.

With these exceptions, it seems that land was not reassessed during this period in Renkōji, and judging from statements by contemporaries that good land was taxed relatively lightly, this was probably also true of many other villages.

Conclusions

(1) In many villages during the Tokugawa period the land tax and *komono-nari* were static or even declined slightly, though the productivity of land was generally rising. Thus a larger and larger "surplus" was left by these two taxes in the hands of peasants. How rapidly the "surplus" was increasing and, consequently, what its absolute size was at any given time, are questions which cannot be answered at present.

(2) Whatever the rate of increase, benefits were probably not spread evenly through the peasant population, but conferred exclusively on peasants who contrived to increase crop yields.

(3) Other types of taxes may have reduced the "surplus," but the reduction was probably not drastic in most cases. The facts of this matter, of course, are obscure. But no one doubts that other taxes were quantitatively much less significant than the land tax, and moreover there was necessarily a tendency to hold them within limits tolerable to the average peasant family. They were therefore unlikely to have offset entirely the increment that accrued to improving peasants from the combination of

---

[20] But one cannot be absolutely sure; it is possible that both a purchase (or sale) *and* a reassessment of land took place in such a way as to obscure the latter. For example, it is conceivable that in 1761 the .0197 of lower upland referred to earlier was not sold but regraded, let us say, as middle upland, and that this does not show in our data because in the same year exactly the same amount of middle upland was sold. This of course is highly unlikely when one figure only has changed during the year, but it is less improbable when several have changed.

rising yields and a static land tax; in no case would they have cancelled the comparative advantage of such peasants.

(4) It seems likely that for a vast number of peasant families in the Tokugawa period farming paid—for some it may even have paid handsomely by the standard of the times. This would help explain certain features of Tokugawa economic and social history that are otherwise puzzling. It would help explain why land ownership tended to concentrate, though generally on a small scale—men sought it because it could be profitably exploited; why tenant farming spread—because with rising yields rent could be added to taxes and still leave the cultivator enough to live; why rural trade and industry developed so powerfully from about 1700 on—because purchasing power in rural areas was expanding proportionately and there were profits from farming to finance new enterprises. Most important, perhaps, it goes far toward explaining the existence of the large class of relatively wealthy, educated, and ambitious peasant families one finds nearly everywhere at the end of the Tokugawa period and who contributed so strikingly to the making of modern Japan.

(5) It is necessary to guard against one possible misunderstanding. I do not wish to suggest that the many contemporary descriptions of agrarian distress are entirely misleading, though considered alone they give a one-sided picture. Not all peasant families were able to increase yields or to increase them fast enough to offset tax increases. Taxes moreover were not the unique cause of peasant distress. Usury, flood, drought, immoderate spending for weddings and funerals, adverse price movements, and deeper involvement in the money economy all contributed to peasant poverty. But widespread poverty—a condition by no means characteristic of all areas—was quite compatible with numerous instances of impressive wealth and elegance. It is a serious mistake to think of the Tokugawa peasantry as even a fairly homogeneous class. The upper strata of peasants were in many respects, not least in respect to standard of life, much nearer to the middle ranks of the warrior class than to the majority of peasants.

(6) Whether the data presented here concerning the land tax require any substantial revision of widely accepted interpretations of Tokugawa economic history is far too large a question to enter on here. It is only fair to confess that I for one suspect so.

Land Tax in the Tokugawa Period

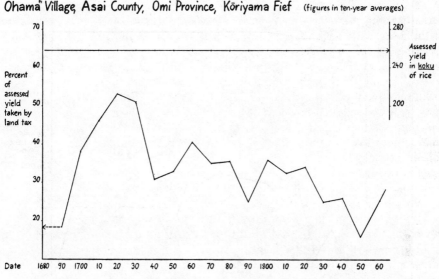

I

Ohama Village, Asai County, Ōmi Province, Kōriyama Fief (figures in ten-year averages)

Percent of assessed yield 50 taken by land tax

Assessed yield in *koku* of rice

Date 1680 90 1700 10 20 30 40 50 60 70 80 90 1800 10 20 30 40 50 60

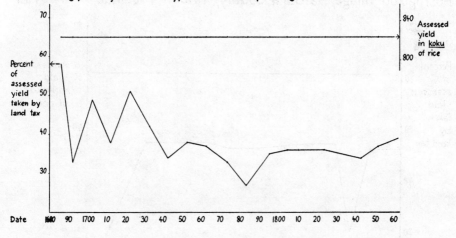

II

Yamabe Village, Murayama County, Dewa Province, Tokugawa Domain

Percent of assessed yield 50 taken by land tax

Assessed yield in *koku* of rice

Date 1680 90 1700 10 20 30 40 50 60 70 80 90 1800 10 20 30 40 50 60

III

Shima Village, Haibara County, Tōtōmi Province, Ōta Fief

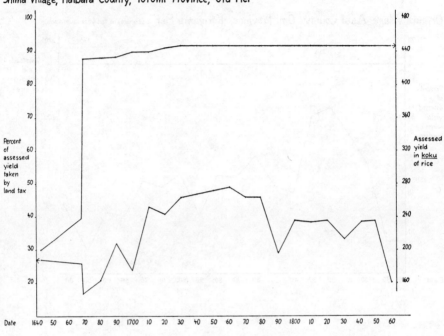

IV

Hoshigubo Village, Haibara County, Tōtōmi Province, ? Fief

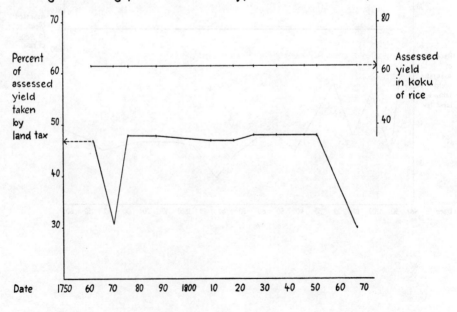

Land Tax in the Tokugawa Period

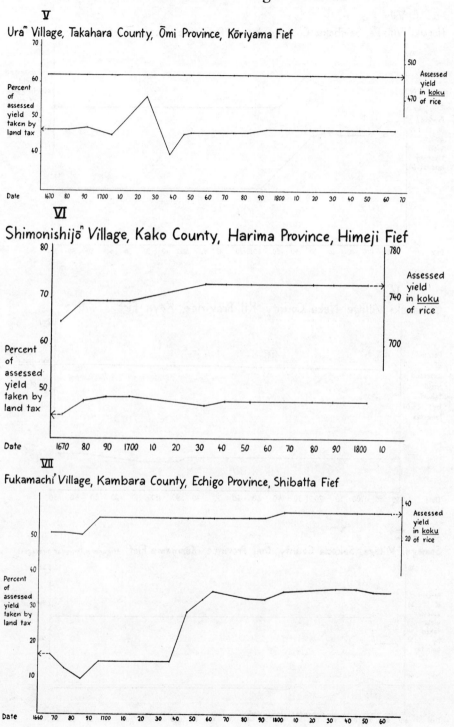

V

Ura⁽ᵐ⁾ Village, Takahara County, Ōmi Province, Kōriyama Fief

VI

Shimonishijō⁽ⁿ⁾ Village, Kako County, Harima Province, Himeji Fief

VII

Fukamachi⁽ʳ⁾ Village, Kambara County, Echigo Province, Shibatta Fief

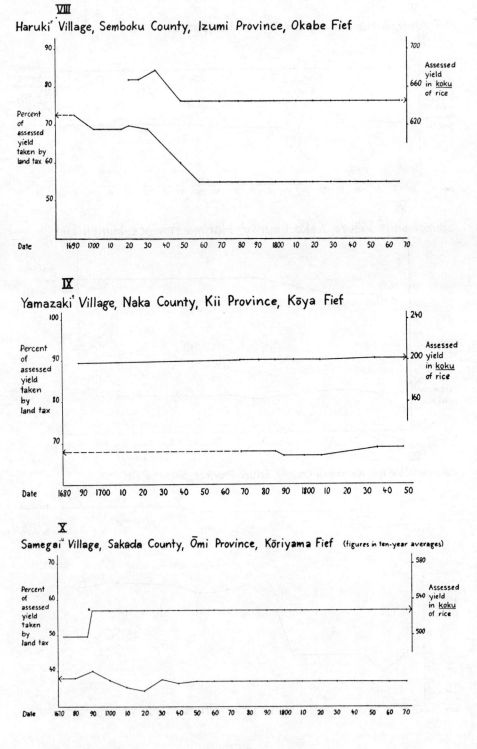

VIII

Haruki Village, Semboku County, Izumi Province, Okabe Fief

IX

Yamazaki Village, Naka County, Kii Province, Kōya Fief

X

Samegai Village, Sakada County, Ōmi Province, Kōriyama Fief (figures in ten-year averages)

Land Tax in the Tokugawa Period

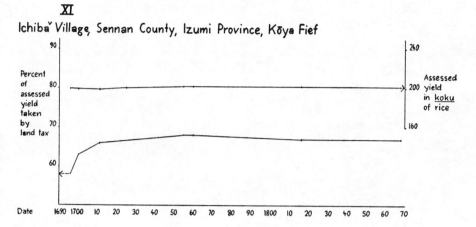

XI

Ichiba Village, Sennan County, Izumi Province, Kōya Fief

The sources of the data contained in the eleven tables are as follows:

I. Documents on Ōhama[h] Village, Shiga University.
II. Documents on Yamabe[i] Village, Shiryōkan, Tokyo.
III. Yamada[k] family documents, Shiryōkan, Tokyo.
IV. Documents on Hoshikubo[l] Village, Meiji University.
V. Documents on Ura[m] Village, Shiga University.
VI. Onishi[o] family documents, Shiryōkan, Tokyo.
VII. Yamaguchi[q] family documents, Shiryōkan, Tokyo.
VIII. Hara[s] family documents, Haruki, Osaka Metropolitan District. In 1800 the assessed yield of Haruki dropped from 646 to 377 *koku* owing to the administrative separation of a part of the village in that year. Since there was no change after that, indicating that no reassessment took place, we have projected the line after 1800 at 646, which was undoubtedly the assessed yield of the whole village.
IX. Documents of Yamazaki[t] Village, Wakayama University.
X. Documents of Samegai[u] Village, Shiga University.
XI. Documents of Ichiba[v], Wakayama University.

a 年貢
b 石高
c 免状
d 割付帳
e 皆済目録
f 鳳至郡村村高免記
g 羽鹿両郡高免記
h 大浜
i 山家
j 嶋
k 山田
l 星久保
m 浦
n 下西條
o 大西
p 深町
q 山口
r 春木
s 原
t 山崎
u 醒井
v 市場
w 小物成
x 郷士
y 蓮光寺
z 富澤

CHAPTER SIXTEEN

VILLAGE AUTONOMY AND ARTICULATION WITH THE STATE

HARUMI BEFU

Reprinted from *Journal of Asian Studies,*
Vol. XXV, No. 1 (November 1965)

WHEN village communities exist in the context of a larger political system, understanding of the system of control at the village level requires analysis both of the system of control imposed on the village by the state and also of that which has evolved within the community through centuries of its existence. These two systems, of course, cannot operate altogether independently of each other but must somehow be articulated with one another. The specific ways in which the two systems articulate differ from society to society. Nonetheless a perusal of the literature suggests a solution to the problem of articulation which is common to many societies. The solution apparently is to maintain a relatively autonomous village community over which the higher authority exercises limited control through certain key agents or agencies, as is, for example, the case with Imperial China, Thailand, Ceylon, and Greece.[1] And this was indeed the solution for Japanese villages of the Tokugawa period, in spite of the tight and rigid control of the military government over the peasantry which historians make much of.[2] (Since our discussion will proceed at a general level at which differences in administration between the Shogunate and daimiate governments are minor, both types of government will be simply referred to as "the government" or "governments" without distinction.)

In what specific ways did the governments of the Tokugawa Shogunate and the daimiate articulate with the village polity?[3] More specifically, what areas of peasant life did these governments attempt to control and why? How was the indigenous

---

[1] See, for example, Hsiao Kung-chuan, *Rural China, Imperial Control in the Nineteenth Century* (Seattle, 1960), p. 269; John E. De Young, *Village Life in Modern Thailand* (Berkeley and Los Angeles, 1955), pp. 1–21; Edmund R. Leach, *Pul Eliya, A Village in Ceylon* (London, 1961), pp. 28–30; Irwin T. Sanders, *Rainbow in the Rock, the People of Rural Greece* (Cambridge, Mass., 1962), pp. 218–240.

[2] This view of rigidly controlled and heavily oppressed peasantry of the Tokugawa period is particularly prevalent among those who interpret history primarily from the point of view of the Shogunate and daimiate administrative system. See, for example, Tokutomi Iichirō, *Kinsei Nihon Kokuminshi [History of the Early Modern Japan]* (Tokyo, 1924), vol. 15, pp. 507–533; Numada Jirō, *Nihon Zenshi [Complete History of Japan]* (Tokyo, 1959), vol. 7, *Kinsei,* part II, pp. 192–194. Not even Sansom was free, at times, from such an interpretation when he speaks of the "heavily oppressed" peasants and cites—in illustrating the condition of the peasants—Honda Masanobu's dictum that the peasant "must be allowed neither too much nor too little, but just enough rice to live on and to keep seed in the following year." George B. Sansom, *A History of Japan, 1615–1867* (Stanford, 1963), pp. 98–100.

[3] It should be noted that for the problem under consideration, the villages of the Tokugawa period are not to be equated with the modern rural communities of Japan, commonly called *buraku.* For the mode of political articulation of the modern Japanese state to the *buraku* is vastly different—due to factors I cannot go into here—from that of the Tokugawa state.

political structure of the village organized in relation to the government? Questions such as these are not easy to answer. For most students of Tokugawa political structure have almost exclusively discussed the political institutions of the military government, ignoring the native village political structure. And those who have analyzed the indigenous village political system have emphasized the autonomous and corporate character of the village, with little regard for the role of imposed government institutions. Consequently, how one is related to the other, how the powerful military government dealt with the supposedly semi-autonomous village has never been made clear.

The burden of this paper is to show that the government to a large measure depended for the implementation of its law on its own system of control which it instituted in the village, but at the same time utilized to a considerable extent the indigenous system of control. The village, on the other hand, relied primarily on its own machinery of control for the execution of regulations which evolved in the local scene, making relatively little use of the government-imposed control system.[4]

The administrative machinery of the Shogunate and daimiate governments consisted, at the village level, of the headman (generally called *shōya* in western Japan and *nanushi* in eastern Japan), the elders (*toshiyori, kumigashira,* etc.), the delegates (*hyakushōdai, yokome,* etc.), and the five-man groups (*goningumi*). Among these the headman was without question the most important official both in terms of the power delegated and the responsibilities assigned by the government.[5] The government held him responsible for keeping accurate and detailed records of the village census, reporting any changes in the village population (through birth, death, migration, marriage, divorce, etc.), apportioning to individual families rice tax levied on the village, collecting the tax in full and on time, maintaining public works in the village, adjudicating disputes arising within the village, reporting any violation of the law, and finally in general assuming the role of the father figure for the village. In addition, he was responsible for the conduct of his villagers, i.e., punishable for their crimes.

There were three or four elders in most villages and it was their duty to assist the headman. The delegates were presumably representatives of ordinary peasants[6] and

---

[4] As Thomas Smith has ably demonstrated in the *Agrarian Origins of Modern Japan* (Stanford, 1959), a great deal of change did take place during the Tokugawa period. Also, it is well known that there were important differences between the Shogunate and daimiate administration. We shall, nonetheless, attempt to generalize about the structure of control at a level of generality applicable throughout the period, both in the Shogunate and daimiate domains.

[5] The nature of the headman's position is discussed more fully by the author in "Duty, Reward, Sanction, and Power—Four-cornered Office of the Tokugawa Village Headman," (Manuscript. 1964).

[6] How effectively the delegates carried out their duties we do not know. Because their historical and economic backgrounds were very similar to those of other officials whom they were to watch, one may suspect that they more often than not allied themselves with the headman and the elders against the common peasants, rather than representing the peasants' interests. An examination of documents on peasant riots in which the village headman was the target of attack shows no clear evidence that delegates tended to side with the ordinary villagers against the headman. For documentation and analysis of peasant riots of Tokugawa period, see Hugh Borton, "Peasant Uprisings in Japan of the Tokugawa Period," *Transactions of the Asiatic Society of Japan,* Ser. 2, XVI (1938), 1–219; Kokushō Iwao, *Hyakushō Ikki no Kenkyū [A Study of Peasant Riots]* (Tokyo, 1928); Aoki Keiichirō, *Nihon Nōmin Undōshi [A History of Peasant Movements in Japan]* (Tokyo, 1959).

according to Asakawa, they were supposed "to keep an eye on the conduct of the village officials, to give counsel and admonition, and generally guard and promote the best interest of the village."[7]

That these officials were in fact held responsible and that these responsibilities were not merely on paper are clear if one examines such sources as the *Oshioki Reiruishū,* criminal records of the Tokugawa period, which list numerous cases in which the officials were punished either for wrong-doings of their own or of their villagers.[8]

The power which the officials needed to execute their responsibilities was derived from the government and tradition of the village. The government empowered the officials to carry out their assigned duties and gave them the right to arrest and report to the magistrate any criminal offenders. But it is important to note at the same time, as Kodama points out,[9] that the officials' ability to carry out their duties effectively was supported by the fact that they represented families which were respected by villagers because they were old, often being among the founding families of the village.

In compensation for their services, the officials received salaries. The headman's salary was roughly one percent or less of the village rice yield, other officials receiving, if anything at all, somewhat less than the headman. The officials' salaries were usually paid in rice, though sometimes a money payment was substituted. The headman's compensation might also have included free use of a piece of tax-exempt land provided by the government, and tax exemption on a certain portion of his own land plus free use of a specified amount of village labor. A point to be noted in this connection is that in whatever form officials were compensated, their salaries came from their own villages. That is, the village was obliged to provide the salaries of officials who were by and large representatives of the government and who did not perform functions important for the maintenance of the internal system of the village. This was one of the ways in which the village acknowledged the power of the state.

In addition, the headman and often other officials, too, were allowed certain privileges denied ordinary peasants, such as the use of surname and bearing of swords, both of which were generally prerogatives reserved for the military class. These officials were also allowed to live in larger and more sumptuously furnished houses and to wear better clothes than ordinary peasants. These privileges served as visible symbols of their status as government officials and of the authority of the government behind them.

As pointed out above, village officials were chosen from among the old and prestigious families of the village whose history often went back to the founding of the village. In some villages, their positions were hereditary; in others they were either selected through an informal agreement among the high ranking villagers or elected by propertied (and therefore tax-paying) villagers (*hombyakushō*). What-

---

[7] Asakawa Ken'ichi, "Notes on Village Government in Japan after 1600, II" *Journal of American Oriental Society,* XXXI (1911), 168.

[8] Elders and delegates, generally received lighter punishment than the headman, if they were punished at all for the same crime as the headman.

[9] Kodama Kōta, *Kinsei nōmin seikatsushi [A History of Peasant Life in the Tokugawa Period]* (Tokyo, 1951), pp. 161–184.

ever the method of selection, officials were always of peasant origin, and almost invariably members of the village.

When a new headman was chosen, by whatever method, the choice had to be approved by the district magistrate—an official of the military class (known as *gundai, daikan,* etc.), who oversaw a large number of villages in an area. This approval was automatic in most cases. The choice of other officials did not require the magistrate's approval in most domains, though the choice had to be reported to him. It is significant that the officials were not outsiders ordinarily, and not warriors. A warrior, because of his superior class identification and because of the prerogatives and power that went with his class vis-à-vis the peasants, would have had a great deal more coercive power to rule than a peasant headman; but he would not have had the confidence of the people that a peasant headman had.

Although the headman was chosen by villagers, power was not delegated to him by villagers. For in the political philosophy of the time, power was reserved by the state and was delegated by the state to administrators.

In addition to the officers of the headman and his assistants, the government instituted the *goningumi,* or five-man group, system for additional security.[10] Though called five-*man* group (*goningumi*), the basic units of the group were always families rather than individuals. The size of the group, although supposedly five families, varied a great deal, from one or two to more than ten.[11] In most villages only the propertied peasants were the full-fledged members of the group, tenants and their families being usually included in the family of their landlord. All peasants were thus required to belong to one five-man group or another (with the exception of village officials, who were sometimes excluded from membership). The group had its head, generally called *kumigashira.* Whether his job was simply to act as the liaison man between the headman of the village and the group, or whether he was in fact held responsible for the conduct of members of his group, we do not know.[12]

The political significance of this institution for control of the peasantry is that it was the unit of group responsibility. A crime committed by a member was a crime of all the others, and concealment of a crime committed by a fellow member was also a crime of all the others. On the other hand, an informer who would report a

---

[10] For documents of the five-man group and discussion of this institution, see Hozumi Nobushige, *Goningumi Hōkishū* [Collection of Five-man Group Codes] (Tokyo, 1921); Hozumi N., *Goningumi Seidoron* [Five-man Group System] (Tokyo, 1921); Hozumi Shigetō, *Goningumi Hōkishū Zokuhen* [Collection of Five-man Group Codes, a Supplement] (Tokyo, 1944); Nomura Kanetarō, *Goningumichō no Kenkyū* [Study of Five-man Group Records] (Tokyo, 1943). For brief discussions in English, see Asakawa, 1911, pp. 196–198; D. B. Simmons and John Wigmore, "Notes on Land Tenure and Local Institutions in Old Japan," *Transactions of Asiatic Society of Japan,* XIX (1891), 95–100; and George B. Sansom, *A History of Japan, 1615–1867* (Stanford, 1963), pp. 101–103.

[11] Such variation was inevitable, in part because of the constant fluctuation in the number of families in any village due to such factors as establishment of branch families, disolution of families through bankruptcy, and migration in and out of the village.

[12] Because both the elders and the heads of five-man groups were sometimes called *kumigashira* in the same village, some writers have regarded these two positions as identical. In some places they were the same, at least in origin; see Hirazawa Kiyoto, "Kumigashira to kinseiteki mura yakunin seido no kakuritsu" ["Kumigashira and the Establishment of Village Offices in the Tokugawa Period"], *Shinano,* V (1958), 696–701. But in some villages there were fewer elders than five-man groups. Also, it is not clear whether some of the heads of the five-man groups also served as elders, or whether the elders were an entirely different group of individuals. For these reasons, when we read in legal documents about *kumigashira,* we are not certain whether they refer to elders or to heads of five-man groups.

violation of law by a fellow member of his five-man group was given a lighter punishment than the others, or sometimes even rewarded.

The membership of the five-man group of a given village was written in a book, generally called *goningumicho,* one copy of which was sent to the district magistrate and another kept in the village. This membership book in most cases contained a preface (*maegaki*), which, varying a great deal in length and contents, listed official edicts and regulations handed down to the village from the Shogunate or daimiate government. The preface usually ended with an oath by all villagers to abide by the preceding regulations.[13] The preface also contained many clauses in which the headman, his assistants, and the five-man groups were explicitly mentioned —perhaps as additional reminders—as being responsible for specific misdemeanors. The government thus attempted to hold responsible not only individuals, but also groups to which they belonged, as well as village officials. Through such double and triple checks, the government attempted to control the peasantry.

By various methods the peasants were reminded of the regulations listed in the five-man group register,[14] such as reading the preface periodically to assembled villagers or using the register as text for penmanship in village schools (*terakoya*). Some historians, such as Hozumi[15] and Hosokawa,[16] tend to interpret the records of the five-man group literally and would have us believe that the group functioned pretty much as was intended. It is, however, a simple truism of methodology that legal prescriptions do not necessarily reflect the reality. Nomura in fact takes an extreme position in this regard, declaring that "organization of the five-man group was almost a mere matter of record keeping, and in practice it scarcely had any meaning."[17]

Though Nomura's scepticism seems too extreme, there are reasons to doubt that the five-man group functioned as effectively as intended. The remoteness of many villages as well as their inaccessibility from the magistrate's office alone must have made effective surveillance difficult, if not impossible. Also, the strong feeling of solidarity of villagers vis-à-vis the ruling elite must have been an effective deterrent in many cases to what amounted to blackmailing of fellow villagers, in case, for example, a fellow *goningumi* member committed a crime against the state. There seems to have been variation in the effectiveness of this institution from domain to domain, also.[18]

There is no doubt that the five-man group was sometimes useful in controlling the peasants. An examination of the above-mentioned *Oshioki Reiruishū,* for example, shows numerous cases in which members of five-man groups were punished for crimes committed by their fellow members.

These government-imposed institutions—the village officials and the five-man group—are predicated upon three concepts of responsibility. First is individual

---

[13] Although Sansom states that the document "was signed by the headman," it was more often "signed" by all members of all five-man groups of the village. Cf. Sansom, 1963, 102.

[14] For a discussion of various methods, see Hozumi N., *Goningumi Hōkishū,* pp. 90–129.

[15] Hozumi N., *Goningumi Seidoron.*

[16] Hosokawa Kiichi, *Rimpo Seidoshi* [History of Neighborhood Association Organization] (Tokyo, 1939).

[17] Nomura, p. 87.

[18] Kodama Kōta, p. 155.

responsibility for one's own action. Second is the concept that the leader of a group is responsible for the action of the members. It is on the basis of this concept that village officials were punished for crimes committed by their villagers. The third concept is that of group responsibility, upon which the five-man group was organized. The concept of group responsibility was utilized in other contexts, too. For example, those living next door and in the three houses across the street from the house where a crime was committed were held responsible for certain crimes, regardless of whether they belonged to the same five-man group. In another application of the same concept the whole village was held responsible, rather than its individual members or five-man groups.

The government capitalized on the indigenous solidarity of the village in instituting group responsibility. For example, levying a lump sum tax on the village, as was usually done, was a far more effective way of collection the full amount of tax than levying t*a*x to individual families, some of which in any village were too poor to meet the quota. In lump-sum taxation, wealthier peasants paid more than their share to help the poorer neighbors. Group responsibility, however had its negative effects, too. The same sense of solidarity—to help and protect one another—impeded the policing function of the group, because villagers were more likely to connive with one another against the government rather than blackmail a fellow villager.

It may be helpful to review briefly the regulations which the government imposed on peasants. To appreciate the types of regulations and their details, we should note several assumptions on which the Shogunate and daimiate governments based their philosophy of ruling the peasantry. First, the state manifestly existed for the benefit of the ruling class, and therefore other classes, including the peasants existed to support the ruling class. Hence the oppressive measures to keep the peasants at the bare subsistence level, taking away every bit of surplus they produced. Second, the peasants were considered by nature stupid, needing detailed regulations for conduct. Third, the society was conceived of in absolutely static terms in which the peasantry had a definite position defined by the ruling elite. Hence the numerous regulations aimed at maintaining and emphasizing the status relation of the peasants to other classes, especially to the ruling class. Fourth, as both Sansom and Asakawa observed,[19] to Tokugawa administrators law and morals were both bound up in the concept of government. Hence the moralistic admonitions intermingled with legal codes and the moralistic tone of legal codes.[20]

It is understandable, given these bases of government, that the Shogunate and daimiate law pertaining to peasants minutely spelled out prescriptions and prohibi-

---

[19] Sansom, George B., *Japan, a Short Cultural History* (New York 1943), p. 461; Asakawa, p. 188.

[20] Space limitations preclude any extended discussion of the legal codes of the Tokugawa period pertaining to the peasantry. Those interested in them will find the following standard documentary sources useful. *Tokugawa Kinreikō Kōshū* [*Prohibitions of the Tokugawa Shogunate, a Supplement*], ed., Kikuchi Shunsuke, (Tokyo, 1931–32); *Kinsei Hampō Shiryō Shūsei* [*Collection of Han Legal Materiel from the Tokugawa Period*], ed., Maki Kenji, (Tokyo, 1944), III, 131–205; *Kinsei Hōsei Shiryō Sōsho* [*Collection of Legal Historical Material from the Tokugawa Period*] ed. Ishii Ryōsuke, (Tokyo, 1938), II, 301–357 and III, 257–276; *Hampōshū II: Tottori-han* [*Collection of Han Laws II: Tottori-han*], ed., Ishii Ryōsuke, (Tokyo, 1961). For examples of such edicts translated into English, see Simmons and Wigmore, "Notes on Land Tenure and. . . . ," 177–210; Asakawa, 1911, 202–216.

Regulations listed in five-man group records are also an excellent source. See footnote 10 for references.

tions, and that it emphasized fiscal matters, status relations, policing, and morality.

Although Asakawa's claim[21] that almost all administrative features were designed to facilitate the collection of taxes is probably an overstatement, we can understand many government regulations in terms of fiscal concern. It explains not only the quantity and detail of the regulations concerning tax assessment and payment, but also the extensive body of law aimed at maximizing agricultural yields[22] and minimizing peasants' expenses beyond basic needs.[23] This is not to say that all prescriptions concerning agriculture were designed expressly to facilitate payment of the tax, but that a great many of them served this function.

Maintenance of status quo was another major concern of the government. Regulations prescribing peasants' behavior toward the warrior, particularly the district magistrate, with whom peasants came into periodic contact for official reasons like cadastral survey and payment of tax, served to define the superior position of the ruling class.[24] Sumptuary regulations mentioned above, which denied peasants the external symbols of well-being, served as much to keep peasants in an underprivileged position appropriate to their social status as to extract surplus wealth from them.

The government attempted to keep as tight a control over the peasants as possible, a third area of the ruler's concern. The five-man group was of course instituted for this very purpose. This policy is also manifested in the control of vagabond warriors (*rōnin*), in the determined attempt to exterminate Christians,[25] in the minute records the headman was required to keep concerning the movement of his villagers, and in the detailed definitions of crimes.

Lastly, government considered itself responsible for moral exhortation. This sense of moral responsibility of the government is evidenced not only in specifically moral precepts—of a Confucian sort in most cases—but also as it pervaded the whole body of law.

The Tokugawa village, however, was not simply an artificial creation for purposes of political control from above. From the point of view of the government, it might indeed have been "an aggregate of peasant holdings and their fiscal values" or a "fictitious entity," as Asakawa and Nakamura, respectively, asserted.[26] But from the point of view of village members, the village was a functioning unit which existed

---

[21] Asakawa Ken'ichi, "Notes on Village Government in Japan after 1600, I," *Journal of American Oriental Society*, XXX (1910), 269.

[22] For example, fields were never to be left fallow and rice fields never to be turned into dry fields or house lots; emigration of peasants was discouraged or prohibited for fear of decrease of crop yields; and severe restrictions were placed on growing luxury crops like tobacco, if it was not outlawed.

[23] For example, ordinary peasants were not allowed to wear silk clothes or *kamishimo*, a formal dress for ceremonial occasions; peasants were to subsist as much as possible on grains other than rice, the premium crop of the state; and as for shelters, the size of house, number of rooms, kinds of furnishings, and materials to be used for construction were all minutely regulated.

[24] The most obvious and visible regulation of this category was the universal law prohibiting peasants (except the village officials) from bearing swords and using surnames. In many domains, the warrior enjoyed the right to execute any peasant who did not behave properly toward him.

[25] Each village was required to prepare a temple registry, called *shūmonchō, shūmon aratamechō*, etc., in which the names of the villagers were listed under the name of the temple of which they were parish members. This list, presumably brought up to date each year, was accompanied by an oath to the effect that none of the villagers espoused Christianity.

[26] Asakawa, 1911, p. 161; Nakamura Kichiji, *Nihon no Sonraku Kyōdōtai* [*Village Community in Japan*] (Tokyo, 1957), pp. 108–112.

with its own raison d'être. That the Tokugawa village was a corporation has been well demonstrated in Nakata's classic essay.[27] The village was a corporate body, a legal entity which owned, bought, and sold property; loaned and borrowed money; and sued, was sued by, and entered into agreements with other villages. The fact that the village had such corporate qualities is important. It indicates the degree of commitment by village members toward the village as a unit and the degree of solidarity they expressed. It is this solidarity which enabled villagers to enforce their self-made laws and invoke sanctions against any members who transgressed them.

The solidarity of this corporate body is best expressed in village codes. These codes contain rules and regulations evolved in the village through centuries of collective living; their purpose was to maintain peace in the village by forbidding disruptive acts and requiring collective defense. The important point is that these codes are a pact agreed upon by all villagers and not something forced upon them from above. Village codes, written in the village codes book, are followed by a statement of oath by all members of the village assembly to abide by the codes.[28]

Whereas the book of the five-man group generally included scores of clauses, sometimes more than one hundred, a book of village codes usually included approximately ten clauses and rarely more than twenty. The great length of the former resulted from the fact that government administrators simply piled edict upon edict, and most of them became incorporated into the book of the five-man group regardless of whether they applied to the village. The village codes, on the other hand, tended to contain only essential items of law.

The village codes are not to be equated with a constitution in the Western sense. They do not contain all the norms of the village in codified form, nor do they fully define the administrative machinery of the village. Inspection of individual books of codes thus gives only a fragmentary picture of the customary law of the village. When we examine codes of many villages, however, we see recurrent themes. In the following, on the basis of Maeda's excellent studies of village codes,[29] we analyze the major characteristics of the codes, comparing them with those of government regulations. Such comparison will reveal functional division of the government and village law as well as overlap, the former complementing each other and the latter reinforcing one another.

Village codes covered such topics as taxation, agriculture, policing, adjudication, civil records (e.g., property transaction), sumptuary regulation, and inter-village agreement. This listing might give the impression that these codes simply reiterate regulations promulgated by the state. To a certain extent they do. For example, there are clauses dealing with handling of the tax levied by the government. Sumptuary regulations, too, seem to be almost direct copies of government edicts. These regulations were included in the village codes because they were relevant to

---

[27] Nakata Kaoru, "Tokugawa jidai ni okeru mura no jinkaku," [The Personality of the Village in Tokugawa Period], *Hōseishi Ronsō*, II (1938), 963–990.

[28] For specimens of village codes, see Maeda Masaharu, *Nihon Kinsei Sompō no Kenkyū* [*A Study of Village Codes of Tokugawa Japan*] (Tokyo, 1950).

[29] Maeda, *Nihon Kinsei Sompō no Kenkyū;* Meada Masaharu, "Hō to sonraku kyōdōtai—Edo jidai ni okeru sompō o chushin to shite," ["Law and Village community—Primarily a Discussion of Village Codes of the Tokugawa Period"], *in Hōken Shakai to Kyōdōtai* [*Feudal Society and Community*], eds. Shimizu Morimitsu and Kaida Yūji (Tokyo, 1961), pp. 169–214.

village life in one way or another. (We shall see later omission from village codes of certain government regulations which are irrelevant to village life.) This is obvious for the government tax. Sumptuary laws, too, made sense to peasants, simply as a means of making ends meet in their tight subsistence economy, although not as a means of maintaining and expressing status symbols as the government intended.[30]

In the areas of policing and security, again village codes overlap with government regulations. But in this case, the former are probably not simply copies of the imposed government regulations; instead they must have evolved independently in the village for its own sake. The reason for this duplication of government and village law regarding local security lies in the relative ineffectiveness of the government law in this regard for two reasons. One, already mentioned above, was the difficulty of reaching the magistrate because primitive transportation and communication made some villages inaccessible. Secondly, there was an implicit assumption in the political philosophy of the time that authorities were not to be disturbed for minor matters or with offenses which could not be definitely demonstrated to the authority's satisfaction.[31] These factors made it necessary for the village to take the law into its own hands, so to speak, even though formally such executions might have been illegal in that they were a prerogative of the state. In short, the village usurped the power of the state in handling matters which vitally affected its internal security or otherwise affected the village as a whole, such as public works and communal lands.

In addition to having regulations overlap with those of the government, village codes show different emphases. While the government law aimed to promote the welfare of the ruling elite, the village codes were designed primarily for the welfare of the village. For example, whereas government laws aimed primarily at increasing production, through encouraging reclamation, maximum use of land, etc., village codes aimed to reduce internal conflicts and disputes by regulating those areas of village life (such as management of communal land, irrigation system, and property boundaries) in which disputes and conflicts were likely to occur. The corporate village is also of prime significance in codes concerned with external affairs. In dealing with higher authorities for such matters as filing of grievances against the district magistrate or in settling disputes with neighboring villagers, villagers were required to present a solid front; anyone who acted contrary to the interest of the village received the severest penalty. The corporateness of the village community is also clearly seen in the sanction system of *mura hachibu* to be discussed below.

Compared with the corporate welfare of the village, individual problems seem to have been relatively unimportant. Matters concerning families or individuals, such as marriage or inheritance, were not generally codified.

Although the government tended indiscriminately to regulate all spheres of life and sometimes even promulgated regulations which were completely irrelevant to a given village, the village codes, having evolved to meet local exigencies, did not include "waste" clauses. A case in point is the government law forbidding Christian worship.

---

[30] It is interesting to note here that there are few sanctions perscribed in village codes against violations of sumptuary laws, indicating that economy and saving were virtues for peasants, but their opposite were not crime in their eyes.

[31] In case a matter was brought to the attention of the magistrate and could not be proved to his satisfaction, the plaintiff was often punished for no other reason than having disturbed the authority without just cause.

After the battle of Shimabara (1637-1638), there were no Christians in most parts of Japan. Yet the five-man group register rarely failed to include a clause about the prohibition of this alien religion. The temple registry, used as a means for controlling Christians, became an anachronism too, although the registry did serve as a convenient census record.

Also almost totally lacking in the village codes are regulations pertaining to relations with members of other classes, particularly warriors, and those having to do with morality. The government was concerned with maintaining a static, stratified society; for this end, the status segregation between classes had to be specified and enforced. Such concern was not shown in the village's indigenous system of law. Also, moralizing was the business of the stateman-philosopher of Confucian persuasion, which Tokugawa administrators invariably were. Peasants, with little or no education, were not concerned with moralizing.

Thus two bodies of law regulated the life of the peasant. But they did so in somewhat different spheres of life because their ultimate objectives were different. The state's objectives were maximum exploitation of the peasants and maintenance of a static and stratified society through both moral and legal legislation. The village wanted primarily to maintain internal peace and protect the village as a corporate entity. The village, of course, was subject to state regulations insofar as peasants were useful in helping the state achieve its goal. This meant that compliance to state law was most important in fiscal matters and status relations and of secondary importance in policing and morality. But the village codes emphasized policing as well as some other aspects of village life which the state did not stress. The next question is how the village executed its own law.

The major political institution for the enactment and enforcement of village codes was the village assembly. In addition, the elite families of the village and the age-grade organization performed important political roles in the village.

The village assembly was the governing body of the village. Although we are not always told who had the right and duty to attend the assembly, it seems that each family—at least the propertied families (*hombyakushō*)—was represented in it. The assembly met from time to time, though not at any regular intervals, for such purposes as drawing up new village codes, selecting village officials (if it had this function), indicting misbehaving officials, deliberating on violations of village codes, and discussing disputes with neighboring villages.

Punishments the assembly decreed varied according to the nature of the crime, but they also varied from village to village for the same crime. Those commonly mentioned in the village codes which Maeda examined are village ostracism, banishment, fine and the demanding of verbal or written apology to the assembly. The best known to present day scholars of rural Japan is village ostracism, or *mura hachibu,* which is still in use.[32] In *mura hachibu* villagers agree not to associate with the culprit's family except possibly in case of fire or death. In these cases villagers would help only in putting out the fire or in conducting funeral services. But in some villages even these occasions are not excepted. *Mura hachibu* was the punishment

---

[32] For a recent discussion of the modern practices, see Robert J. Smith, "The Japanese Rural Community: Norms, Sanctions, and Ostracism," *American Anthropologist,* LXIII (1961), 522-533.

for such crimes as disclosing secret agreements made among villagers; supporting someone who had been purged from office; being incorrigibly intractable; or dissenting from a decision made by the village as a whole.

Banishment from the village probably was more severe punishment than *mura hachibu*. Village codes prescribed banishment for such crimes as stealing lumber from the communal land, stealing crops from the field, harboring gamblers, and committing arson. Punishment by property deprivation—monetary fine, property fine, or loss of the right of access to the communal land—was meted out for theft on communal or private land, theft of farm crops, refusal to provide labor for village corvée, violation of irrigation regulations, gambling, etc. Fines of money or rice were by far the most common form of punishment in Maeda's compilation. When the crime was not grave, the culprit was dismissed after having made a verbal or written apology. According to Takeuchi,[33] confinement was used in some villages. For example, a man from whose house fire spread was required to confine himself in a temple for a certain period of time as an expression of apology for inconveniencing other villagers. Takeuchi lists several other modes of sanction, including corporal punishment, verbal abuse, and making the culprit perform menial tasks such as digging graves. Although Takeuchi's cases are by and large taken from the post-Tokugawa era, it is probably safe to assume that most of these modes of sanction were in practice during the Tokugawa period as well.

In addition to the corporate force of the village bearing on individual wrongdoers, one sees the influence of the government-instituted concept of joint responsibility being utilized by the village. The fellow members of a law-breaker's five-man group were usually, though not always, punished along with him for crimes such as gambling and theft. In another form of joint responsibility, the next-door neighbors on both sides and the three families directly across the street were held punishable in some villages for a crime such as gambling, regardless of whether these families belonged to the five-man group of the culprit.[34]

Although village codes are an agreement of the entire village, a close examination reveals that the actual control, at least some of the time, lay with the elite of the village rather than among all members equally. Miyakawa's analysis of documents from a village in Echizen shows that various rules in the village codes are designed to protect the interests of the elite and to control the lower class peasants.[35] Another illustration of the power elite is given by Andō.[36] At Yuasa in Kinki, there was a group of elite families known as *Toshiyori Sujime Sanjūrokunin* (the thirty-six elders). In this village if there were any disputes between a member of this group and a less privileged member of the village, the latter was judged wrong.

---

[33] Takeuchi Toshimi, "Mura no seisai" ["Village sanctions"] *Shakai Keizai Shigaku*, VIII (1938), no. 6, 603–633, no. 7, 743–772.

[34] The concept of common responsibility, as used by the village assembly, was by and large limited to the cases in which punishment was a fine of money or rice. When *mura hachibu* or banishment was the punishment, the sanction applied only to the culprit and his family.

[35] Miyakawa Mitsuru, "Sonraku kyōdōtai no kinseiteki tenkai" ["Transformation of the Village Community in the Tokugawa period"], in *Hōken Shakai to Kyōdōtai*, ed. Shimizu M. and Kaida Y., pp. 93–168.

[36] Andō Seiichi, *Kinsei Miyaza no Shiteki Kenkyū* [*Historical Study of the Shrine Association in Tokugawa Japan*] (Tokyo, 1960), p. 115.

H. Befu

Elite families generally boasted long historical tradition going back sometimes to the founding of the village. They generally cultivated their own land and also often rented land to tenants in the village. Thus the elite position was defined in terms of historical depth of the family and its economic standing. These families composed the power elite of the village vis-à-vis less privileged families.

It is noteworthy that for the enforcement of village codes, the village headman and other officials did not seem to be empowered to take action, and apparently were not relied upon in internal matters. Rather, the sanction system seems to have operated through coercive power of the village assembly as a corporate body and through other indigenous systems of control.

Elite control of the village is best illustrated in the religious organization known as *miyaza,* or "shrine association."[37] Its membership was limited to old, established families of the village. While *miyaza* was expressly a religious association connected with the village shrine, its members enjoyed many privileges and exercised much power beyond religious functions. For example, it was this organization that chose the village officials; and officials had to be chosen from among its members. In economic spheres, too, members of the *miyaza* had privileges, for example, in possessing exclusive access to the village-owned land.

Miyaza then was a concrete and graphic expression of the power of the elite and served as a reminder for other villagers of the locus of power. I emphasize the fact that *miyaza* as an association functioned as a convenient seat of village power and that in villages where this association was absent, the same pattern of power structure existed.

It is important to note that the headman and other officials were members of the village rather than administrators sent into the village from outside, such as the warrior was, and that they were elite members of the community. The government, in other words, relied on locally influential individuals to enforce its law. From the point of view of the village, selecting as its head and its representative of the government a man who wielded influence in the village, entirely apart from whatever power he acquired as an agent of the government, meant a positive acceptance by the village of the unchallengeable authority of the government. Moreover, the fact that the village officials were normally chosen by the village elite—propertied peasants of the village—meant that the acceptance of the authority of the state could be forced upon the rest of the village through the indigenous political structure.

One last institution to be mentioned in connection with the internal system of control of the village is the age-grade system.[38] Commonly one entered the group sometime in the teens and remained a member until he married or reached some set age in the late twenties or early thirties; membership was compulsory for all those of appropriate ages. Separate groups were organized for the two sexes, the female group being under the strict control of the male group.

---

[37] Andō S., *Edo Jidai no Nōmin* [*Peasants of the Tokugawa Period*] (Tokyo, 1959), pp. 117–156; Andō, S., *Kinsei Miyaza no Shiteki Kenkyū;* Higo Kazuo, *Miyaza no kenkyū* [*A Study of Shrine Associations*] (Tokyo, 1941); Thomas C. Smith, *The Agrarian Origins,* pp. 187–200.

[38] *Wakamono Seido no Kenkyū* [*A Study of the Youth Association*], ed. Dai Nihon Rengō Seinendan, (Tokyo, 1936); *Dainihon Seinendanshi* [*History of the Japanese Youth Association*] ed. Kumagaya Tatsurjirō, (Tokyo, 1943), pp. 13–41; Nakayama Tarō, *Nihon Wakamonon Shi* [*History of the Japanese Youth*], (Tokyo, 1956).

Village Autonomy and Articulation with the State

The group had an internal hierarchy in which older members enjoyed higher status and much authority over younger members, demanding strict obedience from the younger ones. Just as the village elite, rather than the headman, held power in village politics, actual authority in the age group lay in a group of elder and more respected members, the leader of the youth group simply being one among them. This council of elders arbitrated disputes among members, made all important decisions regarding activities of the group, and judged violations of group norms.

The youth group was a powerful control group. There were written and unwritten rules and regulations which everyone was to abide by. These codes concerned gambling, drinking, relations with the opposite sex, etiquette toward the elders, one's work habits, mutual help, and relations with outsiders, particularly women of other villages. The male group possessed exclusive sexual access to the unmarried women of the village. Neither the women themselves nor their parents had the right to deny this right to the group, and no men outside the village were to have access to these women. Conversely, no member of the youth group was allowed to flirt with or marry a woman of another village. Violators of these rules met with some of the severest sanctions. Any commission of severe crimes was publicly punished by the group as a whole, and in extreme cases the culprit was expelled from the group and members were forbidden to associate with him in any way whatsoever. It may be noted that this sanction parallels the *mura hachibu,* discussed above for here one sees the village youth practicing roles they were to play in adulthood. Incorrigible members of the age group were sometimes turned over to the village elders. For less severe cases, lighter punishments were meted out, such as temporary expulsion of the culprit from the group (the duration depending on the seriousness of the offense), temporarily seating him in the junior position, formal inquisition, monetary fine, corporal punishment, and written apologies.

Although the youth group was primarily concerned with internal discipline, they sanctioned outsiders, too—that is, villagers who were not members of the group. On certain nights of the year or month, the youth groups in some regions would gather in front of an offender's home or some other designated place in the village and enumerate all the wrong doings the family was responsible for, and shout abuse at the top of their voices.

It may be instructive to consider the basic reasons why the military government could not rely on the indigenous political system of the village and instead had to create its own legal and administrative structure which it imposed upon the village. The reasons lie in the differences in the goals of the two polities. Village goals were to maintain internal peace and to defend itself against external threat. The goals of the military government, on the other hand, consisted of economic exploitation of the peasants and maintenance of a static society in which the peasantry was given a well defined place. To the village, the welfare of the larger society, of which it was a part, was irrelevant; to the village, too, the exploitative state, represented external threat as much as, or even more than, say a neighboring village trying to steal water.[39]

---

[39] A threatening neighboring village could be dealt with either through appealing to higher authorities for arbitration or through armed conflict, illegal though the latter method might be. These means promised at least some chance of favorable resolution of the conflict. But the state offered no such chance; its law, its demands were absolute as well as unilateral.

It is no wonder, seen in this light, that the indigenous village polity, whose goals did not coincide with those of the state, and whose instruments (political structure and codes) were either indifferent or hostile to the goals of the state, was not particularly useful for the implementation of state goals. For this reason the state had to create separate legal and administrative machinery within the village to achieve its goals.

But the government could not hope to rule the peasantry with coercion alone. It becomes all the more necessary for the state to articulate its political structure with the village structure. The government was successful in controlling the peasants because state-instituted machinery was in fact articulated with village institutions.

We have examined various modes of such articulation throughout this paper. Such articulation is evident in the recruitment of the village officials, in that they had prestige in the village before they assumed government-appointed offices and that they administered at least in part through this "traditional authority." Another mode of articulation is seen in the fact that the village officials were able to perform their duties as government administrators in part because they were chosen by the elite of the village and thereby given the stamp of village approval and promise of support.

On the other hand, this act of choice and approval meant that the village polity acknowledged the legitimacy of the military government's authority. This acknowledgment is symbolized in the village's payment of the tax and also of the salaries of these government officials.

Another mode of articulation is seen in the government's holding the whole village and the five-man group responsible. The concept of group responsibility made a good deal of sense to villagers of Tokugawa Japan. Since the village felt strong solidarity to begin with, and since such practices as mutual cooperation and labor exchange had been indigenous patterns of social organization, the government, by levying tax on the village as a whole and holding the five-man group responsible for any member's crime, was capitalizing on an accepted concept.

There was one area in which the state and the village saw eye to eye, so to speak; this was in the matter of maintenance of internal peace. Because both polities were concerned with peace and security of the village—for different reasons, of course— it appears on the surface that the village cooperated with the state in maintaining peace and punishing any criminal who disturbed the peace of the village. But because the village enforced the law, it usurped the state's prerogative to punish criminals.

The village polity, therefore was obliged to make a major concession in allowing the state to intrude. This meant that in matters of taxation, status relations and policing—areas most sensitive to the state—the village was forced to obey the law of the state. In turn, the state permitted the village to deal with internal matters as it pleased. The latter did adopt some of the institutions of the state, for example, in the concept of joint responsibility and made some use of the village officials for sanctioning purposes. But the indigenous political system by and large remained unaffected.

PART FOUR
LATE TOKUGAWA

CHAPTER SEVENTEEN

TOKUGAWA AND MODERN JAPAN

MARIUS B. JANSEN

Reprinted from *Japan*
Quarterly, Vol. XII (1965), No. 1.

THE INCREASED awareness in recent years of the complexities of the process of modernization has had as one result a new interest in Japan's nineteenth-century transformation. Japan was after all the first, and remains the most successful, Asian country to respond dynamically to the impact of the West, to make successful use of imported technology, and to combine this with its own institutional and intellectual traditions.

Just now we are probably in a better position to view this process dispassionately than ever before. The failures of institutions of constitutional government imported into other countries provide useful perspectives for consideration of the problems of parliamentary government in Japan. Military and authoritarian assaults on political party government, which are denounced as "corrupt" and "self-seeking," have now become a dreary pattern. As a result, Japan's prewar failures no longer look so unique and startling.

On the other hand, it is also possible that America's close and successful relationship with postwar Japan may tend to produce an overly optimistic view of Japan's modernization. It is worth remembering that for some time the political difficulties with militarist Japan made many Western writers concentrate on the militaristic and undesirable features of Japan's recent history. In those days, Japanese writers did their best to assure a skeptical West that their society was not really based upon oppression and aggression. And now our Japanese colleagues temper our enthusiasm for Japan's recent transformation with warnings against overestimation of the new democracy. Perhaps we are fated to disagree. Nevertheless, the changes in perspective at least help to balance the picture for all of us.

Yet no one, optimistic or gloomy, can deny that postwar Japan provides one of the most striking instances of economic and social change in the modern world. Today per capita income stands at U.S.$510. Farming population is 34 per cent of Japan's total; of farm families, one in four own power tillers, and other agricultural machinery is widespread. Modest appliances like automatic rice cookers have revolutionized domestic economy in the most remote areas; in the urban areas, 91 per cent of Japanese homes have television, in rural, 69 per cent. In TV sales, preferences have changed from 12" sets, which led a few years ago, to 14" (1962), 16" last year, and 19" this year. Durables like iceboxes, washing machines, and automobiles, enter the scale of expectation of more families each year. A recent article refers to pianos, room coolers, and automobiles as the "three sacred treasures" of today. Small wonder that one reads sentiments like Irene Tauber's comment, "Feelings of wonder merge into awe as one watches this transformation in an Asian country." (*Foreign Affairs,* July 1962.)

It was tempting for some to credit all of this to the success and foresight of the Occupation authorities. But however great the changes which the Occupation introduced, it is clear that they could have taken root only to the degree that they were appropriate to the setting into which they came. It required, at the very least, readiness—in terms of willingness, know-how, literacy, and organization—to make a go of them. The successes of recent years thus make it necessary to look again at the background, and to seek the real well-springs of Japan's most recent transformation.

For a decade and more most American study of Japan has focused on the changes and personalities involved in the Meiji Period. These were the years when Japan's authorities, who inherited most of the same handicaps of unequal treaties with the West that plagued China, sought "Wisdom throughout the world" in the words of the Imperial Declaration of 1868, and managed to create a modern nation state. They maintained political stability, built a mass education network, an industrial order, and achieved political strength and empire. By the end of the Meiji Period, Japan was one of the world's great powers, the envy of some of her neighbors, and master of others.

These achievements were questioned and downgraded by some. Dr. Hu Shih, for instance, argued persuasively that changes so fast and so carefully directed had to be superficial. Others pointed to contingencies like the collapse of the Chinese and Russian empires, and suggested that the Japanese had in reality been lucky in having prostrate neighbors, on whose backs they had stepped to wealth and power. I doubt this, for it is at least as likely that Japan would have been better off if she had enjoyed stable trading partners as neighbors. The opportunities on the mainland provided profits, to be sure, but even more temptations and diversions—incitations to domestic disorder and confusion, and encouragement for malcontents to question their leaders' priorities and patriotism.

But if the MacArthur changes rested on the developments that came before, so did the Meiji Restoration. What was new in the nineteenth century was the Western impact. But this was experienced by other countries, including China. What responded was there long before the West came. And so, necessarily, Western scholarship is now giving more and more attention to the pre-Meiji picture to see what the preconditions for modernization were. This study was slow in coming for a number of reasons. After the color and excitement of modern Japan, the Tokugawa scene seemed dull and static—a Ming Dynasty, as it were. (And, it is interesting to note that Ming studies and appreciation have risen together with Tokugawa studies.) It must also be granted that the Meiji Japanese did nothing to disabuse us of the unflattering image which we held of the Tokugawa scene. They were so glad to be out of it that they had nothing good to say for it. Fukuzawa could, as Carmen Blacker tells us, remember chiefly the dead hand of the past "I hated the feudal system," he recalled, "as though it were my father's murderer." Poverty, boredom, and social ritual and discipline in personal experience were combined with the consciousness of weakness and humiliation at the hands of the West.

Nor was this without foundation in fact. One has to grant that on one level Tokugawa Japan had been a closed society in a very special sense of the word; a series of garrison states, or a system so warrior-dominated that the sociologist Andrejewski establishes it as a special type, for which he has coined the adjective "bookayan." Tokutomi Sohō pointed out that it was custom, and not Emperor, shogun, or samurai, who ruled. That is why the system seemed so moribund and dull to the Meiji men who looked back on it.

But a system that changed so rapidly had to have internal sources of dynamics and momentum, and however galling the early nineteenth-century conventions may have been for the Meiji leaders, they themselves were the products and beneficiaries of much of the change that had taken place in Japan between 1600 and 1868. And so more and more study is being devoted to the Tokugawa period—its institutions, personalities, its culture and values. And a good many of the papers produced for seminars of the Conference on Modern Japan, which has now met three times and whose first volume is now forthcoming, have centered on the Tokugawa period. It becomes more and more difficult to speak of abstracts like "traditional Japanese society" without going on to explain what part, what period, and what aspect of the premodern scene is meant.

On the other hand, it is equally necessary to define terms like "modern" and "modernization." The definitions popular in Japan today make important inclusion of political values and "democracy," itself by no means easily defined, and those who use them reject much of even postwar Japan as non-modern on these grounds. Studies in the West, on the other hand, have preferred to shy away from this because it leads too easily into an ideological quagmire, and to focus instead on those aspects of the modern world that unite and relate societies whose ideologies would otherwise divide them. To relate, that is, but not to equate, such systems in terms of values—for it obviously makes a great deal of difference what the goals and values of the elites are.

Ambassador Reischauer and other historians have pointed out that the elements which, in combination, characterize modern societies developed first in the Western world. No two countries have them to the same, or perhaps even to the desired, degree, and certainly no East Asian country was at any time without some of them. But if it is the combination that counts, then the presence in Japan of many of them, and of some of them in particularly striking degree, proves of importance for what followed the Western entry.

I propose to concentrate this discussion on two related aspects of the Tokugawa scene, each of which seems to me to have a significant bearing on Japan's rise as a modern state. The first is the clear consciousness of, and allegiance to, the national unit of political organization. A second is the existence of a literate population, capable of articulation and activation into political and economic processes of its society. For reasons of space I will say nothing of many other aspects that might be discussed, although some of what follows will overlap with points of modernity put forth by other writers. Without in any way suggesting that Tokugawa Japan was really very "modern," or without arguing that it was a far more jolly place than Fukuzawa remembered its being, I want only to discuss some ways in which it provided extraordinarily promising preconditions for the modernization movement of the nineteenth century.

NATION AND NATIONALISM

If we begin with the ways in which Tokugawa Japan contributed to the rise of modern nationalism, it is convenient to begin with the uses of Confucianism. Tokugawa Japan has often been called the most Chinese of Japan's historical eras. A complex bureaucratic structure was developed; Chinese was the main fare of scholars, the production of poetry, as of essays, in Chinese was very large, and the inspiration from China in fields of art and literature was important. One might have expected many of the aspects of Confucian thought that operated to slow or divert modernization in China to have shown themselves in Japan, and some of them certainly did. But on the whole the story was one of contrasts, and it reminds us how different the effect of a body of thought can be in different settings.

Confucianism in China produced the view of a Chinese cultural oecumene, which was probably the reverse of modern nationalism. This view was held also in Japan, but with the clear consciousness that Japan was somehow on its fringe. Their feelings might range from adoration to resentment, from emulation to rejection, but the Tokugawa scholars seldom forgot that they did not live in China. "Although ours is a small island" many began their essays, an unspoken reminder of the Chinese colossus on the mainland. Consider the consequence of some of the problems that arose. Yamazaki Ansai asked his students what their duty would be if an army led by Confucius and Mencius were to attack Japan. (The answer was to fight, and to capture them alive in the service of the country. In due course his successors rephrased the problem to show that Japanese armies were going to China to rescue Confucius and Mencius from democracy and communism.) A century later, Ogyū Sorai (although he spoke of himself as an "Eastern barbarian") developed an operational definition of "sage" as dynasty founder and suggested that the "Way" might best be realized in Japan. Nichiren had done the same for Buddhism earlier, and Uchimura Kanzō would approach it for Christianity later. One senses in this strain to indigenize the import an effort to particularize the universal, to identify it and to claim it for Japan. Of course there were also men willing to abase themselves before China as the sacred country, and they were greeted with the eighteenth-century equivalent of the American "If you like it so well, why don't you move there?" It was really the same speech: Arthur

Wright cites Ise Sadatake, an eighteenth-century Japanist, who condemned "wicked Confucians" who "while eating Japanese rice, wearing Japanese clothes, and living on Japanese soil," praised China and scorned Japan. They were, he thought, "of no use to this country. Let them cease eating Japanese rice and starve to death, the sooner the better." Insularity made for national consciousness. Allied with the resurgence of Shinto, it also made for a very strident self-assertion.

Tokugawa Confucianism, whatever its school, was not nearly as "Chinese" as it tried to be. As many writers point out, in a setting in which political, and not family, loyalties were paramount, its thrust was quite different. Chu Hsi's emphasis on loyalty, the practicality of the old text school, and the reformist tendencies of Wang Yang-ming, were all equally remarkable for the way they pointed to political service in Japan rather than speculative or ethical reflection. There is a striking contrast here with much of the Confucian thought of Ch'ing China, which tended increasingly toward interiorization and ethical introspection. In good measure this must have been because application of Confucian learning in China was constrained by the examination system with its official orthodoxy, all in the service of a particular political system. Confucianism in Manchu China was embodied in a concrete political structure and emperor, whose moral and philosophical injunctions were the subject of regular indoctrination even in the villages. Tokugawa Confucianism on the other hand, however compatible with the feudal regimes that encouraged its study, led ultimately to a system not in being, to an emperor not in power, and to goods not yet actualized. Clearly the total impact would be entirely different.

The slogans of nineteenth-century nation building were drawn from the Chinese tradition. "Rich country, strong army"; *fukoku-kyōhei;* these operated as national goals in quite the same way that "peace" and "democracy" did in the years after World War II (until they were temporarily replaced by the Olympics). But Benjamin Schwartz's thoughtful study of Yen Fu (*In Search of Wealth and Power,* 1964) reminds us that these ideas, while Chinese, were not in the heart of the Confucian tradition. They derive from the Han dynasty history's explanation of the way the Ch'in legalists had united the empire by policies of wealth and strength. Until the collapse of dynastic order that followed foreign imperialism in nineteenth-century China, there was some doubt about the propriety of such ideas there. But the Japanese in Tokugawa times were less concerned with distinguishing between parts and nuances of the Chinese intellectual tradition. *Fukoku-kyōhei,* was already a slogan in Tokugawa times well before Perry's appearance, as a policy line for the several fiefs. The principals of maximizing income and restricting consumption in the interests of the political unit had unquestioned currency, and they lay ready at hand for the nineteenth-century reformers. Everything—in politics, in economics, in education, in literature—was to be done "for the sake of the country," and it was with some alarm that leaders noted on the part of their contemporaries in the early twentieth century a readiness to ask what the country might do for them instead. To be sure, most commoners were outside all of this, and farmers showed no particular emotion when the Imperialists bombarded Shimonoseki and Kagoshima in the 1860's. But it is enough that one numerous class did; and that this class was later to instill its views into the masses.

Institutionally, as well as intellectually, Tokugawa Japan served as surprisingly good preparation for the modern world. Competition between the domains resulted in something of a multi-state system, with many invigorating consequences. Ambassador Reischauer and others draw on this to suggest that there may well be a significant relationship between feudalism and successful modernization. Whether or not one chooses to carry it this far, it is nevertheless clear that there was a kind of fief, or domain, nationalism—*han* nationalism, to use Albert Craig's term—in which leaders and activists were determined that their area should not be left behind in wealth or power or influence. One sees it particularly clearly in the maneuvering of the activists in the 1860's, in the desperate urgency with which they warned their superiors and contemporaries that leadership for a competing domain in the politics of exclusion or restoration would bring shame and disgrace to their own realm. These views were the product of generations of contact, and rivalry, between men of many ranks and areas. The rivalry was orderly, for regionalism was tempered—for the ruling class—by the uniformities of life in Edo and castle town.

In a variety of ways the experience of the multi-domain system prepared Japan for its future existence in a multi-state world. There were negotiations of complexity in terms of trade, finance, and above all, politics, which combined to provide a better learning process for the modern world than life in a unitary state could have. Feudal Japan could also afford experimentation. The Restoration activist Nakaoka Shintarō, when he stopped to ask himself whether feudalism was a good thing for Japan or not, concluded that the experimentation with small-scale antiforeignism in Satsuma and Chōshū had been invaluable; it had provided object lessons for the country as a whole, and it had also forced those realms to reorganize and modernize their defense structures after the European guns had knocked them down.

But what of the recollections of the Meiji statesmen of the stagnant politics, in which rank determined office, which they had found so frustrating? Even this, however depressing, provided opportunities, for the very arbitrariness of rank and inherited importance meant that other, lower, and more numerous ranks, came to do the work and learn the lessons.

The reasons for this were very simple. Despite the nominally absolute and autocratic role of the daimyo, the likelihood of an able individual's inheriting the realm seems to have been rather slight. In fact most able daimyo were adopted sons, and quite often the top post was all but vacant. The domain of Fukuoka, for instance, had virtually no daimyo for a century. With the shogun maintaining the peace, this made no difference in terms of national political stability. Nor was the next higher level, of *karō*, limited as it was to three to five families, much more likely to have the time (considering residence in Edo) or ability to do very much. Despite nominal authority at the top, then, each realm found itself with men of considerably lower rank, of whom there were far more, having the exercise (though not the recognition) of power. The pool of talent was constantly larger, and the opportunity for importance consequently greater. Adoption added further openings. Participation in politics was constantly on the increase. So was education for politics, and emphasis on ability and preparation. The 300-odd fiefs needed, used, and trained thousands more than a centralized state might have. This trend reached its peak in the mid-nineteenth century, when men too low on the table of organization for even this sort of eminence began to participate on their own, on a do-it-yourself basis.

This participation, however non-modern and irrational it seemed a generation later, had another very significant aspect. This was the abstract view of authority and authorities that developed. Separated from a daimyo increasingly less important, less in evidence, and less a personality, feudal loyalty shifted to the *concept* of daimyo and authority. What was needed in the nineteenth century was a way of bringing such regional and particular loyalties into central focus and relationships. The symbol of this new attachment, the even more remote and abstract Emperor, served perfectly. The Japanese samurai had had enough of their authorities, but not of authority. And this helped them to change allegiance from one sovereign, seldom seen, to another, without breaking ranks or losing discipline.

It is intriguing to try to estimate the importance of some of these Tokugawa precedents of organization and participation for the development of modern Japan. I think that no one will question the positive values of this sense of authority, related as it was to the unquestioned priority of group and collective goals over those of the individual or family, for the guided modernization of Meiji times. In many ways the continuities outnumbered the discontinuities. The domain governments were strongly paternalistic. Feudal statesmen worked for a kind of autarchy, or perhaps mercantilism, in which they would be less dependent upon "foreign" trade and purchases that might deplete their dwindling stock of money. They instituted monopolies in whatever was profitable for export. It is no accident that one of the great modern firms, that of Mitsubishi, had its origins in such an administrative arrangement; the administrator simply inherited the enterprise.

Merchants and administrators also came to think in terms of a national market and economy. The enforced residence at Edo, and the national market for agricultural products at Osaka where transactions in rice and debts determined many feudal houses' future, and whose merchants invested in land reclamation as far away as northern Japan, made this inevitable.

Government leadership also meant strongly paternalistic measures that foreshadowed the government's leadership in economic development later. In Tosa, to name one example of many, one finds forestry regulated to guarantee a sustained yield as early as the seventeenth century, one finds government orders to farmers (through headmen) instructing them on what they can plant, wear, and do, assigning tasks for the idle months, and warning against consumption of superfluities like tea and tobacco. Thus in 1643: "A farmer . . . who does not keep his rice in stock until spring . . . or who brews *sake* . . . is to be punished. Headmen will report breaches of this rule, and if it is kept secret, they will be punished. No one is to buy and drink *sake*. No one should be a late riser. Violators will be fined in silver for laziness. . . . A useless tree should never be planted. . . . Tea trees, paper mulberry trees, other trees that help in paying tax should be planted. . . ." And in 1662: "Each farmer's behavior should be examined monthly, and his deeds during the month reviewed on the fifth day of the following month. . . . Each village will do this in one unit, and the officials will give rewards where edicts are well observed. . . . During winter, notices reading 'As this is a leisure month for farmers, they should do such and such work and produce such and such an amount' should be posted. . . ." In general, the administrators acted as though they had read about the need for maximizing investment and minimizing consumption in periods of economic development. (That they consumed this themselves, instead of putting it into industrial plants, is for the moment beside the point.) The path to the pilot plants, agricultural testing stations, foreign consultants, and market supervision of the modern period was clearly indicated.

At the last, one has even the daimyo agreeing that his interest and that of the domain may not be identical. When the Tosa daimyo instituted a new and more intensive monopoly and marketing organization in the 1860's, his proclamation, read to his retainers, assured them that the measures proposed were not designed to benefit the Yamauchi house itself, but the entire province.

And then, a final note on the subordination of inferiors to superiors. Professor Maruyama has pointed out that in the sixteenth century, when violence made missteps perilous and fatal, the relation of samurai to lord was far from one of total and abject surrender. The good retainer reproved and argued with his superior. This found echo in some of the Confucian censorate role of retainers in Tokugawa times, but by and large the subordination, if more abstract, became also more absolute. The penalty for daimyo error was no longer so deadly. But in the Restoration decades of the nineteenth century, with danger and action once again in the air, samurai assertion came to the fore again, albeit without the personal relationship between lord and vassal that had conditioned these in the sixteenth century. Hence the striking insubordination of vassals, like those of Chōshū, who knew what was good for their lord's house and provinces, regardless of what he might think himself.

The Meiji period, in which the emperor and a group of consultants and servants worked together in times of danger and tension, reproduced, I suggest, the conditions of the sixteenth century on a larger scale. When one reads of talks between the Emperor and his *genrō,* there is an abundance of trust, responsibility, and a rather sturdy independence. The *genrō,* by the way, also rotated in office, much as the Tokugawa retainers had earlier. What the Emperor thought counted for something, although we will probably never know how much. Thereafter the Emperor became ever more abstract and sacred.

Tokugawa and Modern Japan

The Shōwa emperor of the 1930's was much more like the daimyo of late Tokugawa Japan; he was an idealization, an abstraction seldom seen and never allowed to express an opinion. He could be, and was, dismissed and ignored by young men who knew what was good for Japan, whether he himself did or not, just as their grandfathers and great-grandfathers had ignored their daimyo in the 1860's. He could even be treated with condescension. General Sugiyama, paragon of official rectitude and patriotism as Chief of Staff, is said to have referred to the Emperor as "Tenchan" ("Empie"?) to his subordinates. This remoteness surely had its role to play in the ease with which ideas of imperial sovereignty could be set aside by the MacArthur shogunate.

EDUCATION AND AMBITION

One of the impressive things about modern Japan is the deep commitment to education. Japan has long been known for its mass literacy, and it has one of the world's highest proportions of college-age young people in college. Ninety-nine point nine per cent of all children, the Education Ministry now reports, complete nine year's schooling. One might be inclined to put the enormous proliferation of educational opportunities in recent decades to the success of the economy, but actually Japan began the Meiji Restoration with a proportion of literacy (some estimate it above 35 per cent) which put it close to the most developed parts of the Western world. It is difficult to exaggerate the advantages which this high literacy rate gave the government in its efforts to spread information, make administration uniform, and cajole the nation into doing its will. Novels, prints, official newspapers, opinion journals, all were at hand to be developed and used. The early Meiji government could send out directives which provincial authorities were required to have *in print* within a set and short time.

All of this owed everything to Tokugawa institutions and pressures. The two-and-a-half centuries of peace and order made of an unlettered warrior class a class of bureaucrats. Ronald Dore points out that in Ieyasu's time a literate samurai was unusual, and that a century later Saikaku spoke of an illiterate samurai as badly behind the times. By 1850 he would have been behind a good number of his inferiors as well. Beginning with the shogunate, each fief had established a school for its retainers, and thousands of private schools as well as universally available parish schools had made literacy widely available. On all levels, education grew steadily. As affects the samurai, school building really hit its stride in the latter half of the eighteenth century (only 28 of the 227 domain schools ultimately established were in being in 1750); the early Meiji rush to the schools was a continuation and centralization of existing trends, and not something new.

Learning of some sort had become necessary for the increasing complexity of life for all groups in Tokugawa Japan. Villages had problems of tax computation and allocation, and they were visited by traveling book vendors and lenders. Townsmen, as the literature makes clear, were in constant need of literacy. And the samurai could get nowhere without it. It provided the key, or at least a chance, for success in the competitive pool of manpower from which officials were chosen. All the pressures of modern times were already there; many were born to rank, but few chosen; of those few many were selected arbitrarily, thus increasing the pressure on the others.

Ronald Dore points out another important feature: the authorities approved and promoted education, and had none of the fears of its diffusion which their counterparts in Europe showed. Part of this relates to the fact that there was surprisingly little class hostility, however great the class distinctions. Even more important is the fact that "learning" meant practical tools, and a pattern of morals and ethics (drawn from Confucian classics) which could only make the students better rulers or ruled. The wisdom of the sages was applicable to all branches of society, and no one had to fear its diffusion. In content, as in manner of transmission, it instilled discipline and humility. Every word that fell from the master's lips was true: teachers often exacted a pledge of conformity and obedience before accepting a student. This kind of training certainly did not encourage rash, individual experimentation by men who thought they understood, but really did not. Perhaps it is true, as Dore suggests, that many more boilers and machines would have been wrecked if the Tokugawa educators had stressed initiative and independence of thought.

Is it not to this kind of training, in which the manner and the incidental were taken as seriously as was the core, that we should credit some of the tremendous influence of the Western educators? How else account for the oracular position of men like Clark and Janes? The painstaking, careful notes taken on every occasion by students overseas? Here is what a guide for students abroad, written in the 1870's, had to say: "You must take down everything you see and send it back immediately. What you do not send home you must note carefully in order to report it later." Travel was for the good of the larger unit, and not for personal development.

The main business of Tokugawa higher education was political economy and morality, and this played its role in the fixation with politics and national survival. Dore provides Yamaji Aizan's expression of enthusiasm: "Politics is my mistress. I love politics. I adore politics. I live and breathe politics. My fate is bound up with the fate of the Japanese nation. The governance of the nation, the bringing of peace to the world, have been my study since youth."

These attitudes, expressed in education, had the further assumption that there was some point to it. Not only the learner, but the object, the State, could be improved by application of mind to problem. It was essential for the individual to master himself and to guide others. The path to the early Meiji outlook is a simple one; when the Education Act was issued in 1872, it said flatly that "learning is the key to success in life, and no man can afford to neglect it." And it went on to say, everyone should subordinate all other matters to the education of his children." Again, the preamble to the new school regulations: "Henceforth, throughout the land, without distinction of class and sex, in no village shall there be a house without learning, in no house an ignorant person." Characteristically, Kume Kunitake, the chronicler of the Iwakura Mission in 1872, noted that the problem of the former slaves in America could be solved only if they devoted themselves assiduously to education and self-improvement.

Tokugawa education, however formalistic, had important connotations for the development of abilities and ambition. The note of ambition seems out of consonance with feudal society, and the Meiji leaders complained that one could not have any under the system that had produced them. As Sakamoto Ryōma put it, "In a place like home you can't have any ambition. You waste your time loafing around, and pass the time like an idiot." But the cult of education suggests this is only half the story, or perhaps even less than half. In fact, there was a lot of ambition, a burning desire to bring honor to one's name, and a desire to excel. It is suggested by some that since status was inherited, it became all the more important to achieve success in one's proper status —whether farmer, merchant, samurai, high or low. Whatever the case, ambition was everywhere. The cult of commercial success permeates the novelists' tales of wealth and prudence. The most important folk-god of the times was neither Buddhist nor Shinto, but a curious figure, grotesquely represented, holding sheaves of rice, and usually identified as the God of Wealth. But *Shusse Daikokuten,* to give him his name, should be translated as the God of Success, and his votaries were numerous. Surely it is to this kind of value and obsession that we have to relate the astonishing religion of success that came into Japan in Western form; Samuel Smiles' *Self Help,* nearly the Bible of a generation; its title the inspiration for the first political society, the *Risshisha* in Tosa; Clark's winged words urging his boys to "Be Ambitious" in Hokkaido, and the national pursuit of wealth and strength.

Nor is the story over. If national goals are temporarily out of favor in Japan, individual desire and ambition grow apace. A best-seller of recent months, a multivolume fictionalized biography of the first Tokugawa shogun, is credited with its success because of the way it shows how Ieyasu emerged victorious in an age of warring lords and unified the nation. The Japanese Consulate General newsletter explains in a matter-of-fact tone that "The book provides valuable lessons to businessmen and industrialists who are facing in this modern world competition that is comparable to the time Ieyasu was alive. This historical novel proves that victory or defeat between two opposing armies with equal number of men depends largely on the capability of the commanders-in-chief. The same thing can be applied to the current competition among businessmen and industrialists today."[1] Modern moralists deplore this as callous and materialistic, and the President of Dōshisha responds that the cult of success means "pushing others aside to win fame and high position, and is a manifestation of egotism. . . . Today's college students, I believe, are no longer aiming at standing above others. They should not. Their goal should be, rather, to 'be with and among fellow men, to live in harmony with others as responsible members of the community.'" He would have had a position in the shogun's Confucian academy without difficulty. But even there, as in Dōshisha, his students would be striving to enter, to excel, and to win.

---

[1] A recent American book about executive politics also prefaces its discussion of tactics with a quotation from Field Marshal Montgomery.

M. B. Jansen

More traditional is the spirit, admittedly extreme in its archaism, of a mountain school described by Nagai Michio in 1961. The "Spartan Academy," as it was called, began each day with a pledge of allegiance to its head and a resolve for the utilization of natural gifts to achieve greatness. Frankly aiming at university entrance examinations, the grammar school boys recited in unison their founder's vow: "What someone else reads once, I will read three times; what someone else reads three times, I will read five times. Taking examinations is the student's battle. From this day forth I vow that I will study with the intensity of a madman or like a lunatic in order to achieve my goal." And, lest anyone think this an isolated relic of Tokugawa days, one might quote from recent applications for admission to American universities: "I am determined to kill myself studying if necessary to enter your university." The logic may be imperfect, but the continuity of spirit is clear.

Tokugawa education, then, was less than modern, but it was widely diffused, it produced a fiercely competitive determination to succeed, and it bred a confidence that the individual could improve himself and his society. These were important aids when Japanese authorities called their countrymen to a new challenge in the name of nationalism and progress.

Conclusion

Although the attitudes and institutions of Tokugawa Japan were far removed from the torpor that was later attributed to them, there were nevertheless also respects in which the doubts of Hu Shih deserve consideration; the very rapidity of the change magnified the dislocations, and the aptness of the traditional carryovers guaranteed future strains for modern Japan.

The burst of enthusiasm for national goals helped account for the striking successes of the Meiji reform. But it also carried with it a single-mindedness, an intensity, that could lead to extremism. So long as the national goals were clear and unambiguous, and so long as the politically articulate felt involved and committed to such goals, the problems were relatively few. But the achievement of those same goals—great power status—coincided with an acceleration of social change, economic inequality, shortage of land, and alienation among intellectuals. How pleasant it could be to return to simple goals, and to use them as substitutes for thought, is shown by the psychological function of nation-building that Manchukuo offered, or of empire building that the Greater East Asian Co-prosperity Sphere provided. In postwar days the choices have been fewer, and the substitute goals of the Olympics seem at best poor alternatives. (One might note, in passing, Maruyama's endorsement of Otis Cary's alarm at the response to a victory over the San Francisco Seals by a Japanese team in 1949: "I seriously questioned whether this was the way things ought to be. The Japanese seemed to feel that they had made a 'landing in the face of the enemy' with the instruments of Peace.")

Perhaps this is simply another way of saying that it was easier to make the national adjustment than the personal appropriation of the presumed goals of modernization; rationality, progress, and scientific judgment. The politics, thought, and literature of twentieth-century Japan are full of examples of the difficulty of making this final hurdle. Despite the remarkable achievement of retaining some of the security of rural relationships in the early urban movement, the long-range effect was inevitably the multiplication of very lonely individuals in the world's largest crowds. Intellectuals, as they became more numerous and less esteemed, many with closer contacts to the West as well, were naturally the first to struggle with these issues. More often than not their recourse was a kind of retreat or compartmentalization, and the dislocated and brooding characters of so many modern novels, the intellectuals withdrawn into theory, and the frenetic young extremists of right and left-wing causes, have all been reminders of these difficulties. The deep fissures in thought, in society, and in politics between generations, and between rural and urban environments, the feeling of a lost Eden or perhaps of an oversold Eden, have also been inevitable costs of the process. Hence the importance for recent Japanese intellectuals of the few individuals like Uchimura Kanzō who did seem to work out an individual stand in the name of universal values and beliefs, and of isolated incidents like the Kōtoku trial that brought these conflicts to the forefront of consciousness.

And yet, even when all this is granted, it does not betoken a failure or incompleteness about the modernization process in Japan. Modernization, as Benjamin Schwartz and Cyril Black remind us, has its ambiguities, and its course is by no means toward progress in the sense of better and happier lives. Greater tyranny of state over individual, dislocation of economic and social change, and rootlessness in the face of eroding values and beliefs, have been everywhere the case. They were denied by some of the more doctrinaire social Darwinian advocates of progress, as they are overlooked by their successors, the modern stage theorists of economic development, but they do not therefore cease to be problems. Violence, uneasiness, and unhappiness have everywhere been the companions of modernization processes. Everywhere there is a consciousness of a loss of values, a search for reintegration with new groups. Indeed, to some of us, W. H. Whyte's *Organization Man* was full of reminders of the way American patterns might begin to resemble those of Japan, and David Riesman's intense interest in Japan more recently ought not to surprise us either.

If difficulties of this sort have plagued modernizing societies everywhere, then it is inevitable that they should have been particularly acute in a Japan which was remaking itself with imported technology and ideas. For there the problem was seen less as one of modern vs. tradition, as it was in the West, than of modern vs. Japan; a generation that asked itself whether it was Japanese or modern, Japanese or Christian, experienced a special kind of loneliness and uncertainty.

Most developing nations, of course, would cheerfully exchange some of their problems for Japan's, content to have its growth rate as a harbinger of inevitable good. And it must be admitted, I think, that the solution of so many of the material needs and problems at least opens the way to attack on other problem areas. Hu Shih once suggested scornfully that apologists for "the spiritual civilization of the East," which "tolerates such a terrible form of human slavery as the ricksha coolie" might well contemplate their distinctions and definitions. Not a few countries have experienced some of Japan's problems without its advantages.

A final question that arises is the relevance of Japan's modernization for other countries, and particularly for its neighbors. Can there be models, and if so can Japan serve as one? There are obviously points of technical tutelage, and of economic investment, which Japan has already entered. Reparations and other agreements find Japanese technicians active in many parts of South Asia today.

But even this short look at Japan's preconditions seems to me to indicate the extreme problems about Japan's serving successfully as a "model." Japan entered the modern era scarcely behind the West at all. It had high literacy, and relatively low population; other Asian countries begin with the reverse. Japan's population also followed the "Western" sequence of industrial expansion and death control. In contemporary situations, population control becomes much more difficult. Irene Tauber has pointed out that antibiotics, had they been available, would have complicated Japan's process immeasurably.

In these and many other respects Japan's advantages cannot be shared by the "new nations" of the 1960's. Perhaps the point to make is that *despite* these, despite the relative speed and success of Japan's transformation, the psychological and intellectual dislocation and cost have been high. To turn it around, one might say that insularity and the resultant consciousness of cultural and historical individuality, the diffusion of education and the early production of a self-conscious elite, and the determination to excel—these same elements guaranteed a particularly poignant and sharp awareness of cultural contrast and clash on the part of many Japanese, that in the rush for achievement only a few of their writers and thinkers were inclined to question what was under way, the majority remaining content to stress the material and political achievements of *fukoku-kyōhei*. And that revelation, through defeat and consequent self-analysis brought on a particularly sharp response of self-criticism and dissatisfaction—while the West, now intent on economic growth, pooh-poohs these misgivings.

Whatever the case, few modern histories present us with more throught-provoking questions for the significance of the modernization process, for its interrelationships, and for its amibiguities. Fortunately, it is a story far from over, and one which offers fresh and rewarding insights for the past and future of the West as well. Perhaps, most importantly, Japan's experience sheds new light on the common fate and predicament of twentieth-century man; a situation which includes an abundance of material goods, an atomization of ancient relationships in the new megalapolis, and loneliness in an international order haunted by the fear of the atom. These combine to make more complex the search for autonomy of personality and freedom of choice. It is a search in which there can be no models, and one in which success comes, if at all, only through the self-help so avidly studied by the men of the Meiji era.

CHAPTER EIGHTEEN

TOSA DURING THE LAST CENTURY
OF TOKUGAWA RULE

MARIUS B. JANSEN

As UNDERSTANDING of the dynamics of Tokugawa times grows, new views of periodization develop with it. The traditional view of an unchanging torpor has gone. So also has the opinion that it should be seen as a primitive idyll. Lafcadio Hearn, who probably saw Tokugawa society through the eyes of his ex-samurai father-in-law, thought of it as a society in which "conditions tended to the general happiness . . . there was no need for supreme effort of any sort—no need for the straining of any faculty. Moreover, there was little or nothing to strive after; for the vast majority of the people, there were no prizes to win."[1] Modern scholarship, anxious to see the cracks within the Tokugawa order that would become fissures when subjected to the strains of the Western impact in the nineteenth century, prefers to focus instead on areas of competition, insecurity, and discontent.

If the first century of Tokugawa rule can be seen as one in which the relationship between *bakufu* and *han,* daimyo and retainers, merchants and samurai, officials and farmers became stablized, the last century of that rule, and particularly the period after the 1770's, becomes remarkable for the sharpness with which problems of conflict between groups can be delineated. Local particularity necessarily continued under conditions of local autonomy, but the growth of national and regional interrelationshps bore fruit in problems more uniform and universal.

A recent and challenging discussion of conditions in the late eighteenth century by Hayashi Motoi serves as useful summary of this interpretation.[2] Peasant rebellions, he begins, increased in number and in complexity. Comparison between the complaints of protests in 1717 and in 1786 in Fukui serves to show the complexity of market and economic conditions to which the farmers were responding. Rebellions became national rather than local problems, and the *bakufu* itself led in enunciating and enforcing a hard line of repression and restraint.[3] After the 1750's rebellions were usually domain-wide in extent, in the 1780's and again in the 1840's they were virtually national, following along

---

[1] Lafcadio Hearn, *Japan: An Attempt at Interpretation* (New York, 1907), 386. The Marxist appraisal of a pre-commercial Eden, of course, retains some of this lament.

[2] "Hōreki—Temmeiki no shakai jōsei," Iwanami koza: *Nihon rekishi* (Tokyo, 1963), 12, (*Kinsei,* vol. 4), 104–54.

[3] Hayashi, *op. cit.,* 112, sees the turn in a *bakufu* edict of 1749–1750, "the first time an order for forceful suppression of peasant protests applied to *bakufu* as well as to daimyo realms." Later edicts instructed daimyo to refuse to receive or consider peasant petitions.

the communication routes of commerce and tribute. Cities grew as landless peasants thronged to them in hope of work, and in Edo riots grew from those of 1733, when a few rice wholesalers served as target, to those of 1787, in which whole companies of spear-armed commoners attacked establishments of the rich indiscriminately. Gradually ideas began to be formulated in terms of alternatives; the riots and rebellions of the 1780's were contemporaneous with the loyalist "plotting" of Takeuchi Shikibu and Yamagata Daini, and in some areas sharp disputes broke out within the ruling class itself.[4] Peak years of disorder—the 1780's, 1830's, and 1860's—saw a steady progression of violence. From this, it is concluded that the Tokugawa system was no longer capable of the flexibility required to adjust to problems that had grown within it. Agricultural production had reached its limits under existing technology; population was pressing those limits, and an archaic and inefficient marketing and allocation system was preventing rational utilization of food production. In disaster years the closer interrelationships between areas meant that tremblers in Edo were reflected in the most distant domains. Yet the *bakufu,* with limited administrative control, could deal only with the effects, and not with the local roots of problems. It ruled the metropolis but not the country, and it never approached basic solutions that might threaten the institutional work of the founders it venerated.

This schematization is compelling, but it needs to be qualified in its prediction of inexorable doom. It makes little allowance for the periods of relative stabilization between the several peaks of disorder, and it assumes too insistently the incompatability of money economy with the Tokugawa institutional structure. The *bakufu han* system had survived those inconsistencies for over a century, and some of them were in fact essential to its performance. It required a foreign threat to bring to maturity all the elements of opposition that were present. Yet this too, as well as ideological gropings for alternatives, was coming into being in the 1780's. *Kokugaku,* the national learning, was fully developed by Motoori Norinaga (1730–1801), and by the 1830's his disciple Hirata Atsutane had progressed to criticism of the shogunate that the master never made. "Dutch studies" took on a new lease of life during the 1770's with the discovery of the superiority and practicality of western science, and their influence grew steadily until by the 1830's they were in a positon to incur *bakufu* displeasure and repression. The foreign threat itself, acute in the 1830's with the news that came from China, began in the eighteenth century with fears of Russian advances to the North.

When this schematization is applied to the realm of Tosa, the necessity for distinctions between the main-traveled provinces of Honshu and the southern half of Shikoku becomes clear. The problems the *han* faced during the last century of Tokugawa rule were not new, but they were more acute. Debts to

---

[4] The best discussion of this period in western languages is that of J. W. Hall, *Tanuma Okitsugu (1719–1788): Forerunner of Modern Japan* (Harvard University Press, 1955), 129 f.

Tosa During the Last Century of Tokugawa Rule

Osaka creditors had been a problem as early as 1621, but the eagerness to avoid even more ruinous relationships forced the *han* into repeated controversies with groups whose support it needed most. Agricultural production had grown during the Tokugawa years, but by the end of the eighteenth century good land was occupied and even marginal land scarce, so that the natural limits of production—but not of population—had been reached.[5] The retainer force, too small in the early seventeenth century, was complete, but also more expensive to maintain and for the most part under-employed.[6] Kōchi itself had grown to the point where further immigration into the city was forbidden by edict although common in practice. Yet it would remain far from the size and importance of the great cities of Honshu.[7]

In Kōchi, as elsewhere in Japan, the fissure lines of future faults had been set by solutions to the problems that pressed on the Yamauchi administrators in the seventeenth century. Those dispositions brought trouble when the *han* tried to strengthen its position at the cost of its subordinates. The conflicts that resulted can usually be seen as those between "Kōchi," the *han* administration and principal merchants, and "country," including administrative headmen and rustic samurai who supervised the producer-peasants.

KŌCHI AND COMMONERS: PEASANT REBELLIONS

Examination of the relationship between Kōchi administrators and the population of the countryside makes it clear that the last century of Tokugawa rule saw an acceleration of protest and rebellion, although its proportions and reasons do not suggest words like "crisis" or "widespread." There were measurable protests (organization to present petitions, offer resistance, or plan group flight) four times during the seventeenth century: in 1603, 1663, 1671, and 1682. A lull of almost three-quarters of a century followed, broken in 1751. Then the pace quickened: 1760, 1786, 1787, 1797, and 1809 saw outbreaks, fre-

---

[5] The *bakufu* rated Tosa as 202,626 *koku* throughout the entire Tokugawa period. Actually the Chōsokabe survey showed production at 240,000 *koku*. By the end of Tokugawa rule actual production, including reclaimed land, totaled 512,698 *koku*, of which approximately one half was from "new fields" (*shinden*). By the 1870's documents admitted that further reclamation profits were so marginal that they would be taxed at half of the earlier *shinden* rate. Figures from Hirao Michio, *Tosa han nōgyō keizai shi* (Kōchi, 1958), 52, 66–89 (a province-wide summary, with breakdowns by village), and for 1871, 63.

[6] Population estimates, which must rely upon the imperfect methods used in the religious surveys carried out at *bakufu* orders, many of them lost, show, for the end of the seventeenth century, 379,129, and for the 1840's, 507,095. The retainer force would add about 6,000 family heads; with dependents, perhaps another 30,000. That population pressed upon subsistence is indicated by *han* rules against infanticide issued in 1759. Figures from Hirao Michio, *Kōchi han zaisei shi* (Kōchi, 1953), 5–12.

[7] Kōchi specialties and regulations are described in Hirao Michio, *Tosa han shōgyō keizai shi* (Kōchi, 1960), but population estimates are particularly unsatisfactory. Figures provided, 8–11, would suggest a commoner population of 17,000 to 25,000, but since figures count only adults, and not all of them, the estimate is necessarily rough.

quently with several in each year. Thereafter 1842 and 1860 saw Tosa echoes of the national malaise of those periods.[8]

It would be easy to exaggerate the importance of most of these. Except for the famine year of 1787, which saw Kōchi involved in rice shortages that existed everywhere, most of these rebellions took place in relatively isolated areas, close to the borders of neighboring domains which had served as natural market centers until the imposition of new controls from Kōchi. Four times protesters moved across the frontier, twice in large numbers of several hundred. Nevertheless the rebellions reward study.

Two of the largest, and certainly the most interesting, incidents are important because they show the way *han* efforts to increase official income conflicted with local handicraft and commercial interests in the countryside. Heavily forested and poorly endowed with flatland, Kōchi from the first depended upon lumber. A paper industry received stimulation and protection under the seventeenth century statesman Nonaka Kenzan, whose policies of official monopoly aroused opposition that helped lead to his fall. But by the middle of the eighteenth century paper production was far larger and more important than it had ever been before. The *han* had imported technicians from the Oska area early in the century, and had experimented with a variety of officially-run and merchant-licensed production and purchase bureaus.[9] Whether official or merchant, however, the monopoly system that grew was conducted for the benefit of the castle town and at the expense of the village producers for whom paper production and sale had become an important supplement to a meager agricultural production. Many of their markets were across the frontiers, especially in the neighboring domain of Matsuyama, and closer *han* control of purchase and distribution affected the producers directly and unfavorably. This was shown in the large revolts in the Tsunoyama and Ikegawa areas in 1755 and 1787.

The first of these came three years after the *han* established an Office of Provincial Production in 1752. Although this had been anticipated by several moves earlier in the century, its full implementation struck immediately at the producers of paper, who suddenly found all their products saleable only to authorized buyers for the new monopoly office. Soon complaints were heard that the monopoly was operating solely for the benefit of the favored merchant agents of the *han,* and at the expense of the rural producers. Prices were being forced down, and producers were no longer able to deal with the traders, local and "foreign," who had come to their villages during the periods of free trade. It is indicative of the increased consciousness of central control in Japan that, when the *han* administrators refused to receive their requests and showed signs of punishing them for having presumed to prepare them, the petitioners discussed sending representatives to Edo to complain to the *bakufu* itself. Before it came to violence the *han* dispatched a troop of *ashigaru* to the area,

[8] Chronology from Hirao Michio, *Tosa nōmin ikki shikō* (Kōchi, 1953), 1–7.

[9] Irimajiri Yoshinaga, *Tokugawa bakuhan sei kaitai katei no kenkyū* (Tokyo, 1957), 315 f.

rounded up twenty-two leaders, and after investigation imprisoned eight and released the others. Subsequent prosecution focused on the buyer who had aroused the hostility, and on a *shōya*, Nakahira Zennojō, who had led that hostility. Both were executed. But this did not end the complaints, for others memorialized to question the worth of profits gained in this manner, to warn of popular dismay and unrest, and that the voice of the people was expressing the voice of heaven. Natural phenomena that accompanied the execution of the martyred *shōya* were taken as evidence that his troubled spirit had returned to visit his persecutors.[10]

The *han* retreated a bit. A complaint and petition box placed outside the Kōchi castle brought a flood of new compaints about the monopoly bureau. In 1760 some categories of paper were exempted from official control, and in 1763 the monopoly office was abolished altogether. But after only three years the advantages of securing added revenue for the treasury proved so attractive that the entire establishment was restored in 1766.

The next rebellion, that of Ikegawa in 1785, grew directly from the price differential between what rural paper makers had been receiving and the price they were ordered to accept by the agents of the *han* monopoly. Since outside trade was furthermore cut off more effectively than ever before, the villagers, over five hundred in number (later augmented by another three to four hundred), petitioned for redress and then, receiving no satisfaction, moved across the border into Matsuyama. It seems that the fugitives had every intention of staying in Matsuyama, and when their request to settle was refused they considered asking for permission to move on to the next domain. But *bakufu* regulations made it impossible for any fief to grant such requests by the eighteenth century, and before long Tosa officials were dealing with Matsuyama officials about return of the fugitives. It is interesting to note that they were granted a sort of sanctuary, and that mediators of a temple on the frontier secured from the Tosa administration recognition of seventeen complaints in return for which the fugitives returned to their villages after an absence of a month and a half. Shortly afterward, in 1787, the monopoly system was declared ended once again and open trading in paper revived.[11] The *han* had not given up its intention of controlling and exploiting local products, but tactical requirements had made it necessary to show leniency. Border control stations and instructions to local officials made it apparent that trade across the frontiers continued to be discouraged.[12] Geographical conditions and communication limitations also put the Kōchi officials at a disadvantage in enforcing these.

The other demonstrations of resistance do not require detailed exposition. In 1787, a national famine year, shortages of rice that brought the *bakufu* to demand help from all its vassals also worsened problems in Kōchi. Edo riots

[10] Hirao, *op. cit.,* 19–23; augmented but closely followed by Irimajiri, *op. cit.,* 325–28.
[11] Hirao, *op. cit.,* 32–61.
[12] Hirao Michio, *Kinsei shakai shi kō* (Kōchi, 1962), 151 f, for details on border stations. Also Hirao, *Tosa han shōgyō keizai shi* (Kōchi, 1960), 182 f.

made it hard to get Tosa rice to the Edo garrison, and Tokugawa bureaucrats tried to divert Tosa shipments to municipal relief. In Kōchi, and indeed in all towns of any size in Tosa, rapid increases in the price of rice brought riots and demonstrations. The *han* imported rice from Kyūshū, and devised public works projects to enable urban workers to earn money with which they could buy it.[13]

In 1797, rural protests over corvee required in connection with the daimyo's trip to Edo on *sankin-kūtai* duty were quickly suppressed. And in 1842, when the misrule of a local *shōya* became intolerable, hundreds of villagers from the Nanogawa area protested before crossing the frontier into Matsuyama territory. Once again investigations and negotiations resulted in the return of the aggrieved, with punishment for the offending officials who had caused the difficulty.[14]

It can scarcely be maintained that these incidents reflected Tosa-wide breakdown or even disaffection, but they did relate to the *han's* increasing involvement in the national economy. Fiscal difficulties prompted the repeated attempts at control of handicraft production, despite the known repugnance of villagers for such measures, and national, particularly Edo, rice shortages found speedy echo in disorders in Kōchi. It should not be thought that conditions in Kōchi were particularly severe, or repression unusually successful. There were similar incidents in neighboring *han,* some of which saw villagers moving over the Tosa border, and which required negotiations comparable to those that had been carried out with Matsuyama at the time of the "paper rebellion."

Crisis or not, economic policies and the problems they brought produced a considerable volume of discussion of political economy in Tosa. Mostly prepared as memorials to the daimyo, these documents illustrate the range of alternatives and dissent that was possible under the system.

Questions of monopoly and marketing practices produced several discussions of the effect of price fixing on the volume of production. In 1759, for instance, Tejima Jungo discussed the contradictions for "virtuous government" (*jinsei*) implicit in the monoply edicts. They put the *han* in a position of competing with its people for the profits of their labor. Moreover, they tended to depress production and the resulting scarcity raised prices, and as exports fell the flow of money from neighboring domains diminished. How much better, he thought, not only for producers but for the entire realm, to encourage production by freeing the trade and encouraging private exports to the Osaka area.[15] In 1786, after the end of the paper monopoly, the same writer extended his argument to controls on the manufacture of *sake*. He thought it wrong as well as disadvantageous for the *han* to protect a few large producers at the cost of gain for many traders and challenged the usual arguments about preventing the exodus of money to Bizen. With free trade, money would move in

---

[13] Details and documents in Hirao, *nōmin ikki*, 62–71.

[14] *Ibid.*, 76–91.

[15] Irimajiri, *op. cit.*, 317–18.

both directions, he argued, and *han* customs stations could gain directly from the trade while private dealers carried it on.[16]

Nor was Tejima unique. Ichien Shōan wrote a strong defense of the importance of the merchant role in an economy like the one he knew, and went on to advocate free trade across the borders.[17] Commerce was clearly on the increase, and in 1785 Fukutomi Hannojō noted that "in recent times one sees and hears of many who are leaving agriculture to enter trade." This course was not open to the impoverished, but only to the more successful villagers. That these were nowhere numerous is shown by the occasional village surveys one finds for late Tokugawa Tosa, which show a large proportion of landless labor and relatively few shops.[18] A complaint of 1759 noted that in a village there might be a handful of large farmers, relatively few middle farmers, but mostly small farmers and "of these the landless (*kage* and *mōtō*) are uniformly miserable." [19] Of course there were also conventional theorists who held stoutly to the virtues of agriculture over commerce and denounced merchants as a greedy lot who interfered with the distribution of rice for personal profit at cost to peasant and samurai, and went on to demand suppression of their activities.[20] But in the conditions of the late eighteenth century such sentiments had little relevance.

The Tosa government's problems, like those of other domains, were soluble only to the degree that the *han* could compete successfully with its people for their products and profit. But such steps invariably got in the way of the Confucian rationale for government that was increasingly important to the *han*. As a result, specific suggestions offered the daimyo were moralistic and general, and seldom practical and specific. Kusunose Seiin, who addressed a document to the ninth daimyo, Yamauchi Toyochika, upon his accession to rule in 1769, limited himself to rather patronizing endorsement of the daimyo's announcement of austerity and economy. He held up as example T'ang T'ai Tsung, and commended his paternalism (*mimponhugi*) to the young lord. Far wiser such paternalistic moderation, he wrote, than the harshness of the *bakufu*'s instruction of that year (1769) to daimyo to refuse to receive petitions of complaint and to crush all peasant rebellions ruthlessly. The people should be nurtured with love, and the daimyo should constantly examine his own conduct. And then, to elaborate this point, Kusunose made a specific comment. Toyochika had abandoned the usual sea-borne *sankinkōtai* route on his first trip to Kōchi for an overland procession from northern Shikoku. Peasants along the way had suffered hardship from unnecessary corvee duties just at

---

[16] Hirao, *shōgyō keizai shi,* 115–16. It would be difficult to imagine a policy problem better calculated to prepare Japanese minds for the issues of economic policy that came with the opening of the country.

[17] Hirao, *op. cit.,* 79–80, for text.

[18] For Fukutomi, *ibid,* 80; for a village count, Watanabe Mitsutane, "Bakumatsuki ni okeru Tosa han no nōson jōtai," *Tosa shidan* #64 (1938), 11–28.

[19] Hirao, *nōgyō keizai shi,* 211–12. Hirao's discussion and documentation of village life, 294f, leave one startled that there were not more revolts.

[20] For the views of one such, Otani, in the 1780's, Hirao, *shōgyō keizai shi,* 74–78.

the time of their spring work, while the Tosa maritime power had lost a chance for maneouvers.[21] But economies and paternalism promised no lasting solution, even when an advisor might hold out hope of voluntary contributions to han coffers that might come in response to particularly striking evidence of daimyo virtue.[22]

II. Kōchi and Village Headmen

With the bulk of the retainers force concentrated in the castle town and with the *han* intent on increasing its income from rural handicraft production, cooperation of village heads became ever more important to its purposes. The *shōya* ruled the countryside, and though they might have to share local honors with rural samurai, or *gōshi,* they were unchallenged in their administrative function, and essential to the assessment and collection of taxes. They were the fulcrum of *han* power in the countryside. They could cause great hardship, as in the case of the man whose misgovernment precipitated the revolt in 1842. They could become the object of local affection and legend, as with Nakahira Zennojō, martyred in 1759, whose spirit was credited with responsibility for freak weather and tremblers by the peasants whose cause he had taken up. They were rewarded if revolts were headed off and punished unless they were. In 1751 nine *shōya* were dismissed after the revolt, while one was rewarded with privileges of surname and swords. Needless to say, projects for crossing frontiers in large numbers required cooperation or elimination of *shōya* on both sides of the border.

Shōya were appointed by the district magistrate (*kōri bugyō*), usually from leading families in the area. Their titles, honors, and importance varied with the size of the area they administered, which might range from a single hamlet to a cluster of villages (in the case of an *ōjōya*).[23] Some had privileges of audience, and some headed the entire *shōya* hierarchy with the title *sanban gashira shōya*. Their salary might range from 8 to 140 *koku* of rice. They received labor tax service, "office fields" and a percentage of the tax yield of the area over which they had jurisdiction. They had a number of subordinates. It fell to them to post and, on occasion, to read to heads of mutual responsibility groups the official regulations and injunctions to diligence and morality. They were responsible for all governmental functions within their areas of jurisdiction, from communications, fire, police, livestock sales, corvee or money comutations of it, and festivals, to public morality, which they were to stimulate through search and reward for outstanding examples of virtue and filiality.

---

[21] Nakata Shirō, "Fukenroku ni miru Kusunose Seiin no hansei kaikakuron," *Tosa shidan* #81 (1952), 15–25.

[22] This prediction was made in the famous memorial of Kyūtoku Daihachi (Tokuri), reprinted in *Nihon keizai taiten* (Tokyo, 1928), vol. 5, 597–602.

[23] Yasuoka Dairoku, "Shōya no mibun, shokyū oyobi shokusho," *Tosa shidan* #98 (1960), 27–31.

The towns also had appointed *shōya;* Kōchi had one to each two or three *machi*.[24] But they were overshadowed by higher authority all around them, and not capable of the leadership and self-consciousness of the rural headmen. Moreover the codes, especially the Genroku Ōjōmoku, specified that townsmen should not move to the country without permission (nor was the contrary permitted) and especially forbade urban-rural creditor or commercial relationships.[25] This meant that rural business and official life was likely to remain a world of its own, organized and led by the vigorous, independent headmen. *Han* efforts at greater centralized control ran into their displeasure and sabotage, and commercial developments of the towns confronted *shōya* vested interests and dominance. Although *shōya* undoubtedly became involved in whatever profitable enterprises their districts knew, they thought of themselves as representatives of an early and pure agrarian interest. Together with most *gōshi,* they were educated in private academies scattered throughout the Tosa countryside and conscious of, and pleased with, the things that set them off from town interests and dwellers, military as well as commoner. And as they became familiar with the rudiments of the *kokugaku* loyalist thought of late Tokugawa times, they found in it a rationale for expressing dissatisfaction with changes that were altering the traditional balance between Kōchi and country.[26]

By the 1830's, there were clear signs of sharp dissatisfaction among *shōya* in Tosa. Specific slights were seized on by them as indications of a long-term decline in their prestige and authority, and stirred them to assert their administrative importance and historical inheritance in ringing terms. They used the ideology of loyalism as ultimate source of authority. Recent research has made it possible to move the date for organized expressions of this discontent back almost a decade to 1832, and with comparable research underway in other parts of Japan the importance of this discovery for the mid-nineteenth century political developments seems very great.[27]

In 1832 *shōya* in Takaoka district were found complaining about the way in which their status had declined relative to that of groups to which they did not feel in the least inferior—*jige rōnin, gōshi*. They petitioned for the dignity of surnames and swords and a social position appropriate to the importance of the work they performed. In 1837, when a ceremonial occasion found town officials seated with greater honor than the *shōya* of the locality, the latter protested with a strong affirmation of the priority of country over town. The Tokugawa social order of samurai, farmer, artisan, and merchant, they insisted, placed them above their urban counterparts; moreover, in earlier days farmer-

---

[24] Hirao, *shōgyō keizai shi,* 56.

[25] Article 67 (*Kochi ken shiyō,* Kochi, 1924), supplement.

[26] For the private academies (*shijuku*), cf. M. B. Jansen, *Sakamoto Ryōma and the Meiji Restoration* (Princeton, 1961), 35.

[27] Hirao Michio's chronology and account in *nōmin ikki shikō,* 121f, has been supplemented by new findings reported by Sekita Hidesato, "Shōya dōmei no yōkyū to ishiki," *Tosa shidan* #99 (1960), 27–32.

soldiers had in any case preceded the specialization of warrior and farmer. They traced the origin of their titles and posts to the Kamakura period and the language of the *Taiheiki,* and asserted their preeminence by right of the importance of their tasks and tax and labor privileges. "It is our great task to be entrusted with care of the rice fields, dry fields, mountains, rivers, and ocean. We encourage farming and fishing, we see to the payment of the annual tax and the carrying out of public works, and, if necessary, conscription of workers for military preparations . . . In the final analysis, ours is the office which is entrusted with carrying out all the really important affairs of the realm." The "arrogant behavior of town officials," whose work dealt with conniving merchants who "have never known the hardships of service for their country," and who were robbers in an ordered society, was "a grave offense against the Imperial Way." [28]

Again in 1843, when two *shōya* were accused of embezzling funds intended for public works, examined like commoners, and then vindicated and released, *shōya* found occasion for indignation. Their fellows ought not to be treated like commoners, they said; the investigation should have been discrete, and the men should have been removed from their office and status before being subjected to the indignity of arrest. The authorities had made all *shōya* lose prestige with their people. "The two men, who bear the heavy responsibility of governing the village people, were shamed before the public. And then they were ordered to go home again, in full view, and told to resume their influence over the people." [29]

These incidents were only dramatic examples of what many *shōya* felt was a steady erosion of their position. Their younger colleagues, they feared, no longer realized the importance of the social position their rank had once conveyed. Continued silence would lose them public respect and make them unable to head off rebellion. Continued obsequiousness before petty officials was wasting their time and ruining their influence, and "our collapse is a three-fold loss: for the Emperor, first of all; for his people, and finally for ourselves." [30]

The significant thing about this protest is that it was no longer felt essential to begin with affirmations of the acceptance of samurai priority. The *shōya* sensed that in practical terms the samurai had become an unnecessary nuisance, and from their education in loyalism they had realized that samurai were also a relatively modern encumbrance.

The articles of the Shōya League dating from 1841 provide the fullest statement of this position. The League was formed to petition for the return of former status and procedures, and its members received full statements of why this should be done. The argumentation traced *shōya* office and importance not to Kamakura Japan, but to remote antiquity and the Imperially-authorized

---

[28] For Takaoka, Sekita, *op. cit.* For 1837 and after Hirao, *op. cit.,* 126–27.

[29] *Ibid.,* 146–48.

[30] Hirao, *op. cit.* 127–45, gives the text of the Shōya League petition and the contemporareous internal document cited. I have cited this also in less detail in *Sakamoto Ryōma,* 36–38.

office of *muragimi*. "This is an extremely delicate matter, and we should of course not talk about it; but we can see from this that we were once commissioned directly by the Imperial Court, and if we look at it this way, is not our work anything but humble?" For there was after all "only One who is supreme, the Emperor. The shogun is his deputy, the daimyo are his commanders who head the administration, while the *shōya* are his officers . . ." Samurai had rank, but *shōya* had function, but that was more important; "Should we not say that the *shōya,* who is the head of the commoners, is superior to the retainers who are the hands or feet of the nobles?"

The *shōya* went on to itemize their importance in local administration. It was up to them to control the behavior of *gōshi* and samurai in their areas, to protect their commoners from samurai wrath and unfairness, and to remember that samurai did not own their commoners, but that the latter were "the Emperor's subjects." Nor should they grovel before the samurai and petty officials; Yamauchi Toyochika had ruled that "no one in the realm need prostrate himself before anyone except the lord himself," and although self-important samurai were trying to enforce subservience today they were clearly in the wrong. For the *shōya* required public confidence and esteem. They had to hold to the middle path between poverty and austerity (which would invite scorn) and wealth and ostentation (which would bring unpopularity); and "Since ours is work which easily incurs the suspicion of the *han* administration on the one hand and of the people we rule, who are quick to point up our weaknesses on the other, we must always be on the alert. And above all we must keep in mind the fact that we are always surrounded by the officials."

The specifics of the *shōya* petition were for the most part retrograde in intent. They wanted the authorities to stop appointing as *shōya* men who had been engaged in merchant activities. They wanted barrier keepers rated below themselves. They wanted surname and sword privileges for themselves, regardless of the size of village or length of tenure. They wanted groups formerly subject to them returned to their jurisdiction, and they wanted renewal of the permission to use force in their interrogations. They wanted to be the channels for all reports of religious affiliation, including those of their superiors, and they sought an end to direct appointment of lower village officials (elders, *toshiyori*), since this made them relatively independent of their *shōya* superiors. Their sons, they thought, should have the privileges of surname and swords. Rules of respect should be set and enforced for official correspondence directed to *shōya,* and *gōshi* should grant them the dignity of "esquire" (*dono*) in correspondence. Finally, *shōya* should be permitted to become *gōshi* without having to give up their office.

These indignant protests and requests point to the past and to the future. From the past they draw legitimacy and dignity, and the imperial loyalism that pervades them was a faith that grew in conjunction with the study of Japan's antiquity. The *shōya* therefore seemed intent upon a return to a precommercial, and indeed a pre-feudal, social order. But in another sense, by eliminating a samurai class become irrelevant to daily life throughout most of the Japanese countryside, the *shōya* opened the way for the social reforms of the mid-nineteenth century.[31] The towns whose influence they deplored represented both new currents of commercialism and the stultifying rigidity of the privileged bureaucracy. The return to a purer past was of course doomed, and the Tosa *shōya* class and title were abolished in 1870.[32] But by then their adversaries, the samurai, were already doomed to expropriation.

III. Kōchi and the Rural Retainers

Although the *shōya* wanted to improve their status vis à vis the *gōshi*, in most respects the two groups shared a "country" as opposed to a "Kōchi" outlook. They lived in the same villages, their sons were likely to attend the same schools, and reclamation programs had seen many successful *shōya* rewarded with advancement to *gōshi* rank. Indeed, as the petition made clear, *shōya* hoped to be allowed to retain their office while holding *gōshi* rank, thus combining function with prestige. But on the whole, the *shōya* felt they had declined in status relative to *gōshi;* the latter were no longer under their jurisdiction, they forwarded their statements of religious affiliation to the *han* separately, and they saw no need to extend peer-group privileges to them in correspondence. *Gōshi* were after all samurai. Latecomers came into *gōshi* ranks through reclamation programs carried on in the Hata (1763) and Niida and Kubokawa (1822) districts, but many more *gōshi* families laid claim to a century or more of retainer status.

Although the *gōshi* have to be considered both rustics and retainers, by the last century of Tokugawa rule many of them were neither. Requirements for entry into *gōshi* rank had become more liberal. The first *gōshi* had been Chōsokabe retainers; reclamation programs had broadened qualifications to include families of substance (which probably meant, in practice, *shōya*), but by 1763 regulations specified that even applicants whose ancestors had engaged in trade would be considered. Merchant families might be expected to command the capital to manage reclamation for *gōshi* estates, which were often divided into parcels at some distance from each other. *Gōshi* were thus often absentee landlords, and by the end of Tokugawa times 82 (perhaps one-tenth of the whole) resided in the castle town of Kōchi. Many of these "townsmen *gōshi*" (*chōnin gōshi*), as they were known, had entered the rank laterally, through adoption or transfer purchase of title. One survey for the 1860's comes to the conclusion that of the 742 *gōshi* then listed, 212 had entered the rank since 1830, for the most part by transfer. This would be a very high proportion

---

[31] The most challenging statement of the *shōya* (and *gōshi*) interest as partly "modern" and inherently revolutionary in its disregard of the established order of society is by Ikeda Yoshimasa, "Tempō kaikakuron no saikentō: Tosa han o chūshin ni shite," *Nihon shi kenkyū* #31, 5, and "Tosa han ni okeru Ansei kaikaku to sono hantai ha," *Rekishi gaku kenkyū* #205 (1957), 18–29.

[32] Hirao, *nōgyō keizai shi*, 44–45, for text and discussion of ordinances involved.

indeed, for the *han* was concerned about the martial worth of recruits and periodically barred transfers to townsmen or farmers who had no military background.[33]

These concerns received point especially after the Russian advances in northeast Asia in the late eighteenth century. *Gōshi* were an important part of the *han* military establishment. In the nineteenth century they were shifted from previous dispositions that put them in large contingents directly under the principal *karō* commanders to command local defense units of *jige rōnin* and commoners, so that military ability and standing became more important than ever. By the time of the Restoration wars, the Tosa forces Itagaki led to the north were made up chiefly of *gōshi* and lower ranks.[34]

This being the case, there were naturally numerous complaints about the quality of the new *gōshi*. The older families resented the new. To make it worse, they were the more likely of the two to be permitted to "contribute" to *han* needs. They did their best to get the *han* to rule out transfers of rank and title. "Many of those entering the rank are of no use to the realm," a document of 1839 warns, "and it frightens one to see that a man who was a nobody yesterday has the nerve to appear in style before the lord on a horse today." [35] Worse, others didn't even bother to keep a horse. One complaint of 1768 expressed doubts that more than 60 or 70 *gōshi* out of the presumed 900 could be considered mounted warriors.[36] As complaints continued and danger from abroad neared, these military considerations were central in rulings forbidding more *gōshi* to move into the castle town. Their role in coast defense was upgraded, and at the very end of Tokugawa, new entrance permits were issued for commoners who had served ten years in the special corps (*mimpeitai*) organized after the coming of Perry.

As with the *shōya*, however, commercial activities or even city residence did not produce an urban or commercial orientation by any means. *Gōshi* values, education, and aspirations were securely rural and calculated not to make for rejection of the traditional order of society, but to seek better treatment within that hierarchy. The expressions of *gōshi* discontent, while less spectacular than retainer disputes in some other areas,[37] are nonetheless full of interest for nineteenth-century Japan. They are significant for the evidence of group feeling

---

[33] Ikeda, "Tempo kaikakuron." The usual course of transfer found the impecunious *gōshi* become a *jige rōnin* (retaining swords and surname) or farmer. Hirao, *Tosa han gōshi kiroku* (Kōchi, 1964), 263–76, itemizes 127 *gōshi* families deprived of rank, usually for infractions of discipline, morality, improprieties in landholding reports, etc.; 84 of these cases came after the middle of the eighteenth century.

[34] Hirao, *op. cit.*, 135. See also his breakdown of military dispositions in the 1840's, which provide rosters of units and personnel for 741 *gōshi* and 526 *jige rōnin*, 88–130.

[35] *Ibid.*, 17.

[36] *Ibid.*, 67. This is from one of the documents put into the *han* "complaint box" mentioned earlier.

[37] Hayashi, "Hōreki—Temmeiki no shakai jōsei," 135, notes a 1755 case in which the entire retainer corps of Matsuyama petitioned the *bakufu* to remove their daimyo, who was serving in the Edo Junior Council (*wakadoshiyori*) at the time.

and indignation that could be generated in response to insult or injustice.[38]

One such incident which agitated Tosa *gōshi* for years occurred in 1797. A Yamauchi retainer (*umamawari*, mounted guard) named Inoue was entertaining five of his peers one evening when a *gōshi* neighbor named Takamura dropped in to join them. In the course of the banter that accompanied the *sake*, Inoue proudly showed his prized sword. Takamura scoffed at its quality, only to have Inoue cut him down with it to prove him wrong. Inoue reported the incident immediately; the *han* administration ruled that Inoue had overstepped himself and should exercise more caution, and that his companions, who had apparently helped him, were also out of line. But Takamura had been guilty of disrespect toward a superior, and was posthumously punished with forfeiture of succession privileges and continuity of family line. The *gōshi* response was instant, and the very next month the *han* retreated by demoting Inoue one grade, to *koshōgumi*, with reduction in holdings, meanwhile addressing itself to *gōshi*. It knew, the proclamation went, that they would do nothing so evil as to form a party or plot, but the stories that came to ear were nonetheless alarming. Proper respect for law, authority, and decisions was necessary. But the *gōshi* continued obdurate. The *han* tried addressing more reassurances to them, only to receive new demands for rehabilitation of Takamura and guarantees against new insult in the future. *Gōshi* got up petitions; groups of them came to Kōchi, and there was talk of complaints to Edo. New concessions followed. One official responsible died, and eight others were dismissed or allowed to resign. Not until 1801, four years later, when Inoue was punished a third time by forfeiting *his* family and succession privileges and banishment to the hinterland, did the matter quiet down. Hirao suggests that *gōshi* feelings toward their superiors were never quite the same again.

Another incident came in 1821, when the retainer of a *gōshi* named Ichikawa Ryōemon was felt to have insulted a fencing master's adoptive son. The next day the retainer was cut down by his indignant betters. In the *han's* eyes, his *gōshi* master shared in his condemnation, and Ichikawa was banished and deprived of rank, surname, and swords. When *gōshi* of the area met and visited the site of the unpleasantness, nine of them were also deprived of their rank and its privileges and forbidden access to the vicinity of the castle town. The upper samurai fencer, in turn, was reduced in rank and similarly barred from the Kōchi suburbs, and the fencing master-father lowered in rank. That the *han* punished both parties, despite the considerable differences in rank between them, probably reflected its concern over the previous incident. Even so, the matter was not closed; for the upper samurai involved were not punished immediately. When the *gōshi* Ichikawa decided to resume amicable relations with them, his fellow-*gōshi* forced him to break such relations, themselves withdrawing fencing students (thereby breaking the master-disciple relationship) on grounds the master had put his junior up to the murder.

Gōshi remained disgruntled and quick to take offense. In 1843 the *han*

---

[38] Below I follow Hirao, *gōshi kiroku*, 149–60.

decided they should no longer take part in the annual mounted review at the New Year ceremonies. Wounded dignity and talk of insult brought *gōshi* pouring into Kōchi; over 600 are said to have filed protests, and talk among them spread that they were not required to perform their tasks if they were not accorded traditional privileges of ceremonial prestige. In 1844 they were again permitted to take part in the review.

Gōshi consciousness of membership in an honorable group was thus highly developed, and their resentment of favoritism shown their superiors posed a problem for even obtuse *han* administrators. The *gōshi* did not resent a stratified social structure, but sought revisions within it. It would be erroneous to consider them anti-feudal, or their discontent a real crisis for the feudal order. But it was an embarrassment of some importance for the *han*. When defense crises of the nineteenth century made it necessary to rely more on *gōshi* military contributions, the *han* administrators' freedom of maneouver was further reduced.

IV. Conclusion

I have discussed elsewhere the importance of these developments for politics in nineteenth-century Tosa. In the crisis situation that followed the coming of Perry the *han* government that showed such indecisiveness and weakness in the *gōshi* cases described above was hardly capable of inspiring loyalty or directing policy. Soon after the extent of the emergency was apparent, the traditionalists were replaced by Yoshida Tōyō, a vigorous reformer who resorted to the old and unpopular devices for raising defense money, and added new ones. This stirred *gōshi* and *shōya* anger. It was expressed in loyalist terms, and led to Yoshida's murder in 1862. For a time the *gōshi-shōya* loyalists were the most dynamic element in Kōchi, and they succeeded in adding Kōchi representation to loyalism on the national scene. But they overplayed their hand. The lowly rank of the activists did not qualify them for the posts they needed in order to work their will, and the stage was not yet set for the restoration of imperial rule. The fortuitous return of an able and strong daimyo, and the interval of moderation in national politics that followed the loyalist ascendancy made possible a victory of upper-rank moderation in which the Tosa loyalist leaders were scattered through flight, punishment, and execution. When Tosa reentered national politics in 1867 it was under the leadership of high-ranking loyalists like Itagaki and Gotō, and the *shōya* and *gōshi,* however important the contributions some of them had made as individuals, marched in the armies led by their superiors.[39]

Seen in the national setting, however, Tosa was relatively strong and stable, and its government astute and deliberate in its assessment of and participation on the national scene. It was also remote and relatively backward economically, less subject to the supposedly debilitating effects of national and, after

---

[39] *Sakamoto Ryōma and the Meiji Restoration* (Princeton, 1961); "Takechi Zuizan and the Tosa Loyalist Party", *Journal of Asian Studies,* XVIII, 2, (1959).

1860, foreign commerce. It is not so much the role of Tosa on the late Tokugawa scene that is at question here as it is the effect on Tosa of the late Tokugawa currents with which this essay began. These were, I believe, on the whole less marked and remarkable in social and economic matters than they were in the realm of the thought and in the rhetoric of political discourse.

In respect to general disregard for hereditary holders of authority, Tosa retainers and social leaders were no different from their contemporaries elsewhere in Japan. Several centuries of sheltered life in the Edo mansions had removed the daimyo from action and from sight, and references to incapacity and indifference of men "who never feel the winter's cold," to use the stock phrase, were common in Tosa as they were elsewhere.[40] If an able daimyo, often adoptive, happened to come up through the debilitating system, it was easy to transfer to his collaterals and top retainers—the *mombatsu*—the scorn that some still hesitated to apply to the traditional focus of samurai loyalty. The Tosa *shōya* and *gōshi* loyalists charged their betters with cowardice, laziness, and ignorance, and even claimed they were unable to read documents couched in the formal language of the day.

But more interesting than this, though again by no means unusual to Tosa, was the impact of ideology and education. The influence of Confucian teaching and acceptance of its criteria of government gave petitioners and memorialists an impregnable theoretical base from which to judge and reprove their superiors. They spoke confidently of the Way of Humanity (*jindō*), and the Voice of Heaven (*ten no kuchi*), and while the events of the 1780's doubtless helped them to see and hear these influences, their education had prepared them to identify and classify them. Kusunose's memorial to his daimyo in 1769 could appeal to T'ang T'ai Tsung as authority against the orders of the *bakufu,* and he held up his "people-first-ism" (*mimponshugi,* the phrase later proposed by Yoshino Sakuzō in the 1920's) as a wiser and practical alternative.[41] Fukutomi Hannojō, arguing against the monopoly laws in 1785, argued that the interests of the province and the interests of its farmers were one (*kokka no on tame, hyakushō no tame o hitomichi ni zonjikomitatematsuri*), and then, after due apologies for ignorance and impertinence, began his specifics with: "Is it not the case that all under heaven belongs to all under heaven, and not just to one man? Looked at in this way it cannot be said that the country (province) is one man's either. Does not the ruler's leadership exist because it is over the four classes of the people? If that is so there can be no ruler without the four people." [42] There was something new about the way these sentiments were applied, whether or not the phrasing was original, and that application was a product of the eighteenth century. And the *shōya,*

---

[40] For one famous example, *Hanron,* thought to be a work of Sakamoto's, *Sakamoto Ryōma,* 340f.

[41] Nakata, "Fukenroku ni miru Kusunose Seiin no hansei kaikakuron," *loc. cit.,* 19.

[42] Quoted in Hirao, *et al, Kōchi Shi shi* (Kōchi, 1958), 389. The wording begins, "*Tenka wa tenka no tenka, hitori no tenka ni arazu to ka ya. Kono setsu ni te mireba kuni mo hitori no kuni to wa mosaremajikusōrō.*"

whose confidence derived from an ascription of authority and legitimacy to the imperial throne, could not have made that connection before the work of Motoori Norinaga had provided, and his Tosa followers like Kamochi Masazumi (1791–1858) had popularized, the teachings of *kokugaku*.

If one grants this for the ideologues and advisors, whose courage in application may have developed faster than their thought did in originality, it becomes more striking still to see similar premises and arguments in the complaints of the underprivileged and less-educated. Even a plaintive 1844 petition from *ashigaru,* on the lowest rung of the military ladder, asking for the privileges of adopting family surnames and wearing wooden clogs on rainy days (!), speaks of usages in other areas, contradictory concessions made by the *han* for men when "abroad," cites *ashigaru* service to the realm in time of danger ("as musketmen we have to be the first to sacrifice ourselves in action"), and makes an interesting case for gratitude and service in return for these minimums of human dignity.[43] And the *gōshi,* hardly known as models of compassion themselves, phrased their resentment over the unpunished killing of one of their number in terms of the importance of human life.[44]

It is this tendency, which was clearly on the increase, to see issues in terms of universal principles and to argue requests in terms of such premises that marks, I believe, a different stage in the development of late Tokugawa Tosa and Japan. Not the least of these was the preference for province/country (*kuni*) over lord as basis for policy and argument. A simple farmer (*kage hyakushō*), summing up his care in planting trees and conservation, opines that he "believes it for the good of the province" (*okuni no tame ni ainaru mono to zonjimasu*).[45] These larger, less personal, and more frequently articulated criteria for judgment and action helped provide a setting for the nationalism, the reform, and the ambition of the nineteenth century. In this sense, as Maruyama Masao has put it, the categories of Confucianism served Japan well in an age of transition to modernization.

---

[43] Hirao, *shakai shi kō,* 79f.

[44] Hirao, *gōshi kiroku,* 152.

[45] Hirao, *nōgyō keizai shi,* 217.

CHAPTER NINETEEN

TALENT AND THE SOCIAL ORDER IN TOKUGAWA JAPAN

R. P. DORE

Reprinted with permission of the Past and Present
Society and the author from *Past and Present, a Journal
of historical studies*, No. 21 (April 1962)

THE SOCIAL SYSTEM DEVELOPED BY THE TOKUGAWA SHOGUNS IN THE first half of the seventeenth century was designed to last. Each individual had his proper place as a member of a family — usually, since most younger sons managed to get adopted, of a long-established family. Each family had its proper place in a graded hierarchy knit together by a network of feudal obligations. At the top, the Shogunal family of Tokugawa overlords claimed the allegiance of the fief-owning lords who ranked at the Tokugawa palace according to the size of their fief revenues and the length and nature of their families' services. Each feudal lord in turn had his own samurai retainers, again precisely ranked — sometimes in more than thirty separate categories — according to service and the size of their families' hereditary rice stipends. Each cultivating peasant owned a traditional right to till a portion of his fief-lord's land, and owed a traditional duty to pay heavy rice dues for the privilege. The old Imperial court at Kyoto and the religious foundations had their own smaller, partly independent but similar systems. Only the small world of the merchant and the urban artisan preserved any great fluidity.

The system brought Japan two centuries of peace and relative social stability, and peace and stability in their turn brought a growth in the national income which made possible a growth in educational facilities. At the same time the "civilization" of the militant warrior tradition and the realization that the moral doctrines of the Sung Confucianists offered an excellent doctrinal support for the régime, provided motives for feudal patronage of education. By the first half of the nineteenth century nearly every fief had its own fief school or schools, which admitted — and sometimes required the attendance of — sons of all but the lower ranks of samurai retainers.

This raised certain problems. Systems of formal education are apt to draw attention to the fact that human beings differ widely in their possession of intelligence, judgement, memory and other abilities which are valued in the society. Conflict can easily arise when it is realized that the distribution of these abilities does not necessarily correspond with the distribution of rewards — of income, power and prestige. Educational systems are thus often at the centre of an uneasy tension between the actual and various ideal systems of status. In Tokugawa Japan, educational segregation, whereby higher education was practically limited to samurai while the masses (including, often, the foot-soldiers) went to separate schools to learn the three Rs and read moral treatises encouraging them in habits of piety and diligence, removed any threat to the main division in status between samurai and the rest. But the system of formal education raised acute problems *within* the samurai class with its sharp internal divisions of status. The fief schools were in theory and, by the end of the period usually in practice, attended by all except the lower foot-soldier ranks of the samurai class. This raised obvious problems from the point of view of the school: for instance if the son of a high-ranking fief-elder turned out to be a dunce while the son of a lower samurai was a genius. What devices were adopted to prevent such occurrences becoming too embarrassingly obvious, or to mitigate their social ill-consequences when they did? Similar problems arose in the broader context of society as a whole. Was it, for instance, thought necessary to ensure that men of ability occupied the positions of authority. If so, how closely was the kind of ability demonstrated in school performance felt to be related to the required administrative ability? And how was the need for such ability reconciled with the exigencies of the system of status?

ABILITY AND STATUS IN THE SCHOOLS

As far as the problem of school organization was concerned, its magnitude was considerably lessened by the emphasis on the moral purposes of education. The purely intellectual accomplishment of learning to read Chinese was merely a means to an ethical end. A dull pupil who had difficulty with his books but who nevertheless was virtuous in his conduct, respectful to his superiors, loyal to his lord and filial to his parents had acquired the essentials. These were the qualities which were held up to praise. Mere cleverness was disparaged. The Sunday School approach implied Sunday School criteria of rating. Regularity of attendance was the clearest objective mark of the right moral attitudes. Said one teacher (though, be it noted for later reference, in a tone of sharp complaint):

> A student who attends regularly, even if of only average ability, is rewarded, whereas even an outstandingly good pupil, if he does not attend regularly, even if he is admirably behaved and accomplished, receives no prize.[1]

The fifth Tokugawa Shogun, Tsunayoshi (1680-1709), was largely responsible for the prevalence of this attitude, and that stern upholder of the virtues of intellect, the contemporary Confucian scholar

Ogyū Sorai, is scathing about the decline in intellectual standards which resulted from Tsunayoshi's passion for Confucian sermons[2] — both for listening to them and for giving them in (to paraphrase Gibbon on Marcus Aurelius) a more public manner than was perhaps consistent with the modesty of a sage or the dignity of a Shogun. The pattern of education set by the early schools during Tsunayoshi's reign remained the dominant one throughout the period. Generally, standards of scholarship were not high; little emphasis was placed on wide reading in Chinese history or on the writing of Chinese prose and poetry. Most students could get through the Four Books and some of the Five Classics which were the staple texts, and, where the criteria of excellence were less intellectual ability — the distribution of which rarely corresponds to a scale of hereditary status — than effort, regular attendance and good conduct which training can instil in almost anyone, the danger to the status system was minimal.

In case there should be any mistake, however, some schools went out of their way to emphasise that rank was all-important, and this was the easier in that *rei* — one of the cardinal virtues to be inculcated — was interpreted to mean the meticulous observance of distinctions of status. Some detailed regulations are recorded. At one school, that run by the government of the Kaga fief, for instance, it was laid down that members from the highest families should come to the school accompanied by only two retainers, one additional servant to look after the student's sandals during lectures, and one umbrella-holder on rainy days. The next rank could have one retainer, a sandal-minder and an umbrella-holder. The next, one retainer and a sandal-minder, but they should carry their own umbrellas. Younger sons and those of the lowest rank should come without servants; the school would provide someone to look after their sandals *en masse*.[3] From other schools there survive detailed regulations of seating in the lecture room and the exact place at which swords were to be removed by people of different ranks — at the entrance, in a waiting room, or at their actual seat in the lecture hall.[4] In such schools, tuition methods consisted chiefly of lectures to large classes with little or no give-and-take between teacher and pupils, together with individual tuition alone or in small groups of the same rank. The possibility of differences in ability becoming embarrassingly obvious was thus minimised.

There was no question of education being a selective process designed first to discover intellectual ability and then train it. It was, rather, a means of imparting the degree of moral and intellectual training necessary to all samurai by virtue of their general duty to protect and govern society. It followed that such training was most important for the higher ranks inasmuch as their responsibilities in this regard were heavier. This provided the justification for rules such as those at the school of the Mito fief which set a minimum scale of attendance ranging from fifteen days a month for eldest sons of upper ranks to eight days a month for eldest sons of the lowest rank and younger sons of the next higher ranks.[5]

Such was what might be called the traditional practice which predominated until the end of the eighteenth century. Thereafter, as we shall see, it was subject to some modification, but even so it remained a dominant practice until the end of the period.

It is not, however, the whole story even of educational practices in the early part of the period. In the first place, despite the frequent overt insistence on the greater importance of moral rather than intellectual accomplishments, the scholars who taught in these schools did, after all, owe their positions less to their superior moral qualities than to their superior knowledge. They were intellectual specialists and as such could not be entirely indifferent to the value of intellectual accomplishments.

It is perhaps significant that there is much more emphasis in Japanese Confucian writings on the need for humble respect of the teacher than in the Chinese Confucian tradition. Yoshikawa Kōjirō has recently commented on this as an expression of Japanese "disciplinarianism".[6] It may be so; but it may also be related to the difference in the positions occupied by the scholar in Chinese and Japanese society. The Chinese literati occupied positions of power, prestige, and comparative affluence. The Confucian scholar in Tokugawa Japan rarely exercised power and he earned less. Deference was all he could claim, and it is not surprising that he was jealous of this, his sole form of privilege. He claimed such deference not for himself but for his mastery of the Way of the Sages. In this sense an insistence on the explicit award of recognition to such mastery was a means of bolstering the Confucian scholar's own uncertain claim to deference from society at large.

Secondly, there were certain practical considerations. Scholarship was in itself a distinct profession of which these teachers were the chief exponents, and it was a profession the need for which was recognised by fief authorities, as well as by the scholars themselves. The mediocre level of the ordinary moral education was not such as to train specialists. More intensive and more academic training was necessary if the teachers were to have successors.

This was one of the principal objectives of the widespread practice of selecting a limited number of dormitory students to live in the school for full time study.[7]　In numbers they might range from as few as half a dozen to as many as a hundred, and usually they were students who had shown some taste or aptitude for study.　These students were carried further in their Chinese studies and the teaching methods used — reading and construing texts by turn in class — were such that differences of ability could not be concealed.　It would have been impractical to insist on differences in rank.　Instead, recourse was had to a different criterion of status — relative age.　In the Okayama fief school, for instance, the rule for dormitory students was laid down as follows:

> When you are together in the lecture halls, even if there are only two or three of you, never break the principle of seating by seniority.　If you do the younger will either feel uncomfortable or arrogantly proud.　At the daimyo's court, rank is all-important and the inferior may not vie with the superior.　But in learning seniority is important and the essential thing is to respect the proper relations of senior and junior.[8]

Here was a convenient compromise.　Very roughly age differences corresponded to differences in academic achievement so that the respect for intellectual excellence was, as it were, covertly built into the system.　But it was smuggled in under cover of the respectable Confucian principle of respect for seniors, and had precedents in ancient Chinese educational practice.　In this form, therefore, it was not too subversive of the system of status.　The high-ranking samurai had to defer to his lower-ranking senior, but this was less damaging to his *amour-propre* since no judgement of his merit was implied.　He too would be a senior in his turn.

Some schools used a different criterion for determining status — that of the order of entering the school.　This approximated to the age criterion in effect, but was more closely related to actual achievement.　The rules of the Chōshū fief school at Hagi, for instance, say:

> Among the dormitory students the order of seating shall, irrespective of nobility or baseness of rank, depend on the order of entering the school. In this way, of course, those who are advanced in their studies will provide models for those who are less advanced, and those who are less advanced will respect those who are ahead of them.[9]

The respect for academic achievement as such was most clearly formalised in this device.

The world of scholarship was, thus, a privileged island separated from the outside world, much as the church was in feudal Europe. Privileged, note, but not necessarily of high prestige; some feudal lords treated their Confucian scholars with very much the same kind of condescending disdain as the English gentry accord their vicars in the novels of Jane Austen.　The exact definition of the boundaries of this privileged island was often a ticklish matter which required precise regulation. At the Yonezawa fief school, for instance, apropos of the normal duty of politeness which required students to attend the funerals of parents of their fellow-pupils, the rules say:

> However, although all students are the same within the school, outside the gates there are differences of rank, and hence it is proper for students of high rank simply to send a servant to the funerals of parents of students of low rank.[10]

ABILITY IN ADMINISTRATION

So much for the means whereby, within the schools, the Confucian tradition of respect for scholarship and the need to maintain a scholarly tradition were integrated with the need to maintain the hierarchy of status. What of the problems of running the society, and of the relation of scholastic training to administration? Confucius' insistence on the "rectification of names" — on making sure that the prince was princely and the minister ministerial — was open to two interpretations. One was that embodied in the Chinese examination system — that those who demonstrate virtue and ability should be raised to the status which those qualities warranted. It was the other which, as we have seen, prevailed in Japan — the view that each person should be properly trained to acquire the abilities requisite to his hereditary status. (And it is interesting to note, in passing, that in their discussions on the heredity *versus* environment problem, Tokugawa writers generally come down heavily on the optimistic side of nurture. It was not their genes but their social heredity which justified the superiority of the upper classes.)

The question is whether the acceptance of birth as the main criterion for the distribution of status and authority still permitted the society to operate with reasonable efficiency. By and large it probably did. In the first place, and most important, selection according to ability was not entirely ruled out. The central Tokugawa administration and each fief administration had more samurai retainers available than there were administrative offices to be filled. A system of bureaucratic offices separate from the system of hereditary family ranks but related to it in that each office could only be filled from a limited range of ranks, still, therefore, permitted a certain amount of selection by ability.[11] Secondly, the practice of adopting adolescents into families without heirs or with congenitally deficient sons permitted the occasional importation of ability into high-ranking families. Thirdly, it should not be overlooked that, once the régime was established and its routines worked out, no great administrative skill was required. Those in high positions needed authority rather than intelligence, and authority is more easily acquired by the simple expedient of being born and bred to it. If there were still irreducible defects in those born to command, the extreme formalisation of respectful behaviour helped to compensate for them.[12] Fourthly, the device of allowing able inferiors to do the real work of incompetent superiors further mitigated the possible damage of a hereditary system. And fifthly, in order to ensure that there should be able inferiors it seems that there always was, in practice, and despite the accepted theory, a certain amount of promotion across barriers of rank at the lower levels of the hierarchy.

The professional Confucian scholars and their military equivalents, the teachers of swordsmanship and the use of the lance, were an obvious example.[13] They moved with relative freedom from fief to fief, secured appointments on the basis of their demonstrated talents and were only partially involved in the hierachy of hereditary status. The clerical staffs who did the actual bookwork of administration — men who, as Sorai once complained,[14] were by his standards practically illiterate — were appointed from among the foot-soldiers, or even sometimes from the commoner class.

Given these mitigating factors the hereditary system was not, then, likely to lead to the total breakdown of society, and in the seventeenth century it seems to have been little questioned. By the 1720s, however, when the sense of financial and moral crisis first begins to grip the Tokugawa government, there is a change. The system of *tashidaka* — salary supplements for certain key jobs — was introduced in 1723 with the explicit purpose of opening positions to men of ability in ranks lower than those normally qualified to fill them. Throughout the subsequent reforms, too — in those of Matsudaira Sadanobu at the end of the eighteenth century, in the more short-lived attempts at reform of Mizuno Tadakuni between 1841 and 1843, and in the accelerating upheaval of the 1860s — one can discern a consistent trend towards the modification of the system of official appointments in such a way as to give more scope for honest talents. And this trend in the central Tokugawa administration was paralleled — and stimulated — by similar trends in the administration of some of the major fiefs.

Several factors lay behind these developments. The recurring sense of crisis caused by the spread of administrative corruption and the inability of the fiscal system to adjust itself to the growth of a money economy and spiralling standards of consumption was one; and it was greatly magnified in importance after 1840 when these internal dangers to stability were compounded by the growing external threat posed by the Western powers. Secondly, the growth of scholarship brought a much wider awareness of Chinese and Japanese history; there was the beginning of a science of comparative government, and frequent discussion in scholarly writings of the relative merits of a feudal and a centralized prefectural system of administration. Most writers — aware, as they were, of Chinese criticisms of the Chinese examination system — reached the conclusion that their own feudal system with its stress on loyalty and a sense of personal obligation for the welfare of subordinates was superior to the Chinese system with its reliance on impersonal codes and its temptations to ambitious selfishness.[15] But there were some who argued that to appoint officials by the accident of birth was like "keeping cats to scare burglars and setting dogs to catch mice",[16] and urged at least some modification of the hereditary principle by salary cuts for the grossly incompetent and promotions for those who excelled.[17]

CHANGES IN THE SCHOOLS

The effect on the schools was not automatic. Administrative skills, as they were usually defined, could be identified on the job and their connection with book learning was a matter of dispute. The average Confucian teacher was remote from practical affairs, and although there were occasional suggestions that the schools should introduce vocational training courses designed to teach potential administrators the details of fiscal and judicial administration, of fief protocol or local geography,[18] such suggestions were slow in taking effect. In the main Tokugawa school, for instance, it was not until the 1850s that the Confucian scholars in charge accepted the need for such courses in principle.[19] But by then it was too late for a reform of Confucian education; already the new "Western learning" (or "Dutch learning" as it was usually called) was gradually gaining recognition and incorporation — usually in a separate department or satellite school — into the fief schools. The "Dutch studies" of map-making, strategy, navigation, chemistry, metallurgy, medicine, and eventually political economy, were quite clearly of practical importance, and their incorporation into the school curriculum was an important factor in securing recognition of the schools as training-grounds and selecting mechanisms for administrative talent.

And this necessarily had reciprocal effects on the internal organization of the schools themselves — there was a shifting of the balance achieved between the observance of hereditary status and the recognition of talent, decisively in favour of the latter.

These trends can be traced most clearly in the history of the Hagi school, the school of the Chōshū fief which played a major part in the overthrow of Tokugawa feudalism and the establishment of a centralized government in 1868. From its very beginning in 1719 the school insisted on ranking its pupils according to their date of entry, at the expense of the system of hereditary ranks. There seems, also, to have been an idea that the school would strengthen the fief (it combined, of course, training in military skills with Chinese studies); and this may be the reason why, in what Ogyū Sorai called "the secretive way these Western lords have",[20] the fief tried to prevent the Tokugawa government from learning about the school. The school was, moreover, directed by one of Sorai's pupils and there was, therefore much less insistence on the moral aims of education.

However, in the series of extant documents, the first occurrence of the word *jinzai* — human talent — is probably not earlier than the 1790s. It is a document announcing a fief loan to the school to enable it to take more dormitory pupils. It deplores the decline in standards at the school and goes on:

> In the first place the production of human talent (or of talented men) so that they can serve the fief is the fundamental principle of fief administration. The loan is made in the belief that if there are more pupils then there will be a greater proportion of talented men produced.[21]

But this still did not mean a very widespread search for talent. The number of dormitory pupils was increased to thirty. Since it was a nine-year course this means about seventy-five pupils trained per generation, or one for every thirty-three samurai families in the fief.[22] And it is probable that higher-ranking samurai had better chances of entering the school.

In the nineteenth century the insistence on the production of talent became more strident. In 1840 a memorandum to the school says that graduates will be taken into the feudal lord's service according to the talents they show. It then goes on to urge the school administrators not to keep in the school as dormitory pupils those who fail to show promise in their first three-year period, nor to keep for a third three-year period those whose achievement has fallen off in the second. "The success or failure of the school", it says, "depends entirely on its production of talented men, not on the numbers of students".[23] As might be expected, such a rigorous insistence on the importance of ability ran up against opposition. Another order three months later complains in strong language that despite instructions that the school is to be run on the basis of talent, people are too concerned about rank and are failing to cooperate with each other, the which, it says, is utterly to be deplored.[24]

These complaints were repeated in succeeding years and eventually, in the 1850s, a system of classes was introduced further differentiating students on the grounds of ability. Students were divided into five groups; the high-steppers, the daily improvers, the diligent, the idle and the outcasts: and seating order was to depend on the class and the order of promotion into it. There was no question of sparing anyone's feelings.[25] Two years later it was ordered that a register should be kept of those who had reached the top two classes; students who appeared in the register would have priority in filling official positions.[26] Another order, probably of 1858, again deplores the hindrance to effective cooperative study caused by consciousness of rank and insists that

> Henceforth everything that happens in the school shall be considered as outside the system;[27] differences of rank shall be ignored and in all matters precedence shall depend on the extent of a student's ability and achievement, and on his accomplishments in the various skills.[28]

So the process was complete, and although the first important step in 1840 seems to have been the result of the personal reforms of an innovating fief minister, the trend continued through all the factional tussles which followed. The school had become explicitly an institution for the identification and training of talent and, in order that it could fulfil that function effectively, prestige within the school came to be awarded on the basis of achievement, at the expense of the traditional deference accorded to rank.

There were not many other schools where the object of identifying good administrative timber was made as explicit as in Hagi, though a shift in the same direction is apparent in a good many. For instance, the Kaga school quoted earlier for its regulations about umbrella-holders, changed from seating by rank to seating by age.[29] The Wakayama fief experimented as early as 1803 with a scheme of triennial recruiting examinations for its bureaucracy. The feudal lord posed a practical question concerning fief policy which the students were to answer with judicious citing of historical examples — and also, it was insisted, use of their own judgement. The order announcing this and urging the "education of human talent and learning for practical use" quite clearly promises official positions to those who do well.[30]   One or two other fiefs[31] introduced this kind of examination later, and general school examinations designed primarily to encourage studiousness and to test fitness for promotion within the school became very common after 1800.   If still only a small number of fiefs adopted the Chōshū policy of selecting officials from outstanding students, at the other end of the scale a good many more made certain minimum educational standards a necessary qualification for all official posts, whether in the civil bureaucracies of the fiefs or in their military guards.   Students who failed to reach these (usually rather low) standards were not only debarred from official posts, but sometimes suffered a reduction in their hereditary stipends as well.[32]

The tidy structure of Tokugawa society was thus subject to various and increasing internal pressures, both in the schools and outside. There was, throughout, something of a conflict between the emphasis on hereditary right on which its highly stratified system of status and power was based, and the natural tendency of teachers to find ways of according recognition and reward to achievement and ability.   But this inherent tension was effectively resolved by institutional devices which achieved a considerable measure of compromise.   Towards the end of the period, however, other dynamic factors arose which decisively shifted the balance of that compromise.   There was, firstly, the growing sense of external and internal crisis leading to a demand for ability in leadership and administration.   Secondly, partly as a response to this and partly as a result of the introduction from the West of new branches of learning, there was an increasing incorporation into school curricula of elements of clear vocational relevance to administration.   Thirdly, one should not overlook the effects of the cumulative growth in the *quantity* of education.   The sheer expansion in the size of schools led naturally to the rationalisation of their organisation, the division into grades and the establishment of objective tests of fitness to pass from one grade to the next.   The combination of these three factors operated to reinforce, and give greater scope to, the tendency to stress achievement inherent in the teacher's role.   The hereditary principle was necessarily weakened, both in the school and in the bureaucracies of the fiefs and of the Tokugawa government.   Slowly the barriers of status began to give way.   By the end of the period a man's prestige and his power, if still not his income, was coming to depend less on who he was than on what he could do.

It was a gradual process, though much accelerated in the last decades of the period.   It was also a vital one.   The Meiji Restoration

R. P. Dore

has often seemed a great watershed. And indeed, given the usually accepted picture of Tokugawa society, no change seems more revolutionary than the attack on the system of status in the 1870s, heralded by such resounding declarations as Fukuzawa's opening sentence in *The Encouragement of Learning*: "Heaven did not create men above men, nor put men under men". To emphasise the ancestry of such ideas in the schools and in their subtle subversion of the established hierarchy, is not to deny the boldness of the final challenge; it merely goes some long way towards explaining it.

NOTES

[1] Nakayama Shōrei of Kumamotō, *Gakusei-kō*, (c. 1790) in Mombushō, *NihonKyōikushi Shiryō*, 1880-2 (hereafter *NKSS*), v. p. 614.

[2] *Seidan*, (edn. *Nihon Keizai Taiten*), ix. pp. 191-2.

[3] *NKSS*, ii. p. 87.

[4] *NKSS*, i. p. 744, The Yonezawa school.

[5] *NKSS*, i. p. 351.

[6] *Nihon no Shinjō*, 1960, pp. 148-55.

[7] This was, in fact, often the earlier form, preceding the development of large-class general education. It was an outgrowth, of course, of the scholar's private *juku* where pupil-apprentices gathered at the foot of the master.

[8] Okayama-ken Kyōiku-kai, *Okayama-ken Kyōikushi*, 1937, p. 56.

[9] *NKSS*, ii. p. 661 (1720).

[10] *NKSS*, i. p. 758.

[11] For an excellent illustration of how the system worked in Okayama see Taniguchi Sumio "Han kashindan no keisei to kōzō", *Shigaku Zasshi*, lxvi, No. 6, pp. 594-616.

[12] It is more difficult to withhold deference from those who lack the temperamental weight to command it when the forms of deference required are precisely regulated and deviation becomes obvious and glaring. Moreover, as de Tocqueville remarked, in feudal societies "the master readily obtains prompt, complete, respectful and easy obedience from his servants, because they revere in him not only their master but the whole class of masters. He weighs down their will by the whole weight of the aristocracy." *Democracy in America*, (Vintage edition, 1954), ii. p. 189.

[13] See J. W. Hall, "The Confucian Teacher in Tokugawa Japan", in A. F. Wright and D. S. Nivison, *Confucianism in Action*, Stanford, 1959).

[14] Sorai, writing to Yoshimune, complains of the low quality of official documents which resulted and urged the use of properly trained scholars. Since compilations of legal precedents were written in *kana* rather than in proper Chinese characters they were difficult to run through, and anyone looking for a particular case usually gave it up as a bad job and instead set about finding someone with a good memory. (*Seidan*, edn. *Keizai Taiten*, iv. p. 190).

[15] See, e.g., Nishikawa Joken, *Hayakushō-bukuro*, c. 1700, edn. *Nihon Keizai Sōsho*, (hereafter *NKZS*), v. pp. 169-70; Ogyu Sorai, *Kenen Danyo*, c. 1680 (?), edn. *Nihon Bunko*, iv. p. 17; Hirose Tanso, *Ugen*, 1840, edn.

NKZS, xxxii. p. 99; Endō Yasumichi, *Shigaku Mondō, c.* 1840, edn. *NKZS*, xxvi. p. 237.

¹⁶ Ise Sadatake, *Ansai Zuihitsu, c.* 1770, edn. *Kojitsu Sōsho*, xxvi. p. 127.

¹⁷ See, e.g., Kaiho Seiryo, *Shōridan, c.* 1800, edn. *NKZS*, xxvi. p. 204; Nakai Chikuzan, *Sōbō Kigen*, 1789, edn. *NKZS*, xvi. pp. 320-3; Hirose Tansō, *Ugen*, 1840, *NKZS*, xxxii. pp. 105, 119-120, 130.

¹⁸ See, e.g., Nakayama Shōrei, *Gakusei-kō, c.* 1790, edn. *NKZS*, v. p. 619; and, for a proposal of Tanaka Genshin made in 1787, Ogawa Wataru, Aizu-han Kyoiku-kō, 1941, p. 105.   ¹⁹ *NKSS*, vii. pp. 99, 101-5.

²⁰ *Seidan*, edn. Keizai Taiten, ix. pp. 189/93.   ²¹ *NKSS*, ii. p. 665.

²² Suematsu Kenchō, *Bōchō Kaitenshi*, (revised edn. 1921), i. pp. 42-6 gives a total of 2,599 samurai families of all grades in 1852 (excluding foot-soldiers and retainers of retainers).   ²³ *NKSS*, ii. p. 676.   ²⁴ *NKSS*, ii. p. 677.

²⁵ *NKSS*, ii. p. 748. This was started in Feb. 1859 according to *Bōchō Kaitenshi*, (ii. p. 564). The terms were *kōsoku* (an old Confucian word for a "prize pupil") *nisshin, senshin, yūtai* and *hinseki*.

²⁶ *Bōchō Kaitenshi*, iv. p. 535.

²⁷ *Seigai* is the term used. Interestingly, an almost contemporary edict to the pupils of the Kagoshima school uses the same term to describe what the school is *not*. Learning, it says, is for the good of the fief, and those who look on it as *seigai* just like Buddhism are guilty of grievous error.

²⁸ *NKSS*, ii. p. 706.   ²⁹ *NKSS*, ii. p. 176: above p. 62.

³⁰ *NKSS*, ii. p. 816.

³¹ e.g. Kurume (*NKSS*, iii. p. 41) Iwamura (*NKSS*, i. p. 479) and the Tokugawa government itself after 1853 (*NKSS*, vii. p. 87).

³² The fiefs of Aizu, Saga and Tosa are only three among many, (*NKSS*, iii. p. 123; ii. p. 906; i. p. 680).

CHAPTER TWENTY

THE RESTORATION MOVEMENT IN CHŌSHŪ

ALBERT CRAIG

Reprinted from *Journal of Asian Studies,*
Vol. XVIII, No. 2 (February 1959)

UNTIL recent times, and to a certain extent, even at the present, most historians have spoken of the movements which led to the Meiji Restoration as lower samurai movements. It is my aim in this article to show that they were not. First, negatively, I hope to show by a consideration of what is meant by the term "lower samurai" and by the application of this to the Chōshū scene that the early Restoration movement or *sonnō jōi* (Honor the Emperor, Expel the Barbarian) movement[1] cannot be described as a lower samurai movement. Second, positively, I will attempt an alternate characterization in terms of the different groups participating in this movement in Chōshū from its inception in 1858 until its culmination in the Chōshū Civil War in 1865.

The first reason why the *sonnō jōi* movement should not be termed a "lower samurai movement" is that the phrase "lower samurai movement" is so ambiguous and so vague as to be more of a hindrance than a help in characterizing the groups which were active on the eve of the Meiji Restoration. Definitions of what is meant by "lower samurai" vary from writer to writer. Some will define it in such a manner that ninety to ninety-five per cent of the military class are lower samurai; others define it such that only about fifty per cent of the samurai class are called lower samurai. Such widely variant characterizations result from the great number of different criteria used in these definitions. Some writers define "lower samurai" in terms of the gradations of feudal rank; others have said that those samurai who did not have the right to an audience with their daimyo were lower samurai. Max Weber held that samurai without fiefs were lower samurai;[2] still other historians have defined "lower samurai" in terms of arbitrary income brackets. As an example of the latter, one historian has suggested that all samurai with fiefs or stipends of less than one hundred *koku* were lower samurai, those with fiefs or stipends ranging from one hundred to two hundred and fifty *koku* were middle samurai, and those with more than two hundred and fifty *koku*, upper samurai.[3]

However varied the above criteria may be, each contains a certain truth concerning the status of samurai during the Tokugawa period. In the appropriate context, each can be used as a working definition, and as such, each has certain advantages and certain disadvantages. Unfortunately, however, many writers blithely use "lower samurai" without bothering to define the term at all. This is inexcusable: where a

---

[1] It is well to distinguish between *sonnō* and *jōi* as ideas and *sonnō jōi* as the name of a movement. Both *sonnō* and, to a lesser extent *jōi*, continued down to, and even after 1868. The *sonnō jōi* movement, on the other hand, ended early in 1865; or, alternatively, one might say in 1865 it underwent a metamorphosis emerging as the *tōbaku* (Overthrow the Bakufu) movement.

[2] Shimmi Kikiji, *Kakyū shizoku no kenkyū* [*A Study of Lower Samurai*] (Tokyo, 1953), p. 2.

[3] Tanaka Akira, "Chōshū-han no Tempō kaikaku" ["The Tempō Reform in Chōshū"], *Historia*, No. 18 (1957), pp. 28–29.

A. Craig

variety of definitions makes "lower samurai" vague, a lack of definition reduces the term to an absurdity. Consequently, one finds writers lumping together men of diverse rank and status (Saigō, Ōkubo, Kido, Takasugi, Itō, Yamagata, Ōkuma, Gotō, Itagaki, etc.) as if all were equal or almost equal in station.

Further, what is more significant for the purpose of this article is that even when "lower samurai" is rigorously defined, it is still impossible to apply it to the *sonnō jōi* movement in such a way that it becomes valid to call the movement a lower samurai movement. This can be illustrated by an application to the Chōshū *sonnō jōi* movement of the two most common, and perhaps most valid, definitions of "lower samurai."

The first definition distinguishes between *shi*[a] (alternately *shizoku*[b] or *shibun*[c] or *shikaku*[d]) and *sotsu*[e] (alternately *keihai*[f] or *keisotsu*[g]).[4] That is to say, it distinguishes between samurai and soldier, or, since "samurai" is used in English to denote the entire military class, between knight and soldier.[5] By this definition, "lower samurai" is defined as *sotsu* or soldier. In terms of the realities of Tokugawa society, this is one of the best possible definitions. Throughout the Tokugawa period the distinction

---

[4] It should be noted that there is a difference between *shi* and *sotsu* when they are used as general terms roughly equivalent in their denotation to *shikaku* and *keihai*, and *shi* (or *shizoku*) and *sotsu* (or *sotsuzoku*[i]) as names given to administrative categories after the Meiji Restoration. *Shizoku* as an administrative category was first established in 1869 (Meiji 2.6). It was set up as a new national class beneath the *kazoku*[m] (nobles and former daimyo) and above the commoners at the same time that the daimyo gave up their fiefs and vassals to the Emperor (*hanseki hōkan*[n]). Six months later the Meiji government set up the distinction between *shizoku* and *sotsu;* originally this was to apply only to the former retainers of the Shogun. Actually, however, this distinction was picked up and used by almost all of the *han*. In fact, in most cases, the *han* went on to make many finer distinctions within these two major categories, mirroring the many fine distinctions of rank of the Tokugawa period. As a consequence, in 1870 (Meiji 3.9), the government issued an order legitimizing the *han*'s usage of these two categories but prohibiting the various finer distinctions. The difficulty with this order was that the decision as to who should be placed in the *shizoku* and who in the *sotsu*, was left to the various *han*. As a result, groups that in one *han* were made *shizoku* were in another, made *sotsu*. Some, for example, put the stratum of *kachi* in the *shizoku* and others put them in the class of *sotsu*. Some such as Mita-*han* said that samurai living outside of the castle town (*chishi*[o], literally, "country samurai") should be *sotsu;* others such as Takamatsu-*han* said they should be *shizoku*. Some *han* included *baishin* among the *sotsu*, while others made up an entirely new category, *baisotsu*[p], for the rear vassals. (See Shimmi, pp. 1–8.) Because of these many irregularities, an order was issued by the Meiji government in 1872 (Meiji 5.1) abolishing the category of *sotsu*. The *han* were instructed to include all *sotsu* who had been hereditary retainers in the class of *shizoku* and to register all others, such as commoners who had been permitted to wear swords and to bear a name, single generation samurai, peasant officials, and the like, as commoners (*heimin*). This immediately gave rise to protests from those newly registered as commoners and a "Restore Rank Movement" (*fukuzoku undō*[q]) began which continued until 1887. Moreover, the older distinctions were unofficially continued: the old class or *shi* applied the pejorative "upstart *shizoku*" (*nari agari shizoku*[r]) to those newly elevated from the *sotsu* to the *shizoku*, in much the same way that the former nobles of the Court (*kuge kazoku*[s]) looked down on the newly ennobled daimyo as "upstart nobles" (*shin kazoku*[t], literally, "new nobles"). Consequently, it must be kept in mind that *shi* or *shikaku* in the Tokugawa sense is not strictly the same as *shi* or *shizoku* in the 1869–72 administrative sense, and that *sotsu* or *keihai* in the Tokugawa sense is not exactly the same as *sotsu* or *sotsuzoku* in the early Meiji sense. Yet, in spite of the lack of perfect congruence, the Meiji administrative categories were obviously intended to mirror the Tokugawa classes and were substantially the same except for borderline cases, and therefore I felt justified in treating them together under one definition.

[5] In English the use of "samurai" is both broader and narrower than in Japanese: broader in that it designates the entire *bushi* class and not just its upper levels, and narrower in that it fails to include Court or temple samurai who were not *bushi*.

between *shi* and *sotsu* (or between *shikaku* and *keihai*) was the fundamental cleavage within the military class. In Chōshū, for example, there were seventeen ranks or strata within the class of *shi* or knights, and twenty-three of *sotsu* or soldiers.[6] Within each of these two divisions there was a certain limited measure of mobility; between them there was almost none.

This distinction, moreover, was not limited to Chōshū alone but it was fundamental in most of the *han* in Japan. Shimazu Hisamitsu of Satsuma, for example, criticized the early Meiji conscription law saying that it "lowered *shi* making *sotsu* of them."[7] A contemporary Japanese scholar, Shimmi Kikiji, in his work on the "lower samurai" of Owari-*han* writes that "in the period of the military houses there was a strict status distinction between *shi* and *sotsu*," and he limited his study to an investigation of the latter.[8]

In Chōshū at the beginning of the Bakumatsu period in 1853 there were about 11,000 samurai; this is, of course, the number of samurai families and not the number of individuals within the samurai class. Of these 11,000 samurai about 5,600 were direct vassals and the remaining 5,400 were *baishin*[h] or rear vassals.[9] Of the direct vassals, about fifty-two per cent were *shi* and forty-eight per cent, *sotsu*. Comparably exact figures are unavailable for the class of rear vassals but known examples suggest that the proportion of *shi* to *sotsu* was roughly the same among rear vassals as among direct vassals.[10] That the distinction between *shi* and *sotsu* was even more fundamental than the one between direct and rear vassal can be seen by the fact that while a direct vassal *shi* was higher in social status than a rear vassal *shi*, a rear vassal *shi* was higher than a direct vassal *sotsu*.[11]

When this first definition is applied to the *sonnō jōi* movement in Chōshū we can immediately see that it was not a lower samurai movement, a movement of *sotsu*. Even excluding the Elders and others of the highest strata of *shi* who were a part of the movement after 1862, we find that a large number of the *sonnō jōi* intellectuals, those in Chōshū associated with the school of Yoshida Shōin, were not lower samurai. Yoshida Shōin himself, Kido Kōin, Takasugi Shinsaku, Kusaka Genzui, Inoue Kaoru, Maebara Issei, Hirozawa Saneomi, and perhaps even Ōmura Masujirō, to mention only a few of the more prominent figures, were all *shi*, all upper samurai.

A second definition of the term "lower samurai," one which also has considerable merit, is substantially different from the first. This second definition limits the use of the term "upper samurai" to the top two strata, and a part of the third, out of a total of seventeen strata of *shi*. It then discerns an intermediary class of middle samurai consisting of the other part of the third stratum and the next four strata of *shi*; and finally, it lumps together the remaining ten ranks of *shi*, twenty-three ranks of *sotsu*,

---

[6] Suematsu Kenchō, *Bōchō kaiten shi* [*A History of Chōshū and the Meiji Restoration*] (Tokyo, 1921), I, 36–39.

[7] Shimmi, p. 1.

[8] Shimmi, p. 1.

[9] Umetani Noboru, "Meiji ishin ni okeru kiheitai no mondai" ["The Problem of the Kiheitai in the History of the Meiji Restoration"], *Jimbun gakuhō*, No. 3 (1953), pp. 17–18. Other records have placed the number of families of rear vassals as high as 6,000.

[10] Kimura Motoi of Meiji University has kindly given me figures which he obtained from the *Kerai kyūroku chō*[u] of 1870 showing the breakdown of the retainers (rear vassals) of Masuda Uemon, an Elder of Chōshū. Of a total of 538 retainers, 263 were *shi* and 275 *sotsu*.

[11] *Bōchō kaiten shi*, I, 41.

and the entire body of rear vassals, into one great class of lower samurai. Like the first, this definition is very common: it was used by the Chōshū government in the administrative reform of the first year of Meiji;[12] it was used in the *Bōchō kaiten shi*, the comprehensive history of Bakumatsu Chōshū;[13] and a definition very close to this was implied by Fukuzawa Yukichi when in his autobiography he spoke of himself as a lower samurai,[14] or in his work *Kyūhanjō*, he spoke of those of the rank of *kachi*[i] and below as lower samurai.[15]

Even apart from its widespread use there is almost as much to be said for this second definition as there is for the first. Though the distinction between *shi* and *sotsu* was primary during the Tokugawa period, there were immense differences between the upper and lower strata of *shi*. Socially and economically the upper *shi* and the low-ranking *shi* were almost in two separate worlds: the highest-ranking *shi* in Chōshū had a fief of 16,000 *koku*, larger than that of many daimyo; on the other hand, hundreds of lower *shi* received stipends of less than forty *koku*. Throughout the Tokugawa period and even during the Bakumatsu period, bureaucratic position in the *han* was limited almost exclusively to the top four strata of *shi*. However superior the lower *shi* might have felt towards the *sotsu*, when viewed from the vantage ground of an upper *shi*, his situation was not vastly different from that of the *sotsu*. Sufu Masanosuke, a *shi* of the fourth highest rank and the leader of the activist bureaucratic clique that controlled the Chōshū government from 1858 to 1864, once lamented during a period of crisis in 1864 that he could do nothing since his rank was so low.[16] This statement was made in unusual circumstances; nevertheless, it indicates the great differences in position and power existing even within the top strata of *shi*.

Upon applying this second definition to the Chōshū samurai class, we find that less than one per cent of the samurai are upper samurai; about fourteen per cent are middle samurai, and eighty-five per cent are lower samurai.[17] By this definition al-

---

[12] Kimura Motoi, "Hagi-han zaichi kashindan ni tsuite" ["Country Vassal Groups in Chōshū"], *SZ*, LXII, No. 8 (1953), 34.

[13] *Bōchō kaiten shi*, I, 35, 47. This second definition is implicit when, for example, the *mukyūdōri*[w] or *kachi* are referred to as lower samurai. This may well reflect the early Meiji use of the term. The *Bōchō kaiten shi* also recognizes the distinction between *shi* and *sotsu* as fundamental throughout the Tokugawa period.

[14] Fukuzawa Yukichi, *The Autobiography of Fukuzawa Yukichi*, trans. Kiyooka Eiichi (Tokyo, 1948), p. 19. "Children of lower samurai families like ours were obliged to use a respectful manner of address in speaking to the children of high samurai families. . . ."

[15] Fukuzawa Yukichi, *Kyūhanjō*, trans. Carmen Blacker, *MN*, IX (1953), p. 311. Fukuzawa's distinction between *kyūnin*[w], those with fiefs, and *kachi*, which often refers specifically to those who march in the cortege of their daimyo, but here used in its more general sense as foot soldier, is clearly not the same as our distinction between *shi* and *sotsu*. And yet Fukuzawa refers to it as the fundamental cleavage in the samurai class in Nakatsu-*han*. Therefore, it may be that this should be taken as an illustration of the diversity of samurai class structure during the Tokugawa period. Certainly most *han* would consider Fukuzawa, a member of the *nakakoshō*[w] as a *shi* and not as a *sotsu*. When we consider that Fukuzawa's description of Nakatsu samurai class structure excluded *baishin*, then the *kyūnin* class may really have comprised only one-sixth or fourteen per cent of the total class, about the same as the middle and upper samurai in Chōshū by our second definition. It is to be hoped that someone will analyze Fukuzawa's *Kyūhanjō* in relation to more universal terms which must appear in the documents of Nakatsu-*han*.

[16] *Bōchō kaiten shi*, VI, 57–58.

[17] By this definition only the highest two and a part of the third stratum of *shi* were upper samurai. The top two strata contained the eight *karō* families. The third stratum of *shi*, the so-called *yorigumi*[w],

most any large movement of samurai would of necessity be a lower samurai movement unless it were made up from the ranks of those already in power. The *sonnō jōi* movement is no exception: by this definition it can indeed be called a lower samurai movement but to call it that is to say very little about it. Given this definition what now become important are the finer distinctions within the larger class of lower samurai. Which of the subgroups within the class of lower samurai were active in the movement and why, or what type of person within which subgroup was the most active, and so on. Moreover, even by this inclusive definition which designates eighty-five per cent of Chōshū's military class as lower samurai, many of the most important *sonnō jōi* leaders, men such as Kido Kōin, Takasugi Shinsaku, Inoue Kaoru, Sufu Masanosuke, etc., were still either middle or upper samurai.

Thus, neither of these two most common definitions of "lower samurai" can be satisfactorily applied to the *sonnō jōi* movement. By the first, it is false to call it a lower samurai movement; by the second, it is closer to the truth but the truth is no longer meaningful.

Perhaps even more dangerous than the ambiguity inherent in the common use of the term "lower samurai" is the fact that the term implies, or at least suggests, certain assumptions concerning the motivations of those who participated in the movement that are not true. "Lower samurai movement" suggests a single class united by common economic and political frustrations and moved by a common resentment against the Tokugawa system under which they lived. It suggests an impoverished military class suffering from both the demands of their *han* government and the demands of a new and rising commercial economy to which their traditional way of life could not adjust; a class of samurai who, by participating in the *sonnō jōi* movement, were somehow striking out at their feudal fetters; samurai who, finding no outlet for their ambitions within the existing society, were willing to turn tradition upside down to create a new order. This is a very seductive picture and one not completely untrue; yet, it is a distortion.

First, the *sonnō jōi* movement in Chōshū was not the work of a single group with a single set of motivations; it was supported by at least three distinct groups within the *han* and its nature was as complex as that of these different groups. Second, economically, it is not clear that the conditions of the Chōshū samurai were any worse in the Bakumatsu period than they had been fifty or one hundred years earlier. Reforms had been carried out during the 1840's and 1850's, the debts of the samurai had been reduced or taken over by the *han,* and the amount "borrowed" from the stipend of the samurai to supplement the Chōshū budget had been curtailed. Moreover, the rising price of rice during the Bakumatsu period made their fixed income worth considerably more than at an earlier period. Until these changes are studied in relation to the prices of other goods and services, one cannot simply assume that their condition was steadily deteriorating. Third, even if the conditions of the samurai can be shown to have grown worse during the Bakumatsu period—and it is very unlikely that this was the case in Chōshū—one may not infer automatically that they had become disenchanted with the old society. Rather, there are many indications that the vast majority of those participating in the movements of the Bakumatsu period were in-

---

had sixty-two members with incomes ranging from 5,000 to 250 *koku*. Of these 62 families, only those with fiefs greater than 1,000 *koku* were rated as upper samurai by this definition.

tent on recreating the virtues of the old society and not on creating a new order. Even commoners joining the movement seem to have done so to obtain the coveted status of the military class rather than from an anti-feudal position. Finally, the strength and nature of the *sonnō jōi* movement varied, or appeared to vary from area to area. In Saga or Mito or Tosa, the movement seemed to transcend *han* borders: the loyalty of the "loyalist" samurai appeared to pass from a local to a national focus. On the other hand, in Chōshū, and possibly Satsuma, the loyalty of certain *sonnō* factions to the Emperor was inextricably linked with their loyalty to the daimyo.

The difficulties of definition and assumptions involved in calling the *sonnō jōi* movement a "lower samurai movement" may appear as a verbal quibble. Its significance, however, is much greater. If the movement cannot truthfully or meaningfully be called a lower samurai movement, and if the nature of the movement was not that suggested by the term, then one is forced to seek an alternative characterization. The razing of one construct must lead to the formulation of others.

In Chōshū the *sonnō jōi* movement as it developed from 1858 to 1865 was supported by three major groups each with a different character: the *sonnō jōi* intellectuals, the activist bureaucratic clique, and the auxiliary militia. The differing natures of these three groups can be seen by discussing phase by phase the movement as it emerged in Chōshū.[18]

The first phase of the movement was the incubation period of the *sonnō jōi* ideology and ideologists, centering on the school of Yoshida Shōin. It is this aspect of the movement in Chōshū that has been given the fullest treatment by Western historians. In terms of class origins the backgrounds of Shōin's students were various: some were high-ranking *shi* such as Takasugi, others *sotsu* such as Itō, and some were the sons of well-to-do peasants (perhaps it is significant that there are no famous names to mention in this last category). In spite of their diverse origins, were these students impelled by a common motivation? Judging from their own remarks, some were attracted by the person of Shōin, some came to imbibe of what in Hagi in 1857 could be thought of as progressive education, others came simply because as *sotsu* or *baishin* they were ineligible to enter the official Chōshū "college," the Meirinkan. One of Shōin's former students, recollecting his own motives, wrote: "At the time the reputation of Master Shōin was high and everyone was going to his school; it was the fashion. Besides, I thought that I might be able to find [official] employment if I attended the school."[19] And yet, however diverse their material motivations may have been, those of Shōin's students who went on to participate actively in the *sonnō jōi* movement seem to have been singularly devoted to certain key concepts in his teachings. It is this common attachment to doctrine that enables us to refer to them as "*sonnō jōi* intellectuals," although "*sonnō jōi* moralists" might be a better description if it did not have other connotations as well.[20]

---

[18] Most of the materials in the second part of this article have been culled from within the depths of the *Bōchō kaiten shi*. I did not feel it necessary to footnote materials that are readily available in standard secondary works.

[19] *Yoshida Shōin zenshū* [*The Collected Works of Yoshida Shōin*], XII (Tokyo, 1940), 206.

[20] Many extremely important questions still remain concerning the relation between Shōin's school and the later rise of the Chōshū *sonnō jōi* intellectuals: how many students passed through his school, of these how many later became politically active, how many were inactive, how many who were active were not associated with the school, and so on. The answers to these and other related questions will shed considerable light on the nature of the early movement in Chōshū.

Restoration Movement in Chōshū

If any of the groups in Chōshū which contributed to the movement can be thought of as possessing a loyalty which transcended the boundaries of the *han* it was undoubtedly this group, yet even this group seems from time to time to have been moved by what can only be called "*han* nationalism." Shōin's disciples, for example, once suggested that they join with like-minded samurai of Echizen, Owari, Mito, and Satsuma to assassinate the Bakufu Tairō, Ii Naosuke. Shōin responded: "It would be a good thing to join with the others to punish the evil Ii; yet if the other *han* are the leaders and ours the follower, would this not be shameful"?[21] Shōin subsequently proposed an alternative assassination by which the Chōshū group could demonstrate their merit and open the way for later joint action in which Chōshū could participate as an equal.

A second instance of the force of *han* nationalism occurred in the spring of 1859 when Takasugi, Kusaka, and others of Shōin's closest disciples broke with their teacher on the grounds that his plots would bring disaster to Chōshū. Rebuffed by *han* officials, Shōin had become increasingly fanatic throughout 1858; at one point he was told by *han* officials "to stop acting like a reckless student."[22] By early 1859 he had determined to sacrifice himself to his cause and began to plot wild and fantastic schemes, acts of terror and peasant uprisings with no hope of success. His students may have broken with him as much from self-preservation as from loyalty to the *han*, yet they spoke only of the latter. In 1859 loyalty to the *han* was functional while loyalty to a national Emperor was a dream cherishable only by extreme idealists.

The second phase of Chōshū's *sonnō jōi* movement began in 1861 after the execution of Yoshida Shōin and the assassination of the Bakufu Tairō Ii. This second phase was a sort of transitional phase linking the intellectual *sonnō jōi*-ism of 1858 and 1859 with the bureaucratic *sonnō jōi*-ism of 1862. By 1861 the activist bureaucratic clique, the dominant clique within the *han* bureaucracy, had decided that Chōshū should embark on a policy of mediation between the Bakufu and the Court. The specific policy on which it hoped to mediate was heavily weighted in favor of the Bakufu. Consequently, it was attacked from two sides within Chōshū: on the one hand the conservative bureaucratic clique (the *Zokurontō* referred to by E. Herbert Norman)[23] argued that any involvement in national politics was dangerous to the *han;* on the other hand the *sonnō jōi* intellectuals contended that it was not in accord with the pro-Emperor traditions of Chōshū. The activist bureaucratic clique was little affected by these criticisms and continued with its negotiations between the Court and the Bakufu.

The third phase of the Chōshū *sonnō jōi* movement began in 1862 when Satsuma, by adopting a position slightly more favorable to the Court than that of Chōshū, was able to supplant Chōshū as mediator between the Bakufu and the Court. This was a crucial point in the development of the Chōshū *sonnō jōi* movement. At this point the activist bureaucratic clique in charge of the Chōshū government adopted the pro-Court *sonnō jōi* position of the loyalist intellectuals. It did this not because of any intrinsic merits the doctrine might possess, not because the activist bureaucrats were convinced of its truth (since barely a year before they had been advocating an almost opposite policy), not because of the agitation of the *sonnō jōi* intellectuals to whom

---

[21] Naramoto Tatsuya, *Yoshida Shōin* (Tokyo, 1955), p. 132.

[22] *Bōchō kaiten shi*, II, 263.

[23] E. Herbert Norman, *Japan's Emergence as a Modern State* (New York, 1948), pp. 64–66.

they had been almost indifferent, but solely as a means to regain the lead in national politics that Chōshū had lost to Satsuma. This proved effective. The Court which had dropped Chōshū's mediation in favor of that of Satsuma now dropped Satsuma and once again took up with Chōshū.

Who were these activist bureaucrats responsible for throwing Chōshū's weight behind the *sonnō jōi* movement? They were samurai from the fourth highest rank of *shi* with fiefs or stipends averaging about one hundred *koku*.[24] Since only 661 of Chōshū's 11,000 samurai had income of one hundred *koku* or more, this placed them roughly in the upper six per cent of the Chōshū samurai class.[25] It cannot be over-emphasized that it was the military power of Chōshū controlled by this activist clique of bureaucrats which enabled the *sonnō jōi* movement to grow as it did in Kyoto in 1862 and 1863. Had they not been backed by Chōshū, the *sonnō jōi* intellectuals would have been scattered as chaff before the wind by any of the powerful *han* advocating more moderate policies.

It should also be mentioned that the adoption of the *sonnō jōi* policy by the Chōshū government did not mean the inclusion of the *sonnō jōi* intellectuals in the government. For the most part, the relationship between these intellectuals and the activist bureaucrats was essentially symbiotic: the bureaucrats used the intellectuals for their contacts with the samurai of other *han* and the intellectuals used the official Chōshū position in Kyoto as a shield behind which they could spread their ideas and forward the position of the Court. The only exception to the separation of the two groups was the appointment of Kido Kōin to a fairly important position in the *han* government. While his appointment may have been facilitated by the new *sonnō jōi* policy of Chōshū it must be stressed that Kido rose through the usual channels of bureaucratic advancement and that he was a high-ranking samurai with a stipend of one hundred and fifty *koku*, a stipend higher than the average of one hundred *koku* of the activist bureaucrats.

The fourth phase of the *sonnō jōi* movement, a period of decline, began in the summer of 1863 when two profound changes took place in the forces and fortunes of the movement. The first was the formation in Chōshū of an auxiliary militia; the second was the expulsion of Chōshū and the *sonnō jōi* forces from Kyoto. The auxiliary militia or *shotai*[j] were formed in response to a bombardment of Shimonoseki by foreign warships. They were formed by the orders of the activist bureaucrats, organized by Takasugi Shinsaku (a samurai with a stipend or fief of two hundred *koku*) who was given official position at this time, and, for the most part, led by the *sonnō jōi* intellectuals. The composition of these auxiliary militia was mixed: part samurai and part commoner in varying proportions. The most famous if not the largest of the *shotai*, the *Kiheitai*, contained more samurai than commoners. Several others whose composition have been analyzed contained about seventy per cent commoners and thirty per cent samurai.[26] A few of the smaller units may have contained an even larger percentage of commoners but they were not peasant militia by any means. The samurai component was made up mostly of rear vassals, *ashigaru*[k], and

---

[24] Tanaka Akira, "Tōbakuha no keisei katei" ["The Process of Formation of the Anti-Tokugawa Party"], *Rekishigaku kenkyū*, No. 205 (March 1957), p. 4.

[25] *Bōchō kaiten shi*, I, 42.

[26] Tanaka Akira, "Chōshū-*han* kaikakuha no kiban" ["Foundation of Reformers in the Chōshū Clan"], *Shichō*, No. 51 (1954), pp. 12–13.

the like, but they also contained a leaven of upper samurai, that is to say, *shi* as well. The commoner component was even more heterogeneous: peasants, hunters, merchants, priests, and even professional wrestlers were present in their ranks. In almost every case the commoners seem to have been motivated by a desire for the symbols and status of the samurai. These auxiliary militia were the third force supporting the *sonnō jōi* movement in Chōshū.

The second profound change in the fortunes of the movement was the expulsion of Chōshū and the *sonnō jōi* intellectuals from Kyoto by a Satsuma-Aizu *coup d'état* in the summer of 1863. By this coup Satsuma once again regained the leadership in national politics which she had lost a year earlier; Chōshū and the *sonnō jōi* movement were once again relegated to the periphery of national politics. In reaction to this each of the three groups in Chōshū that had supported the *sonnō jōi* policies felt the need for a new and determined action to regain Chōshū's former position. The activist bureaucratic clique needed national position to justify their own past policies and to maintain themselves in office (they were criticized more and more by the conservative clique for having exposed the *han* to the dangers of national politics). The auxiliary militia wanted a chance to prove their mettle as warriors. And the *sonnō jōi* intellectuals wished to restore both Chōshū and the Court to their rightful position in national affairs. Since the national struggle was no longer one of words or policies, it was decided to launch a counter-coup. This was attempted in the summer of 1864 but it failed and Chōshū was declared the "Enemy of the Court" for having tried to storm the Imperial Palace. The First Chōshū Expedition was proclaimed, orders were sent out by the Bakufu for the mobilization of the troops of the various *han,* and by the late fall of 1864 Chōshū was surrounded by a Bakufu army awaiting the order to attack.

This led to the fifth and final phase of the *sonnō jōi* movement in Chōshū. The threat posed by the imminent attack of the poised Bakufu army led to the dissolution of the *sonnō jōi* coalition first formed in 1862, and in a sense the dissolution of this coalition marked the end of the *sonnō jōi* movement. One partner to the coalition, the activist bureaucratic clique, lost control of the *han* government which came into the hands of the conservative bureaucratic clique. The conservative clique then charged their opposition with the responsibility for the 1864 attack in Kyoto and executed seventeen of the activist clique (among them three Elders who were perhaps not members of any clique in a strict sense but who had led the attack on Kyoto). The conservative clique then ordered the auxiliary militia to disband: a few did but most of them merely withdrew to isolated spots in the *han* to await further action. If the *sonnō jōi* movement shorn of its governmental support can be thought to have continued at all it was in the militia. The third group, the *sonnō jōi* intellectuals, having no status in the official hierarchy of the *han,* were considered too insignificant to be punished along with the active bureaucrats and most of them withdrew with the militia. Only Kido and Takasugi who had held official position as well as having been disciples of Yoshida Shōin were forced to remain outside the *han.*

Satisfied with these measures and confident that Chōshū under the conservative government was neutralized and would no longer aspire to a role in national politics, the Bakufu army withdrew. This was the signal for an uprising by the militia. It marked the beginning of the Chōshū Civil War. It was perhaps the most crucial moment in Chōshū Bakumatsu history. It marked the point at which the *sonnō jōi* movement became the *tōbaku* (overthrow the Bakufu) movement. It marked a new distribution of forces within the *han*.

It also marked a battle between two extremes. No longer restrained by the rational calculations of the activist bureaucratic clique, undaunted by the prospects of a second Bakufu expedition against Chōshū, the militia led by the *sonnō jōi* intellectuals set out to unseat the conservative government. The conservative government also represented an extreme of a sort. It was relatively unpopular and had long been out of power. It could command the allegiance of only a part of the regular *han* army. The nature of the Civil War is not yet completely clear but it seems to have been fought between units of the auxiliary militia and small sections of the regular *han* army. But a large number of important military groups such as rear vassals, a good number of the regular *han* army, and most peasant militia, remained neutral. Had these neutral groups supported the conservatives, the uprising of the militia would undoubtedly have been crushed. As it was the militia was victorious.

Was the Civil War in any sense a struggle between upper and lower samurai? The nature and composition of the militia and *sonnō jōi* intellectuals (now *tōbaku* intellectuals) have already been discussed; how do they compare with the conservative clique or bureaucrats and their military support? As measured in terms of rank and stipend, the conservative clique was of almost exactly the same status as the former activist clique. That is to say, the average stipend or fief of its members was about one hundred *koku*, placing them in the upper six per cent of the Chōshū military class.[27] Their military support was various: some samurai from high-ranking families of the castle town of Hagi, some samurai who resented the inclusion of commoners in the militia, and some who fought solely because the conservative government could issue orders in the name of the daimyo. Since the fighting took place between extremes, and since most of the activist clique—the high-ranking *sonnō jōi* supporters—had been executed, in a certain sense one can say that a class differential existed in the Civil War that had not existed earlier. However, one must remember that several of the Elders, the highest-ranking samurai of all, still favored the pro-Court forces while the conservatives used peasant troops to the extent that they could muster them. Even at this late stage, the common image of anti-feudal lower samurai (or lower samurai and peasants) fighting against a feudal aristocracy is a distortion of historical fact.

In conclusion, it seems clear that the usual uncritical and undefined use of "lower samurai" has thrown more shadow than light on the study of Bakumatsu history. Therefore, it must be abandoned except when rigorously defined, and when so defined it can no longer be used to characterize the political movements of the period.

In place of the class concept of "lower samurai" we have substituted a characterization in terms of three groups: the activist bureaucrats, the *sonnō jōi* intellectuals, and the auxiliary militia. This is a more detailed analysis than the above, but it is also a different kind of analysis and we must be careful not to impute to these three groups the inflexible character which hitherto has all too often been attributed to the class of "lower samurai." First, it should be made clear that none of the above groups were monoliths with a single set of class or group determinants. On the contrary, each had many facets and further research must explain which facet, or which combination of facets, was crucial at which times. There was also a great deal of variation within any

---

[27] Tanaka Akira, "Tōbakuha no keisei katei," p. 4.

one group. The activist bureaucrats split over the question of whether or not to adopt the *sonnō jōi* policy in 1864. Both bureaucrats and intellectuals split over the question of the 1864 Kyoto counter-coup. Moreover, both in personnel and policies these groups were fluid, changing considerably over a period of time. The *sonnō jōi* intellectuals who repudiated Yoshida Shōin in 1858 were quite different from those who began the *han* civil war in 1865.

We must also emphasize that the actions of any group are not explicable in terms of the group alone (in contrast to the class concept of lower samurai with its fixed set of built-in motivations). The identity of the activist bureaucrats as bureaucrats, for example, is only one among many, and it becomes significant for the *sonnō jōi* movement primarily at those points where it articulates with their identities as samurai of Chōshū, inhabitants of Japan, and so on. They exist within the structured field of Chōshū and it is chiefly the nature of this field and not the nature of the group that differentiates them from roughly comparable bureaucratic cliques in other *han*.

To illustrate concretely the sense in which the success or failure of any group is due largely to the configuration of forces within which it is set, let us take the case of the Chōshū *sonnō jōi* intellectuals. The ultimate triumph of this group in Chōshū does not mean that the group itself was stronger than similar groups in other *han*. Rather it was an indirect consequence of a decision by a traditional bureaucratic clique of upper-ranking samurai to launch Chōshū into the uncertain waters of national politics. This led to Chōshū's competition with Satsuma which in turn led to the adoption of the *sonnō jōi* policy as the official policy of Chōshū. In time the national struggle over policy led to military struggles from which the pro-Court forces eventually emerged victorious. This victory, however, was based on the total strength of the *han* and not solely on the *sonnō jōi* intellectuals.

Finally, although this article has been limited to a consideration of merely one phase of an extremely complex question, the process indicated above suggests at least one possible line of inquiry into the problem of why certain *han* emerged to play important roles in the Restoration while others did not. If in any given *han* one can show the nature of its bureaucratic cliques, their position within the power structure of the *han*, and the factors influencing policy decisions in that *han*, then the position of the *han* in national politics will be understood. And this may further explain why the *sonnō jōi* group in that particular *han* did or did not become important. Only by comparing the experiences of those *han* remaining inactive with those which were active will we be able to explain definitively the successes of the latter.

a 士	f 軽輩	k 足軽	p 倍卒	u 家来給禄帳
b 士族	g 軽卒	l 卒族	q 復族運動	v 無給通
c 士分	h 倍臣	m 華族	r 成リ上リ士族	w 給人
d 士格	i 徒士	n 版籍奉還	s 公卿華族	x 中小姓
e 卒	j 諸隊	o 地士	t 新華族	y 寄組

CHAPTER TWENTY-ONE

FROM TOKUGAWA TO MEIJI IN JAPANESE LOCAL ADMINISTRATION

JOHN WHITNEY HALL

JAPAN converted itself from a country of widely fragmented political divisions into a unified nation state with seemingly little effort after the Meiji Restoration of 1868. The transition from Tokugawa decentralization to Meiji centralization was accomplished with surprisingly little difficulty and with even less fanfare. What in other countries has taken decades of bloody civil war to achieve, was apparently carried out in Japan as an orderly process which offered almost no resistance to the authority of a newly formed central power. There was, to be sure, some separatist resistance, first from displaced elements of the Tokugawa faction and then by disillusioned members of the original Meiji leadership. But in the main, once the political competition at the center of the stage had been decided, the country at large fell in behind the new government. It is this willingness of what we have assumed to be relatively independent local territories to follow the lead of an essentially revolutionary central authority (often to their own apparent disadvantage) which has so astonished the historians of the period.

As with so many aspects of the Meiji Restoration movement a good deal of the mystery which surrounds questions of this kind stems from the historian's initial exaggeration of the conditions of decentralization existing at the end of the Tokugawa period. If one assumes, for instances, that Tokugawa Japan was feudal in the full sense of the term, then the sudden jump from feudalism to centralized monarchy seems incomprehensible. If the daimyo are thought of as fully independent territorial rulers, then it becomes equally difficult to imagine how they could have given up their powers without a prolonged struggle. Some of the mystery is dispelled, then, if we realize that in the latter days of the Tokugawa period Japan was feudal only in a very limited sense and that a uniformity of administrative practice had penetrated much more deeply and widely into local affairs than is commonly assumed. All of the vast Tokugawa territories, were centrally administered, of course, and to large extent the territories of the *fudai* daimyo were subordinate to the policies or the inertia of the shogunate. Even the *tozama* daimyo, theoretically peers of the shogun, were autonomous only insofar as they were expected to administer their territories without necessitating interference from the shogun. Certainly all daimyo were well-accustomed to receive and act upon instructions from the shogun, and all had well-defined bureaucratic means to handle liaison with the *bakufu*. Moreover, all daimyo conceived of themselves as existing under the superior (though mainly nominal) authority of the emperor who stood as symbol of a real, though admittedly ill-defined, sense of national unity. The problems of unification from the Tokugawa base were much less severe than, say, those faced by Italy or Germany in the same century.

Thus to some extent it is more correct to think of Japan in the 1860's as being overdue for unification rather than as an unruly welter of sovereign territorial units.[1] Nonetheless between the political system of Tokugawa regime and the centralized local administration which supported the Meiji government, a vast effort at reorganization was required. The new government was obliged to merge roughly 280 daimyo domains, the widely scattered Tokugawa territories, nearly 5,000 separate fiefs held by the shogun's lesser retainers (chiefly *hatamoto*), and many thousands of ecclesiastical holdings into a single unified administration. This was no simple task, and it had to be achieved in different manner from section to section of the country depending upon the local mix between types of daimyo (*fudai* or *tozama*), amount of Tokugawa territory, and other political considerations.

In this paper I shall describe the process of consolidation as it transpired in the section of Japan which eventually took shape as Okayama Prefecture, in other words the territory consisting of the old provinces of Bizen, Bitchū, and Mimasaka. The example of Okayama is informative, though it should not be looked upon as necessarily representative. The area is not necessarily typical of all Japan, but neither is it marked by gross extremes. To this extent it provides something of a median example for the purposes of most studies, including this.

At the end of the Tokugawa period the area which later became Okayama Prefecture consisted of 47 separate administrative jurisdictions made up of over 120 separate pieces of territory many of them widely separated from each other. A political map of the period shows a patchwork of administrative units distributed in seeming defiance of any rational system of local government.[2] This was the base upon which unification was imposed. Yet it came about rapidly between 1868 and 1877, the result of a number of quite separate stages of consolidation which appear to have been fairly typical for those parts of Japan where no particular military action either pro- or anti-shogunate took place in 1868 and 1869. At the expense of some slight oversimplification I will take up the Okayama story in terms of these stages.

I. Administrative Simplification During the Tokugawa Period

Despite the seeming complexity of administrative districts revealed by the Tokugawa political map, we must assume that some simplification and rationalization of local administration had taken place by the end of the Tokugawa period. In the first place the areas on the map which showed the greatest

---

[1] Edwin O. Reischauer has popularized the view. Commenting on the Tokugawa regime he says, "Since the political system had been basically reactionary even in the early seventeenth century, it was by now more than two hundred years out of date." *Japan Past and Present* (New York, 1953), 108.

[2] See the map based on one prepared by Professor Taniguchi Sumio from data in "Okayama-ken gunjishi." The count of 47 divisions comes from Okayama-ken, *Okayama-ken tōkei nempō* (Okayama, 1951), 9–12. Also listed are 30 temple and shrine holdings.

confusion of small jurisdictions consisted of territories held directly by the shogun (*tenryō*), by minor retainers of the shogun, or by *fudai* daimyo whose headquarters and main holdings were located in some other part of the country. After 1642, all shogunal territory in Bitchū was administered through the office of the Tokugawa intendent (*daikan-sho*) established at the town of Kurashiki. Similar offices were created in 1689 to superintend the *tenryō* in Mimasaka.[3] We can assume that some degree of administrative rationalization was imposed on the *hatamoto* fiefs through these offices. At least the shogunal intendent (*daikan*) exercised a superior local jurisdiction in the name of the shogun. If, then, we subsume these many small holdings under the authority of the shogunate, then we are left with only 25 strictly independent systems of authority in the area.[4] These were, in addition to shogunal jurisdictions, territories under daimyo administration. The most important of these were seven: Okayama, Matsuyama (renamed Takahashi), Ashimori, Tsuyama, Nariwa, Majima (formerly Katsuyama), and Niwase. But in terms of real regional influence backed by military power, since the intendent headquarters were purely administrative and had no military forces, the only significant centers in the area were Okayama, Matsuyama, and Tsuyama. Among these, moreover, Okayama, which held all of Bizen and parts of Bitchū, stood out above the rest. Its holdings, and hence its military potential, were over half again as large as all of the other daimyo of the region combined.

II. POLITICAL NEUTRALIZATION ON THE EVE OF THE RESTORATION

The most significant feature of the Okayama area just prior to the Meiji Restoration was the stalemate which inhibited political action on the part of even the larger daimyo domains. Once the fear of foreign invasion had shaken the Tokugawa system, and once the control system of the shogunate had been eased, all of the daimyo of Japan felt to greater or lesser degree the impending crisis in national affairs. Yet we know that in this atmosphere of crisis a very few of the domains, primarily because of the energy of a few active leaders, became direct participants in the political struggle. The Ikeda House of Okayama and the other lesser daimyo of the area were among the vast majority which remained inactive. And the reason that the Okayama domains remained immobile may explain why so few other sections of the country joined in the Restoration movement. Immobility did not necessarily indicate lethargy but rather resulted from certain neutralizing conditions which precluded determined action either for or against the Tokugawa shogun.

Beginning with the Okayama domain, we find that in 1863 the ninth son of Tokugawa Nariaki (the controversial head of the Mito branch of the Tokugawa house) had been adopted as heir to the Ikeda family and so had become daimyo of Okayama. This man, known as Ikeda Mochimasa, brought

---

[3] Nagayama Usaburō, *Okayama-ken tsūshi*, 2 vols. (Okayama, 1930), vol. 2, 231.

[4] In fact in 1869, when the first effort at administrative simplification was made, the area of the three provinces remained divided into 25 jurisdictions. *Okayama-ken tōkei nempō*, 9–12.

with him a predisposition to put the national interest (as symbolized by loyalty to the emperor) before shogunal interests. Thus at crucial points in his years as daimyo of Okayama, he demonstrated his sympathy to the imperial cause. For example he made only a token contribution of military forces to the first Tokugawa expedition against Chōshū and claimed inability (on the grounds of his own illness) to send support for the second expedition. It is quite obvious that despite the fact that Mochimasa was a blood member of the Tokugawa house, he had no intention of supporting the shogun at any cost. And he even permitted his senior officers to memorialize the shogunate from time to time on the necessity of political reforms to counter the foreign threat. Thus when Mochimasa's brother Yoshinobu became shogun in 1866, the tension between his desire to part company with shogunal policy and the desire to demonstrate family loyalty made decisions of any kind extremely difficult. Probably only the strong family relationship between Mochimasa and Yoshinobu prevented Okayama's active participation in some sort of anti-Tokugawa alliance, and meanwhile a good deal of covert negotiation was going on between the men of Bizen and the loyalist faction, particularly the men of Chōshū.[5]

Turning to Tsuyama, governed by a cadet branch of the Tokugawa house, we should expect vigorous support for the shogun. Yet Tsuyama was also immobilized by a split which developed between the young daimyo who was pro-emperor and the retired daimyo who remained pro-shogunate. Again the test of Tsuyama's stand came during the two expeditions against Chōshū when the performance of the young daimyo was reluctant and largely nominal.[6]

Of all the daimyo of the region only the head of the Matsyama domain appears publically to have asserted a pro-shogunal position. Itakura Katsukiyo, the daimyo, had been appointed senior councilor (rōjū) in the shogun's government and so could hardly have behaved differently. Yet he himself was seldom in Matsuyama, being obliged to remain at the shogun's side, and the officers he left behind in his domain, being surrounded by territories which had expressed reluctance or open hostility to following the shogunal dictates, were not inclined to play the hero in a lost cause. This then was how things stood in the Okayama area prior to January 1868: the entire area was neutral or predisposed to the imperial cause except for Matsuyama and the headquarters of the shogunal intendent.

III. RESPONSE TO THE RESTORATION

News of the Restoration broke upon a scene of comparative quiet in the Okayama area. There was no noticeable breakdown of local order, there was no panic or mobilization for possible civil war, simply apprehensive waiting.

---

[5] Taniguchi Sumio, "Meiji Ishin-shi ni okeru Okayama-han no seiji katei," in Sakata Yoshio, Meiji Ishin-shi mondai ten (Tokyo, 1962), 377–400.

[6] Okayama-ken, ed., Okayama-ken no rekishi (Okayama, 1962), 491–492.

From Tokugawa to Meiji in Local Administration

Not until the new government declared the Tokugawa rebels and their territory confiscated did a brief scramble take place for realignment of loyalties. There had not been at the time of the Restoration, nor even after the confiscation of Tokugawa properties, a general call to defend the Tokugawa cause. And since the shogun had resigned his office in 1867, there was obviously confusion as to where primary loyalties lay between ex-shogun and emperor, shogunate and newly declared imperial government. The shift in the center of political authority from Edo to Kyoto was not sudden but had been coming gradually as the shogun entered into negotiations with the imperial court and permitted the formation of the so-called *kōbu-gattai* coalition under the emperor. It was from about 1862 when the *sankin-kōtai* system was relaxed that daimyo began to receive communications from both Edo and Kyoto. Certainly as of January 1868 it seemed possible for the daimyo of Okayama to accept orders from Kyoto without in any way betraying the Tokugawa house. Loyalty to imperial command was not immediately made inconsistent with loyalty to the former shogun, and even the Restoration did not at first pose an absolute threat to the Tokugawa partisans.

The battle of Fushimi-Toba on January 27, 1868, however, polarized the political atmosphere and drew a rigid line between the Tokugawa and imperial causes. Immediately, not only the Tokugawa house but the *fudai* daimyo and the *hatamoto* were designated rebels and obliged to throw themselves on the mercy of the new government. Fortunately for Japan, Tokugawa Keiki, the ex-shogun, decided against resistance. But in northeastern Japan, where the saturation of loyal Tokugawa houses was greatest, several of the daimyo refused to capitulate and took up arms against the decision against them. In western Japan the possibility of military resistance by pro-Tokugawa daimyo seemed almost out of the question. What happened in Okayama illustrates why.

IV. Victory of the Imperial Case

In the Okayama area, the Ikeda domain played an immediate and crucial role in securing the area for the imperial cause. Despite the fact that the Ikeda daimyo was a brother of the ex-shogun, leaders of the Restoration had already assured themselves that the domain would prove loyal to them when the test came.[7] Thus the domain officials received both public and secret orders to mobilize forces in order to hold down the Okayama area and to proceed immediately to block any move by presumably pro-shogunal Matsuyama *han*. Apparently Ikeda Mochimasa, brother of the ex-shogun Keiki, readily followed these orders, though we must imagine with considerable personal anguish. For he soon resigned as daimyo of Okayama in favor of Ikeda Massaki, the former daimyo of the Kamogata branch of the Ikeda house. Massaki had already

---

[7] Taniguchi, *op.cit.,* 400–401. Discussions between Kido Kōin and various Okayama officials were at the bottom of this.

shown himself to be pro-loyalist and had urged an anti-Tokugawa policy on Mochimasa during the time of the second Chōshū expediton. His appearance as daimyo of Okayama quickly converted Okayama into a bulwark of the imperial cause in central Japan.[8]

In the first months after the coup d'etat of January 1868, the Okayama establishment was used in two ways to the advantage of the Restoration government. First the daimyo of Okayama was directed to hold down the three provinces of Bizen, Bitchū, and Mimasaka, and particularly to neutralize the possible pro-Tokugawa moves of the Matsuyama domain. In addition units of the Okayama armed forces were drawn upon to support various military thrusts against Tokugawa resistance in central and eastern Japan. The latter military activity is of less concern to us and can be disposed of first. In early 1868 a unit of roughly 300 Okayama men joined the imperial forces moving from Kyoto toward Edo. Their farthest advance was Nagoya. About the same time a force of over 1,000 men moved into Harima to assure the loyalty of the domains in that province. Later in the year forces of a few hundred each were sent into the Wakamatsu and the Hakodate engagements to the north and far north.[9]

The really significant service which the Okayama domain rendered the new leaders in Kyoto was that of stabilizing the Okayama region in the initial weeks after the announcement of the Restoration. The fighting between the loyalist and the Tokugawa forces at Toba-Fushimi had broken out on January 27, 1868. A week later the general announcement calling for chastisement of the ex-shogun and the Tokugawa adherents was issued. It was at this time that the Tokugawa domains and holdings in the Okayama area were declared confiscated and the daimyo of Okayama was instructed to accept the submission of the various *hatamoto* in Bitchū and Mimasaka and to pacify the domains of Matsuyama, Tsuyama, Katsuyama, as well as Tatsuno in Harima province. Accompanying the orders to the daimyo were two banners bearing the imperial crest which served to symbolize the legitimation of his cause. The daimyo of Okayama had very little difficulty in achieving his mission. In quick succession the smaller domains of the region pledged their alliance to the new government, while forces sent against Matsuyama, Tsuyama, and Tatsuno had no difficulty in securing the submission of the castle headquarters of these territories. The force of roughly 1,500 men sent against Matsuyama saw no action whatever. The daimyo of Matsuyama was unable to return to his castle because he was accompanying the ex-shogun in Edo, and his retainers took little time in professing their support of the Restoraton, giving up their arms, and turning over hostages to the Okayama force. At about this time also the daimyo of Okayama was instructed to take over temporarily the administration of the Tokugawa territories which had been in the jurisdiction of the Kurashiki headquarters. Thus without a struggle the entire Okayama area was secured for the new government, and the daimyo of Okayama had

---

[8] *Okayama-ken no rekishi,* 494–499.
[9] Taniguchi, *op.cit.,* 407.

stepped in to serve as the main stabilizing force in the area as well as interim administrator for all vacated jurisdictions.[10]

V. Initial Efforts at Centralization

From the early months of 1868 until early 1869 the major daimyo domains and other territorial divisions in the Okayama area were left pretty much as they had been under the Tokugawa shogunate. The one major change was the incorporation of all former Tokugawa territory (including Matsuyama *han*) into a new unit called Kurashiki-ken (Kurashiki Prefecture) which was administered by a governor sent out from Kyoto. Here was a clear foreshadowing of the eventual conversion of all *han* into prefectures within a few years. Outside of Kurashiki-ken how long the officials of Okayama *han* superintended the administration of the other territorial units is not certain. For several months at least, Okayama forces were maintained in the castle headquarters of Tsuyama, Matsuyama, Katsuyama, and at Kurashiki. But the Okayama officials were soon replaced by agents sent out from the central government.

It is remarkable, in fact, that the central administration was able to move as rapidly as it did to affect a centralization and standardization of local administration throughout Japan. Liaison officials were quickly dispatched from Kyoto to discuss with the various daimyo officials the problems of uniformity in local administration. The announcement of the Seitaisho, Japan's first systematic plan for government, in June of 1868, actually specified a simplified form of local administration which was to be adopted by the several daimyo. But even more significant, it obliged the daimyo to accept restrictions on their freedom of action by virtue of the fact that they now existed under a constitutional document promulgated by the empeor. Moreover this document for the first time clarified in legal terminology the daimyo's local powers and authorities, and made provison for the central government to interfere in the affairs of the daimyo domain, primarily in fiscal matters. In other words, the local territories were now treated as though they were units of a central administration.[11]

VI. Retrocession of the Han

How the daimyo could possibly have agreed peaceably to return their territories to the emperor has been one of the great mysteries of the Restoration era. The case of the Okayama domain provides some answers. But fundamentally it was a matter of not having any reason to resist the transfer of what was essentially a nominal authority. The daimyo by this time had so expended their resources in military buildup (and some action) and in *han* administrative reforms, and their administration had been so interfered with

---

[10] *Okayama-ken no rekishi,* 499–500.

[11] Ishii Ryōsuke, *Meiji bunka shi Hōsei hen* (Tokyo, 1954), 66–68. This was the beginning, in fact, of the term *han* in reference to the daimyo territories.

by liaison officers from the central administration, that they must have welcomed the opportunity to return to the central government whatever independent political authority they presumably had in the form of land and tax registers. By this time the daimyo were only nominal rulers and their territories could claim little room for independent activity. In February of 1869 the daimyo of Okayama turned back his domain grants to the imperial government. These were the documents of enfeoffment received from the shogun with the accompanying cadastral registers. Thereafter, though the domain retained its territorial identity, it became a unit of local government administratively identical with the new prefectures. The daimyo, though retained as governors of their former domains, were legally appointees of the central government. In fact they were called Chiji, and the name of the domain was changed to coincide with the name of the castle town.[12]

Throughout 1869 and 1870, further pressures were applied to bring domain administration under uniform procedure. The domain governments were reorganized, new names were applied to offices and personnel, and new systems of rank, salary, and appointment were instituted. Toward the end of 1870 Okayama *han* underwent a major administrative revision under the command of the central government. There was now a clear definition of the functions of the *han* governor, a specific annual salary, and a streamlined administration which was to be staffed according to merit. The former military ranks were abolished, and status was determined by rank within the new bureaucracy.[13]

VII. ABOLITION OF THE HAN AND ESTABLISHMENT OF THE KEN

That the attempt to standardize local administration by enforcing uniformities upon the former daimyo domains did not prove particularly satisfactory is clear from the writings of the leaders in the central government. The proposal that the *han* be converted into prefectures had been in the air for some time. It was eventually picked up by such leaders as Ōkubo and Kido who finally convinced their colleagues and their daimyo.[14] With the assembling of an imperial army of some size in the spring of 1871, the central government felt strong enough to call for the abolition of the daimyo system. On August 29, 1871, the former domains were declared converted into *ken,* and the former daimyo were completely separated from their old territorial authority.[15]

The abolition of the *han* and the formation of *ken* still left the Okayama region cut up into a complicated patchwork of jurisdictions.[16] In all, 25 *ken,* with boundaries which were still those of the former *han* territories, had been created. The main achievement of the abolition of the *han* had been the elim-

---

[12] Okayama-ken, *Okayama kenseishi,* 2 vols. (Tokyo, 1941), vol. 1, 16.

[13] See Ardath W. Burks "Administrative Transition from *Han* to *Ken:* The Example of Okayama," *Far Eastern Quarterly,* vol. 15, No. 3 (May 1956), 371–382.

[14] Masakazu Iwata, *Ōkubo Toshimichi* (Berkeley, 1965), 143–147.

[15] *Okayama kenseishi,* vol. 1, 21–22.

[16] *Okayama-ken tōkei nempō,* 9–12.

ination of the daimyo as territorial governors and their replacement by perfectural officials appointed directly by the central government. Localism in local administration had been eliminated as new personnel were sent out from Kyoto to take over the new *ken,* and as men of lower status were raised to office on the basis of ability. In the new Okayama prefecture, the change of personnel may have moved somewhat more slowly than elsewhere. With the departure of the daimyo for Tokyo the former chief councilor, Shinjō Atsunobu, a former Okayama samurai official of middle rank, became governor, thus making some continuity in policy and vested local interest inevitable.[17]

VIII. Initial Consolidation of the *Ken*

It is obvious that the retention of the territorial divisions of the Tokugawa period could not last for long even though a systematic administrational machinery had been thrown over them. Before the end of 1871, therefore, the 25 scattered jurisdictions were merged and their place taken by three large new prefectures. The most interesting feature of this first stage in prefectural consolidation was its reliance on territorial boundaries which derived from a remote period of Japanese history. The new *ken* were based on boundaries which coincided almost exactly with those of the old provinces (*kuni*) which had been brought into being during the eighth century and had fallen into disuse during the fifteenth century. In addition the old district subdivisions (*gun*) were also made use of. Thus the three new prefectures were Okayama (equivalent to the old province of Bizen), Fukatsu (containing Bitchū and two districts of Bingo), and Hōjō (equivalent to the province of Mimasaka). On the fifteenth day of the eleventh month of Meiji four, identical orders were dispatched to the existing *ken* headquarters instructing the governors of the consolidation plans. Within a period of four to five months the governors of each of the disbanded prefectures proceeded to the new prefectural headquarters with his official papers containing the land and population registers and financial accounts.[18]

By the spring of 1872, the three new prefectural headquarters were in a position to serve as the administrative centers of their greatly enlarged areas of jurisdiction. Concurrently, procedures were undertaken to take care of the members of the samuri class dismissed from office by these moves, and legal clarification was made regarding the property of the former daimyo and their retainers. In Okayama prefecture the administrative offices were now moved out of the former castle headquarters into space which had formerly been the office of the magistrate of rural affairs. Eventually of course a new prefectural building was erected. The old governor functioned for a few months but was eventually replaced by an appointee whose home domain had been Satsuma. The other two new prefectures were from the outset placed under governors from Satsuma and Chōshū.[19]

---

[17] *Okayama-ken tsūshi,* vol. 2, appendix "Kenkan ichiran," 16.

[18] *Okayama kenseishi,* vol. 1, 26 ff.

[19] *Okayama-ken no rekishi,* 503–507.

J. W. Hall

IX. Final Consolidation of Local Administration

The years 1873 to 1877 provided another critical turning point in the local administration of Okayama. In January of 1873, a new governor was sent out from Tokyo. Ishibe Seichū, a former Satsuma samurai, began administrative reforms and the initial stages of land reform. At the end of the year a new Home Ministry (Naimushō) was established in Tokyo with more effective powers over the prefecture. Then in October 1875, the man who really hammered Okayama into a modern prefecture arrived as governor. Takasaki Goroku, a former Satsuma samurai, immediately dismissed all prefectural employees (111 persons in all) and appointed an entirely new staff of officials. Many were drawn from Tokyo. In another six months Takasaki had presided over the amalgamation of the three prefectures into the larger single entity which persists today. He also completed the land reform, ruthlessly dispatching surveyors into the countryside to modernize the cadastral records. The result was a new and efficient tax system based on a land base which was more than 40% expanded over the old Tokugawa figures. By 1884, when Takasaki retired, Okayama-ken was solidly integrated into the national system of prefectual administration and taxation.[20]

X. Conclusion

The modern Japanese prefecture proved a remarkably effective and durable unit of local administration for the modern Japanese state. The Okayama example illustrates how, in one sector of the country, a scattering of separate local jurisdictions was first placed under uniform regulation and then compressed into a systematic prefectural administration. The process was pragmatic and used whatever means were at hand. Later on of course the details of local administrative law came under French and Prussian influence. But the essential base had already been laid. The Japanese name for what they created, the so-called *gun-ken* system, had its inspiration in Japan's early imperial administration and needed no external model. The central government planners had taken what had proved to be a most cumbersome system of local administration under the Tokugawa regime and had pulled it together bit by bit, using at a crucial stage in the process the preexisting but largely inoperative boundaries of the pre-Tokugawa provincial and district systems, moving step by step from small to large units. Probably it would be an exaggeration to say that the hazy remembrance of an old provincial system helped to make consolidation into provincial units acceptable to men who had nonetheless become accustomed to the less rational Tokugawa system. Yet merely the ideal of unity under an imperial system had proved inspirational to many Japanese of the time. Given the problem of local administration faced by the new government in 1868, the prefectural solution seems logical and almost inevitable.

[20] *Ibid.*, 512–520.

From Tokugawa to Meiji in Local Administration

But the question still remains as to how it was possible to refashion Japanese local administration without prolonged struggle or military coercion. Perhaps the fact which stands out most clearly in this respect is that the entire transfer from Tokugawa *han* to Meiji *ken*, though rapid, was accomplished in easy stages, no increment of which was sufficiently drastic to arouse the fear or antagonism of any major sector or group within the political elite. Thus as far as areas like Okayama were concerned, there was no revolutionry threat during any stage in the process. It is only as we lay the final result back upon the starting point that we can see that a revolution had actually occurred. Throughout the crucial stages of transition the structure of authority and administrative process had remained sufficiently intact so that changes were carried out within the framework of existing institutions. This was particularly apparent in the months immediately after the Restoration when with slightly more push the entire Tokugawa system could well have dissolved into chaos and civil war on a grand scale. Instead, a sufficient order was maintained, and sufficient numbers of daimyo and *han* officials stayed at their posts so that the solution could be worked out within the confines of the conventional political order. Hence although military force played a part in the loyalist takeover, a relatively few units did the work. In Okayama a few hundred men sent to the local daimyo headquarters managed to stabilize the area. And the 1,500 men sent against Matsuyama never saw action. Throughout this entire period the rules of the game were maintained, and no revolutionary leadership tried to turn chaos to their advantage. Thus if we think of the formation of the modern prefecture as primarily a tightening and centralizing process, then the continuity of authority and the ability of the central government to legitimize itself and assert its authority through the remnants of the very system it was about to discard becomes the critical factor.

But there is another dimension to what happened which was certainly of equal, though of somewhat less obvious importance, namely that throughout the Restoration era the incentive to resist change was somehow muted. This is to some degree explained by what we have already said about the weak economic position of the samurai class as a whole and the daimyo in particular. But this was not the only factor. For in contrast to the forces of consolidation and simplification which brought the *ken* out of the *han*, there were also contrapuntal forces at work which offered new opportunities and rewards to those men of ambition who might otherwise have turned revolutionary. The life of the samurai under the late Tokugawa regime had been stultifying and frustrating to most. The new imperial order gave promise of new opportunities for the ambitious. And in fact the turnover in the official personnel of local government was most drastic. In Okayama by 1875, for example, fewer than one-quarter of the officials of the prefectural office were carry-overs from the old domain. A large number of men from other parts of the country and some from outside of the samurai class itself had been taken in. The ex-samurai of Okayama could certainly not have taken this casually had the influx of new personnel represented simply a super-imposition of men from Chōshū or Sat-

suma over their heads or in their place. But the fact was that for men of Okayama opportunities had opened up elsewhere. The most ambitious had gone
on to the stage of national service or politics. Thus while the old structure was
being shaken down, the men who had once filled the overstaffed domain bureaucracies were able to aspire to new jobs higher up in the central government
or in other prefectures. While many samurai were by-passed and fell into poverty, those who had the competitive instinct were not denied a future. It is this
upward mobility of talent matching the consolidating efforts of the central government that is so well-described for the former Tokugawa domain of Fukui
by William Griffis in 1877:

"Great changes have taken place in the city since the departure of the
prince. . . . Most of the high officers have been called by the Imperial Government to Tōkiō. Mitsuoka is now mayor of Tōkiō. Ogasawara, Tsutsumi,
and several others have been made officials of other *ken*. It is the policy of
the government to send the men of one *ken* to act as officers in another, and
thus break up local prejudices. It is a grand idea. Sasaki Gonroku has been
called to a position in the Department of Public Works. Many of the best
teachers in the school have been given official places in the capital. My best
friends and helpers have left Fukui; and now my advanced students, their
support at home being no longer sufficient, are leaving to seek their fortune
in Yokohama or Tōkiō. . . . Since the summer—so I am told—over seven
hundred families have left Fukui. Tōkiō is making up in population the
loss of Yedo in 1862, when the daimios withdrew. . . . The military school
has been disbanded, and the gunpower works and the rifle factory removed.
Three companies of imperial troops, in uniform of French style, with the
mikado's crest on their caps, and the national flag (a red sun in a white
field) as their standard, now occupy the city barracks.[21]

---

[21] William E. Griffis, *The Mikado's Empire* (New York, 1906), 536.

LIST OF CONTRIBUTORS

HARUMI BEFU, Assistant Professor of Anthropology at Stanford University, is the author of several studies of Tokugawa village structure, including "Duty, Reward, Sanction: Four-cornered Office of the Tokugawa Village Headman," in *Modern Japanese Leadership,* ed. B. S. Silberman and H. D. Harootunian (1966).

ALBERT M. CRAIG, Professor of History at Harvard University, is the author of *Chōshū in the Meiji Restoration* (1961) and co-author (with J. K. Fairbank and E. O. Reischauer) of *East Asia: The Modern Transformation* (1965).

E. SYDNEY CRAWCOUR, Professor and Head of the Department of Japanese at the Australian National University at Canberra, is the author of articles on Japanese economic history, including "Some Observations on Merchants: A Translation of Mitsui Takafusa's *Chōnin koken roku,* with an Introduction and Notes," *Transactions of the Asiatic Society of Japan* (1962).

R. P. DORE, Professor of Sociology with special reference to the Far East at the London School of Economics and Political Science, and the School of Oriental and African Studies, University of London, is the author of *City Life in Japan* (1958), *Land Reform in Japan* (1959), *Education in Tokugawa Japan* (1964), and editor of *Aspects of Social Change in Modern Japan* (1967).

JOHN W. HALL, Alfred Whitney Griswold Professor of History at Yale University, is the author of *Tanuma Okitsugu (1719–1788), Forerunner of Modern Japan* (1955), *Japanese History, a Guide to Japanese Research and Reference Materials,* co-author (with R. E. Ward and R. K. Beardsley) of *Village Japan* (1959), co-author (with R. K. Beardsley) of *Twelve Doors to Japan* (1965), and author of *Government and Local Power in Japan, 500–1700: A Study Based on Bizen Province* (1966).

DAN FENNO HENDERSON, Professor of Law and Director of the Asian Law Program at the University of Washington, is the author of *Conciliation and Japanese Law: Tokugawa and Modern* (2 vols., 1965).

MARIUS B. JANSEN, Professor of History at Princeton University, is the author of *The Japanese and Sun Yat-sen* (1954), *Sakamoto Ryōma and the Meiji Restoration* (1961), and editor of *Changing Japanese Attitudes toward Modernization* (1965).

ROBERT K. SAKAI, Professor of History and Chairman of the Asian Studies Program at the University of Hawaii, is the author of several studies of Satsuma and editor of *Studies of Asia* from 1960 to 1966.

List of Contributors

DONALD H. SHIVELY, Professor of Japanese History and Literature at Harvard University, a former editor of the *Journal of Asian Studies,* is the author of *The Love Suicide at Amijima* (1953) and other studies in intellectual and cultural history, and editor of *Tradition and Modernization in Japanese Culture* (forthcoming).

THOMAS C. SMITH, Professor of History at Stanford University, is the author of *Political Change and Industrial Development in Japan, 1868–1880* (1955), *The Agrarian Origins of Modern Japan* (1959), and editor of *City and Village in Japan* (*Economic Development and Cultural Change,* 1960).

JOSEPH R. STRAYER, Dayton Stockton Professor of History at Princeton University, is President of the Mediaeval Academy of America, and the author of *Feudalism* (1965), *Studies in Early French Taxation* (1939), and *The Administration of Normandy under St. Louis* (1932).

INDEX

Index

Index

Index

Index

Index

Index

395

Index

village (*continued*)
310; nayosechō, 137; tax register, 287; temple registry, 310; waritsukechō, 265-66, 271-73, 278, 284, 291, 293
  miyaza, 312. See also shrine association
  mura hachibu, 309-311, 313
  tax: dashimai, 135; komono-nari, 288-91, 293; land tax, 294, 306; nengu (menjō), 284
  village assembly, 310, 312

Wakamatsu, 380
wakashū kabuki, 236
warriors, see samurai

yakuban, 217
Yakusha hyōbanki, 241
Yamagata Daini, 332, 364
Yamaguchi, 147, 171
Yamamura-za, 253-54, 257
Yamanoguchi, 137

Yamashiro, 201
Yamauchi, 100, 115-16, 118-21, 123-25, 333, 344; Kazutoyo, 116-18; Tadayoshi, 119-20, 122, 124, 126-27; Toyochika, 337, 341; Yasutomo, 117, 119
Yamazaki Ansai, 126, 320
yarō kabuki, 238
yarō mushi, 240
Yodoya, 194; Keian, 191; Saburōemon, 194
Yokohama, 386
yoriki, 226
yori-ko, 50
yori-oya, 50
Yoritomo, see Minamoto-no-Yoritomo
Yoshida, 81
Yoshida Shōin, 365, 368-69, 371, 373
Yoshida Tōyō, 345
Yoshino Sakuzō, 346
Yoshiwara, 234, 248

Zen, 126
Zeniya Gohei, 200
Zōjōji, 253